DART'S

FREIGHT COMPUTATIONS:

A COMPLETE WORK,

EMBRACING EIGHTY-EIGHT THOUSAND TWO HUNDRED AND TWENTY-THREE CALCULATIONS,

FROM ONE CUBIC INCH TO FOUR THOUSAND FEET,

AT RATES FROM

TWENTY-FIVE CENTS TO TWENTY DOLLARS PER TON OF FORTY CUBIC FEET, AND EQUIVALENT RATES PER FOOT MEASUREMENT.

CALCULATED FOR EVERY MODE OF TRANSPORTATION,

COASTWISE AND INLAND, THROUGHOUT THE UNITED STATES,

AND ALSO FOR EVERY CLASS OF STORAGE.

BY P. C. DART.

ELECTROTYPE EDITION.

NEW YORK:
D. APPLETON & CO., 90, 92 & 94 GRAND STREET.
1868.

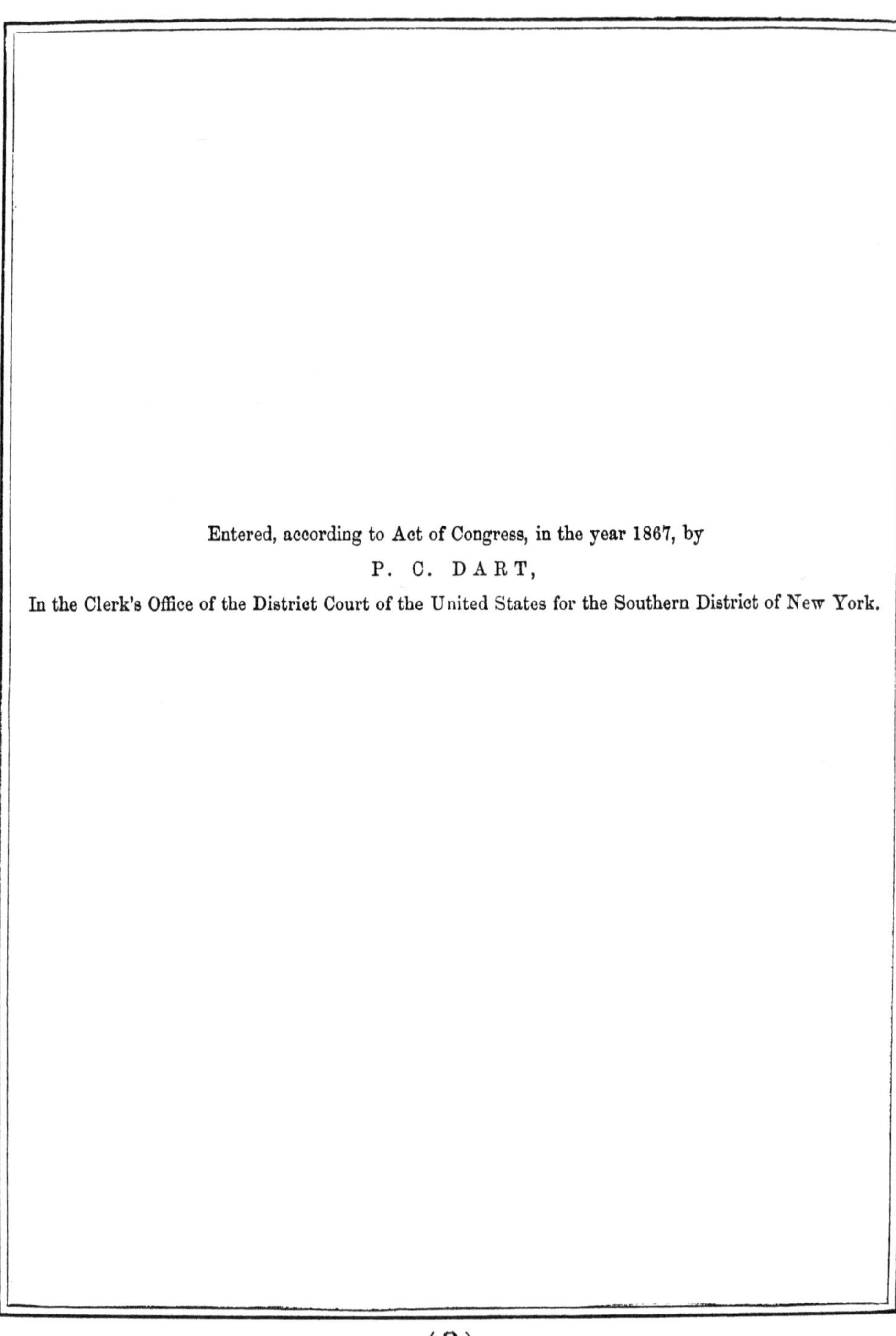

NOTICE.

To Shipping Merchants, Forwarding Houses, Ship Masters, Canal, River, and Lake Transportation Companies, Railroad Companies, Army Quartermasters, Bonded and Free Warehousemen, throughout the United States and Territories:

THE character of the following work is such as to commend itself directly to the attention of a large class of the business men of the country.

The author, having been engaged for many years in the transportation of merchandise, and thoroughly versed in the business, has, for the last five years, devoted much time and study to perfect and arrange a set of Practical Tables intended to do away with the labor and time, and also to avoid the inaccuracies of calculating freights in the CARGO BOOK, MANIFEST, BILL OF LADING, and FREIGHT LIST.

In all Shipping Houses the computations of freight by the various lines of transportation, and at the different prices, is well understood to be an intricate work; and this part of the business generally comes at the time when dispatch is required, and when the errors of hurried work can least be tolerated. By the aid of these Tables, NO MULTIPLICATIONS OR CALCULATIONS WHATEVER ARE REQUIRED to determine at a view the EXACT sum of any amount of cubic freight, from ONE INCH TO FOUR THOUSAND FEET, at prices from TWENTY-FIVE CENTS TO TWENTY DOLLARS PER TON; comprehending the lowest to any required quantity, at every rate in use, by every mode of transportation, coastwise or inland; enabling the clerk to do the same work accurately in ONE-TENTH THE TIME required by multiplications in the old way.

The principle upon which the Tables have been made does not admit the possibility of error; and the author, knowing that no favors whatever can be expected, CORDIALLY INVITES CRITICISM of his work, and submits it with ENTIRE CONFIDENCE to a discriminating public.

P. C. DART.

SAN FRANCISCO, *Sept.*, 1867.

EXPLANATION.

Throughout this work, it will be observed, that, at the top of each page, the rates of freight are uniform, or exactly the same on each page — viz.: 25 cts., 50 cts., $1, $2, and so on to $20. *Directly under* these, commencing with the $1 column, are *equivalent rates per foot,* as follow: 2½ cts., 5 cts., 7½ cts., 10 cts., on to 50 cts.

On the *left* of each page is the column indicating the *quantity;* as, for instance, on the first page of Tables, the left column is from 1 to 11 *inches;* the next page is from 1 to 50 *feet;* the next, from 51 to 100 *feet.* Observe, the *column of quantity is on each page.*

The *Index* is abbreviated, for convenience, running from 1 to 40—meaning from 100 feet to 4000 feet.

EXAMPLES.

Question.—What is the *freight* on 193 ft. 11 inches, at $18 per ton?

Answer.—Turn to 2 in the index (200 feet), on the $18 column; opposite 193 ft. is $86.85. Then on the page of inches, in the same manner, you find 41 cts.; the two added make $87.26, the correct answer.

Question.—What is the *freight* on 2763 feet, at $16 per ton?

Answer.—Turn to 28 in the Index; on the $16 column, opposite 2763 feet, is $1105.20, the answer.

Question.—1906 feet 10 inches, at 35 cts. per foot?

Answer.—$667.39.

Question.—What is the *storage* on 3779 feet, at 25 cts. per ton?

Answer.—See column for 25 cts.; opposite 3779 feet, $23.62.

Question.—What is the *storage* on 2876 feet, at 50 cts. per ton?

Answer.—$35.95.

TABLE OF INCHES.

Per Ton.	25c.	50c.	$1	$2	$3	$4	$5	$6	$7	$8	$9	$10	$11	$12	$13	$14	$15	$16	$17	$18	$19	$20
Per Foot.			2½c.	5c.	7½c.	10c.	12½c.	15c.	17½c.	20c.	22½c.	25c.	27½c.	30c.	32½c.	35c.	37½c.	40c.	42½c.	45c.	47½c.	50c.
1					1	1	1	1	1	2	2	2	2	2	3	3	3	3	4	4	4	4
2				1	1	2	2	2	3	3	4	4	5	5	5	6	6	7	7	7	8	8
3			1	1	2	2	3	4	4	5	6	6	7	7	8	9	9	10	11	11	12	12
4			1	2	2	3	4	5	6	7	7	8	9	10	11	12	12	13	14	15	16	17
5			1	2	3	4	5	6	7	8	9	10	11	12	13	14	15	16	17	19	19	21
6			1	2	4	5	6	7	9	10	11	12	14	15	16	17	19	20	21	22	24	25
7		1	1	3	4	6	7	9	10	12	13	15	16	17	19	20	22	23	25	26	28	29
8		1	2	3	5	7	8	10	12	13	15	17	18	20	22	23	25	27	28	30	31	33
9		1	2	4	6	7	9	11	13	15	17	19	21	22	24	26	28	30	32	34	36	37
10		1	2	4	6	8	10	12	15	17	19	21	23	25	27	29	31	33	35	37	40	42
11	1	1	2	5	7	9	11	14	16	18	21	23	25	27	30	32	34	37	39	41	43	46

50 FEET.

Per Ton,	25c.	50c.	$1	$2	$3	$4	$5	$6	$7	$8	$9	$10
Per Foot,			2½ cts.	5 cts.	7½ cts.	10 cts.	12½ cts.	15 cts.	17½ cts.	20 cts.	22½ cts.	25 cts.
Feet.												
1	1	1	2	5	7	10	12	15	17	20	22	25
2	1	2	5	10	15	20	25	30	35	40	45	50
3	2	4	7	15	22	30	37	45	52	60	67	75
4	2	5	10	20	30	40	50	60	70	80	90	1.00
5	3	6	12	25	37	50	62	75	87	1.00	1.12	1.25
6	4	7	15	30	45	60	75	90	1.05	1.20	1.35	1.50
7	4	9	17	35	52	70	87	1.05	1.22	1.40	1.57	1.75
8	5	10	20	40	60	80	1.00	1.20	1.40	1.60	1.80	2.00
9	6	11	22	45	67	90	1.12	1.35	1.57	1.80	2.02	2.25
10	6	12	25	50	75	1.00	1.25	1.50	1.75	2.00	2.25	2.50
11	7	14	27	55	82	1.10	1.37	1.65	1.92	2.20	2.47	2.75
12	7	15	30	60	90	1.20	1.50	1.80	2.10	2.40	2.70	3.00
13	8	16	32	65	97	1.30	1.62	1.95	2.27	2.60	2.92	3.25
14	9	17	35	70	1.05	1.40	1.75	2.10	2.45	2.80	3.15	3.50
15	9	19	37	75	1.12	1.50	1.87	2.25	2.62	3.00	3.37	3.75
16	10	20	40	80	1.20	1.60	2.00	2.40	2.80	3.20	3.60	4.00
17	11	21	42	85	1.27	1.70	2.12	2.55	2.97	3.40	3.82	4.25
18	11	22	45	90	1.35	1.80	2.25	2.70	3.15	3.60	4.05	4.50
19	12	24	47	95	1.42	1.90	2.37	2.85	3.32	3.80	4.27	4.75
20	12	25	50	1.00	1.50	2.00	2.50	3.00	3.50	4.00	4.50	5.00
21	13	26	52	1.05	1.57	2.10	2.62	3.15	3.67	4.20	4.72	5.25
22	14	27	55	1.10	1.65	2.20	2.75	3.30	3.85	4.40	4.95	5.50
23	14	29	57	1.15	1.72	2.30	2.87	3.45	4.02	4.60	5.17	5.75
24	15	30	60	1.20	1.80	2.40	3.00	3.60	4.20	4.80	5.40	6.00
25	16	31	62	1.25	1.87	2.50	3.12	3.75	4.37	5.00	5.62	6.25
26	16	32	65	1.30	1.95	2.60	3.25	3.90	4.55	5.20	5.85	6.50
27	17	34	67	1.35	2.02	2.70	3.37	4.05	4.72	5.40	6.07	6.75
28	17	35	70	1.40	2.10	2.80	3.50	4.20	4.90	5.60	6.30	7.00
29	18	36	72	1.45	2.17	2.90	3.62	4.35	5.07	5.80	6.52	7.25
30	19	37	75	1.50	2.25	3.00	3.75	4.50	5.25	6.00	6.75	7.50
31	19	39	77	1.55	2.32	3.10	3.87	4.65	5.42	6.20	6.97	7.75
32	20	40	80	1.60	2.40	3.20	4.00	4.80	5.60	6.40	7.20	8.00
33	21	41	82	1.65	2.47	3.30	4.12	4.95	5.77	6.60	7.42	8.25
34	21	42	85	1.70	2.55	3.40	4.25	5.10	5.95	6.80	7.65	8.50
35	22	44	87	1.75	2.62	3.50	4.37	5.25	6.12	7.00	7.87	8.75
36	22	45	90	1.80	2.70	3.60	4.50	5.40	6.30	7.20	8.10	9.00
37	23	46	92	1.85	2.77	3.70	4.62	5.55	6.47	7.40	8.32	9.25
38	24	47	95	1.90	2.85	3.80	4.75	5.70	6.65	7.60	8.55	9.50
39	24	49	97	1.95	2.92	3.90	4.87	5.85	6.82	7.80	8.77	9.75
40	25	50	1.00	2.00	3.00	4.00	5.00	6.00	7.00	8.00	9.00	10.00
41	26	51	1.02	2.05	3.07	4.10	5.12	6.15	7.17	8.20	9.22	10.25
42	26	52	1.05	2.10	3.15	4.20	5.25	6.30	7.35	8.40	9.45	10.50
43	27	54	1.07	2.15	3.22	4.30	5.37	6.45	7.52	8.60	9.67	10.75
44	27	55	1.10	2.20	3.30	4.40	5.50	6.60	7.70	8.80	9.90	11.00
45	28	56	1.12	2.25	3.37	4.50	5.62	6.75	7.87	9.00	10.12	11.25
46	29	57	1.15	2.30	3.45	4.60	5.75	6.90	8.05	9.20	10.35	11.50
47	29	59	1.17	2.35	3.52	4.70	5.87	7.05	8.22	9.40	10.57	11.75
48	30	60	1.20	2.40	3.60	4.80	6.00	7.20	8.40	9.60	10.80	12.00
49	31	61	1.22	2.45	3.67	4.90	6.12	7.35	8.57	9.80	11.02	12.25
50	31	62	1.25	2.50	3.75	5.00	6.25	7.50	8.75	10.00	11.25	12.50

50 FEET.

Per Ton, Per Foot,	$11 27½ cts.	$12 30 cts.	$13 32½ cts.	$14 35 cts.	$15 37½ cts.	$16 40 cts.	$17 42½ cts.	$18 45 cts.	$19 47½ cts.	$20 50 cts.
Feet. 1	27	30	32	35	37	40	42	45	47	50
2	55	60	65	70	75	80	85	90	95	1.00
3	82	90	97	1.05	1.12	1.20	1.27	1.35	1.42	1.50
4	1.10	1.20	1.30	1.40	1.50	1.60	1.70	1.80	1.90	2.00
5	1.37	1.50	1.62	1.75	1.87	2.00	2.12	2.25	2.37	2.50
6	1.65	1.80	1.95	2.10	2.25	2.40	2.55	2.70	2.85	3.00
7	1.92	2.10	2.27	2.45	2.62	2.80	2.97	3.15	3.32	3.50
8	2.20	2.40	2.60	2.80	3.00	3.20	3.40	3.60	3.80	4.00
9	2.47	2.70	2.92	3.15	3.37	3.60	3.82	4.05	4.27	4.50
10	2.75	3.00	3.25	3.50	3.75	4.00	4.25	4.50	4.75	5.00
11	3.02	3.30	3.57	3.85	4.12	4.40	4.67	4.95	5.22	5.50
12	3.30	3.60	3.90	4.20	4.50	4.80	5.10	5.40	5.70	6.00
13	3.57	3.90	4.22	4.55	4.87	5.20	5.52	5.85	6.17	6.50
14	3.85	4.20	4.55	4.90	5.25	5.60	5.95	6.30	6.65	7.00
15	4.12	4.50	4.87	5.25	5.62	6.00	6.37	6.75	7.12	7.50
16	4.40	4.80	5.20	5.60	6.00	6.40	6.80	7.20	7.60	8.00
17	4.67	5.10	5.52	5.95	6.37	6.80	7.22	7.65	8.07	8.50
18	4.95	5.40	5.85	6.30	6.75	7.20	7.65	8.10	8.55	9.00
19	5.22	5.70	6.17	6.65	7.12	7.60	8.07	8.55	9.02	9.50
20	5.50	6.00	6.50	7.00	7.50	8.00	8.50	9.00	9.50	10.00
21	5.77	6.30	6.82	7.35	7.87	8.40	8.92	9.45	9.97	10.50
22	6.05	6.60	7.15	7.70	8.25	8.80	9.35	9.90	10.45	11.00
23	6.32	6.90	7.47	8.05	8.62	9.20	9.77	10.35	10.92	11.50
24	6.60	7.20	7.80	8.40	9.00	9.60	10.20	10.80	11.40	12.00
25	6.87	7.50	8.12	8.75	9.37	10.00	10.62	11.25	11.87	12.50
26	7.15	7.80	8.45	9.10	9.75	10.40	11.05	11.70	12.35	13.00
27	7.42	8.10	8.77	9.45	10.12	10.80	11.47	12.15	12.82	13.50
28	7.70	8.40	9.10	9.80	10.50	11.20	11.90	12.60	13.30	14.00
29	7.97	8.70	9.42	10.15	10.87	11.60	12.32	13.05	13.77	14.50
30	8.25	9.00	9.75	10.50	11.25	12.00	12.75	13.50	14.25	15.00
31	8.52	9.30	10.07	10.85	11.62	12.40	13.17	13.95	14.72	15.50
32	8.80	9.60	10.40	11.20	12.00	12.80	13.60	14.40	15.20	16.00
33	9.07	9.90	10.72	11.55	12.37	13.20	14.02	14.85	15.67	16.50
34	9.35	10.20	11.05	11.90	12.75	13.60	14.45	15.30	16.15	17.00
35	9.62	10.50	11.37	12.25	13.12	14.00	14.87	15.75	16.62	17.50
36	9.90	10.80	11.70	12.60	13.50	14.40	15.30	16.20	17.10	18.00
37	10.17	11.10	12.02	12.95	13.87	14.80	15.72	16.65	17.57	18.50
38	10.45	11.40	12.35	13.30	14.25	15.20	16.15	17.10	18.05	19.00
39	10.72	11.70	12.67	13.65	14.62	15.60	16.57	17.55	18.52	19.50
40	11.00	12.00	13.00	14.00	15.00	16.00	17.00	18.00	19.00	20.00
41	11.27	12.30	13.32	14.35	15.37	16.40	17.42	18.45	19.47	20.50
42	11.55	12.60	13.65	14.70	15.75	16.80	17.85	18.90	19.95	21.00
43	11.82	12.90	13.97	15.05	16.12	17.20	18.27	19.35	20.42	21.50
44	12.10	13.20	14.30	15.40	16.50	17.60	18.70	19.80	20.90	22.00
45	12.37	13.50	14.62	15.75	16.87	18.00	19.12	20.25	21.37	22.50
46	12.65	13.80	14.95	16.10	17.25	18.40	19.55	20.70	21.85	23.00
47	12.92	14.10	15.27	16.45	17.62	18.80	19.97	21.15	22.32	23.50
48	13.20	14.40	15.60	16.80	18.00	19.20	20.40	21.60	22.80	24.00
49	13.47	14.70	15.92	17.15	18.37	19.60	20.82	22.05	23.27	24.50
50	13.75	15.00	16.25	17.50	18.75	20.00	21.25	22.50	23.75	25.00

100 FEET.

Per Ton,	25c.	50c.	$1	$2	$3	$4	$5	$6	$7	$8	$9	$10
Per Foot,			2½ cts.	5 cts.	7½ cts.	10 cts.	12½ cts.	15 cts.	17½ cts.	20 cts.	22½ cts.	25 cts.
Feet.												
51	32	64	1.27	2.55	3.82	5.10	6.37	7.65	8.92	10.20	11.47	12.75
52	32	65	1.30	2.60	3.90	5.20	6.50	7.80	9.10	10.40	11.70	13.00
53	33	66	1.32	2.65	3.97	5.30	6.62	7.95	9.27	10.60	11.92	13.25
54	34	67	1.35	2.70	4.05	5.40	6.75	8.10	9.45	10.80	12.15	13.50
55	34	69	1.37	2.75	4.12	5.50	6.87	8.25	9.62	11.00	12.37	13.75
56	35	70	1.40	2.80	4.20	5.60	7.00	8.40	9.80	11.20	12.60	14.00
57	36	71	1.42	2.85	4.27	5.70	7.12	8.55	9.97	11.40	12.82	14.25
58	36	72	1.45	2.90	4.35	5.80	7.25	8.70	10.15	11.60	13.05	14.50
59	37	74	1.47	2.95	4.42	5.90	7.37	8.85	10.32	11.80	13.27	14.75
60	37	75	1.50	3.00	4.50	6.00	7.50	9.00	10.50	12.00	13.50	15.00
61	38	76	1.52	3.05	4.57	6.10	7.62	9.15	10.67	12.20	13.72	15.25
62	39	77	1.55	3.10	4.65	6.20	7.75	9.30	10.85	12.40	13.95	15.50
63	39	79	1.57	3.15	4.72	6.30	7.87	9.45	11.02	12.60	14.17	15.75
64	40	80	1.60	3.20	4.80	6.40	8.00	9.60	11.20	12.80	14.40	16.00
65	41	81	1.62	3.25	4.87	6.50	8.12	9.75	11.37	13.00	14.62	16.25
66	41	82	1.65	3.30	4.95	6.60	8.25	9.90	11.55	13.20	14.85	16.50
67	42	84	1.67	3.35	5.02	6.70	8.37	10.05	11.72	13.40	15.07	16.75
68	42	85	1.70	3.40	5.10	6.80	8.50	10.20	11.90	13.60	15.30	17.00
69	43	86	1.72	3.45	5.17	6.90	8.62	10.35	12.07	13.80	15.52	17.25
70	44	87	1.75	3.50	5.25	7.00	8.75	10.50	12.25	14.00	15.75	17.50
71	44	89	1.77	3.55	5.32	7.10	8.87	10.65	12.42	14.20	15.97	17.75
72	45	90	1.80	3.60	5.40	7.20	9.00	10.80	12.60	14.40	16.20	18.00
73	46	91	1.82	3.65	5.47	7.30	9.12	10.95	12.77	14.60	16.42	18.25
74	46	92	1.85	3.70	5.55	7.40	9.25	11.10	12.95	14.80	16.65	18.50
75	47	94	1.87	3.75	5.62	7.50	9.37	11.25	13.12	15.00	16.87	18.75
76	47	95	1.90	3.80	5.70	7.60	9.50	11.40	13.30	15.20	17.10	19.00
77	48	96	1.92	3.85	5.77	7.70	9.62	11.55	13.47	15.40	17.32	19.25
78	49	97	1.95	3.90	5.85	7.80	9.75	11.70	13.65	15.60	17.55	19.50
79	49	99	1.97	3.95	5.92	7.90	9.87	11.85	13.82	15.80	17.77	19.75
80	50	1.00	2.00	4.00	6.00	8.00	10.00	12.00	14.00	16.00	18.00	20.00
81	51	1.01	2.02	4.05	6.07	8.10	10.12	12.15	14.17	16.20	18.22	20.25
82	51	1.02	2.05	4.10	6.15	8.20	10.25	12.30	14.35	16.40	18.45	20.50
83	52	1.04	2.07	4.15	6.22	8.30	10.37	12.45	14.52	16.60	18.67	20.75
84	52	1.05	2.10	4.20	6.30	8.40	10.50	12.60	14.70	16.80	18.90	21.00
85	53	1.06	2.12	4.25	6.37	8.50	10.62	12.75	14.87	17.00	19.12	21.25
86	54	1.07	2.15	4.30	6.45	8.60	10.75	12.90	15.05	17.20	19.35	21.50
87	54	1.09	2.17	4.35	6.52	8.70	10.87	13.05	15.22	17.40	19.57	21.75
88	55	1.10	2.20	4.40	6.60	8.80	11.00	13.20	15.40	17.60	19.80	22.00
89	56	1.11	2.22	4.45	6.67	8.90	11.12	13.35	15.57	17.80	20.02	22.25
90	56	1.12	2.25	4.50	6.75	9.00	11.25	13.50	15.75	18.00	20.25	22.50
91	57	1.14	2.27	4.55	6.82	9.10	11.37	13.65	15.92	18.20	20.47	22.75
92	57	1.15	2.30	4.60	6.90	9.20	11.50	13.80	16.10	18.40	20.70	23.00
93	58	1.16	2.32	4.65	6.97	9.30	11.62	13.95	16.27	18.60	20.92	23.25
94	59	1.17	2.35	4.70	7.05	9.40	11.75	14.10	16.45	18.80	21.15	23.50
95	59	1.19	2.37	4.75	7.12	9.50	11.87	14.25	16.62	19.00	21.37	23.75
96	60	1.20	2.40	4.80	7.20	9.60	12.00	14.40	16.80	19.20	21.60	24.00
97	61	1.21	2.42	4.85	7.27	9.70	12.12	14.55	16.97	19.40	21.82	24.25
98	61	1.22	2.45	4.90	7.35	9.80	12.25	14.70	17.15	19.60	22.05	24.50
99	62	1.24	2.47	4.95	7.42	9.90	12.37	14.85	17.32	19.80	22.27	24.75
100	62	1.25	2.50	5.00	7.50	10.00	12.50	15.00	17.50	20.00	22.50	25.00

100 FEET.

Per Ton,	$11	$12	$13	$14	$15	$16	$17	$18	$19	$20
Per Foot,	27½ cts.	30 cts.	32½ cts.	35 cts.	37½ cts.	40 cts.	42½ cts.	45 cts.	47½ cts.	50 cts.
Feet.										
51	14.02	15.30	16.57	17.85	19.12	20.40	21.67	22.95	24.22	25.50
52	14.30	15.60	16.90	18.20	19.50	20.80	22.10	23.40	24.70	26.00
53	14.57	15.90	17.22	18.55	19.87	21.20	22.52	23.85	25.17	26.50
54	14.85	16.20	17.55	18.90	20.25	21.60	22.95	24.30	25.65	27.00
55	15.12	16.50	17.87	19.25	20.62	22.00	23.37	24.75	26.12	27.50
56	15.40	16.80	18.20	19.60	21.00	22.40	23.80	25.20	26.60	28.00
57	15.67	17.10	18.52	19.95	21.37	22.80	24.22	25.65	27.07	28.50
58	15.95	17.40	18.85	20.30	21.75	23.20	24.65	26.10	27.55	29.00
59	16.22	17.70	19.17	20.65	22.12	23.60	25.07	26.55	28.02	29.50
60	16.50	18.00	19.50	21.00	22.50	24.00	25.50	27.00	28.50	30.00
61	16.77	18.30	19.82	21.35	22.87	24.40	25.92	27.45	28.97	30.50
62	17.05	18.60	20.15	21.70	23.25	24.80	26.35	27.90	29.45	31.00
63	17.32	18.90	20.47	22.05	23.62	25.20	26.77	28.35	29.92	31.50
64	17.60	19.20	20.80	22.40	24.00	25.60	27.20	28.80	30.40	32.00
65	17.87	19.50	21.12	22.75	24.37	26.00	27.62	29.25	30.87	32.50
66	18.15	19.80	21.45	23.10	24.75	26.40	28.05	29.70	31.35	33.00
67	18.42	20.10	21.77	23.45	25.12	26.80	28.47	30.15	31.82	33.50
68	18.70	20.40	22.10	23.80	25.50	27.20	28.90	30.60	32.30	34.00
69	18.97	20.70	22.42	24.15	25.87	27.60	29.32	31.05	32.77	34.50
70	19.25	21.00	22.75	24.50	26.25	28.00	29.75	31.50	33.25	35.00
71	19.52	21.30	23.07	24.85	26.62	28.40	30.17	31.95	33.72	35.50
72	19.80	21.60	23.40	25.20	27.00	28.80	30.60	32.40	34.20	36.00
73	20.07	21.90	23.72	25.55	27.37	29.20	31.02	32.85	34.67	36.50
74	20.35	22.20	24.05	25.90	27.75	29.60	31.45	33.30	35.15	37.00
75	20.62	22.50	24.37	26.25	28.12	30.00	31.87	33.75	35.62	37.50
76	20.90	22.80	24.70	26.60	28.50	30.40	32.30	34.20	36.10	38.00
77	21.17	23.10	25.02	26.95	28.87	30.80	32.72	34.65	36.57	38.50
78	21.45	23.40	25.35	27.30	29.25	31.20	33.15	35.10	37.05	39.00
79	21.72	23.70	25.67	27.65	29.62	31.60	33.57	35.55	37.52	39.50
80	22.00	24.00	26.00	28.00	30.00	32.00	34.00	36.00	38.00	40.00
81	22.27	24.30	26.32	28.35	30.37	32.40	34.42	36.45	38.47	40.50
82	22.55	24.60	26.65	28.70	30.75	32.80	34.85	36.90	38.95	41.00
83	22.82	24.90	26.97	29.05	31.12	33.20	35.27	37.35	39.42	41.50
84	23.10	25.20	27.30	29.40	31.50	33.60	35.70	37.80	39.90	42.00
85	23.37	25.50	27.62	29.75	31.87	34.00	36.12	38.25	40.37	42.50
86	23.65	25.80	27.95	30.10	32.25	34.40	36.55	38.70	40.85	43.00
87	23.92	26.10	28.27	30.45	32.62	34.80	36.97	39.15	41.32	43.50
88	24.20	26.40	28.60	30.80	33.00	35.20	37.40	39.60	41.80	44.00
89	24.47	26.70	28.92	31.15	33.37	35.60	37.82	40.05	42.27	44.50
90	24.75	27.00	29.25	31.50	33.75	36.00	38.25	40.50	42.75	45.00
91	25.02	27.30	29.57	31.85	34.12	36.40	38.67	40.95	43.22	45.50
92	25.30	27.60	29.90	32.20	34.50	36.80	39.10	41.40	43.70	46.00
93	25.57	27.90	30.22	32.55	34.87	37.20	39.52	41.85	44.17	46.50
94	25.85	28.20	30.55	32.90	35.25	37.60	39.95	42.30	44.65	47.00
95	26.12	28.50	30.87	33.25	35.62	38.00	40.37	42.75	45.12	47.50
96	26.40	28.80	31.20	33.60	36.00	38.40	40.80	43.20	45.60	48.00
97	26.67	29.10	31.52	33.95	36.37	38.80	41.22	43.65	46.07	48.50
98	26.95	29.40	31.85	34.30	36.75	39.20	41.65	44.10	46.55	49.00
99	27.22	29.70	32.17	34.65	37.12	39.60	42.07	44.55	47.02	49.50
100	27.50	30.00	32.50	35.00	37.50	40.00	42.50	45.00	47.50	50.00

150 FEET.

Per Ton,	25c.	50c.	$1	$2	$3	$4	$5	$6	$7	$8	$9	$10
Per Foot,			2½ cts.	5 cts.	7½ cts.	10 cts.	12½ cts.	15 cts.	17½ cts.	20 cts.	22½ cts.	25 cts.
Feet.												
101	63	1.26	2.52	5.05	7.57	10.10	12.62	15.15	17.67	20.20	22.72	25.25
102	64	1.27	2.55	5.10	7.65	10.20	12.75	15.30	17.85	20.40	22.95	25.50
103	64	1.29	2.57	5.15	7.72	10.30	12.87	15.45	18.02	20.60	23.17	25.75
104	65	1.30	2.60	5.20	7.80	10.40	13.00	15.60	18.20	20.80	23.40	26.00
105	66	1.31	2.62	5.25	7.87	10.50	13.12	15.75	18.37	21.00	23.62	26.25
106	66	1.32	2.65	5.30	7.95	10.60	13.25	15.90	18.55	21.20	23.85	26.50
107	67	1.34	2.67	5.35	8.02	10.70	13.37	16.05	18.72	21.40	24.07	26.75
108	67	1.35	2.70	5.40	8.10	10.80	13.50	16.20	18.90	21.60	24.30	27.00
109	68	1.36	2.72	5.45	8.17	10.90	13.62	16.35	19.07	21.80	24.52	27.25
110	69	1.37	2.75	5.50	8.25	11.00	13.75	16.50	19.25	22.00	24.75	27.50
111	69	1.39	2.77	5.55	8.32	11.10	13.87	16.65	19.42	22.20	24.97	27.75
112	70	1.40	2.80	5.60	8.40	11.20	14.00	16.80	19.60	22.40	25.20	28.00
113	71	1.41	2.82	5.65	8.47	11.30	14.12	16.95	19.77	22.60	25.42	28.25
114	71	1.42	2.85	5.70	8.55	11.40	14.25	17.10	19.95	22.80	25.65	28.50
115	72	1.44	2.87	5.75	8.62	11.50	14.37	17.25	20.12	23.00	25.87	28.75
116	72	1.45	2.90	5.80	8.70	11.60	14.50	17.40	20.30	23.20	26.10	29.00
117	73	1.46	2.92	5.85	8.77	11.70	14.62	17.55	20.47	23.40	26.32	29.25
118	74	1.47	2.95	5.90	8.85	11.80	14.75	17.70	20.65	23.60	26.55	29.50
119	74	1.49	2.97	5.95	8.92	11.90	14.87	17.85	20.82	23.80	26.77	29.75
120	75	1.50	3.00	6.00	9.00	12.00	15.00	18.00	21.00	24.00	27.00	30.00
121	76	1.51	3.02	6.05	9.07	12.10	15.12	18.15	21.17	24.20	27.22	30.25
122	76	1.52	3.05	6.10	9.15	12.20	15.25	18.30	21.35	24.40	27.45	30.50
123	77	1.54	3.07	6.15	9.22	12.30	15.37	18.45	21.52	24.60	27.67	30.75
124	77	1.55	3.10	6.20	9.30	12.40	15.50	18.60	21.70	24.80	27.90	31.00
125	78	1.56	3.12	6.25	9.37	12.50	15.62	18.75	21.87	25.00	28.12	31.25
126	79	1.57	3.15	6.30	9.45	12.60	15.75	18.90	22.05	25.20	28.35	31.50
127	79	1.59	3.17	6.35	9.52	12.70	15.87	19.05	22.22	25.40	28.57	31.75
128	80	1.60	3.20	6.40	9.60	12.80	16.00	19.20	22.40	25.60	28.80	32.00
129	81	1.61	3.22	6.45	9.67	12.90	16.12	19.35	22.57	25.80	29.02	32.25
130	81	1.62	3.25	6.50	9.75	13.00	16.25	19.50	22.75	26.00	29.25	32.50
131	82	1.64	3.27	6.55	9.82	13.10	16.37	19.65	22.92	26.20	29.47	32.75
132	82	1.65	3.30	6.60	9.90	13.20	16.50	19.80	23.10	26.40	29.70	33.00
133	83	1.66	3.32	6.65	9.97	13.30	16.62	19.95	23.27	26.60	29.92	33.25
134	84	1.67	3.35	6.70	10.05	13.40	16.75	20.10	23.45	26.80	30.15	33.50
135	84	1.69	3.37	6.75	10.12	13.50	16.87	20.25	23.62	27.00	30.37	33.75
136	85	1.70	3.40	6.80	10.20	13.60	17.00	20.40	23.80	27.20	30.60	34.00
137	86	1.71	3.42	6.85	10.27	13.70	17.12	20.55	23.97	27.40	30.82	34.25
138	86	1.72	3.45	6.90	10.35	13.80	17.25	20.70	24.15	27.60	31.05	34.50
139	87	1.74	3.47	6.95	10.42	13.90	17.37	20.85	24.32	27.80	31.27	34.75
140	87	1.75	3.50	7.00	10.50	14.00	17.50	21.00	24.50	28.00	31.50	35.00
141	88	1.76	3.52	7.05	10.57	14.10	17.62	21.15	24.67	28.20	31.72	35.25
142	89	1.77	3.55	7.10	10.65	14.20	17.75	21.30	24.85	28.40	31.95	35.50
143	89	1.79	3.57	7.15	10.72	14.30	17.87	21.45	25.02	28.60	32.17	35.75
144	90	1.80	3.60	7.20	10.80	14.40	18.00	21.60	25.20	28.80	32.40	36.00
145	91	1.81	3.62	7.25	10.87	14.50	18.12	21.75	25.37	29.00	32.62	36.25
146	91	1.82	3.65	7.30	10.95	14.60	18.25	21.90	25.55	29.20	32.85	36.50
147	92	1.84	3.67	7.35	11.02	14.70	18.37	22.05	25.72	29.40	33.07	36.75
148	92	1.85	3.70	7.40	11.10	14.80	18.50	22.20	25.90	29.60	33.30	37.00
149	93	1.86	3.72	7.45	11.17	14.90	18.62	22.35	26.07	29.80	33.52	37.25
150	94	1.87	3.75	7.50	11.25	15.00	18.75	22.50	26.25	30.00	33.75	37.50

150 FEET.

Per Ton, / Per Foot, Feet.	$11 27½ cts.	$12 30 cts.	$13 32½ cts.	$14 35 cts.	$15 37½ cts.	$16 40 cts.	$17 42½ cts.	$18 45 cts.	$19 47½ cts.	$20 50 cts.
101	27.77	30.30	32.82	35.35	37.87	40.40	42.92	45.45	47.97	50.50
102	28.05	30.60	33.15	35.70	38.25	40.80	43.35	45.90	48.45	51.00
103	28.32	30.90	33.47	36.05	38.62	41.20	43.77	46.35	48.92	51.50
104	28.60	31.20	33.80	36.40	39.00	41.60	44.20	46.80	49.40	52.00
105	28.87	31.50	34.12	36.75	39.37	42.00	44.62	47.25	49.87	52.50
106	29.15	31.80	34.45	37.10	39.75	42.40	45.05	47.70	50.35	53.00
107	29.42	32.10	34.77	37.45	40.12	42.80	45.47	48.15	50.82	53.50
108	29.70	32.40	35.10	37.80	40.50	43.20	45.90	48.60	51.30	54.00
109	29.97	32.70	35.42	38.15	40.87	43.60	46.32	49.05	51.77	54.50
110	30.25	33.00	35.75	38.50	41.25	44.00	46.75	49.50	52.25	55.00
111	30.52	33.30	36.07	38.85	41.62	44.40	47.17	49.95	52.72	55.50
112	30.80	33.60	36.40	39.20	42.00	44.80	47.60	50.40	53.20	56.00
113	31.07	33.90	36.72	39.55	42.37	45.20	48.02	50.85	53.67	56.50
114	31.35	34.20	37.05	39.90	42.75	45.60	48.45	51.30	54.15	57.00
115	31.62	34.50	37.37	40.25	43.12	46.00	48.87	51.75	54.62	57.50
116	31.90	34.80	37.70	40.60	43.50	46.40	49.30	52.20	55.10	58.00
117	32.17	35.10	38.02	40.95	43.87	46.80	49.72	52.65	55.57	58.50
118	32.45	35.40	38.35	41.30	44.25	47.20	50.15	53.10	56.05	59.00
119	32.72	35.70	38.67	41.65	44.62	47.60	50.57	53.55	56.52	59.50
120	33.00	36.00	39.00	42.00	45.00	48.00	51.00	54.00	57.00	60.00
121	33.27	36.30	39.32	42.35	45.37	48.40	51.42	54.45	57.47	60.50
122	33.55	36.60	39.65	42.70	45.75	48.80	51.85	54.90	57.95	61.00
123	33.82	36.90	39.97	43.05	46.12	49.20	52.27	55.35	58.42	61.50
124	34.10	37.20	40.30	43.40	46.50	49.60	52.70	55.80	58.90	62.00
125	34.37	37.50	40.62	43.75	46.87	50.00	53.12	56.25	59.37	62.50
126	34.65	37.80	40.95	44.10	47.25	50.40	53.55	56.70	59.85	63.00
127	34.92	38.10	41.27	44.45	47.62	50.80	53.97	57.15	60.32	63.50
128	35.20	38.40	41.60	44.80	48.00	51.20	54.40	57.60	60.80	64.00
129	35.47	38.70	41.92	45.15	48.37	51.60	54.82	58.05	61.27	64.50
130	35.75	39.00	42.25	45.50	48.75	52.00	55.25	58.50	61.75	65.00
131	36.02	39.30	42.57	45.85	49.12	52.40	55.67	58.95	62.22	65.50
132	36.30	39.60	42.90	46.20	49.50	52.80	56.10	59.40	62.70	66.00
133	36.57	39.90	43.22	46.55	49.87	53.20	56.52	59.85	63.17	66.50
134	36.85	40.20	43.55	46.90	50.25	53.60	56.95	60.30	63.65	67.00
135	37.12	40.50	43.87	47.25	50.62	54.00	57.37	60.75	64.12	67.50
136	37.40	40.80	44.20	47.60	51.00	54.40	57.80	61.20	64.60	68.00
137	37.67	41.10	44.52	47.95	51.37	54.80	58.22	61.65	65.07	68.50
138	37.95	41.40	44.85	48.30	51.75	55.20	58.65	62.10	65.55	69.00
139	38.22	41.70	45.17	48.65	52.12	55.60	59.07	62.55	66.02	69.50
140	38.50	42.00	45.50	49.00	52.50	56.00	59.50	63.00	66.50	70.00
141	38.77	42.30	45.82	49.35	52.87	56.40	59.92	63.45	66.97	70.50
142	39.05	42.60	46.15	49.70	53.25	56.80	60.35	63.90	67.45	71.00
143	39.32	42.90	46.47	50.05	53.62	57.20	60.77	64.35	67.92	71.50
144	39.60	43.20	46.80	50.40	54.00	57.60	61.20	64.80	68.40	72.00
145	39.87	43.50	47.12	50.75	54.37	58.00	61.62	65.25	68.87	72.50
146	40.15	43.80	47.45	51.10	54.75	58.40	62.05	65.70	69.35	73.00
147	40.42	44.10	47.77	51.45	55.12	58.80	62.47	66.15	69.82	73.50
148	40.70	44.40	48.10	51.80	55.50	59.20	62.90	66.60	70.30	74.00
149	40.97	44.70	48.42	52.15	55.87	59.60	63.32	67.05	71.77	74.50
150	41.25	45.00	48.75	52.50	56.25	60.00	63.75	67.50	71.25	75.00

200 FEET.

Per Ton,	25c.	50c.	$1	$2	$3	$4	$5	$6	$7	$8	$9	$10
Per Foot,			2¼ cts.	5 cts.	7½ cts.	10 cts.	12½ cts.	15 cts.	17½ cts.	20 cts.	22½ cts.	25 cts.
Feet.												
151	94	1.89	3.77	7.55	11.32	15.10	18.87	22.65	26.42	30.20	33.97	37.75
152	95	1.90	3.80	7.60	11.40	15.20	19.00	22.80	26.60	30.40	34.20	38.00
153	96	1.91	3.82	7.65	11.47	15.30	19.12	22.95	26.77	30.60	34.42	38.25
154	96	1.92	3.85	7.70	11.55	15.40	19.25	23.10	26.95	30.80	34.65	38.50
155	97	1.94	3.87	7.75	11.62	15.50	19.37	23.25	27.12	31.00	34.87	38.75
156	97	1.95	3.90	7.80	11.70	15.60	19.50	23.40	27.30	31.20	35.10	39.00
157	98	1.96	3.92	7.85	11.77	15.70	19.62	23.55	27.47	31.40	35.32	39.25
158	99	1.97	3.95	7.90	11.85	15.80	19.75	23.70	27.65	31.60	35.55	39.50
159	99	1.99	3.97	7.95	11.92	15.90	19.87	23.85	27.82	31.80	35.77	39.75
160	1.00	2.00	4.00	8.00	12.00	16.00	20.00	24.00	28.00	32.00	36.00	40.00
161	1.01	2.01	4.02	8.05	12.07	16.10	20.12	24.15	28.17	32.20	36.22	40.25
162	1.01	2.02	4.05	8.10	12.15	16.20	20.25	24.30	28.35	32.40	36.45	40.50
163	1.02	2.04	4.07	8.15	12.22	16.30	20.37	24.45	28.52	32.60	36.67	40.75
164	1.02	2.05	4.10	8.20	12.30	16.40	20.50	24.60	28.70	32.80	36.90	41.00
165	1.03	2.06	4.12	8.25	12.37	16.50	20.62	24.75	28.87	33.00	37.12	41.25
166	1.04	2.07	4.15	8.30	12.45	16.60	20.75	24.90	29.05	33.20	37.35	41.50
167	1.04	2.09	4.17	8.35	12.52	16.70	20.87	25.05	29.22	33.40	37.57	41.75
168	1.05	2.10	4.20	8.40	12.60	16.80	21.00	25.20	29.40	33.60	37.80	42.00
169	1.06	2.11	4.22	8.45	12.67	16.90	21.12	25.35	29.57	33.80	38.02	42.25
170	1.06	2.12	4.25	8.50	12.75	17.00	21.25	25.50	29.75	34.00	38.25	42.50
171	1.07	2.14	4.27	8.55	12.82	17.10	21.37	25.65	29.92	34.20	38.47	42.75
172	1.07	2.15	4.30	8.60	12.90	17.20	21.50	25.80	30.10	34.40	38.70	43.00
173	1.08	2.16	4.32	8.65	12.97	17.30	21.62	25.95	30.27	34.60	38.92	43.25
174	1.09	2.17	4.35	8.70	13.05	17.40	21.75	26.10	30.45	34.80	39.15	43.50
175	1.09	2.19	4.37	8.75	13.12	17.50	21.87	26.25	30.62	35.00	39.37	43.75
176	1.10	2.20	4.40	8.80	13.20	17.60	22.00	26.40	30.80	35.20	39.60	44.00
177	1.11	2.21	4.42	8.85	13.27	17.70	22.12	26.55	30.97	35.40	39.82	44.25
178	1.11	2.22	4.45	8.90	13.35	17.80	22.25	26.70	31.15	35.60	40.05	44.50
179	1.12	2.24	4.47	8.95	13.42	17.90	22.37	26.85	31.32	35.80	40.27	44.75
180	1.12	2.25	4.50	9.00	13.50	18.00	22.50	27.00	31.50	36.00	40.50	45.00
181	1.13	2.26	4.52	9.05	13.57	18.10	22.62	27.15	31.67	36.20	40.72	45.25
182	1.14	2.27	4.55	9.10	13.65	18.20	22.75	27.30	31.85	36.40	40.95	45.50
183	1.14	2.29	4.57	9.15	13.72	18.30	22.87	27.45	32.02	36.60	41.17	45.75
184	1.15	2.30	4.60	9.20	13.80	18.40	23.00	27.60	32.20	36.80	41.40	46.00
185	1.16	2.31	4.62	9.25	13.87	18.50	23.12	27.75	32.37	37.00	41.62	46.25
186	1.16	2.32	4.65	9.30	13.95	18.60	23.25	27.90	32.55	37.20	41.85	46.50
187	1.17	2.34	4.67	9.35	14.02	18.70	23.37	28.05	32.72	37.40	42.07	46.75
188	1.17	2.35	4.70	9.40	14.10	18.80	23.50	28.20	32.90	37.60	42.30	47.00
189	1.18	2.36	4.72	9.45	14.17	18.90	23.62	28.35	33.07	37.80	42.52	47.25
190	1.19	2.37	4.75	9.50	14.25	19.00	23.75	28.50	33.25	38.00	42.75	47.50
191	1.19	2.39	4.77	9.55	14.32	19.10	23.87	28.65	33.42	38.20	42.97	47.75
192	1.20	2.40	4.80	9.60	14.40	19.20	24.00	28.80	33.60	38.40	43.20	48.00
193	1.21	2.41	4.82	9.65	14.47	19.30	24.12	28.95	33.77	38.60	43.42	48.25
194	1.21	2.42	4.85	9.70	14.55	19.40	24.25	29.10	33.95	38.80	43.65	48.50
195	1.22	2.44	4.87	9.75	14.62	19.50	24.37	29.25	34.12	39.00	43.87	48.75
196	1.22	2.45	4.90	9.80	14.70	19.60	24.50	29.40	34.30	39.20	44.10	49.00
197	1.23	2.46	4.92	9.85	14.77	19.70	24.62	29.55	34.47	39.40	44.32	49.25
198	1.24	2.47	4.95	9.90	14.85	19.80	24.75	29.70	34.65	39.60	44.55	49.50
199	1.24	2.49	4.97	9.95	14.92	19.90	24.87	29.85	34.82	39.80	44.77	46.75
200	1.25	2.50	5.00	10.00	15.00	20.00	25.00	30.00	35.00	40.00	45.00	50.00

200 FEET.

Per Ton, / Per Foot,	$11 / 27½ cts.	$12 / 30 cts.	$13 / 32½ cts.	$14 / 35 cts.	$15 / 37½ cts.	$16 / 40 cts.	$17 / 42½ cts.	$18 / 45 cts.	$19 / 47½ cts.	$20 / 50 cts.
Feet.										
151	41.52	45.30	49.07	52.85	56.62	60.40	64.17	67.95	71.72	75.50
152	41.80	45.60	49.40	53.20	57.00	60.80	64.60	68.40	72.20	76.00
153	42.07	45.90	49.72	53.55	57.37	61.20	65.02	68.85	72.67	76.50
154	42.35	46.20	50.05	53.90	57.75	61.60	65.45	69.30	73.15	77.00
155	42.62	46.50	50.37	54.25	58.12	62.00	65.87	69.75	73.62	77.50
156	42.90	46.80	50.70	54.60	58.50	62.40	66.30	70.20	74.10	78.00
157	43.17	47.10	51.02	54.95	58.87	62.80	66.72	70.65	74.57	78.50
158	43.45	47.40	51.35	55.30	59.25	63.20	67.15	71.10	75.05	79.00
159	43.72	47.70	51.67	55.65	59.62	63.60	67.57	71.55	75.52	79.50
160	44.00	48.00	52.00	56.00	60.00	64.00	68.00	72.00	76.00	80.00
161	44.27	48.30	52.32	56.35	60.37	64.40	68.42	72.45	76.47	80.50
162	44.55	48.60	52.65	56.70	60.75	64.80	68.85	72.90	76.95	81.00
163	44.82	48.90	52.97	57.05	61.12	65.20	69.27	73.35	77.42	81.50
164	45.10	49.20	53.30	57.40	61.50	65.60	69.70	73.80	77.90	82.00
165	45.37	49.50	53.62	57.75	61.87	66.00	70.12	74.25	78.37	82.50
166	45.65	49.80	53.95	58.10	62.25	66.40	70.55	74.70	78.85	83.00
167	45.92	50.10	54.27	58.45	62.62	66.80	70.97	75.15	79.32	83.50
168	46.20	50.40	54.60	58.80	63.00	67.20	71.40	75.60	79.80	84.00
169	46.47	50.70	54.92	59.15	63.37	67.60	71.82	76.05	80.27	84.50
170	46.75	51.00	55.25	59.50	63.75	68.00	72.25	76.50	80.75	85.00
171	47.02	51.30	55.57	59.85	64.12	68.40	72.67	76.95	81.22	85.50
172	47.30	51.60	55.90	60.20	64.50	68.80	73.10	77.40	81.70	86.00
173	47.57	51.90	56.22	60.55	64.87	69.20	73.52	77.85	82.17	86.50
174	47.85	52.20	56.55	60.90	65.25	69.60	73.95	78.30	82.65	87.00
175	48.12	52.50	56.87	61.25	65.62	70.00	74.37	78.75	83.12	87.50
176	48.40	52.80	57.20	61.60	66.00	70.40	74.80	79.20	83.60	88.00
177	48.67	53.10	57.52	61.95	66.37	70.80	75.22	79.65	84.07	88.50
178	48.95	53.40	57.85	62.30	66.75	71.20	75.65	80.10	84.55	89.00
179	49.22	53.70	58.17	62.65	67.12	71.60	76.07	80.55	85.02	89.50
180	49.50	54.00	58.50	63.00	67.50	72.00	76.50	81.00	85.50	90.00
181	49.77	54.30	58.82	63.35	67.87	72.40	76.92	81.45	85.97	90.50
182	50.05	54.60	59.15	63.70	68.25	72.80	77.35	81.90	86.45	91.00
183	50.32	54.90	59.47	64.05	68.62	73.20	77.77	82.35	86.92	91.50
184	50.60	55.20	59.80	64.40	69.00	73.60	78.20	82.80	87.40	92.00
185	50.87	55.50	60.12	64.75	69.37	74.00	78.62	83.25	87.87	92.50
186	51.15	55.80	60.45	65.10	69.75	74.40	79.05	83.70	88.35	93.00
187	51.42	56.10	60.77	65.45	70.12	74.80	79.47	84.15	88.82	93.50
188	51.70	56.40	61.10	65.80	70.50	75.20	79.90	84.60	89.30	94.00
189	51.97	56.70	61.42	66.15	70.87	75.60	80.32	85.05	89.77	94.50
190	52.25	57.00	61.75	66.50	71.25	76.00	80.75	85.50	90.25	95.00
191	52.52	57.30	62.07	66.85	71.62	76.40	81.17	85.95	90.72	95.50
192	52.80	57.60	62.40	67.20	72.00	76.80	81.60	86.40	91.20	96.00
193	53.07	57.90	62.72	67.55	72.37	77.20	82.02	86.85	91.67	96.50
194	53.35	58.20	63.05	67.90	72.75	77.60	82.45	87.30	92.15	97.00
195	53.62	58.50	63.37	68.25	73.12	78.00	82.87	87.75	92.62	97.50
196	53.90	58.80	63.70	68.60	73.50	78.40	83.30	88.20	93.10	98.00
197	54.17	59.10	64.02	68.95	73.87	78.80	83.72	88.65	93.57	98.50
198	54.45	59.40	64.35	69.30	74.25	79.20	84.15	89.10	94.05	99.00
199	54.72	59.70	64.67	69.65	74.62	79.60	84.57	89.55	94.52	99.50
200	55.00	60.00	65.00	70.00	75.00	80.00	85.00	90.00	95.00	100.00

250 FEET.

Per Ton, Per Foot, Feet.	25c.	50c.	$1 2½ cts.	$2 5 cts.	$3 7½ cts.	$4 10 cts.	$5 12½ cts.	$6 15 cts.	$7 17½ cts.	$8 20 cts.	$9 22½ cts.	$10 25 cts.
201	1.26	2.51	5.02	10.05	15.07	20.10	25.12	30.15	35.17	40.20	45.22	50.25
202	1.26	2.52	5.05	10.10	15.15	20.20	25.25	30.30	35.35	40.40	45.45	50.50
203	1.27	2.54	5.07	10.15	15.22	20.30	25.37	30.45	35.52	40.60	45.67	50.75
204	1.27	2.55	5.10	10.20	15.30	20.40	25.50	30.60	35.70	40.80	45.90	51.00
205	1.28	2.56	5.12	10.25	15.37	20.50	25.62	30.75	35.87	41.00	46.12	51.25
206	1.29	2.57	5.15	10.30	15.45	20.60	25.75	30.90	36.05	41.20	46.35	51.50
207	1.29	2.59	5.17	10.35	15.52	20.70	25.87	31.05	36.22	41.40	46.57	51.75
208	1.30	2.60	5.20	10.40	15.60	20.80	26.00	31.20	36.40	41.60	46.80	52.00
209	1.31	2.61	5.22	10.45	15.67	20.90	26.12	31.35	36.57	41.80	47.02	52.25
210	1.31	2.62	5.25	10.50	15.75	21.00	26.25	31.50	36.75	42.00	47.25	52.50
211	1.32	2.64	5.27	10.55	15.82	21.10	26.37	31.65	36.92	42.20	47.47	52.75
212	1.32	2.65	5.30	10.60	15.90	21.20	26.50	31.80	37.10	42.40	47.70	53.00
213	1.33	2.66	5.32	10.65	15.97	21.30	26.62	31.95	37.27	42.60	47.92	53.25
214	1.34	2.67	5.35	10.70	16.05	21.40	26.75	32.10	37.45	42.80	48.15	53.50
215	1.34	2.69	5.37	10.75	16.12	21.50	26.87	32.25	37.62	43.00	48.37	53.75
216	1.35	2.70	5.40	10.80	16.20	21.60	27.00	32.40	37.80	43.20	48.60	54.00
217	1.36	2.71	5.42	10.85	16.27	21.70	27.12	32.55	37.97	43.40	48.82	54.25
218	1.36	2.72	5.45	10.90	16.35	21.80	27.25	32.70	38.15	43.60	49.05	54.50
219	1.37	2.74	5.47	10.95	16.42	21.90	27.37	32.85	38.32	43.80	49.27	54.75
220	1.37	2.75	5.50	11.00	16.50	22.00	27.50	33.00	38.50	44.00	49.50	55.00
221	1.38	2.76	5.52	11.05	16.57	22.10	27.62	33.15	38.67	44.20	49.72	55.25
222	1.39	2.77	5.55	11.10	16.65	22.20	27.75	33.30	38.85	44.40	49.95	55.50
223	1.39	2.79	5.57	11.15	16.72	22.30	27.87	33.45	39.02	44.60	50.17	55.75
224	1.40	2.80	5.60	11.20	16.80	22.40	28.00	33.60	39.20	44.80	50.40	56.00
225	1.41	2.81	5.62	11.25	16.87	22.50	28.12	33.75	39.37	45.00	50.62	56.25
226	1.41	2.82	5.65	11.30	16.95	22.60	28.25	33.90	39.55	45.20	50.85	56.50
227	1.42	2.84	5.67	11.35	17.02	22.70	28.37	34.05	39.72	45.40	51.07	56.75
228	1.42	2.85	5.70	11.40	17.10	22.80	28.50	34.20	39.90	45.60	51.30	57.00
229	1.43	2.86	5.72	11.45	17.17	22.90	28.62	34.35	40.07	45.80	51.52	57.25
230	1.44	2.87	5.75	11.50	17.25	23.00	28.75	34.50	40.25	46.00	51.75	57.50
231	1.44	2.89	5.77	11.55	17.32	23.10	28.87	34.65	40.42	46.20	51.97	57.75
232	1.45	2.90	5.80	11.60	17.40	23.20	29.00	34.80	40.60	46.40	52.20	58.00
233	1.46	2.91	5.82	11.65	17.47	23.30	29.12	34.95	40.77	46.60	52.42	58.25
234	1.46	2.92	5.85	11.70	17.55	23.40	29.25	35.10	40.95	46.80	52.65	58.50
235	1.47	2.94	5.87	11.75	17.62	23.50	29.37	35.25	41.12	47.00	52.87	58.75
236	1.47	2.95	5.90	11.80	17.70	23.60	29.50	35.40	41.30	47.20	53.10	59.00
237	1.48	2.96	5.92	11.85	17.77	23.70	29.62	35.55	41.47	47.40	53.32	59.25
238	1.49	2.97	5.95	11.90	17.85	23.80	29.75	35.70	41.65	47.60	53.55	59.50
239	1.49	2.99	5.97	11.95	17.92	23.90	29.87	35.85	41.82	47.80	53.77	59.75
240	1.50	3.00	6.00	12.00	18.00	24.00	30.00	36.00	42.00	48.00	54.00	60.00
241	1.51	3.01	6.02	12.05	18.07	24.10	30.12	36.15	42.17	48.20	54.22	60.25
242	1.51	3.02	6.05	12.10	18.15	24.20	30.25	36.30	42.35	48.40	54.45	60.50
243	1.52	3.04	6.07	12.15	18.22	24.30	30.37	36.45	42.52	48.60	54.67	60.75
244	1.52	3.05	6.10	12.20	18.30	24.40	30.50	36.60	42.70	48.80	54.90	61.00
245	1.53	3.06	6.12	12.25	18.37	24.50	30.62	36.75	42.87	49.00	55.12	61.25
246	1.54	3.07	6.15	12.30	18.45	24.60	30.75	36.90	43.05	49.20	55.35	61.50
247	1.54	3.09	6.17	12.35	18.52	24.70	30.87	37.05	43.22	49.40	55.57	61.75
248	1.55	3.10	6.20	12.40	18.60	24.80	31.00	37.20	43.40	49.60	55.80	62.00
249	1.56	3.11	6.22	12.45	18.67	24.90	31.12	37.25	43.57	49.80	56.02	62.25
250	1.56	3.12	6.25	12.50	18.75	25.00	31.25	37.50	43.75	50.00	56.25	62.50

250 FEET.

Per Ton, Per Foot,	$11 27½ cts.	$12 30 cts.	$13 32½ cts.	$14 35 cts.	$15 37½ cts.	$16 40 cts.	$17 42½ cts.	$18 45 cts.	$19 47½ cts.	$20 50 cts.
Feet.										
201	55.27	60.30	65.32	70.35	75.37	80.40	85.42	90.45	95.47	100.50
202	55.55	60.60	65.65	70.70	75.75	80.80	85.85	90.90	95.95	101.00
203	55.82	60.90	65.97	71.05	76.12	81.20	86.27	91.35	96.42	101.50
204	56.10	61.20	66.30	71.40	76.50	81.60	86.70	91.80	96.90	102.00
205	56.37	61.50	66.62	71.75	76.87	82.00	87.12	92.25	97.37	102.50
206	56.65	61.80	66.95	72.10	77.25	82.40	87.55	92.70	97.85	103.00
207	56.92	62.10	67.27	72.45	77.62	82.80	87.97	93.15	98.32	103.50
208	57.20	62.40	67.60	72.80	78.00	83.20	88.40	93.60	98.80	104.00
209	57.47	62.70	67.92	73.15	78.37	83.60	88.82	94.05	99.27	104.50
210	57.75	63.00	68.25	73.50	78.75	84.00	89.25	94.50	99.75	105.00
211	58.02	63.30	68.57	73.85	79.12	84.40	89.67	94.95	100.22	105.50
212	58.30	63.60	68.90	74.20	79.50	84.80	90.10	95.40	100.70	106.00
213	58.57	63.90	69.22	74.55	79.87	85.20	90.52	95.85	101.17	106.50
214	58.85	64.20	69.55	74.90	80.25	85.60	90.95	96.30	101.65	107.00
215	59.12	64.50	69.87	75.25	80.62	86.00	91.37	96.75	102.12	107.50
216	59.40	64.80	70.20	75.60	81.00	86.40	91.80	97.20	102.60	108.00
217	59.67	65.10	70.52	75.95	81.37	86.80	92.22	97.65	103.07	108.50
218	59.95	65.40	70.85	76.30	81.75	87.20	92.65	98.10	103.55	109.00
219	60.22	65.70	71.17	76.65	82.12	87.60	93.07	98.55	104.02	109.50
220	60.50	66.00	71.50	77.00	82.50	88.00	93.50	99.00	104.50	110.00
221	60.77	66.30	71.82	77.35	82.87	88.40	93.92	99.45	104.97	110.50
222	61.05	66.60	72.15	77.70	83.25	88.80	94.35	99.90	105.45	111.00
223	61.32	66.90	72.47	78.05	83.62	89.20	94.77	100.35	105.92	111.50
224	61.60	67.20	72.80	78.40	84.00	89.60	95.20	100.80	106.40	112.00
225	61.87	67.50	73.12	78.75	84.37	90.00	95.62	101.25	106.87	112.50
226	62.15	67.80	73.45	79.10	84.75	90.40	96.05	101.70	107.35	113.00
227	62.42	68.10	73.77	79.45	85.12	90.80	96.47	102.15	107.82	113.50
228	62.70	68.40	74.10	79.80	85.50	91.20	96.90	102.60	108.30	114.00
229	62.97	68.70	74.42	80.15	85.87	91.60	97.32	103.05	108.77	114.50
230	63.25	69.00	74.75	80.50	86.25	92.00	97.75	103.50	109.25	115.00
231	63.52	69.30	75.07	80.85	86.62	92.40	98.17	103.95	109.72	115.50
232	63.80	69.60	75.40	81.20	87.00	92.80	98.60	104.40	110.20	116.00
233	64.07	69.90	75.72	81.55	87.37	93.20	99.02	104.85	110.67	116.50
234	64.35	70.20	76.05	81.90	87.75	93.60	99.45	105.30	111.15	117.00
235	64.62	70.50	76.37	82.25	88.12	94.00	99.87	105.75	111.62	117.50
236	64.90	70.80	76.70	82.60	88.50	94.40	100.30	106.20	112.10	118.00
237	65.17	71.10	77.02	82.95	88.87	94.80	100.72	106.65	112.57	118.50
238	65.45	71.40	77.35	83.30	89.25	95.20	101.15	107.10	113.05	119.00
239	65.72	71.70	77.67	83.65	89.62	95.60	101.57	107.55	113.52	119.50
240	66.00	72.00	78.00	84.00	90.00	96.00	102.00	108.00	114.00	120.00
241	66.27	72.30	78.32	84.35	90.37	96.40	102.42	108.45	114.47	120.50
242	66.55	72.60	78.65	84.70	90.75	96.80	102.85	108.90	114.95	121.00
243	66.82	72.90	78.97	85.05	91.12	97.20	103.27	109.35	115.42	121.50
244	67.10	73.20	79.30	85.40	91.50	97.60	103.70	109.80	115.90	122.00
245	67.37	73.50	79.62	85.75	91.87	98.00	104.12	110.25	116.37	122.50
246	67.65	73.80	79.95	86.10	92.25	98.40	104.55	110.70	116.85	123.00
247	67.92	74.10	80.27	86.45	92.62	98.80	104.97	111.15	117.32	123.50
248	68.20	74.40	80.60	86.80	93.00	99.20	105.40	111.60	117.80	124.00
249	68.47	74.70	80.92	87.15	93.37	99.60	105.82	112.05	118.27	124.50
250	68.75	75.00	81.25	87.50	93.75	100.00	106.25	112.50	118.75	125.00

2

300 FEET.

Per Ton, Per Foot, Feet.	25c.	50c.	$1 2¼ cts.	$2 5 cts.	$3 7½ cts.	$4 10 cts.	$5 12½ cts.	$6 15 cts.	$7 17½ cts.	$8 20 cts.	$9 22½ cts.	$10 25 cts.
251	1.57	3.14	6.27	12.55	18.82	25.10	31.37	37.65	43.92	50.20	56.47	62.75
252	1.57	3.15	6.30	12.60	18.90	25.20	31.50	37.80	44.10	50.40	56.70	63.00
253	1.58	3.16	6.32	12.65	18.97	25.30	31.62	37.95	44.27	50.60	56.92	63.25
254	1.59	3.17	6.35	12.70	19.05	25.40	31.75	38.10	44.45	50.80	57.15	63.50
255	1.59	3.19	6.37	12.75	19.12	25.50	31.87	38.25	44.62	51.00	57.37	63.75
256	1.60	3.20	6.40	12.80	19.20	25.60	32.00	38.40	44.80	51.20	57.60	64.00
257	1.61	3.21	6.42	12.85	19.27	25.70	32.12	38.55	44.97	51.40	57.82	64.25
258	1.61	3.22	6.45	12.90	19.35	25.80	32.25	38.70	45.15	51.60	58.05	64.50
259	1.62	3.24	6.47	12.95	19.42	25.90	32.37	38.85	45.32	51.80	58.27	64.75
260	1.62	3.25	6.50	13.00	19.50	26.00	32.50	39.00	45.50	52.00	58.50	65.00
261	1.63	3.26	6.52	13.05	19.57	26.10	32.62	39.15	45.67	52.20	58.72	65.25
262	1.64	3.27	6.55	13.10	19.65	26.20	32.75	39.30	45.85	52.40	58.95	65.50
263	1.64	3.29	6.57	13.15	19.72	26.30	32.87	39.45	46.02	52.60	59.17	65.75
264	1.65	3.30	6.60	13.20	19.80	26.40	33.00	39.60	46.20	52.80	59.40	66.00
265	1.66	3.31	6.62	13.25	19.87	26.50	33.12	39.75	46.37	53.00	59.62	66.25
266	1.66	3.32	6.65	13.30	19.95	26.60	33.25	39.90	46.55	53.20	59.85	66.50
267	1.67	3.34	6.67	13.35	20.02	26.70	33.37	40.05	46.72	53.40	60.07	66.75
268	1.67	3.35	6.70	13.40	20.10	26.80	33.50	40.20	46.90	53.60	60.30	67.00
269	1.68	3.36	6.72	13.45	20.17	26.90	33.62	40.35	47.07	53.80	60.52	67.25
270	1.69	3.37	6.75	13.50	20.25	27.00	33.75	40.50	47.25	54.00	60.75	67.50
271	1.69	3.39	6.77	13.55	20.32	27.10	33.87	40.65	47.42	54.20	60.97	67.75
272	1.70	3.40	6.80	13.60	20.40	27.20	34.00	40.80	47.60	54.40	61.20	68.00
273	1.71	3.41	6.82	13.65	20.47	27.30	34.12	40.95	47.77	54.60	61.42	68.25
274	1.71	3.42	6.85	13.70	20.55	27.40	34.25	41.10	47.95	54.80	61.65	68.50
275	1.72	3.44	6.87	13.75	20.62	27.50	34.37	41.25	48.12	55.00	61.87	68.75
276	1.72	3.45	6.90	13.80	20.70	27.60	34.50	41.40	48.30	55.20	62.10	69.00
277	1.73	3.46	6.92	13.85	20.77	27.70	34.62	41.55	48.47	55.40	62.32	69.25
278	1.74	3.47	6.95	13.90	20.85	27.80	34.75	41.70	48.65	55.60	62.55	69.50
279	1.74	3.49	6.97	13.95	20.92	27.90	34.87	41.85	48.82	55.80	62.77	69.75
280	1.75	3.50	7.00	14.00	21.00	28.00	35.00	42.00	49.00	56.00	63.00	70.00
281	1.76	3.51	7.02	14.05	21.07	28.10	35.12	42.15	49.17	56.20	63.22	70.25
282	1.76	3.52	7.05	14.10	21.15	28.20	35.25	42.30	49.35	56.40	63.45	70.50
283	1.77	3.54	7.07	14.15	21.22	28.30	35.37	42.45	49.52	56.60	63.67	70.75
284	1.77	3.55	7.10	14.20	21.30	28.40	35.50	42.60	49.70	56.80	63.90	71.00
285	1.78	3.56	7.12	14.25	21.37	28.50	35.62	42.75	49.87	57.00	64.12	71.25
286	1.79	3.57	7.15	14.30	21.45	28.60	35.75	42.90	50.05	57.20	64.35	71.50
287	1.79	3.59	7.17	14.35	21.52	28.70	35.87	43.05	50.22	57.40	64.57	71.75
288	1.80	3.60	7.20	14.40	21.60	28.80	36.00	43.20	50.40	57.60	64.80	72.00
289	1.81	3.61	7.22	14.45	21.67	28.90	36.12	43.35	50.57	57.80	65.02	72.25
290	1.81	3.62	7.25	14.50	21.75	29.00	36.25	43.50	50.75	58.00	65.25	72.50
291	1.82	3.64	7.27	14.55	21.82	29.10	36.37	43.65	50.92	58.20	65.47	72.75
292	1.82	3.65	7.30	14.60	21.90	29.20	36.50	43.80	51.10	58.40	65.70	73.00
293	1.83	3.66	7.32	14.65	21.97	29.30	36.62	43.95	51.27	58.60	65.92	73.25
294	1.84	3.67	7.35	14.70	22.05	29.40	36.75	44.10	51.45	58.80	66.15	73.50
295	1.84	3.69	7.37	14.75	22.12	29.50	36.87	44.25	51.62	59.00	66.37	73.75
296	1.85	3.70	7.40	14.80	22.20	29.60	37.00	44.40	51.80	59.20	66.60	74.00
297	1.86	3.71	7.42	14.85	22.27	29.70	37.12	44.55	51.97	59.40	66.82	74.25
298	1.86	3.72	7.45	14.90	22.35	29.80	37.25	44.70	52.15	59.60	67.05	74.50
299	1.87	3.74	7.47	14.95	22.42	29.90	37.37	44.85	52.32	59.80	67.27	74.75
300	1.87	3.75	7.50	15.00	22.50	30.00	37.50	45.00	52.50	60.00	67.50	75.00

300 FEET.

Per Ton,	$11	$12	$13	$14	$15	$16	$17	$18	$19	$20
Per Foot,	27½ cts.	30 cts.	32½ cts.	35 cts.	37½ cts.	40 cts.	42½ cts.	45 cts.	47½ cts.	50 cts.
Feet.										
251	69.02	75.30	81.57	87.85	94.12	100.40	106.67	112.95	119.22	125.50
252	69.30	75.60	81.90	88.20	94.50	100.80	107.10	113.40	119.70	126.00
253	69.57	75.90	82.22	88.55	94.87	101.20	107.52	113.85	120.17	126.50
254	69.85	76.20	82.55	88.90	95.25	101.60	107.95	114.30	120.65	127.00
255	70.12	76.50	82.87	89.25	95.62	102.00	108.37	114.75	121.12	127.50
256	70.40	76.80	83.20	89.60	96.00	102.40	108.80	115.20	121.60	128.00
257	70.67	77.10	83.52	89.95	96.37	102.80	109.22	115.65	122.07	128.50
258	70.95	77.40	83.85	90.30	96.75	103.20	109.65	116.10	122.55	129.00
259	71.22	77.70	84.17	90.65	97.12	103.60	110.07	116.55	123.02	129.50
260	71.50	78.00	84.50	91.00	97.50	104.00	110.50	117.00	123.50	130.00
261	71.77	78.30	84.82	91.35	97.87	104.40	110.92	117.45	123.97	130.50
262	72.05	78.60	85.15	91.70	98.25	104.80	111.35	117.90	124.45	131.00
263	72.32	78.90	85.47	92.05	98.62	105.20	111.77	118.35	124.92	131.50
264	72.60	79.20	85.80	92.40	99.00	105.60	112.20	118.80	125.40	132.00
265	72.87	79.50	86.12	92.75	99.37	106.00	112.62	119.25	125.87	132.50
266	73.15	79.80	86.45	93.10	99.75	106.40	113.05	119.70	126.35	133.00
267	73.42	80.10	86.77	93.45	100.12	106.80	113.47	120.15	126.82	133.50
268	73.70	80.40	87.10	93.80	100.50	107.20	113.90	120.60	127.30	134.00
269	73.97	80.70	87.42	94.15	100.87	107.60	114.32	121.05	127.77	134.50
270	74.25	81.00	87.75	94.50	101.25	108.00	114.75	121.50	128.25	135.00
271	74.52	81.30	88.07	94.85	101.62	108.40	115.17	121.95	128.72	135.50
272	74.80	81.60	88.40	95.20	102.00	108.80	115.60	122.40	129.20	136.00
273	75.07	81.90	88.72	95.55	102.37	109.20	116.02	122.85	129.67	136.50
274	75.35	82.20	89.05	95.90	102.75	109.60	116.45	123.30	130.15	137.00
275	75.62	82.50	89.37	96.25	103.12	110.00	116.87	123.75	130.62	137.50
276	75.90	82.80	89.70	96.60	103.50	110.40	117.30	124.20	131.10	138.00
277	76.17	83.10	90.02	96.95	103.87	110.80	117.72	124.65	131.57	138.50
278	76.45	83.40	90.35	97.30	104.25	111.20	118.15	125.10	132.05	139.00
279	76.72	83.70	90.67	97.65	104.62	111.60	118.57	125.55	132.52	139.50
280	77.00	84.00	91.00	98.00	105.00	112.00	119.00	126.00	133.00	140.00
281	77.27	84.30	91.32	98.35	105.37	112.40	119.42	126.45	133.47	140.50
282	77.55	84.60	91.65	98.70	105.75	112.80	119.85	126.90	133.95	141.00
283	77.82	84.90	91.97	99.05	106.12	113.20	120.27	127.35	134.42	141.50
284	78.10	85.20	92.30	99.40	106.50	113.60	120.70	127.80	134.90	142.00
285	78.37	85.50	92.62	99.75	106.87	114.00	121.12	128.25	135.37	142.50
286	78.65	85.80	92.95	100.10	107.25	114.40	121.55	128.70	135.85	143.00
287	78.92	86.10	93.27	100.45	107.62	114.80	121.97	129.15	136.32	143.50
288	79.20	86.40	93.60	100.80	108.00	115.20	122.40	129.60	136.80	144.00
289	79.47	86.70	93.92	101.15	108.37	115.60	122.82	130.05	137.27	144.50
290	79.75	87.00	94.25	101.50	108.75	116.00	123.25	130.50	137.75	145.00
291	80.02	87.30	94.57	101.85	109.12	116.40	123.67	130.95	138.22	145.50
292	80.30	87.60	94.90	102.20	109.50	116.80	124.10	131.40	138.70	146.00
293	80.57	87.90	95.22	102.55	109.87	117.20	124.52	131.85	139.17	146.50
294	80.85	88.20	95.55	102.90	110.25	117.60	124.95	132.30	139.65	147.00
295	81.12	88.50	95.87	103.25	110.62	118.00	125.37	132.75	140.12	147.50
296	81.40	88.80	96.20	103.60	111.00	118.40	125.80	133.20	140.60	148.00
297	81.67	89.10	96.52	103.95	111.37	118.80	126.22	133.65	141.07	148.50
298	81.95	89.40	96.85	104.30	111.75	119.20	126.65	134.10	141.55	149.00
299	82.22	89.70	97.17	104.65	112.12	119.60	127.07	134.55	142.02	149.50
300	82.50	90.00	97.50	105.00	112.50	120.00	127.50	135.00	142.50	150.00

350 FEET.

Per Ton,	25c.	50c.	$1	$2	$3	$4	$5	$6	$7	$8	$9	$10
Per Foot,			2½ cts.	5 cts.	7½ cts.	10 cts.	12½ cts.	15 cts.	17½ cts.	20 cts.	22½ cts.	25 cts.
Feet.												
301	1.88	3.76	7.52	15.05	22.57	30.10	37.62	45.15	52.67	60.20	67.72	75.25
302	1.89	3.77	7.55	15.10	22.65	30.20	37.75	45.30	52.85	60.40	67.95	75.50
303	1.89	3.79	7.57	15.15	22.72	30.30	37.87	45.45	53.02	60.60	68.17	75.75
304	1.90	3.80	7.60	15.20	22.80	30.40	38.00	45.60	53.20	60.80	68.40	76.00
305	1.91	3.81	7.62	15.25	22.87	30.50	38.12	45.75	53.37	61.00	68.62	76.25
306	1.91	3.82	7.65	15.30	22.95	30.60	38.25	45.90	53.55	61.20	68.85	76.50
307	1.92	3.84	7.67	15.35	23.02	30.70	38.37	46.05	53.72	61.40	69.07	76.75
308	1.92	3.85	7.70	15.40	23.10	30.80	38.50	46.20	53.90	61.60	69.30	77.00
309	1.93	3.86	7.72	15.45	23.17	30.90	38.62	46.35	54.07	61.80	69.52	77.25
310	1.94	3.87	7.75	15.50	23.25	31.00	38.75	46.50	54.25	62.00	69.75	77.50
311	1.94	3.89	7.77	15.55	23.32	31.10	38.87	46.65	54.42	62.20	69.97	77.75
312	1.95	3.90	7.80	15.60	23.40	31.20	39.00	46.80	54.60	62.40	70.20	78.00
313	1.96	3.91	7.82	15.65	23.47	31.30	39.12	46.95	54.77	62.60	70.42	78.25
314	1.96	3.92	7.85	15.70	23.55	31.40	39.25	47.10	54.95	62.80	70.65	78.50
315	1.97	3.94	7.87	15.75	23.62	31.50	39.37	47.25	55.12	63.00	70.87	78.75
316	1.97	3.95	7.90	15.80	23.70	31.60	39.50	47.40	55.30	63.20	71.10	79.00
317	1.98	3.96	7.92	15.85	23.77	31.70	39.62	47.55	55.47	63.40	71.32	79.25
318	1.99	3.97	7.95	15.90	23.85	31.80	39.75	47.70	55.65	63.60	71.55	79.50
319	1.99	3.99	7.97	15.95	23.92	31.90	39.87	47.85	55.82	63.80	71.77	79.75
320	2.00	4.00	8.00	16.00	24.00	32.00	40.00	48.00	56.00	64.00	72.00	80.00
321	2.01	4.01	8.02	16.05	24.07	32.10	40.12	48.15	56.17	64.20	72.22	80.25
322	2.01	4.02	8.05	16.10	24.15	32.20	40.25	48.30	56.35	64.40	72.45	80.50
323	2.02	4.04	8.07	16.15	24.22	32.30	40.37	48.45	56.52	64.60	72.67	80.75
324	2.02	4.05	8.10	16.20	24.30	32.40	40.50	48.60	56.70	64.80	72.90	81.00
325	2.03	4.06	8.12	16.25	24.37	32.50	40.62	48.75	56.87	65.00	73.12	81.25
326	2.04	4.07	8.15	16.30	24.45	32.60	40.75	48.90	57.05	65.20	73.35	81.50
327	2.04	4.09	8.17	16.35	24.52	32.70	40.87	49.05	57.22	65.40	73.57	81.75
328	2.05	4.10	8.20	16.40	24.60	32.80	41.00	49.20	57.40	65.60	73.80	82.00
329	2.06	4.11	8.22	16.45	24.67	32.90	41.12	49.35	57.57	65.80	74.02	82.25
330	2.06	4.12	8.25	16.50	24.75	33.00	41.25	49.50	57.75	66.00	74.25	82.50
331	2.07	4.14	8.27	16.55	24.82	33.10	41.37	49.65	57.92	66.20	74.47	82.75
332	2.07	4.15	8.30	16.60	24.90	33.20	41.50	49.80	58.10	66.40	74.70	83.00
333	2.08	4.16	8.32	16.65	24.97	33.30	41.62	49.95	58.27	66.60	74.92	83.25
334	2.09	4.17	8.35	16.70	25.05	33.40	41.75	50.10	58.45	66.80	75.15	83.50
335	2.09	4.19	8.37	16.75	25.12	33.50	41.87	50.25	58.62	67.00	75.37	83.75
336	2.10	4.20	8.40	16.80	25.20	33.60	42.00	50.40	58.80	67.20	75.60	84.00
337	2.11	4.21	8.42	16.85	25.27	33.70	42.12	50.55	58.97	67.40	75.82	84.25
338	2.11	4.22	8.45	16.90	25.35	33.80	42.25	50.70	59.15	67.60	76.05	84.50
339	2.12	4.24	8.47	16.95	25.42	33.90	42.37	50.85	59.32	67.80	76.27	84.75
340	2.12	4.25	8.50	17.00	25.50	34.00	42.50	51.00	59.50	68.00	76.50	85.00
341	2.13	4.26	8.52	17.05	25.57	34.10	42.62	51.15	59.67	68.20	76.72	85.25
342	2.14	4.27	8.55	17.10	25.65	34.20	42.75	51.30	59.85	68.40	76.95	85.50
343	2.14	4.29	8.57	17.15	25.72	34.30	42.87	51.45	60.02	68.60	77.17	85.75
344	2.15	4.30	8.60	17.20	25.80	34.40	43.00	51.60	60.20	68.80	77.40	86.00
345	2.16	4.31	8.62	17.25	25.87	34.50	43.12	51.75	60.37	69.00	77.62	86.25
346	2.16	4.32	8.65	17.30	25.95	34.60	43.25	51.90	60.55	69.20	77.85	86.50
347	2.17	4.34	8.67	17.35	26.02	34.70	43.37	52.05	60.72	69.40	78.07	86.75
348	2.17	4.35	8.70	17.40	26.10	34.80	43.50	52.20	60.90	69.60	78.30	87.00
349	2.18	4.36	8.72	17.45	26.17	34.90	43.62	52.35	61.07	69.80	78.52	87.25
350	2.19	4.37	8.75	17.50	26.25	35.00	43.75	52.50	61.25	70.00	78.75	87.50

350 FEET.

Per Ton, Per Foot,	$11 27½ cts.	$12 30 cts.	$13 32½ cts.	$14 35 cts.	$15 37½ cts.	$16 40 cts.	$17 42½ cts.	$18 45 cts.	$19 47½ cts.	$20 50 cts.
Feet.										
301	82.77	90.30	97.82	105.35	112.87	120.40	127.92	135.45	142.97	150.50
302	83.05	90.60	98.15	105.70	113.25	120.80	128.35	135.90	143.45	151.00
303	83.32	90.90	98.47	106.05	113.62	121.20	128.77	136.35	143.92	151.50
304	83.60	91.20	98.80	106.40	114.00	121.60	129.20	136.80	144.40	152.00
305	83.87	91.50	99.12	106.75	114.37	122.00	129.62	137.25	144.87	152.50
306	84.15	91.80	99.45	107.10	114.75	122.40	130.05	137.70	145.35	153.00
307	84.42	92.10	99.77	107.45	115.12	122.80	130.47	138.15	145.82	153.50
308	84.70	92.40	100.10	107.80	115.50	123.20	130.90	138.60	146.30	154.00
309	84.97	92.70	100.42	108.15	115.87	123.60	131.32	139.05	146.77	154.50
310	85.25	93.00	100.75	108.50	116.25	124.00	131.75	139.50	147.25	155.00
311	85.52	93.30	101.07	108.85	116.62	124.40	132.17	139.95	147.72	155.50
312	85.80	93.60	101.40	109.20	117.00	124.80	132.60	140.40	148.20	156.00
313	86.07	93.90	101.72	109.55	117.37	125.20	133.02	140.85	148.67	156.50
314	86.35	94.20	102.05	109.90	117.75	125.60	133.45	141.30	149.15	157.00
315	86.62	94.50	102.37	110.25	118.12	126.00	133.87	141.75	149.62	157.50
316	86.90	94.80	102.70	110.60	118.50	126.40	134.30	142.20	150.10	158.00
317	87.17	95.10	103.02	110.95	118.87	126.80	134.72	142.65	150.57	158.50
318	87.45	95.40	103.35	111.30	119.25	127.20	135.15	143.10	151.05	159.00
319	87.72	95.70	103.67	111.65	119.62	127.60	135.57	143.55	151.52	159.50
320	88.00	96.00	104.00	112.00	120.00	128.00	136.00	144.00	152.00	160.00
321	88.27	96.30	104.32	112.35	120.37	128.40	136.42	144.45	152.47	160.50
322	88.55	96.60	104.65	112.70	120.75	128.80	136.85	144.90	152.95	161.00
323	88.82	96.90	104.97	113.05	121.12	129.20	137.27	145.35	153.42	161.50
324	89.10	97.20	105.30	113.40	121.50	129.60	137.70	145.80	153.90	162.00
325	89.37	97.50	105.62	113.75	121.87	130.00	138.12	146.25	154.37	162.50
326	89.65	97.80	105.95	114.10	122.25	130.40	138.55	146.70	154.85	163.00
327	89.92	98.10	106.27	114.45	122.62	130.80	138.97	147.15	155.32	163.50
328	90.20	98.40	106.60	114.80	123.00	131.20	139.40	147.60	155.80	164.00
329	90.47	98.70	106.92	115.15	123.37	131.60	139.82	148.05	156.27	164.50
330	90.75	99.00	107.25	115.50	123.75	132.00	140.25	148.50	156.75	165.00
331	91.02	99.30	107.57	115.85	124.12	132.40	140.67	148.95	157.22	165.50
332	91.30	99.60	107.90	116.20	124.50	132.80	141.10	149.40	157.70	166.00
333	91.57	99.90	108.22	116.55	124.87	133.20	141.52	149.85	158.17	166.50
334	91.85	100.20	108.55	116.90	125.25	133.60	141.95	150.30	158.65	167.00
335	92.12	100.50	108.87	117.25	125.62	134.00	142.37	150.75	159.12	167.50
336	92.40	100.80	109.20	117.60	126.00	134.40	142.80	151.20	159.60	168.00
337	92.67	101.10	109.52	117.95	126.37	134.80	143.22	151.65	160.07	168.50
338	92.95	101.40	109.85	118.30	126.75	135.20	143.65	152.10	160.55	169.00
339	93.22	101.70	110.17	118.65	127.12	135.60	144.07	152.55	161.02	169.50
340	93.50	102.00	110.50	119.00	127.50	136.00	144.50	153.00	161.50	170.00
341	93.77	102.30	110.82	119.35	127.87	136.40	144.92	153.45	161.97	170.50
342	94.05	102.60	111.15	119.70	128.25	136.80	145.35	153.90	162.45	171.00
343	94.32	102.90	111.47	120.05	128.62	137.20	145.77	154.35	162.92	171.50
344	94.60	103.20	111.80	120.40	129.00	137.60	146.20	154.80	163.40	172.00
345	94.87	103.50	112.12	120.75	129.37	138.00	146.62	155.25	163.87	172.50
346	95.15	103.80	112.45	121.10	129.75	138.40	147.05	155.70	164.35	173.00
347	95.42	104.10	112.77	121.45	130.12	138.80	147.47	156.15	164.82	173.50
348	95.70	104.40	113.10	121.80	130.50	139.20	147.90	156.60	165.30	174.00
349	95.97	104.70	113.42	122.15	130.87	139.60	148.32	157.05	165.77	174.50
350	96.25	105.00	113.75	122.50	131.25	140.00	148.75	157.50	166.25	175.00

400 FEET.

Per Ton,	25c.	50c.	$1	$2	$3	$4	$5	$6	$7	$8	$9	$10
Per Foot,			2½ cts.	5 cts.	7½ cts.	10 cts.	12½ cts.	15 cts.	17½ cts.	20 cts.	22½ cts.	25 cts.
Feet.												
351	2.19	4.39	8.77	17.55	26.32	35.10	43.87	52.65	61.42	70.20	78.97	87.75
352	2.20	4.40	8.80	17.60	26.40	35.20	44.00	52.80	61.60	70.40	79.20	88.00
353	2.21	4.41	8.82	17.65	26.47	35.30	44.12	52.95	61.77	70.60	79.42	88.25
354	2.21	4.42	8.85	17.70	26.55	35.40	44.25	53.10	61.95	70.80	79.65	88.50
355	2.22	4.44	8.87	17.75	26.62	35.50	44.37	53.25	62.12	71.00	79.87	88.75
356	2.22	4.45	8.90	17.80	26.70	35.60	44.50	53.40	62.30	71.20	80.10	89.00
357	2.23	4.46	8.92	17.85	26.77	35.70	44.62	53.55	62.47	71.40	80.32	89.25
358	2.24	4.47	8.95	17.90	26.85	35.80	44.75	53.70	62.65	71.60	80.55	89.50
359	2.24	4.49	8.97	17.95	26.92	35.90	44.87	53.85	62.82	71.80	80.77	89.75
360	2.25	4.50	9.00	18.00	27.00	36.00	45.00	54.00	63.00	72.00	81.00	90.00
361	2.26	4.51	9.02	18.05	27.07	36.10	45.12	54.15	63.17	72.20	81.22	90.25
362	2.26	4.52	9.05	18.10	27.15	36.20	45.25	54.30	63.35	72.40	81.45	90.50
363	2.27	4.54	9.07	18.15	27.22	36.30	45.37	54.45	63.52	72.60	81.67	90.75
364	2.27	4.55	9.10	18.20	27.30	36.40	45.50	54.60	63.70	72.80	81.90	91.00
365	2.28	4.56	9.12	18.25	27.37	36.50	45.62	54.75	63.87	73.00	82.12	91.25
366	2.29	4.57	9.15	18.30	27.45	36.60	45.75	54.90	64.05	73.20	82.35	91.50
367	2.29	4.59	9.17	18.35	27.52	36.70	45.87	55.05	64.22	73.40	82.57	91.75
368	2.30	4.60	9.20	18.40	27.60	36.80	46.00	55.20	64.40	73.60	82.80	92.00
369	2.31	4.61	9.22	18.45	27.67	36.90	46.12	55.35	64.57	73.80	83.02	92.25
370	2.31	4.62	9.25	18.50	27.75	37.00	46.25	55.50	64.75	74.00	83.25	92.50
371	2.32	4.64	9.27	18.55	27.82	37.10	46.37	55.65	64.92	74.20	83.47	92.75
372	2.32	4.65	9.30	18.60	27.90	37.20	46.50	55.80	65.10	74.40	83.70	93.00
373	2.33	4.66	9.32	18.65	27.97	37.30	46.62	55.95	65.27	74.60	83.92	93.25
374	2.34	4.67	9.35	18.70	28.05	37.40	46.75	56.10	65.45	74.80	84.15	93.50
375	2.34	4.69	9.37	18.75	28.12	37.50	46.87	56.25	65.62	75.00	84.37	93.75
376	2.35	4.70	9.40	18.80	28.20	37.60	47.00	56.40	65.80	75.20	84.60	94.00
377	2.36	4.71	9.42	18.85	28.27	37.70	47.12	56.55	65.97	75.40	84.82	94.25
378	2.36	4.72	9.45	18.90	28.35	37.80	47.25	56.70	66.15	75.60	85.05	94.50
379	2.37	4.74	9.47	18.95	28.42	37.90	47.37	56.85	66.32	75.80	85.27	94.75
380	2.37	4.75	9.50	19.00	28.50	38.00	47.50	57.00	66.50	76.00	85.50	95.00
381	2.38	4.76	9.52	19.05	28.57	38.10	47.62	57.15	66.67	76.20	85.72	95.25
382	2.39	4.77	9.55	19.10	28.65	38.20	47.75	57.30	66.85	76.40	85.95	95.50
383	2.39	4.79	9.57	19.15	28.72	38.30	47.87	57.45	67.02	76.60	86.17	95.75
384	2.40	4.80	9.60	19.20	28.80	38.40	48.00	57.60	67.20	76.80	86.40	96.00
385	2.41	4.81	9.62	19.25	28.87	38.50	48.12	57.75	67.37	77.00	86.62	96.25
386	2.41	4.82	9.65	19.30	28.95	38.60	48.25	57.90	67.55	77.20	86.85	96.50
387	2.42	4.84	9.67	19.35	29.02	38.70	48.37	58.05	67.72	77.40	87.07	96.75
388	2.42	4.85	9.70	19.40	29.10	38.80	48.50	58.20	67.90	77.60	87.30	97.00
389	2.43	4.86	9.72	19.45	29.17	38.90	48.62	58.35	68.07	77.80	87.52	97.25
390	2.44	4.87	9.75	19.50	29.25	39.00	48.75	58.50	68.25	78.00	87.75	97.50
391	2.44	4.89	9.77	19.55	29.32	39.10	48.87	58.65	68.42	78.20	88.97	97.75
392	2.45	4.90	9.80	19.60	29.40	39.20	49.00	58.80	68.60	78.40	88.20	98.00
393	2.46	4.91	9.82	19.65	29.47	39.30	49.12	59.95	68.77	78.60	88.42	98.25
394	2.46	4.92	9.85	19.70	29.55	39.40	49.25	59.10	68.95	78.80	88.65	98.50
395	2.47	4.94	9.87	19.75	29.62	39.50	49.37	59.25	69.12	79.00	88.87	98.75
396	2.47	4.95	9.90	19.80	29.70	39.60	49.50	59.40	69.30	79.20	89.10	99.00
397	2.48	4.96	9.92	19.85	29.77	39.70	49.62	59.55	69.47	79.40	89.32	99.25
398	2.49	4.97	9.95	19.90	29.85	39.80	49.75	59.70	69.65	79.60	89.55	99.50
399	2.49	4.99	9.97	19.95	29.92	39.90	49.87	59.85	69.82	79.80	89.77	99.75
400	2.50	5.00	10.00	20.00	30.00	40.00	50.00	60.00	70.00	80.00	90.00	100.00

400 FEET.

Per Ton,	$11	$12	$13	$14	$15	$16	$17	$18	$19	$20
Per Foot,	27½ cts.	30 cts.	32½ cts.	35 cts.	37½ cts.	40 cts.	42½ cts.	45 cts.	47½ cts.	50 cts.
Feet.										
351	96.52	105.30	114.07	122.85	131.62	140.40	149.17	157.95	166.72	175.50
352	96.80	105.60	114.40	123.20	132.00	140.80	149.60	158.40	167.20	176.00
353	97.07	105.90	114.72	123.55	132.37	141.20	150.02	158.85	167.67	176.50
354	97.35	106.20	115.05	123.90	132.75	141.60	150.45	159.30	168.15	177.00
355	97.62	106.50	115.37	124.25	133.12	142.00	150.87	159.75	168.62	177.50
356	97.90	106.80	115.70	124.60	133.50	142.40	151.30	160.20	169.10	178.00
357	98.17	107.10	116.02	124.95	133.87	142.80	151.72	160.65	169.57	178.50
358	98.45	107.40	116.35	125.30	134.25	143.20	152.15	161.10	170.05	179.00
359	98.72	107.70	116.67	125.65	134.62	143.60	152.57	161.55	170.52	179.50
360	99.00	108.00	117.00	126.00	135.00	144.00	153.00	162.00	171.00	180.00
361	99.27	108.30	117.32	126.35	135.37	144.40	153.42	162.45	171.47	180.50
362	99.55	108.60	117.65	126.70	135.75	144.80	153.85	162.90	171.95	181.00
363	99.82	108.90	117.97	127.05	136.12	145.20	154.27	163.35	172.42	181.50
364	100.10	109.20	118.30	127.40	136.50	145.60	154.70	163.80	172.90	182.00
365	100.37	109.50	118.62	127.75	136.87	146.00	155.12	164.25	173.37	182.50
366	100.65	109.80	118.95	128.10	137.25	146.40	155.55	164.70	173.85	183.00
367	100.92	110.10	119.27	128.45	137.62	146.80	155.97	165.15	174.32	183.50
368	101.20	110.40	119.60	128.80	138.00	147.20	156.40	165.60	174.80	184.00
369	101.47	110.70	119.92	129.15	138.37	147.60	156.82	166.05	175.27	184.50
370	101.75	111.00	120.25	129.50	138.75	148.00	157.25	166.50	175.75	185.00
371	102.02	111.30	120.57	129.85	139.12	148.40	157.67	166.95	176.22	185.50
372	102.30	111.60	120.90	130.20	139.50	148.80	158.10	167.40	176.70	186.00
373	102.57	111.90	121.22	130.55	139.87	149.20	158.52	167.85	177.17	186.50
374	102.85	112.20	121.55	130.90	140.25	149.60	158.95	168.30	177.65	187.00
375	103.12	112.50	121.87	131.25	140.62	150.00	159.37	168.75	178.12	187.50
376	103.40	112.80	122.20	131.60	141.00	150.40	159.80	169.20	178.60	188.00
377	103.67	113.10	122.52	131.95	141.37	150.80	160.22	169.65	179.07	188.50
378	103.95	113.40	122.85	132.30	141.75	151.20	160.65	170.10	179.55	189.00
379	104.22	113.70	123.17	132.65	142.12	151.60	161.07	170.55	180.02	189.50
380	104.50	114.00	123.50	133.00	142.50	152.00	161.50	171.00	180.50	190.00
381	104.77	114.30	123.82	133.35	142.87	152.40	161.92	171.45	180.97	190.50
382	105.05	114.60	124.15	133.70	143.25	152.80	162.35	171.90	181.45	191.00
383	105.32	114.90	124.47	134.05	143.62	153.20	162.77	172.35	181.92	191.50
384	105.60	115.20	124.80	134.40	144.00	153.60	163.20	172.80	182.40	192.00
385	105.87	115.50	125.12	134.75	144.37	154.00	163.62	173.25	182.87	192.50
386	106.15	115.80	125.45	135.10	144.75	154.40	164.05	173.70	183.35	193.00
387	106.42	116.10	125.77	135.45	145.12	154.80	164.47	174.15	183.82	193.50
388	106.70	116.40	126.10	135.80	145.50	155.20	164.90	174.60	184.30	194.00
389	106.97	116.70	126.42	136.15	145.87	155.60	165.32	175.05	184.77	194.50
390	107.25	117.00	126.75	136.50	146.25	156.00	165.75	175.50	185.25	195.00
391	107.52	117.30	127.07	136.85	146.62	156.40	166.17	175.95	185.72	195.50
392	107.80	117.60	127.40	137.20	147.00	156.80	166.60	176.40	186.20	196.00
393	108.07	117.90	127.72	137.55	147.37	157.20	167.02	176.85	186.67	196.50
394	108.35	118.20	128.05	137.90	147.75	157.60	167.45	177.30	187.15	197.00
395	108.62	118.50	128.37	138.25	148.12	158.00	167.87	177.75	187.62	197.50
396	108.90	118.80	128.70	138.60	148.50	158.40	168.30	178.20	188.10	198.00
397	109.17	119.10	129.02	138.95	148.87	158.80	168.72	178.65	188.57	198.50
398	109.45	119.40	129.35	139.30	149.25	159.20	169.15	179.10	189.05	199.00
399	109.72	119.70	129.67	139.65	149.62	159.60	169.57	179.55	189.52	199.50
400	110.00	120.00	130.00	140.00	150.00	160.00	170.00	180.00	190.00	200.00

450 FEET.

Per Ton,	25c.	50c.	$1	$2	$3	$4	$5	$6	$7	$8	$9	$10
Per Foot,			2½ cts.	5 cts.	7½ cts.	10 cts.	12½ cts.	15 cts.	17½ cts.	20 cts.	22½ cts.	25 cts.
Feet.												
401	2.51	5.01	10.02	20.05	30.07	40.10	50.12	60.15	70.17	80.20	90.22	100.25
402	2.51	5.02	10.05	20.10	30.15	40.20	50.25	60.30	70.35	80.40	90.45	100.50
403	2.52	5.04	10.07	20.15	30.22	40.30	50.37	60.45	70.52	80.60	90.67	100.75
404	2.52	5.05	10.10	20.20	30.30	40.40	50.50	60.60	70.70	80.80	90.90	101.00
405	2.53	5.06	10.12	20.25	30.37	40.50	50.62	60.75	70.87	81.00	91.12	101.25
406	2.54	5.07	10.15	20.30	30.45	40.60	50.75	60.90	71.05	81.20	91.35	101.50
407	2.54	5.09	10.17	20.35	30.52	40.70	50.87	61.05	71.22	81.40	91.57	101.75
408	2.55	5.10	10.20	20.40	30.60	40.80	51.00	61.20	71.40	81.60	91.80	102.00
409	2.56	5.11	10.22	20.45	30.67	40.90	51.12	61.35	71.57	81.80	92.02	102.25
410	2.56	5.12	10.25	20.50	30.75	41.00	51.25	61.50	71.75	82.00	92.25	102.50
411	2.57	5.14	10.27	20.55	30.82	41.10	51.37	61.65	71.92	82.20	92.47	102.75
412	2.57	5.15	10.30	20.60	30.90	41.20	51.50	61.80	72.10	82.40	92.70	103.00
413	2.58	5.16	10.32	20.65	30.97	41.30	51.62	61.95	72.27	82.60	92.92	103.25
414	2.59	5.17	10.35	20.70	31.05	41.40	51.75	62.10	72.45	82.80	93.15	103.50
415	2.59	5.19	10.37	20.75	31.12	41.50	51.87	62.25	72.62	83.00	93.37	103.75
416	2.60	5.20	10.40	20.80	31.20	41.60	52.00	62.40	72.80	83.20	93.60	104.00
417	2.61	5.21	10.42	20.85	31.27	41.70	52.12	62.55	72.97	83.40	93.82	104.25
418	2.61	5.22	10.45	20.90	31.35	41.80	52.25	62.70	73.15	83.60	94.05	104.50
419	2.62	5.24	10.47	20.95	31.42	41.90	52.37	62.85	73.32	83.80	94.27	104.75
420	2.62	5.25	10.50	21.00	31.50	42.00	52.50	63.00	73.50	84.00	94.50	105.00
421	2.63	5.26	10.52	21.05	31.57	42.10	52.62	63.15	73.67	84.20	94.72	105.25
422	2.64	5.27	10.55	21.10	31.65	42.20	52.75	63.30	73.85	84.40	94.95	105.50
423	2.64	5.29	10.57	21.15	31.72	42.30	52.87	63.45	74.02	84.60	95.17	105.75
424	2.65	5.30	10.60	21.20	31.80	42.40	53.00	63.60	74.20	84.80	95.40	106.00
425	2.66	5.31	10.62	21.25	31.87	42.50	53.12	63.75	74.37	85.00	95.62	106.25
426	2.66	5.32	10.65	21.30	31.95	42.60	53.25	63.90	74.55	85.20	95.85	106.50
427	2.67	5.34	10.67	21.35	32.02	42.70	53.37	64.05	74.72	85.40	96.07	106.75
428	2.67	5.35	10.70	21.40	32.10	42.80	53.50	64.20	74.90	85.60	96.30	107.00
429	2.68	5.36	10.72	21.45	32.17	42.90	53.62	64.35	75.07	85.80	96.52	107.25
430	2.69	5.37	10.75	21.50	32.25	43.00	53.75	64.50	75.25	86.00	96.75	107.50
431	2.69	5.39	10.77	21.55	32.32	43.10	53.87	64.65	75.42	86.20	96.97	107.75
432	2.70	5.40	10.80	21.60	32.40	43.20	54.00	64.80	75.60	86.40	97.20	108.00
433	2.71	5.41	10.82	21.65	32.47	43.30	54.12	64.95	75.77	86.60	97.42	108.25
434	2.71	5.42	10.85	21.70	32.55	43.40	54.25	65.10	75.95	86.80	97.65	108.50
435	2.72	5.44	10.87	21.75	32.62	43.50	54.37	65.25	76.12	87.00	97.87	108.75
436	2.72	5.45	10.90	21.80	32.70	43.60	54.50	65.40	76.30	87.20	98.10	109.00
437	2.73	5.46	10.92	21.85	32.77	43.70	54.62	65.55	76.47	87.40	98.32	109.25
438	2.74	5.47	10.95	21.90	32.85	43.80	54.75	65.70	76.65	87.60	98.55	109.50
439	2.74	5.49	10.97	21.95	32.92	43.90	54.87	65.85	76.82	87.80	98.77	109.75
440	2.75	5.50	11.00	22.00	33.00	44.00	55.00	66.00	77.00	88.00	99.00	110.00
441	2.76	5.51	11.02	22.05	33.07	44.10	55.12	66.15	77.17	88.20	99.22	110.25
442	2.76	5.52	11.05	22.10	33.15	44.20	55.25	66.30	77.35	88.40	99.45	110.50
443	2.77	5.54	11.07	22.15	33.22	44.30	55.37	66.45	77.52	88.60	99.67	110.75
444	2.77	5.55	11.10	22.20	33.30	44.40	55.50	66.60	77.70	88.80	99.90	111.00
445	2.78	5.56	11.12	22.25	33.37	44.50	55.62	66.75	77.87	89.00	100.12	111.25
446	2.79	5.57	11.15	22.30	33.45	44.60	55.75	66.90	78.05	89.20	100.35	111.50
447	2.79	5.59	11.17	22.35	33.52	44.70	55.87	67.05	78.22	89.40	100.57	111.75
448	2.80	5.60	11.20	22.40	33.60	44.80	56.00	67.20	78.40	89.60	100.80	112.00
449	2.81	5.61	11.22	22.45	33.67	44.90	56.12	67.35	78.57	89.80	101.02	112.25
450	2.81	5.62	11.25	22.50	33.75	45.00	56.25	67.50	78.75	90.00	101.25	112.50

450 FEET.

Per Ton,	$11	$12	$13	$14	$15	$16	$17	$18	$19	$20
Per Foot,	27½ cts.	30 cts.	32½ cts.	35 cts.	37½ cts.	40 cts.	42½ cts.	45 cts.	47½ cts.	50 cts.
Feet.										
401	110.27	120.30	130.32	140.35	150.37	160.40	170.42	180.45	190.47	200.50
402	110.55	120.60	130.65	140.70	150.75	160.80	170.85	180.90	190.95	201.00
403	110.82	120.90	130.97	141.05	151.12	161.20	171.27	181.35	191.42	201.50
404	111.10	121.20	131.30	141.40	151.50	161.60	171.70	181.80	191.90	202.00
405	111.37	121.50	131.62	141.75	151.87	162.00	172.12	182.25	192.37	202.50
406	111.65	121.80	131.95	142.10	152.25	162.40	172.55	182.70	192.85	203.00
407	111.92	122.10	132.27	142.45	152.62	162.80	172.97	183.15	193.32	203.50
408	112.20	122.40	132.60	142.80	153.00	163.20	173.40	183.60	193.80	204.00
409	112.47	122.70	132.92	143.15	153.37	163.60	173.82	184.05	194.27	204.50
410	112.75	123.00	133.25	143.50	153.75	164.00	174.25	184.50	194.75	205.00
411	113.02	123.30	133.57	143.85	154.12	164.40	174.67	184.95	195.22	205.50
412	113.30	123.60	133.90	144.20	154.50	164.80	175.10	185.40	195.70	206.00
413	113.57	123.90	134.22	144.55	154.87	165.20	175.52	185.85	196.17	206.50
414	113.85	124.20	134.55	144.90	155.25	165.60	175.95	186.30	196.65	207.00
415	114.12	124.50	134.87	145.25	155.62	166.00	176.37	186.75	197.12	207.50
416	114.40	124.80	135.20	145.60	156.00	166.40	176.80	187.20	197.60	208.00
417	114.67	125.10	135.52	145.95	156.37	166.80	177.22	187.65	198.07	208.50
418	114.95	125.40	135.85	146.30	156.75	167.20	177.65	188.10	198.55	209.00
419	115.22	125.70	136.17	146.65	157.12	167.60	178.07	188.55	199.02	209.50
420	115.50	126.00	136.50	147.00	157.50	168.00	178.50	189.00	199.50	210.00
421	115.77	126.30	136.82	147.35	157.87	168.40	178.92	189.45	199.97	210.50
422	116.05	126.60	137.15	147.70	158.25	168.80	179.35	189.90	200.45	211.00
423	116.32	126.90	137.47	148.05	158.62	169.20	179.77	190.35	200.92	211.50
424	116.60	127.20	137.80	148.40	159.00	169.60	180.20	190.80	201.40	212.00
425	116.87	127.50	138.12	148.75	159.37	170.00	180.62	191.25	201.87	212.50
426	117.15	127.80	138.45	149.10	159.75	170.40	181.05	191.70	202.35	213.00
427	117.42	128.10	138.77	149.45	160.12	170.80	181.47	192.15	202.82	213.50
428	117.70	128.40	139.10	149.80	160.50	171.20	181.90	192.60	203.30	214.00
429	117.97	128.70	139.42	150.15	160.87	171.60	182.32	193.05	203.77	214.50
430	118.25	129.00	139.75	150.50	161.25	172.00	182.75	193.50	204.25	215.00
431	118.52	129.30	140.07	150.85	161.62	172.40	183.17	193.95	204.72	215.50
432	118.80	129.60	140.40	151.20	162.00	172.80	183.60	194.40	205.20	216.00
433	119.07	129.90	140.72	151.55	162.37	173.20	184.02	194.85	205.67	216.50
434	119.35	130.20	141.05	151.90	162.75	173.60	184.45	195.30	206.15	217.00
435	119.62	130.50	141.37	152.25	163.12	174.00	184.87	195.75	206.62	217.50
436	119.90	130.80	141.70	152.60	163.50	174.40	185.30	196.20	207.10	218.00
437	120.17	131.10	142.02	152.95	163.87	174.80	185.72	196.65	207.57	218.50
438	120.45	131.40	142.35	153.30	164.25	175.20	186.15	197.10	208.05	219.00
439	120.72	131.70	142.67	153.65	164.62	175.60	186.57	197.55	208.52	219.50
440	121.00	132.00	143.00	154.00	165.00	176.00	187.00	198.00	209.00	220.00
441	121.27	132.30	143.32	154.35	165.37	176.40	187.42	198.45	209.47	220.50
442	121.55	132.60	143.65	154.70	165.75	176.80	187.85	198.90	209.95	221.00
443	121.82	132.90	143.97	155.05	166.12	177.20	188.27	199.35	210.42	221.50
444	122.10	133.20	144.30	155.40	166.50	177.60	188.70	199.80	210.90	222.00
445	122.37	133.50	144.62	155.75	166.87	178.00	189.12	200.25	211.37	222.50
446	122.65	133.80	144.95	156.10	167.25	178.40	189.55	200.70	211.85	223.00
447	122.92	134.10	145.27	156.45	167.62	178.80	189.97	201.15	212.32	223.50
448	123.20	134.40	145.60	156.80	168.00	179.20	190.40	201.60	212.80	224.00
449	123.47	134.70	145.92	157.15	168.37	179.60	190.82	202.05	213.27	224.50
450	123.75	135.00	146.25	157.50	168.75	180.00	191.25	202.50	213.75	225.00

500 FEET.

Per Ton, Per Foot, Feet.	25c.	50c.	$1 2½ cts.	$2 5 cts.	$3 7½ cts.	$4 10 cts.	$5 12½ cts.	$6 15 cts.	$7 17½ cts.	$8 20 cts.	$9 22½ cts.	$10 25 cts.
451	2.82	5.64	11.27	22.55	33.82	45.10	56.37	67.65	78.92	90.20	101.47	112.75
452	2.82	5.65	11.30	22.60	33.90	45.20	56.50	67.80	79.10	90.40	101.70	113.00
453	2.83	5.66	11.32	22.65	33.97	45.30	56.62	67.95	79.27	90.60	101.92	113.25
454	2.84	5.67	11.35	22.70	34.05	45.40	56.75	68.10	79.45	90.80	102.15	113.50
455	2.84	5.69	11.37	22.75	34.12	45.50	56.87	68.25	79.62	91.00	102.37	113.75
456	2.85	5.70	11.40	22.80	34.20	45.60	57.00	68.40	79.80	91.20	102.60	114.00
457	2.86	5.71	11.42	22.85	34.27	45.70	57.12	68.55	79.97	91.40	102.82	114.25
458	2.86	5.72	11.45	22.90	34.35	45.80	57.25	68.70	80.15	91.60	103.05	114.50
459	2.87	5.74	11.47	22.95	34.42	45.90	57.37	68.85	80.32	91.80	103.27	114.75
460	2.87	5.75	11.50	23.00	34.50	46.00	57.50	69.00	80.50	92.00	103.50	115.00
461	2.88	5.76	11.52	23.05	34.57	46.10	57.62	69.15	80.67	92.20	103.72	115.25
462	2.89	5.77	11.55	23.10	34.65	46.20	57.75	69.30	80.85	92.40	103.95	115.50
463	2.89	5.79	11.57	23.15	34.72	46.30	57.87	69.45	81.02	92.60	104.17	115.75
464	2.90	5.80	11.60	23.20	34.80	46.40	58.00	69.60	81.20	92.80	104.40	116.00
465	2.91	5.81	11.62	23.25	34.87	46.50	58.12	69.75	81.37	93.00	104.62	116.25
466	2.91	5.82	11.65	23.30	34.95	46.60	58.25	69.90	81.55	93.20	104.85	116.50
467	2.92	5.84	11.67	23.35	35.02	46.70	58.37	70.05	81.72	93.40	105.07	116.75
468	2.92	5.85	11.70	23.40	35.10	46.80	58.50	70.20	81.90	93.60	105.30	117.00
469	2.93	5.86	11.72	23.45	35.17	46.90	58.62	70.35	82.07	93.80	105.52	117.25
470	2.94	5.87	11.75	23.50	35.25	47.00	58.75	70.50	82.25	94.00	105.75	117.50
471	2.94	5.89	11.77	23.55	35.32	47.10	58.87	70.65	82.42	94.20	105.97	117.75
472	2.95	5.90	11.80	23.60	35.40	47.20	59.00	70.80	82.60	94.40	106.20	118.00
473	2.96	5.91	11.82	23.65	35.47	47.30	59.12	70.95	82.77	94.60	106.42	118.25
474	2.96	5.92	11.85	23.70	35.55	47.40	59.25	71.10	82.95	94.80	106.65	118.50
475	2.97	5.94	11.87	23.75	35.62	47.50	59.37	71.25	83.12	95.00	106.87	118.75
476	2.97	5.95	11.90	23.80	35.70	47.60	59.50	71.40	83.30	95.20	107.10	119.00
477	2.98	5.96	11.92	23.85	35.77	47.70	59.62	71.55	83.47	95.40	107.32	119.25
478	2.99	5.97	11.95	23.90	35.85	47.80	59.75	71.70	83.65	95.60	107.55	119.50
479	2.99	5.99	11.97	23.95	35.92	47.90	59.87	71.85	83.82	95.80	107.77	119.75
480	3.00	6.00	12.00	24.00	36.00	48.00	60.00	72.00	84.00	96.00	108.00	120.00
481	3.01	6.01	12.02	24.05	36.07	48.10	60.12	72.15	84.17	96.20	108.22	120.25
482	3.01	6.02	12.05	24.10	36.15	48.20	60.25	72.30	84.35	96.40	108.45	120.50
483	3.02	6.04	12.07	24.15	36.22	48.30	60.37	72.45	84.52	96.60	108.67	120.75
484	3.02	6.05	12.10	24.20	36.30	48.40	60.50	72.60	84.70	96.80	108.90	121.00
485	3.03	6.06	12.12	24.25	36.37	48.50	60.62	72.75	84.87	97.00	109.12	121.25
486	3.04	6.07	12.15	24.30	36.45	48.60	60.75	72.90	85.05	97.20	109.35	121.50
487	3.04	6.09	12.17	24.35	36.52	48.70	60.87	73.05	85.22	97.40	109.57	121.75
488	3.05	6.10	12.20	24.40	36.60	48.80	61.00	73.20	85.40	97.60	109.80	122.00
489	3.06	6.11	12.22	24.45	36.67	48.90	61.12	73.35	85.57	97.80	110.02	122.25
490	3.06	6.12	12.25	24.50	36.75	49.00	61.25	73.50	85.75	98.00	110.25	122.50
491	3.07	6.14	12.27	24.55	36.82	49.10	61.37	73.65	85.92	98.20	110.47	122.75
492	3.07	6.15	12.30	24.60	36.90	49.20	61.50	73.80	86.10	98.40	110.70	123.00
493	3.08	6.16	12.32	24.65	36.97	49.30	61.62	73.95	86.27	98.60	110.92	123.25
494	3.09	6.17	12.35	24.70	37.05	49.40	61.75	74.10	86.45	98.80	111.15	123.50
495	3.09	6.19	12.37	24.75	37.12	49.50	61.87	74.25	86.62	99.00	111.37	123.75
496	3.10	6.20	12.40	24.80	37.20	49.60	62.00	74.40	86.80	99.20	111.60	124.00
497	3.11	6.21	12.42	24.85	37.27	49.70	62.12	74.55	86.97	99.40	111.82	124.25
498	3.11	6.22	12.45	24.90	37.35	49.80	62.25	74.70	87.15	99.60	112.05	124.50
499	3.12	6.24	12.47	24.95	37.42	49.90	62.37	74.85	87.32	99.80	112.27	124.75
500	3.12	6.25	12.50	25.00	37.50	50.00	62.50	75.00	87.50	100.00	112.50	125.00

500 FEET.

Per Ton,	$11	$12	$13	$14	$15	$16	$17	$18	$19	$20
Per Foot,	27½ cts.	30 cts.	32½ cts.	35 cts.	37½ cts.	40 cts.	42½ cts.	45 cts.	47½ cts.	50 cts.
Feet.										
451	124.02	135.30	146.57	157.85	169.12	180.40	191.67	202.95	214.22	225.50
452	124.30	135.60	146.90	158.20	169.50	180.80	192.10	203.40	214.70	226.00
453	124.57	135.90	147.22	158.55	169.87	181.20	192.52	203.85	215.17	226.50
454	124.85	136.20	147.55	158.90	170.25	181.60	192.95	204.30	215.65	227.00
455	125.12	136.50	147.87	159.25	170.62	182.00	193.37	204.75	216.12	227.50
456	125.40	136.80	148.20	159.60	171.00	182.40	193.80	205.20	216.60	228.00
457	125.67	137.10	148.52	159.95	171.37	182.80	194.22	205.65	217.07	228.50
458	125.95	137.40	148.85	160.30	171.75	183.20	194.65	206.10	217.55	229.00
459	126.22	137.70	149.17	160.65	172.12	183.60	195.07	206.55	218.02	229.50
460	126.50	138.00	149.50	161.00	172.50	184.00	195.50	207.00	218.50	230.00
461	126.77	138.30	149.82	161.35	172.87	184.40	195.92	207.45	218.97	230.50
462	127.05	138.60	150.15	161.70	173.25	184.80	196.35	207.90	219.45	231.00
463	127.32	138.90	150.47	162.05	173.62	185.20	196.77	208.35	219.92	231.50
464	127.60	139.20	150.80	162.40	174.00	185.60	197.20	208.80	220.40	232.00
465	127.87	139.50	151.12	162.75	174.37	186.00	197.62	209.25	220.87	232.50
466	128.15	139.80	151.45	163.10	174.75	186.40	198.05	209.70	221.35	233.00
467	128.42	140.10	151.77	163.45	175.12	186.80	198.47	210.15	221.82	233.50
468	128.70	140.40	152.10	163.80	175.50	187.20	198.90	210.60	222.30	234.00
469	128.97	140.70	152.42	164.15	175.87	187.60	199.32	211.05	222.77	234.50
470	129.25	141.00	152.75	164.50	176.25	188.00	199.75	211.50	223.25	235.00
471	129.52	141.30	153.07	164.85	176.62	188.40	200.17	211.95	223.72	235.50
472	129.80	141.60	153.40	165.20	177.00	188.80	200.60	212.40	224.20	236.00
473	130.07	141.90	153.72	165.55	177.37	189.20	201.02	212.85	224.67	236.50
474	130.35	142.20	154.05	165.90	177.75	189.60	201.45	213.30	225.15	237.00
475	130.62	142.50	154.37	166.25	178.12	190.00	201.87	213.75	225.62	237.50
476	130.90	142.80	154.70	166.60	178.50	190.40	202.30	214.20	226.10	238.00
477	131.17	143.10	155.02	166.95	178.87	190.80	202.72	214.65	226.57	238.50
478	131.45	143.40	155.35	167.30	179.25	191.20	203.15	215.10	227.05	239.00
479	131.72	143.70	155.67	167.65	179.62	191.60	203.57	215.55	227.52	239.50
480	132.00	144.00	156.00	168.00	180.00	192.00	204.00	216.00	228.00	240.00
481	132.27	144.30	156.32	168.35	180.37	192.40	204.42	216.45	228.47	240.50
482	132.55	144.60	156.65	168.70	180.75	192.80	204.85	216.90	228.95	241.00
483	132.82	144.90	156.97	169.05	181.12	193.20	205.27	217.35	229.42	241.50
484	133.10	145.20	157.30	169.40	181.50	193.60	205.70	217.80	229.90	242.00
485	133.37	145.50	157.62	169.75	181.87	194.00	206.12	218.25	230.37	242.50
486	133.65	145.80	157.95	170.10	182.25	194.40	206.55	218.70	230.85	243.00
487	133.92	146.10	158.27	170.45	182.62	194.80	206.97	219.15	231.32	243.50
488	134.20	146.40	158.60	170.80	183.00	195.20	207.40	219.60	231.80	244.00
489	134.47	146.70	158.92	171.15	183.37	195.60	207.82	220.05	232.27	244.50
490	134.75	147.00	159.25	171.50	183.75	196.00	208.25	220.50	232.75	245.00
491	135.02	147.30	159.57	171.85	184.12	196.40	208.67	220.95	233.22	245.50
492	135.30	147.60	159.90	172.20	184.50	196.80	209.10	221.40	233.70	246.00
493	135.57	147.90	160.22	172.55	184.87	197.20	209.52	221.85	234.17	246.50
494	135.85	148.20	160.55	172.90	185.25	197.60	209.95	222.30	234.65	247.00
495	136.12	148.50	160.87	173.25	185.62	198.00	210.37	222.75	235.12	247.50
496	136.40	148.80	161.20	173.60	186.00	198.40	210.80	223.20	235.60	248.00
497	136.67	149.10	161.52	173.95	186.37	198.80	211.22	223.65	236.07	248.50
498	136.95	149.40	161.85	174.30	186.75	199.20	211.65	224.10	236.55	249.00
499	137.22	149.70	162.17	174.65	187.12	199.60	212.07	224.55	237.02	249.50
500	137.50	150.00	162.50	175.00	187.50	200.00	212.50	225.00	237.50	250.00

550 FEET.

Per Ton,	25c.	50c.	$1	$2	$3	$4	$5	$6	$7	$8	$9	$10
Per Foot,			2½ cts.	5 cts.	7½ cts.	10 cts.	12½ cts.	15 cts.	17½ cts.	20 cts.	22½ cts.	25 cts.
Feet.												
501	3.13	6.26	12.52	25.05	37.57	50.10	62.62	75.15	87.67	100.20	112.72	125.25
502	3.14	6.27	12.55	25.10	37.65	50.20	62.75	75.30	87.85	100.40	112.95	125.50
503	3.14	6.29	12.57	25.15	37.72	50.30	62.87	75.45	88.02	100.60	113.17	125.75
504	3.15	6.30	12.60	25.20	37.80	50.40	63.00	75.60	88.20	100.80	113.40	126.00
505	3.16	6.31	12.62	25.25	37.87	50.50	63.12	75.75	88.37	101.00	113.62	126.25
506	3.16	6.32	12.65	25.30	37.95	50.60	63.25	75.90	88.55	101.20	113.85	126.50
507	3.17	6.34	12.67	25.35	38.02	50.70	63.37	76.05	88.72	101.40	114.07	126.75
508	3.17	6.35	12.70	25.40	38.10	50.80	63.50	76.20	88.90	101.60	114.30	127.00
509	3.18	6.36	12.72	25.45	38.17	50.90	63.62	76.35	89.07	101.80	114.52	127.25
510	3.19	6.37	12.75	25.50	38.25	51.00	63.75	76.50	89.25	102.00	114.75	127.50
511	3.19	6.39	12.77	25.55	38.32	51.10	63.87	76.65	89.42	102.20	114.97	127.75
512	3.20	6.40	12.80	25.60	38.40	51.20	64.00	76.80	89.60	102.40	115.20	128.00
513	3.21	6.41	12.82	25.65	38.47	51.30	64.12	76.95	89.77	102.60	115.42	128.25
514	3.21	6.42	12.85	25.70	38.55	51.40	64.25	77.10	89.95	102.80	115.65	128.50
515	3.22	6.44	12.87	25.75	38.62	51.50	64.37	77.25	90.12	103.00	115.87	128.75
516	3.22	6.45	12.90	25.80	38.70	51.60	64.50	77.40	90.30	103.20	116.10	129.00
517	3.23	6.46	12.92	25.85	38.77	51.70	64.62	77.55	90.47	103.40	116.32	129.25
518	3.24	6.47	12.95	25.90	38.85	51.80	64.75	77.70	90.65	103.60	116.55	129.50
519	3.24	6.49	12.97	25.95	38.92	51.90	64.87	77.85	90.82	103.80	116.77	129.75
520	3.25	6.50	13.00	26.00	39.00	52.00	65.00	78.00	91.00	104.00	117.00	130.00
521	3.26	6.51	13.02	26.05	39.07	52.10	65.12	78.15	91.17	104.20	117.22	130.25
522	3.26	6.52	13.05	26.10	39.15	52.20	65.25	78.30	91.35	104.40	117.45	130.50
523	3.27	6.54	13.07	26.15	39.22	52.30	65.37	78.45	91.52	104.60	117.67	130.75
524	3.27	6.55	13.10	26.20	39.30	52.40	65.50	78.60	91.70	104.80	117.90	131.00
525	3.28	6.56	13.12	26.25	39.37	52.50	65.62	78.75	91.87	105.00	118.12	131.25
526	3.29	6.57	13.15	26.30	39.45	52.60	65.75	78.90	92.05	105.20	118.35	131.50
527	3.29	6.59	13.17	26.35	39.52	52.70	65.87	79.05	92.22	105.40	118.57	131.75
528	3.30	6.60	13.20	26.40	39.60	52.80	66.00	79.20	92.40	105.60	118.80	132.00
529	3.31	6.61	13.22	26.45	39.67	52.90	66.12	79.35	92.57	105.80	119.02	132.25
530	3.31	6.62	13.25	26.50	39.75	53.00	66.25	79.50	92.75	106.00	119.25	132.50
531	3.32	6.64	13.27	26.55	39.82	53.10	66.37	79.65	92.92	106.20	119.47	132.75
532	3.32	6.65	13.30	26.60	39.90	53.20	66.50	79.80	93.10	106.40	119.70	133.00
533	3.33	6.66	13.32	26.65	39.97	53.30	66.62	79.95	93.27	106.60	119.92	133.25
534	3.34	6.67	13.35	26.70	40.05	53.40	66.75	80.10	93.45	106.80	120.15	133.50
535	3.34	6.69	13.37	26.75	40.12	53.50	66.87	80.25	93.62	107.00	120.37	133.75
536	3.35	6.70	13.40	26.80	40.20	53.60	67.00	80.40	93.80	107.20	120.60	134.00
537	3.36	6.71	13.42	26.85	40.27	53.70	67.12	80.55	93.97	107.40	120.82	134.25
538	3.36	6.72	13.45	26.90	40.35	53.80	67.25	80.70	94.15	107.60	121.05	134.50
539	3.37	6.74	13.47	26.95	40.42	53.90	67.37	80.85	94.32	107.80	121.27	134.75
540	3.37	6.75	13.50	27.00	40.50	54.00	67.50	81.00	94.50	108.00	121.50	135.00
541	3.38	6.76	13.52	27.05	40.57	54.10	67.62	81.15	94.67	108.20	121.72	135.25
542	3.39	6.77	13.55	27.10	40.65	54.20	67.75	81.30	94.85	108.40	121.95	135.50
543	3.39	6.79	13.57	27.15	40.72	54.30	67.87	81.45	95.02	108.60	122.17	135.75
544	3.40	6.80	13.60	27.20	40.80	54.40	68.00	81.60	95.20	108.80	122.40	136.00
545	3.41	6.81	13.62	27.25	40.87	54.50	68.12	81.75	95.37	109.00	122.62	136.25
546	3.41	6.82	13.65	27.30	40.95	54.60	68.25	81.90	95.55	109.20	122.85	136.50
547	3.42	6.84	13.67	27.35	41.02	54.70	68.37	82.05	95.72	109.40	123.07	136.75
548	3.42	6.85	13.70	27.40	41.10	54.80	68.50	82.20	95.90	109.60	123.30	137.00
549	3.43	6.86	13.72	27.45	41.17	54.90	68.62	82.35	96.07	109.80	123.52	137.25
550	3.44	6.87	13.75	27.50	41.25	55.00	68.75	82.50	96.25	110.00	123.75	137.50

550 FEET.

Per Ton,	$11	$12	$13	$14	$15	$16	$17	$18	$19	$20
Per Foot,	27½ cts.	30 cts.	32½ cts.	35 cts.	37½ cts.	40 cts.	42½ cts.	45 cts.	47½ cts.	50 cts.
Feet.										
501	137.77	150.30	162.82	175.35	187.87	200.40	212.92	225.45	237.97	250.50
502	138.05	150.60	163.15	175.70	188.25	200.80	213.35	225.90	238.45	251.00
503	138.32	150.90	163.47	176.05	188.62	201.20	213.77	226.35	238.92	251.50
504	138.60	151.20	163.80	176.40	189.00	201.60	214.20	226.80	239.40	252.00
505	138.87	151.50	164.12	176.75	189.37	202.00	214.62	227.25	239.87	252.50
506	139.15	151.80	164.45	177.10	189.75	202.40	215.05	227.70	240.35	253.00
507	139.42	152.10	164.77	177.45	190.12	202.80	215.47	228.15	240.82	253.50
508	139.70	152.40	165.10	177.80	190.50	203.20	215.90	228.60	241.30	254.00
509	139.97	152.70	165.42	178.15	190.87	203.60	216.32	229.05	241.77	254.50
510	140.25	153.00	165.75	178.50	191.25	204.00	216.75	229.50	242.25	255.00
511	140.52	153.30	166.07	178.85	191.62	204.40	217.17	229.95	242.72	255.50
512	140.80	153.60	166.40	179.20	192.00	204.80	217.60	230.40	243.20	256.00
513	141.07	153.90	166.72	179.55	192.37	205.20	218.02	230.85	243.67	256.50
514	141.35	154.20	167.05	179.90	192.75	205.60	218.45	231.30	244.15	257.00
515	141.62	154.50	167.37	180.25	193.12	206.00	218.87	231.75	244.62	257.50
516	141.90	154.80	167.70	180.60	193.50	206.40	219.30	232.20	245.10	258.00
517	142.17	155.10	168.02	180.95	193.87	206.80	219.72	232.65	245.57	258.50
518	142.45	155.40	168.35	181.30	194.25	207.20	220.15	233.10	246.05	259.00
519	142.72	155.70	168.67	181.65	194.62	207.60	220.57	233.55	246.52	259.50
520	143.00	156.00	169.00	182.00	195.00	208.00	221.00	234.00	247.00	260.00
521	143.27	156.30	169.32	182.35	195.37	208.40	221.42	234.45	247.47	260.50
522	143.55	156.60	169.65	182.70	195.75	208.80	221.85	234.90	247.95	261.00
523	143.82	156.90	169.97	183.05	196.12	209.20	222.27	235.35	248.42	261.50
524	144.10	157.20	170.30	183.40	196.50	209.60	222.70	235.80	248.90	262.00
525	144.37	157.50	170.62	183.75	196.87	210.00	223.12	236.25	249.37	262.50
526	144.65	157.80	170.95	184.10	197.25	210.40	223.55	236.70	249.85	263.00
527	144.92	158.10	171.27	184.45	197.62	210.80	223.97	237.15	250.32	263.50
528	145.20	158.40	171.60	184.80	198.00	211.20	224.40	237.60	250.80	264.00
529	145.47	158.70	171.92	185.15	198.37	211.60	224.82	238.05	251.27	264.50
530	145.75	159.00	172.25	185.50	198.75	212.00	225.25	238.50	251.75	265.00
531	146.02	159.30	172.57	185.85	199.12	212.40	225.67	238.95	252.22	265.50
532	146.30	159.60	172.90	186.20	199.50	212.80	226.10	239.40	252.70	266.00
533	146.57	159.90	173.22	186.55	199.87	213.20	226.52	239.85	253.17	266.50
534	146.85	160.20	173.55	186.90	200.25	213.60	226.95	240.30	253.65	267.00
535	147.12	160.50	173.87	187.25	200.62	214.00	227.37	240.75	254.12	267.50
536	147.40	160.80	174.20	187.60	201.00	214.40	227.80	241.20	254.60	268.00
537	147.67	161.10	174.52	187.95	201.37	214.80	228.22	241.65	255.07	268.50
538	147.95	161.40	174.85	188.30	201.75	215.20	228.65	242.10	255.55	269.00
539	148.22	161.70	175.17	188.65	202.12	215.60	229.07	242.55	256.02	269.50
540	148.50	162.00	175.50	189.00	202.50	216.00	229.50	243.00	256.50	270.00
541	148.77	162.30	175.82	189.35	202.87	216.40	229.92	243.45	256.97	270.50
542	149.05	162.60	176.15	189.70	203.25	216.80	230.35	243.90	257.45	271.00
543	149.32	162.90	176.47	190.05	203.62	217.20	230.77	244.35	257.92	271.50
544	149.60	163.20	176.80	190.40	204.00	217.60	231.20	244.80	258.40	272.00
545	149.87	163.50	177.12	190.75	204.37	218.00	231.62	245.25	258.87	272.50
546	150.15	163.80	177.45	191.10	204.75	218.40	232.05	245.70	259.35	273.00
547	150.42	164.10	177.77	191.45	205.12	218.80	232.47	246.15	259.82	273.50
548	150.70	164.40	178.10	191.80	205.50	219.20	232.90	246.60	260.30	274.00
549	150.97	164.70	178.42	192.15	205.87	219.60	233.32	247.05	260.77	274.50
550	151.25	165.00	178.75	192.50	206.25	220.00	233.75	247.50	261.25	275.00

600 FEET.

Per Ton,	25c.	50c.	$1	$2	$3	$4	$5	$6	$7	$8	$9	$10
Per Foot,			2½ cts.	5 cts.	7½ cts.	10 cts.	12½ cts.	15 cts.	17½ cts.	20 cts.	22½ cts.	25 cts.
Feet.												
551	3.44	6.89	13.77	27.55	41.32	55.10	68.87	82.65	96.42	110.20	123.97	137.75
552	3.45	6.90	13.80	27.60	41.40	55.20	69.00	82.80	96.60	110.40	124.20	138.00
553	3.46	6.91	13.82	27.65	41.47	55.30	69.12	82.95	96.77	110.60	124.42	138.25
554	3.46	6.92	13.85	27.70	41.55	55.40	69.25	83.10	96.95	110.80	124.65	138.50
555	3.47	6.94	13.87	27.75	41.62	55.50	69.37	83.25	97.12	111.00	124.87	138.75
556	3.47	6.95	13.90	27.80	41.70	55.60	69.50	83.40	97.30	111.20	125.10	139.00
557	3.48	6.96	13.92	27.85	41.77	55.70	69.62	83.55	97.47	111.40	125.32	139.25
558	3.49	6.97	13.95	27.90	41.85	55.80	69.75	83.70	97.65	111.60	125.55	139.50
559	3.49	6.99	13.97	27.95	41.92	55.90	69.87	83.85	97.82	111.80	125.77	139.75
560	3.50	7.00	14.00	28.00	42.00	56.00	70.00	84.00	98.00	112.00	126.00	140.00
561	3.51	7.01	14.02	28.05	42.07	56.10	70.12	84.15	98.17	112.20	126.22	140.25
562	3.51	7.02	14.05	28.10	42.15	56.20	70.25	84.30	98.35	112.40	126.45	140.50
563	3.52	7.04	14.07	28.15	42.22	56.30	70.37	84.45	98.52	112.60	126.67	140.75
564	3.52	7.05	14.10	28.20	42.30	56.40	70.50	84.60	98.70	112.80	126.90	141.00
565	3.53	7.06	14.12	28.25	42.37	56.50	70.62	84.75	98.87	113.00	127.12	141.25
566	3.54	7.07	14.15	28.30	42.45	56.60	70.75	84.90	99.05	113.20	127.35	141.50
567	3.54	7.09	14.17	28.35	42.52	56.70	70.87	85.05	99.22	113.40	127.57	141.75
568	3.55	7.10	14.20	28.40	42.60	56.80	71.00	85.20	99.40	113.60	127.80	142.00
569	3.56	7.11	14.22	28.45	42.67	56.90	71.12	85.35	99.57	113.80	128.02	142.25
570	3.56	7.12	14.25	28.50	42.75	57.00	71.25	85.50	99.75	114.00	128.25	142.50
571	3.57	7.14	14.27	28.55	42.82	57.10	71.37	85.65	99.92	114.20	128.47	142.75
572	3.57	7.15	14.30	28.60	42.90	57.20	71.50	85.80	100.10	114.40	128.70	143.00
573	3.58	7.16	14.32	28.65	42.97	57.30	71.62	85.95	100.27	114.60	128.92	143.25
574	3.59	7.17	14.35	28.70	43.05	57.40	71.75	86.10	100.45	114.80	129.15	143.50
575	3.59	7.19	14.37	28.75	43.12	57.50	71.87	86.25	100.62	115.00	129.37	143.75
576	3.60	7.20	14.40	28.80	43.20	57.60	72.00	86.40	100.80	115.20	129.60	144.00
577	3.61	7.21	14.42	28.85	43.27	57.70	72.12	86.55	100.97	115.40	129.82	144.25
578	3.61	7.22	14.45	28.90	43.35	57.80	72.25	86.70	101.15	115.60	130.05	144.50
579	3.62	7.24	14.47	28.95	43.42	57.90	72.37	86.85	101.32	115.80	130.27	144.75
580	3.62	7.25	14.50	29.00	43.50	58.00	72.50	87.00	101.50	116.00	130.50	145.00
581	3.63	7.26	14.52	29.05	43.57	58.10	72.62	87.15	101.67	116.20	130.72	145.25
582	3.64	7.27	14.55	29.10	43.65	58.20	72.75	87.30	101.85	116.40	130.95	145.50
583	3.64	7.29	14.57	29.15	43.72	58.30	72.87	87.45	102.02	116.60	131.17	145.75
584	3.65	7.30	14.60	29.20	43.80	58.40	73.00	87.60	102.20	116.80	131.40	146.00
585	3.66	7.31	14.62	29.25	43.87	58.50	73.12	87.75	102.37	117.00	131.62	146.25
586	3.66	7.32	14.65	29.30	43.95	58.60	73.25	87.90	102.55	117.20	131.85	146.50
587	3.67	7.34	14.67	29.35	44.02	58.70	73.37	88.05	102.72	117.40	132.07	146.75
588	3.67	7.35	14.70	29.40	44.10	58.80	73.50	88.20	102.90	117.60	132.30	147.00
589	3.68	7.36	14.72	29.45	44.17	58.90	73.62	88.35	103.07	117.80	132.52	147.25
590	3.69	7.37	14.75	29.50	44.25	59.00	73.75	88.50	103.25	118.00	132.75	147.50
591	3.69	7.39	14.77	29.55	44.32	59.10	73.87	88.65	103.42	118.20	132.97	147.75
592	3.70	7.40	14.80	29.60	44.40	59.20	74.00	88.80	103.60	118.40	133.20	148.00
593	3.71	7.41	14.82	29.65	44.47	59.30	74.12	88.95	103.77	118.60	133.42	148.25
594	3.71	7.42	14.85	29.70	44.55	59.40	74.25	89.10	103.95	118.80	133.65	148.50
595	3.72	7.44	14.87	29.75	44.62	59.50	74.37	89.25	104.12	119.00	133.87	148.75
596	3.72	7.45	14.90	29.80	44.70	59.60	74.50	89.40	104.30	119.20	134.10	149.00
597	3.73	7.46	14.92	29.85	44.77	59.70	74.62	89.55	104.47	119.40	134.32	149.25
598	3.74	7.47	14.95	29.90	44.85	59.80	74.75	89.70	104.65	119.60	134.55	149.50
599	3.74	7.49	14.97	29.95	44.92	59.90	74.87	89.85	104.82	119.80	134.77	149.75
600	3.75	7.50	15.00	30.00	45.00	60.00	75.00	90.00	105.00	120.00	135.00	150.00

600 FEET.

Per Ton,	$11	$12	$13	$14	$15	$16	$17	$18	$19	$20
Per Foot,	27½ cts.	30 cts.	32½ cts.	35 cts.	37½ cts.	40 cts.	42½ cts.	45 cts.	47½ cts.	50 cts.
Feet.										
551	151.52	165.30	179.07	192.85	206.62	220.40	234.17	247.95	261.72	275.50
552	151.80	165.60	179.40	193.20	207.00	220.80	234.60	248.40	262.20	276.00
553	152.07	165.90	179.72	193.55	207.37	221.20	235.02	248.85	262.67	276.50
554	152.35	166.20	180.05	193.90	207.75	221.60	235.45	249.30	263.15	277.00
555	152.62	166.50	180.37	194.25	208.12	222.00	235.87	249.75	263.62	277.50
556	152.90	166.80	180.70	194.60	208.50	222.40	236.30	250.20	264.10	278.00
557	153.17	167.10	181.02	194.95	208.87	222.80	236.72	250.65	264.57	278.50
558	153.45	167.40	181.35	195.30	209.25	223.20	237.15	251.10	265.05	279.00
559	153.72	167.70	181.67	195.65	209.62	223.60	237.57	251.55	265.52	279.50
560	154.00	168.00	182.00	196.00	210.00	224.00	238.00	252.00	266.00	280.00
561	154.27	168.30	182.32	196.35	210.37	224.40	238.42	252.45	266.47	280.50
562	154.55	168.60	182.65	196.70	210.75	224.80	238.85	252.90	266.95	281.00
563	154.82	168.90	182.97	197.05	211.12	225.20	239.27	253.35	267.42	281.50
564	155.10	169.20	183.30	197.40	211.50	225.60	239.70	253.80	267.90	282.00
565	155.37	169.50	183.62	197.75	211.87	226.00	240.12	254.25	268.37	282.50
566	155.65	169.80	183.95	198.10	212.25	226.40	240.55	254.70	268.85	283.00
567	155.92	170.10	184.27	198.45	212.62	226.80	240.97	255.15	269.32	283.50
568	156.20	170.40	184.60	198.80	213.00	227.20	241.40	255.60	269.80	284.00
569	156.47	170.70	184.92	199.15	213.37	227.60	241.82	256.05	270.27	284.50
570	156.75	171.00	185.25	199.50	213.75	228.00	242.25	256.50	270.75	285.00
571	157.02	171.30	185.57	199.85	214.12	228.40	242.67	256.95	271.22	285.50
572	157.30	171.60	185.90	200.20	214.50	228.80	243.10	257.40	271.70	286.00
573	157.57	171.90	186.22	200.55	214.87	229.20	243.52	257.85	272.17	286.50
574	157.85	172.20	186.55	200.90	215.25	229.60	243.95	258.30	272.65	287.00
575	158.12	172.50	186.87	201.25	215.62	230.00	244.37	258.75	273.12	287.50
576	158.40	172.80	187.20	201.60	216.00	230.40	244.80	259.20	273.60	288.00
577	158.67	173.10	187.52	201.95	216.37	230.80	245.22	259.65	274.07	288.50
578	158.95	173.40	187.85	202.30	216.75	231.20	245.65	260.10	274.55	289.00
579	159.22	173.70	188.17	202.65	217.12	231.60	246.07	260.55	275.02	289.50
580	159.50	174.00	188.50	203.00	217.50	232.00	246.50	261.00	275.50	290.00
581	159.77	174.30	188.82	203.35	217.87	232.40	246.92	261.45	275.97	290.50
582	160.05	174.60	189.15	203.70	218.25	232.80	247.35	261.90	276.45	291.00
583	160.32	174.90	189.47	204.05	218.62	233.20	247.77	262.35	276.92	291.50
584	160.60	175.20	189.80	204.40	219.00	233.60	248.20	262.80	277.40	292.00
585	160.87	175.50	190.12	204.75	219.37	234.00	248.62	263.25	277.87	292.50
586	161.15	175.80	190.45	205.10	219.75	234.40	249.05	263.70	278.35	293.00
587	161.42	176.10	190.77	205.45	220.12	234.80	249.47	264.15	278.82	293.50
588	161.70	176.40	191.10	205.80	220.50	235.20	249.90	264.60	279.30	294.00
589	161.97	176.70	191.42	206.15	220.87	235.60	250.32	265.05	279.77	294.50
590	162.25	177.00	191.75	206.50	221.25	236.00	250.75	265.50	280.25	295.00
591	162.52	177.30	192.07	206.85	221.62	236.40	251.17	265.95	280.72	295.50
592	162.80	177.60	192.40	207.20	222.00	236.80	251.60	266.40	281.20	296.00
593	163.07	177.90	192.72	207.55	222.37	237.20	252.02	266.85	281.67	296.50
594	163.35	178.20	193.05	207.90	222.75	237.60	252.45	267.30	282.15	297.00
595	163.62	178.50	193.37	208.25	223.12	238.00	252.87	267.75	282.62	297.50
596	163.90	178.80	193.70	208.60	223.50	238.40	253.30	268.20	283.10	298.00
597	164.17	179.10	194.02	208.95	223.87	238.80	253.72	268.65	283.57	298.50
598	164.45	179.40	194.35	209.30	224.25	239.20	254.15	269.10	284.05	299.00
599	164.72	179.70	194.67	209.65	224.62	239.60	254.57	269.55	284.52	299.50
600	165.00	180.00	195.00	210.00	225.00	240.00	255.00	270.00	285.00	300.00

Per Ton, Per Foot, Feet.	25c.	50c.	$1 2½ cts.	$2 5 cts.	$3 7½ cts.	$4 10 cts.	$5 12½ cts.	$6 15 cts.	$7 17½ cts.	$8 20 cts.	$9 22½ cts.	$10 25 cts.
601	3.76	7.51	15.02	30.05	45.07	60.10	75.12	90.15	105.17	120.20	135.22	150.25
602	3.76	7.52	15.05	30.10	45.15	60.20	75.25	90.30	105.35	120.40	135.45	150.50
603	3.77	7.54	15.07	30.15	45.22	60.30	75.37	90.45	105.52	120.60	135.67	150.75
604	3.77	7.55	15.10	30.20	45.30	60.40	75.50	90.60	105.70	120.80	135.90	151.00
605	3.78	7.56	15.12	30.25	45.37	60.50	75.62	90.75	105.87	121.00	136.12	151.25
606	3.79	7.57	15.15	30.30	45.45	60.60	75.75	90.90	106.05	121.20	136.35	151.50
607	3.79	7.59	15.17	30.35	45.52	60.70	75.87	91.05	106.22	121.40	136.57	151.75
608	3.80	7.60	15.20	30.40	45.60	60.80	76.00	91.20	106.40	121.60	136.80	152.00
609	3.81	7.61	15.22	30.45	45.67	60.90	76.12	91.35	106.57	121.80	137.02	152.25
610	3.81	7.62	15.25	30.50	45.75	61.00	76.25	91.50	106.75	122.00	137.25	152.50
611	3.82	7.64	15.27	30.55	45.82	61.10	76.37	91.65	106.92	122.20	137.47	152.75
612	3.82	7.65	15.30	30.60	45.90	61.20	76.50	91.80	107.10	122.40	137.70	153.00
613	3.83	7.66	15.32	30.65	45.97	61.30	76.62	91.95	107.27	122.60	137.92	153.25
614	3.84	7.67	15.35	30.70	46.05	61.40	76.75	92.10	107.45	122.80	138.15	153.50
615	3.84	7.69	15.37	30.75	46.12	61.50	76.87	92.25	107.62	123.00	138.37	153.75
616	3.85	7.70	15.40	30.80	46.20	61.60	77.00	92.40	107.80	123.20	138.60	154.00
617	3.86	7.71	15.42	30.85	46.27	61.70	77.12	92.55	107.97	123.40	138.82	154.25
618	3.86	7.72	15.45	30.90	46.35	61.80	77.25	92.70	108.15	123.60	139.05	154.50
619	3.87	7.74	15.47	30.95	46.42	61.90	77.37	92.85	108.32	123.80	139.27	154.75
620	3.87	7.75	15.50	31.00	46.50	62.00	77.50	93.00	108.50	124.00	139.50	155.00
621	3.88	7.76	15.52	31.05	46.57	62.10	77.62	93.15	108.67	124.20	139.72	155.25
622	3.89	7.77	15.55	31.10	46.65	62.20	77.75	93.30	108.85	124.40	139.95	155.50
623	3.89	7.79	15.57	31.15	46.72	62.30	77.87	93.45	109.02	124.60	140.17	155.75
624	3.90	7.80	15.60	31.20	46.80	62.40	78.00	93.60	109.20	124.80	140.40	156.00
625	3.91	7.81	15.62	31.25	46.87	62.50	78.12	93.75	109.37	125.00	140.62	156.25
626	3.91	7.82	15.65	31.30	46.95	62.60	78.25	93.90	109.55	125.20	140.85	156.50
627	3.92	7.84	15.67	31.35	47.02	62.70	78.37	94.05	109.72	125.40	141.07	156.75
628	3.92	7.85	15.70	31.40	47.10	62.80	78.50	94.20	109.90	125.60	141.30	157.00
629	3.93	7.86	15.72	31.45	47.17	62.90	78.62	94.35	110.07	125.80	141.52	157.25
630	3.94	7.87	15.75	31.50	47.25	63.00	78.75	94.50	110.25	126.00	141.75	157.50
631	3.94	7.89	15.77	31.55	47.32	63.10	78.87	94.65	110.42	126.20	141.97	157.75
632	3.95	7.90	15.80	31.60	47.40	63.20	79.00	94.80	110.60	126.40	142.20	158.00
633	3.96	7.91	15.82	31.65	47.47	63.30	79.12	94.95	110.77	126.60	142.42	158.25
634	3.96	7.92	15.85	31.70	47.55	63.40	79.25	95.10	110.95	126.80	142.65	158.50
635	3.97	7.94	15.87	31.75	47.62	63.50	79.37	95.25	111.12	127.00	142.87	158.75
636	3.97	7.95	15.90	31.80	47.70	63.60	79.50	95.40	111.30	127.20	143.10	159.00
637	3.98	7.96	15.92	31.85	47.77	63.70	79.62	95.55	111.47	127.40	143.32	159.25
638	3.99	7.97	15.95	31.90	47.85	63.80	79.75	95.70	111.65	127.60	143.55	159.50
639	3.99	7.99	15.97	31.95	47.92	63.90	79.87	95.85	111.82	127.80	143.77	159.75
640	4.00	8.00	16.00	32.00	48.00	64.00	80.00	96.00	112.00	128.00	144.00	160.00
641	4.01	8.01	16.02	32.05	48.07	64.10	80.12	96.15	112.17	128.20	144.22	160.25
642	4.01	8.02	16.05	32.10	48.15	64.20	80.25	96.30	112.35	128.40	144.45	160.50
643	4.02	8.04	16.07	32.15	48.22	64.30	80.37	96.45	112.52	128.60	144.67	160.75
644	4.02	8.05	16.10	32.20	48.30	64.40	80.50	96.60	112.70	128.80	144.90	161.00
645	4.03	8.06	16.12	32.25	48.37	64.50	80.62	96.75	112.87	129.00	145.12	161.25
646	4.04	8.07	16.15	32.30	48.45	64.60	80.75	96.90	113.05	129.20	145.35	161.50
647	4.04	8.09	16.17	32.35	48.52	64.70	80.87	97.05	113.22	129.40	145.57	161.75
648	4.05	8.10	16.20	32.40	48.60	64.80	81.00	97.20	113.40	129.60	145.80	162.00
649	4.06	8.11	16.22	32.45	48.67	64.90	81.12	97.35	113.57	129.80	146.02	162.25
650	4.06	8.12	16.25	32.50	48.75	65.00	81.25	97.50	113.75	130.00	146.25	162.50

650 FEET.

Per Ton,	$11	$12	$13	$14	$15	$16	$17	$18	$19	$20
Per Foot,	27½ cts.	30 cts.	32½ cts.	35 cts.	37½ cts.	40 cts.	42½ cts.	45 cts.	47½ cts.	50 cts.
Feet.										
601	165.27	180.30	195.32	210.35	225.37	240.40	255.42	270.45	285.47	300.50
602	165.55	180.60	195.65	210.70	225.75	240.80	255.85	270.90	285.95	301.00
603	165.82	180.90	195.97	211.05	226.12	241.20	256.27	271.35	286.42	301.50
604	166.10	181.20	196.30	211.40	226.50	241.60	256.70	271.80	286.90	302.00
605	166.37	181.50	196.62	211.75	226.87	242.00	257.12	272.25	287.37	302.50
606	166.65	181.80	196.95	212.10	227.25	242.40	257.55	272.70	287.85	303.00
607	166.92	182.10	197.27	212.45	227.62	242.80	257.97	273.15	288.32	303.50
608	167.20	182.40	197.60	212.80	228.00	243.20	258.40	273.60	288.80	304.00
609	167.47	182.70	197.92	213.15	228.37	243.60	258.82	274.05	289.27	304.50
610	167.75	183.00	198.25	213.50	228.75	244.00	259.25	274.50	289.75	305.00
611	168.02	183.30	198.57	213.85	229.12	244.40	259.67	274.95	290.22	305.50
612	168.30	183.60	198.90	214.20	229.50	244.80	260.10	275.40	290.70	306.00
613	168.57	183.90	199.22	214.55	229.87	245.20	260.52	275.85	291.17	306.50
614	168.85	184.20	199.55	214.90	230.25	245.60	260.95	276.30	291.65	307.00
615	169.12	184.50	199.87	215.25	230.62	246.00	261.37	276.75	292.12	307.50
616	169.40	184.80	200.20	215.60	231.00	246.40	261.80	277.20	292.60	308.00
617	169.67	185.10	200.52	215.95	231.37	246.80	262.22	277.65	293.07	308.50
618	169.95	185.40	200.85	216.30	231.75	247.20	262.65	278.10	293.55	309.00
619	170.22	185.70	201.17	216.65	232.12	247.60	263.07	278.55	294.02	309.50
620	170.50	186.00	201.50	217.00	232.50	248.00	263.50	279.00	294.50	310.00
621	170.77	186.30	201.82	217.35	232.87	248.40	263.92	279.45	294.97	310.50
622	171.05	186.60	202.15	217.70	233.25	248.80	264.35	279.90	295.45	311.00
623	171.32	186.90	202.47	218.05	233.62	249.20	264.77	280.35	295.92	311.50
624	171.60	187.20	202.80	218.40	234.00	249.60	265.20	280.80	296.40	312.00
625	171.87	187.50	203.12	218.75	234.37	250.00	265.62	281.25	296.87	312.50
626	172.15	187.80	203.45	219.10	234.75	250.40	266.05	281.70	297.35	313.00
627	172.42	188.10	203.77	219.45	235.12	250.80	266.47	282.15	297.82	313.50
628	172.70	188.40	204.10	219.80	235.50	251.20	266.90	282.60	298.30	314.00
629	172.97	188.70	204.42	220.15	235.87	251.60	267.32	283.05	298.77	314.50
630	173.25	189.00	204.75	220.50	236.25	252.00	267.75	283.50	299.25	315.00
631	173.52	189.30	205.07	220.85	236.62	252.40	268.17	283.95	299.72	315.50
632	173.80	189.60	205.40	221.20	237.00	252.80	268.60	284.40	300.20	316.00
633	174.07	189.90	205.72	221.55	237.37	253.20	269.02	284.85	300.67	316.50
634	174.35	190.20	206.05	221.90	237.75	253.60	269.45	285.30	301.15	317.00
635	174.62	190.50	206.37	222.25	238.12	254.00	269.87	285.75	301.62	317.50
636	174.90	190.80	206.70	222.60	238.50	254.40	270.30	286.20	302.10	318.00
637	175.17	191.10	207.02	222.95	238.87	254.80	270.72	286.65	302.57	318.50
638	175.45	191.40	207.35	223.30	239.25	255.20	271.15	287.10	303.05	319.00
639	175.72	191.70	207.67	223.65	239.62	255.60	271.57	287.55	303.52	319.50
640	176.00	192.00	208.00	224.00	240.00	256.00	272.00	288.00	304.00	320.00
641	176.27	192.30	208.32	224.35	240.37	256.40	272.42	288.45	304.47	320.50
642	176.55	192.60	208.65	224.70	240.75	256.80	272.85	288.90	304.95	321.00
643	176.82	192.90	208.97	225.05	241.12	257.20	273.27	289.35	305.42	321.50
644	177.10	193.20	209.30	225.40	241.50	257.60	273.70	289.80	305.90	322.00
645	177.37	193.50	209.62	225.75	241.87	258.00	274.12	290.25	306.37	322.50
646	177.65	193.80	209.95	226.10	242.25	258.40	274.55	290.70	306.85	323.00
647	177.92	194.10	210.27	226.45	242.62	258.80	274.97	291.15	307.32	323.50
648	178.20	194.40	210.60	226.80	243.00	259.20	275.40	291.60	307.80	324.00
649	178.47	194.70	210.92	227.15	243.37	259.60	275.82	292.05	308.27	324.50
650	178.75	195.00	211.25	227.50	243.75	260.00	276.25	292.50	308.75	325.00

700 FEET.

Per Ton,	25c.	50c.	$1	$2	$3	$4	$5	$6	$7	$8	$9	$10
Per Foot,			2½ cts.	5 cts.	7½ cts.	10 cts.	12½ cts.	15 cts.	17½ cts.	20 cts.	22½ cts.	25 cts.
Feet.												
651	4.07	8.14	16.27	32.55	48.82	65.10	81.37	97.65	113.92	130.20	146.47	162.75
652	4.07	8.15	16.30	32.60	48.90	65.20	81.50	97.80	114.10	130.40	146.70	163.00
653	4.08	8.16	16.32	32.65	48.97	65.30	81.62	97.95	114.27	130.60	146.92	163.25
654	4.09	8.17	16.35	32.70	49.05	65.40	81.75	98.10	114.45	130.80	147.15	163.50
655	4.09	8.19	16.37	32.75	49.12	65.50	81.87	98.25	114.62	131.00	147.37	163.75
656	4.10	8.20	16.40	32.80	49.20	65.60	82.00	98.40	114.80	131.20	147.60	164.00
657	4.11	8.21	16.42	32.85	49.27	65.70	82.12	98.55	114.97	131.40	147.82	164.25
658	4.11	8.22	16.45	32.90	49.35	65.80	82.25	98.70	115.15	131.60	148.05	164.50
659	4.12	8.24	16.47	32.95	49.42	65.90	82.37	98.85	115.32	131.80	148.27	164.75
660	4.12	8.25	16.50	33.00	49.50	66.00	82.50	99.00	115.50	132.00	148.50	165.00
661	4.13	8.26	16.52	33.05	49.57	66.10	82.62	99.15	115.67	132.20	148.72	165.25
662	4.14	8.27	16.55	33.10	49.65	66.20	82.75	99.30	115.85	132.40	148.95	165.50
663	4.14	8.29	16.57	33.15	49.72	66.30	82.87	99.45	116.02	132.60	149.17	165.75
664	4.15	8.30	16.60	33.20	49.80	66.40	83.00	99.60	116.20	132.80	149.40	166.00
665	4.16	8.31	16.62	33.25	49.87	66.50	83.12	99.75	116.37	133.00	149.62	166.25
666	4.16	8.32	16.65	33.30	49.95	66.60	83.25	99.90	116.55	133.20	149.85	166.50
667	4.17	8.34	16.67	33.35	50.02	66.70	83.37	100.05	116.72	133.40	150.07	166.75
668	4.17	8.35	16.70	33.40	50.10	66.80	83.50	100.20	116.90	133.60	150.30	167.00
669	4.18	8.36	16.72	33.45	50.17	66.90	83.62	100.35	117.07	133.80	150.52	167.25
670	4.19	8.37	16.75	33.50	50.25	67.00	83.75	100.50	117.25	134.00	150.75	167.50
671	4.19	8.39	16.77	33.55	50.32	67.10	83.87	100.65	117.42	134.20	150.97	167.75
672	4.20	8.40	16.80	33.60	50.40	67.20	84.00	100.80	117.60	134.40	151.20	168.00
673	4.21	8.41	16.82	33.65	50.47	67.30	84.12	100.95	117.77	134.60	151.42	168.25
674	4.21	8.42	16.85	33.70	50.55	67.40	84.25	101.10	117.95	134.80	151.65	168.50
675	4.22	3.44	16.87	33.75	50.62	67.50	84.37	101.25	118.12	135.00	151.87	168.75
676	4.22	8.45	16.90	33.80	50.70	67.60	84.50	101.40	118.30	135.20	152.10	169.00
677	4.23	8.46	16.92	33.85	50.77	67.70	84.62	101.55	118.47	135.40	152.32	169.25
678	4.24	8.47	16.95	33.90	50.85	67.80	84.75	101.70	118.65	135.60	152.55	169.50
679	4.24	8.49	16.97	33.95	50.92	67.90	84.87	101.85	118.82	135.80	152.77	169.75
680	4.25	8.50	17.00	34.00	51.00	68.00	85.00	102.00	119.00	136.00	153.00	170.00
681	4.26	8.51	17.02	34.05	51.07	68.10	85.12	102.15	119.17	136.20	153.22	170.25
682	4.26	8.52	17.05	34.10	51.15	68.20	85.25	102.30	119.35	136.40	153.45	170.50
683	4.27	8.54	17.07	34.15	51.22	68.30	85.37	102.45	119.52	136.60	153.67	170.75
684	4.27	8.55	17.10	34.20	51.30	68.40	85.50	102.60	119.70	136.80	153.90	171.00
685	4.28	8.56	17.12	34.25	51.37	68.50	85.62	102.75	119.87	137.00	154.12	171.25
686	4.29	8.57	17.15	34.30	51.45	68.60	85.75	102.90	120.05	137.20	154.35	171.50
687	4.29	8.59	17.17	34.35	51.52	68.70	85.87	103.05	120.22	137.40	154.57	171.75
688	4.30	8.60	17.20	34.40	51.60	68.80	86.00	103.20	120.40	137.60	154.80	172.00
689	4.31	8.61	17.22	34.45	51.67	68.90	86.12	103.35	120.57	137.80	155.02	172.25
690	4.31	8.62	17.25	34.50	51.75	69.00	86.25	103.50	120.75	138.00	155.25	172.50
691	4.32	8.64	17.27	34.55	51.82	69.10	86.37	103.65	120.92	138.20	155.47	172.75
692	4.32	8.65	17.30	34.60	51.90	69.20	86.50	103.80	121.10	138.40	155.70	173.00
693	4.33	8.66	17.32	34.65	51.97	69.30	86.62	103.95	121.27	138.60	155.92	173.25
694	4.34	8.67	17.35	34.70	52.05	69.40	86.75	104.10	121.45	138.80	156.15	173.50
695	4.34	8.69	17.37	34.75	52.12	69.50	86.87	104.25	121.62	139.00	156.37	173.75
696	4.35	8.70	17.40	34.80	52.20	69.60	87.00	104.40	121.80	139.20	156.60	174.00
697	4.36	8.71	17.42	34.85	52.27	69.70	87.12	104.55	121.97	139.40	156.82	174.25
698	4.36	8.72	17.45	34.90	52.35	69.80	87.25	104.70	122.15	139.60	157.05	174.50
699	4.37	8.74	17.47	34.95	52.42	69.90	87.37	104.85	122.32	139.80	157.27	174.75
700	4.37	8.75	17.50	35.00	52.50	70.00	87.50	105.00	122.50	140.00	157.50	175.00

700 FEET.

Per Ton,	$11	$12	$13	$14	$15	$16	$17	$18	$19	$20
Per Foot,	27½ cts.	30 cts.	32½ cts.	35 cts.	37½ cts.	40 cts.	42½ cts.	45 cts.	47½ cts.	50 cts.
Feet.										
651	179.02	195.30	211.57	227.85	244.12	260.40	276.67	292.95	309.22	325.50
652	179.30	195.60	211.90	228.20	244.50	260.80	277.10	293.40	309.70	326.00
653	179.57	195.90	212.22	228.55	244.87	261.20	277.52	293.85	310.17	326.50
654	179.85	196.20	212.55	228.90	245.25	261.60	277.95	294.30	310.65	327.00
655	180.12	196.50	212.87	229.25	245.62	262.00	278.37	294.75	311.12	327.50
656	180.40	196.80	213.20	229.60	246.00	262.40	278.80	295.20	311.60	328.00
657	180.67	197.10	213.52	229.95	246.37	262.80	279.22	295.65	312.07	328.50
658	180.95	197.40	213.85	230.30	246.75	263.20	279.65	296.10	312.55	329.00
659	181.22	197.70	214.17	230.65	247.12	263.60	280.07	296.55	313.02	329.50
660	181.50	198.00	214.50	231.00	247.50	264.00	280.50	297.00	313.50	330.00
661	181.77	198.30	214.82	231.35	247.87	264.40	280.92	297.45	313.97	330.50
662	182.05	198.60	215.15	231.70	248.25	264.80	281.35	297.90	314.45	331.00
663	182.32	198.90	215.47	232.05	248.62	265.20	281.77	298.35	314.92	331.50
664	182.60	199.20	215.80	232.40	249.00	265.60	282.20	298.80	315.40	332.00
665	182.87	199.50	216.12	232.75	249.37	266.00	282.62	299.25	315.87	332.50
666	183.15	199.80	216.45	233.10	249.75	266.40	283.05	299.70	316.35	333.00
667	183.42	200.10	216.77	233.45	250.12	266.80	283.47	300.15	316.82	333.50
668	183.70	200.40	217.10	233.80	250.50	267.20	283.90	300.60	317.30	334.00
669	183.97	200.70	217.42	234.15	250.87	267.60	284.32	301.05	317.77	334.50
670	184.25	201.00	217.75	234.50	251.25	268.00	284.75	301.50	318.25	335.00
671	184.52	201.30	218.07	234.85	251.62	268.40	285.17	301.95	318.72	335.50
672	184.80	201.60	218.40	235.20	252.00	268.80	285.60	302.40	319.20	336.00
673	185.07	201.90	218.72	235.55	252.37	269.20	286.02	302.85	319.67	336.50
674	185.35	202.20	219.05	235.90	252.75	269.60	286.45	303.30	320.15	337.00
675	185.62	202.50	219.37	236.25	253.12	270.00	286.87	303.75	320.62	337.50
676	185.90	202.80	219.70	236.60	253.50	270.40	287.30	304.20	321.10	338.00
677	186.17	203.10	220.02	236.95	253.87	270.80	287.72	304.65	321.57	338.50
678	186.45	203.40	220.35	237.30	254.25	271.20	288.15	305.10	322.05	339.00
679	186.72	203.70	220.67	237.65	254.62	271.60	288.57	305.55	322.52	339.50
680	187.00	204.00	221.00	238.00	255.00	272.00	289.00	306.00	323.00	340.00
681	187.27	204.30	221.32	238.35	255.37	272.40	289.42	306.45	323.47	340.50
682	187.55	204.60	221.65	238.70	255.75	272.80	289.85	306.90	323.95	341.00
683	187.82	204.90	221.97	239.05	256.12	273.20	290.27	307.35	324.42	341.50
684	188.10	205.20	222.30	239.40	256.50	273.60	290.70	307.80	324.90	342.00
685	188.37	205.50	222.62	239.75	256.87	274.00	291.12	308.25	325.37	342.50
686	188.65	205.80	222.95	240.10	257.25	274.40	291.55	308.70	325.85	343.00
687	188.92	206.10	223.27	240.45	257.62	274.80	291.97	309.15	326.32	343.50
688	189.20	206.40	223.60	240.80	258.00	275.20	292.40	309.60	326.80	344.00
689	189.47	206.70	223.92	241.15	258.37	275.60	292.82	310.05	327.27	344.50
690	189.75	207.00	224.25	241.50	258.75	276.00	293.25	310.50	327.75	345.00
691	190.02	207.30	224.57	241.85	259.12	276.40	293.67	310.95	328.22	345.50
692	190.30	207.60	224.90	242.20	259.50	276.80	294.10	311.40	328.70	346.00
693	190.57	207.90	225.22	242.55	259.87	277.20	294.52	311.85	329.17	346.50
694	190.85	208.20	225.55	242.90	260.25	277.60	294.95	312.30	329.65	347.00
695	191.12	208.50	225.87	243.25	260.62	278.00	295.37	312.75	330.12	347.50
696	191.40	208.80	226.20	243.60	261.00	278.40	295.80	313.20	330.60	348.00
697	191.67	209.10	226.52	243.95	261.37	278.80	296.22	313.65	331.07	348.50
698	191.95	209.40	226.85	244.30	261.75	279.20	296.65	314.10	331.55	349.00
699	192.22	209.70	227.17	244.65	262.12	279.60	297.07	314.55	332.02	349.50
700	192.50	210.00	227.50	245.00	262.50	280.00	297.50	315.00	332.50	350.00

750 FEET.

Per Ton,	25c.	50c.	$1	$2	$3	$4	$5	$6	$7	$8	$9	$10
Per Foot,			2½ cts.	5 cts.	7½ cts.	10 cts.	12½ cts.	15 cts.	17½ cts.	20 cts.	22½ cts	25 cts.
Feet.												
701	4.38	8.76	17.52	35.05	52.57	70.10	87.62	105.15	122.67	140.20	157.72	175.25
702	4.39	8.77	17.55	35.10	52.65	70.20	87.75	105.30	122.85	140.40	157.95	175.50
703	4.39	8.79	17.57	35.15	52.72	70.30	87.87	105.45	123.02	140.60	158.17	175.75
704	4.40	8.80	17.60	35.20	52.80	70.40	88.00	105.60	123.20	140.80	158.40	176.00
705	4.41	8.81	17.62	35.25	52.87	70.50	88.12	105.75	123.37	141.00	158.62	176.25
706	4.41	8.82	17.65	35.30	52.95	70.60	88.25	105.90	123.55	141.20	158.85	176.50
707	4.42	8.84	17.67	35.35	53.02	70.70	88.37	106.05	123.72	141.40	159.07	176.75
708	4.42	8.85	17.70	35.40	53.10	70.80	88.50	106.20	123.90	141.60	159.30	177.00
709	4.43	8.86	17.72	35.45	53.17	70.90	88.62	106.35	124.07	141.80	159.52	177.25
710	4.44	8.87	17.75	35.50	53.25	71.00	88.75	106.50	124.25	142.00	159.75	177.50
711	4.44	8.89	17.77	35.55	53.32	71.10	88.87	106.65	124.42	142.20	159.97	177.75
712	4.45	8.90	17.80	35.60	53.40	71.20	89.00	106.80	124.60	142.40	160.20	178.00
713	4.46	8.91	17.82	35.65	53.47	71.30	89.12	106.95	124.77	142.60	160.42	178.25
714	4.46	8.92	17.85	35.70	53.55	71.40	89.25	107.10	124.95	142.80	160.65	178.50
715	4.47	8.94	17.87	35.75	53.62	71.50	89.37	107.25	125.12	143.00	160.87	178.75
716	4.47	8.95	17.90	35.80	53.70	71.60	89.50	107.40	125.30	143.20	161.10	179.00
717	4.48	8.96	17.92	35.85	53.77	71.70	89.62	107.55	125.47	143.40	161.32	179.25
718	4.49	8.97	17.95	35.90	53.85	71.80	89.75	107.70	125.65	143.60	161.55	179.50
719	4.49	8.99	17.97	35.95	53.92	71.90	89.87	107.85	125.82	143.80	161.77	179.75
720	4.50	9.00	18.00	36.00	54.00	72.00	90.00	108.00	126.00	144.00	162.00	180.00
721	4.51	9.01	18.02	36.05	54.07	72.10	90.12	108.15	126.17	144.20	162.22	180.25
722	4.51	9.02	18.05	36.10	54.15	72.20	90.25	108.30	126.35	144.40	162.45	180.50
723	4.52	9.04	18.07	36.15	54.22	72.30	90.37	108.45	126.52	144.60	162.67	180.75
724	4.52	9.05	18.10	36.20	54.30	72.40	90.50	108.60	126.70	144.80	162.90	181.00
725	4.53	9.06	18.12	36.25	54.37	72.50	90.62	108.75	126.87	145.00	163.12	181.25
726	4.54	9.07	18.15	36.30	54.45	72.60	90.75	108.90	127.05	145.20	163.35	181.50
727	4.54	9.09	18.17	36.35	54.52	72.70	90.87	109.05	127.22	145.40	163.57	181.75
728	4.55	9.10	18.20	36.40	54.60	72.80	91.00	109.20	127.40	145.60	163.80	182.00
729	4.56	9.11	18.22	36.45	54.67	72.90	91.12	109.35	127.57	145.80	164.02	182.25
730	4.56	9.12	18.25	36.50	54.75	73.00	91.25	109.50	127.75	146.00	164.25	182.50
731	4.57	9.14	18.27	36.55	54.82	73.10	91.37	109.65	127.92	146.20	164.47	182.75
732	4.57	9.15	18.30	36.60	54.90	73.20	91.50	109.80	128.10	146.40	164.70	183.00
733	4.58	9.16	18.32	36.65	54.97	73.30	91.62	109.95	128.27	146.60	164.92	183.25
734	4.59	9.17	18.35	36.70	55.05	73.40	91.75	110.10	128.45	146.80	165.15	183.50
735	4.59	9.19	18.37	36.75	55.12	73.50	91.87	110.25	128.62	147.00	165.37	183.75
736	4.60	9.20	18.40	36.80	55.20	73.60	92.00	110.40	128.80	147.20	165.60	184.00
737	4.61	9.21	18.42	36.85	55.27	73.70	92.12	110.55	128.97	147.40	165.82	184.25
738	4.61	9.22	18.45	36.90	55.35	73.80	92.25	110.70	129.15	147.60	166.05	184.50
739	4.62	9.24	18.47	36.95	55.42	73.90	92.37	110.85	129.32	147.80	166.27	184.75
740	4.62	9.25	18.50	37.00	55.50	74.00	92.50	111.00	129.50	148.00	166.50	185.00
741	4.63	9.26	18.52	37.05	55.57	74.10	92.62	111.15	129.67	148.20	166.72	185.25
742	4.64	9.27	18.55	37.10	55.65	74.20	92.75	111.30	129.85	148.40	166.95	185.50
743	4.64	9.29	18.57	37.15	55.72	74.30	92.87	111.45	130.02	148.60	167.17	185.75
744	4.65	9.30	18.60	37.20	55.80	74.40	93.00	111.60	130.20	148.80	167.40	186.00
745	4.66	9.31	18.62	37.25	55.87	74.50	93.12	111.75	130.37	149.00	167.62	186.25
746	4.66	9.32	18.65	37.30	55.95	74.60	93.25	111.90	130.55	149.20	167.85	186.50
747	4.67	9.34	18.67	37.35	56.02	74.70	93.37	112.05	130.72	149.40	168.07	186.75
748	4.67	9.35	18.70	37.40	56.10	74.80	93.50	112.20	130.90	149.60	168.30	187.00
749	4.68	9.36	18.72	37.45	56.17	74.90	93.62	112.35	131.07	149.80	168.52	187.25
750	4.69	9.37	18.75	37.50	56.25	75.00	93.75	112.50	131.25	150.00	168.75	187.50

750 FEET.

Per Ton,	$11	$12	$13	$14	$15	$16	$17	$18	$19	$20
Per Foot,	27½ cts.	30 cts.	32½ cts.	35 cts.	37½ cts.	40 cts.	42½ cts.	45 cts.	47½ cts.	50 cts.
Feet.										
701	192.77	210.30	227.82	245.35	262.87	280.40	297.92	315.45	332.97	350.50
702	193.05	210.60	228.15	245.70	263.25	280.80	298.35	315.90	333.45	351.00
703	193.32	210.90	228.47	246.05	263.62	281.20	298.77	316.35	333.92	351.50
704	193.60	211.20	228.80	246.40	264.00	281.60	299.20	316.80	334.40	352.00
705	193.87	211.50	229.12	246.75	264.37	282.00	299.62	317.25	334.87	352.50
706	194.15	211.80	229.45	247.10	264.75	282.40	300.05	317.70	335.35	353.00
707	194.42	212.10	229.77	247.45	265.12	282.80	300.47	318.15	335.82	353.50
708	194.70	212.40	230.10	247.80	265.50	283.20	300.90	318.60	336.30	354.00
709	194.97	212.70	230.42	248.15	265.87	283.60	301.32	319.05	336.77	354.50
710	195.25	213.00	230.75	248.50	266.25	284.00	301.75	319.50	337.25	355.00
711	195.52	213.30	231.07	248.85	266.62	284.40	302.17	319.95	337.72	355.50
712	195.80	213.60	231.40	249.20	267.00	284.80	302.60	320.40	338.20	356.00
713	196.07	213.90	231.72	249.55	267.37	285.20	303.02	320.85	338.67	356.50
714	196.35	214.20	232.05	249.90	267.75	285.60	303.45	321.30	339.15	357.00
715	196.62	214.50	232.37	250.25	268.12	286.00	303.87	321.75	339.62	357.50
716	196.90	214.80	232.70	250.60	268.50	286.40	304.30	322.20	340.10	358.00
717	197.17	215.10	233.02	250.95	268.87	286.80	304.72	322.65	340.57	358.50
718	197.45	215.40	233.35	251.30	269.25	287.20	305.15	323.10	341.05	359.00
719	197.72	215.70	233.67	251.65	269.62	287.60	305.57	323.55	341.52	359.50
720	198.00	216.00	234.00	252.00	270.00	288.00	306.00	324.00	342.00	360.00
721	198.27	216.30	234.32	252.35	270.37	288.40	306.42	324.45	342.47	360.50
722	198.55	216.60	234.65	252.70	270.75	288.80	306.85	324.90	342.95	361.00
723	198.82	216.90	234.97	253.05	271.12	289.20	307.27	325.35	343.42	361.50
724	199.10	217.20	235.30	253.40	271.50	289.60	307.70	325.80	343.90	362.00
725	199.37	217.50	235.62	253.75	271.87	290.00	308.12	326.25	344.37	362.50
726	199.65	217.80	235.95	254.10	272.25	290.40	308.55	326.70	344.85	363.00
727	199.92	218.10	236.27	254.45	272.62	290.80	308.97	327.15	345.32	363.50
728	200.20	218.40	236.60	254.80	273.00	291.20	309.40	327.60	345.80	364.00
729	200.47	218.70	236.92	255.15	273.37	291.60	309.82	328.05	346.27	364.50
730	200.75	219.00	237.25	255.50	273.75	292.00	310.25	328.50	346.75	365.00
731	201.02	219.30	237.57	255.85	274.12	292.40	310.67	328.95	347.22	365.50
732	201.30	219.60	237.90	256.20	274.50	292.80	311.10	329.40	347.70	366.00
733	201.57	219.90	238.22	256.55	274.87	293.20	311.52	329.85	348.17	366.50
734	201.85	220.20	238.55	256.90	275.25	293.60	311.95	330.30	348.65	367.00
735	202.12	220.50	238.87	257.25	275.62	294.00	312.37	330.75	349.12	367.50
736	202.40	220.80	239.20	257.60	276.00	294.40	312.80	331.20	349.60	368.00
737	202.67	221.10	239.52	257.95	276.37	294.80	313.22	331.65	350.07	368.50
738	202.95	221.40	239.85	258.30	276.75	295.20	313.65	332.10	350.55	369.00
739	203.22	221.70	240.17	258.65	277.12	295.60	314.07	332.55	351.02	369.50
740	203.50	222.00	240.50	259.00	277.50	296.00	314.50	333.00	351.50	370.00
741	203.77	222.30	240.82	259.35	277.87	296.40	314.92	333.45	351.97	370.50
742	204.05	222.60	241.15	259.70	278.25	296.80	315.35	333.90	352.45	371.00
743	204.32	222.90	241.47	260.05	278.62	297.20	315.77	334.35	352.92	371.50
744	204.60	223.20	241.80	260.40	279.00	297.60	316.20	334.80	353.40	372.00
745	204.87	223.50	242.12	260.75	279.37	298.00	316.62	335.25	353.87	372.50
746	205.15	223.80	242.45	261.10	279.75	298.40	317.05	335.70	354.35	373.00
747	205.42	224.10	242.77	261.45	280.12	298.80	317.47	336.15	354.82	373.50
748	205.70	224.40	243.10	261.80	280.50	299.20	317.90	336.60	355.30	374.00
749	205.97	224.70	243.42	262.15	280.87	299.60	318.32	337.05	355.77	374.50
750	206.25	225.00	243.75	262.50	281.25	300.00	318.75	337.50	356.25	375.00

800 FEET.

Per Ton,	25c.	50c.	$1	$2	$3	$4	$5	$6	$7	$8	$9	$10
Per Foot,			2½ cts.	5 cts.	7½ cts.	10 cts.	12½ cts.	15 cts.	17½ cts.	20 cts.	22½ cts.	25 cts.
Feet.												
751	4.69	9.39	18.77	37.55	56.32	75.10	93.87	112.65	131.42	150.20	168.97	187.75
752	4.70	9.40	18.80	37.60	56.40	75.20	94.00	112.80	131.60	150.40	169.20	188.00
753	4.71	9.41	18.82	37.65	56.47	75.30	94.12	112.95	131.77	150.60	169.42	188.25
754	4.71	9.42	18.85	37.70	56.55	75.40	94.25	113.10	131.95	150.80	169.65	188.50
755	4.72	9.44	18.87	37.75	56.62	75.50	94.37	113.25	132.12	151.00	169.87	188.75
756	4.72	9.45	18.90	37.80	56.70	75.60	94.50	113.40	132.30	151.20	170.10	189.00
757	4.73	9.46	18.92	37.85	56.77	75.70	94.62	113.55	132.47	151.40	170.32	189.25
758	4.74	9.47	18.95	37.90	56.85	75.80	94.75	113.70	132.65	151.60	170.55	189.50
759	4.74	9.49	18.97	37.95	56.92	75.90	94.87	113.85	132.82	151.80	170.77	189.75
760	4.75	9.50	19.00	38.00	57.00	76.00	95.00	114.00	133.00	152.00	171.00	190.00
761	4.76	9.51	19.02	38.05	57.07	76.10	95.12	114.15	133.17	152.20	171.22	190.25
762	4.76	9.52	19.05	38.10	57.15	76.20	95.25	114.30	133.35	152.40	171.45	190.50
763	4.77	9.54	19.07	38.15	57.22	76.30	95.37	114.45	133.52	152.60	171.67	190.75
764	4.77	9.55	19.10	38.20	57.30	76.40	95.50	114.60	133.70	152.80	171.90	191.00
765	4.78	9.56	19.12	38.25	57.37	76.50	95.62	114.75	133.87	153.00	172.12	191.25
766	4.79	9.57	19.15	38.30	57.45	76.60	95.75	114.90	134.05	153.20	172.35	191.50
767	4.79	9.59	19.17	38.35	57.52	76.70	95.87	115.05	134.22	153.40	172.57	191.75
768	4.80	9.60	19.20	38.40	57.60	76.80	96.00	115.20	134.40	153.60	172.80	192.00
769	4.81	9.61	19.22	38.45	57.67	76.90	96.12	115.35	134.57	153.80	173.02	192.25
770	4.81	9.62	19.25	38.50	57.75	77.00	96.25	115.50	134.75	154.00	173.25	192.50
771	4.82	9.64	19.27	38.55	57.82	77.10	96.37	115.65	134.92	154.20	173.47	192.75
772	4.82	9.65	19.30	38.60	57.90	77.20	96.50	115.80	135.10	154.40	173.70	193.00
773	4.83	9.66	19.32	38.65	57.97	77.30	96.62	115.95	135.27	154.60	173.92	193.25
774	4.84	9.67	19.35	38.70	58.05	77.40	96.75	116.10	135.45	154.80	174.15	193.50
775	4.84	9.69	19.37	38.75	58.12	77.50	96.87	116.25	135.62	155.00	174.37	193.75
776	4.85	9.70	19.40	38.80	58.20	77.60	97.00	116.40	135.80	155.20	174.60	194.00
777	4.86	9.71	19.42	38.85	58.27	77.70	97.12	116.55	135.97	155.40	174.82	194.25
778	4.86	9.72	19.45	38.90	58.35	77.80	97.25	116.70	136.15	155.60	175.05	194.50
779	4.87	9.74	19.47	38.95	58.42	77.90	97.37	116.85	136.32	155.80	175.27	194.75
780	4.87	9.75	19.50	39.00	58.50	78.00	97.50	117.00	136.50	156.00	175.50	195.00
781	4.88	9.76	19.52	39.05	58.57	78.10	97.62	117.15	136.67	156.20	175.72	195.25
782	4.89	9.77	19.55	39.10	58.65	78.20	97.75	117.30	136.85	156.40	175.95	195.50
783	4.89	9.79	19.57	39.15	58.72	78.30	97.87	117.45	137.02	156.60	176.17	195.75
784	4.90	9.80	19.60	39.20	58.80	78.40	98.00	117.60	137.20	156.80	176.40	196.00
785	4.91	9.81	19.62	39.25	58.87	78.50	98.12	117.75	137.37	157.00	176.62	196.25
786	4.91	9.82	19.65	39.30	58.95	78.60	98.25	117.90	137.55	157.20	176.85	196.50
787	4.92	9.84	19.67	39.35	59.02	78.70	98.37	118.05	137.72	157.40	177.07	196.75
788	4.92	9.85	19.70	39.40	59.10	78.80	98.50	118.20	137.90	157.60	177.30	197.00
789	4.93	9.86	19.72	39.45	59.17	78.90	98.62	118.35	138.07	157.80	177.52	197.25
790	4.94	9.87	19.75	39.50	59.25	79.00	98.75	118.50	138.25	158.00	177.75	197.50
791	4.94	9.89	19.77	39.55	59.32	79.10	98.87	118.65	138.42	158.20	177.97	197.75
792	4.95	9.90	19.80	39.60	59.40	79.20	99.00	118.80	138.60	158.40	178.20	198.00
793	4.96	9.91	19.82	39.65	59.47	79.30	99.12	118.95	138.77	158.60	178.42	198.25
794	4.96	9.92	19.85	39.70	59.55	79.40	99.25	119.10	138.95	158.80	178.65	198.50
795	4.97	9.94	19.87	39.75	59.62	79.50	99.37	119.25	139.12	159.00	178.87	198.75
796	4.97	9.95	19.90	39.80	59.70	79.60	99.50	119.40	139.30	159.20	179.10	199.00
797	4.98	9.96	19.92	39.85	59.77	79.70	99.62	119.55	139.47	159.40	179.32	199.25
798	4.99	9.97	19.95	39.90	59.85	79.80	99.75	119.70	139.65	159.60	179.55	199.50
799	4.99	9.99	19.97	39.95	59.92	79.90	99.87	119.85	139.82	159.80	179.77	199.75
800	5.00	10.00	20.00	40.00	60.00	80.00	100.00	120.00	140.00	160.00	180.00	200.00

800 FEET.

Per Ton,	$11	$12	$13	$14	$15	$16	$17	$18	$19	$20
Per Foot,	27½ cts.	30 cts.	32½ cts.	35 cts.	37½ cts.	40 cts.	42½ cts.	45 cts.	47½ cts.	50 cts.
Feet.										
751	206.52	225.30	244.07	262.85	281.62	300.40	319.17	337.95	356.72	375.50
752	206.80	225.60	244.40	263.20	282.00	300.80	319.60	338.40	357.20	376.00
753	207.07	225.90	244.72	263.55	282.37	301.20	320.02	338.85	357.67	376.50
754	207.35	226.20	245.05	263.90	282.75	301.60	320.45	339.30	358.15	377.00
755	207.62	226.50	245.37	264.25	283.12	302.00	320.87	339.75	358.62	377.50
756	207.90	226.80	245.70	264.60	283.50	302.40	321.30	340.20	359.10	378.00
757	208.17	227.10	246.02	264.95	283.87	302.80	321.72	340.65	359.57	378.50
758	208.45	227.40	246.35	265.30	284.25	303.20	322.15	341.10	360.05	379.00
759	208.72	227.70	246.67	265.65	284.62	303.60	322.57	341.55	360.52	379.50
760	209.00	228.00	247.00	266.00	285.00	304.00	323.00	342.00	361.00	380.00
761	209.27	228.30	247.32	266.35	285.37	304.40	323.42	342.45	361.47	380.50
762	209.55	228.60	247.65	266.70	285.75	304.80	323.85	342.90	361.95	381.00
763	209.82	228.90	247.97	267.05	286.12	305.20	324.27	343.35	362.42	381.50
764	210.10	229.20	248.30	267.40	286.50	305.60	324.70	343.80	362.90	382.00
765	210.37	229.50	248.62	267.75	286.87	306.00	325.12	344.25	363.37	382.50
766	210.65	229.80	248.95	268.10	287.25	306.40	325.55	344.70	363.85	383.00
767	210.92	230.10	249.27	268.45	287.62	306.80	325.97	345.15	364.32	383.50
768	211.20	230.40	249.60	268.80	288.00	307.20	326.40	345.60	364.80	384.00
769	211.47	230.70	249.92	269.15	288.37	307.60	326.82	346.05	365.27	384.50
770	211.75	231.00	250.25	269.50	288.75	308.00	327.25	346.50	365.75	385.00
771	212.02	231.30	250.57	269.85	289.12	308.40	327.67	346.95	366.22	385.50
772	212.30	231.60	250.90	270.20	289.50	308.80	328.10	347.40	366.70	386.00
773	212.57	231.90	251.22	270.55	289.87	309.20	328.52	347.85	367.17	386.50
774	212.85	232.20	251.55	270.90	290.25	309.60	328.95	348.30	367.65	387.00
775	213.12	232.50	251.87	271.25	290.62	310.00	329.37	348.75	368.12	387.50
776	213.40	232.80	252.20	271.60	291.00	310.40	329.80	349.20	368.60	388.00
777	213.67	233.10	252.52	271.95	291.37	310.80	330.22	349.65	369.07	388.50
778	213.95	233.40	252.85	272.30	291.75	311.20	330.65	350.10	369.55	389.00
779	214.22	233.70	253.17	272.65	292.12	311.60	331.07	350.55	370.02	389.50
780	214.50	234.00	253.50	273.00	292.50	312.00	331.50	351.00	370.50	390.00
781	214.77	234.30	253.82	273.35	292.87	312.40	331.92	351.45	370.97	390.50
782	215.05	234.60	254.15	273.70	293.25	312.80	332.35	351.90	371.45	391.00
783	215.32	234.90	254.47	274.05	293.62	313.20	332.77	352.35	371.92	391.50
784	215.60	235.20	254.80	274.40	294.00	313.60	333.20	352.80	372.40	392.00
785	215.87	235.50	255.12	274.75	294.37	314.00	333.62	353.25	372.87	392.50
786	216.15	235.80	255.45	275.10	294.75	314.40	334.05	353.70	373.35	393.00
787	216.42	236.10	255.77	275.45	295.12	314.80	334.47	354.15	373.82	393.50
788	216.70	236.40	256.10	275.80	295.50	315.20	334.90	354.60	374.30	394.00
789	216.97	236.70	256.42	276.15	295.87	315.60	335.32	355.05	374.77	394.50
790	217.25	237.00	256.75	276.50	296.25	316.00	335.75	355.50	375.25	395.00
791	217.52	237.30	257.07	276.85	296.62	316.40	336.17	355.95	375.72	395.50
792	217.80	237.60	257.40	277.20	297.00	316.80	336.60	356.40	376.20	396.00
793	218.07	237.90	257.72	277.55	297.37	317.20	337.02	356.85	376.67	396.50
794	218.35	238.20	258.05	277.90	297.75	317.60	337.45	357.30	377.15	397.00
795	218.62	238.50	258.37	278.25	298.12	318.00	337.87	357.75	377.62	397.50
796	218.90	238.80	258.70	278.60	298.50	318.40	338.30	358.20	378.10	398.00
797	219.17	239.10	259.02	278.95	298.87	318.80	338.72	358.65	378.57	398.50
798	219.45	239.40	259.35	279.30	299.25	319.20	339.15	359.10	379.05	399.00
799	219.72	239.70	259.67	279.65	299.62	319.60	339.57	359.55	379.52	399.50
800	220.00	240.00	260.00	280.00	300.00	320.00	340.00	360.00	380.00	400.00

850 FEET.

Per Ton,	25c.	50c.	$1	$2	$3	$4	$5	$6	$7	$8	$9	$10
Per Foot,			2½ cts.	5 cts.	7½ cts.	10 cts.	12½ cts.	15 cts.	17½ cts.	20 cts.	22½ cts.	25 cts.
Feet.												
801	5.01	10.01	20.02	40.05	60.07	80.10	100.12	120.15	140.17	160.20	180.22	200.25
802	5.01	10.02	20.05	40.10	60.15	80.20	100.25	120.30	140.35	160.40	180.45	200.50
803	5.02	10.04	20.07	40.15	60.22	80.30	100.37	120.45	140.52	160.60	180.67	200.75
804	5.02	10.05	20.10	40.20	60.30	80.40	100.50	120.60	140.70	160.80	180.90	201.00
805	5.03	10.06	20.12	40.25	60.37	80.50	100.62	120.75	140.87	161.00	181.12	201.25
806	5.04	10.07	20.15	40.30	60.45	80.60	100.75	120.90	141.05	161.20	181.35	201.50
807	5.04	10.09	20.17	40.35	60.52	80.70	100.87	121.05	141.22	161.40	181.57	201.75
808	5.05	10.10	20.20	40.40	60.60	80.80	101.00	121.20	141.40	161.60	181.80	202.00
809	5.06	10.11	20.22	40.45	60.67	80.90	101.12	121.35	141.57	161.80	182.02	202.25
810	5.06	10.12	20.25	40.50	60.75	81.00	101.25	121.50	141.75	162.00	182.25	202.50
811	5.07	10.14	20.27	40.55	60.82	81.10	101.37	121.65	141.92	162.20	182.47	202.75
812	5.07	10.15	20.30	40.60	60.90	81.20	101.50	121.80	142.10	162.40	182.70	203.00
813	5.08	10.16	20.32	40.65	60.97	81.30	101.62	121.95	142.27	162.60	182.92	203.25
814	5.09	10.17	20.35	40.70	61.05	81.40	101.75	122.10	142.45	162.80	183.15	203.50
815	5.09	10.19	20.37	40.75	61.12	81.50	101.87	122.25	142.62	163.00	183.37	203.75
816	5.10	10.20	20.40	40.80	61.20	81.60	102.00	122.40	142.80	163.20	183.60	204.00
817	5.11	10.21	20.42	40.85	61.27	81.70	102.12	122.55	142.97	163.40	183.82	204.25
818	5.11	10.22	20.45	40.90	61.35	81.80	102.25	122.70	143.15	163.60	184.05	204.50
819	5.12	10.24	20.47	40.95	61.42	81.90	102.37	122.85	143.32	163.80	184.27	204.75
820	5.12	10.25	20.50	41.00	61.50	82.00	102.50	123.00	143.50	164.00	184.50	205.00
821	5.13	10.26	20.52	41.05	61.57	82.10	102.62	123.15	143.67	164.20	184.72	205.25
822	5.14	10.27	20.55	41.10	61.65	82.20	102.75	123.30	143.85	164.40	184.95	205.50
823	5.14	10.29	20.57	41.15	61.72	82.30	102.87	123.45	144.02	164.60	185.17	205.75
824	5.15	10.30	20.60	41.20	61.80	82.40	103.00	123.60	144.20	164.80	185.40	206.00
825	5.16	10.31	20.62	41.25	61.87	82.50	103.12	123.75	144.37	165.00	185.62	206.25
826	5.16	10.32	20.65	41.30	61.95	82.60	103.25	123.90	144.55	165.20	185.85	206.50
827	5.17	10.34	20.67	41.35	62.02	82.70	103.37	124.05	144.72	165.40	186.07	206.75
828	5.17	10.35	20.70	41.40	62.10	82.80	103.50	124.20	144.90	165.60	186.30	207.00
829	5.18	10.36	20.72	41.45	62.17	82.90	103.62	124.35	145.07	165.80	186.52	207.25
830	5.19	10.37	20.75	41.50	62.25	83.00	103.75	124.50	145.25	166.00	186.75	207.50
831	5.19	10.39	20.77	41.55	62.32	83.10	103.87	124.65	145.42	166,20	186.97	207.75
832	5.20	10.40	20.80	41.60	62.40	83.20	104.00	124.80	145.60	166.40	187.20	208.00
833	5.21	10.41	20.82	41.65	62.47	83.30	104.12	124.95	145.77	166.60	187.42	208.25
834	5.21	10.42	20.85	41.70	62.55	83.40	104.25	125.10	145.95	166.80	187.65	208.50
835	5.22	10.44	20.87	41.75	62.62	83.50	104.37	125.25	146.12	167.00	187.87	208.75
836	5.22	10.45	20.90	41.80	62.70	83.60	104.50	125.40	146.30	167.20	188.10	209.00
837	5.23	10.46	20.92	41.85	62.77	83.70	104.62	125.55	146.47	167.40	188.32	209.25
838	5.24	10.47	20.95	41.90	62.85	83.80	104.75	125.70	146.65	167.60	188.55	209.50
839	5.24	10.49	20.97	41.95	62.92	83.90	104.87	125.85	146.82	167.80	188.77	209.75
840	5.25	10.50	21.00	42.00	63.00	84.00	105.00	126.00	147.00	168.00	189.00	210.00
841	5.26	10.51	21.02	42.05	63.07	84.10	105.12	126.15	147.17	168.20	189.22	210.25
842	5.26	10.52	21.05	42.10	63.15	84.20	105.25	126.30	147.35	168.40	189.45	210.50
843	5.27	10.54	21.07	42.15	63.22	84.30	105.37	126.45	147.52	168.60	189.67	210.75
844	5.27	10.55	21.10	42.20	63.30	84.40	105.50	126.60	147.70	168.80	189.90	211.00
845	5.28	10.56	21.12	42.25	63.37	84.50	105.62	126.75	147.87	169.00	190.12	211.25
846	5.29	10.57	21.15	42.30	63.45	84.60	105.75	126.90	148.05	169.20	190.35	211.50
847	5.29	10.59	21.17	42.35	63.52	84.70	105.87	127.05	148.22	169.40	190.57	211.75
848	5.30	10.60	21.20	42.40	63.60	84.80	106.00	127.20	148.40	169.60	190.80	212.00
849	5.31	10.61	21.22	42.45	63.67	84.90	106.12	127.35	148.57	169.80	191.02	212.25
850	5.31	10.62	21.25	42.50	63.75	85.00	106.25	127.50	148.75	170.00	191.25	212.50

850 FEET.

Per Ton, / Per Foot,	$11 / 27½ cts.	$12 / 30 cts.	$13 / 32½ cts.	$14 / 35 cts.	$15 / 37½ cts.	$16 / 40 cts.	$17 / 42½ cts.	$18 / 45 cts.	$19 / 47½ cts.	$20 / 50 cts.
Feet.										
801	220.27	240.30	260.32	280.35	300.37	320.40	340.42	360.45	380.47	400.50
802	220.55	240.60	260.65	280.70	300.75	320.80	340.85	360.90	380.95	401.00
803	220.82	240.90	260.97	281.05	301.12	321.20	341.27	361.35	381.42	401.50
804	221.10	241.20	261.30	281.40	301.50	321.60	341.70	361.80	381.90	402.00
805	221.37	241.50	261.62	281.75	301.87	322.00	342.12	362.25	382.37	402.50
806	221.65	241.80	261.95	282.10	302.25	322.40	342.55	362.70	382.85	403.00
807	221.92	242.10	262.27	282.45	302.62	322.80	342.97	363.15	383.32	403.50
808	222.20	242.40	262.60	282.80	303.00	323.20	343.40	363.60	383.80	404.00
809	222.47	242.70	262.92	283.15	303.37	323.60	343.82	364.05	384.27	404.50
810	222.75	243.00	263.25	283.50	303.75	324.00	344.25	364.50	384.75	405.00
811	223.02	243.30	263.57	283.85	304.12	324.40	344.67	364.95	385.22	405.50
812	223.30	243.60	263.90	284.20	304.50	324.80	345.10	365.40	385.70	406.00
813	223.57	243.90	264.22	284.55	304.87	325.20	345.52	365.85	386.17	406.50
814	223.85	244.20	264.55	284.90	305.25	325.60	345.95	366.30	386.65	407.00
815	224.12	244.50	264.87	285.25	305.62	326.00	346.37	366.75	387.12	407.50
816	224.40	244.80	265.20	285.60	306.00	326.40	346.80	367.20	387.60	408.00
817	224.67	245.10	265.52	285.95	306.37	326.80	347.22	367.65	388.07	408.50
818	224.95	245.40	265.85	286.30	306.75	327.20	347.65	368.10	388.55	409.00
819	225.22	245.70	266.17	286.65	307.12	327.60	348.07	368.55	389.02	409.50
820	225.50	246.00	266.50	287.00	307.50	328.00	348.50	369.00	389.50	410.00
821	225.77	246.30	266.82	287.35	307.87	328.40	348.92	369.45	389.97	410.50
822	226.05	246.60	267.15	287.70	308.25	328.80	349.35	369.90	390.45	411.00
823	226.32	246.90	267.47	288.05	308.62	329.20	349.77	370.35	390.92	411.50
824	226.60	247.20	267.80	288.40	309.00	329.60	350.20	370.80	391.40	412.00
825	226.87	247.50	268.12	288.75	309.37	330.00	350.62	371.25	391.87	412.50
826	227.15	247.80	268.45	289.10	309.75	330.40	351.05	371.70	392.35	413.00
827	227.42	248.10	268.77	289.45	310.12	330.80	351.47	372.15	392.82	413.50
828	227.70	248.40	269.10	289.80	310.50	331.20	351.90	372.60	393.30	414.00
829	227.97	248.70	269.42	290.15	310.87	331.60	352.32	373.05	393.77	414.50
830	228.25	249.00	269.75	290.50	311.25	332.00	352.75	373.50	394.25	415.00
831	228.52	249.30	270.07	290.85	311.62	332.40	353.17	373.95	394.72	415.50
832	228.80	249.60	270.40	291.20	312.00	332.80	353.60	374.40	395.20	416.00
833	229.07	249.90	270.72	291.55	312.37	333.20	354.02	374.85	395.67	416.50
834	229.35	250.20	271.05	291.90	312.75	333.60	354.45	375.30	396.15	417.00
835	229.62	250.50	271.37	292.25	313.12	334.00	354.87	375.75	396.62	417.50
836	229.90	250.80	271.70	292.60	313.50	334.40	355.30	376.20	397.10	418.00
837	230.17	251.10	272.02	292.95	313.87	334.80	355.72	376.65	397.57	418.50
838	230.45	251.40	272.35	293.30	314.25	335.20	356.15	377.10	398.05	419.00
839	230.72	251.70	272.67	293.65	314.62	335.60	356.57	377.55	398.52	419.50
840	231.00	252.00	273.00	294.00	315.00	336.00	357.00	378.00	399.00	420.00
841	231.27	252.30	273.32	294.35	315.37	336.40	357.42	378.45	399.47	420.50
842	231.55	252.60	273.65	294.70	315.75	336.80	357.85	378.90	399.95	421.00
843	231.82	252.90	273.97	295.05	316.12	337.20	358.27	379.35	400.42	421.50
844	232.10	253.20	274.30	295.40	316.50	337.60	358.70	379.80	400.90	422.00
845	232.37	253.50	274.62	295.75	316.87	338.00	359.12	380.25	401.37	422.50
846	232.65	253.80	274.95	296.10	317.25	338.40	359.55	380.70	401.85	423.00
847	232.92	254.10	275.27	296.45	317.62	338.80	359.97	381.15	402.32	423.50
848	233.20	254.40	275.60	296.80	318.00	339.20	360.40	381.60	402.80	424.00
849	233.47	254.70	275.92	297.15	318.37	339.60	360.82	382.05	403.27	424.50
850	233.75	255.00	276.25	297.50	318.75	340.00	361.25	382.50	403.75	425.00

900 FEET.

Per Ton,	25c.	50c.	$1	$2	$3	$4	$5	$6	$7	$8	$9	$10
Per Foot,			2½ cts.	5 cts.	7½ cts.	10 cts.	12½ cts.	15 cts.	17½ cts.	20 cts.	22½ cts.	25 cts.
Feet.												
851	5.32	10.64	21.27	42.55	63.82	85.10	106.37	127.65	148.92	170.20	191.47	212.75
852	5.32	10.65	21.30	42.60	63.90	85.20	106.50	127.80	149.10	170.40	191.70	213.00
853	5.33	10.66	21.32	42.65	63.97	85.30	106.62	127.95	149.27	170.60	191.92	213.25
854	5.34	10.67	21.35	42.70	64.05	85.40	106.75	128.10	149.45	170.80	192.15	213.50
855	5.34	10.69	21.37	42.75	64.12	85.50	106.87	128.25	149.62	171.00	192.37	213.75
856	5.35	10.70	21.40	42.80	64.20	85.60	107.00	128.40	149.80	171.20	192.60	214.00
857	5.36	10.71	21.42	42.85	64.27	85.70	107.12	128.55	149.97	171.40	192.82	214.25
858	5.36	10.72	21.45	42.90	64.35	85.80	107.25	128.70	150.15	171.60	193.05	214.50
859	5.37	10.74	21.47	42.95	64.42	85.90	107.37	128.85	150.32	171.80	193.27	214.75
860	5.37	10.75	21.50	43.00	64.50	86.00	107.50	129.00	150.50	172.00	193.50	215.00
861	5.38	10.76	21.52	43.05	64.57	86.10	107.62	129.15	150.67	172.20	193.72	215.25
862	5.39	10.77	21.55	43.10	64.65	86.20	107.75	129.30	150.85	172.40	193.95	215.50
863	5.39	10.79	21.57	43.15	64.72	86.30	107.87	129.45	151.02	172.60	194.17	215.75
864	5.40	10.80	21.60	43.20	64.80	86.40	108.00	129.60	151.20	172.80	194.40	216.00
865	5.41	10.81	21.62	43.25	64.87	86.50	108.12	129.75	151.37	173.00	194.62	216.25
866	5.41	10.82	21.65	43.30	64.95	86.60	108.25	129.90	151.55	173.20	194.85	216.50
867	5.42	10.84	21.67	43.35	65.02	86.70	108.37	130.05	151.72	173.40	195.07	216.75
868	5.42	10.85	21.70	43.40	65.10	86.80	108.50	130.20	151.90	173.60	195.30	217.00
869	5.43	10.86	21.72	43.45	65.17	86.90	108.62	130.35	152.07	173.80	195.52	217.25
870	5.44	10.87	21.75	43.50	65.25	87.00	108.75	130.50	152.25	174.00	195.75	217.50
871	5.44	10.89	21.77	43.55	65.32	87.10	108.87	130.65	152.42	174.20	195.97	217.75
872	5.45	10.90	21.80	43.60	65.40	87.20	109.00	130.80	152.60	174.40	196.20	218.00
873	5.46	10.91	21.82	43.65	65.47	87.30	109.12	130.95	152.77	174.60	196.42	218.25
874	5.46	10.92	21.85	43.70	65.55	87.40	109.25	131.10	152.95	174.80	196.65	218.50
875	5.47	10.94	21.87	43.75	65.62	87.50	109.37	131.25	153.12	175.00	196.87	218.75
876	5.47	10.95	21.90	43.80	65.70	87.60	109.50	131.40	153.30	175.20	197.10	219.00
877	5.48	10.96	21.92	43.85	65.77	87.70	109.62	131.55	153.47	175.40	197.32	219.25
878	5.49	10.97	21.95	43.90	65.85	87.80	109.75	131.70	153.65	175.60	197.55	219.50
879	5.49	10.99	21.97	43.95	65.92	87.90	109.87	131.85	153.82	175.80	197.77	219.75
880	5.50	11.00	22.00	44.00	66.00	88.00	110.00	132.00	154.00	176.00	198.00	220.00
881	5.51	11.01	22.02	44.05	66.07	88.10	110.12	132.15	154.17	176.20	198.22	220.25
882	5.51	11.02	22.05	44.10	66.15	88.20	110.25	132.30	154.35	176.40	198.45	220.50
883	5.52	11.04	22.07	44.15	66.22	88.30	110.37	132.45	154.52	176.60	198.67	220.75
884	5.52	11.05	22.10	44.20	66.30	88.40	110.50	132.60	154.70	176.80	198.90	221.00
885	5.53	11.06	22.12	44.25	66.37	88.50	110.62	132.75	154.87	177.00	199.12	221.25
886	5.54	11.07	22.15	44.30	66.45	88.60	110.75	132.90	155.05	177.20	199.35	221.50
887	5.54	11.09	22.17	44.35	66.52	88.70	110.87	133.05	155.22	177.40	199.57	221.75
888	5.55	11.10	22.20	44.40	66.60	88.80	111.00	133.20	155.40	177.60	199.80	222.00
889	5.56	11.11	22.22	44.45	66.67	88.90	111.12	133.35	155.57	177.80	200.02	222.25
890	5.56	11.12	22.25	44.50	66.75	89.00	111.25	133.50	155.75	178.00	200.25	222.50
891	5.57	11.14	22.27	44.55	66.82	89.10	111.37	133.65	155.92	178.20	200.47	222.75
892	5.57	11.15	22.30	44.60	66.90	89.20	111.50	133.80	156.10	178.40	200.70	223.00
893	5.58	11.16	22.32	44.65	66.97	89.30	111.62	133.95	156.27	178.60	200.92	223.25
894	5.59	11.17	22.35	44.70	67.05	89.40	111.75	134.10	156.45	178.80	201.15	223.50
895	5.59	11.19	22.37	44.75	67.12	89.50	111.87	134.25	156.62	179.00	201.37	223.75
896	5.60	11.20	22.40	44.80	67.20	89.60	112.00	134.40	156.80	179.20	201.60	224.00
897	5.61	11.21	22.42	44.85	67.27	89.70	112.12	134.55	156.97	179.40	201.82	224.25
898	5.61	11.22	22.45	44.90	67.35	89.80	112.25	134.70	157.15	179.60	202.05	224.50
899	5.62	11.24	22.47	44.95	67.42	89.90	112.37	134.85	157.32	179.80	202.27	224.75
900	5.62	11.25	22.50	45.00	67.50	90.00	112.50	135.00	157.50	180.00	202.50	225.00

900 FEET.

Per Ton,	$11	$12	$13	$14	$15	$16	$17	$18	$19	$20
Per Foot,	27½ cts.	30 cts.	32½ cts.	35 cts.	37½ cts.	40 cts.	42½ cts.	45 cts.	47½ cts.	50 cts.
Feet.										
851	234.02	255.30	276.57	297.85	319.12	340.40	361.67	382.95	404.22	425.50
852	234.30	255.60	276.90	298.20	319.50	340.80	362.10	383.40	404.70	426.00
853	234.57	255.90	277.22	298.55	319.87	341.20	362.52	383.85	405.17	426.50
854	234.85	256.20	277.55	298.90	320.25	341.60	362.95	384.30	405.65	427.00
855	235.12	256.50	277.87	299.25	320.62	342.00	363.37	384.75	406.12	427.50
856	235.40	256.80	278.20	299.60	321.00	342.40	363.80	385.20	406.60	428.00
857	235.67	257.10	278.52	299.95	321.37	342.80	364.22	385.65	407.07	428.50
858	235.95	257.40	278.85	300.30	321.75	343.20	364.65	386.10	407.55	429.00
859	236.22	257.70	279.17	300.65	322.12	343.60	365.07	386.55	408.02	429.50
860	236.50	258.00	279.50	301.00	322.50	344.00	365.50	387.00	408.50	430.00
861	236.77	258.30	279.82	301.35	322.87	344.40	365.92	387.45	408.97	430.50
862	237.05	258.60	280.15	301.70	323.25	344.80	366.35	387.90	409.45	431.00
863	237.32	258.90	280.47	302.05	323.62	345.20	366.77	388.35	409.92	431.50
864	237.60	259.20	280.80	302.40	324.00	345.60	367.20	388.80	410.40	432.00
865	237.87	259.50	281.12	302.75	324.37	346.00	367.62	389.25	410.87	432.50
866	238.15	259.80	281.45	303.10	324.75	346.40	368.05	389.70	411.35	433.00
867	238.42	260.10	281.77	303.45	325.12	346.80	368.47	390.15	411.82	433.50
868	238.70	260.40	282.10	303.80	325.50	347.20	368.90	390.60	412.30	434.00
869	238.97	260.70	282.42	304.15	325.87	347.60	369.32	391.05	412.77	434.50
870	239.25	261.00	282.75	304.50	326.25	348.00	369.75	391.50	413.25	435.00
871	239.52	261.30	283.07	304.85	326.62	348.40	370.17	391.95	413.72	435.50
872	239.80	261.60	283.40	305.20	327.00	348.80	370.60	392.40	414.20	436.00
873	240.07	261.90	283.72	305.55	327.37	349.20	371.02	392.85	414.67	436.50
874	240.35	262.20	284.05	305.90	327.75	349.60	371.45	393.30	415.15	437.00
875	240.62	262.50	284.37	306.25	328.12	350.00	371.87	393.75	415.62	437.50
876	240.90	262.80	284.70	306.60	328.50	350.40	372.30	394.20	416.10	438.00
877	241.17	263.10	285.02	306.95	328.87	350.80	372.72	394.65	416.57	438.50
878	241.45	263.40	285.35	307.30	329.25	351.20	373.15	395.10	417.05	439.00
879	241.72	263.70	285.67	307.65	329.62	351.60	373.57	395.55	417.52	439.50
880	242.00	264.00	286.00	308.00	330.00	352.00	374.00	396.00	418.00	440.00
881	242.27	264.30	286.32	308.35	330.37	352.40	374.42	396.45	418.47	440.50
882	242.55	264.60	286.65	308.70	330.75	352.80	374.85	396.90	418.95	441.00
883	242.82	264.90	286.97	309.05	331.12	353.20	375.27	397.35	419.42	441.50
884	243.10	265.20	287.30	309.40	331.50	353.60	375.70	397.80	419.90	442.00
885	243.37	265.50	287.62	309.75	331.87	354.00	376.12	398.25	420.37	442.50
886	243.65	265.80	287.95	310.10	332.25	354.40	376.55	398.70	420.85	443.00
887	243.92	266.10	288.27	310.45	332.62	354.80	376.97	399.15	421.32	443.50
888	244.20	266.40	288.60	310.80	333.00	355.20	377.40	399.60	421.80	444.00
889	244.47	266.70	288.92	311.15	333.37	355.60	377.82	400.05	422.27	444.50
890	244.75	267.00	289.25	311.50	333.75	356.00	378.25	400.50	422.75	445.00
891	245.02	267.30	289.57	311.85	334.12	356.40	378.67	400.95	423.22	445.50
892	245.30	267.60	289.90	312.20	334.50	356.80	379.10	401.40	423.70	446.00
893	245.57	267.90	290.22	312.55	334.87	357.20	379.52	401.85	424.17	446.50
894	245.85	268.20	290.55	312.90	335.25	357.60	379.95	402.30	424.65	447.00
895	246.12	268.50	290.87	313.25	335.62	358.00	380.37	402.75	425.12	447.50
896	246.40	268.80	291.20	313.60	336.00	358.40	380.80	403.20	425.60	448.00
897	246.67	269.10	291.52	313.95	336.37	358.80	381.22	403.65	426.07	448.50
898	246.95	269.40	291.85	314.30	336.75	359.20	381.65	404.10	426.55	449.00
899	247.22	269.70	292.17	314.65	337.12	359.60	382.07	404.55	427.02	449.50
900	247.50	270.00	292.50	315.00	337.50	360.00	382.50	405.00	427.50	450.00

950 FEET.

Per Ton,	25c.	50c.	$1	$2	$3	$4	$5	$6	$7	$8	$9	$10
Per Foot,			2½ cts.	5 cts.	7½ cts.	10 cts.	12½ cts.	15 cts.	17½ cts.	20 cts.	22½ cts.	25 cts.
Feet.												
901	5.63	11.26	22.52	45.05	67.57	90.10	112.62	135.15	157.67	180.20	202.72	225.25
902	5.64	11.27	22.55	45.10	67.65	90.20	112.75	135.30	157.85	180.40	202.95	225.50
903	5.64	11.29	22.57	45.15	67.72	90.30	112.87	135.45	158.02	180.60	203.17	225.75
904	5.65	11.30	22.60	45.20	67.80	90.40	113.00	135.60	158.20	180.80	203.40	226.00
905	5.66	11.31	22.62	45.25	67.87	90.50	113.12	135.75	158.37	181.00	203.62	226.25
906	5.66	11.32	22.65	45.30	67.95	90.60	113.25	135.90	158.55	181.20	203.85	226.50
907	5.67	11.34	22.67	45.35	68.02	90.70	113.37	136.05	158.72	181.40	204.07	226.75
908	5.67	11.35	22.70	45.40	68.10	90.80	113.50	136.20	158.90	181.60	204.30	227.00
909	5.68	11.36	22.72	45.45	68.17	90.90	113.62	136.35	159.07	181.80	204.52	227.25
910	5.69	11.37	22.75	45.50	68.25	91.00	113.75	136.50	159.25	182.00	204.75	227.50
911	5.69	11.39	22.77	45.55	68.32	91.10	113.87	136.65	159.42	182.20	204.97	227.75
912	5.70	11.40	22.80	45.60	68.40	91.20	114.00	136.80	159.60	182.40	205.20	228.00
913	5.71	11.41	22.82	45.65	68.47	91.30	114.12	136.95	159.77	182.60	205.42	228.25
914	5.71	11.42	22.85	45.70	68.55	91.40	114.25	137.10	159.95	182.80	205.65	228.50
915	5.72	11.44	22.87	45.75	68.62	91.50	114.37	137.25	160.12	183.00	205.87	228.75
916	5.72	11.45	22.90	45.80	68.70	91.60	114.50	137.40	160.30	183.20	206.10	229.00
917	5.73	11.46	22.92	45.85	68.77	91.70	114.62	137.55	160.47	183.40	206.32	229.25
918	5.74	11.47	22.95	45.90	68.85	91.80	114.75	137.70	160.65	183.60	206.55	229.50
919	5.74	11.49	22.97	45.95	68.92	91.90	114.87	137.85	160.82	183.80	206.77	229.75
920	5.75	11.50	23.00	46.00	69.00	92.00	115.00	138.00	161.00	184.00	207.00	230.00
921	5.76	11.51	23.02	46.05	69.07	92.10	115.12	138.15	161.17	184.20	207.22	230.25
922	5.76	11.52	23.05	46.10	69.15	92.20	115.25	138.30	161.35	184.40	207.45	230.50
923	5.77	11.54	23.07	46.15	69.22	92.30	115.37	138.45	161.52	184.60	207.67	230.75
924	5.77	11.55	23.10	46.20	69.30	92.40	115.50	138.60	161.70	184.80	207.90	231.00
925	5.78	11.56	23.12	46.25	69.37	92.50	115.62	138.75	161.87	185.00	208.12	231.25
926	5.79	11.57	23.15	46.30	69.45	92.60	115.75	138.90	162.05	185.20	208.35	231.50
927	5.79	11.59	23.17	46.35	69.52	92.70	115.87	139.05	162.22	185.40	208.57	231.75
928	5.80	11.60	23.20	46.40	69.60	92.80	116.00	139.20	162.40	185.60	208.80	232.00
929	5.81	11.61	23.22	46.45	69.67	92.90	116.12	139.35	162.57	185.80	209.02	232.25
930	5.81	11.62	23.25	46.50	69.75	93.00	116.25	139.50	162.75	186.00	209.25	232.50
931	5.82	11.64	23.27	46.55	69.82	93.10	116.37	139.65	162.92	186.20	209.47	232.75
932	5.82	11.65	23.30	46.60	69.90	93.20	116.50	139.80	163.10	186.40	209.70	233.00
933	5.83	11.66	23.32	46.65	69.97	93.30	116.62	139.95	163.27	186.60	209.92	233.25
934	5.84	11.67	23.35	46.70	70.05	93.40	116.75	140.10	163.45	186.80	210.15	233.50
935	5.84	11.69	23.37	46.75	70.12	93.50	116.87	140.25	163.62	187.00	210.37	233.75
936	5.85	11.70	23.40	46.80	70.20	93.60	117.00	140.40	163.80	187.20	210.60	234.00
937	5.86	11.71	23.42	46.85	70.27	93.70	117.12	140.55	163.97	187.40	210.82	234.25
938	5.86	11.72	23.45	46.90	70.35	93.80	117.25	140.70	164.15	187.60	211.05	234.50
939	5.87	11.74	23.47	46.95	70.42	93.90	117.37	140.85	164.32	187.80	211.27	234.75
940	5.87	11.75	23.50	47.00	70.50	94.00	117.50	141.00	164.50	188.00	211.50	235.00
941	5.88	11.76	23.52	47.05	70.57	94.10	117.62	141.15	164.67	188.20	211.72	235.25
942	5.89	11.77	23.55	47.10	70.65	94.20	117.75	141.30	164.85	188.40	211.95	235.50
943	5.89	11.79	23.57	47.15	70.72	94.30	117.87	141.45	165.02	188.60	212.17	235.75
944	5.90	11.80	23.60	47.20	70.80	94.40	118.00	141.60	165.20	188.80	212.40	236.00
945	5.91	11.81	23.62	47.25	70.87	94.50	118.12	141.75	165.37	189.00	212.62	236.25
946	5.91	11.82	23.65	47.30	70.95	94.60	118.25	141.90	165.55	189.20	212.85	236.50
947	5.92	11.84	23.67	47.35	71.02	94.70	118.37	142.05	165.72	189.40	213.07	236.75
948	5.92	11.85	23.70	47.40	71.10	94.80	118.50	142.20	165.90	189.60	213.30	237.00
949	5.93	11.86	23.72	47.45	71.17	94.90	118.62	142.35	166.07	189.80	213.52	237.25
950	5.94	11.87	23.75	47.50	71.25	95.00	118.75	142.50	166.25	190.00	213.75	237.50

950 FEET.

Per Ton,	$11	$12	$13	$14	$15	$16	$17	$18	$19	$20
Per Foot,	27½ cts.	30 cts.	32½ cts.	35 cts.	37½ cts.	40 cts.	42½ cts.	45 cts.	47½ cts.	50 cts.
Feet.										
901	247.77	270.30	292.82	315.35	337.87	360.40	382.92	405.45	427.97	450.50
902	248.05	270.60	293.15	315.70	338.25	360.80	383.35	405.90	428.45	451.00
903	248.32	270.90	293.47	316.05	338.62	361.20	383.77	406.35	428.92	451.50
904	248.60	271.20	293.80	316.40	339.00	361.60	384.20	406.80	429.40	452.00
905	248.87	271.50	294.12	316.75	339.37	362.00	384.62	407.25	429.87	452.50
906	249.15	271.80	294.45	317.10	339.75	362.40	385.05	407.70	430.35	453.00
907	249.42	272.10	294.77	317.45	340.12	362.80	385.47	408.15	430.82	453.50
908	249.70	272.40	295.10	317.80	340.50	363.20	385.90	408.60	431.30	454.00
909	249.97	272.70	295.42	318.15	340.87	363.60	386.32	409.05	431.77	454.50
910	250.25	273.00	295.75	318.50	341.25	364.00	386.75	409.50	432.25	455.00
911	250.52	273.30	296.07	318.85	341.62	364.40	387.17	409.95	432.72	455.50
912	250.80	273.60	296.40	319.20	342.00	364.80	387.60	410.40	433.20	456.00
913	251.07	273.90	296.72	319.55	342.37	365.20	388.02	410.85	433.67	456.50
914	251.35	274.20	297.05	319.90	342.75	365.60	388.45	411.30	434.15	457.00
915	251.62	274.50	297.37	320.25	343.12	366.00	388.87	411.75	434.62	457.50
916	251.90	274.80	297.70	320.60	343.50	366.40	389.30	412.20	435.10	458.00
917	252.17	275.10	298.02	320.95	343.87	366.80	389.72	412.65	435.57	458.50
918	252.45	275.40	298.35	321.30	344.25	367.20	390.15	413.10	436.05	459.00
919	252.72	275.70	298.67	321.65	344.62	367.60	390.57	413.55	436.52	459.50
920	253.00	276.00	299.00	322.00	345.00	368.00	391.00	414.00	437.00	460.00
921	253.27	276.30	299.32	322.35	345.37	368.40	391.42	414.45	437.47	460.50
922	253.55	276.60	299.65	322.70	345.75	368.80	391.85	414.90	437.95	461.00
923	253.82	276.90	299.97	323.05	346.12	369.20	392.27	415.35	438.42	461.50
924	254.10	277.20	300.30	323.40	346.50	369.60	392.70	415.80	438.90	462.00
925	254.37	277.50	300.62	323.75	346.87	370.00	393.12	416.25	439.37	462.50
926	254.65	277.80	300.95	324.10	347.25	370.40	393.55	416.70	439.85	463.00
927	254.92	278.10	301.27	324.45	347.62	370.80	393.97	417.15	440.32	463.50
928	255.20	278.40	301.60	324.80	348.00	371.20	394.40	417.60	440.80	464.00
929	255.47	278.70	301.92	325.15	348.37	371.60	394.82	418.05	441.27	464.50
930	255.75	279.00	302.25	325.50	348.75	372.00	395.25	418.50	441.75	465.00
931	256.02	279.30	302.57	325.85	349.12	372.40	395.67	418.95	442.22	465.50
932	256.30	279.60	302.90	326.20	349.50	372.80	396.10	419.40	442.70	466.00
933	256.57	279.90	303.22	326.55	349.87	373.20	396.52	419.85	443.17	466.50
934	256.85	280.20	303.55	326.90	350.25	373.60	396.95	420.30	443.65	467.00
935	257.12	280.50	303.87	327.25	350.62	374.00	397.37	420.75	444.12	467.50
936	257.40	280.80	304.20	327.60	351.00	374.40	397.80	421.20	444.60	468.00
937	257.67	281.10	304.52	327.95	351.37	374.80	398.22	421.65	445.07	468.50
938	257.95	281.40	304.85	328.30	351.75	375.20	398.65	422.10	445.55	469.00
939	258.22	281.70	305.17	328.65	352.12	375.60	399.07	422.55	446.02	469.50
940	258.50	282.00	305.50	329.00	352.50	376.00	399.50	423.00	446.50	470.00
941	258.77	282.30	305.82	329.35	352.87	376.40	399.92	423.45	446.97	470.50
942	259.05	282.60	306.15	329.70	353.25	376.80	400.35	423.90	447.45	471.00
943	259.32	282.90	306.47	330.05	353.62	377.20	400.77	424.35	447.92	471.50
944	259.60	283.20	306.80	330.40	354.00	377.60	401.20	424.80	448.40	472.00
945	259.87	283.50	307.12	330.75	354.37	378.00	401.62	425.25	448.87	472.50
946	260.15	283.80	307.45	331.10	354.75	378.40	402.05	425.70	449.35	473.00
947	260.42	284.10	307.77	331.45	355.12	378.80	402.47	426.15	449.82	473.50
948	260.70	284.40	308.10	331.80	355.50	379.20	402.90	426.60	450.30	474.00
949	260.97	284.70	308.42	332.15	355.87	379.60	403.32	427.05	450.77	474.50
950	261.25	285.00	308.75	332.50	356.25	380.00	403.75	427.50	451.25	475.00

1000 FEET.

Per Ton,	25c.	50c.	$1	$2	$3	$4	$5	$6	$7	$8	$9	$10
Per Foot,			2½ cts.	5 cts.	7½ cts.	10 cts.	12½ cts.	15 cts.	17½ cts.	20 cts.	22½ cts.	25 cts.
Feet.												
951	5.94	11.89	23.77	47.55	71.32	95.10	118.87	142.65	166.42	190.20	213.97	237.75
952	5.95	11.90	23.80	47.60	71.40	95.20	119.00	142.80	166.60	190.40	214.20	238.00
953	5.96	11.91	23.82	47.65	71.47	95.30	119.12	142.95	166.77	190.60	214.42	238.25
954	5.96	11.92	23.85	47.70	71.55	95.40	119.25	143.10	166.95	190.80	214.65	238.50
955	5.97	11.94	23.87	47.75	71.62	95.50	119.37	143.25	167.12	191.00	214.87	238.75
956	5.97	11.95	23.90	47.80	71.70	95.60	119.50	143.40	167.30	191.20	215.10	239.00
957	5.98	11.96	23.92	47.85	71.77	95.70	119.62	143.55	167.47	191.40	215.32	239.25
958	5.99	11.97	23.95	47.90	71.85	95.80	119.75	143.70	167.65	191.60	215.55	239.50
959	5.99	11.99	23.97	47.95	71.92	95.90	119.87	143.85	167.82	191.80	215.77	239.75
960	6.00	12.00	24.00	48.00	72.00	96.00	120.00	144.00	168.00	192.00	216.00	240.00
961	6.01	12.01	24.02	48.05	72.07	96.10	120.12	144.15	168.17	192.20	216.22	240.25
962	6.01	12.02	24.05	48.10	72.15	96.20	120.25	144.30	168.35	192.40	216.45	240.50
963	6.02	12.04	24.07	48.15	72.22	96.30	120.37	144.45	168.52	192.60	216.67	240.75
964	6.02	12.05	24.10	48.20	72.30	96.40	120.50	144.60	168.70	192.80	216.90	241.00
965	6.03	12.06	24.12	48.25	72.37	96.50	120.62	144.75	168.87	193.00	217.12	241.25
966	6.04	12.07	24.15	48.30	72.45	96.60	120.75	144.90	169.05	193.20	217.35	241.50
967	6.04	12.09	24.17	48.35	72.52	96.70	120.87	145.05	169.22	193.40	217.57	241.75
968	6.05	12.10	24.20	48.40	72.60	96.80	121.00	145.20	169.40	193.60	217.80	242.00
969	6.06	12.11	24.22	48.45	72.67	96.90	121.12	145.35	169.57	193.80	218.02	242.25
970	6.06	12.12	24.25	48.50	72.75	97.00	121.25	145.50	169.75	194.00	218.25	242.50
971	6.07	12.14	24.27	48.55	72.82	97.10	121.37	145.65	169.92	194.20	218.47	242.75
972	6.07	12.15	24.30	48.60	72.90	97.20	121.50	145.80	170.10	194.40	218.70	243.00
973	6.08	12.16	24.32	48.65	72.97	97.30	121.62	145.95	170.27	194.60	218.92	243.25
974	6.09	12.17	24.35	48.70	73.05	97.40	121.75	146.10	170.45	194.80	219.15	243.50
975	6.09	12.19	24.37	48.75	73.12	97.50	121.87	146.25	170.62	195.00	219.37	243.75
976	6.10	12.20	24.40	48.80	73.20	97.60	122.00	146.40	170.80	195.20	219.60	244.00
977	6.11	12.21	24.42	48.85	73.27	97.70	122.12	146.55	170.97	195.40	219.82	244.25
978	6.11	12.22	24.45	48.90	73.35	97.80	122.25	146.70	171.15	195.60	220.05	244.50
979	6.12	12.24	24.47	48.95	73.42	97.90	122.37	146.85	171.32	195.80	220.27	244.75
980	6.12	12.25	24.50	49.00	73.50	98.00	122.50	147.00	171.50	196.00	220.50	245.00
981	6.13	12.26	24.52	49.05	73.57	98.10	122.62	147.15	171.67	196.20	220.72	245.25
982	6.14	12.27	24.55	49.10	73.65	98.20	122.75	147.30	171.85	196.40	220.95	245.50
983	6.14	12.29	24.57	49.15	73.72	98.30	122.87	147.45	172.02	196.60	221.17	245.75
984	6.15	12.30	24.60	49.20	73.80	98.40	123.00	147.60	172.20	196.80	221.40	246.00
985	6.16	12.31	24.62	49.25	73.87	98.50	123.12	147.75	172.37	197.00	221.62	246.25
986	6.16	12.32	24.65	49.30	73.95	98.60	123.25	147.90	172.55	197.20	221.85	246.50
987	6.17	12.34	24.67	49.35	74.02	98.70	123.37	148.05	172.72	197.40	222.07	246.75
988	6.17	12.35	24.70	49.40	74.10	98.80	123.50	148.20	172.90	197.60	222.30	247.00
989	6.18	12.36	24.72	49.45	74.17	98.90	123.62	148.35	173.07	197.80	222.52	247.25
990	6.19	12.37	24.75	49.50	74.25	99.00	123.75	148.50	173.25	198.00	222.75	247.50
991	6.19	12.39	24.77	49.55	74.32	99.10	123.87	148.65	173.42	198.20	222.97	247.75
992	6.20	12.40	24.80	49.60	74.40	99.20	124.00	148.80	173.60	198.40	223.20	248.00
993	6.21	12.41	24.82	49.65	74.47	99.30	124.12	148.95	173.77	198.60	223.42	248.25
994	6.21	12.42	24.85	49.70	74.55	99.40	124.25	149.10	173.95	198.80	223.65	248.50
995	6.22	12.44	24.87	49.75	74.62	99.50	124.37	149.25	174.12	199.00	223.87	248.75
996	6.22	12.45	24.90	49.80	74.70	99.60	124.50	149.40	174.30	199.20	224.10	249.00
997	6.23	12.46	24.92	49.85	74.77	99.70	124.62	149.55	174.47	199.40	224.32	249.25
998	6.24	12.47	24.95	49.90	74.85	99.80	124.75	149.70	174.65	199.60	224.55	249.50
999	6.24	12.49	24.97	49.95	74.92	99.90	124.87	149.85	174.82	199.80	224.77	249.75
1000	6.25	12.50	25.00	50.00	75.00	100.00	125.00	150.00	175.00	200.00	225.00	250.00

1000 FEET.

Per Ton,	$11	$12	$13	$14	$15	$16	$17	$18	$19	$20
Per Foot,	27½ cts.	30 cts.	32½ cts.	35 cts.	37½ cts.	40 cts.	42½ cts.	45 cts.	47½ cts.	50 cts.
Feet.										
951	261.52	285.30	309.07	332.85	356.62	380.40	404.17	427.95	451.72	475.50
952	261.80	285.60	309.40	333.20	357.00	380.80	404.60	428.40	452.20	476.00
953	262.07	285.90	309.72	333.55	357.37	381.20	405.02	428.85	452.67	476.50
954	262.35	286.20	310.05	333.90	357.75	381.60	405.45	429.30	453.15	477.00
955	262.62	286.50	310.37	334.25	358.12	382.00	405.87	429.75	453.62	477.50
956	262.90	286.80	310.70	334.60	358.50	382.40	406.30	430.20	454.10	478.00
957	263.17	287.10	311.02	334.95	358.87	382.80	406.72	430.65	454.57	478.50
958	263.45	287.40	311.35	335.30	359.25	383.20	407.15	431.10	455.05	479.00
959	263.72	287.70	311.67	335.65	359.62	383.60	407.57	431.55	455.52	479.50
960	264.00	288.00	312.00	336.00	360.00	384.00	408.00	432.00	456.00	480.00
961	264.27	288.30	312.32	336.35	360.37	384.40	408.42	432.45	456.47	480.50
962	264.55	288.60	312.65	336.70	360.75	384.80	408.85	432.90	456.95	481.00
963	264.82	288.90	312.97	337.05	361.12	385.20	409.27	433.35	457.42	481.50
964	265.10	289.20	313.30	337.40	361.50	385.60	409.70	433.80	457.90	482.00
965	265.37	289.50	313.62	337.75	361.87	386.00	410.12	434.25	458.37	482.50
966	265.65	289.80	313.95	338.10	362.25	386.40	410.55	434.70	458.85	483.00
967	265.92	290.10	314.27	338.45	362.62	386.80	410.97	435.15	459.32	483.50
968	266.20	290.40	314.60	338.80	363.00	387.20	411.40	435.60	459.80	484.00
969	266.47	290.70	314.92	339.15	363.37	387.60	411.82	436.05	460.27	484.50
970	266.75	291.00	315.25	339.50	363.75	388.00	412.25	436.50	460.75	485.00
971	267.02	291.30	315.57	339.85	364.12	388.40	412.67	436.95	461.22	485.50
972	267.30	291.60	315.90	340.20	364.50	388.80	413.10	437.40	461.70	486.00
973	267.57	291.90	316.22	340.55	364.87	389.20	413.52	437.85	462.17	486.50
974	267.85	292.20	316.55	340.90	365.25	389.60	413.95	438.30	462.65	487.00
975	268.12	292.50	316.87	341.25	365.62	390.00	414.37	438.75	463.12	487.50
976	268.40	292.80	317.20	341.60	366.00	390.40	414.80	439.20	463.60	488.00
977	268.67	293.10	317.52	341.95	366.37	390.80	415.22	439.65	464.07	488.50
978	268.95	293.40	317.85	342.30	366.75	391.20	415.65	440.10	464.55	489.00
979	269.22	293.70	318.17	342.65	367.12	391.60	416.07	440.55	465.02	489.50
980	269.50	294.00	318.50	343.00	367.50	392.00	416.50	441.00	465.50	490.00
981	269.77	294.30	318.82	343.35	367.87	392.40	416.92	441.45	465.97	490.50
982	270.05	294.60	319.15	343.70	368.25	392.80	417.35	441.90	466.45	491.00
983	270.32	294.90	319.47	344.05	368.62	393.20	417.77	442.35	466.92	491.50
984	270.60	295.20	319.80	344.40	369.00	393.60	418.20	442.80	467.40	492.00
985	270.87	295.50	320.12	344.75	369.37	394.00	418.62	443.25	467.87	492.50
986	271.15	295.80	320.45	345.10	369.75	394.40	419.05	443.70	468.35	493.00
987	271.42	296.10	320.77	345.45	370.12	394.80	419.47	444.15	468.82	493.50
988	271.70	296.40	321.10	345.80	370.50	395.20	419.90	444.60	469.30	494.00
989	271.97	296.70	321.42	346.15	370.87	395.60	420.32	445.05	469.77	494.50
990	272.25	297.00	321.75	346.50	371.25	396.00	420.75	445.50	470.25	495.00
991	272.52	297.30	322.07	346.85	371.62	396.40	421.17	445.95	470.72	495.50
992	272.80	297.60	322.40	347.20	372.00	396.80	421.60	446.40	471.20	496.00
993	273.07	297.90	322.72	347.55	372.37	397.20	422.02	446.85	471.67	496.50
994	273.35	298.20	323.05	347.90	372.75	397.60	422.45	447.30	472.15	497.00
995	273.62	298.50	323.37	348.25	373.12	398.00	422.87	447.75	472.62	497.50
996	273.90	298.80	323.70	348.60	373.50	398.40	423.30	448.20	473.10	498.00
997	274.17	299.10	324.02	348.95	373.87	398.80	423.72	448.65	473.57	498.50
998	274.45	299.40	324.35	349.30	374.25	399.20	424.15	449.10	474.05	499.00
999	274.72	299.70	324.67	349.65	374.62	399.60	424.57	449.55	474.52	499.50
1000	275.00	300.00	325.00	350.00	375.00	400.00	425.00	450.00	475.00	500.00

1050 FEET.

Per Ton,	25c.	50c.	$1	$2	$3	$4	$5	$6	$7	$8	$9	$10
Per Foot,			2½ cts.	5 cts.	7½ cts.	10 cts.	12½ cts.	15 cts.	17½ cts.	20 cts.	22½ cts.	25 cts.
Feet.												
1001	6.26	12.51	25.02	50.05	75.07	100.10	125.12	150.15	175.17	200.20	225.22	250.25
1002	6.26	12.52	25.05	50.10	75.15	100.20	125.25	150.30	175.35	200.40	225.45	250.50
1003	6.27	12.54	25.07	50.15	75.22	100.30	125.37	150.45	175.52	200.60	225.67	250.75
1004	6.27	12.55	25.10	50.20	75.30	100.40	125.50	150.60	175.70	200.80	225.90	251.00
1005	6.28	12.56	25.12	50.25	75.37	100.50	125.62	150.75	175.87	201.00	226.12	251.25
1006	6.29	12.57	25.15	50.30	75.45	100.60	125.75	150.90	176.05	201.20	226.35	251.50
1007	6.29	12.59	25.17	50.35	75.52	100.70	125.87	151.05	176.22	201.40	226.57	251.75
1008	6.30	12.60	25.20	50.40	75.60	100.80	126.00	151.20	176.40	201.60	226.80	252.00
1009	6.31	12.61	25.22	50.45	75.67	100.90	126.12	151.35	176.57	201.80	227.02	252.25
1010	6.31	12.62	25.25	50.50	75.75	101.00	126.25	151.50	176.75	202.00	227.25	252.50
1011	6.32	12.64	25.27	50.55	75.82	101.10	126.37	151.65	176.92	202.20	227.47	252.75
1012	6.32	12.65	25.30	50.60	75.90	101.20	126.50	151.80	177.10	202.40	227.70	253.00
1013	6.33	12.66	25.32	50.65	75.97	101.30	126.62	151.95	177.27	202.60	227.92	253.25
1014	6.34	12.67	25.35	50.70	76.05	101.40	126.75	152.10	177.45	202.80	228.15	253.50
1015	6.34	12.69	25.37	50.75	76.12	101.50	126.87	152.25	177.62	203.00	228.37	253.75
1016	6.35	12.70	25.40	50.80	76.20	101.60	127.00	152.40	177.80	203.20	228.60	254.00
1017	6.36	12.71	25.42	50.85	76.27	101.70	127.12	152.55	177.97	203.40	228.82	254.25
1018	6.36	12.72	25.45	50.90	76.35	101.80	127.25	152.70	178.15	203.60	229.05	254.50
1019	6.37	12.74	25.47	50.95	76.42	101.90	127.37	152.85	178.32	203.80	229.27	254.75
1020	6.37	12.75	25.50	51.00	76.50	102.00	127.50	153.00	178.50	204.00	229.50	255.00
1021	6.38	12.76	25.52	51.05	76.57	102.10	127.62	153.15	178.67	204.20	229.72	255.25
1022	6.39	12.77	25.55	51.10	76.65	102.20	127.75	153.30	178.85	204.40	229.95	255.50
1023	6.39	12.79	25.57	51.15	76.72	102.30	127.87	153.45	179.02	204.60	230.17	255.75
1024	6.40	12.80	25.60	51.20	76.80	102.40	128.00	153.60	179.20	204.80	230.40	256.00
1025	6.41	12.81	25.62	51.25	76.87	102.50	128.12	153.75	179.37	205.00	230.62	256.25
1026	6.41	12.82	25.65	51.30	76.95	102.60	128.25	153.90	179.55	205.20	230.85	256.50
1027	6.42	12.84	25.67	51.35	77.02	102.70	128.37	154.05	179.72	205.40	231.07	256.75
1028	6.42	12.85	25.70	51.40	77.10	102.80	128.50	154.20	179.90	205.60	231.30	257.00
1029	6.43	12.86	25.72	51.45	77.17	102.90	128.62	154.35	180.07	205.80	231.52	257.25
1030	6.44	12.87	25.75	51.50	77.25	103.00	128.75	154.50	180.25	206.00	231.75	257.50
1031	6.44	12.89	25.77	51.55	77.32	103.10	128.87	154.65	180.42	206.20	231.97	257.75
1032	6.45	12.90	25.80	51.60	77.40	103.20	129.00	154.80	180.60	206.40	232.20	258.00
1033	6.46	12.91	25.82	51.65	77.47	103.30	129.12	154.95	180.77	206.60	232.42	258.25
1034	6.46	12.92	25.85	51.70	77.55	103.40	129.25	155.10	180.95	206.80	232.65	258.50
1035	6.47	12.94	25.87	51.75	77.62	103.50	129.37	155.25	181.12	207.00	232.87	258.75
1036	6.47	12.95	25.90	51.80	77.70	103.60	129.50	155.40	181.20	207.20	233.10	259.00
1037	6.48	12.96	25.92	51.85	77.77	103.70	129.62	155.55	181.47	207.40	233.32	259.25
1038	6.49	12.97	25.95	51.90	77.85	103.80	129.75	155.70	181.65	207.60	233.55	259.50
1039	6.49	12.99	25.97	51.95	77.92	103.90	129.87	155.85	181.82	207.80	233.77	259.75
1040	6.50	13.00	26.00	52.00	78.00	104.00	130.00	156.00	182.00	208.00	234.00	260.00
1041	6.51	13.01	26.02	52.05	78.07	104.10	130.12	156.15	182.17	208.20	234.22	260.25
1042	6.51	13.02	26.05	52.10	78.15	104.20	130.25	156.30	182.35	208.40	234.45	260.50
1043	6.52	13.04	26.07	52.15	78.22	104.30	130.37	156.45	182.52	208.60	234.67	260.75
1044	6.52	13.05	26.10	52.20	78.30	104.40	130.50	156.60	182.70	208.80	234.90	261.00
1045	6.53	13.06	26.12	52.25	78.37	104.50	130.62	156.75	182.87	209.00	235.12	261.25
1046	6.54	13.07	26.15	52.30	78.45	104.60	130.75	156.90	183.05	209.20	235.35	261.50
1047	6.54	13.09	26.17	52.35	78.52	104.70	130.87	157.05	183.22	209.40	235.57	261.75
1048	6.55	13.10	26.20	52.40	78.60	104.80	131.00	157.20	183.40	209.60	235.80	262.00
1049	6.55	13.11	26.22	52.45	78.67	104.90	131.12	157.35	183.57	209.80	236.02	262.25
1050	6.56	13.12	26.25	52.50	88.75	105.00	131.25	157.50	183.75	210.00	236.25	262.50

1050 FEET.

Per Ton,	$11	$12	$13	$14	$15	$16	$17	$18	$19	$20
Per Foot,	27½ cts.	30 cts.	32½ cts.	35 cts.	37½ cts.	40 cts.	42½ cts.	45 cts.	47½ cts.	50 cts.
Feet.										
1001	275.27	300.30	325.32	350.35	375.37	400.40	425.42	450.45	475.47	500.50
1002	275.55	300.60	325.65	350.70	375.75	400.80	425.85	450.90	475.95	501.00
1003	275.82	300.90	325.97	351.05	376.12	401.20	426.27	451.35	476.42	501.50
1004	276.10	301.20	326.30	351.40	376.50	401.60	426.70	451.80	476.90	502.00
1005	276.37	301.50	326.62	351.75	376.87	402.00	427.12	452.25	477.37	502.50
1006	276.65	301.80	326.95	352.10	377.25	402.40	427.55	452.70	477.85	503.00
1007	276.92	302.10	327.27	352.45	377.62	402.80	427.97	453.15	478.32	503.50
1008	277.20	302.40	327.60	352.80	378.00	403.20	428.40	453.60	478.80	504.00
1009	277.47	302.70	327.92	353.15	378.37	403.60	428.82	454.05	479.27	504.50
1010	277.75	303.00	328.25	353.50	378.75	404.00	429.25	454.50	479.75	505.00
1011	278.02	303.30	328.57	353.85	379.12	404.40	429.67	454.95	480.22	505.50
1012	278.30	303.60	328.90	354.20	379.50	404.80	430.10	455.40	480.70	506.00
1013	278.57	303.90	329.22	354.55	379.87	405.20	430.52	455.85	481.17	506.50
1014	278.85	304.20	329.55	354.90	380.25	405.60	430.95	456.30	481.65	507.00
1015	279.12	304.50	329.87	355.25	380.62	406.00	431.37	456.75	482.12	507.50
1016	279.40	304.80	330.20	355.60	381.00	406.40	431.80	457.20	482.60	508.00
1017	279.67	305.10	330.52	355.95	381.37	406.80	432.22	457.65	483.07	508.50
1018	279.95	305.40	330.85	356.30	381.75	407.20	432.65	458.10	483.55	509.00
1019	280.22	305.70	331.17	356.65	382.12	407.60	433.07	458.55	484.02	509.50
1020	280.50	306.00	331.50	357.00	382.50	408.00	433.50	459.00	484.50	510.00
1021	280.77	306.30	331.82	357.35	382.87	408.40	433.92	459.45	484.97	510.50
1022	281.05	306.60	332.15	357.70	383.25	408.80	434.35	459.90	485.45	511.00
1023	281.32	306.90	332.47	358.05	383.62	409.20	434.77	460.35	485.92	511.50
1024	281.60	307.20	332.80	358.40	384.00	409.60	435.20	460.80	486.40	512.00
1025	281.87	307.50	333.12	358.75	384.37	410.00	435.62	461.25	486.87	512.50
1026	282.15	307.80	333.45	359.10	384.75	410.40	436.05	461.70	487.35	513.00
1027	282.42	308.10	333.77	359.45	385.12	410.80	436.47	462.15	487.82	513.50
1028	282.70	308.40	334.10	359.80	385.50	411.20	436.90	462.60	488.30	514.00
1029	282.97	308.70	334.42	360.15	385.87	411.60	437.32	463.05	488.77	514.50
1030	283.25	309.00	334.75	360.50	386.25	412.00	437.75	463.50	489.25	515.00
1031	283.52	309.30	335.07	360.85	386.62	412.40	438.17	463.95	489.72	515.50
1032	283.80	309.60	335.40	361.20	387.00	412.80	438.60	464.40	490.20	516.00
1033	284.07	309.90	335.72	361.55	387.37	413.20	439.02	464.85	490.67	516.50
1034	284.35	310.20	336.05	361.90	387.75	413.60	439.45	465.30	491.15	517.00
1035	284.62	310.50	336.37	362.25	388.12	414.00	439.87	465.75	491.62	517.50
1036	284.90	310.80	336.70	362.60	388.50	414.40	440.30	466.20	492.10	518.00
1037	285.17	311.10	337.02	362.95	388.87	414.80	440.72	466.65	492.57	518.50
1038	285.45	311.40	337.35	363.30	389.25	415.20	441.15	467.10	493.05	519.00
1039	285.72	311.70	337.67	363.65	389.62	415.60	441.57	467.55	493.52	519.50
1040	286.00	312.00	338.00	364.00	390.00	416.00	442.00	468.00	494.00	520.00
1041	286.27	312.30	338.32	364.35	390.37	416.40	442.42	468.45	494.47	520.50
1042	286.55	312.60	338.65	364.70	390.75	416.80	442.85	468.90	494.95	521.00
1043	286.82	312.90	338.97	365.05	391.12	417.20	443.27	469.35	495.42	521.50
1044	287.10	313.20	339.30	365.40	391.50	417.60	443.70	469.80	495.90	522.00
1045	287.37	313.50	339.62	365.75	391.87	418.00	444.12	470.25	496.37	522.50
1046	287.65	313.80	339.95	366.10	392.25	418.40	444.55	470.70	496.85	523.00
1047	287.92	314.10	340.27	366.45	392.62	418.80	444.97	471.15	497.32	523.50
1048	288.20	314.40	340.60	366.80	393.00	419.20	445.40	471.60	497.80	524.00
1049	288.47	314.70	340.92	367.15	393.37	419.60	445.82	472.05	498.27	524.50
1050	288.75	315.00	341.25	367.50	393.75	420.00	446.25	472.50	498.75	525.00

1100 FEET.

Per Ton,	25c.	50c.	$1	$2	$3	$4	$5	$6	$7	$8	$9	$10
Per Foot,			2½ cts.	5 cts.	7½ cts.	10 cts.	12½ cts.	15 cts.	17½ cts.	20 cts.	22½ cts.	25 cts.
Feet.												
1051	6.57	13.14	26.27	52.55	78.82	105.10	131.37	157.65	183.92	210.20	236.47	262.75
1052	6.57	13.15	26.30	52.60	78.90	105.20	131.50	157.80	184.10	210.40	236.70	263.00
1053	6.58	13.16	26.32	52.65	78.97	105.30	131.62	157.95	184.27	210.60	236.92	263.25
1054	6.59	13.17	26.35	52.70	79.05	105.40	131.75	158.10	184.45	210.80	237.15	263.50
1055	6.59	13.19	26.37	52.75	79.12	105.50	131.87	158.25	184.62	211.00	237.37	263.75
1056	6.60	13.20	26.40	52.80	79.20	105.60	132.00	158.40	184.80	211.20	237.60	264.00
1057	6.61	13.21	26.42	52.85	79.27	105.70	132.12	158.55	184.97	211.40	237.82	264.25
1058	6.61	13.22	26.45	52.90	79.35	105.80	132.25	158.70	185.15	211.60	238.05	264.50
1059	6.62	13.24	26.47	52.95	79.42	105.90	132.37	158.85	185.32	211.80	238.27	264.75
1060	6.62	13.25	26.50	53.00	79.50	106.00	132.50	159.00	185.50	212.00	238.50	265.00
1061	6.63	13.26	26.52	53.05	79.57	106.10	132.62	159.15	185.67	212.20	238.72	265.25
1062	6.64	13.27	26.55	53.10	79.65	106.20	132.75	159.30	185.85	212.40	238.95	265.50
1063	6.64	13.29	26.57	53.15	79.72	106.30	132.87	159.45	186.02	212.60	239.17	265.75
1064	6.65	13.30	26.60	53.20	79.80	106.40	133.00	159.60	186.20	212.80	239.40	266.00
1065	6.66	13.31	26.62	53.25	79.87	106.50	133.12	159.75	186.37	213.00	239.62	266.25
1066	6.66	13.32	26.65	53.30	79.95	106.60	133.25	159.90	186.55	213.20	239.85	266.50
1067	6.67	13.34	26.67	53.35	80.02	106.70	133.37	160.05	186.72	213.40	240.07	266.75
1068	6.67	13.35	26.70	53.40	80.10	106.80	133.50	160.20	186.90	213.60	240.30	267.00
1069	6.68	13.36	26.72	53.45	80.17	106.90	133.62	160.35	187.07	213.80	240.52	267.25
1070	6.69	13.37	26.75	53.50	80.25	107.00	133.75	160.50	187.25	214.00	240.75	267.50
1071	6.69	13.39	26.77	53.55	80.32	107.10	133.87	160.65	187.42	214.20	240.97	267.75
1072	6.70	13.40	26.80	53.60	80.40	107.20	134.00	160.80	187.60	214.40	241.20	268.00
1073	6.71	13.41	26.82	53.65	80.47	107.30	134.12	160.95	187.77	214.60	241.42	268.25
1074	6.71	13.42	26.85	53.70	80.55	107.40	134.25	161.10	187.95	214.80	241.65	268.50
1075	6.72	13.44	26.87	53.75	80.62	107.50	134.37	161.25	188.12	215.00	241.87	268.75
1076	6.72	13.45	26.90	53.80	80.70	107.60	134.50	161.40	188.30	215.20	242.10	269.00
1077	6.73	13.46	26.92	53.85	80.77	107.70	134.62	161.55	188.47	215.40	242.32	269.25
1078	6.74	13.47	26.95	53.90	80.85	107.80	134.75	161.70	188.65	215.60	242.55	269.50
1079	6.74	13.49	26.97	53.95	80.92	107.90	134.87	161.85	188.82	215.80	242.77	269.75
1080	6.75	13.50	27.00	54.00	81.00	108.00	135.00	162.00	189.00	216.00	243.00	270.00
1081	6.76	13.51	27.02	54.05	81.07	108.10	135.12	162.15	189.17	216.20	243.22	270.25
1082	6.76	13.52	27.05	54.10	81.15	108.20	135.25	162.30	189.35	216.40	243.45	270.50
1083	6.77	13.54	27.07	54.15	81.22	108.30	135.37	162.45	189.52	216.60	243.67	270.75
1084	6.77	13.55	27.10	54.20	81.30	108.40	135.50	162.60	189.70	216.80	243.90	271.00
1085	6.78	13.56	27.12	54.25	81.37	108.50	135.62	162.75	189.87	217.00	244.12	271.25
1086	6.79	13.57	27.15	54.30	81.45	108.60	135.75	162.90	190.05	217.20	244.35	271.50
1087	6.79	13.59	27.17	54.35	81.52	108.70	135.87	163.05	190.22	217.40	244.57	271.75
1088	6.80	13.60	27.20	54.40	81.60	108.80	136.00	163.20	190.40	217.60	244.80	272.00
1089	6.81	13.61	27.22	54.45	81.67	108.90	136.12	163.35	190.57	217.80	245.02	272.25
1090	6.81	13.62	27.25	54.50	81.75	109.00	136.25	163.50	190.75	218.00	245.25	272.50
1091	6.82	13.64	27.27	54.55	81.82	109.10	136.37	163.65	190.92	218.20	245.47	272.75
1092	6.82	13.65	27.30	54.60	81.90	109.20	136.50	163.80	191.10	218.40	245.70	273.00
1093	6.83	13.66	27.32	54.65	81.97	109.30	136.62	163.95	191.27	218.60	245.92	273.25
1094	6.84	13.67	27.35	54.70	82.05	109.40	136.75	164.10	191.45	218.80	246.15	273.50
1095	6.84	13.69	27.37	54.75	82.12	109.50	136.87	164.25	191.62	219.00	246.37	273.75
1096	6.85	13.70	27.40	54.80	82.20	109.60	137.00	164.40	191.80	219.20	246.60	274.00
1097	6.86	13.71	27.42	54.85	82.27	109.70	137.12	164.55	191.97	219.40	246.82	274.25
1098	6.86	13.72	27.45	54.90	82.35	109.80	137.25	164.70	192.15	219.60	247.05	274.50
1099	6.87	13.74	27.47	54.95	82.42	109.90	137.37	164.85	192.32	219.80	247.27	274.75
1100	6.87	13.75	27.50	55.00	82.50	110.00	137.50	165.00	192.50	220.00	247.50	275.00

1100 FEET.

Per Ton,	$11	$12	$13	$14	$15	$16	$17	$18	$19	$20
Per Foot,	27½ cts.	30 cts.	32½ cts.	35 cts.	37½ cts.	40 cts.	42½ cts.	45 cts.	47½ cts.	50 cts.
Feet.										
1051	289.02	315.30	341.57	367.85	394.12	420.40	446.67	472.95	499.22	525.50
1052	289.30	315.60	341.90	368.20	394.50	420.80	447.10	473.40	499.70	526.00
1053	289.57	315.90	342.22	368.55	394.87	421.20	447.52	473.85	500.17	526.50
1054	289.85	316.20	342.55	368.90	395.25	421.60	447.95	474.30	500.65	527.00
1055	290.12	316.50	342.87	369.25	395.62	422.00	448.37	474.75	501.12	527.50
1056	290.40	316.80	343.20	369.60	396.00	422.40	448.80	475.20	501.60	528.00
1057	290.67	317.10	343.52	369.95	396.37	422.80	449.22	475.65	502.07	528.50
1058	290.95	317.40	343.85	370.30	396.75	423.20	449.65	476.10	502.55	529.00
1059	291.22	317.70	344.17	370.65	397.12	423.60	450.07	476.55	503.02	529.50
1060	291.50	318.00	344.50	371.00	397.50	424.00	450.50	477.00	503.50	530.00
1061	291.77	318.30	344.82	371.35	397.87	424.40	450.92	477.45	503.97	530.50
1062	292.05	318.60	345.15	371.70	398.25	424.80	451.35	477.90	504.45	531.00
1063	292.32	318.90	345.47	372.05	398.62	425.20	451.77	478.35	504.92	531.50
1064	292.60	319.20	345.80	372.40	399.00	425.60	452.20	478.80	505.40	532.00
1065	292.87	319.50	346.12	372.75	399.37	426.00	452.62	479.25	505.87	532.50
1066	293.15	319.80	346.45	373.10	399.75	426.40	453.05	479.70	506.35	533.00
1067	293.42	320.10	346.77	373.45	400.12	426.80	453.47	480.15	506.82	533.50
1068	293.70	320.40	347.10	373.80	400.50	427.20	453.90	480.60	507.30	534.00
1069	293.97	320.70	347.42	374.15	400.87	427.60	454.32	481.05	507.77	534.50
1070	294.25	321.00	347.75	374.50	401.25	428.00	454.75	481.50	508.25	535.00
1071	294.52	321.30	348.07	374.85	401.62	428.40	455.17	481.95	508.72	535.50
1072	294.80	321.60	348.40	375.20	402.00	428.80	455.60	482.40	509.20	536.00
1073	295.07	321.90	348.72	375.55	402.37	429.20	456.02	482.85	509.67	536.50
1074	295.35	322.20	349.05	375.90	402.75	429.60	456.45	483.30	510.15	537.00
1075	295.62	322.50	349.37	376.25	403.12	430.00	456.87	483.75	510.62	537.50
1076	295.90	322.80	349.70	376.60	403.50	430.40	457.30	484.20	511.10	538.00
1077	296.17	323.10	350.02	376.95	403.87	430.80	457.72	484.65	511.57	538.50
1078	296.45	323.40	350.35	377.30	404.25	431.20	458.15	485.10	512.05	539.00
1079	296.72	323.70	350.67	377.65	404.62	431.60	458.57	485.55	512.52	539.50
1080	297.00	324.00	351.00	378.00	405.00	432.00	459.00	486.00	513.00	540.00
1081	297.27	324.30	351.32	378.35	405.37	432.40	459.42	486.45	513.47	540.50
1082	297.55	324.60	351.65	378.70	405.75	432.80	459.85	486.90	513.95	541.00
1083	297.82	324.90	351.97	379.05	406.12	433.20	460.27	487.35	514.42	541.50
1084	298.10	325.20	352.30	379.40	406.50	433.60	460.70	487.80	514.90	542.00
1085	298.37	325.50	352.62	379.75	406.87	434.00	461.12	488.25	515.37	542.50
1086	298.65	325.80	352.95	380.10	407.25	434.40	461.55	488.70	515.85	543.00
1087	298.92	326.10	353.27	380.45	407.62	434.80	461.97	489.15	516.32	543.50
1088	299.20	326.40	353.60	380.80	408.00	435.20	462.40	489.60	516.80	544.00
1089	299.47	326.70	353.92	381.15	408.37	435.60	462.82	490.05	517.27	544.50
1090	299.75	327.00	354.25	381.50	408.75	436.00	463.25	490.50	517.75	545.00
1091	300.02	327.30	354.57	381.85	409.12	436.40	463.67	490.95	518.22	545.50
1092	300.30	327.60	354.90	382.20	409.50	436.80	464.10	491.40	518.70	546.00
1093	300.57	327.90	355.22	382.55	409.87	437.20	464.52	491.85	519.17	546.50
1094	300.85	328.20	355.55	382.90	410.25	437.60	464.95	492.30	519.65	547.00
1095	301.12	328.50	355.87	383.25	410.62	438.00	465.37	492.75	520.12	547.50
1096	301.40	328.80	356.20	383.60	411.00	438.40	465.80	493.20	520.60	548.00
1097	301.67	329.10	356.52	383.95	411.37	438.80	466.22	493.65	521.07	548.50
1098	301.95	329.40	356.85	384.30	411.75	439.20	466.65	494.10	521.55	549.00
1099	302.22	329.70	357.17	384.65	412.12	439.60	467.07	494.55	522.02	549.50
1100	302.50	330.00	357.50	385.00	412.50	440.00	467.50	495.00	522.50	550.00

1150 FEET.

Per Ton,	25c.	50c.	$1	$2	$3	$4	$5	$6	$7	$8	$9	$10
Per Foot,			2½ cts.	5 cts.	7½ cts.	10 cts.	12½ cts.	15 cts.	17½ cts.	20 cts.	22½ cts.	25 cts.
Feet.												
1101	6.88	13.76	27.52	55.05	82.57	110.10	137.62	165.15	192.67	220.20	247.72	275.25
1102	6.89	13.77	27.55	55.10	82.65	110.20	137.75	165.30	192.85	220.40	247.95	275.50
1103	6.89	13.79	27.57	55.15	82.72	110.30	137.87	165.45	193.02	220.60	248.17	275.75
1104	6.90	13.80	27.60	55.20	82.80	110.40	138.00	165.60	193.20	220.80	248.40	276.00
1105	6.91	13.81	27.62	55.25	82.87	110.50	138.12	165.75	193.37	221.00	248.62	276.25
1106	6.91	13.82	27.65	55.30	82.95	110.60	138.25	165.90	193.55	221.20	248.85	276.50
1107	6.92	13.84	27.67	55.35	83.02	110.70	138.37	166.05	193.72	221.40	249.07	276.75
1108	6.92	13.85	27.70	55.40	83.10	110.80	138.50	166.20	193.90	221.60	249.30	277.00
1109	6.93	13.86	27.72	55.45	83.17	110.90	138.62	166.35	194.07	221.80	249.52	277.25
1110	6.94	13.87	27.75	55.50	83.25	111.00	138.75	166.50	194.25	222.00	249.75	277.50
1111	6.94	13.89	27.77	55.55	83.32	111.10	138.87	166.65	194.42	222.20	249.97	277.75
1112	6.95	13.90	27.80	55.60	83.40	111.20	139.00	166.80	194.60	222.40	250.20	278.00
1113	6.96	13.91	27.82	55.65	83.47	111.30	139.12	166.95	194.77	222.60	250.42	278.25
1114	6.96	13.92	27.85	55.70	83.55	111.40	139.25	167.10	194.95	222.80	250.65	278.50
1115	6.97	13.94	27.87	55.75	83.62	111.50	139.37	167.25	195.12	223.00	250.87	278.75
1116	6.97	13.95	27.90	55.80	83.70	111.60	139.50	167.40	195.30	223.20	251.10	279.00
1117	6.98	13.96	27.92	55.85	83.77	111.70	139.62	167.55	195.47	223.40	251.32	279.25
1118	6.99	13.97	27.95	55.90	83.85	111.80	139.75	167.70	195.65	223.60	251.55	279.50
1119	6.99	13.99	27.97	55.95	83.92	111.90	139.87	167.85	195.82	223.80	251.77	279.75
1120	7.00	14.00	28.00	56.00	84.00	112.00	140.00	168.00	196.00	224.00	252.00	280.00
1121	7.01	14.01	28.02	56.05	84.07	112.10	140.12	168.15	196.17	224.20	252.22	280.25
1122	7.01	14.02	28.05	56.10	84.15	112.20	140.25	168.30	196.35	224.40	252.45	280.50
1123	7.02	14.04	28.07	56.15	84.22	112.30	140.37	168.45	196.52	224.60	252.67	280.75
1124	7.02	14.05	28.10	56.20	84.30	112.40	140.50	168.60	196.70	224.80	252.90	281.00
1125	7.03	14.06	28.12	56.25	84.37	112.50	140.62	168.75	196.87	225.00	253.12	281.25
1126	7.04	14.07	28.15	56.30	84.45	112.60	140.75	168.90	197.05	225.20	253.35	281.50
1127	7.04	14.09	28.17	56.35	84.52	112.70	140.87	169.05	197.22	225.40	253.57	281.75
1128	7.05	14.10	28.20	56.40	84.60	112.80	141.00	169.20	197.40	225.60	253.80	282.00
1129	7.06	14.11	28.22	56.45	84.67	112.90	141.12	169.35	197.57	225.80	254.02	282.25
1130	7.06	14.12	28.25	56.50	84.75	113.00	141.25	169.50	197.75	226.00	254.25	282.50
1131	7.07	14.14	28.27	56.55	84.82	113.10	141.37	169.65	197.92	226.20	254.47	282.75
1132	7.07	14.15	28.30	56.60	84.90	113.20	141.50	169.80	198.10	226.40	254.70	283.00
1133	7.08	14.16	28.32	56.65	84.97	113.30	141.62	169.95	198.27	226.60	254.92	283.25
1134	7.09	14.17	28.35	56.70	85.05	113.40	141.75	170.10	198.45	226.80	255.15	283.50
1135	7.09	14.19	28.37	56.75	85.12	113.50	141.87	170.25	198.62	227.00	255.37	283.75
1136	7.10	14.20	28.40	56.80	85.20	113.60	142.00	170.40	198.80	227.20	255.60	284.00
1137	7.11	14.21	28.42	56.85	85.27	113.70	142.12	170.55	198.97	227.40	255.82	284.25
1138	7.11	14.22	28.45	56.90	85.35	113.80	142.25	170.70	199.15	227.60	256.05	284.50
1139	7.12	14.24	28.47	56.95	85.42	113.90	142.37	170.85	199.32	227.80	256.27	284.75
1140	7.12	14.25	28.50	57.00	85.50	114.00	142.50	171.00	199.50	228.00	256.50	285.00
1141	7.13	14.26	28.52	57.05	85.57	114.10	142.62	171.15	199.67	228.20	256.72	285.25
1142	7.14	14.27	28.55	57.10	85.65	114.20	142.75	171.30	199.85	228.40	256.95	285.50
1143	7.14	14.29	28.57	57.15	85.72	114.30	142.87	171.45	200.02	228.60	257.17	285.75
1144	7.15	14.30	28.60	57.20	85.80	114.40	143.00	171.60	200.20	228.80	257.40	286.00
1145	7.16	14.31	28.62	57.25	85.87	114.50	143.12	171.75	200.37	229.00	257.62	286.25
1146	7.16	14.32	28.65	57.30	85.95	114.60	143.25	171.90	200.55	229.20	257.85	286.50
1147	7.17	14.34	28.67	57.35	86.02	114.70	143.37	172.05	200.72	229.40	258.07	286.75
1148	7.17	14.35	28.70	57.40	86.10	114.80	143.50	172.20	200.90	229.60	258.30	287.00
1149	7.18	14.36	28.72	57.45	86.17	114.90	143.62	172.35	201.07	229.80	258.52	287.25
1150	7.19	14.37	28.75	57.50	86.25	115.00	143.75	172.50	201.25	230.00	258.75	287.50

1150 FEET.

Per Ton,	$11	$12	$13	$14	$15	$16	$17	$18	$19	$20
Per Foot,	27½ cts.	30 cts.	32½ cts.	35 cts.	37½ cts.	40 cts.	42½ cts.	45 cts.	47½ cts.	50 cts.
Feet.										
1101	302.77	330.30	357.82	385.35	412.87	440.40	467.92	495.45	522.97	550.50
1102	303.05	330.60	358.15	385.70	413.25	440.80	468.35	495.90	523.45	551.00
1103	303.32	330.90	358.47	386.05	413.62	441.20	468.77	496.35	523.92	551.50
1104	303.60	331.20	358.80	386.40	414.00	441.60	469.20	496.80	524.40	552.00
1105	303.87	331.50	359.12	386.75	414.37	442.00	469.62	497.25	524.87	552.50
1106	304.15	331.80	359.45	387.10	414.75	442.40	470.05	497.70	525.35	553.00
1107	304.42	332.10	359.77	387.45	415.12	442.80	470.47	498.15	525.82	553.50
1108	304.70	332.40	360.10	387.80	415.50	443.20	470.90	498.60	526.30	554.00
1109	304.97	332.70	360.42	388.15	415.87	443.60	471.32	499.05	526.77	554.50
1110	305.25	333.00	360.75	388.50	416.25	444.00	471.75	499.50	527.25	555.00
1111	305.52	333.30	361.07	388.85	416.62	444.40	472.17	499.95	527.72	555.50
1112	305.80	333.60	361.40	389.20	417.00	444.80	472.60	500.40	528.20	556.00
1113	306.07	333.90	361.72	389.55	417.37	445.20	473.02	500.85	528.67	556.50
1114	306.35	334.20	362.05	389.90	417.75	445.60	473.45	501.30	529.15	557.00
1115	306.62	334.50	362.37	390.25	418.12	446.00	473.87	501.75	529.62	557.50
1116	306.90	334.80	362.70	390.60	418.50	446.40	474.30	502.20	530.10	558.00
1117	307.17	335.10	363.02	390.95	418.87	446.80	474.72	502.65	530.57	558.50
1118	307.45	335.40	363.35	391.30	419.25	447.20	475.15	503.10	531.05	559.00
1119	307.72	335.70	363.67	391.65	419.62	447.60	475.57	503.55	531.52	559.50
1120	308.00	336.00	364.00	392.00	420.00	448.00	476.00	504.00	532.00	560.00
1121	308.27	336.30	364.32	392.35	420.37	448.40	476.42	504.45	532.47	560.50
1122	308.55	336.60	364.65	392.70	420.75	448.80	476.85	504.90	532.95	561.00
1123	308.82	336.90	364.97	393.05	421.12	449.20	477.27	505.35	533.42	561.50
1124	309.10	337.20	365.30	393.40	421.50	449.60	477.70	505.80	533.90	562.00
1125	309.37	337.50	365.62	393.75	421.87	450.00	478.12	506.25	534.37	562.50
1126	309.65	337.80	365.95	394.10	422.25	450.40	478.55	506.70	534.85	563.00
1127	309.92	338.10	366.27	394.45	422.62	450.80	478.97	507.15	535.32	563.50
1128	310.20	338.40	366.60	394.80	423.00	451.20	479.40	507.60	535.80	564.00
1129	310.47	338.70	366.92	395.15	423.37	451.60	479.82	508.05	536.27	564.50
1130	310.75	339.00	367.25	395.50	423.75	452.00	480.25	508.50	536.75	565.00
1131	311.02	339.30	367.57	395.85	424.12	452.40	480.67	508.95	537.22	565.50
1132	311.30	339.60	367.90	396.20	424.50	452.80	481.10	509.40	537.70	566.00
1133	311.57	339.90	368.22	396.55	424.87	453.20	481.52	509.85	538.17	566.50
1134	311.85	340.20	368.55	396.90	425.25	453.60	481.95	510.30	538.65	567.00
1135	312.12	340.50	368.87	397.25	425.62	454.00	482.37	510.75	539.12	567.50
1136	312.40	340.80	369.20	397.60	426.00	454.40	482.80	511.20	539.60	568.00
1137	312.67	341.10	369.52	397.95	426.37	454.80	483.22	511.65	540.07	568.50
1138	312.95	341.40	369.85	398.30	426.75	455.20	483.65	512.10	540.55	569.00
1139	313.22	341.70	370.17	398.65	427.12	455.60	484.07	512.55	541.02	569.50
1140	313.50	342.00	370.50	399.00	427.50	456.00	484.50	513.00	541.50	570.00
1141	313.77	342.30	370.82	399.35	427.87	456.40	484.92	513.45	541.97	570.50
1142	314.05	342.60	371.15	399.70	428.25	456.80	485.35	513.90	542.45	571.00
1143	314.32	342.90	371.47	400.05	428.62	457.20	485.77	514.35	542.92	571.50
1144	314.60	343.20	371.80	400.40	429.00	457.60	486.20	514.80	543.40	572.00
1145	314.87	343.50	372.12	400.75	429.37	458.00	486.62	515.25	543.87	572.50
1146	315.15	343.80	372.45	401.10	429.75	458.40	487.05	515.70	544.35	573.00
1147	315.42	344.10	372.77	401.45	430.12	458.80	487.47	516.15	544.82	573.50
1148	315.70	344.40	373.10	401.80	430.50	459.20	487.90	516.60	545.30	574.00
1149	315.97	344.70	373.42	402.15	430.87	459.60	488.32	517.05	545.77	574.50
1150	316.25	345.00	373.75	402.50	431.25	460.00	488.75	517.50	546.25	575.00

1200 FEET.

Per Ton, Per Foot,	25c.	50c.	$1 2½ cts.	$2 5 cts.	$3 7½ cts.	$4 10 cts.	$5 12½ cts.	$6 15 cts.	$7 17½ cts.	$8 20 cts.	$9 22½ cts.	$10 25 cts.
Feet.												
1151	7.19	14.39	28.77	57.55	86.32	115.10	143.87	172.65	201.42	230.20	258.97	287.75
1152	7.20	14.40	28.80	57.60	86.40	115.20	144.00	172.80	201.60	230.40	259.20	288.00
1153	7.21	14.41	28.82	57.65	86.47	115.30	144.12	172.95	201.77	230.60	259.42	288.25
1154	7.21	14.42	28.85	57.70	86.55	115.40	144.25	173.10	201.95	230.80	259.65	288.50
1155	7.22	14.44	28.87	57.75	86.62	115.50	144.37	173.25	202.12	231.00	259.87	288.75
1156	7.22	14.45	28.90	57.80	86.70	115.60	144.50	173.40	202.30	231.20	260.10	289.00
1157	7.23	14.46	28.92	57.85	86.77	115.70	144.62	173.55	202.47	231.40	260.32	289.25
1158	7.24	14.47	28.95	57.90	86.85	115.80	144.75	173.70	202.65	231.60	260.55	289.50
1159	7.24	14.49	28.97	57.95	86.92	115.90	144.87	173.85	202.82	231.80	260.77	289.75
1160	7.25	14.50	29.00	58.00	87.00	116.00	145.00	174.00	203.00	232.00	261.00	290.00
1161	7.26	14.51	29.02	58.05	87.07	116.10	145.12	174.15	203.17	232.20	261.22	290.25
1162	7.26	14.52	29.05	58.10	87.15	116.20	145.25	174.30	203.35	232.40	261.45	290.50
1163	7.27	14.54	29.07	58.15	87.22	116.30	145.37	174.45	203.52	232.60	261.67	290.75
1164	7.27	14.55	29.10	58.20	87.30	116.40	145.50	174.60	203.70	232.80	261.90	291.00
1165	7.28	14.56	29.12	58.25	87.37	116.50	145.62	174.75	203.87	233.00	262.12	291.25
1166	7.29	14.57	29.15	58.30	87.45	116.60	145.75	174.90	204.05	233.20	262.35	291.50
1167	7.29	14.59	29.17	58.35	87.52	116.70	145.87	175.05	204.22	233.40	262.57	291.75
1168	7.30	14.60	29.20	58.40	87.60	116.80	146.00	175.20	204.40	233.60	262.80	292.00
1169	7.31	14.61	29.22	58.45	87.67	116.90	146.12	175.35	204.57	233.80	263.02	292.25
1170	7.31	14.62	29.25	58.50	87.75	117.00	146.25	175.50	204.75	234.00	263.25	292.50
1171	7.32	14.64	29.27	58.55	87.82	117.10	146.37	175.65	204.92	234.20	263.47	292.75
1172	7.32	14.65	29.30	58.60	87.90	117.20	146.50	175.80	205.10	234.40	263.70	293.00
1173	7.33	14.66	29.32	58.65	87.97	117.30	146.62	175.95	205.27	234.60	263.92	293.25
1174	7.34	14.67	29.35	58.70	88.05	117.40	146.75	176.10	205.45	234.80	264.15	293.50
1175	7.34	14.69	29.37	58.75	88.12	117.50	146.87	176.25	205.62	235.00	264.37	293.75
1176	7.35	14.70	29.40	58.80	88.20	117.60	147.00	176.40	205.80	235.20	264.60	294.00
1177	7.36	14.71	29.42	58.85	88.27	117.70	147.12	176.55	205.97	235.40	264.82	294.25
1178	7.36	14.72	29.45	58.90	88.35	117.80	147.25	176.70	206.15	235.60	265.05	294.50
1179	7.37	14.74	29.47	58.95	88.42	117.90	147.37	176.85	206.32	235.80	265.27	294.75
1180	7.37	14.75	29.50	59.00	88.50	118.00	147.50	177.00	206.50	236.00	265.50	295.00
1181	7.38	14.76	29.52	59.05	88.57	118.10	147.62	177.15	206.67	236.20	265.72	295.25
1182	7.39	14.77	29.55	59.10	88.65	118.20	147.75	177.30	206.85	236.40	265.95	295.50
1183	7.39	14.79	29.57	59.15	88.72	118.30	147.87	177.45	207.02	236.60	266.17	295.75
1184	7.40	14.80	29.60	59.20	88.80	118.40	148.00	177.60	207.20	236.80	266.40	296.00
1185	7.41	14.81	29.62	59.25	88.87	118.50	148.12	177.75	207.37	237.00	266.62	296.25
1186	7.41	14.82	29.65	59.30	88.95	118.60	148.25	177.90	207.55	237.20	266.85	296.50
1187	7.42	14.84	29.67	59.35	89.02	118.70	148.37	178.05	207.72	237.40	267.07	296.75
1188	7.42	14.85	29.70	59.40	89.10	118.80	148.50	178.20	207.90	237.60	267.30	297.00
1189	7.43	14.86	29.72	59.45	89.17	118.90	148.62	178.35	208.07	237.80	267.52	297.25
1190	7.44	14.87	29.75	59.50	89.25	119.00	148.75	178.50	208.25	238.00	267.75	297.50
1191	7.44	14.89	29.77	59.55	89.32	119.10	148.87	178.65	208.42	238.20	267.97	297.75
1192	7.45	14.90	29.80	59.60	89.40	119.20	149.00	178.80	208.60	238.40	268.20	298.00
1193	7.46	14.91	29.82	59.65	89.47	119.30	149.12	178.95	208.77	238.60	268.42	298.25
1194	7.46	14.92	29.85	59.70	89.55	119.40	149.25	179.10	208.95	238.80	268.65	298.50
1195	7.47	14.94	29.87	59.75	89.62	119.50	149.37	179.25	209.12	239.00	268.87	298.75
1196	7.47	14.95	29.90	59.80	89.70	119.60	149.50	179.40	209.30	239.20	269.10	299.00
1197	7.48	14.96	29.92	59.85	89.77	119.70	149.62	179.55	209.47	239.40	269.32	299.25
1198	7.49	14.97	29.95	59.90	89.85	119.80	149.75	179.70	209.65	239.60	269.55	299.50
1199	7.49	14.99	29.97	59.95	89.92	119.90	149.87	179.85	209.82	239.80	269.77	299.75
1200	7.50	15.00	30.00	60.00	90.00	120.00	150.00	180.00	210.00	240.00	270.00	300.00

1200 FEET.

Per Ton, Per Foot,	$11 27½ cts.	$12 30 cts.	$13 32½ cts.	$14 35 cts.	$15 37½ cts.	$16 40 cts.	$17 42½ cts.	$18 45 cts.	$19 47½ cts.	$20 50 cts.
Feet.										
1151	316.52	345.30	374.07	402.85	431.62	460.40	489.17	517.95	546.72	575.50
1152	316.80	345.60	374.40	403.20	432.00	460.80	489.60	518.40	547.20	576.00
1153	317.07	345.90	374.72	403.55	432.37	461.20	490.02	518.85	547.67	576.50
1154	317.35	346.20	375.05	403.90	432.75	461.60	490.45	519.30	548.15	577.00
1155	317.62	346.50	375.37	404.25	433.12	462.00	490.87	519.75	548.62	577.50
1156	317.90	346.80	375.70	404.60	433.50	462.40	491.30	520.20	549.10	578.00
1157	318.17	347.10	376.02	404.95	433.87	462.80	491.72	520.65	549.57	578.50
1158	318.45	347.40	376.35	405.30	434.25	463.20	492.15	521.10	550.05	579.00
1159	318.72	347.70	376.67	405.65	434.62	463.60	492.57	521.55	550.52	579.50
1160	319.00	348.00	377.00	406.00	435.00	464.00	493.00	522.00	551.00	580.00
1161	319.27	348.30	377.32	406.35	435.37	464.40	493.42	522.45	551.47	580.50
1162	319.55	348.60	377.65	406.70	435.75	464.80	493.85	522.90	551.95	581.00
1163	319.82	348.90	377.97	407.05	436.12	465.20	494.27	523.35	552.42	581.50
1164	320.10	349.20	378.30	407.40	436.50	465.60	494.70	523.80	552.90	582.00
1165	320.37	349.50	378.62	407.75	436.87	466.00	495.12	524.25	553.37	582.50
1166	320.65	349.80	378.95	408.10	437.25	466.40	495.55	524.70	553.85	583.00
1167	320.92	350.10	379.27	408.45	437.62	466.80	495.97	525.15	554.32	583.50
1168	321.20	350.40	379.60	408.80	438.00	467.20	496.40	525.60	554.80	584.00
1169	321.47	350.70	379.92	409.15	438.37	467.60	496.82	526.05	555.27	584.50
1170	321.75	351.00	380.25	409.50	438.75	468.00	497.25	526.50	555.75	585.00
1171	322.02	351.30	380.57	409.85	439.12	468.40	497.67	526.95	556.22	585.50
1172	322.30	351.60	380.90	410.20	439.50	468.80	498.10	527.40	556.70	586.00
1173	322.57	351.90	381.22	410.55	439.87	469.20	498.52	527.85	557.17	586.50
1174	322.85	352.20	381.55	410.90	440.25	469.60	498.95	528.30	557.65	587.00
1175	323.12	352.50	381.87	411.25	440.62	470.00	499.37	528.75	558.12	587.50
1176	323.40	352.80	382.20	411.60	441.00	470.40	499.80	529.20	558.60	588.00
1177	323.67	353.10	382.52	411.95	441.37	470.80	500.22	529.65	559.07	588.50
1178	323.95	353.40	382.85	412.30	441.75	471.20	500.65	530.10	559.55	589.00
1179	324.22	353.70	383.17	412.65	442.12	471.60	501.07	530.55	560.02	589.50
1180	324.50	354.00	383.50	413.00	442.50	472.00	501.50	531.00	560.50	590.00
1181	324.77	354.30	383.82	413.35	442.87	472.40	501.92	531.45	560.97	590.50
1182	325.05	354.60	384.15	413.70	443.25	472.80	502.35	531.90	561.45	591.00
1183	325.32	354.90	384.47	414.05	443.62	473.20	502.77	532.35	561.92	591.50
1184	325.60	355.20	384.80	414.40	444.00	473.60	503.20	532.80	562.40	592.00
1185	325.87	355.50	385.12	414.75	444.37	474.00	503.62	533.25	562.87	592.50
1186	326.15	355.80	385.45	415.10	444.75	474.40	504.05	533.70	563.35	593.00
1187	326.42	356.10	385.77	415.45	445.12	474.80	504.47	534.15	563.82	593.50
1188	326.70	356.40	386.10	415.80	445.50	475.20	504.90	534.60	564.30	594.00
1189	326.97	356.70	386.42	416.15	445.87	475.60	505.32	535.05	564.77	594.50
1190	327.25	357.00	386.75	416.50	446.25	476.00	505.75	535.50	565.25	595.00
1191	327.52	357.30	387.07	416.85	446.62	476.40	506.17	535.95	565.72	595.50
1192	327.80	357.60	387.40	417.20	447.00	476.80	506.60	536.40	566.20	596.00
1193	328.07	357.90	387.72	417.55	447.37	477.20	507.02	536.85	566.67	596.50
1194	328.35	358.20	388.05	417.90	447.75	477.60	507.45	537.30	567.15	597.00
1195	328.62	358.50	388.37	418.25	448.12	478.00	507.87	537.75	567.62	597.50
1196	328.90	358.80	388.70	418.60	448.50	478.40	508.30	538.20	568.10	598.00
1197	329.17	359.10	389.02	418.95	448.87	478.80	508.72	538.65	568.57	598.50
1198	329.45	359.40	389.35	419.30	449.25	479.20	509.15	539.10	569.05	599.00
1199	329.72	359.70	389.67	419.65	449.62	479.60	509.57	539.55	569.52	599.50
1200	330.00	360.00	390.00	420.00	450.00	480.00	510.00	540.00	570.00	600.00

1250 FEET.

Per Ton, 25c.		50c.	$1	$2	$3	$4	$5	$6	$7	$8	$9	$10
Per Foot,			2½ cts.	5 cts.	7½ cts.	10 cts.	12½ cts.	15 cts.	17½ cts.	20 cts.	22½ cts.	25 cts.
Feet.												
1201	7.51	15.01	30.02	60.05	90.07	120.10	150.12	180.15	210.17	240.20	270.22	300.25
1202	7.51	15.02	30.05	60.10	90.15	120.20	150.25	180.30	210.35	240.40	270.45	300.50
1203	7.52	15.04	30.07	60.15	90.22	120.30	150.37	180.45	210.52	240.60	270.67	300.75
1204	7.52	15.05	30.10	60.20	90.30	120.40	150.50	180.60	210.70	240.80	270.90	301.00
1205	7.53	15.06	30.12	60.25	90.37	120.50	150.62	180.75	210.87	241.00	271.12	301.25
1206	7.54	15.07	30.15	60.30	90.45	120.60	150.75	180.90	211.05	241.20	271.35	301.50
1207	7.54	15.09	30.17	60.35	90.52	120.70	150.87	181.05	211.22	241.40	271.57	301.75
1208	7.55	15.10	30.20	60.40	90.60	120.80	151.00	181.20	211.40	241.60	271.80	302.00
1209	7.56	15.11	30.22	60.45	90.67	120.90	151.12	181.35	211.57	241.80	272.02	302.25
1210	7.56	15.12	30.25	60.50	90.75	121.00	151.25	181.50	211.75	242.00	272.25	302.50
1211	7.57	15.14	30.27	60.55	90.82	121.10	151.37	181.65	211.92	242.20	272.47	302.75
1212	7.57	15.15	30.30	60.60	90.90	121.20	151.50	181.80	212.10	242.40	272.70	303.00
1213	7.58	15.16	30.32	60.65	90.97	121.30	151.62	181.95	212.27	242.60	272.92	303.25
1214	7.59	15.17	30.35	60.70	91.05	121.40	151.75	182.10	212.45	242.80	273.15	303.50
1215	7.59	15.19	30.37	60.75	91.12	121.50	151.87	182.25	212.62	243.00	273.37	303.75
1216	7.60	15.20	30.40	60.80	91.20	121.60	152.00	182.40	212.80	243.20	273.60	304.00
1217	7.61	15.21	30.42	60.85	91.27	121.70	152.12	182.55	212.97	243.40	273.82	304.25
1218	7.61	15.22	30.45	60.90	91.35	121.80	152.25	182.70	213.15	243.60	274.05	304.50
1219	7.62	15.24	30.47	60.95	91.42	121.90	152.37	182.85	213.32	243.80	274.27	304.75
1220	7.62	15.25	30.50	61.00	91.50	122.00	152.50	183.00	213.50	244.00	274.50	305.00
1221	7.63	15.26	30.52	61.05	91.57	122.10	152.62	183.15	213.67	244.20	274.72	305.25
1222	7.64	15.27	30.55	61.10	91.65	122.20	152.75	183.30	213.85	244.40	274.95	305.50
1223	7.64	15.29	30.57	61.15	91.72	122.30	152.87	183.45	214.02	244.60	275.17	305.75
1224	7.65	15.30	30.60	61.20	91.80	122.40	153.00	183.60	214.20	244.80	275.40	306.00
1225	7.66	15.31	30.62	61.25	91.87	122.50	153.12	183.75	214.37	245.00	275.62	306.25
1226	7.66	15.32	30.65	61.30	91.95	122.60	153.25	183.90	214.55	245.20	275.85	306.50
1227	7.67	15.34	30.67	61.35	92.02	122.70	153.37	184.05	214.72	245.40	276.07	306.75
1228	7.67	15.35	30.70	61.40	92.10	122.80	153.50	184.20	214.90	245.60	276.30	307.00
1229	7.68	15.36	30.72	61.45	92.17	122.90	153.62	184.35	215.07	245.80	276.52	307.25
1230	7.69	15.37	30.75	61.50	92.25	123.00	153.75	184.50	215.25	246.00	276.75	307.50
1231	7.69	15.39	30.77	61.55	92.32	123.10	153.87	184.65	215.42	246.20	276.97	307.75
1232	7.70	15.40	30.80	61.60	92.40	123.20	154.00	184.80	215.60	246.40	277.20	308.00
1233	7.71	15.41	30.82	61.65	92.47	123.30	154.12	184.95	215.77	246.60	277.42	308.25
1234	7.71	15.42	30.85	61.70	92.55	123.40	154.25	185.10	215.95	246.80	277.65	308.50
1235	7.72	15.44	30.87	61.75	92.62	123.50	154.37	185.25	216.12	247.00	277.87	308.75
1236	7.72	15.45	30.90	61.80	92.70	123.60	154.50	185.40	216.30	247.20	278.10	309.00
1237	7.73	15.46	30.92	61.85	92.77	123.70	154.62	185.55	216.47	247.40	278.32	309.25
1238	7.74	15.47	30.95	61.90	92.85	123.80	154.75	185.70	216.65	247.60	278.55	309.50
1239	7.74	15.49	30.97	61.95	92.92	123.90	154.87	185.85	216.82	247.80	278.77	309.75
1240	7.75	15.50	31.00	62.00	93.00	124.00	155.00	186.00	217.00	248.00	279.00	310.00
1241	7.76	15.51	31.02	62.05	93.07	124.10	155.12	186.15	217.17	248.20	279.22	310.25
1242	7.76	15.52	31.05	62.10	93.15	124.20	155.25	186.30	217.35	248.40	279.45	310.50
1243	7.77	15.54	31.07	62.15	93.22	124.30	155.37	186.45	217.52	248.60	279.67	310.75
1244	7.77	15.55	31.10	62.20	93.30	124.40	155.50	186.60	217.70	248.80	279.90	311.00
1245	7.78	15.56	31.12	62.25	93.37	124.50	155.62	186.75	217.87	249.00	280.12	311.25
1246	7.79	15.57	31.15	62.30	93.45	124.60	155.75	186.90	218.05	249.20	280.35	311.50
1247	7.79	15.59	31.17	62.35	93.52	124.70	155.87	187.05	218.22	249.40	280.57	311.75
1248	7.80	15.60	31.20	62.40	93.60	124.80	156.00	187.20	218.40	249.60	280.80	312.00
1249	7.81	15.61	31.22	62.45	93.67	124.90	156.12	187.35	218.57	249.80	281.02	312.25
1250	7.81	15.62	31.25	62.50	93.75	125.00	156.25	187.50	218.75	250.00	281.25	312.50

1250 FEET.

Per Ton, / Per Foot,	$11 27½ cts.	$12 30 cts.	$13 32½ cts.	$14 35 cts.	$15 37½ cts.	$16 40 cts.	$17 42½ cts.	$18 45 cts.	$19 47½ cts.	$20 50 cts.
Feet.										
1201	330.27	360.30	390.32	420.35	450.37	480.40	510.42	540.45	570.47	600.50
1202	330.55	360.60	390.65	420.70	450.75	480.80	510.85	540.90	570.95	601.00
1203	330.82	360.90	390.97	421.05	451.12	481.20	511.27	541.35	571.42	601.50
1204	331.10	361.20	391.30	421.40	451.50	481.60	511.70	541.80	571.90	602.00
1205	331.37	361.50	391.62	421.75	451.87	482.00	512.12	542.25	572.37	602.50
1206	331.65	361.80	391.95	422.10	452.25	482.40	512.55	542.70	572.85	603.00
1207	331.92	362.10	392.27	422.45	452.62	482.80	512.97	543.15	573.32	603.50
1208	332.20	362.40	392.60	422.80	453.00	483.20	513.40	543.60	573.80	604.00
1209	332.47	362.70	392.92	423.15	453.37	483.60	513.82	544.05	574.27	604.50
1210	332.75	363.00	393.25	423.50	453.75	484.00	514.25	544.50	574.75	605.00
1211	333.02	363.30	393.57	423.85	454.12	484.40	514.67	544.95	575.22	605.50
1212	333.30	363.60	393.90	424.20	454.50	484.80	515.10	545.40	575.70	606.00
1213	333.57	363.90	394.22	424.55	454.87	485.20	515.52	545.85	576.17	606.50
1214	333.85	364.20	394.55	424.90	455.25	485.60	515.95	546.30	576.65	607.00
1215	334.12	364.50	394.87	425.25	455.62	486.00	516.37	546.75	577.12	607.50
1216	334.40	364.80	395.20	425.60	456.00	486.40	516.80	547.20	577.60	608.00
1217	334.67	365.10	395.52	425.95	456.37	486.80	517.22	547.65	578.07	608.50
1218	334.95	365.40	395.85	426.30	456.75	487.20	517.65	548.10	578.55	609.00
1219	335.22	365.70	396.17	426.65	457.12	487.60	518.07	548.55	579.02	609.50
1220	335.50	366.00	396.50	427.00	457.50	488.00	518.50	549.00	579.50	610.00
1221	335.77	366.30	396.82	427.35	457.87	488.40	518.92	549.45	579.97	610.50
1222	336.05	366.60	397.15	427.70	458.25	488.80	519.35	549.90	580.45	611.00
1223	336.32	366.90	397.47	428.05	458.62	489.20	519.77	550.35	580.92	611.50
1224	336.60	367.20	397.80	428.40	459.00	489.60	520.20	550.80	581.40	612.00
1225	336.87	367.50	398.12	428.75	459.37	490.00	520.62	551.25	581.87	612.50
1226	337.15	367.80	398.45	429.10	459.75	490.40	521.05	551.70	582.35	613.00
1227	337.42	368.10	398.77	429.45	460.12	490.80	521.47	552.15	582.82	613.50
1228	337.70	368.40	399.10	429.80	460.50	491.20	521.90	552.60	583.30	614.00
1229	337.97	368.70	399.42	430.15	460.87	491.60	522.32	553.05	583.77	614.50
1230	338.25	369.00	399.75	430.50	461.25	492.00	522.75	553.50	584.25	615.00
1231	338.52	369.30	400.07	430.85	461.62	492.40	523.17	553.95	584.72	615.50
1232	338.80	369.60	400.40	431.20	462.00	492.80	523.60	554.40	585.20	616.00
1233	339.07	369.90	400.72	431.55	462.37	493.20	524.02	554.85	585.67	616.50
1234	339.35	370.20	401.05	431.90	462.75	493.60	524.45	555.30	586.15	617.00
1235	339.62	370.50	401.37	432.25	463.12	494.00	524.87	555.75	586.62	617.50
1236	339.90	370.80	401.70	432.60	463.50	494.40	525.30	556.20	587.10	618.00
1237	340.17	371.10	402.02	432.95	463.87	494.80	525.72	556.65	587.57	618.50
1238	340.45	371.40	402.35	433.30	464.25	495.20	526.15	557.10	588.05	619.00
1239	340.72	371.70	402.67	433.65	464.62	495.60	526.57	557.55	588.52	619.50
1240	341.00	372.00	403.00	434.00	465.00	496.00	527.00	558.00	589.00	620.00
1241	341.27	372.30	403.32	434.35	465.37	496.40	527.42	558.45	589.47	620.50
1242	341.55	372.60	403.65	434.70	465.75	496.80	527.85	558.90	589.95	621.00
1243	341.82	372.90	403.97	435.05	466.12	497.20	528.27	559.35	590.42	621.50
1244	342.10	373.20	404.30	435.40	466.50	497.60	528.70	559.80	590.90	622.00
1245	342.37	373.50	404.62	435.75	466.87	498.00	529.12	560.25	591.37	622.50
1246	342.65	373.80	404.95	436.10	467.25	498.40	529.55	560.70	591.85	623.00
1247	342.92	374.10	405.27	436.45	467.62	498.80	529.97	561.15	592.32	623.50
1248	343.20	374.40	405.60	436.80	468.00	499.20	530.40	561.60	592.80	624.00
1249	343.47	374.70	405.92	437.15	468.37	499.60	530.82	562.05	593.27	624.50
1250	343.75	375.00	406.25	437.50	468.75	500.00	531.25	562.50	593.75	625.00

1300 FEET.

Per Ton,	25c.	50c.	$1	$2	$3	$4	$5	$6	$7	$8	$9	$10
Per Foot,			2½ cts.	5 cts.	7½ cts.	10 cts.	12½ cts.	15 cts.	17½ cts.	20 cts.	22½ cts.	25 cts.
Feet.												
1251	7.82	15.64	31.27	62.55	93.82	125.10	156.37	187.65	218.92	250.20	281.47	312.75
1252	7.82	15.65	31.30	62.60	93.90	125.20	156.50	187.80	219.10	250.40	281.70	313.00
1253	7.83	15.66	31.32	62.65	93.97	125.30	156.62	187.95	219.27	250.60	281.92	313.25
1254	7.84	15.67	31.35	62.70	94.05	125.40	156.75	188.10	219.45	250.80	282.15	313.50
1255	7.84	15.69	31.37	62.75	94.12	125.50	156.87	188.25	219.62	251.00	282.37	313.75
1256	7.85	15.70	31.40	62.80	94.20	125.60	157.00	188.40	219.80	251.20	282.60	314.00
1257	7.86	15.71	31.42	62.85	94.27	125.70	157.12	188.55	219.97	251.40	282.82	314.25
1258	7.86	15.72	31.45	62.90	94.35	125.80	157.25	188.70	220.15	251.60	283.05	314.50
1259	7.87	15.74	31.47	62.95	94.42	125.90	157.37	188.85	220.32	251.80	283.27	314.75
1260	7.87	15.75	31.50	63.00	94.50	126.00	157.50	189.00	220.50	252.00	283.50	315.00
1261	7.88	15.76	31.52	63.05	94.57	126.10	157.62	189.15	220.67	252.20	283.72	315.25
1262	7.89	15.77	31.55	63.10	94.65	126.20	157.75	189.30	220.85	252.40	283.95	315.50
1263	7.89	15.79	31.57	63.15	94.72	126.30	157.87	189.45	221.02	252.60	284.17	315.75
1264	7.90	15.80	31.60	63.20	94.80	126.40	158.00	189.60	221.20	252.80	284.40	316.00
1265	7.91	15.81	31.62	63.25	94.87	126.50	158.12	189.75	221.37	253.00	284.62	316.25
1266	7.91	15.82	31.65	63.30	94.95	126.60	158.25	189.90	221.55	253.20	284.85	316.50
1267	7.92	15.84	31.67	63.35	95.02	126.70	158.37	190.05	221.72	253.40	285.07	316.75
1268	7.92	15.85	31.70	63.40	95.10	126.80	158.50	190.20	221.90	253.60	285.30	317.00
1269	7.93	15.86	31.72	63.45	95.17	126.90	158.62	190.35	222.07	253.80	285.52	317.25
1270	7.94	15.87	31.75	63.50	95.25	127.00	158.75	190.50	222.25	254.00	285.75	317.50
1271	7.94	15.89	31.77	63.55	95.32	127.10	158.87	190.65	222.42	254.20	285.97	317.75
1272	7.95	15.90	31.80	63.60	95.40	127.20	159.00	190.80	222.60	254.40	286.20	318.00
1273	7.96	15.91	31.82	63.65	95.47	127.30	159.12	190.95	222.77	254.60	286.42	318.25
1274	7.96	15.92	31.85	63.70	95.55	127.40	159.25	191.10	222.95	254.80	286.65	318.50
1275	7.97	15.94	31.87	63.75	95.62	127.50	159.37	191.25	223.12	255.00	286.87	318.75
1276	7.97	15.95	31.90	63.80	95.70	127.60	159.50	191.40	223.30	255.20	287.10	319.00
1277	7.98	15.96	31.92	63.85	95.77	127.70	159.62	191.55	223.47	255.40	287.32	319.25
1278	7.99	15.97	31.95	63.90	95.85	127.80	159.75	191.70	223.65	255.60	287.55	319.50
1279	7.99	15.99	31.97	63.95	95.92	127.90	159.87	191.85	223.82	255.80	287.77	319.75
1280	8.00	16.00	32.00	64.00	96.00	128.00	160.00	192.00	224.00	256.00	288.00	320.00
1281	8.01	16.01	32.02	64.05	96.07	128.10	160.12	192.15	224.17	256.20	288.22	320.25
1282	8.01	16.02	32.05	64.10	96.15	128.20	160.25	192.30	224.35	256.40	288.45	320.50
1283	8.02	16.04	32.07	64.15	96.22	128.30	160.37	192.45	224.52	256.60	288.67	320.75
1284	8.02	16.05	32.10	64.20	96.30	128.40	160.50	192.60	224.70	256.80	288.90	321.00
1285	8.03	16.06	32.12	64.25	96.37	128.50	160.62	192.75	224.87	257.00	289.12	321.25
1286	8.04	16.07	32.15	64.30	96.45	128.60	160.75	192.90	225.05	257.20	289.35	321.50
1287	8.04	16.09	32.17	64.35	96.52	128.70	160.87	193.05	225.22	257.40	289.57	321.75
1288	8.05	16.10	32.20	64.40	96.60	128.80	161.00	193.20	225.40	257.60	289.80	322.00
1289	8.06	16.11	32.22	64.45	96.67	128.90	161.12	193.35	225.57	257.80	290.02	322.25
1290	8.06	16.12	32.25	64.50	96.75	129.00	161.25	193.50	225.75	258.00	290.25	322.50
1291	8.07	16.14	32.27	64.55	96.82	129.10	161.37	193.65	225.92	258.20	290.47	322.75
1292	8.07	16.15	32.30	64.60	96.90	129.20	161.50	193.80	226.10	258.40	290.70	323.00
1293	8.08	16.16	32.32	64.65	96.97	129.30	161.62	193.95	226.27	258.60	290.92	323.25
1294	8.09	16.17	32.35	64.70	97.05	129.40	161.75	194.10	226.45	258.80	291.15	323.50
1295	8.09	16.19	32.37	64.75	97.12	129.50	161.87	194.25	226.62	259.00	291.37	323.75
1296	8.10	16.20	32.40	64.80	97.20	129.60	162.00	194.40	226.80	259.20	291.60	324.00
1297	8.11	16.21	32.42	64.85	97.27	129.70	162.12	194.55	226.97	259.40	291.82	324.25
1298	8.11	16.22	32.45	64.90	97.35	129.80	162.25	194.70	227.15	259.60	292.05	324.50
1299	8.12	16.24	32.47	64.95	97.42	129.90	162.37	194.85	227.32	259.80	292.27	324.75
1300	8.12	16.25	32.50	65.00	97.50	130.00	162.50	195.00	227.50	260.00	292.50	325.00

1300 FEET.

Per Ton,	$11	$12	$13	$14	$15	$16	$17	$18	$19	$20
Per Foot,	27½ cts.	30 cts.	32½ cts.	35 cts.	37½ cts.	40 cts.	42½ cts.	45 cts.	47½ cts.	50 cts.
Feet.										
1251	344.02	375.30	406.57	437.85	469.12	500.40	531.67	562.95	594.22	625.50
1252	344.30	375.60	406.90	438.20	469.50	500.80	532.10	563.40	594.70	626.00
1253	344.57	375.90	407.22	438.55	469.87	501.20	532.52	563.85	595.17	626.50
1254	344.85	376.20	407.55	438.90	470.25	501.60	532.95	564.30	595.65	627.00
1255	345.12	376.50	407.87	439.25	470.62	502.00	533.37	564.75	596.12	627.50
1256	345.40	376.80	408.20	439.60	471.00	502.40	533.80	565.20	596.60	628.00
1257	345.67	377.10	408.52	439.95	471.37	502.80	534.22	565.65	597.07	628.50
1258	345.95	377.40	408.85	440.30	471.75	503.20	534.65	566.10	597.55	629.00
1259	346.22	377.70	409.17	440.65	472.12	503.60	535.07	566.55	598.02	629.50
1260	346.50	378.00	409.50	441.00	472.50	504.00	535.50	567.00	598.50	630.00
1261	346.77	378.30	409.82	441.35	472.87	504.40	535.92	567.45	598.97	630.50
1262	347.05	378.60	410.15	441.70	473.25	504.80	536.35	567.90	599.45	631.00
1263	347.32	378.90	410.47	442.05	473.62	505.20	536.77	568.35	599.92	631.50
1264	347.60	379.20	410.80	442.40	474.00	505.60	537.20	568.80	600.40	632.00
1265	347.87	379.50	411.12	442.75	474.37	506.00	537.62	569.25	600.87	632.50
1266	348.15	379.80	411.45	443.10	474.75	506.40	538.05	569.70	601.35	633.00
1267	348.42	380.10	411.77	443.45	475.12	506.80	538.47	570.15	601.82	633.50
1268	348.70	380.40	412.10	443.80	475.50	507.20	538.90	570.60	602.30	634.00
1269	348.97	380.70	412.42	444.15	475.87	507.60	539.32	571.05	602.77	634.50
1270	349.25	381.00	412.75	444.50	476.25	508.00	539.75	571.50	603.25	635.00
1271	349.52	381.30	413.07	444.85	476.62	508.40	540.17	571.95	603.72	635.50
1272	349.80	381.60	413.40	445.20	477.00	508.80	540.60	572.40	604.20	636.00
1273	350.07	381.90	413.72	445.55	477.37	509.20	541.02	572.85	604.67	636.50
1274	350.35	382.20	414.05	445.90	477.75	509.60	541.45	573.30	605.15	637.00
1275	350.62	382.50	414.37	446.25	478.12	510.00	541.87	573.75	605.62	637.50
1276	350.90	382.80	414.70	446.60	478.50	510.40	542.30	574.20	606.10	638.00
1277	351.17	383.10	415.02	446.95	478.87	510.80	542.72	574.65	606.57	638.50
1278	351.45	383.40	415.35	447.30	479.25	511.20	543.15	575.10	607.05	639.00
1279	351.72	383.70	415.67	447.65	479.62	511.60	543.57	575.55	607.52	639.50
1280	352.00	384.00	416.00	448.00	480.00	512.00	544.00	576.00	608.00	640.00
1281	352.27	384.30	416.32	448.35	480.37	512.40	544.42	576.45	608.47	640.50
1282	352.55	384.60	416.65	448.70	480.75	512.80	544.85	576.90	608.95	641.00
1283	352.82	384.90	416.97	449.05	481.12	513.20	545.27	577.35	609.42	641.50
1284	353.10	385.20	417.30	449.40	481.50	513.60	545.70	577.80	609.90	642.00
1285	353.37	385.50	417.62	449.75	481.87	514.00	546.12	578.25	610.37	642.50
1286	353.65	385.80	417.95	450.10	482.25	514.40	546.55	578.70	610.85	643.00
1287	353.92	386.10	418.27	450.45	482.62	514.80	546.97	579.15	611.32	643.50
1288	354.20	386.40	418.60	450.80	483.00	515.20	547.40	579.60	611.80	644.00
1289	354.47	386.70	418.92	451.15	483.37	515.60	547.82	580.05	612.27	644.50
1290	354.75	387.00	419.25	451.50	483.75	516.00	548.25	580.50	612.75	645.00
1291	355.02	387.30	419.57	451.85	484.12	516.40	548.67	580.95	613.22	645.50
1292	355.30	387.60	419.90	452.20	484.50	516.80	549.10	581.40	613.70	646.00
1293	355.57	387.90	420.22	452.55	484.87	517.20	549.52	581.85	614.17	646.50
1294	355.85	388.20	420.55	452.90	485.25	517.60	549.95	582.30	614.65	647.00
1295	356.12	388.50	420.87	453.25	485.62	518.00	550.37	582.75	615.12	647.50
1296	356.40	388.80	421.20	453.60	486.00	518.40	550.80	583.20	615.60	648.00
1297	356.67	389.10	421.52	453.95	486.37	518.80	551.22	583.65	616.07	648.50
1298	356.95	389.40	421.85	454.30	486.75	519.20	551.65	584.10	616.55	649.00
1299	357.22	389.70	422.17	454.65	487.12	519.60	552.07	584.55	617.02	649.50
1300	357.50	390.00	422.50	455.00	487.50	520.00	552.50	585.00	617.50	650.00

1350 FEET.

Per Ton,	25c.	50c.	$1	$2	$3	$4	$5	$6	$7	$8	$9	$10
Per Foot,			2½ cts.	5 cts.	7½ cts.	10 cts.	12½ cts.	15 cts.	17½ cts.	20 cts.	22½ cts.	25 cts.
Feet.												
1301	8.13	16.26	32.52	65.05	97.57	130.10	162.62	195.15	227.67	260.20	292.72	325.25
1302	8.14	16.27	32.55	65.10	97.65	130.20	162.75	195.30	227.85	260.40	292.95	325.50
1303	8.14	16.29	32.57	65.15	97.72	130.30	162.87	195.45	228.02	260.60	293.17	325.75
1304	8.15	16.30	32.60	65.20	97.80	130.40	163.00	195.60	228.20	260.80	293.40	326.00
1305	8.16	16.31	32.62	65.25	97.87	130.50	163.12	195.75	228.37	261.00	293.62	326.25
1306	8.16	16.32	32.65	65.30	97.95	130.60	163.25	195.90	228.55	261.20	293.85	326.50
1307	8.17	16.34	32.67	65.35	98.02	130.70	163.37	196.05	228.72	261.40	294.07	326.75
1308	8.17	16.35	32.70	65.40	98.10	130.80	163.50	196.20	228.90	261.60	294.30	327.00
1309	8.18	16.36	32.72	65.45	98.17	130.90	163.62	196.35	229.07	261.80	294.52	327.25
1310	8.19	16.37	32.75	65.50	98.25	131.00	163.75	196.50	229.25	262.00	294.75	327.50
1311	8.19	16.39	32.77	65.55	98.32	131.10	163.87	196.65	229.42	262.20	294.97	327.75
1312	8.20	16.40	32.80	65.60	98.40	131.20	164.00	196.80	229.60	262.40	295.20	328.00
1313	8.21	16.41	32.82	65.65	98.47	131.30	164.12	196.95	229.77	262.60	295.42	328.25
1314	8.21	16.42	32.85	65.70	98.55	131.40	164.25	197.10	229.95	262.80	295.65	328.50
1315	8.22	16.44	32.87	65.75	98.62	131.50	164.37	197.25	230.12	263.00	295.87	328.75
1316	8.22	16.45	32.90	65.80	98.70	131.60	164.50	197.40	230.30	263.20	296.10	329.00
1317	8.23	16.46	32.92	65.85	98.77	131.70	164.62	197.55	230.47	263.40	296.32	329.25
1318	8.24	16.47	32.95	65.90	98.85	131.80	164.75	197.70	230.65	263.60	296.55	329.50
1319	8.24	16.49	32.97	65.95	98.92	131.90	164.87	197.85	230.82	263.80	296.77	329.75
1320	8.25	16.50	33.00	66.00	99.00	132.00	165.00	198.00	231.00	264.00	297.00	330.00
1321	8.26	16.51	33.02	66.05	99.07	132.10	165.12	198.15	231.17	264.20	297.22	330.25
1322	8.26	16.52	33.05	66.10	99.15	132.20	165.25	198.30	231.35	264.40	297.45	330.50
1323	8.27	16.54	33.07	66.15	99.22	132.30	165.37	198.45	231.52	264.60	297.67	330.75
1324	8.27	16.55	33.10	66.20	99.30	132.40	165.50	198.60	231.70	264.80	297.90	331.00
1325	8.28	16.56	33.12	66.25	99.37	132.50	165.62	198.75	231.87	265.00	298.12	331.25
1326	8.29	16.57	33.15	66.30	99.45	132.60	165.75	198.90	232.05	265.20	298.35	331.50
1327	8.29	16.59	33.17	66.35	99.52	132.70	165.87	199.05	232.22	265.40	298.57	331.75
1328	8.30	16.60	33.20	66.40	99.60	132.80	166.00	199.20	232.40	265.60	298.80	332.00
1329	8.31	16.61	33.22	66.45	99.67	132.90	166.12	199.35	232.57	265.80	299.02	332.25
1330	8.31	16.62	33.25	66.50	99.75	133.00	166.25	199.50	232.75	266.00	299.25	332.50
1331	8.32	16.64	33.27	66.55	99.82	133.10	166.37	199.65	232.92	266.20	299.47	332.75
1332	8.32	16.65	33.30	66.60	99.90	133.20	166.50	199.80	233.10	266.40	299.70	333.00
1333	8.33	16.66	33.32	66.65	99.97	133.30	166.62	199.95	233.27	266.60	299.92	333.25
1334	8.34	16.67	33.35	66.70	100.05	133.40	166.75	200.10	233.45	266.80	300.15	333.50
1335	8.34	16.69	33.37	66.75	100.12	133.50	166.87	200.25	233.62	267.00	300.37	333.75
1336	8.35	16.70	33.40	66.80	100.20	133.60	167.00	200.40	233.80	267.20	300.60	334.00
1337	8.36	16.71	33.42	66.85	100.27	133.70	167.12	200.55	233.97	267.40	300.82	334.25
1338	8.36	16.72	33.45	66.90	100.35	133.80	167.25	200.70	234.15	267.60	301.05	334.50
1339	8.37	16.74	33.47	66.95	100.42	133.90	167.37	200.85	234.32	267.80	301.27	334.75
1340	8.37	16.75	33.50	67.00	100.50	134.00	167.50	201.00	234.50	268.00	301.50	335.00
1341	8.38	16.76	33.52	67.05	100.57	134.10	167.62	201.15	234.67	268.20	301.72	335.25
1342	8.39	16.77	33.55	67.10	100.65	134.20	167.75	201.30	234.85	268.40	301.95	335.50
1343	8.39	16.79	33.57	67.15	100.72	134.30	167.87	201.45	235.02	268.60	302.17	335.75
1344	8.40	16.80	33.60	67.20	100.80	134.40	168.00	201.60	235.20	268.80	302.40	336.00
1345	8.41	16.81	33.62	67.25	100.87	134.50	168.12	201.75	235.37	269.00	302.62	336.25
1346	8.41	16.82	33.65	67.30	100.95	134.60	168.25	201.90	235.55	269.20	302.85	336.50
1347	8.42	16.84	33.67	67.35	101.02	134.70	168.37	202.05	235.72	269.40	303.07	336.75
1348	8.42	16.85	33.70	67.40	101.10	134.80	168.50	202.20	235.90	269.60	303.30	337.00
1349	8.43	16.86	33.72	67.45	101.17	134.90	168.62	202.35	236.07	269.80	303.52	337.25
1350	8.44	16.87	33.75	67.50	101.25	135.00	168.75	202.50	236.25	270.00	303.75	337.50

1350 FEET.

Per Ton,	$11	$12	$13	$14	$15	$16	$17	$18	$19	$20
Per Foot,	27½ cts.	30 cts.	32½ cts.	35 cts.	37½ cts.	40 cts.	42½ cts.	45 cts.	47½ cts.	50 cts.
Feet.										
1301	357.77	390.30	422.82	455.35	487.87	520.40	552.92	585.45	617.97	650.50
1302	358.05	390.60	423.15	455.70	488.25	520.80	553.35	585.90	618.45	651.00
1303	358.32	390.90	423.47	456.05	488.62	521.20	553.77	586.35	618.92	651.50
1304	358.60	391.20	423.80	456.40	489.00	521.60	554.20	586.80	619.40	652.00
1305	358.87	391.50	424.12	456.75	489.37	522.00	554.62	587.25	619.87	652.50
1306	359.15	391.80	424.45	457.10	489.75	522.40	555.05	587.70	620.35	653.00
1307	359.42	392.10	424.77	457.45	490.12	522.80	555.47	588.15	620.82	653.50
1308	359.70	392.40	425.10	457.80	490.50	523.20	555.90	588.60	621.30	654.00
1309	359.97	392.70	425.42	458.15	490.87	523.60	556.32	589.05	621.77	654.50
1310	360.25	393.00	425.75	458.50	491.25	524.00	556.75	589.50	622.25	655.00
1311	360.52	393.30	426.07	458.85	491.62	524.40	557.17	589.95	622.72	655.50
1312	360.80	393.60	426.40	459.20	492.00	524.80	557.60	590.40	623.20	656.00
1313	361.07	393.90	426.72	459.55	492.37	525.20	558.02	590.85	623.67	656.50
1314	361.35	394.20	427.05	459.90	492.75	525.60	558.45	591.30	624.15	657.00
1315	361.62	394.50	427.37	460.25	493.12	526.00	558.87	591.75	624.62	657.50
1316	361.90	394.80	427.70	460.60	493.50	526.40	559.30	592.20	625.10	658.00
1317	362.17	395.10	428.02	460.95	493.87	526.80	559.72	592.65	625.57	658.50
1318	362.45	395.40	428.35	461.30	494.25	527.20	560.15	593.10	626.05	659.00
1319	362.72	395.70	428.67	461.65	494.62	527.60	560.57	593.55	626.52	659.50
1320	363.00	396.00	429.00	462.00	495.00	528.00	561.00	594.00	627.00	660.00
1321	363.27	396.30	429.32	462.35	495.37	528.40	561.42	594.45	627.47	660.50
1322	363.55	396.60	429.65	462.70	495.75	528.80	561.85	594.90	627.95	661.00
1323	363.82	396.90	429.97	463.05	496.12	529.20	562.27	595.35	628.42	661.50
1324	364.10	397.20	430.30	463.40	496.50	529.60	562.70	595.80	628.90	662.00
1325	364.37	397.50	430.62	463.75	496.87	530.00	563.12	596.25	629.37	662.50
1326	364.65	397.80	430.95	464.10	497.25	530.40	563.55	596.70	629.85	663.00
1327	364.92	398.10	431.27	464.45	497.62	530.80	563.97	597.15	630.32	663.50
1328	365.20	398.40	431.60	464.80	498.00	531.20	564.40	597.60	630.80	664.00
1329	365.47	398.70	431.92	465.15	498.37	531.60	564.82	598.05	631.27	664.50
1330	365.75	399.00	432.25	465.50	498.75	532.00	565.25	598.50	631.75	665.00
1331	366.02	399.30	432.57	465.85	499.12	532.40	565.67	598.95	632.22	665.50
1332	366.30	399.60	432.90	466.20	499.50	532.80	566.10	599.40	632.70	666.00
1333	366.57	399.90	433.22	466.55	499.87	533.20	566.52	599.85	633.17	666.50
1334	366.85	400.20	433.55	466.90	500.25	533.60	566.95	600.30	633.65	667.00
1335	367.12	400.50	433.87	467.25	500.62	534.00	567.37	600.75	634.12	667.50
1336	367.40	400.80	434.20	467.60	501.00	534.40	567.80	601.20	634.60	668.00
1337	367.67	401.10	434.52	467.95	501.37	534.80	568.22	601.65	635.07	668.50
1338	367.95	401.40	434.85	468.30	501.75	535.20	568.65	602.10	635.55	669.00
1339	368.22	401.70	435.17	468.65	502.12	535.60	569.07	602.55	636.02	669.50
1340	368.50	402.00	435.50	469.00	502.50	536.00	569.50	603.00	636.50	670.00
1341	368.77	402.30	435.82	469.35	502.87	536.40	569.92	603.45	636.97	670.50
1342	369.05	402.60	436.15	469.70	503.25	536.80	570.35	603.90	637.45	671.00
1343	369.32	402.90	436.47	470.05	503.62	537.20	570.77	604.35	637.92	671.50
1344	369.60	403.20	436.80	470.40	504.00	537.60	571.20	604.80	638.40	672.00
1345	369.87	403.50	437.12	470.75	504.37	538.00	571.62	605.25	638.87	672.50
1346	370.15	403.80	437.45	471.10	504.75	538.40	572.05	605.70	639.35	673.00
1347	370.42	404.10	437.77	471.45	505.12	538.80	572.47	606.15	639.82	673.50
1348	370.70	404.40	438.10	471.80	505.50	539.20	572.90	606.60	640.30	674.00
1349	370.97	404.70	438.42	472.15	505.87	539.60	573.32	607.05	640.77	674.50
1350	371.25	405.00	438.75	472.50	506.25	540.00	573.75	607.50	641.25	675.00

1400 FEET.

Per Ton,	25c.	50c.	$1	$2	$3	$4	$5	$6	$7	$8	$9	$10
Per Foot,			2½ cts.	5 cts.	7½ cts.	10 cts.	12½ cts.	15 cts.	17½ cts.	20 cts.	22½ cts.	25 cts.
Feet.												
1351	8.44	16.89	33.77	67.55	101.32	135.10	168.87	202.65	236.42	270.20	303.97	337.75
1352	8.45	16.90	33.80	67.60	101.40	135.20	169.00	202.80	236.60	270.40	304.20	338.00
1353	8.46	16.91	33.82	67.65	101.47	135.30	169.12	202.95	236.77	270.60	304.42	338.25
1354	8.46	16.92	33.85	67.70	101.55	135.40	169.25	203.10	236.95	270.80	304.65	338.50
1355	8.47	16.94	33.87	67.75	101.62	135.50	169.37	203.25	237.12	271.00	304.87	338.75
1356	8.47	16.95	33.90	67.80	101.70	135.60	169.50	203.40	237.30	271.20	305.10	339.00
1357	8.48	16.96	33.92	67.85	101.77	135.70	169.62	203.55	237.47	271.40	305.32	339.25
1358	8.49	16.97	33.95	67.90	101.85	135.80	169.75	203.70	237.65	271.60	305.55	339.50
1359	8.49	16.99	33.97	67.95	101.92	135.90	169.87	203.85	237.82	271.80	305.77	339.75
1360	8.50	17.00	34.00	68.00	102.00	136.00	170.00	204.00	238.00	272.00	306.00	340.00
1361	8.51	17.01	34.02	68.05	102.07	136.10	170.12	204.15	238.17	272.20	306.22	340.25
1362	8.51	17.02	34.05	68.10	102.15	136.20	170.25	204.30	238.35	272.40	306.45	340.50
1363	8.52	17.04	34.07	68.15	102.22	136.30	170.37	204.45	238.52	272.60	306.67	340.75
1364	8.52	17.05	34.10	68.20	102.30	136.40	170.50	204.60	238.70	272.80	306.90	341.00
1365	8.53	17.06	34.12	68.25	102.37	136.50	170.62	204.75	238.87	273.00	307.12	341.25
1366	8.54	17.07	34.15	68.30	102.45	136.60	170.75	204.90	239.05	273.20	307.35	341.50
1367	8.54	17.09	34.17	68.35	102.52	136.70	170.87	205.05	239.22	273.40	307.57	341.75
1368	8.55	17.10	34.20	68.40	102.60	136.80	171.00	205.20	239.40	273.60	307.80	342.00
1369	8.56	17.11	34.22	68.45	102.67	136.90	171.12	205.35	239.57	273.80	308.02	342.25
1370	8.56	17.12	34.25	68.50	102.75	137.00	171.25	205.50	239.75	274.00	308.25	342.50
1371	8.57	17.14	34.27	68.55	102.82	137.10	171.37	205.65	239.92	274.20	308.47	342.75
1372	8.57	17.15	34.30	68.60	102.90	137.20	171.50	205.80	240.10	274.40	308.70	343.00
1373	8.58	17.16	34.32	68.65	102.97	137.30	171.62	205.95	240.27	274.60	308.92	343.25
1374	8.59	17.17	34.35	68.70	103.05	137.40	171.75	206.10	240.45	274.80	309.15	343.50
1375	8.59	17.19	34.37	68.75	103.12	137.50	171.87	206.25	240.62	275.00	309.37	343.75
1376	8.60	17.20	34.40	68.80	103.20	137.60	172.00	206.40	240.80	275.20	309.60	344.00
1377	8.61	17.21	34.42	68.85	103.27	137.70	172.12	206.55	240.97	275.40	309.82	344.25
1378	8.61	17.22	34.45	68.90	103.35	137.80	172.25	206.70	241.15	275.60	310.05	344.50
1379	8.62	17.24	34.47	68.95	103.42	137.90	172.37	206.85	241.32	275.80	310.27	344.75
1380	8.62	17.25	34.50	69.00	103.50	138.00	172.50	207.00	241.50	276.00	310.50	345.00
1381	8.63	17.26	34.52	69.05	103.57	138.10	172.62	207.15	241.67	276.20	310.72	345.25
1382	8.64	17.27	34.55	69.10	103.65	138.20	172.75	207.30	241.85	276.40	310.95	345.50
1383	8.64	17.29	34.57	69.15	103.72	138.30	172.87	207.45	242.02	276.60	311.17	345.75
1384	8.65	17.30	34.60	69.20	103.80	138.40	173.00	207.60	242.20	276.80	311.40	346.00
1385	8.66	17.31	34.62	69.25	103.87	138.50	173.12	207.75	242.37	277.00	311.62	346.25
1386	8.66	17.32	34.65	69.30	103.95	138.60	173.25	207.90	242.55	277.20	311.85	346.50
1387	8.67	17.34	34.67	69.35	104.02	138.70	173.37	208.05	242.72	277.40	312.07	346.75
1388	8.67	17.35	34.70	69.40	104.10	138.80	173.50	208.20	242.90	277.60	312.30	347.00
1389	8.68	17.36	34.72	69.45	104.17	138.90	173.62	208.35	243.07	277.80	312.52	347.25
1390	8.69	17.37	34.75	69.50	104.25	139.00	173.75	208.50	243.25	278.00	312.75	347.50
1391	8.69	17.39	34.77	69.55	104.32	139.10	173.87	208.65	243.42	278.20	312.97	347.75
1392	8.70	17.40	34.80	69.60	104.40	139.20	174.00	208.80	243.60	278.40	313.20	348.00
1393	8.71	17.41	34.82	69.65	104.47	139.30	174.12	208.95	243.77	278.60	313.42	348.25
1394	8.71	17.42	34.85	69.70	104.55	139.40	174.25	209.10	243.95	278.80	313.65	348.50
1395	8.72	17.44	34.87	69.75	104.62	139.50	174.37	209.25	244.12	279.00	313.87	348.75
1396	8.72	17.45	34.90	69.80	104.70	139.60	174.50	209.40	244.30	279.20	314.10	349.00
1397	8.73	17.46	34.92	69.85	104.77	139.70	174.62	209.55	244.47	279.40	314.32	349.25
1398	8.74	17.47	34.95	69.90	104.85	139.80	174.75	209.70	244.65	279.60	314.55	349.50
1399	8.74	17.49	34.97	69.95	104.92	139.90	174.87	209.85	244.82	279.80	314.77	349.75
1400	8.75	17.50	35.00	70.00	105.00	140.00	175.00	210.00	245.00	280.00	315.00	350.00

1400 FEET.

Per Ton,	$11	$12	$13	$14	$15	$16	$17	$18	$19	$20
Per Foot,	27½ cts.	30 cts.	32½ cts.	35 cts.	37½ cts.	40 cts.	42½ cts.	45 cts.	47½ cts.	50 cts.
Feet.										
1351	371.52	405.30	439.07	472.85	506.62	540.40	574.17	607.95	641.72	675.50
1352	371.80	405.60	439.40	473.20	507.00	540.80	574.60	608.40	642.20	676.00
1353	372.07	405.90	439.72	473.55	507.37	541.20	575.02	608.85	642.67	676.50
1354	372.35	406.20	440.05	473.90	507.75	541.60	575.45	609.30	643.15	677.00
1355	372.62	406.50	440.37	474.25	508.12	542.00	575.87	609.75	643.62	677.50
1356	372.90	406.80	440.70	474.60	508.50	542.40	576.30	610.20	644.10	678.00
1357	373.17	407.10	441.02	474.95	508.87	542.80	576.72	610.65	644.57	678.50
1358	373.45	407.40	441.35	475.30	509.25	543.20	577.15	611.10	645.05	679.00
1359	373.72	407.70	441.67	475.65	509.62	543.60	577.57	611.55	645.52	679.50
1360	374.00	408.00	442.00	476.00	510.00	544.00	578.00	612.00	646.00	680.00
1361	374.27	408.30	442.32	476.35	510.37	544.40	578.42	612.45	646.47	680.50
1362	374.55	408.60	442.65	476.70	510.75	544.80	578.85	612.90	646.95	681.00
1363	374.82	409.90	442.97	477.05	511.12	545.20	579.27	613.35	647.42	681.50
1364	375.10	409.20	443.30	477.40	511.50	545.60	579.70	613.80	647.90	682.00
1365	375.37	409.50	443.62	477.75	511.87	546.00	580.12	614.25	648.37	682.50
1366	375.65	409.80	443.95	478.10	512.25	546.40	580.55	614.70	648.85	683.00
1367	375.92	410.10	444.27	478.45	512.62	546.80	580.97	615.15	649.32	683.50
1368	376.20	410.40	444.60	478.80	513.00	547.20	581.40	615.60	649.80	684.00
1369	376.47	410.70	444.92	479.15	513.37	547.60	581.82	616.05	650.27	684.50
1370	376.75	411.00	445.25	479.50	513.75	548.00	582.25	616.50	650.75	685.00
1371	377.02	411.30	445.57	479.85	514.12	548.40	582.67	616.95	651.22	685.50
1372	377.30	411.60	445.90	480.20	514.50	548.80	583.10	617.40	651.70	686.00
1373	377.57	411.90	446.22	480.55	514.87	549.20	583.52	617.85	652.17	686.50
1374	377.85	412.20	446.55	480.90	515.25	549.60	583.95	618.30	652.65	687.00
1375	378.12	412.50	446.87	481.25	515.62	550.00	584.37	618.75	653.12	687.50
1376	378.40	412.80	447.20	481.60	516.00	550.40	584.80	619.20	653.60	688.00
1377	378.67	413.10	447.52	481.95	516.37	550.80	585.22	619.65	654.07	688.50
1378	378.95	413.40	447.85	482.30	516.75	551.20	585.65	620.10	654.55	689.00
1379	379.22	413.70	448.17	482.65	517.12	551.60	586.07	620.55	655.02	689.50
1380	379.50	414.00	448.50	483.00	517.50	552.00	586.50	621.00	655.50	690.00
1381	379.77	414.30	448.82	483.35	517.87	552.40	586.92	621.45	655.97	690.50
1382	380.05	414.60	449.15	483.70	518.25	552.80	587.35	621.90	656.45	691.00
1383	380.32	414.90	449.47	484.05	518.62	553.20	587.77	622.35	656.92	691.50
1384	380.60	415.20	449.80	484.40	519.00	553.60	588.20	622.80	657.40	692.00
1385	380.87	415.50	450.12	484.75	519.37	554.00	588.62	623.25	657.87	692.50
1386	381.15	415.80	450.45	485.10	519.75	554.40	589.05	623.70	658.35	693.00
1387	381.42	416.10	450.77	485.45	520.12	554.80	589.47	624.15	658.82	693.50
1388	381.70	416.40	451.10	485.80	520.50	555.20	589.90	624.60	659.30	694.00
1389	381.97	416.70	451.42	486.15	520.87	555.60	590.32	625.05	659.77	694.50
1390	382.25	417.00	451.75	486.50	521.25	556.00	590.75	625.50	660.25	695.00
1391	382.52	417.30	452.07	486.85	521.62	556.40	591.17	625.95	660.72	695.50
1392	382.80	417.60	452.30	487.20	522.00	556.80	591.60	626.40	661.20	696.00
1393	383.07	417.90	452.72	487.55	522.37	557.20	592.02	626.85	661.67	696.50
1394	383.35	418.20	453.05	487.90	522.75	557.60	592.45	627.30	662.15	697.00
1395	383.62	418.50	453.37	488.25	523.12	558.00	592.87	627.75	662.62	697.50
1396	383.90	418.80	453.70	488.60	523.50	558.40	593.30	628.20	663.10	698.00
1397	384.17	419.10	454.02	488.95	523.87	558.80	593.72	628.65	663.57	698.50
1398	384.45	419.40	454.35	489.30	524.25	559.20	594.15	629.10	664.05	699.00
1399	384.72	419.70	454.67	489.65	524.62	559.60	594.57	629.55	664.52	699.50
1400	385.00	420.00	455.00	490.00	525.00	560.00	595.00	630.00	665.00	700.00

1450 FEET.

Per Ton,	25c.	50c.	$1	$2	$3	$4	$5	$6	$7	$8	$9	$10
Per Foot,			2½ cts.	5 cts.	7½ cts.	10 cts.	12½ cts.	15 cts.	17½ cts.	20 cts.	22½ cts.	25 cts.
Feet.												
1401	8.76	17.51	35.02	70.05	105.07	140.10	175.12	210.15	245.17	280.20	315.22	350.25
1402	8.76	17.52	35.05	70.10	105.15	140.20	175.25	210.30	245.35	280.40	315.45	350.50
1403	8.77	17.54	35.07	70.15	105.22	140.30	175.37	210.45	245.52	280.60	315.67	350.75
1404	8.77	17.55	35.10	70.20	105.30	140.40	175.50	210.60	245.70	280.80	315.90	351.00
1405	8.78	17.56	35.12	70.25	105.37	140.50	175.62	210.75	245.87	281.00	316.12	351.25
1406	8.79	17.57	35.15	70.30	105.45	140.60	175.75	210.90	246.05	281.20	316.35	351.50
1407	8.79	17.59	35.17	70.35	105.52	140.70	175.87	211.05	246.22	281.40	316.57	351.75
1408	8.80	17.60	35.20	70.40	105.60	140.80	176.00	211.20	246.40	281.60	316.80	352.00
1409	8.81	17.61	35.22	70.45	105.67	140.90	176.12	211.35	246.57	281.80	317.02	352.25
1410	8.81	17.62	35.25	70.50	105.75	141.00	176.25	211.50	246.75	282.00	317.25	352.50
1411	8.82	17.64	35.27	70.55	105.82	141.10	176.37	211.65	246.92	282.20	317.47	352.75
1412	8.82	17.65	35.30	70.60	105.90	141.20	176.50	211.80	247.10	282.40	317.70	353.00
1413	8.83	17.66	35.32	70.65	105.97	141.30	176.62	211.95	247.27	282.60	317.92	353.25
1414	8.84	17.67	35.35	70.70	106.05	141.40	176.75	212.10	247.45	282.80	318.15	353.50
1415	8.84	17.69	35.37	70.75	106.12	141.50	176.87	212.25	247.62	283.00	318.37	353.75
1416	8.85	17.70	35.40	70.80	106.20	141.60	177.00	212.40	247.80	283.20	318.60	354.00
1417	8.86	17.71	35.42	70.85	106.27	141.70	177.12	212.55	247.97	283.40	318.82	354.25
1418	8.86	17.72	35.45	70.90	106.35	141.80	177.25	212.70	248.15	283.60	319.05	354.50
1419	8.87	17.74	35.47	70.95	106.42	141.90	177.37	212.85	248.32	283.80	319.27	354.75
1420	8.87	17.75	35.50	71.00	106.50	142.00	177.50	213.00	248.50	284.00	319.50	355.00
1421	8.88	17.76	35.52	71.05	106.57	142.10	177.62	213.15	248.67	284.20	319.72	355.25
1422	8.89	17.77	35.55	71.10	106.65	142.20	177.75	213.30	248.85	284.40	319.95	355.50
1423	8.89	17.79	35.57	71.15	106.72	142.30	177.87	213.45	249.02	284.60	320.17	355.75
1424	8.90	17.80	35.60	71.20	106.80	142.40	178.00	213.60	249.20	284.80	320.40	356.00
1425	8.91	17.81	35.62	71.25	106.87	142.50	178.12	213.75	249.37	285.00	320.62	356.25
1426	8.91	17.82	35.65	71.30	106.95	142.60	178.25	213.90	249.55	285.20	320.85	356.50
1427	8.92	17.84	35.67	71.35	107.02	142.70	178.37	214.05	249.72	285.40	321.07	356.75
1428	8.92	17.85	35.70	71.40	107.10	142.80	178.50	214.20	249.90	285.60	321.30	357.00
1429	8.93	17.86	35.72	71.45	107.17	142.90	178.62	214.35	250.07	285.80	321.52	357.25
1430	8.94	17.87	35.75	71.50	107.25	143.00	178.75	214.50	250.25	286.00	321.75	357.50
1431	8.94	17.89	35.77	71.55	107.32	143.10	178.87	214.65	250.42	286.20	321.97	357.75
1432	8.95	17.90	35.80	71.60	107.40	143.20	179.00	214.80	250.60	286.40	322.20	358.00
1433	8.96	17.91	35.82	71.65	107.47	143.30	179.12	214.95	250.77	286.60	322.42	358.25
1434	8.96	17.92	35.85	71.70	107.55	143.40	179.25	215.10	250.95	286.80	322.65	358.50
1435	8.97	17.94	35.87	71.75	107.62	143.50	179.37	215.25	251.12	287.00	322.87	358.75
1436	8.97	17.95	35.90	71.80	107.70	143.60	179.50	215.40	251.30	287.20	323.10	359.00
1437	8.98	17.96	35.92	71.85	107.77	143.70	179.62	215.55	251.47	287.40	323.32	359.25
1438	8.99	17.97	35.95	71.90	107.85	143.80	179.75	215.70	251.65	287.60	323.55	359.50
1439	8.99	17.99	35.97	71.95	107.92	143.90	179.87	215.85	251.82	287.80	323.77	359.75
1440	9.00	18.00	36.00	72.00	108.00	144.00	180.00	216.00	252.00	288.00	324.00	360.00
1441	9.01	18.01	36.02	72.05	108.07	144.10	180.12	216.15	252.17	288.20	324.22	360.25
1442	9.01	18.02	36.05	72.10	108.15	144.20	180.25	216.30	252.35	288.40	324.45	360.50
1443	9.02	18.04	36.07	72.15	108.22	144.30	180.37	216.45	252.52	288.60	324.67	360.75
1444	9.02	18.05	36.10	72.20	108.30	144.40	180.50	216.60	252.70	288.80	324.90	361.00
1445	9.03	18.06	36.12	72.25	108.37	144.50	180.62	216.75	252.87	289.00	325.12	361.25
1446	9.04	18.07	36.15	72.30	108.45	144.60	180.75	216.90	253.05	289.20	325.35	361.50
1447	9.04	18.09	36.17	72.35	108.52	144.70	180.87	217.05	253.22	289.40	325.57	361.75
1448	9.05	18.10	36.20	72.40	108.60	144.80	181.00	217.20	253.40	289.60	325.80	362.00
1449	9.06	18.11	36.22	72.45	108.67	144.90	181.12	217.35	253.57	289.80	326.02	362.25
1450	9.06	18.12	36.25	72.50	108.75	145.00	181.25	217.50	253.75	290.00	326.25	362.50

1450 FEET.

Per Ton,	$11	$12	$13	$14	$15	$16	$17	$18	$19	$20
Per Foot,	27½ cts.	30 cts.	32½ cts.	35 cts.	37½ cts.	40 cts.	42½ cts.	45 cts.	47½ cts.	50 cts.
Feet.										
1401	385.27	420.30	455.32	490.35	525.37	560.40	595.42	630.45	665.47	700.50
1402	385.55	420.60	455.65	490.70	525.75	560.80	595.85	630.90	665.95	701.00
1403	385.82	420.90	455.97	491.05	526.12	561.20	596.27	631.35	666.42	701.50
1404	386.10	421.20	456.30	491.40	526.50	561.60	596.70	631.80	666.90	702.00
1405	386.37	421.50	456.62	491.75	526.87	562.00	597.12	632.25	667.37	702.50
1406	386.65	421.80	456.95	492.10	527.25	562.40	597.55	632.70	667.85	703.00
1407	386.92	422.10	457.27	492.45	527.62	562.80	597.97	633.15	668.32	703.50
1408	387.20	422.40	457.60	492.80	528.00	563.20	598.40	633.60	668.80	704.00
1409	387.47	422.70	457.92	493.15	528.37	563.60	598.82	634.05	669.27	704.50
1410	387.75	423.00	458.25	493.50	528.75	564.00	599.25	634.50	669.75	705.00
1411	388.02	423.30	458.57	493.85	529.12	564.40	599.67	634.95	670.22	705.50
1412	388.30	423.60	458.90	494.20	529.50	564.80	600.10	635.40	670.70	706.00
1413	388.57	423.90	459.22	494.55	529.87	565.20	600.52	635.85	671.17	706.50
1414	388.85	424.20	459.55	494.90	530.25	565.60	600.95	636.30	671.65	707.00
1415	389.12	424.50	459.87	495.25	530.62	566.00	601.37	636.75	672.12	707.50
1416	389.40	424.80	460.20	495.60	531.00	566.40	601.80	637.20	672.60	708.00
1417	389.67	425.10	460.52	495.95	531.37	566.80	602.22	637.65	673.07	708.50
1418	389.95	425.40	460.85	496.30	531.75	567.20	602.65	638.10	673.55	709.00
1419	390.22	425.70	461.17	496.65	532.12	567.60	603.07	638.55	674.02	709.50
1420	390.50	426.00	461.50	497.00	532.50	568.00	603.50	639.00	674.50	710.00
1421	390.77	426.30	461.82	497.35	532.87	568.40	603.92	639.45	674.97	710.50
1422	391.05	426.60	462.15	497.70	533.25	568.80	604.35	639.90	675.45	711.00
1423	391.32	426.90	462.47	498.05	533.62	569.20	604.77	640.35	675.92	711.50
1424	391.60	427.20	462.80	498.40	534.00	569.60	605.20	640.80	676.40	712.00
1425	391.87	427.50	463.12	498.75	534.37	570.00	605.62	641.25	676.87	712.50
1426	392.15	427.80	463.45	499.10	534.75	570.40	606.05	641.70	677.35	713.00
1427	392.42	428.10	463.77	499.45	535.12	570.80	606.47	642.15	677.82	713.50
1428	392.70	428.40	464.10	499.80	535.50	571.20	606.90	642.60	678.30	714.00
1429	392.97	428.70	464.42	500.15	535.87	571.60	607.32	643.05	678.77	714.50
1430	393.25	429.00	464.75	500.50	536.25	572.00	607.75	643.50	679.25	715.00
1431	393.52	429.30	465.07	500.85	536.62	572.40	608.17	643.95	679.72	715.50
1432	393.80	429.60	465.40	501.20	537.00	572.80	608.60	644.40	680.20	716.00
1433	394.07	429.90	465.72	501.55	537.37	573.20	609.02	644.85	680.67	716.50
1434	394.35	430.20	466.05	501.90	537.75	573.60	609.45	645.30	681.15	717.00
1435	394.62	430.50	466.37	502.25	538.12	574.00	609.87	645.75	681.62	717.50
1436	394.90	430.80	466.70	502.60	538.50	574.40	610.30	646.20	682.10	718.00
1437	395.17	431.10	467.02	502.95	538.87	574.80	610.72	646.65	682.57	718.50
1438	395.45	431.40	467.35	503.30	539.25	575.20	611.15	647.10	683.05	719.00
1439	395.72	431.70	467.67	503.65	539.62	575.60	611.57	647.55	683.52	719.50
1440	396.00	432.00	468.00	504.00	540.00	576.00	612.00	648.00	684.00	720.00
1441	396.27	432.30	468.32	504.35	540.37	576.40	612.42	648.45	684.47	720.50
1442	396.55	432.60	468.65	504.70	540.75	576.80	612.85	648.90	684.95	721.00
1443	396.82	432.90	468.97	505.05	541.12	577.20	613.27	649.35	685.42	721.50
1444	397.10	433.20	469.30	505.40	541.50	577.60	613.70	649.80	685.90	722.00
1445	397.37	433.50	469.62	505.75	541.87	578.00	614.12	650.25	686.37	722.50
1446	397.65	433.80	469.95	506.10	542.25	578.40	614.55	650.70	686.85	723.00
1447	397.92	434.10	470.27	506.45	542.62	578.80	614.97	651.15	687.32	723.50
1448	398.20	434.40	470.60	506.80	543.00	579.20	615.40	651.60	687.80	724.00
1449	398.47	434.70	470.92	507.15	543.37	579.60	615.82	652.05	688.27	724.50
1450	398.75	435.00	471.25	507.50	543.75	580.00	616.25	652.50	688.75	725.00

1500 FEET.

Per Ton,	25c.	50c.	$1	$2	$3	$4	$5	$6	$7	$8	$9	$10
Per Foot,			2½ cts.	5 cts.	7½ cts.	10 cts.	12½ cts.	15 cts.	17½ cts.	20 cts.	22½ cts.	25 cts.
Feet.												
1451	9.07	18.14	36.27	72.55	108.82	145.10	181.37	217.65	253.92	290.20	326.47	362.75
1452	9.07	18.15	36.30	72.60	108.90	145.20	181.50	217.80	254.10	290.40	326.70	363.00
1453	9.08	18.16	36.32	72.65	108.97	145.30	181.62	217.95	254.27	290.60	326.92	363.25
1454	9.09	18.17	36.35	72.70	109.05	145.40	181.75	218.10	254.45	290.80	327.15	363.50
1455	9.09	18.19	36.37	72.75	109.12	145.50	181.87	218.25	254.62	291.00	327.37	363.75
1456	9.10	18.20	36.40	72.80	109.20	145.60	182.00	218.40	254.80	291.20	327.60	364.00
1457	9.11	18.21	36.42	72.85	109.27	145.70	182.12	218.55	254.97	291.40	327.82	364.25
1458	9.11	18.22	36.45	72.90	109.35	145.80	182.25	218.70	255.15	291.60	328.05	364.50
1459	9.12	18.24	36.47	72.95	109.42	145.90	182.37	218.85	255.32	291.80	328.27	364.75
1460	9.12	18.25	36.50	73.00	109.50	146.00	182.50	219.00	255.50	292.00	328.50	365.00
1461	9.13	18.26	36.52	73.05	109.57	146.10	182.62	219.15	255.67	292.20	328.72	365.25
1462	9.14	18.27	36.55	73.10	109.65	146.20	182.75	219.30	255.85	292.40	328.95	365.50
1463	9.14	18.29	36.57	73.15	109.72	146.30	182.87	219.45	256.02	292.60	329.17	365.75
1464	9.15	18.30	36.60	73.20	109.80	146.40	183.00	219.60	256.20	292.80	329.40	366.00
1465	9.16	18.31	36.62	73.25	109.87	146.50	183.12	219.75	256.37	293.00	329.62	366.25
1466	9.16	18.32	36.65	73.30	109.95	146.60	183.25	219.90	256.55	293.20	329.85	366.50
1467	9.17	18.34	36.67	73.35	110.02	146.70	183.37	220.05	256.72	293.40	330.07	366.75
1468	9.17	18.35	36.70	73.40	110.10	146.80	183.50	220.20	256.90	293.60	330.30	367.00
1469	9.18	18.36	36.72	73.45	110.17	146.90	183.62	220.35	257.07	293.80	330.52	367.25
1470	9.19	18.37	36.75	73.50	110.25	147.00	183.75	220.50	257.25	294.00	330.75	367.50
1471	9.19	18.39	36.77	73.55	110.32	147.10	183.87	220.65	257.42	294.20	330.97	367.75
1472	9.20	18.40	36.80	73.60	110.40	147.20	184.00	220.80	257.60	294.40	331.20	368.00
1473	9.21	18.41	36.82	73.65	110.47	147.30	184.12	220.95	257.77	294.60	331.42	368.25
1474	9.21	18.42	36.85	73.70	110.55	147.40	184.25	221.10	257.95	294.80	331.65	368.50
1475	9.22	18.44	36.87	73.75	110.62	147.50	184.37	221.25	258.12	295.00	331.87	368.75
1476	9.22	18.45	36.90	73.80	110.70	147.60	184.50	221.40	258.30	295.20	332.10	369.00
1477	9.23	18.46	36.92	73.85	110.77	147.70	184.62	221.55	258.47	295.40	332.32	369.25
1478	9.24	18.47	36.95	73.90	110.85	147.80	184.75	221.70	258.65	295.60	332.55	369.50
1479	9.24	18.49	36.97	73.95	110.92	147.90	184.87	221.85	258.82	295.80	332.77	369.75
1480	9.25	18.50	37.00	74.00	111.00	148.00	185.00	222.00	259.00	296.00	333.00	370.00
1481	9.26	18.51	37.02	74.05	111.07	148.10	185.12	222.15	259.17	296.20	333.22	370.25
1482	9.26	18.52	37.05	74.10	111.15	148.20	185.25	222.30	259.35	296.40	333.45	370.50
1483	9.27	18.54	37.07	74.15	111.22	148.30	185.37	222.45	259.52	296.60	333.67	370.75
1484	9.27	18.55	37.10	74.20	111.30	148.40	185.50	222.60	259.70	296.80	333.90	371.00
1485	9.28	18.56	37.12	74.25	111.37	148.50	185.62	222.75	259.87	297.00	334.12	371.25
1486	9.29	18.57	37.15	74.30	111.45	148.60	185.75	222.90	260.05	297.20	334.35	371.50
1487	9.29	18.59	37.17	74.35	111.52	148.70	185.87	223.05	260.22	297.40	334.57	371.75
1488	9.30	18.60	37.20	74.40	111.60	148.80	186.00	223.20	260.40	297.60	334.80	372.00
1489	9.31	18.61	37.22	74.45	111.67	148.90	186.12	223.35	260.57	297.80	335.02	372.25
1490	9.31	18.62	37.25	74.50	111.75	149.00	186.25	223.50	260.75	298.00	335.25	372.50
1491	9.32	18.64	37.27	74.55	111.82	149.10	186.37	223.65	260.92	298.20	335.47	372.75
1492	9.32	18.65	37.30	74.60	111.90	149.20	186.50	223.80	261.10	298.40	335.70	373.00
1493	9.33	18.66	37.32	74.65	111.97	149.30	186.62	223.95	261.27	298.60	335.92	373.25
1494	9.34	18.67	37.35	74.70	112.05	149.40	186.75	224.10	261.45	298.80	336.15	373.50
1495	9.34	18.69	37.37	74.75	112.12	149.50	186.87	224.25	261.62	299.00	336.37	373.75
1496	9.35	18.70	37.40	74.80	112.20	149.60	187.00	224.40	261.80	299.20	336.60	374.00
1497	9.36	18.71	37.42	74.85	112.27	149.70	187.12	224.55	261.97	299.40	336.82	374.25
1498	9.36	18.72	37.45	74.90	112.35	149.80	187.25	224.70	262.15	299.60	337.05	374.50
1499	9.37	18.74	37.47	74.95	112.42	149.90	187.37	224.85	262.32	299.80	337.27	374.75
1500	9.37	18.75	37.50	75.00	112.50	150.00	187.50	225.00	262.50	300.00	337.50	375.00

1500 FEET.

Per Ton,	$11	$12	$13	$14	$15	$16	$17	$18	$19	$20
Per Foot,	27½ cts.	30 cts.	32½ cts.	35 cts.	37½ cts.	40 cts.	42½ cts.	45 cts.	47½ cts.	50 cts.
Feet.										
1451	399.02	435.30	471.57	507.85	544.12	580.40	616.67	652.95	689.22	725.50
1452	399.30	435.60	471.90	508.20	544.50	580.80	617.10	653.40	689.70	726.00
1453	399.57	435.90	472.22	508.55	544.87	581.20	617.52	653.85	690.17	726.50
1454	399.85	436.20	472.55	508.90	545.25	581.60	617.95	654.30	690.65	727.00
1455	400.12	436.50	472.87	509.25	545.62	582.00	618.37	654.75	691.12	727.50
1456	400.40	436.80	473.20	509.60	546.00	582.40	618.80	655.20	691.60	728.00
1457	400.67	437.10	473.52	509.95	546.37	582.80	619.22	655.65	692.07	728.50
1458	400.95	437.40	473.85	510.30	546.75	583.20	619.65	656.10	692.55	729.00
1459	401.22	437.70	474.17	510.65	547.12	583.60	620.07	656.55	693.02	729.50
1460	401.50	438.00	474.50	511.00	547.50	584.00	620.50	657.00	693.50	730.00
1461	401.77	438.30	474.82	511.35	547.87	584.40	620.92	657.45	693.97	730.50
1462	402.05	438.60	475.15	511.70	548.25	584.80	621.35	657.90	694.45	731.00
1463	402.32	438.90	475.47	512.05	548.62	585.20	621.77	658.35	694.92	731.50
1464	402.60	439.20	475.80	512.40	549.00	585.60	622.20	658.80	695.40	732.00
1465	402.87	439.50	476.12	512.75	549.37	586.00	622.62	659.25	695.87	732.50
1466	403.15	439.80	476.45	513.10	549.75	586.40	623.05	659.70	696.35	733.00
1467	403.42	440.10	476.77	513.45	550.12	586.80	623.47	660.15	696.82	733.50
1468	403.70	440.40	477.10	513.80	550.50	587.20	623.90	660.60	697.30	734.00
1469	403.97	440.70	477.42	514.15	550.87	587.60	624.32	661.05	697.77	734.50
1470	404.25	441.00	477.75	514.50	551.25	588.00	624.75	661.50	698.25	735.00
1471	404.52	441.30	478.07	514.85	551.62	588.40	625.17	661.95	698.72	735.50
1472	404.80	441.60	478.40	515.20	552.00	588.80	625.60	662.40	699.20	736.00
1473	405.07	441.90	478.72	515.55	552.37	589.20	626.02	662.85	699.67	736.50
1474	405.35	442.20	479.05	515.90	552.75	589.60	626.45	663.30	700.15	737.00
1475	405.62	442.50	479.37	516.25	553.12	590.00	626.87	663.75	700.62	737.50
1476	405.90	442.80	479.70	516.60	553.50	590.40	627.30	664.20	701.10	738.00
1477	406.17	443.10	480.02	516.95	553.87	590.80	627.72	664.65	701,57	738.50
1478	406.45	443.40	480.35	517.30	554.25	591.20	628.15	665.10	702.05	739.00
1479	406.72	443.70	480.67	517.65	554.62	591.60	628.57	665.55	702.52	739.50
1480	407.00	444.00	481.00	518.00	555.00	592.00	629.00	666.00	703.00	740.00
1481	407.27	444.30	481.32	518.35	555.37	592.40	629.42	666.45	703.47	740.50
1482	407.55	444.60	481.65	518.70	555.75	592.80	629.85	666.90	703,95	741.00
1483	407.82	444.90	481.97	519.05	556.12	593.20	630.27	667.35	704.42	741.50
1484	408.10	445.20	482.30	519.40	556.50	593.60	630.70	667.80	704.90	742.00
1485	408.37	445.50	482.62	519.75	556.87	594.00	631.12	668.25	705.37	742.50
1486	408.65	445.80	482.95	520.10	557.25	594.40	631.55	668.70	705.85	743.00
1487	408.92	446.10	483.27	520.45	557.62	594.80	631.97	669.15	706.32	743.50
1488	409.20	446.40	483.60	520.80	558.00	595.20	632.40	669.60	706.80	744.00
1489	409.47	446.70	483.92	521.15	558.37	595.60	632.82	670.05	707.27	744.50
1490	409.75	447.00	484.25	521.50	558.75	596.00	633.25	670.50	707.75	745.00
1491	410.02	447.30	484.57	521.85	559.12	596.40	633.67	670.95	708.22	745.50
1492	410.30	447.60	484.90	522.20	559.50	596.80	634.10	671.40	708.70	746.00
1493	410.57	447.90	485.22	522.55	559.87	597.20	634.52	671.85	709.17	746.50
1494	410.85	448.20	485.55	522.90	560.25	597.60	634.95	672.30	709.65	747.00
1495	411.12	448.50	485.87	523.25	560.62	598.00	635.37	672.75	710.12	747.50
1496	411.40	448.80	486.20	523.60	561.00	598.40	635.80	673.20	710.60	748.00
1497	411.67	449.10	486.52	523.95	561.37	598.80	636.22	673.65	711.07	748.50
1498	411.95	449.40	486.85	524.30	561.75	599.20	636.65	674.10	711.55	749.00
1499	412.22	449.70	487.17	524.65	562.12	599.60	637.07	674.55	712.02	749.50
1500	412.50	450.00	487.50	525.00	562.50	600.00	637.50	675.00	712.50	750.00

1550 FEET.

Per Ton,	25c.	50c.	$1	$2	$3	$4	$5	$6	$7	$8	$9	$10
Per Foot,			2½ cts.	5 cts.	7½ cts.	10 cts.	12½ cts.	15 cts.	17½ cts.	20 cts.	22½ cts.	25 cts.
Feet.												
1501	9.38	18.76	37.52	75.05	112.57	150.10	187.62	225.15	262.67	300.20	337.72	375.25
1502	9.39	18.77	37.55	75.10	112.65	150.20	187.75	225.30	262.85	300.40	337.95	375.50
1503	9.39	18.79	37.57	75.15	112.72	150.30	187.87	225.45	263.02	300.60	338.17	375.75
1504	9.40	18.80	37.60	75.20	112.80	150.40	188.00	225.60	263.20	300.80	338.40	376.00
1505	9.41	18.81	37.62	75.25	112.87	150.50	188.12	225.75	263.37	301.00	338.62	376.25
1506	9.41	18.82	37.65	75.30	112.95	150.60	188.25	225.90	263.55	301.20	338.85	376.50
1507	9.42	18.84	37.67	75.35	113.02	150.70	188.37	226.05	263.72	301.40	339.07	376.75
1508	9.42	18.85	37.70	75.40	113.10	150.80	188.50	226.20	263.90	301.60	339.30	377.00
1509	9.43	18.86	37.72	75.45	113.17	150.90	188.62	226.35	264.07	301.80	339.52	377.25
1510	9.44	18.87	37.75	75.50	113.25	151.00	188.75	226.50	264.25	302.00	339.75	377.50
1511	9.44	18.89	37.77	75.55	113.32	151.10	188.87	226.65	264.42	302.20	339.97	377.75
1512	9.45	18.90	37.80	75.60	113.40	151.20	189.00	226.80	264.60	302.40	340.20	378.00
1513	9.46	18.91	37.82	75.65	113.47	151.30	189.12	226.95	264.77	302.60	340.42	378.25
1514	9.46	18.92	37.85	75.70	113.55	151.40	189.25	227.10	264.95	302.80	340.65	378.50
1515	9.47	18.94	37.87	75.75	113.62	151.50	189.37	227.25	265.12	303.00	340.87	378.75
1516	9.47	18.95	37.90	75.80	113.70	151.60	189.50	227.40	265.30	303.20	341.10	379.00
1517	9.48	18.96	37.92	75.85	113.77	151.70	189.62	227.55	265.47	303.40	341.32	379.25
1518	9.49	18.97	37.95	75.90	113.85	151.80	189.75	227.70	265.65	303.60	341.55	379.50
1519	9.49	18.99	37.97	75.95	113.92	151.90	189.87	227.85	265.82	303.80	341.77	379.75
1520	9.50	19.00	38.00	76.00	114.00	152.00	190.00	228.00	266.00	304.00	342.00	380.00
1521	9.51	19.01	38.02	76.05	114.07	152.10	190.12	228.15	266.17	304.20	342.22	380.25
1522	9.51	19.02	38.05	76.10	114.15	152.20	190.25	228.30	266.35	304.40	342.45	380.50
1523	9.52	19.04	38.07	76.15	114.22	152.30	190.37	228.45	266.52	304.60	342.67	380.75
1524	9.52	19.05	38.10	76.20	114.30	152.40	190.50	228.60	266.70	304.80	342.90	381.00
1525	9.53	19.06	38.12	76.25	114.37	152.50	190.62	228.75	266.87	305.00	343.12	381.25
1526	9.54	19.07	38.15	76.30	114.45	152.60	190.75	228.90	267.05	305.20	343.35	381.50
1527	9.54	19.09	38.17	76.35	114.52	152.70	190.87	229.05	267.22	305.40	343.57	381.75
1528	9.55	19.10	38.20	76.40	114.60	152.80	191.00	229.20	267.40	305.60	343.80	382.00
1529	9.56	19.11	38.22	76.45	114.67	152.90	191.12	229.35	267.57	305.80	344.02	382.25
1530	9.56	19.12	38.25	76.50	114.75	153.00	191.25	229.50	267.75	306.00	344.25	382.50
1531	9.57	19.14	38.27	76.55	114.82	153.10	191.37	229.65	267.92	306.20	344.47	382.75
1532	9.57	19.15	38.30	76.60	114.90	153.20	191.50	229.80	268.10	306.40	344.70	383.00
1533	9.58	19.16	38.32	76.65	114.97	153.30	191.62	229.95	268.27	306.60	344.92	383.25
1534	9.59	19.17	38.35	76.70	115.05	153.40	191.75	230.10	268.45	306.80	345.15	383.50
1535	9.59	19.19	38.37	76.75	115.12	153.50	191.87	230.25	268.62	307.00	345.37	383.75
1536	9.60	19.20	38.40	76.80	115.20	153.60	192.00	230.40	268.80	307.20	345.60	384.00
1537	9.61	19.21	38.42	76.85	115.27	153.70	192.12	230.55	268.97	307.40	345.82	384.25
1538	9.61	19.22	38.45	76.90	115.35	153.80	192.25	230.70	269.15	307.60	346.05	384.50
1539	9.62	19.24	38.47	76.95	115.42	153.90	192.37	230.85	269.32	307.80	346.27	384.75
1540	9.62	19.25	38.50	77.00	115.50	154.00	192.50	231.00	269.50	308.00	346.50	385.00
1541	9.63	19.26	38.52	77.05	115.57	154.10	192.62	231.15	269.67	308.20	346.72	385.25
1542	9.64	19.27	38.55	77.10	115.65	154.20	192.75	231.30	269.85	308.40	346.95	385.50
1543	9.64	19.29	38.57	77.15	115.72	154.30	192.87	231.45	270.02	308.60	347.17	385.75
1544	9.65	19.30	38.60	77.20	115.80	154.40	193.00	231.60	270.20	308.80	347.40	386.00
1545	9.66	19.31	38.62	77.25	115.87	154.50	193.12	231.75	270.37	309.00	347.62	386.25
1546	9.66	19.32	38.65	77.30	115.95	154.60	193.25	231.90	270.55	309.20	347.85	386.50
1547	9.67	19.34	38.67	77.35	116.02	154.70	193.37	232.05	270.72	309.40	348.07	386.75
1548	9.67	19.35	38.70	77.40	116.10	154.80	193.50	232.20	270.90	309.60	348.30	387.00
1549	9.68	19.36	38.72	77.45	116.17	154.90	193.62	232.35	271.07	309.80	348.52	387.25
1550	9.69	19.37	38.75	77.50	116.25	155.00	193.75	232.50	271.25	310.00	348.75	387.50

1550 FEET.

Per Ton,	$11	$12	$13	$14	$15	$16	$17	$18	$19	$20
Per Foot,	27½ cts.	30 cts.	32½ cts.	35 cts.	37½ cts.	40 cts.	42½ cts.	45 cts.	47½ cts.	50 cts.
Feet.										
1501	412.77	450.30	487.82	525.35	562.87	600.40	637.92	675.45	712.97	750.50
1502	413.05	450.60	488.15	525.70	563.25	600.80	638.35	675.90	713.45	751.00
1503	413.32	450.90	488.47	526.05	563.62	601.20	638.77	676.35	713.92	751.50
1504	413.60	451.20	488.80	526.40	564.00	601.60	639.20	676.80	714.40	752.00
1505	413.87	451.50	489.12	526.75	564.37	602.00	639.62	677.25	714.87	752.50
1506	414.15	451.80	489.45	527.10	564.75	602.40	640.05	677.70	715.35	753.00
1507	414.42	452.10	489.77	527.45	565.12	602.80	640.47	678.15	715.82	753.50
1508	414.70	452.40	490.10	527.80	565.50	603.20	640.90	678.60	716.30	754.00
1509	414.97	452.70	490.42	528.15	565.87	603.60	641.32	679.05	716.77	754.50
1510	415.25	453.00	490.75	528.50	566.25	604.00	641.75	679.50	717.25	755.00
1511	415.52	453.30	491.07	528.85	566.62	604.40	642.17	679.95	717.72	755.50
1512	415.80	453.60	491.40	529.20	567.00	604.80	642.60	680.40	718.20	756.00
1513	416.07	453.90	491.72	529.55	567.37	605.20	643.02	680.85	718.67	756.50
1514	416.35	454.20	492.05	529.90	567.75	605.60	643.45	681.30	719.15	757.00
1515	416.62	454.50	492.37	530.25	568.12	606.00	643.87	681.75	719.62	757.50
1516	416.90	454.80	492.70	530.60	568.50	606.40	644.30	682.20	720.10	758.00
1517	417.17	455.10	493.02	530.95	568.87	606.80	644.72	682.65	720.57	758.50
1518	417.45	455.40	493.35	531.30	569.25	607.20	645.15	683.10	721.05	759.00
1519	417.72	455.70	493.67	531.65	569.62	607.60	645.57	683.55	721.52	759.50
1520	418.00	456.00	494.00	532.00	570.00	608.00	646.00	684.00	722.00	760.00
1521	418.27	456.30	494.32	532.35	570.37	608.40	646.42	684.45	722.47	760.50
1522	418.55	456.60	494.65	532.70	570.75	608.80	646.85	684.90	722.95	761.00
1523	418.82	456.90	494.97	533.05	571.12	609.20	647.27	685.35	723.42	761.50
1524	419.10	457.20	495.30	533.40	571.50	609.60	647.70	685.80	723.90	762.00
1525	419.37	457.50	495.62	533.75	571.87	610.00	648.12	686.25	724.37	762.50
1526	419.65	457.80	495.95	534.10	572.25	610.40	648.55	686.70	724.85	763.00
1527	419.92	458.10	496.27	534.45	572.62	610.80	648.97	687.15	725.32	763.50
1528	420.20	458.40	496.60	534.80	573.00	611.20	649.40	687.60	725.80	764.00
1529	420.47	458.70	496.92	535.15	573.37	611.60	649.82	688.05	726.27	764.50
1530	420.75	459.00	497.25	535.50	573.75	612.00	650.25	688.50	726.75	765.00
1531	421.02	459.30	497.57	535.85	574.12	612.40	650.67	688.95	727.22	765.50
1532	421.30	459.60	497.90	536.20	574.50	612.80	651.10	689.40	727.70	766.00
1533	421.57	459.90	498.22	536.55	574.87	613.20	651.52	689.85	728.17	766.50
1534	421.85	460.20	498.55	536.90	575.25	613.60	651.95	690.30	728.65	767.00
1535	422.12	460.50	498.87	537.25	575.62	614.00	652.37	690.75	729.12	767.50
1536	422.40	460.80	499.20	537.60	576.00	614.40	652.80	691.20	729.60	768.00
1537	422.67	461.10	499.52	537.95	576.37	614.80	653.22	691.65	730.07	768.50
1538	422.95	461.40	499.85	538.30	576.75	615.20	653.65	692.10	730.55	769.00
1539	423.22	461.70	500.17	538.65	577.12	615.60	654.07	692.55	731.02	769.50
1540	423.50	462.00	500.50	539.00	577.50	616.00	654.50	693.00	731.50	770.00
1541	423.77	462.30	500.82	539.35	577.87	616.40	654.92	693.45	731.97	770.50
1542	424.05	462.60	501.15	539.70	578.25	616.80	655.35	693.90	732.45	771.00
1543	424.32	462.90	501.47	540.05	578.62	617.20	655.77	694.35	732.92	771.50
1544	424.60	463.20	501.80	540.40	579.00	617.60	656.20	694.80	733.40	772.00
1545	424.87	463.50	502.12	540.75	579.37	618.00	656.62	695.25	733.87	772.50
1546	425.15	463.80	502.45	541.10	579.75	618.40	657.05	695.70	734.35	773.00
1547	425.42	464.10	502.77	541.45	580.12	618.80	657.47	696.15	734.82	773.50
1548	425.70	464.40	503.10	541.80	580.50	619.20	657.90	696.60	735.30	774.00
1549	425.97	464.70	503.42	542.15	580.87	619.60	658.32	697.05	735.77	774.50
1550	426.25	465.00	503.75	542.50	581.25	620.00	658.75	697.50	736.25	775.00

1600 FEET.

Per Ton,	25c.	50c.	$1	$2	$3	$4	$5	$6	$7	$8	$9	$10
Per Foot,			2½ cts.	5 cts.	7½ cts.	10 cts.	12½ cts.	15 cts.	17½ cts.	20 cts.	22½ cts.	25 cts.
Feet.												
1551	9.69	19.39	38.77	77.55	116.32	155.10	193.87	232.65	271.42	310.20	348.97	387.75
1552	9.70	19.40	38.80	77.60	116.40	155.20	194.00	232.80	271.60	310.40	349.20	388.00
1553	9.71	19.41	38.82	77.65	116.47	155.30	194.12	232.95	271.77	310.60	349.42	388.25
1554	9.71	19.42	38.85	77.70	116.55	155.40	194.25	233.10	271.95	310.80	349.65	388.50
1555	9.72	19.44	38.87	77.75	116.62	155.50	194.37	233.25	272.12	311.00	349.87	388.75
1556	9.72	19.45	38.90	77.80	116.70	155.60	194.50	233.40	272.30	311.20	350.10	389.00
1557	9.73	19.46	38.92	77.85	116.77	155.70	194.62	233.55	272.47	311.40	350.32	389.25
1558	9.74	19.47	38.95	77.90	116.85	155.80	194.75	233.70	272.65	311.60	350.55	389.50
1559	9.74	19.49	38.97	77.95	116.92	155.90	194.87	233.85	272.82	311.80	350.77	389.75
1560	9.75	19.50	39.00	78.00	117.00	156.00	195.00	234.00	273.00	312.00	351.00	390.00
1561	9.76	19.51	39.02	78.05	117.07	156.10	195.12	234.15	273.17	312.20	351.22	390.25
1562	9.76	19.52	39.05	78.10	117.15	156.20	195.25	234.30	273.35	312.40	351.45	390.50
1563	9.77	19.54	39.07	78.15	117.22	156.30	195.37	234.45	273.52	312.60	351.67	390.75
1564	9.77	19.55	39.10	78.20	117.30	156.40	195.50	234.60	273.70	312.80	351.90	391.00
1565	9.78	19.56	39.12	78.25	117.37	156.50	195.62	234.75	273.87	313.00	352.12	391.25
1566	9.79	19.57	39.15	78.30	117.45	156.60	195.75	234.90	274.05	313.20	352.35	391.50
1567	9.79	19.59	39.17	78.35	117.52	156.70	195.87	235.05	274.22	313.40	352.57	391.75
1568	9.80	19.60	39.20	78.40	117.60	156.80	196.00	235.20	274.40	313.60	352.80	392.00
1569	9.81	19.61	39.22	78.45	117.67	156.90	196.12	235.35	274.57	313.80	353.02	392.25
1570	9.81	19.62	39.25	78.50	117.75	157.00	196.25	235.50	274.75	314.00	353.25	392.50
1571	9.82	19.64	39.27	78.55	117.82	157.10	196.37	235.65	274.92	314.20	353.47	392.75
1572	9.82	19.65	39.30	78.60	117.90	157.20	196.50	235.80	275.10	314.40	353.70	393.00
1573	9.83	19.66	39.32	78.65	117.97	157.30	196.62	235.95	275.27	314.60	353.92	393.25
1574	9.84	19.67	39.35	78.70	118.05	157.40	196.75	236.10	275.45	314.80	354.15	393.50
1575	9.84	19.69	39.37	78.75	118.12	157.50	196.87	236.25	275.62	315.00	354.37	393.75
1576	9.85	19.70	39.40	78.80	118.20	157.60	197.00	236.40	275.80	315.20	354.60	394.00
1577	9.86	19.71	39.42	78.85	118.27	157.70	197.12	236.55	275.97	315.40	354.82	394.25
1578	9.86	19.72	39.45	78.90	118.35	157.80	197.25	236.70	276.15	315.60	355.05	394.50
1579	9.87	19.74	39.47	78.95	118.42	157.90	197.37	236.85	276.32	315.80	355.27	394.75
1580	9.87	19.75	39.50	79.00	118.50	158.00	197.50	237.00	276.50	316.00	355.50	395.00
1581	9.88	19.76	39.52	79.05	118.57	158.10	197.62	237.15	276.67	316.20	355.72	395.25
1582	9.89	19.77	39.55	79.10	118.65	158.20	197.75	237.30	276.85	316.40	355.95	395.50
1583	9.89	19.79	39.57	79.15	118.72	158.30	197.87	237.45	277.02	316.60	356.17	395.75
1584	9.90	19.80	39.60	79.20	118.80	158.40	198.00	237.60	277.20	316.80	356.40	396.00
1585	9.91	19.81	39.62	79.25	118.87	158.50	198.12	237.75	277.37	317.00	356.62	396.25
1586	9.91	19.82	39.65	79.30	118.95	158.60	198.25	237.90	277.55	317.20	356.85	396.50
1587	9.92	19.84	39.67	79.35	119.02	158.70	198.37	238.05	277.72	317.40	357.07	396.75
1588	9.92	19.85	39.70	79.40	119.10	158.80	198.50	238.20	277.90	317.60	357.30	397.00
1589	9.93	19.86	39.72	79.45	119.17	158.90	198.62	238.35	278.07	317.80	357.52	397.25
1590	9.94	19.87	39.75	79.50	119.25	159.00	198.75	238.50	278.25	318.00	357.75	397.50
1591	9.94	19.89	39.77	79.55	119.32	159.10	198.87	238.65	278.42	318.20	357.97	397.75
1592	9.95	19.90	39.80	79.60	119.40	159.20	199.00	238.80	278.60	318.40	358.20	398.00
1593	9.96	19.91	39.82	79.65	119.47	159.30	199.12	238.95	278.77	318.60	358.42	398.25
1594	9.96	19.92	39.85	79.70	119.55	159.40	199.25	239.10	278.95	318.80	358.65	398.50
1595	9.97	19.94	39.87	79.75	119.62	159.50	199.37	239.25	279.12	319.00	358.87	398.75
1596	9.97	19.95	39.90	79.80	119.70	159.60	199.50	239.40	279.30	319.20	359.10	399.00
1597	9.98	19.96	39.92	79.85	119.77	159.70	199.62	239.55	279.47	319.40	359.32	399.25
1598	9.99	19.97	39.95	79.90	119.85	159.80	199.75	239.70	279.65	319.60	359.55	399.50
1599	9.99	19.99	39.97	79.95	119.92	159.90	199.80	239.85	279.82	319.80	359.77	399.75
1600	10.00	20.00	40.00	80.00	120.00	160.00	200.00	240.00	280.00	320.00	360.00	400.00

1600 FEET.

Per Ton,	$11	$12	$13	$14	$15	$16	$17	$18	$19	$20
Per Foot,	27½ cts.	30 cts.	32½ cts.	35 cts.	37½ cts.	40 cts.	42½ cts.	45 cts.	47½ cts.	50 cts.
Feet.										
1551	426.52	465.30	504.07	542.85	581.62	620.40	659.17	697.95	736.72	775.50
1552	426.80	465.60	504.40	543.20	582.00	620.80	659.60	698.40	737.20	776.00
1553	427.07	465.90	504.72	543.55	582.37	621.20	660.02	698.85	737.67	776.50
1554	427.35	466.20	505.05	543.90	582.75	621.60	660.45	699.30	738.15	777.00
1555	427.62	466.50	505.37	544.25	583.12	622.00	660.87	699.75	738.62	777.50
1556	427.90	466.80	505.70	544.60	583.50	622.40	661.30	700.20	739.10	778.00
1557	428.17	467.10	506.02	544.95	583.87	622.80	661.72	700.65	739.57	778.50
1558	428.45	467.40	506.35	545.30	584.25	623.20	662.15	701.10	740.05	779.00
1559	428.72	467.70	506.67	545.65	584.62	623.60	662.57	701.55	740.52	779.50
1560	429.00	468.00	507.00	546.00	585.00	624.00	663.00	702.00	741.00	780.00
1561	429.27	468.30	507.32	546.35	585.37	624.40	663.42	702.45	741.47	780.50
1562	429.55	468.60	507.65	546.70	585.75	624.80	663.85	702.90	741.95	781.00
1563	429.82	468.90	507.97	547.05	586.12	625.20	664.27	703.35	742.42	781.50
1564	430.10	469.20	508.30	547.40	586.50	625.60	664.70	703.80	742.90	782.00
1565	430.37	469.50	508.62	547.75	586.87	626.00	665.12	704.25	743.37	782.50
1566	430.65	469.80	508.95	548.10	587.25	626.40	665.55	704.70	743.85	783.00
1567	430.92	470.10	509.27	548.45	587.62	626.80	665.97	705.15	744.32	783.50
1568	431.20	470.40	509.60	548.80	588.00	627.20	666.40	705.60	744.80	784.00
1569	431.47	470.70	509.92	549.15	588.37	627.60	666.82	706.05	745.27	784.50
1570	431.75	471.00	510.25	549.50	588.75	628.00	667.25	706.50	745.75	785.00
1571	432.02	471.30	510.57	549.85	589.12	628.40	667.67	706.95	746.22	785.50
1572	432.30	471.60	510.90	550.20	589.50	628.80	668.10	707.40	746.70	786.00
1573	432.57	471.90	511.22	550.55	589.87	629.20	668.52	707.85	747.17	786.50
1574	432.85	472.20	511.55	550.90	590.25	629.60	668.95	708.30	747.65	787.00
1575	433.12	472.50	511.87	551.25	590.62	630.00	669.37	708.75	748.12	787.50
1576	433.40	472.80	512.20	551.60	591.00	630.40	669.80	709.20	748.60	788.00
1577	433.67	473.10	512.52	551.95	591.37	630.80	670.22	709.65	749.07	788.50
1578	433.95	473.40	512.85	552.30	591.75	631.20	670.65	710.10	749.55	789.00
1579	434.22	473.70	513.17	552.65	592.12	631.60	671.07	710.55	750.02	789.50
1580	434.50	474.00	513.50	553.00	592.50	632.00	671.50	711.00	750.50	790.00
1581	434.77	474.30	513.82	553.35	592.87	632.40	671.92	711.45	750.97	790.50
1582	435.05	474.60	514.15	553.70	593.25	632.80	672.35	711.90	751.45	791.00
1583	435.32	474.90	514.47	554.05	593.62	633.20	672.77	712.35	751.92	791.50
1584	435.60	475.20	514.80	554.40	594.00	633.60	673.20	712.80	752.40	792.00
1585	435.87	475.50	515.12	554.75	594.37	634.00	673.62	713.25	752.87	792.50
1586	436.15	475.80	515.45	555.10	594.75	634.40	674.05	713.70	753.35	793.00
1587	436.42	476.10	515.77	555.45	595.12	634.80	674.47	714.15	753.82	793.50
1588	436.70	476.40	516.10	555.80	595.50	635.20	674.90	714.60	754.30	794.00
1589	436.97	476.70	516.42	556.15	595.87	635.60	675.32	715.05	754.77	794.50
1590	437.25	477.00	516.75	556.50	596.25	636.00	675.75	715.50	755.25	795.00
1591	437.52	477.30	517.07	556.85	596.62	636.40	676.17	715.95	755.72	795.50
1592	437.80	477.60	517.40	557.20	597.00	636.80	676.60	716.40	756.20	796.00
1593	438.07	477.90	517.72	557.55	597.37	637.20	677.02	716.85	756.67	796.50
1594	438.35	478.20	518.05	557.90	597.75	637.60	677.45	717.30	757.15	797.00
1595	438.62	478.50	518.37	558.25	598.12	638.00	677.87	717.75	757.62	797.50
1596	438.90	478.80	518.70	558.60	598.50	638.40	678.30	718.20	758.10	798.00
1597	439.17	479.10	519.02	558.95	598.87	638.80	678.72	718.65	758.57	798.50
1598	439.45	479.40	519.35	559.30	599.25	639.20	679.15	719.10	759.05	799.00
1599	439.72	479.70	519.67	559.65	599.62	639.60	679.57	719.55	759.52	799.50
1600	440.00	480.00	520.00	560.00	600.00	640.00	680.00	720.00	760.00	800.00

1650 FEET.

Per Ton, Per Foot,	25c.	50c.	$1 2½ cts.	$2 5 cts.	$3 7½ cts.	$4 10 cts.	$5 12½ cts.	$6 15 cts.	$7 17½ cts.	$8 20 cts.	$9 22½ cts.	$10 25 cts.
Feet.												
1601	10.01	20.01	40.02	80.05	120.07	160.10	200.12	240.15	280.17	320.20	360.22	400.25
1602	10.01	20.02	40.05	80.10	120.15	160.20	200.25	240.30	280.35	320.40	360.45	400.50
1603	10.02	20.04	40.07	80.15	120.22	160.30	200.37	240.45	280.52	320.60	360.67	400.75
1604	10.02	20.05	40.10	80.20	120.30	160.40	200.50	240.60	280.70	320.80	360.90	401.00
1605	10.03	20.06	40.12	80.25	120.37	160.50	200.62	240.75	280.87	321.00	361.12	401.25
1606	10.04	20.07	40.15	80.30	120.45	160.60	200.75	240.90	281.05	321.20	361.35	401.50
1607	10.04	20.09	40.17	80.35	120.52	160.70	200.87	241.05	281.22	321.40	361.57	401.75
1608	10.05	20.10	40.20	80.40	120.60	160.80	201.00	241.20	281.40	321.60	361.80	402.00
1609	10.06	20.11	40.22	80.45	120.67	160.90	201.12	241.35	281.57	321.80	362.02	402.25
1610	10.06	20.12	40.25	80.50	120.75	161.00	201.25	241.50	281.75	322.00	362.25	402.50
1611	10.07	20.14	40.27	80.55	120.82	161.10	201.37	241.65	281.92	322.20	362.47	402.75
1612	10.07	20.15	40.30	80.60	120.90	161.20	201.50	241.80	282.10	322.40	362.70	403.00
1613	10.08	20.16	40.32	80.65	120.97	161.30	201.62	241.95	282.27	322.60	362.92	403.25
1614	10.09	20.17	40.35	80.70	121.05	161.40	201.75	242.10	282.45	322.80	363.15	403.50
1615	10.09	20.19	40.37	80.75	121.12	161.50	201.87	242.25	282.62	323.00	363.37	403.75
1616	10.10	20.20	40.40	80.80	121.20	161.60	202.00	242.40	282.80	323.20	363.60	404.00
1617	10.11	20.21	40.42	80.85	121.27	161.70	202.12	242.55	282.97	323.40	363.82	404.25
1618	10.11	20.22	40.45	80.90	121.35	161.80	202.25	242.70	283.15	323.60	364.05	404.50
1619	10.12	20.24	40.47	80.95	121.42	161.90	202.37	242.85	283.32	323.80	364.27	404.75
1620	10.12	20.25	40.50	81.00	121.50	162.00	202.50	243.00	283.50	324.00	364.50	405.00
1621	10.13	20.26	40.52	81.05	121.57	162.10	202.62	243.15	283.67	324.20	364.72	405.25
1622	10.14	20.27	40.55	81.10	121.65	162.20	202.75	243.30	283.85	324.40	364.95	405.50
1623	10.14	20.29	40.57	81.15	121.72	162.30	202.87	243.45	284.02	324.60	365.17	405.75
1624	10.15	20.30	40.60	81.20	121.80	162.40	203.00	243.60	284.20	324.80	365.40	406.00
1625	10.16	20.31	40.62	81.25	121.87	162.50	203.12	243.75	284.37	325.00	365.62	406.25
1626	10.16	20.32	40.65	81.30	121.95	162.60	203.25	243.90	284.55	325.20	365.85	406.50
1627	10.17	20.34	40.67	81.35	122.02	162.70	203.37	244.05	284.72	325.40	366.07	406.75
1628	10.17	20.35	40.70	81.40	122.10	162.80	203.50	244.20	284.90	325.60	366.30	407.00
1629	10.18	20.36	40.72	81.45	122.17	162.90	203.62	244.35	285.07	325.80	366.52	407.25
1630	10.19	20.37	40.75	81.50	122.25	163.00	203.75	244.50	285.25	326.00	366.75	407.50
1631	10.19	20.39	40.77	81.55	122.32	163.10	203.87	244.65	285.42	326.20	366.97	407.75
1632	10.20	20.40	40.80	81.60	122.40	163.20	204.00	244.80	285.60	326.40	367.20	408.00
1633	10.21	20.41	40.82	81.65	122.47	163.30	204.12	244.95	285.77	326.60	367.42	408.25
1634	10.21	20.42	40.85	81.70	122.55	163.40	204.25	245.10	285.95	326.80	367.65	408.50
1635	10.22	20.44	40.87	81.75	122.62	163.50	204.37	245.25	286.12	327.00	367.87	408.75
1636	10.22	20.45	40.90	81.80	122.70	163.60	204.50	245.40	286.30	327.20	368.10	409.00
1637	10.23	20.46	40.92	81.85	122.77	163.70	204.62	245.55	286.47	327.40	368.32	409.25
1638	10.24	20.47	40.95	81.90	122.85	163.80	204.75	245.70	286.65	327.60	368.55	409.50
1639	10.24	20.49	40.97	81.95	122.92	163.90	204.87	245.85	286.82	327.80	368.77	409.75
1640	10.25	20.50	41.00	82.00	123.00	164.00	205.00	246.00	287.00	328.00	369.00	410.00
1641	10.26	20.51	41.02	82.05	123.07	164.10	205.12	246.15	287.17	328.20	369.22	410.25
1642	10.26	20.52	41.05	82.10	123.15	164.20	205.25	246.30	287.35	328.40	369.45	410.50
1643	10.27	20.54	41.07	82.15	123.22	164.30	205.37	246.45	287.52	328.60	369.67	410.75
1644	10.27	20.55	41.10	82.20	123.30	164.40	205.50	246.60	287.70	328.80	369.90	411.00
1645	10.28	20.56	41.12	82.25	123.37	164.50	205.62	246.75	287.87	329.00	370.12	411.25
1646	10.29	20.57	41.15	82.30	123.45	164.60	205.75	246.90	288.05	329.20	370.35	411.50
1647	10.29	20.59	41.17	82.35	123.52	164.70	205.87	247.05	288.22	329.40	370.57	411.75
1648	10.30	20.60	41.20	82.40	123.60	164.80	206.00	247.20	288.40	329.60	370.80	412.00
1649	10.31	20.61	41.22	82.45	123.67	164.90	206.12	247.35	288.57	329.80	371.02	412.25
1650	10.31	20.62	41.25	82.50	123.75	165.00	206.25	247.50	288.75	330.00	371.25	412.50

1650 FEET.

Per Ton, / Feet.	$11	$12	$13	$14	$15	$16	$17	$18	$19	$20
Per Foot,	27½ cts.	30 cts.	32½ cts.	35 cts.	37½ cts.	40 cts.	42½ cts.	45 cts.	47½ cts.	50 cts.
1601	440.27	480.30	520.32	560.35	600.37	640.40	680.42	720.45	760.47	800.50
1602	440.55	480.60	520.65	560.70	600.75	640.80	680.85	720.90	760.95	801.00
1603	440.82	480.90	520.97	561.05	601.12	641.20	681.27	721.35	761.42	801.50
1604	441.10	481.20	521.30	561.40	601.50	641.60	681.70	721.80	761.90	802.00
1605	441.37	481.50	521.62	561.75	601.87	642.00	682.12	722.25	762.37	802.50
1606	441.65	481.80	521.95	562.10	602.25	642.40	682.55	722.70	762.85	803.00
1607	441.92	482.10	522.27	562.45	602.62	642.80	682.97	723.15	763.32	803.50
1608	442.20	482.40	522.60	562.80	603.00	643.20	683.40	723.60	763.80	804.00
1609	442.47	482.70	522.92	563.15	603.37	643.60	683.82	724.05	764.27	804.50
1610	442.75	483.00	523.25	563.50	603.75	644.00	684.25	724.50	764.75	805.00
1611	443.02	483.30	523.57	563.85	604.12	644.40	684.67	724.95	765.22	805.50
1612	443.30	483.60	523.90	564.20	604.50	644.80	685.10	725.40	765.70	806.00
1613	443.57	483.90	524.22	564.55	604.87	645.20	685.52	725.85	766.17	806.50
1614	443.85	484.20	524.55	564.90	605.25	645.60	685.95	726.30	766.65	807.00
1615	444.12	484.50	524.87	565.25	605.62	646.00	686.37	726.75	767.12	807.50
1616	444.40	484.80	525.20	565.60	606.00	646.40	686.80	727.20	767.60	808.00
1617	444.67	485.10	525.52	565.95	606.37	646.80	687.22	727.65	768.07	808.50
1618	444.95	485.40	525.85	566.30	606.75	647.20	687.65	728.10	768.55	809.00
1619	445.22	485.70	526.17	566.65	607.12	647.60	688.07	728.55	769.02	809.50
1620	445.50	486.00	526.50	567.00	607.50	648.00	688.50	729.00	769.50	810.00
1621	445.77	486.30	526.82	567.35	607.87	648.40	688.92	729.45	769.97	810.50
1622	446.05	486.60	527.15	567.70	608.25	648.80	689.35	729.90	770.45	811.00
1623	446.32	486.90	527.47	568.05	608.62	649.20	689.77	730.35	770.92	811.50
1624	446.60	487.20	527.80	568.40	609.00	649.60	690.20	730.80	771.40	812.00
1625	446.87	487.50	528.12	568.75	609.37	650.00	690.62	731.25	771.87	812.50
1626	447.15	487.80	528.45	569.10	609.75	650.40	691.05	731.70	772.35	813.00
1627	447.42	488.10	528.77	569.45	610.12	650.80	691.47	732.15	772.82	813.50
1628	447.70	488.40	529.10	569.80	610.50	651.20	691.90	732.60	773.30	814.00
1629	447.97	488.70	529.42	570.15	610.87	651.60	692.32	733.05	773.77	814.50
1630	448.25	489.00	529.75	570.50	611.25	652.00	692.75	733.50	774.25	815.00
1631	448.52	489.30	530.07	570.85	611.62	652.40	693.17	733.95	774.72	815.50
1632	448.80	489.60	530.40	571.20	612.00	652.80	693.60	734.40	775.20	816.00
1633	449.07	489.90	530.72	571.55	612.37	653.20	694.02	734.85	775.67	816.50
1634	449.35	490.20	531.05	571.90	612.75	653.60	694.45	735.30	776.15	817.00
1635	449.62	490.50	531.37	572.25	613.12	654.00	694.87	735.75	776.62	817.50
1636	449.90	490.80	531.70	572.60	613.50	654.40	695.30	736.20	777.10	818.00
1637	450.17	491.10	532.02	572.95	613.87	654.80	695.72	736.65	777.57	818.50
1638	450.45	491.40	532.35	573.30	614.25	655.20	696.15	737.10	778.05	819.00
1639	450.72	491.70	532.67	573.65	614.62	655.60	696.57	737.55	778.52	819.50
1640	451.00	492.00	533.00	574.00	615.00	656.00	697.00	738.00	779.00	820.00
1641	451.27	492.30	533.32	574.35	615.37	656.40	697.42	738.45	779.47	820.50
1642	451.55	492.60	533.65	574.70	615.75	656.80	697.85	738.90	779.95	821.00
1643	451.82	492.90	533.97	575.05	616.12	657.20	698.27	739.35	780.42	821.50
1644	452.10	493.20	534.30	575.40	616.50	657.60	698.70	739.80	780.90	822.00
1645	452.37	493.50	534.62	575.75	616.87	658.00	699.12	740.25	781.37	822.50
1646	452.65	493.80	534.95	576.10	617.25	658.40	699.55	740.70	781.85	823.00
1647	452.92	494.10	535.27	576.45	617.62	658.80	699.97	741.15	782.32	823.50
1648	453.20	494.40	535.60	576.80	618.00	659.20	700.40	741.60	782.80	824.00
1649	453.47	494.70	535.92	577.15	618.37	659.60	700.82	742.05	783.27	824.50
1650	453.75	495.00	536.25	577.50	618.75	660.00	701.25	742.50	783.75	825.00

1700 FEET.

Per Ton,	25c.	50c.	$1	$2	$3	$4	$5	$6	$7	$8	$9	$10
Per Foot,			2½ cts.	5 cts.	7½ cts.	10 cts.	12½ cts.	15 cts.	17½ cts.	20 cts.	22½ cts.	25 cts.
Feet.												
1651	10.32	20.64	41.27	82.55	123.82	165.10	206.37	247.65	288.92	330.20	371.47	412.75
1652	10.32	20.65	41.30	82.60	123.90	165.20	206.50	247.80	289.10	330.40	371.70	413.00
1653	10.33	20.66	41.32	82.65	123.97	165.30	206.62	247.95	289.27	330.60	371.92	413.25
1654	10.34	20.67	41.35	82.70	124.05	165.40	206.75	248.10	289.45	330.80	372.15	413.50
1655	10.34	20.69	41.37	82.75	124.12	165.50	206.87	248.25	289.62	331.00	372.37	413.75
1656	10.35	20.70	41.40	82.80	124.20	165.60	207.00	248.40	289.80	331.20	372.60	414.00
1657	10.36	20.71	41.42	82.85	124.27	165.70	207.12	248.55	289.97	331.40	372.82	414.25
1658	10.36	20.72	41.45	82.90	124.35	165.80	207.25	248.70	290.15	331.60	373.05	414.50
1659	10.37	20.74	41.47	82.95	124.42	165.90	207.37	248.85	290.32	331.80	373.27	414.75
1660	10.37	20.75	41.50	83.00	124.50	166.00	207.50	249.00	290.50	332.00	373.50	415.00
1661	10.38	20.76	41.52	83.05	124.57	166.10	207.62	249.15	290.67	332.20	373.72	415.25
1662	10.39	20.77	41.55	83.10	124.65	166.20	207.75	249.30	290.85	332.40	373.95	415.50
1663	10.39	20.79	41.57	83.15	124.72	166.30	207.87	249.45	291.02	332.60	374.17	415.75
1664	10.40	20.80	41.60	83.20	124.80	166.40	208.00	249.60	291.20	332.80	374.40	416.00
1665	10.41	20.81	41.62	83.25	124.87	166.50	208.12	249.75	291.37	333.00	374.62	416.25
1666	10.41	20.82	41.65	83.30	124.95	166.60	208.25	249.90	291.55	333.20	374.85	416.50
1667	10.42	20.84	41.67	83.35	125.02	166.70	208.37	250.05	291.72	333.40	375.07	416.75
1668	10.42	20.85	41.70	83.40	125.10	166.80	208.50	250.20	291.90	333.60	375.30	417.00
1669	10.43	20.86	41.72	83.45	125.17	166.90	208.62	250.35	292.07	333.80	375.52	417.25
1670	10.44	20.87	41.75	83.50	125.25	167.00	208.75	250.50	292.25	334.00	375.75	417.50
1671	10.44	20.89	41.77	83.55	125.32	167.10	208.87	250.65	292.42	334.20	375.97	417.75
1672	10.45	20.90	41.80	83.60	125.40	167.20	209.00	250.80	292.60	334.40	376.20	418.00
1673	10.46	20.91	41.82	83.65	125.47	167.30	209.12	250.95	292.77	334.60	376.42	418.25
1674	10.46	20.92	41.85	83.70	125.55	167.40	209.25	251.10	292.95	334.80	376.65	418.50
1675	10.47	20.94	41.87	83.75	125.62	167.50	209.37	251.25	293.12	335.00	376.87	418.75
1676	10.47	20.95	41.90	83.80	125.70	167.60	209.50	251.40	293.30	335.20	377.10	419.00
1677	10.48	20.96	41.92	83.85	125.77	167.70	209.62	251.55	293.47	335.40	377.32	419.25
1678	10.49	20.97	41.95	83.90	125.85	167.80	209.75	251.70	293.65	335.60	377.55	419.50
1679	10.49	20.99	41.97	83.95	125.92	167.90	209.87	251.85	293.82	335.80	377.77	419.75
1680	10.50	21.00	42.00	84.00	126.00	168.00	210.00	252.00	294.00	336.00	378.00	420.00
1681	10.51	21.01	42.02	84.05	126.07	168.10	210.12	252.15	294.17	336.20	378.22	420.25
1682	10.51	21.02	42.05	84.10	126.15	168.20	210.25	252.30	294.35	336.40	378.45	420.50
1683	10.52	21.04	42.07	84.15	126.22	168.30	210.37	252.45	294.52	336.60	378.67	420.75
1684	10.52	21.05	42.10	84.20	126.30	168.40	210.50	252.60	294.70	336.80	378.90	421.00
1685	10.53	21.06	42.12	84.25	126.37	168.50	210.62	252.75	294.87	337.00	379.12	421.25
1686	10.54	21.07	42.15	84.30	126.45	168.60	210.75	252.90	295.05	337.20	379.35	421.50
1687	10.54	21.09	42.17	84.35	126.52	168.70	210.87	253.05	295.22	337.40	379.57	421.75
1688	10.55	21.10	42.20	84.40	126.60	168.80	211.00	253.20	295.40	337.60	379.80	422.00
1689	10.56	21.11	42.22	84.45	126.67	168.90	211.12	253.35	295.57	337.80	380.02	422.25
1690	10.56	21.12	42.25	84.50	126.75	169.00	211.25	253.50	295.75	338.00	380.25	422.50
1691	10.57	21.14	42.27	84.55	126.82	169.10	211.37	253.65	295.92	338.20	380.47	422.75
1692	10.57	21.15	42.30	84.60	126.90	169.20	211.50	253.80	296.10	338.40	380.70	423.00
1693	10.58	21.16	42.32	84.65	126.97	169.30	211.62	253.95	296.27	338.60	380.92	423.25
1694	10.59	21.17	42.35	84.70	127.05	169.40	211.75	254.10	296.45	338.80	381.15	423.50
1695	10.59	21.19	42.37	84.75	127.12	169.50	211.87	254.25	296.62	339.00	381.37	423.75
1696	10.60	21.20	42.40	84.80	127.20	169.60	212.00	254.40	296.80	339.20	381.60	424.00
1697	10.61	21.21	42.42	84.85	127.27	169.70	212.12	254.55	296.97	339.40	381.82	424.25
1698	10.61	21.22	42.45	84.90	127.35	169.80	212.25	254.70	297.15	339.60	382.05	424.50
1699	10.62	21.24	42.47	84.95	127.42	169.90	212.37	254.85	297.32	339.80	382.27	424.75
1700	10.62	21.25	42.50	85.00	127.50	170.00	212.50	255.00	297.50	340.00	382.50	425.00

1700 FEET.

Per Ton,	$11	$12	$13	$14	$15	$16	$17	$18	$19	$20
Per Foot,	27½ cts.	30 cts.	32½ cts.	35 cts.	37½ cts.	40 cts.	42½ cts.	45 cts.	47½ cts.	50 cts.
Feet.										
1651	454.02	495.30	536.57	577.85	619.12	660.40	701.67	742.95	784.22	825.50
1652	454.30	495.60	536.90	578.20	619.50	660.80	702.10	743.40	784.70	826.00
1653	454.57	495.90	537.22	578.55	619.87	661.20	702.52	743.85	785.17	826.50
1654	454.85	496.20	537.55	578.90	620.25	661.60	702.95	744.30	785.65	827.00
1655	455.12	496.50	537.87	579.25	620.62	662.00	703.37	744.75	786.12	827.50
1656	455.40	496.80	538.20	579.60	621.00	662.40	703.80	745.20	786.60	828.00
1657	455.67	497.10	538.52	579.95	621.37	662.80	704.22	745.65	787.07	828.50
1658	455.95	497.40	538.85	580.30	621.75	663.20	704.65	746.10	787.55	829.00
1659	456.22	497.70	539.17	580.65	622.12	663.60	705.07	746.55	788.02	829.50
1660	456.50	498.00	539.50	581.00	622.50	664.00	705.50	747.00	788.50	830.00
1661	456.77	498.30	539.82	581.35	622.87	664.40	705.92	747.45	788.97	830.50
1662	457.05	498.60	540.15	581.70	623.25	664.80	706.35	747.90	789.45	831.00
1663	457.32	498.90	540.47	582.05	623.62	665.20	706.77	748.35	789.92	831.50
1664	457.60	499.20	540.80	582.40	624.00	665.60	707.20	748.80	790.40	832.00
1665	457.87	499.50	541.12	582.75	624.37	666.00	707.62	749.25	790.87	832.50
1666	458.15	499.80	541.45	583.10	624.75	666.40	708.05	749.70	791.35	833.00
1667	458.42	500.10	541.77	583.45	625.12	666.80	708.47	750.15	791.82	833.50
1668	458.70	500.40	542.10	583.80	625.50	667.20	708.90	750.60	792.30	834.00
1669	458.97	500.70	542.42	584.15	625.87	667.60	709.32	751.05	792.77	834.50
1670	459.25	501.00	542.75	584.50	626.25	668.00	709.75	751.50	793.25	835.00
1671	459.52	501.30	543.07	584.85	626.62	668.40	710.17	751.95	793.72	835.50
1672	459.80	501.60	543.40	585.20	627.00	668.80	710.60	752.40	794.20	836.00
1673	460.07	501.90	543.72	585.55	627.37	669.20	711.02	752.85	794.67	836.50
1674	460.35	502.20	544.05	585.90	627.75	669.60	711.45	753.30	795.15	837.00
1675	460.62	502.50	544.37	586.25	628.12	670.00	711.87	753.75	795.62	837.50
1676	460.90	502.80	544.70	586.60	628.50	670.40	712.30	754.20	796.10	838.00
1677	461.17	503.10	545.02	586.95	628.87	670.80	712.72	754.65	796.57	838.50
1678	461.45	503.40	545.35	587.30	629.25	671.20	713.15	755.10	797.05	839.00
1679	461.72	503.70	545.67	587.65	629.62	671.60	713.57	755.55	797.52	839.50
1680	462.00	504.00	546.00	588.00	630.00	672.00	714.00	756.00	798.00	840.00
1681	462.27	504.30	546.32	588.35	630.37	672.40	714.42	756.45	798.47	840.50
1682	462.55	504.60	546.65	588.70	630.75	672.80	714.85	756.90	798.95	841.00
1683	462.82	504.90	546.97	589.05	631.12	673.20	715.27	757.35	799.42	841.50
1684	463.10	505.20	547.30	589.40	631.50	673.60	715.70	757.80	799.90	842.00
1685	463.37	505.50	547.62	589.75	631.87	674.00	716.12	758.25	800.37	842.50
1686	463.65	505.80	547.95	590.10	632.25	674.40	716.55	758.70	800.85	843.00
1687	463.92	506.10	548.27	590.45	632.62	674.80	716.97	759.15	801.32	843.50
1688	464.20	506.40	548.60	590.80	633.00	675.20	717.40	759.60	801.80	844.00
1689	464.47	506.70	548.92	591.15	633.37	675.60	717.82	760.05	802.27	844.50
1690	464.75	507.00	549.25	591.50	633.75	676.00	718.25	760.50	802.75	845.00
1691	465.02	507.30	549.57	591.85	634.12	676.40	718.67	760.95	803.22	845.50
1692	465.30	507.60	549.90	592.20	634.50	676.80	719.10	761.40	803.70	846.00
1693	465.57	507.90	550.22	592.55	634.87	677.20	719.52	761.85	804.17	846.50
1694	465.85	508.20	550.55	592.90	635.25	677.60	719.95	762.30	804.65	847.00
1695	466.12	508.50	550.87	593.25	635.62	678.00	720.37	762.75	805.12	847.50
1696	466.40	508.80	551.20	593.60	636.00	678.40	720.80	763.20	805.60	848.00
1697	466.67	509.10	551.52	593.95	636.37	678.80	721.22	763.65	806.07	848.50
1698	466.95	509.40	551.85	594.30	636.75	679.20	721.65	764.10	806.55	849.00
1699	467.22	509.70	552.17	594.65	637.12	679.60	722.07	764.55	807.02	849.50
1700	467.50	510.00	552.50	595.00	637.50	680.00	722.50	765.00	807.50	850.00

1750 FEET.

Per Ton, Per Foot,	25c.	50c.	$1 2½ cts.	$2 5 cts.	$3 7½ cts.	$4 10 cts.	$5 12½ cts.	$6 15 cts.	$7 17½ cts.	$8 20 cts.	$9 22½ cts.	$10 25 cts.
Feet.												
1701	10.63	21.26	42.52	85.05	127.57	170.10	212.62	255.15	297.67	340.20	382.72	425.25
1702	10.64	21.27	42.55	85.10	127.65	170.20	212.75	255.30	297.85	340.40	382.95	425.50
1703	10.64	21.29	42.57	85.15	127.72	170.30	212.87	255.45	298.02	340.60	383.17	425.75
1704	10.65	21.30	42.60	85.20	127.80	170.40	213.00	255.60	298.20	340.80	383.40	426.00
1705	10.66	21.31	42.62	85.25	127.87	170.50	213.12	255.75	298.37	341.00	383.62	426.25
1706	10.66	21.32	42.65	85.30	127.95	170.60	213.25	255.90	298.55	341.20	383.85	426.50
1707	10.67	21.34	42.67	85.35	128.02	170.70	213.37	256.05	298.72	341.40	384.07	426.75
1708	10.67	21.35	42.70	85.40	128.10	170.80	213.50	256.20	298.90	341.60	384.30	427.00
1709	10.68	21.36	42.72	85.45	128.17	170.90	213.62	256.35	299.07	341.80	384.52	427.25
1710	10.69	21.37	42.75	85.50	128.25	171.00	213.75	256.50	299.25	342.00	384.75	427.50
1711	10.69	21.39	42.77	85.55	128.32	171.10	213.87	256.65	299.42	342.20	384.97	427.75
1712	10.70	21.40	42.80	85.60	128.40	171.20	214.00	256.80	299.60	342.40	385.20	428.00
1713	10.71	21.41	42.82	85.65	128.47	171.30	214.12	256.95	299.77	342.60	385.42	428.25
1714	10.71	21.42	42.85	85.70	128.55	171.40	214.25	257.10	299.95	342.80	385.65	428.50
1715	10.72	21.44	42.87	85.75	128.62	171.50	214.37	257.25	300.12	343.00	385.87	428.75
1716	10.72	21.45	42.90	85.80	128.70	171.60	214.50	257.40	300.30	343.20	386.10	429.00
1717	10.73	21.46	42.92	85.85	128.77	171.70	214.62	257.55	300.47	343.40	386.32	429.25
1718	10.74	21.47	42.95	85.90	128.85	171.80	214.75	257.70	300.65	343.60	386.55	429.50
1719	10.74	21.49	42.97	85.95	128.92	171.90	214.87	257.85	300.82	343.80	386.77	429.75
1720	10.75	21.50	43.00	86.00	129.00	172.00	215.00	258.00	301.00	344.00	387.00	430.00
1721	10.76	21.51	43.02	86.05	129.07	172.10	215.12	258.15	301.17	344.20	387.22	430.25
1722	10.76	21.52	43.05	86.10	129.15	172.20	215.25	258.30	301.35	344.40	387.45	430.50
1723	10.77	21.54	43.07	86.15	129.22	172.30	215.37	258.45	301.52	344.60	387.67	430.75
1724	10.77	21.55	43.10	86.20	129.30	172.40	215.50	258.60	301.70	344.80	387.90	431.00
1725	10.78	21.56	43.12	86.25	129.37	172.50	215.62	258.75	301.87	345.00	388.12	431.25
1726	10.79	21.57	43.15	86.30	129.45	172.60	215.75	258.90	302.05	345.20	388.35	431.50
1727	10.79	21.59	43.17	86.35	129.52	172.70	215.87	259.05	302.22	345.40	388.57	431.75
1728	10.80	21.60	43.20	86.40	129.60	172.80	216.00	259.20	302.40	345.60	388.80	432.00
1729	10.81	21.61	43.22	86.45	129.67	172.90	216.12	259.35	302.57	345.80	389.02	432.25
1730	10.81	21.62	43.25	86.50	129.75	173.00	216.25	259.50	302.75	346.00	389.25	432.50
1731	10.82	21.64	43.27	86.55	129.82	173.10	216.37	259.65	302.92	346.20	389.47	432.75
1732	10.82	21.65	43.30	86.60	129.90	173.20	216.50	259.80	303.10	346.40	389.70	433.00
1733	10.83	21.66	43.32	86.65	129.97	173.30	216.62	260.95	303.27	346.60	389.92	433.25
1734	10.84	21.67	43.35	86.70	130.05	173.40	216.75	260.10	303.45	346.80	390.15	433.50
1735	10.84	21.69	43.37	86.75	130.12	173.50	216.87	260.25	303.62	347.00	390.37	433.75
1736	10.85	21.70	43.40	86.80	130.20	173.60	217.00	260.40	303.80	347.20	390.60	434.00
1737	10.86	21.71	43.42	86.85	130.27	173.70	217.12	260.55	303.97	347.40	390.82	434.25
1738	10.86	21.72	43.45	86.90	130.35	173.80	217.25	260.70	304.15	347.60	391.05	434.50
1739	10.87	21.74	43.47	86.95	130.42	173.90	217.37	260.85	304.32	347.80	391.27	434.75
1740	10.87	21.75	43.50	87.00	130.50	174.00	217.50	261.00	304.50	348.00	391.50	435.00
1741	10.88	21.76	43.52	87.05	130.57	174.10	217.62	261.15	304.67	348.20	391.72	435.25
1742	10.89	21.77	43.55	87.10	130.65	174.20	217.75	261.30	304.85	348.40	391.95	435.50
1743	10.89	21.79	43.57	87.15	130.72	174.30	217.87	261.45	805.02	348.60	392.17	435.75
1744	10.90	21.80	43.60	87.20	130.80	174.40	218.00	261.60	305.20	348.80	392.40	436.00
1745	10.91	21.81	43.62	87.25	130.87	174.50	218.12	261.75	305.37	349.00	392.62	436.25
1746	10.91	21.82	43.65	87.30	130.95	174.60	218.25	261.90	305.55	349.20	392.85	436.50
1747	10.92	21.84	43.67	87.35	131.02	174.70	218.37	262.05	305.72	349.40	393.07	436.75
1748	10.92	21.85	43.70	87.40	131.10	174.80	218.50	262.20	305.90	349.60	393.30	437.00
1749	10.93	21.86	43.72	87.45	131.17	174.90	218.62	262.35	306.07	349.80	393.52	437.25
1750	10.94	21.87	43.75	87.50	131.25	175.00	218.75	262.50	306.25	350.00	393.75	437.50

1750 FEET.

Feet.	Per Ton, $11 Per Foot, 27½ cts.	$12 30 cts.	$13 32½ cts.	$14 35 cts.	$15 37½ cts.	$16 40 cts.	$17 42½ cts.	$18 45 cts.	$19 47½ cts.	$20 50 cts.
1701	467.77	510.30	552.82	595.35	637.87	680.40	722.92	765.45	807.97	850.50
1702	468.05	510.60	553.15	595.70	638.25	680.80	723.35	765.90	808.45	851.00
1703	468.32	510.90	553.47	596.05	638.62	681.20	723.77	766.35	808.92	851.50
1704	468.60	511.20	553.80	596.40	639.00	681.60	724.20	766.80	809.40	852.00
1705	468.87	511.50	554.12	596.75	639.37	682.00	724.62	767.25	809.87	852.50
1706	469.15	511.80	554.45	597.10	639.75	682.40	725.05	767.70	810.35	853.00
1707	469.42	512.10	554.77	597.45	640.12	682.80	725.47	768.15	810.82	853.50
1708	469.70	512.40	555.10	597.80	640.50	683.20	725.90	768.60	811.30	854.00
1709	469.97	512.70	555.42	598.15	640.87	683.60	726.32	769.05	811.77	854.50
1710	470.25	513.00	555.75	598.50	641.25	684.00	726.75	769.50	812.25	855.00
1711	470.52	513.30	556.07	598.85	641.62	684.40	727.17	769.95	812.72	855.50
1712	470.80	513.60	556.40	599.20	642.00	684.80	727.60	770.40	813.20	856.00
1713	471.07	513.90	556.72	599.55	642.37	685.20	728.02	770.85	813.67	856.50
1714	471.35	514.20	557.05	599.90	642.75	685.60	728.45	771.30	814.15	857.00
1715	471.62	514.50	557.37	600.25	643.12	686.00	728.87	771.75	814.62	857.50
1716	471.90	514.80	557.70	600.60	643.50	686.40	729.30	772.20	815.10	858.00
1717	472.17	515.10	558.02	600.95	643.87	686.80	729.72	772.65	815.57	858.50
1718	472.45	515.40	558.35	601.30	644.25	687.20	730.15	773.10	816.05	859.00
1719	472.72	515.70	558.67	601.65	644.62	687.60	730.57	773.55	816.52	859.50
1720	473.00	516.00	559.00	602.00	645.00	688.00	731.00	774.00	817.00	860.00
1721	473.27	516.30	559.32	602.35	645.37	688.40	731.42	774.45	817.47	860.50
1722	473.55	516.60	559.65	602.70	645.75	688.80	731.85	774.90	817.95	861.00
1723	473.82	516.90	559.97	603.05	646.12	689.20	732.27	775.35	818.42	861.50
1724	474.10	517.20	560.30	603.40	646.50	689.60	732.70	775.80	818.90	862.00
1725	474.37	517.50	560.62	603.75	646.87	690.00	733.12	776.25	819.37	862.50
1726	474.65	517.80	560.95	604.10	647.25	690.40	733.55	776.70	819.85	863.00
1727	474.92	518.10	561.27	604.45	647.62	690.80	733.97	777.15	820.32	863.50
1728	475.20	518.40	561.60	604.80	648.00	691.20	734.40	777.60	820.80	864.00
1729	475.47	518.70	561.92	605.15	648.37	691.60	734.82	778.05	821.27	864.50
1730	475.75	519.00	562.25	605.50	648.75	692.00	735.25	778.50	821.75	865.00
1731	476.02	519.30	562.57	605.85	649.12	692.40	735.67	778.95	822.22	865.50
1732	476.30	519.60	562.90	606.20	649.50	692.80	736.10	779.40	822.70	866.00
1733	476.57	519.90	563.22	606.55	649.87	693.20	736.52	779.85	823.17	866.50
1734	476.85	520.20	563.55	606.90	650.25	693.60	736.95	780.30	823.65	867.00
1735	477.12	520.50	563.87	607.25	650.62	694.00	737.37	780.75	824.12	867.50
1736	477.40	520.80	564.20	607.60	651.00	694.40	737.80	781.20	824.60	868.00
1737	477.67	521.10	564.52	607.95	651.37	694.80	738.22	781.65	825.07	868.50
1738	477.95	521.40	564.85	608.30	651.75	695.20	738.65	782.10	825.55	869.00
1739	478.22	521.70	565.17	608.65	652.12	695.60	739.07	782.55	826.02	869.50
1740	478.50	522.00	565.50	609.00	652.50	696.00	739.50	783.00	826.50	870.00
1741	478.77	522.30	565.82	609.35	652.87	696.40	739.92	783.45	826.97	870.50
1742	479.05	522.60	566.15	609.70	653.25	696.80	740.35	783.90	827.45	871.00
1743	479.32	522.90	566.47	610.05	653.62	697.20	740.77	784.35	827.92	871.50
1744	479.60	523.20	566.80	610.40	654.00	697.60	741.20	784.80	828.40	872.00
1745	479.87	523.50	567.12	610.75	654.37	698.00	741.62	785.25	828.87	872.50
1746	480.15	523.80	567.45	611.10	654.75	698.40	742.05	785.70	829.35	873.00
1747	480.42	524.10	567.77	611.45	655.12	698.80	742.47	786.15	829.82	873.50
1748	480.70	524.40	568.10	611.80	655.50	699.20	742.90	786.60	830.30	874.00
1749	480.97	524.70	568.42	612.15	655.87	699.60	743.32	787.05	830.77	874.50
1750	481.25	525.00	568.75	612.50	656.25	700.00	743.75	787.50	831.25	875.00

1800 FEET.

Per Ton,	25c.	50c.	$1	$2	$3	$4	$5	$6	$7	$8	$9	$10
Per Foot,			2½ cts.	5 cts.	7½ cts.	10 cts.	12½ cts.	15 cts.	17½ cts.	20 cts.	22½ cts.	25 cts.
Feet.												
1751	10.94	21.89	43.77	87.55	131.32	175.10	218.87	262.65	306.42	350.20	393.97	437.75
1752	10.95	21.90	43.80	87.60	131.40	175.20	219.00	262.80	306.60	350.40	394.20	438.00
1753	10.96	21.91	43.82	87.65	131.47	175.30	219.12	262.95	306.77	350.60	394.42	438.25
1754	10.96	21.92	43.85	87.70	131.55	175.40	219.25	263.10	306.95	350.80	394.65	438.50
1755	10.97	21.94	43.87	87.75	131.62	175.50	219.37	263.25	807.12	351.00	394.87	438.75
1756	10.97	21.95	43.90	87.80	131.70	175.60	219.50	263.40	307.30	351.20	395.10	439.00
1757	10.98	21.96	43.92	87.85	131.77	175.70	219.62	263.55	307.47	351.40	395.32	439.25
1758	10.99	21.97	43.95	87.90	131.85	175.80	219.75	263.70	307.65	351.60	395.55	439.50
1759	10.99	21.99	43.97	87.95	131.92	175.90	219.87	263.85	307.82	351.80	395.77	439.75
1760	11.00	22.00	44.00	88.00	132.00	176.00	220.00	264.00	308.00	352.00	396.00	440.00
1761	11.01	22.01	44.02	88.05	132.07	176.10	220.12	264.15	308.17	352.20	396.22	440.25
1762	11.01	22.02	44.05	88.10	132.15	176.20	220.25	264.30	308.35	352.40	396.45	440.50
1763	11.02	22.04	44.07	88.15	132.22	176.30	220.37	264.45	308.52	352.60	396.67	440.75
1764	11.02	22.05	44.10	88.20	132.30	176.40	220.50	264.60	308.70	352.80	396.90	441.00
1765	11.03	22.06	44.12	88.25	132.37	176.50	220.62	264.75	308.87	353.00	397.12	441.25
1766	11.04	22.07	44.15	88.30	132.45	176.60	220.75	264.90	309.05	353.20	397.35	441.50
1767	11.04	22.09	44.17	88.35	132.52	176.70	220.87	265.05	309.22	353.40	397.57	441.75
1768	11.05	22.10	44.20	88.40	132.60	176.80	221.00	265.20	309.40	353.60	397.80	442.00
1769	11.06	22.11	44.22	88.45	132.67	176.90	221.12	265.35	309.57	353.80	398.02	442.25
1770	11.06	22.12	44.25	88.50	132.75	177.00	221.25	265.50	309.75	354.00	398.25	442.50
1771	11.07	22.14	44.27	88.55	132.82	177.10	221.37	265.65	309.92	354.20	398.47	442.75
1772	11.07	22.15	44.30	88.60	132.90	177.20	221.50	265.80	310.10	354.40	398.70	443.00
1773	11.08	22.16	44.32	88.65	132.97	177.30	221.62	265.95	310.27	354.60	398.92	443.25
1774	11.09	22.17	44.35	88.70	133.05	177.40	221.75	266.10	310.45	354.80	399.15	443.50
1775	11.09	22.19	44.37	88.75	133.12	177.50	221.87	266.25	310.62	355.00	399.37	443.75
1776	11.10	22.20	44.40	88.80	133.20	177.60	222.00	266.40	310.80	355.20	399.60	444.00
1777	11.11	22.21	44.42	88.85	133.27	177.70	222.12	266.55	310.97	355.40	399.82	444.25
1778	11.11	22.22	44.45	88.90	133.35	177.80	222.25	266.70	311.15	355.60	400.05	444.50
1779	11.12	22.24	44.47	88.95	133.42	177.90	222.37	266.85	311.32	355.80	400.27	444.75
1780	11.12	22.25	44.50	89.00	133.50	178.00	222.50	267.00	311.50	356.00	400.50	445.00
1781	11.13	22.26	44.52	89.05	133.57	178.10	222.62	267.15	311.67	356.20	400.72	445.25
1782	11.14	22.27	44.55	89.10	133.65	178.20	222.75	267.30	311.85	356.40	400.95	445.50
1783	11.14	22.29	44.57	89.15	133.72	178.30	222.87	267.45	312.02	356.60	401.17	445.75
1784	11.15	22.30	44.60	89.20	133.80	178.40	223.00	267.60	312.20	356.80	401.40	446.00
1785	11.16	22.31	44.62	89.25	133.87	178.50	223.12	267.75	312.37	357.00	401.62	446.25
1786	11.16	22.32	44.65	89.30	133.95	178.60	223.25	267.90	312.55	357.20	401.85	446.50
1787	11.17	22.34	44.67	89.35	134.02	178.70	223.37	268.05	312.72	357.40	402.07	446.75
1788	11.17	22.35	44.70	89.40	134.10	178.80	223.50	268.20	312.90	357.60	402.30	447.00
1789	11.18	22.36	44.72	89.45	134.17	178.90	223.62	268.35	313.07	357.80	402.52	447.25
1790	11.19	22.37	44.75	89.50	134.25	179.00	223.75	268.50	313.25	358.00	402.75	447.50
1791	11.19	22.39	44.77	89.55	134.32	179.10	223.87	268.65	313.42	358.20	402.97	447.75
1792	11.20	22.40	44.80	89.60	134.40	179.20	224.00	268.80	313.60	358.40	403.20	448.00
1793	11.21	22.41	44.82	89.65	134.47	179.30	224.12	268.95	313.77	358.60	403.42	448.25
1794	11.21	22.42	44.85	89.70	134.55	179.40	224.25	269.10	313.95	358.80	403.65	448.50
1795	11.22	22.44	44.87	89.75	134.62	179.50	224.37	269.25	314.12	359.00	403.87	448.75
1796	11.22	22.45	44.90	89.80	134.70	179.60	224.50	269.40	314.30	359.20	404.10	449.00
1797	11.23	22.46	44.92	89.85	134.77	179.70	224.62	269.55	314.47	359.40	404.32	449.25
1798	11.24	22.47	44.95	89.90	134.85	179.80	224.75	269.70	314.65	359.60	404.55	449.50
1799	11.24	22.49	44.97	89.95	134.92	179.90	224.87	269.85	314.82	359.80	404.77	449.75
1800	11.25	22.50	45.00	90.00	135.00	180.00	225.00	270.00	315.00	360.00	405.00	450.00

1800 FEET.

Per Ton,	$11	$12	$13	$14	$15	$16	$17	$18	$19	$20
Per Foot,	27½ cts.	30 cts.	32½ cts.	35 cts.	37½ cts.	40 cts.	42½ cts.	45 cts.	47½ cts.	50 cts.
Feet.										
1751	481.52	525.30	569.07	612.85	656.62	700.40	744.17	787.95	831.72	875.50
1752	481.80	525.60	569.40	613.20	657.00	700.80	744.60	788.40	832.20	876.00
1753	482.07	525.90	569.72	613.55	657.37	701.20	745.02	788.85	832.67	876.50
1754	482.35	526.20	570.05	613.90	657.75	701.60	745.45	789.30	833.15	877.00
1755	482.62	526.50	570.37	614.25	658.12	702.00	745.87	789.75	833.62	877.50
1756	482.90	526.80	570.70	614.60	658.50	702.40	746.30	790.20	834.10	878.00
1757	483.17	527.10	571.02	614.95	658.87	702.80	746.72	790.65	834.57	878.50
1758	483.45	527.40	571.35	615.30	659.25	703.20	747.15	791.10	835.05	879.00
1759	483.72	527.70	571.67	615.65	659.62	703.60	747.57	791.55	835.52	879.50
1760	484.00	528.00	572.00	616.00	660.00	704.00	748.00	792.00	836.00	880.00
1761	484.27	528.30	572.32	616.35	660.37	704.40	748.42	792.45	836.47	880.50
1762	484.55	528.60	572.65	616.70	660.75	704.80	748.85	792.90	836.95	881.00
1763	484.82	528.90	572.97	617.05	661.12	705.20	749.27	793.35	837.42	881.50
1764	485.10	529.20	573.30	617.40	661.50	705.60	749.70	793.80	837.90	882.00
1765	485.37	529.50	573.62	617.75	661.87	706.00	750.12	794.25	838.37	882.50
1766	485.65	529.80	573.95	618.10	662.25	706.40	750.55	794.70	838.85	883.00
1767	485.92	530.10	574.27	618.45	662.62	706.80	750.97	795.15	839.32	883.50
1768	486.20	530.40	574.60	618.80	663.00	707.20	751.40	795.60	839.80	884.00
1769	486.47	530.70	574.92	619.15	663.37	707.60	751.82	796.05	840.27	884.50
1770	486.75	531.00	575.25	619.50	663.75	708.00	752.25	796.50	840.75	885.00
1771	487.02	531.30	575.57	619.85	664.12	708.40	752.67	796.95	841.22	885.50
1772	487.30	531.60	575.90	620.20	664.50	708.80	753.10	797.40	841.70	886.00
1773	487.57	531.90	576.22	620.55	664.87	709.20	753.52	797.85	842.17	886.50
1774	487.85	532.20	576.55	620.90	665.25	709.60	753.95	798.30	842.65	887.00
1775	488.12	532.50	576.87	621.25	665.62	710.00	754.37	798.75	843.12	887.50
1776	488.40	532.80	577.20	621.60	666.00	710.40	754.80	799.20	843.60	888.00
1777	488.67	533.10	577.52	621.95	666.37	710.80	755.22	799.65	844.07	888.50
1778	488.95	533.40	577.85	622.30	666.75	711.20	755.65	800.10	844.55	889.00
1779	489.22	533.70	578.17	622.65	667.12	711.60	756.07	800.55	845.02	889.50
1780	489.50	534.00	578.50	623.00	667.50	712.00	756.50	801.00	845.50	890.00
1781	489.77	534.30	578.82	623.35	667.87	712.40	756.92	801.45	845.97	890.50
1782	490.05	534.60	579.15	623.70	668.25	712.80	757.35	801.90	846.45	891.00
1783	490.32	534.90	579.47	624.05	668.62	713.20	757.77	802.35	846.92	891.50
1784	490.60	535.20	579.80	624.40	669.00	713.60	758.20	802.80	847.40	892.00
1785	490.87	535.50	580.12	624.75	669.37	714.00	758.62	803.25	847.87	892.50
1786	491.15	535.80	580.45	625.10	669.75	714.40	759.05	803.70	848.35	893.00
1787	491.42	536.10	580.77	625.45	670.12	714.80	759.47	804.15	848.82	893.50
1788	491.70	536.40	581.10	625.80	670.50	715.20	759.90	804.60	849.30	894.00
1789	491.97	536.70	581.42	626.15	670.87	715.60	760.32	805.05	849.77	894.50
1790	492.25	537.00	581.75	626.50	671.25	716.00	760.75	805.50	850.25	895.00
1791	492.52	537.30	582.07	626.85	671.62	716.40	761.17	805.95	850.72	895.50
1792	492.80	537.60	582.40	627.20	672.00	716.80	761.60	806.40	851.20	896.00
1793	493.07	537.90	582.72	627.55	672.37	717.20	762.02	806.85	851.67	896.50
1794	493.35	538.20	583.05	627.90	672.75	717.60	762.45	807.30	852.15	897.00
1795	493.62	538.50	583.37	628.25	673.12	718.00	762.87	807.75	852.62	897.50
1796	493.90	538.80	583.70	628.60	673.50	718.40	763.30	808.20	853.10	898.00
1797	494.17	539.10	584.02	628.95	673.87	718.80	763.72	808.65	853.57	898.50
1798	494.45	539.40	584.35	629.30	674.25	719.20	764.15	809.10	854.05	899.00
1799	494.72	539.70	584.67	629.65	674.62	719.60	764.57	809.55	854.52	899.50
1800	495.00	540.00	585.00	630.00	675.00	720.00	765.00	810.00	855.00	900.00

1850 FEET.

Per Ton, Per Foot, Feet.	25c.	50c.	$1 2¼ cts.	$2 5 cts.	$3 7½ cts.	$4 10 cts.	$5 12½ cts.	$6 15 cts.	$7 17½ cts.	$8 20 cts.	$9 22½ cts.	$10 25 cts.
1801	11.26	22.51	45.02	90.05	135.07	180.10	225.12	270.15	315.17	360.20	405.22	450.25
1802	11.26	22.52	45.05	90.10	135.15	180.20	225.25	270.30	315.35	360.40	405.45	450.50
1803	11.27	22.54	45.07	90.15	135.22	180.30	225.37	270.45	315.52	360.60	405.67	450.75
1804	11.27	22.55	45.10	90.20	135.30	180.40	225.50	270.60	315.70	360.80	405.90	451.00
1805	11.28	22.56	45.12	90.25	135.37	180.50	225.62	270.75	315.87	361.00	406.12	451.25
1806	11.29	22.57	45.15	90.30	135.45	180.60	225.75	270.90	316.05	361.20	406.35	451.50
1807	11.29	22.59	45.17	90.35	135.52	180.70	225.87	271.05	316.22	361.40	406.57	451.75
1808	11.30	22.60	45.20	90.40	135.60	180.80	226.00	271.20	316.40	361.60	406.80	452.00
1809	11.31	22.61	45.22	90.45	135.67	180.90	226.12	271.35	316.57	361.80	407.02	452.25
1810	11.31	22.62	45.25	90.50	135.75	181.00	226.25	271.50	316.75	362.00	407.25	452.50
1811	11.32	22.64	45.27	90.55	135.82	181.10	226.37	271.65	316.92	362.20	407.47	452.75
1812	11.32	22.65	45.30	90.60	135.90	181.20	226.50	271.80	317.10	362.40	407.70	453.00
1813	11.33	22.66	45.32	90.65	135.97	181.30	226.62	271.95	317.27	362.60	407.92	453.25
1814	11.34	22.67	45.35	90.70	136.05	181.40	226.75	272.10	317.45	362.80	408.15	453.50
1815	11.34	22.69	45.37	90.75	136.12	181.50	226.87	272.25	317.62	363.00	408.37	453.75
1816	11.35	22.70	45.40	90.80	136.20	181.60	227.00	272.40	317.80	363.20	408.60	454.00
1817	11.36	22.71	45.42	90.85	136.27	181.70	227.12	272.55	317.97	363.40	408.82	454.25
1818	11.36	22.72	45.45	90.90	136.35	181.80	227.25	272.70	318.15	363.60	409.05	454.50
1819	11.37	22.74	45.47	90.95	136.42	181.90	227.37	272.85	318.32	363.80	409.27	454.75
1820	11.37	22.75	45.50	91.00	136.50	182.00	227.50	273.00	318.50	364.00	409.50	455.00
1821	11.38	22.76	45.52	91.05	136.57	182.10	227.62	273.15	318.67	364.20	409.72	455.25
1822	11.39	22.77	45.55	91.10	136.65	182.20	227.75	273.30	318.85	364.40	409.95	455.50
1823	11.39	22.79	45.57	91.15	136.72	182.30	227.87	273.45	319.02	364.60	410.17	455.75
1824	11.40	22.80	45.60	91.20	136.80	182.40	228.00	273.60	319.20	364.80	410.40	456.00
1825	11.41	22.81	45.62	91.25	136.87	182.50	228.12	273.75	319.37	365.00	410.62	456.25
1826	11.41	22.82	45.65	91.30	136.95	182.60	228.25	273.90	319.55	365.20	410.85	456.50
1827	11.42	22.84	45.67	91.35	137.02	182.70	228.37	274.05	319.72	365.40	411.07	456.75
1828	11.42	22.85	45.70	91.40	137.10	182.80	228.50	274.20	319.90	365.60	411.30	457.00
1829	11.43	22.86	45.72	91.45	137.17	182.90	228.62	274.35	320.07	365.80	411.52	457.25
1830	11.44	22.87	45.75	91.50	137.25	183.00	228.75	274.50	320.25	366.00	411.75	457.50
1831	11.44	22.89	45.77	91.55	137.32	183.10	228.87	274.65	320.42	366.20	411.97	457.75
1832	11.45	22.90	45.80	91.60	137.40	183.20	229.00	274.80	320.60	366.40	412.20	458.00
1833	11.46	22.91	45.82	91.65	137.47	183.30	229.12	274.95	320.77	366.60	412.42	458.25
1834	11.46	22.92	45.85	91.70	137.55	183.40	229.25	275.10	320.95	366.80	412.65	458.50
1835	11.47	22.94	45.87	91.75	137.62	183.50	229.37	275.25	321.12	367.00	412.87	458.75
1836	11.47	22.95	45.90	91.80	137.70	183.60	229.50	275.40	321.30	367.20	413.10	459.00
1837	11.48	22.96	45.92	91.85	137.77	183.70	229.62	275.55	321.47	367.40	413.32	459.25
1838	11.49	22.97	45.95	91.90	137.85	183.80	229.75	275.70	321.65	367.60	413.55	459.50
1839	11.49	22.99	45.97	91.95	137.92	183.90	229.87	275.85	321.82	367.80	413.77	459.75
1840	11.50	23.00	46.00	92.00	138.00	184.00	230.00	276.00	322.00	368.00	414.00	460.00
1841	11.51	23.01	46.02	92.05	138.07	184.10	230.12	276.15	322.17	368.20	414.22	460.25
1842	11.51	23.02	46.05	92.10	138.15	184.20	230.25	276.30	322.35	368.40	414.45	460.50
1843	11.52	23.04	46.07	92.15	138.22	184.30	230.37	276.45	322.52	368.60	414.67	460.75
1844	11.52	23.05	46.10	92.20	138.30	184.40	230.50	276.60	322.70	368.80	414.90	461.00
1845	11.53	23.06	46.12	92.25	138.37	184.50	230.62	276.75	322.87	369.00	415.12	461.25
1846	11.54	23.07	46.15	92.30	138.45	184.60	230.75	276.90	323.05	369.20	415.35	461.50
1847	11.54	23.09	46.17	92.35	138.52	184.70	230.87	277.05	323.22	369.40	415.57	461.75
1848	11.55	23.10	46.20	92.40	138.60	184.80	231.00	277.20	323.40	369.60	415.80	462.00
1849	11.56	23.11	46.22	92.45	138.67	184.90	231.12	277.35	323.57	369.80	416.02	462.25
1850	11.56	23.12	46.25	92.50	138.75	185.00	231.25	277.50	323.75	370.00	416.25	462.50

1850 FEET.

Per Ton,	$11	$12	$13	$14	$15	$16	$17	$18	$19	$20
Per Foot,	27½ cts.	30 cts.	32½ cts.	35 cts.	37½ cts.	40 cts.	42½ cts.	45 cts.	47½ cts.	50 cts.
Feet.										
1801	495.27	540.30	585.32	630.35	675.37	720.40	765.42	810.45	855.47	900.50
1802	495.55	540.60	585.65	630.70	675.75	720.80	765.85	810.90	855.95	901.00
1803	495.82	540.90	585.97	631.05	676.12	721.20	766.27	811.35	856.42	901.50
1804	496.10	541.20	586.30	631.40	676.50	721.60	766.70	811.80	856.90	902.00
1805	496.37	541.50	586.62	631.75	676.87	722.00	767.12	812.25	857.37	902.50
1806	496.65	541.80	586.95	632.10	677.25	722.40	767.55	812.70	857.85	903.00
1807	496.92	542.10	587.27	632.45	677.62	722.80	767.97	813.15	858.32	903.50
1808	497.20	542.40	587.60	632.80	678.00	723.20	768.40	813.60	858.80	904.00
1809	497.47	542.70	587.92	633.15	678.37	723.60	768.82	814.05	859.27	904.50
1810	497.75	543.00	588.25	633.50	678.75	724.00	769.25	814.50	859.75	905.00
1811	498.02	543.30	588.57	633.85	679.12	724.40	769.67	814.95	860.22	905.50
1812	498.30	543.60	588.90	634.20	679.50	724.80	770.10	815.40	860.70	906.00
1813	498.57	543.90	589.22	634.55	679.87	725.20	770.52	815.85	861.17	906.50
1814	498.85	544.20	589.55	634.90	680.25	725.60	770.95	816.30	861.65	907.00
1815	499.12	544.50	589.87	635.25	680.62	726.00	771.37	816.75	862.12	907.50
1816	499.40	544.80	590.20	635.60	681.00	726.40	771.80	817.20	862.60	908.00
1817	499.67	545.10	590.52	635.95	681.37	726.80	772.22	817.65	863.07	908.50
1818	499.95	545.40	590.85	636.30	681.75	727.20	772.65	818.10	863.55	909.00
1819	500.22	545.70	591.17	636.65	682.12	727.60	773.07	818.55	864.02	909.50
1820	500.50	546.00	591.50	637.00	682.50	728.00	773.50	819.00	864.50	910.00
1821	500.77	546.30	591.82	637.35	682.87	728.40	773.92	819.45	864.97	910.50
1822	501.05	546.60	592.15	637.70	683.25	728.80	774.35	819.90	865.45	911.00
1823	501.32	546.90	592.47	638.05	683.62	729.20	774.77	820.35	865.92	911.50
1824	501.60	547.20	592.80	638.40	684.00	729.60	775.20	820.80	866.40	912.00
1825	501.87	547.50	593.12	638.75	684.37	730.00	775.62	821.25	866.87	912.50
1826	502.15	547.80	593.45	639.10	684.75	730.40	776.05	821.70	867.35	913.00
1827	502.42	548.10	593.77	639.45	685.12	730.80	776.47	822.15	867.82	913.50
1828	502.70	548.40	594.10	639.80	685.50	731.20	776.90	822.60	868.30	914.00
1829	502.97	548.70	594.42	640.15	685.87	731.60	777.32	823.05	868.77	914.50
1830	503.25	549.00	594.75	640.50	686.25	732.00	777.75	823.50	869.25	915.00
1831	503.52	549.30	595.07	640.85	686.62	732.40	778.17	823.95	869.72	915.50
1832	503.80	549.60	595.40	641.20	687.00	732.80	778.60	824.40	870.20	916.00
1833	504.07	549.90	595.72	641.55	687.37	733.20	779.02	824.85	870.67	916.50
1834	504.35	550.20	596.05	641.90	687.75	733.60	779.45	825.30	871.15	917.00
1835	504.62	550.50	596.37	642.25	688.12	734.00	779.87	825.75	871.62	917.50
1836	504.90	550.80	596.70	642.60	688.50	734.40	780.30	826.20	872.10	918.00
1837	505.17	551.10	597.02	642.95	688.87	734.80	780.72	826.65	872.57	918.50
1838	505.45	551.40	597.35	643.30	689.25	735.20	781.15	827.10	873.05	919.00
1839	505.72	551.70	597.67	643.65	689.62	735.60	781.57	827.55	873.52	919.50
1840	506.00	552.00	598.00	644.00	690.00	736.00	782.00	828.00	874.00	920.00
1841	506.27	552.30	598.32	644.35	690.37	736.40	782.42	828.45	874.47	920.50
1842	506.55	552.60	598.65	644.70	690.75	736.80	782.85	828.90	874.95	921.00
1843	506.82	552.90	598.97	645.05	691.12	737.20	783.27	829.35	875.42	921.50
1844	507.10	553.20	599.30	645.40	691.50	737.60	783.70	829.80	875.90	922.00
1845	507.37	553.50	599.62	645.75	691.87	738.00	784.12	830.25	876.37	922.50
1846	507.65	553.80	599.95	646.10	692.25	738.40	784.55	830.70	876.85	923.00
1847	507.92	554.10	600.27	646.45	692.62	738.80	784.97	831.15	877.32	923.50
1848	508.20	554.40	600.60	646.80	693.00	739.20	785.40	831.60	877.80	924.00
1849	508.47	554.70	600.92	647.15	693.37	739.60	785.82	832.05	878.27	924.50
1850	508.75	555.00	601.25	647.50	693.75	740.00	786.25	832.50	878.75	925.00

1900 FEET.

Per Ton, Per Foot, Feet.	25c.	50c.	$1 2¼ cts.	$2 5 cts.	$3 7½ cts.	$4 10 cts.	$5 12½ cts.	$6 15 cts.	$7 17½ cts.	$8 20 cts.	$9 22½ cts.	$10 25 cts.
1851	11.57	23.14	46.27	92.55	138.82	185.10	231.37	277.65	323.92	370.20	416.47	462.75
1852	11.57	23.15	46.30	92.60	138.90	185.20	231.50	277.80	324.10	370.40	416.70	463.00
1853	11.58	23.16	46.32	92.65	138.97	185.30	231.62	277.95	324.27	370.60	416.92	463.25
1854	11.59	23.17	46.35	92.70	139.05	185.40	231.75	278.10	324.45	370.80	417.15	463.50
1855	11.59	23.19	46.37	92.75	139.12	185.50	231.87	278.25	324.62	371.00	417.37	463.75
1856	11.60	23.20	46.40	92.80	139.20	185.60	232.00	278.40	324.80	371.20	417.60	464.00
1857	11.61	23.21	46.42	92.85	139.27	185.70	232.12	278.55	324.97	371.40	417.82	464.25
1858	11.61	23.22	46.45	92.90	139.35	185.80	232.25	278.70	325.15	371.60	418.05	464.50
1859	11.62	23.24	46.47	92.95	139.42	185.90	232.37	278.85	325.32	371.80	418.27	464.75
1860	11.62	23.25	46.50	93.00	139.50	186.00	232.50	279.00	325.50	372.00	418.50	465.00
1861	11.63	23.26	46.52	93.05	139.57	186.10	232.62	279.15	325.67	372.20	418.72	465.25
1862	11.64	23.27	46.55	93.10	139.65	186.20	232.75	279.30	325.85	372.40	418.95	465.50
1863	11.64	23.29	46.57	93.15	139.72	186.30	232.87	279.45	326.02	372.60	419.17	465.75
1864	11.65	23.30	46.60	93.20	139.80	186.40	233.00	279.60	326.20	372.80	419.40	466.00
1865	11.66	23.31	46.62	93.25	139.87	186.50	233.12	279.75	326.37	373.00	419.62	466.25
1866	11.66	23.32	46.65	93.30	139.95	186.60	233.25	279.90	326.55	373.20	419.85	466.50
1867	11.67	23.34	46.67	93.35	140.02	186.70	233.37	280.05	326.72	373.40	420.07	466.75
1868	11.67	23.35	46.70	93.40	140.10	186.80	233.50	280.20	326.90	373.60	420.30	467.00
1869	11.68	23.36	46.72	93.45	140.17	186.90	233.62	280.35	327.07	373.80	420.52	467.25
1870	11.69	23.37	46.75	93.50	140.25	187.00	233.75	280.50	327.25	374.00	420.75	467.50
1871	11.69	23.39	46.77	93.55	140.32	187.10	233.87	280.65	327.42	374.20	420.97	467.75
1872	11.70	23.40	46.80	93.60	140.40	187.20	234.00	280.80	327.60	374.40	421.20	468.00
1873	11.71	23.41	46.82	93.65	140.47	187.30	234.12	280.95	327.77	374.60	421.42	468.25
1874	11.71	23.42	46.85	93.70	140.55	187.40	234.25	281.10	327.95	374.80	421.65	468.50
1875	11.72	23.44	46.87	93.75	140.62	187.50	234.37	281.25	328.12	375.00	421.87	468.75
1876	11.72	23.45	46.90	93.80	140.70	187.60	234.50	281.40	328.30	375.20	422.10	469.00
1877	11.73	23.46	46.92	93.85	140.77	187.70	234.62	281.55	328.47	375.40	422.32	469.25
1878	11.74	23.47	46.95	93.90	140.85	187.80	234.75	281.70	328.65	375.60	422.55	469.50
1879	11.74	23.49	46.97	93.95	140.92	187.90	234.87	281.85	328.82	375.80	422.77	469.75
1880	11.75	23.50	47.00	94.00	141.00	188.00	235.00	282.00	329.00	376.00	423.00	470.00
1881	11.76	23.51	47.02	94.05	141.07	188.10	235.12	282.15	329.17	376.20	423.22	470.25
1882	11.76	23.52	47.05	94.10	141.15	188.20	235.25	282.30	329.35	376.40	423.45	470.50
1883	11.77	23.54	47.07	94.15	141.22	188.30	235.37	282.45	329.52	376.60	423.67	470.75
1884	11.77	23.55	47.10	94.20	141.30	188.40	235.50	282.60	329.70	376.80	423.90	471.00
1885	11.78	23.56	47.12	94.25	141.37	188.50	235.62	282.75	329.87	377.00	424.12	471.25
1886	11.79	23.57	47.15	94.30	141.45	188.60	235.75	282.90	330.05	377.20	424.35	471.50
1887	11.79	23.59	47.17	94.35	141.52	188.70	235.87	283.05	330.22	377.40	424.57	471.75
1888	11.80	23.60	47.20	94.40	141.60	188.80	236.00	283.20	330.40	377.60	424.80	472.00
1889	11.81	23.61	47.22	94.45	141.67	188.90	236.12	283.35	330.57	377.80	425.02	472.25
1890	11.81	23.62	47.25	94.50	141.75	189.00	236.25	283.50	330.75	378.00	425.25	472.50
1891	11.82	23.64	47.27	94.55	141.82	189.10	236.37	283.65	330.92	378.20	425.47	472.75
1892	11.82	23.65	47.30	94.60	141.90	189.20	236.50	283.80	331.10	378.40	425.70	473.00
1893	11.83	23.66	47.32	94.65	141.97	189.30	236.62	283.95	331.27	378.60	425.92	473.25
1894	11.84	23.67	47.35	94.70	142.05	189.40	236.75	284.10	331.45	378.80	426.15	473.50
1895	11.84	23.69	47.37	94.75	142.12	189.50	236.87	284.25	331.62	379.00	426.37	473.75
1896	11.85	23.70	47.40	94.80	142.20	189.60	237.00	284.40	331.80	379.20	426.60	474.00
1897	11.86	23.71	47.42	94.85	142.27	189.70	237.12	284.55	331.97	379.40	426.82	474.25
1898	11.86	23.72	47.45	94.90	142.35	189.80	237.25	284.70	332.15	379.60	427.05	474.50
1899	11.87	23.74	47.47	94.95	142.42	189.90	237.37	284.85	332.32	379.80	427.27	474.75
1900	11.87	23.75	47.50	95.00	142.50	190.00	237.50	285.00	332.50	380.00	427.50	475.00

1900 FEET.

Per Ton,	$11	$12	$13	$14	$15	$16	$17	$18	$19	$20
Per Foot,	27½ cts.	30 cts.	32½ cts.	35 cts.	37½ cts.	40 cts.	42½ cts.	45 cts.	47½ cts.	50 cts.
Feet.										
1851	509.02	555.30	601.57	647.85	694.12	740.40	786.67	832.95	879.22	925.50
1852	509.30	555.60	601.90	648.20	694.50	740.80	787.10	833.40	879.70	926.00
1853	509.57	555.90	602.22	648.55	694.87	741.20	787.52	833.85	880.17	926.50
1854	509.85	556.20	602.55	648.90	695.25	741.60	787.95	834.30	880.65	927.00
1855	510.12	556.50	602.87	649.25	695.62	742.00	788.37	834.75	881.12	927.50
1856	510.40	556.80	603.20	649.60	696.00	742.40	788.80	835.20	881.60	928.00
1857	510.67	557.10	603.52	649.95	696.37	742.80	789.22	835.65	882.07	928.50
1858	510.95	557.40	603.85	650.30	696.75	743.20	789.65	836.10	882.55	929.00
1859	511.22	557.70	604.17	650.65	697.12	743.60	790.07	836.55	883.02	929.50
1860	511.50	558.00	604.50	651.00	697.50	744.00	790.50	837.00	883.50	930.00
1861	511.77	558.30	604.82	651.35	697.87	744.40	790.92	837.45	883.97	930.50
1862	512.05	558.60	605.15	651.70	698.25	744.80	791.35	837.90	884.45	931.00
1863	512.32	558.90	605.47	652.05	698.62	745.20	791.77	838.35	884.92	931.50
1864	512.60	559.20	605.80	652.40	699.00	745.60	792.20	838.80	885.40	932.00
1865	512.87	559.50	606.12	652.75	699.37	746.00	792.62	839.25	885.87	932.50
1866	513.15	559.80	606.45	653.10	699.75	746.40	793.05	839.70	886.35	933.00
1867	513.42	560.10	606.77	653.45	700.12	746.80	793.47	840.15	886.82	933.50
1868	513.70	560.40	607.10	653.80	700.50	747.20	793.90	840.60	887.30	934.00
1869	513.97	560.70	607.42	654.15	700.87	747.60	794.32	841.05	887.77	934.50
1870	514.25	561.00	607.75	654.50	701.25	748.00	794.75	841.50	888.25	935.00
1871	514.52	561.30	608.07	654.85	701.62	748.40	795.17	841.95	888.72	935.50
1872	514.80	561.60	608.40	655.20	702.00	748.80	795.60	842.40	889.20	936.00
1873	515.07	561.90	608.72	655.55	702.37	749.20	796.02	842.85	889.67	936.50
1874	515.35	562.20	609.05	655.90	702.75	749.60	796.45	843.30	890.15	937.00
1875	515.62	562.50	609.37	656.25	703.12	750.00	796.87	843.75	890.62	937.50
1876	515.90	562.80	609.70	656.60	703.50	750.40	797.30	844.20	891.10	938.00
1877	516.17	563.10	610.02	656.95	703.87	750.80	797.72	844.65	891.57	938.50
1878	516.45	563.40	610.35	657.30	704.25	751.20	798.15	845.10	892.05	939.00
1879	516.72	563.70	610.67	657.65	704.62	751.60	798.57	845.55	892.52	939.50
1880	517.00	564.00	611.00	658.00	705.00	752.00	799.00	846.00	893.00	940.00
1881	517.27	564.30	611.32	658.35	705.37	752.40	799.42	846.45	893.47	940.50
1882	517.55	564.60	611.65	658.70	705.75	752.80	799.85	846.90	893.95	941.00
1883	517.82	564.90	611.97	659.05	706.12	753.20	800.27	847.35	894.42	941.50
1884	518.10	565.20	612.30	659.40	706.50	753.60	800.70	847.80	894.90	942.00
1885	518.37	565.50	612.62	659.75	706.87	754.00	801.12	848.25	895.37	942.50
1886	518.65	565.80	612.95	660.10	707.25	754.40	801.55	848.70	895.85	943.00
1887	518.92	566.10	613.27	660.45	707.62	754.80	801.97	849.15	896.32	943.50
1888	519.20	566.40	613.60	660.80	708.00	755.20	802.40	849.60	896.80	944.00
1889	519.47	566.70	613.92	661.15	708.37	755.60	802.82	850.05	897.27	944.50
1890	519.75	567.00	614.25	661.50	708.75	756.00	803.25	850.50	897.75	945.00
1891	520.02	567.30	614.57	661.85	709.12	756.40	803.67	850.95	898.22	945.50
1892	520.30	567.60	614.90	662.20	709.50	756.80	804.10	851.40	898.70	946.00
1893	520.57	567.90	615.22	662.55	709.87	757.20	804.52	851.85	899.17	946.50
1894	520.85	568.20	615.55	662.90	710.25	757.60	804.95	852.30	899.65	947.00
1895	521.12	568.50	615.87	663.25	710.62	758.00	805.37	852.75	900.12	947.50
1896	521.40	568.80	616.20	663.60	711.00	758.40	805.80	853.20	900.60	948.00
1897	521.67	569.10	616.52	663.95	711.37	758.80	806.22	853.65	901.07	948.50
1898	521.95	569.40	616.85	664.30	711.75	759.20	806.65	854.10	901.55	949.00
1899	522.22	569.70	617.17	664.65	712.12	759.60	807.07	854.55	902.02	949.50
1900	522.50	570.00	617.50	665.00	712.50	760.00	807.50	855.00	902.50	950.00

1950 FEET.

Per Ton,	25c.	50c.	$1	$2	$3	$4	$5	$6	$7	$8	$9	$10
Per Foot,			2½ cts.	5 cts.	7½ cts.	10 cts.	12½ cts.	15 cts.	17½ cts.	20 cts.	22½ cts.	25 cts.
Feet.												
1901	11.88	23.76	47.52	95.05	142.57	190.10	237.62	285.15	332.67	380.20	427.72	475.25
1902	11.89	23.77	47.55	95.10	142.65	190.20	237.75	285.30	332.85	380.40	427.95	475.50
1903	11.89	23.79	47.57	95.15	142.72	190.30	237.87	285.45	333.02	380.60	428.17	475.75
1904	11.90	23.80	47.60	95.20	142.80	190.40	238.00	285.60	333.20	380.80	428.40	476.00
1905	11.91	23.81	47.62	95.25	142.87	190.50	238.12	285.75	333.37	381.00	428.62	476.25
1906	11.91	23.82	47.65	95.30	142.95	190.60	238.25	285.90	333.55	381.20	428.85	476.50
1907	11.92	23.84	47.67	95.35	143.02	190.70	238.37	286.05	333.72	381.40	429.07	476.75
1908	11.92	23.85	47.70	95.40	143.10	190.80	238.50	286.20	333.90	381.60	429.30	477.00
1909	11.93	23.86	47.72	95.45	143.17	190.90	238.62	286.35	334.07	381.80	429.52	477.25
1910	11.94	23.87	47.75	95.50	143.25	191.00	238.75	286.50	334.25	382.00	429.75	477.50
1911	11.94	23.89	47.77	95.55	143.32	191.10	238.87	286.65	334.42	382.20	429.97	477.75
1912	11.95	23.90	47.80	95.60	143.40	191.20	239.00	286.80	334.60	382.40	430.20	478.00
1913	11.96	23.91	47.82	95.65	143.47	191.30	239.12	286.95	334.77	382.60	430.42	478.25
1914	11.96	23.92	47.85	95.70	143.55	191.40	239.25	287.10	334.95	382.80	430.65	478.50
1915	11.97	23.94	47.87	95.75	143.62	191.50	239.37	287.25	335.12	383.00	430.87	478.75
1916	11.97	23.95	47.90	95.80	143.70	191.60	239.50	287.40	335.30	383.20	431.10	479.00
1917	11.98	23.96	47.92	95.85	143.77	191.70	239.62	287.55	335.47	383.40	431.32	479.25
1918	11.99	23.97	47.95	95.90	143.85	191.80	239.75	287.70	335.65	383.60	431.55	479.50
1919	11.99	23.99	47.97	95.95	143.92	191.90	239.87	287.85	335.82	383.80	431.77	479.75
1920	12.00	24.00	48.00	96.00	144.00	192.00	240.00	288.00	336.00	384.00	432.00	480.00
1921	12.01	24.01	48.02	96.05	144.07	192.10	240.12	288.15	336.17	384.20	432.22	480.25
1922	12.01	24.02	48.05	96.10	144.15	192.20	240.25	288.30	336.35	384.40	432.45	480.50
1923	12.02	24.04	48.07	96.15	144.22	192.30	240.37	288.45	336.52	384.60	432.67	480.75
1924	12.02	24.05	48.10	96.20	144.30	192.40	240.50	288.60	336.70	384.80	432.90	481.00
1925	12.03	24.06	48.12	96.25	144.37	192.50	240.62	288.75	336.87	385.00	433.12	481.25
1926	12.04	24.07	48.15	96.30	144.45	192.60	240.75	288.90	337.05	385.20	433.35	481.50
1927	12.04	24.09	48.17	96.35	144.52	192.70	240.87	289.05	337.22	385.40	433.57	481.75
1928	12.05	24.10	48.20	96.40	144.60	192.80	241.00	289.20	337.40	385.60	433.80	482.00
1929	12.06	24.11	48.22	96.45	144.67	192.90	241.12	289.35	337.57	385.80	434.02	482.25
1930	12.06	24.12	48.25	96.50	144.75	193.00	241.25	289.50	337.75	386.00	434.25	482.50
1931	12.07	24.14	48.27	96.55	144.82	193.10	241.37	289.65	337.92	386.20	434.47	482.75
1932	12.07	24.15	48.30	96.60	144.90	193.20	241.50	289.80	338.10	386.40	434.70	483.00
1933	12.08	24.16	48.32	96.65	144.97	193.30	241.62	289.95	338.27	386.60	434.92	483.25
1934	12.09	24.17	48.35	96.70	145.05	193.40	241.75	290.10	338.45	386.80	435.15	483.50
1935	12.09	24.19	48.37	96.75	145.12	193.50	241.87	290.25	338.62	387.00	435.37	483.75
1936	12.10	24.20	48.40	96.80	145.20	193.60	242.00	290.40	338.80	387.20	435.60	484.00
1937	12.11	24.21	48.42	96.85	145.27	193.70	242.12	290.55	338.97	387.40	435.82	484.25
1938	12.11	24.22	48.45	96.90	145.35	193.80	242.25	290.70	339.15	387.60	436.05	484.50
1939	12.12	24.24	48.47	96.95	145.42	193.90	242.37	290.85	339.32	387.80	436.27	484.75
1940	12.12	24.25	48.50	97.00	145.50	194.00	242.50	291.00	339.50	388.00	436.50	485.00
1941	12.13	24.26	48.52	97.05	145.57	194.10	242.62	291.15	339.67	388.20	436.72	485.25
1942	12.14	24.27	48.55	97.10	145.65	194.20	242.75	291.30	339.85	388.40	436.95	485.50
1943	12.14	24.29	48.57	97.15	145.72	194.30	242.87	291.45	340.02	388.60	437.17	485.75
1944	12.15	24.30	48.60	97.20	145.80	194.40	243.00	291.60	340.20	388.80	437.40	486.00
1945	12.16	24.31	48.62	97.25	145.87	194.50	243.12	291.75	340.37	389.00	437.62	486.25
1946	12.16	24.32	48.65	97.30	145.95	194.60	243.25	291.90	340.55	389.20	437.85	486.50
1947	12.17	24.34	48.67	97.35	146.02	194.70	243.37	292.05	340.72	389.40	438.07	486.75
1948	12.17	24.35	48.70	97.40	146.10	194.80	243.50	292.20	340.90	389.60	438.30	487.00
1949	12.18	24.36	48.72	97.45	146.17	194.90	243.62	292.35	341.07	389.80	438.52	487.25
1950	12.19	24.37	48.75	97.50	146.25	195.00	243.75	292.50	341.25	390.00	438.75	487.50

1950 FEET.

Per Ton,	$11	$12	$13	$14	$15	$16	$17	$18	$19	$20
Per Foot,	27½ cts.	30 cts.	32½ cts.	35 cts.	37½ cts.	40 cts.	42½ cts.	45 cts.	47½ cts.	50 cts.
Feet.										
1901	522.77	570.30	617.82	665.35	712.87	760.40	807.92	855.45	902.97	950.50
1902	523.05	570.60	618.15	665.70	713.25	760.80	808.35	855.90	903.45	951.00
1903	523.32	570.90	618.47	666.05	713.62	761.20	808.77	856.35	903.92	951.50
1904	523.60	571.20	618.80	666.40	714.00	761.60	809.20	856.80	904.40	952.00
1905	523.87	571.50	619.12	666.75	714.37	762.00	809.62	857.25	904.87	952.50
1906	524.15	571.80	619.45	667.10	714.75	762.40	810.05	857.70	905.35	953.00
1907	524.42	572.10	619.77	667.45	715.12	762.80	810.47	858.15	905.82	953.50
1908	524.70	572.40	620.10	667.80	715.50	763.20	810.90	858.60	906.30	954.00
1909	524.97	572.70	620.42	668.15	715.87	763.60	811.32	859.05	906.77	954.50
1910	525.25	573.00	620.75	668.50	716.25	764.00	811.75	859.50	907.25	955.00
1911	525.52	573.30	621.07	668.85	716.62	764.40	812.17	859.95	907.72	955.50
1912	525.80	573.60	621.40	669.20	717.00	764.80	812.60	860.40	908.20	956.00
1913	526.07	573.90	621.72	669.55	717.37	765.20	813.02	860.85	908.67	956.50
1914	526.35	574.20	622.05	669.90	717.75	765.60	813.45	861.30	909.15	957.00
1915	526.62	574.50	622.37	670.25	718.12	766.00	813.87	861.75	909.62	957.50
1916	526.90	574.80	622.70	670.60	718.50	766.40	814.30	862.20	910.10	958.00
1917	527.17	575.10	623.02	670.95	718.87	766.80	814.72	862.65	910.57	958.50
1918	527.45	575.40	623.35	671.30	719.25	767.20	815.15	863.10	911.05	959.00
1919	527.72	575.70	623.67	671.65	719.62	767.60	815.57	863.55	911.52	959.50
1920	528.00	576.00	624.00	672.00	720.00	768.00	816.00	864.00	912.00	960.00
1921	528.27	576.30	624.32	672.35	720.37	768.40	816.42	864.45	912.47	960.50
1922	528.55	576.60	624.65	672.70	720.75	768.80	816.85	864.90	912.95	961.00
1923	528.82	576.90	624.97	673.05	721.12	769.20	817.27	865.35	913.42	961.50
1924	529.10	577.20	625.30	673.40	721.50	769.60	817.70	865.80	913.90	962.00
1925	529.37	577.50	625.62	673.75	721.87	770.00	818.12	866.25	914.37	962.50
1926	529.65	577.80	625.95	674.10	722.25	770.40	818.55	866.70	914.85	963.00
1927	529.92	578.10	626.27	674.45	722.62	770.80	818.97	867.15	915.32	963.50
1928	530.20	578.40	626.60	674.80	723.00	771.20	819.40	867.60	915.80	964.00
1929	530.47	578.70	626.92	675.15	723.37	771.60	819.82	868.05	916.27	964.50
1930	530.75	579.00	627.25	675.50	723.75	772.00	820.25	868.50	916.75	965.00
1931	531.02	579.30	627.57	675.85	724.12	772.40	820.67	868.95	917.22	965.50
1932	531.30	579.60	627.90	676.20	724.50	772.80	821.10	869.40	917.70	966.00
1933	531.57	579.90	628.22	676.55	724.87	773.20	821.52	869.85	918.17	966.50
1934	531.85	580.20	628.55	676.90	725.25	773.60	821.95	870.30	918.65	967.00
1935	532.12	580.50	628.87	677.25	725.62	774.00	822.37	870.75	919.12	967.50
1936	532.40	580.80	629.20	677.60	726.00	774.40	822.80	871.20	919.60	968.00
1937	532.67	581.10	629.52	677.95	726.37	774.80	823.22	871.65	920.07	968.50
1938	532.95	581.40	629.85	678.30	726.75	775.20	823.65	872.10	920.55	969.00
1939	533.22	581.70	630.17	678.65	727.12	775.60	824.07	872.55	921.02	969.50
1940	533.50	582.00	630.50	679.00	727.50	776.00	824.50	873.00	921.50	970.00
1941	533.77	582.30	630.82	679.35	727.87	776.40	824.92	873.45	921.97	970.50
1942	534.05	582.60	631.15	679.70	728.25	776.80	825.35	873.90	922.45	971.00
1943	534.32	582.90	631.47	680.05	728.62	777.20	825.77	874.35	922.92	971.50
1944	534.60	583.20	631.80	680.40	729.00	777.60	826.20	874.80	923.40	972.00
1945	534.87	583.50	632.12	680.75	729.37	778.00	826.62	875.25	923.87	972.50
1946	535.15	583.80	632.45	681.10	729.75	778.40	827.05	875.70	924.35	973.00
1947	535.42	584.10	632.77	681.45	730.12	778.80	827.47	876.15	924.82	973.50
1948	535.70	584.40	633.10	681.80	730.50	779.20	827.90	876.60	925.30	974.00
1949	535.97	584.70	633.42	682.15	730.87	779.60	828.32	877.05	925.77	974.50
1950	536.25	585.00	633.75	682.50	731.25	780.00	828.75	877.50	926.25	975.00

2000 FEET.

Per Ton, Per Foot,	25c.	50c.	$1 2½ cts.	$2 5 cts.	$3 7½ cts.	$4 10 cts.	$5 12½ cts.	$6 15 cts.	$7 17½ cts.	$8 20 cts.	$9 22½ cts.	$10 25 cts.
Feet.												
1951	12.19	24.39	48.77	97.55	146.32	195.10	243.87	292.65	341.42	390.20	438.97	487.75
1952	12.20	24.40	48.80	97.60	146.40	195.20	244.00	292.80	341.60	390.40	439.20	488.00
1953	12.21	24.41	48.82	97.65	146.47	195.30	244.12	292.95	341.77	390.60	439.42	488.25
1954	12.21	24.42	48.85	97.70	146.55	195.40	244.25	293.10	341.95	390.80	439.65	488.50
1955	12.22	24.44	48.87	97.75	146.62	195.50	244.37	293.25	342.12	391.00	439.87	488.75
1956	12.22	24.45	48.90	97.80	146.70	195.60	244.50	293.40	342.30	391.20	440.10	489.00
1957	12.23	24.46	48.92	97.85	146.77	195.70	244.62	293.55	342.47	391.40	440.32	489.25
1958	12.24	24.47	48.95	97.90	146.85	195.80	244.75	293.70	342.65	391.60	440.55	489.50
1959	12.24	24.49	48.97	97.95	146.92	195.90	244.87	293.85	342.82	391.80	440.77	489.75
1960	12.25	24.50	49.00	98.00	147.00	196.00	245.00	294.00	343.00	392.00	441.00	490.00
1961	12.26	24.51	49.02	98.05	147.07	196.10	245.12	294.15	343.17	392.20	441.22	490.25
1962	12.26	24.52	49.05	98.10	147.15	196.20	245.25	294.30	343.35	392.40	441.45	490.50
1963	12.27	24.54	49.07	98.15	147.22	196.30	245.37	294.45	343.52	392.60	441.67	490.75
1964	12.27	24.55	49.10	98.20	147.30	196.40	245.50	294.60	343.70	392.80	441.90	491.00
1965	12.28	24.56	49.12	98.25	147.37	196.50	245.62	294.75	343.87	393.00	442.12	491.25
1966	12.29	24.57	49.15	98.30	147.45	196.60	245.75	294.90	344.05	393.20	442.35	491.50
1967	12.29	24.59	49.17	98.35	147.52	196.70	245.87	295.05	344.22	393.40	442.57	491.75
1968	12.30	24.60	49.20	98.40	147.60	196.80	246.00	295.20	344.40	393.60	442.80	492.00
1969	12.31	24.61	49.22	98.45	147.67	196.90	246.12	295.35	344.57	393.80	443.02	492.25
1970	12.31	24.62	49.25	98.50	147.75	197.00	246.25	295.50	344.75	394.00	443.25	492.50
1971	12.32	24.64	49.27	98.55	147.82	197.10	246.37	295.65	344.92	394.20	443.47	492.75
1972	12.32	24.65	49.30	98.60	147.90	197.20	246.50	295.80	345.10	394.40	443.70	493.00
1973	12.33	24.66	49.32	98.65	147.97	197.30	246.62	295.95	345.27	394.60	443.92	493.25
1974	12.34	24.67	49.35	98.70	148.05	197.40	246.75	296.10	345.45	394.80	444.15	493.50
1975	12.34	24.69	49.37	98.75	148.12	197.50	246.87	296.25	345.62	395.00	444.37	493.75
1976	12.35	24.70	49.40	98.80	148.20	197.60	247.00	296.40	345.80	395.20	444.60	494.00
1977	12.36	24.71	49.42	98.85	148.27	197.70	247.12	296.55	345.97	395.40	444.82	494.25
1978	12.36	24.72	49.45	98.90	148.35	197.80	247.25	296.70	346.15	395.60	445.05	494.50
1979	12.37	24.74	49.47	98.95	148.42	197.90	247.37	296.85	346.32	395.80	445.27	494.75
1980	12.37	24.75	49.50	99.00	148.50	198.00	247.50	297.00	346.50	396.00	445.50	495.00
1981	12.38	24.76	49.52	99.05	148.57	198.10	247.62	297.15	346.67	396.20	445.72	495.25
1982	12.39	24.77	49.55	99.10	148.65	198.20	247.75	297.30	346.85	396.40	445.95	495.50
1983	12.39	24.79	49.57	99.15	148.72	198.30	247.87	297.45	347.02	396.60	446.17	495.75
1984	12.40	24.80	49.60	99.20	148.80	198.40	248.00	297.60	347.20	396.80	446.40	496.00
1985	12.41	24.81	49.62	99.25	148.87	198.50	248.12	297.75	347.37	397.00	446.62	496.25
1986	12.41	24.82	49.65	99.30	148.95	198.60	248.25	297.90	347.55	397.20	446.85	496.50
1987	12.42	24.84	49.67	99.35	149.02	198.70	248.37	298.05	347.72	397.40	447.07	496.75
1988	12.42	24.85	49.70	99.40	149.10	198.80	248.50	298.20	347.90	397.60	447.30	497.00
1989	12.43	24.86	49.72	99.45	149.17	198.90	248.62	298.35	348.07	397.80	447.52	497.25
1990	12.44	24.87	49.75	99.50	149.25	199.00	248.75	298.50	348.25	398.00	447.75	497.50
1991	12.44	24.89	49.77	99.55	149.32	199.10	248.87	298.65	348.42	398.20	447.97	497.75
1992	12.45	24.90	49.80	99.60	149.40	199.20	249.00	298.80	348.60	398.40	448.20	498.00
1993	12.46	24.91	49.82	99.65	149.47	199.30	249.12	298.95	348.77	398.60	448.42	498.25
1994	12.46	24.92	49.85	99.70	149.55	199.40	249.25	299.10	348.95	398.80	448.65	498.50
1995	12.47	24.94	49.87	99.75	149.62	199.50	249.37	299.25	349.12	399.00	448.87	498.75
1996	12.47	24.95	49.90	99.80	149.70	199.60	249.50	299.40	349.20	399.20	449.10	499.00
1997	12.48	24.96	49.92	99.85	149.77	199.70	249.62	299.55	349.47	399.40	449.32	499.25
1998	12.49	24.97	49.95	99.90	149.85	199.80	249.75	299.70	349.65	399.60	449.55	499.50
1999	12.49	24.99	49.97	99.95	149.92	199.90	249.87	299.85	349.82	399.80	449.77	499.75
2000	12.50	25.00	50.00	100.00	150.00	200.00	250.00	300.00	350.00	400.00	450.00	500.00

2000 FEET.

Per Ton, Per Foot, Feet.	$11 27½ cts.	$12 30 cts.	$13 32½ cts.	$14 35 cts.	$15 37½ cts.	$16 40 cts.	$17 42½ cts.	$18 45 cts.	$19 47½ cts.	$20 50 cts.
1951	536.52	585.30	634.07	682.85	731.62	780.40	829.17	877.95	926.72	975.50
1952	536.80	585.60	634.40	683.20	732.00	780.80	829.60	878.40	927.20	976.00
1953	537.07	585.90	634.72	683.55	732.37	781.20	830.02	878.85	927.67	976.50
1954	537.35	586.20	635.05	683.90	732.75	781.60	830.45	879.30	928.15	977.00
1955	537.62	586.50	635.37	684.25	733.12	782.00	830.87	879.75	928.62	977.50
1956	537.90	586.80	635.70	684.60	733.50	782.40	831.30	880.20	929.10	978.00
1957	538.17	587.10	636.02	684.95	733.87	782.80	831.72	880.65	929.57	978.50
1958	538.45	587.40	636.35	685.30	734.25	783.20	832.15	881.10	930.05	979.00
1959	538.72	587.70	636.67	685.65	734.62	783.60	832.57	881.55	930.52	979.50
1960	539.00	588.00	637.00	686.00	735.00	784.00	833.00	882.00	931.00	980.00
1961	539.27	588.30	637.32	686.35	735.37	784.40	833.42	882.45	931.47	980.50
1962	539.55	588.60	637.65	686.70	735.75	784.80	833.85	882.90	931.95	981.00
1963	539.82	588.90	637.97	687.05	736.12	785.20	834.27	883.35	932.42	981.50
1964	540.10	589.20	638.30	687.40	736.50	785.60	834.70	883.80	932.90	982.00
1965	540.37	589.50	638.62	687.75	736.87	786.00	835.12	884.25	933.37	982.50
1966	540.65	589.80	638.95	688.10	737.25	786.40	835.55	884.70	933.85	983.00
1967	540.92	590.10	639.27	688.45	737.62	786.80	835.97	885.15	934.32	983.50
1968	541.20	590.40	639.60	688.80	738.00	787.20	836.40	885.60	934.80	984.00
1969	541.47	590.70	639.92	689.15	738.37	787.60	836.82	836.05	935.27	984.50
1970	541.75	591.00	640.25	689.50	738.75	788.00	837.25	886.50	935.75	985.00
1971	542.02	591.30	640.57	689.85	739.12	788.40	837.67	886.95	936.22	985.50
1972	542.30	591.60	640.90	690.20	739.50	788.80	838.10	887.40	936.70	986.00
1973	542.57	591.90	641.22	690.55	739.87	789.20	838.52	887.85	937.17	986.50
1974	542.85	592.20	641.55	690.90	740.25	789.60	838.95	888.30	937.65	987.00
1975	543.12	592.50	641.87	691.25	740.62	790.00	839.37	888.75	938.12	987.50
1976	543.40	592.80	642.20	691.60	741.00	790.40	839.80	889.20	938.60	988.00
1977	543.67	593.10	642.52	691.95	741.37	790.80	840.22	889.65	939.07	988.50
1978	543.95	593.40	642.85	692.30	741.75	791.20	840.65	890.10	939.55	989.00
1979	544.22	593.70	643.17	692.65	742.12	791.60	841.07	890.55	940.02	989.50
1980	544.50	594.00	643.50	693.00	742.50	792.00	841.50	891.00	940.50	990.00
1981	544.77	594.30	643.82	693.35	742.87	792.40	841.92	891.45	940.97	990.50
1982	545.05	594.60	644.15	693.70	743.25	792.80	842.35	891.90	941.45	991.00
1983	545.32	594.90	644.47	694.05	743.62	793.20	842.77	892.35	941.92	991.50
1984	545.60	595.20	644.80	694.40	744.00	793.60	843.20	892.80	942.40	992.00
1985	545.87	595.50	645.12	694.75	744.37	794.00	843.62	893.25	942.87	992.50
1986	546.15	595.80	645.45	695.10	744.75	794.40	844.05	893.70	943.35	993.00
1987	546.42	596.10	645.77	695.45	745.12	794.80	844.47	894.15	943.82	993.50
1988	546.70	596.40	646.10	695.80	745.50	795.20	844.90	894.60	944.30	994.00
1989	546.97	596.70	646.42	696.15	745.87	795.60	845.32	895.05	944.77	994.50
1990	547.25	597.00	646.75	696.50	746.25	796.00	845.75	895.50	945.25	995.00
1991	547.52	597.30	647.07	696.85	746.62	796.40	846.17	895.95	945.72	995.50
1992	547.80	597.60	647.40	697.20	747.00	796.80	846.60	896.40	946.20	996.00
1993	548.07	597.90	647.72	697.55	747.37	797.20	847.02	896.85	946.67	996.50
1994	548.35	598.20	648.05	697.90	747.75	797.60	847.45	897.30	947.15	997.00
1995	548.62	598.50	648.37	698.25	748.12	798.00	847.87	897.75	947.62	997.50
1996	548.90	598.80	648.70	698.60	748.50	798.40	848.30	898.20	948.10	998.00
1997	549.17	599.10	649.02	698.95	748.87	798.80	848.72	898.65	948.57	998.50
1998	549.45	599.40	649.35	699.30	749.25	799.20	849.15	899.10	949.05	999.00
1999	549.72	599.70	649.67	699.65	749.62	799.60	849.57	899.55	949.52	999.50
2000	550.00	600.00	650.00	700.00	750.00	800.00	850.00	900.00	950.00	1000.00

2050 FEET.

Per Ton,	25c.	50c.	$1	$2	$3	$4	$5	$6	$7	$8	$9	$10
Per Foot,			2¼ cts.	5 cts.	7½ cts.	10 cts.	12½ cts.	15 cts.	17½ cts.	20 cts.	22½ cts.	25 cts.
Feet.												
2001	12.51	25.01	50.02	100.05	150.07	200.10	250.12	300.15	350.17	400.20	450.22	500.25
2002	12.51	25.02	50.05	100.10	150.15	200.20	250.25	300.30	350.35	400.40	450.45	500.50
2003	12.52	25.04	50.07	100.15	150.22	200.30	250.37	300.45	350.52	400.60	450.67	500.75
2004	12.52	25.05	50.10	100.20	150.30	200.40	250.50	300.60	350.70	400.80	450.90	501.00
2005	12.53	25.06	50.12	100.25	150.37	200.50	250.62	300.75	350.87	401.00	451.12	501.25
2006	12.54	25.07	50.15	100.30	150.45	200.60	250.75	300.90	351.05	401.20	451.35	501.50
2007	12.54	25.09	50.17	100.35	150.52	200.70	250.87	301.05	351.22	401.40	451.57	501.75
2008	12.55	25.10	50.20	100.40	150.60	200.80	251.00	301.20	351.40	401.60	451.80	502.00
2009	12.56	25.11	50.22	100.45	150.67	200.90	251.12	301.35	351.57	401.80	452.02	502.25
2010	12.56	25.12	50.25	100.50	150.75	201.00	251.25	301.50	351.75	402.00	452.25	502.50
2011	12.57	25.14	50.27	100.55	150.82	201.10	251.37	301.65	351.92	402.20	452.47	502.75
2012	12.57	25.15	50.30	100.60	150.90	201.20	251.50	301.80	352.10	402.40	452.70	503.00
2013	12.58	25.16	50.32	100.65	150.97	201.30	251.62	301.95	352.27	402.60	452.92	503.25
2014	12.59	25.17	50.35	100.70	151.05	201.40	251.75	302.10	352.45	402.80	453.15	503.50
2015	12.59	25.19	50.37	100.75	151.12	201.50	251.87	302.25	352.62	403.00	453.37	503.75
2016	12.60	25.20	50.40	100.80	151.20	201.60	252.00	302.40	352.80	403.20	453.60	504.00
2017	12.61	25.21	50.42	100.85	151.27	201.70	252.12	302.55	352.97	403.40	453.82	504.25
2018	12.61	25.22	50.45	100.90	151.35	201.80	252.25	302.70	353.15	403.60	454.05	504.50
2019	12.62	25.24	50.47	100.95	151.42	201.90	252.37	302.85	353.32	403.80	454.27	504.75
2020	12.62	25.25	50.50	101.00	151.50	202.00	252.50	303.00	353.50	404.00	454.50	505.00
2021	12.63	25.26	50.52	101.05	151.57	202.10	252.62	303.15	353.67	404.20	454.72	505.25
2022	12.64	25.27	50.55	101.10	151.65	202.20	252.75	303.30	353.85	404.40	454.95	505.50
2023	12.64	25.29	50.57	101.15	151.72	202.30	252.87	303.45	354.02	404.60	455.17	505.75
2024	12.65	25.30	50.60	101.20	151.80	202.40	253.00	303.60	354.20	404.80	455.40	506.00
2025	12.66	25.31	50.62	101.25	151.87	202.50	253.12	303.75	354.37	405.00	455.62	506.25
2026	12.66	25.32	50.65	101.30	151.95	202.60	253.25	303.90	354.55	405.20	455.85	506.50
2027	12.67	25.34	50.67	101.35	152.02	202.70	253.37	304.05	354.72	405.40	456.07	506.75
2028	12.67	25.35	50.70	101.40	152.10	202.80	253.50	304.20	354.90	405.60	456.30	507.00
2029	12.68	25.36	50.72	101.45	152.17	202.90	253.62	304.35	355.07	405.80	456.52	507.25
2030	12.69	25.37	50.75	101.50	152.25	203.00	253.75	304.50	355.25	406.00	456.75	507.50
2031	12.69	25.39	50.77	101.55	152.32	203.10	253.87	304.65	355.42	406.20	456.97	507.75
2032	12.70	25.40	50.80	101.60	152.40	203.20	254.00	304.80	355.60	406.40	457.20	508.00
2033	12.71	25.41	50.82	101.65	152.47	203.30	254.12	304.95	355.77	406.60	457.42	508.25
2034	12.71	25.42	50.85	101.70	152.55	203.40	254.25	305.10	355.95	406.80	457.65	508.50
2035	12.72	25.44	50.87	101.75	152.62	203.50	254.37	305.25	356.12	407.00	457.87	508.75
2036	12.72	25.45	50.90	101.80	152.70	203.60	254.50	305.40	356.30	407.20	458.10	509.00
2037	12.73	25.46	50.92	101.85	152.77	203.70	254.62	305.55	356.47	407.40	458.32	509.25
2038	12.74	25.47	50.95	101.90	152.85	203.80	254.75	305.70	356.65	407.60	458.55	509.50
2039	12.74	25.49	50.97	101.95	152.92	203.90	254.87	305.85	356.82	407.80	458.77	509.75
2040	12.75	25.50	51.00	102.00	153.00	204.00	255.00	306.00	357.00	408.00	459.00	510.00
2041	12.76	25.51	51.02	102.05	153.07	204.10	255.12	306.15	357.17	408.20	459.22	510.25
2042	12.76	25.52	51.05	102.10	153.15	204.20	255.25	306.30	357.35	408.40	459.45	510.50
2043	12.77	25.54	51.07	102.15	153.22	204.30	255.37	306.45	357.52	408.60	459.67	510.75
2044	12.77	25.55	51.10	102.20	153.30	204.40	255.50	306.60	357.70	408.80	459.90	511.00
2045	12.78	25.56	51.12	102.25	153.37	204.50	255.62	306.75	357.87	409.00	460.12	511.25
2046	12.79	25.57	51.15	102.30	153.45	204.60	255.75	306.90	358.05	409.20	460.35	511.50
2047	12.79	25.59	51.17	102.35	153.52	204.70	255.87	307.05	358.22	409.40	460.57	511.75
2048	12.80	25.60	51.20	102.40	153.60	204.80	256.00	307.20	358.40	409.60	460.80	512.00
2049	12.81	25.61	51.22	102.45	153.67	204.90	256.12	307.35	358.57	409.80	461.02	512.25
2050	12.81	25.62	51.25	102.50	153.75	205.00	256.25	307.50	358.75	410.00	461.25	512.50

2050 FEET.

Per Ton, / Per Foot,	$11 / 27½ cts.	$12 / 30 cts.	$13 / 32½ cts.	$14 / 35 cts.	$15 / 37½ cts.	$16 / 40 cts.	$17 / 42½ cts.	$18 / 45 cts.	$19 / 47½ cts.	$20 / 50 cts.
Feet.										
2001	550.27	600.30	650.32	700.35	750.37	800.40	850.42	900.45	950.47	1000.50
2002	550.55	600.60	650.65	700.70	750.75	800.80	850.85	900.90	950.95	1001.00
2003	550.82	600.90	650.97	701.05	751.12	801.20	851.27	901.35	951.42	1001.50
2004	551.10	601.20	651.30	701.40	751.50	801.60	851.70	901.80	951.90	1002.00
2005	551.37	601.50	651.62	701.75	751.87	802.00	852.12	902.25	952.37	1002.50
2006	551.65	601.80	651.95	702.10	752.25	802.40	852.55	902.70	952.85	1003.00
2007	551.92	602.10	652.27	702.45	752.62	802.80	852.97	903.15	953.32	1003.50
2008	552.20	602.40	652.60	702.80	753.00	803.20	853.40	903.60	953.80	1004.00
2009	552.47	602.70	652.92	703.15	753.37	803.60	853.82	904.05	954.27	1004.50
2010	552.75	603.00	653.25	703.50	753.75	804.00	854.25	904.50	954.75	1005.00
2011	553.02	603.30	653.57	703.85	754.12	804.40	854.67	904.95	955.22	1005.50
2012	553.30	603.60	653.90	704.20	754.50	804.80	855.10	905.40	955.70	1006.00
2013	553.57	603.90	654.22	704.55	754.87	805.20	855.52	905.85	956.17	1006.50
2014	553.85	604.20	654.55	704.90	755.25	805.60	855.95	906.30	956.65	1007.00
2015	554.12	604.50	654.87	705.25	755.62	806.00	856.37	906.75	957.12	1007.50
2016	554.40	604.80	655.20	705.60	756.00	806.40	856.80	907.20	957.60	1008.00
2017	554.67	605.10	655.52	705.95	756.37	806.80	857.22	907.65	958.07	1008.50
2018	554.95	605.40	655.85	706.30	756.75	807.20	857.65	908.10	958.55	1009.00
2019	555.22	605.70	656.17	706.65	757.12	807.60	858.07	908.55	959.02	1009.50
2020	555.50	606.00	656.50	707.00	757.50	808.00	858.50	909.00	959.50	1010.00
2021	555.77	606.30	656.82	707.35	757.87	808.40	858.92	909.45	959.97	1010.50
2022	556.05	606.60	657.15	707.70	758.25	808.80	859.35	909.90	960.45	1011.00
2023	556.32	606.90	657.47	708.05	758.62	809.20	859.77	910.35	960.92	1011.50
2024	556.60	607.20	657.80	708.40	759.00	809.60	860.20	910.80	961.40	1012.00
2025	556.87	607.50	658.12	708.75	759.37	810.00	860.62	911.25	961.87	1012.50
2026	557.15	607.80	658.45	709.10	759.75	810.40	861.05	911.70	962.35	1013.00
2027	557.42	608.10	658.77	709.45	760.12	810.80	861.47	912.15	962.82	1013.50
2028	557.70	608.40	659.10	709.80	760.50	811.20	861.90	912.60	963.30	1014.00
2029	557.97	608.70	659.42	710.15	760.87	811.60	862.32	913.05	963.77	1014.50
2030	558.25	609.00	659.75	710.50	761.25	812.00	862.75	913.50	964.25	1015.00
2031	558.52	609.30	660.07	710.85	761.62	812.40	863.17	913.95	964.72	1015.50
2032	558.80	609.60	660.40	711.20	762.00	812.80	863.60	914.40	965.20	1016.00
2033	559.07	609.90	660.72	711.55	762.37	813.20	864.02	914.85	965.67	1016.50
2034	559.35	610.20	661.05	711.90	762.75	813.60	864.45	915.30	966.15	1017.00
2035	559.62	610.50	661.37	712.25	763.12	814.00	864.87	915.75	966.62	1017.50
2036	559.90	610.80	661.70	712.60	763.50	814.40	865.30	916.20	967.10	1018.00
2037	560.17	611.10	662.02	712.95	763.87	814.80	865.72	916.65	967.57	1018.50
2038	560.45	611.40	662.35	713.30	764.25	815.20	866.15	917.10	968.05	1019.00
2039	560.72	611.70	662.67	713.65	764.62	815.60	866.57	917.55	968.52	1019.50
2040	561.00	612.00	663.00	714.00	765.00	816.00	867.00	918.00	969.00	1020.00
2041	561.27	612.30	663.32	714.35	765.37	816.40	867.42	918.45	969.47	1020.50
2042	561.55	612.60	663.65	714.70	765.75	816.80	867.85	918.90	969.95	1021.00
2043	561.82	612.90	663.97	715.05	766.12	817.20	868.27	919.35	970.42	1021.50
2044	562.10	613.20	664.30	715.40	766.50	817.60	868.70	919.80	970.90	1022.00
2045	562.37	613.50	664.62	715.75	766.87	818.00	869.12	920.25	971.37	1022.50
2046	562.65	613.80	664.95	716.10	767.25	818.40	869.55	920.70	971.85	1023.00
2047	562.92	614.10	665.27	716.45	767.62	818.80	869.97	921.15	972.32	1023.50
2048	563.20	614.40	665.60	716.80	768.00	819.20	870.40	921.60	972.80	1024.00
2049	563.47	614.70	665.92	717.15	768.37	819.60	870.82	922.05	973.27	1024.50
2050	563.75	615.00	666.25	717.50	768.75	820.00	871.25	922.50	973.75	1025.00

2100 FEET.

Per Ton, Per Foot, Feet.	25c.	50c.	$1 2½ cts.	$2 5 cts.	$3 7½ cts.	$4 10 cts.	$5 12½ cts.	$6 15 cts.	$7 17½ cts.	$8 20 cts.	$9 22½ cts.	$10 25 cts.
2051	12.82	25.64	51.27	102.55	153.82	205.10	256.37	307.65	358.92	410.20	461.47	512.75
2052	12.82	25.65	51.30	102.60	153.90	205.20	256.50	307.80	359.10	410.40	461.70	513.00
2053	12.83	25.66	51.32	102.65	153.97	205.30	256.62	307.95	359.27	410.60	461.92	513.25
2054	12.84	25.67	51.35	102.70	154.05	205.40	256.75	308.10	359.45	410.80	462.15	513.50
2055	12.84	25.69	51.37	102.75	154.12	205.50	256.87	308.25	359.62	411.00	462.37	513.75
2056	12.85	25.70	51.40	102.80	154.20	205.60	257.00	308.40	359.80	411.20	462.60	514.00
2057	12.86	25.71	51.42	102.85	154.27	205.70	257.12	308.55	359.97	411.40	462.82	514.25
2058	12.86	25.72	51.45	102.90	154.35	205.80	257.25	308.70	360.15	411.60	463.05	514.50
2059	12.87	25.74	51.47	102.95	154.42	205.90	257.37	308.85	360.32	411.80	463.27	514.75
2060	12.87	25.75	51.50	103.00	154.50	206.00	257.50	309.00	360.50	412.00	463.50	515.00
2061	12.88	25.76	51.52	103.05	154.57	206.10	257.62	309.15	360.67	412.20	463.72	515.25
2062	12.89	25.77	51.55	103.10	154.65	206.20	257.75	309.30	360.85	412.40	463.95	515.50
2063	12.89	25.79	51.57	103.15	154.72	206.30	257.87	309.45	361.02	412.60	464.17	515.75
2064	12.90	25.80	51.60	103.20	154.80	206.40	258.00	309.60	361.20	412.80	464.40	516.00
2065	12.91	25.81	51.62	103.25	154.87	206.50	258.12	309.75	361.37	413.00	464.62	516.25
2066	12.91	25.82	51.65	103.30	154.95	206.60	258.25	309.90	361.55	413.20	464.85	516.50
2067	12.92	25.84	51.67	103.35	155.02	206.70	258.37	310.05	361.72	413.40	465.07	516.75
2068	12.92	25.85	51.70	103.40	155.10	206.80	258.50	310.20	361.90	413.60	465.30	517.00
2069	12.93	25.86	51.72	103.45	155.17	206.90	258.62	310.35	362.07	413.80	465.52	517.25
2070	12.94	25.87	51.75	103.50	155.25	207.00	258.75	310.50	362.25	414.00	465.75	517.50
2071	12.94	25.89	51.77	103.55	155.32	207.10	258.87	310.65	362.42	414.20	465.97	517.75
2072	12.95	25.90	51.80	103.60	155.40	207.20	259.00	310.80	362.60	414.40	466.20	518.00
2073	12.96	25.91	51.82	103.65	155.47	207.30	259.12	310.95	362.77	414.60	466.42	518.25
2074	12.96	25.92	51.85	103.70	155.55	207.40	259.25	311.10	362.95	414.80	466.65	518.50
2075	12.97	25.94	51.87	103.75	155.62	207.50	259.37	311.25	363.12	415.00	466.87	518.75
2076	12.97	25.95	51.90	103.80	155.70	207.60	259.50	311.40	363.30	415.20	467.10	519.00
2077	12.98	25.96	51.92	103.85	155.77	207.70	259.62	311.55	363.47	415.40	467.32	519.25
2078	12.99	25.97	51.95	103.90	155.85	207.80	259.75	311.70	363.65	415.60	467.55	519.50
2079	13.99	25.99	51.97	103.95	155.92	207.90	259.87	311.85	363.82	415.80	467.77	519.75
2080	13.00	26.00	52.00	104.00	156.00	208.00	260.00	312.00	364.00	416.00	468.00	520.00
2081	13.01	26.01	52.02	104.05	156.07	208.10	260.12	312.15	364.17	416.20	468.22	520.25
2082	13.01	26.02	52.05	104.10	156.15	208.20	260.25	312.30	364.35	416.40	468.45	520.50
2083	13.02	26.04	52.07	104.15	156.22	208.30	260.37	312.45	364.52	416.60	468.67	520.75
2084	13.02	26.05	52.10	104.20	156.30	208.40	260.50	312.60	364.70	416.80	468.90	521.00
2085	13.03	26.06	52.12	104.25	156.37	208.50	260.62	312.75	364.87	417.00	469.12	521.25
2086	13.04	26.07	52.15	104.30	156.45	208.60	260.75	312.90	365.05	417.20	469.35	521.50
2087	13.04	26.09	52.17	104.35	156.52	208.70	260.87	313.05	365.22	417.40	469.57	521.75
2088	13.05	26.10	52.20	104.40	156.60	208.80	261.00	313.20	365.40	417.60	469.80	522.00
2089	13.06	26.11	52.22	104.45	156.67	208.90	261.12	313.35	365.57	417.80	470.02	522.25
2090	13.06	26.12	52.25	104.50	156.75	209.00	261.25	313.50	365.75	418.00	470.25	522.50
2091	13.07	26.14	52.27	104.55	156.82	209.10	261.37	313.65	365.92	418.20	470.47	522.75
2092	13.07	26.15	52.30	104.60	156.90	209.20	261.50	313.80	366.10	418.40	470.70	523.00
2093	13.08	26.16	52.32	104.65	156.97	209.30	261.62	313.95	366.27	418.60	470.92	523.25
2094	13.09	26.17	52.35	104.70	157.05	209.40	261.75	314.10	366.45	418.80	471.15	523.50
2095	13.09	26.19	52.37	104.75	157.12	209.50	261.87	314.25	366.62	419.00	471.37	523.75
2096	13.10	26.20	52.40	104.80	157.20	209.60	262.00	314.40	366.80	419.20	471.60	524.00
2097	13.11	26.21	52.42	104.85	157.27	209.70	262.12	314.55	366.97	419.40	471.82	524.25
2098	13.11	26.22	52.45	104.90	157.35	209.80	262.25	314.70	367.15	419.60	472.05	524.50
2099	13.12	26.24	52.47	104.95	157.42	209.90	262.37	314.85	367.32	419.80	472.27	524.75
2100	13.12	26.25	52.50	105.00	157.50	210.00	262.50	315.00	367.50	420.00	472.50	525.00

2100 FEET.

Per Ton, / Per Foot, / Feet.	$11 / 27½ cts.	$12 / 30 cts.	$13 / 32½ cts.	$14 / 35 cts.	$15 / 37½ cts.	$16 / 40 cts.	$17 / 42½ cts.	$18 / 45 cts.	$19 / 47½ cts.	$20 / 50 cts.
2051	564.02	615.30	666.57	717.85	769.12	820.40	871.67	922.95	974.22	1025.50
2052	564.30	615.60	666.90	718.20	769.50	820.80	872.10	923.40	974.70	1026.00
2053	564.57	615.90	667.22	718.55	769.87	821.20	872.52	923.85	975.17	1026.50
2054	564.85	616.20	667.55	718.90	770.25	821.60	872.95	924.30	975.65	1027.00
2055	565.12	616.50	667.87	719.25	770.62	822.00	873.37	924.75	976.12	1027.50
2056	565.40	616.80	668.20	719.60	771.00	822.40	873.80	925.20	976.60	1028.00
2057	565.67	617.10	668.52	719.95	771.37	822.80	874.22	925.65	977.07	1028.50
2058	565.95	617.40	668.85	720.30	771.75	823.20	874.65	926.10	977.55	1029.00
2059	566.22	617.70	669.17	720.65	772.12	823.60	875.07	926.55	978.02	1029.50
2060	566.50	618.00	669.50	721.00	772.50	824.00	875.50	927.00	978.50	1030.00
2061	566.77	618.30	669.82	721.35	772.87	824.40	875.92	927.45	978.97	1030.50
2062	567.05	618.60	670.15	721.70	773.25	824.80	876.35	927.90	979.45	1031.00
2063	567.32	618.90	670.47	722.05	773.62	825.20	876.77	928.35	979.92	1031.50
2064	567.60	619.20	670.80	722.40	774.00	825.60	877.20	928.80	980.40	1032.00
2065	567.87	619.50	671.12	722.75	774.37	826.00	877.62	929.25	980.87	1032.50
2066	568.15	619.80	671.45	723.10	774.75	826.40	878.05	929.70	981.35	1033.00
2067	568.42	620.10	671.77	723.45	775.12	826.80	878.47	930.15	981.82	1033.50
2068	568.70	620.40	672.10	723.80	775.50	827.20	878.90	930.60	982.30	1034.00
2069	568.97	620.70	672.42	724.15	775.87	827.60	879.32	931.05	982.77	1034.50
2070	569.25	621.00	672.75	724.50	776.25	828.00	879.75	931.50	983.25	1035.00
2071	569.52	621.30	673.07	724.85	776.62	828.40	880.17	931.95	983.72	1035.50
2072	569.80	621.60	673.40	725.20	777.00	828.80	880.60	932.40	984.20	1036.00
2073	570.07	621.90	673.72	725.55	777.37	829.20	881.02	932.85	984.67	1036.50
2074	570.35	622.20	674.05	725.90	777.75	829.60	881.45	933.30	985.15	1037.00
2075	570.62	622.50	674.37	726.25	778.12	830.00	881.87	933.75	985.62	1037.50
2076	570.90	622.80	674.70	726.60	778.50	830.40	882.30	934.20	986.10	1038.00
2077	571.17	623.10	675.02	726.95	778.87	830.80	882.72	934.65	986.57	1038.50
2078	571.45	623.40	675.35	727.30	779.25	831.20	883.15	935.10	987.05	1039.00
2079	571.72	623.70	675.67	727.65	779.62	831.60	883.57	935.55	987.52	1039.50
2080	572.00	624.00	676.00	728.00	780.00	832.00	884.00	936.00	988.00	1040.00
2081	572.27	624.30	676.32	728.35	780.37	832.40	884.42	936.45	988.47	1040.50
2082	572.55	624.60	676.65	728.70	780.75	832.80	884.85	936.90	988.95	1041.00
2083	572.82	624.90	676.97	729.05	781.12	833.20	885.27	937.35	989.42	1041.50
2084	573.10	625.20	677.30	729.40	781.50	833.60	885.70	937.80	989.90	1042.00
2085	573.37	625.50	677.62	729.75	781.87	834.00	886.12	938.25	990.37	1042.50
2086	573.65	625.80	677.95	730.10	782.25	834.40	886.55	938.70	990.85	1043.00
2087	573.92	626.10	678.27	730.45	782.62	834.80	886.97	939.15	991.32	1043.50
2088	574.20	626.40	678.60	730.80	783.00	835.20	887.40	939.60	991.80	1044.00
2089	574.47	626.70	678.92	731.15	783.37	835.60	887.82	940.05	992.27	1044.50
2090	574.75	627.00	679.25	731.50	783.75	836.00	888.25	940.50	992.75	1045.00
2091	575.02	627.30	679.57	731.85	784.12	836.40	888.67	940.95	993.22	1045.50
2092	575.30	627.60	679.90	732.20	784.50	836.80	889.10	941.40	993.70	1046.00
2093	575.57	627.90	680.22	732.55	784.87	837.20	889.52	941.85	994.17	1046.50
2094	575.85	628.20	680.55	732.90	785.25	837.60	889.95	942.30	994.65	1047.00
2095	576.12	628.50	680.87	733.25	785.62	838.00	890.37	942.75	995.12	1047.50
2096	576.40	628.80	681.20	733.60	786.00	838.40	890.80	943.20	995.60	1048.00
2097	576.67	629.10	681.52	733.95	786.37	838.80	891.22	943.65	996.07	1048.50
2098	576.95	629.40	681.85	734.30	786.75	839.20	891.65	944.10	996.55	1049.00
2099	577.22	629.70	682.17	734.65	787.12	839.60	892.07	944.55	997.02	1049.50
2100	577.50	630.00	682.50	735.00	787.50	840.00	892.50	945.00	997.50	1050.00

Per Ton,	25c.	50c.	$1	$2	$3	$4	$5	$6	$7	$8	$9	$10
Per Foot,			2½ cts.	5 cts.	7½ cts.	10 cts.	12½ cts.	15 cts.	17½ cts.	20 cts.	22½ cts.	25 cts.
Feet.												
2101	13.13	26.26	52.52	105.05	157.57	210.10	262.62	315.15	367.67	420.20	472.72	525.25
2102	13.14	26.27	52.55	105.10	157.65	210.20	262.75	315.30	367.85	420.40	472.95	525.50
2103	13.14	26.29	52.57	105.15	157.72	210.30	262.87	315.45	368.02	420.60	473.17	525.75
2104	13.15	26.30	52.60	105.20	157.80	210.40	263.00	315.60	368.20	420.80	473.40	526.00
2105	13.16	26.31	52.62	105.25	157.87	210.50	263.12	315.75	368.37	421.00	473.62	526.25
2106	13.16	26.32	52.65	105.30	157.95	210.60	263.25	315.90	368.55	421.20	473.85	526.50
2107	13.17	26.34	52.67	105.35	158.02	210.70	263.37	316.05	368.72	421.40	474.07	526.75
2108	13.17	26.35	52.70	105.40	158.10	210.80	263.50	316.20	368.90	421.60	474.30	527.00
2109	13.18	26.36	52.72	105.45	158.17	210.90	263.62	316.35	369.07	421.80	474.52	527.25
2110	13.19	26.37	52.75	105.50	158.25	211.00	263.75	316.50	369.25	422.00	474.75	527.50
2111	13.19	26.39	52.77	105.55	158.32	211.10	263.87	316.65	369.42	422.20	474.97	527.75
2112	13.20	26.40	52.80	105.60	158.40	211.20	264.00	316.80	369.60	422.40	475.20	528.00
2113	13.21	26.41	52.82	105.65	158.47	211.30	264.12	316.95	369.77	422.60	475.42	528.25
2114	13.21	26.42	52.85	105.70	158.55	211.40	264.25	317.10	369.95	422.80	475.65	528.50
2115	13.22	26.44	52.87	105.75	158.62	211.50	264.37	317.25	370.12	423.00	475.87	528.75
2116	13.22	26.45	52.90	105.80	158.70	211.60	264.50	317.40	370.30	423.20	476.10	529.00
2117	13.23	26.46	52.92	105.85	158.77	211.70	264.62	317.55	370.47	423.40	476.32	529.25
2118	13.24	26.47	52.95	105.90	158.85	211.80	264.75	317.70	370.65	423.60	476.55	529.50
2119	13.24	26.49	52.97	105.95	158.92	211.90	264.87	317.85	370.82	423.80	476.77	529.75
2120	13.25	26.50	53.00	106.00	159.00	212.00	265.00	318.00	371.00	424.00	477.00	530.00
2121	13.26	26.51	53.02	106.05	159.07	212.10	265.12	318.15	371.17	424.20	477.22	530.25
2122	13.26	26.52	53.05	106.10	159.15	212.20	265.25	318.30	371.35	424.40	477.45	530.50
2123	13.27	26.54	53.07	106.15	159.22	212.30	265.37	318.45	371.52	424.60	477.67	530.75
2124	13.27	26.55	53.10	106.20	159.30	212.40	265.50	318.60	371.70	424.80	477.90	531.00
2125	13.28	26.56	53.12	106.25	159.37	212.50	265.62	318.75	371.87	425.00	478.12	531.25
2126	13.29	26.57	53.15	106.30	159.45	212.60	265.75	318.90	372.05	425.20	478.35	531.50
2127	13.29	26.59	53.17	106.35	159.52	212.70	265.87	319.05	372.22	425.40	478.57	531.75
2128	13.30	26.60	53.20	106.40	159.60	212.80	266.00	319.20	372.40	425.60	478.80	532.00
2129	13.31	26.61	53.22	106.45	159.67	212.90	266.12	319.35	372.57	425.80	479.02	532.25
2130	13.31	26.62	53.25	106.50	159.75	213.00	266.25	319.50	372.75	426.00	479.25	532.50
2131	13.32	26.64	53.27	106.55	159.82	213.10	266.37	319.65	372.92	426.20	479.47	532.75
2132	13.32	26.65	53.30	106.60	159.90	213.20	266.50	319.80	373.10	426.40	479.70	533.00
2133	13.33	26.66	53.32	106.65	159.97	213.30	266.62	319.95	373.27	426.60	479.92	533.25
2134	13.34	26.67	53.35	106.70	160.05	213.40	266.75	320.10	373.45	426.80	480.15	533.50
2135	13.34	26.69	53.37	106.75	160.12	213.50	266.87	320.25	373.62	427.00	480.37	533.75
2136	13.35	26.70	53.40	106.80	160.20	213.60	267.00	320.40	373.80	427.20	480.60	534.00
2137	13.36	26.71	53.42	106.85	160.27	213.70	267.12	320.55	373.97	427.40	480.82	534.25
2138	13.36	26.72	53.45	106.90	160.35	213.80	267.25	320.70	374.15	427.60	481.05	534.50
2139	13.37	26.74	53.47	106.95	160.42	213.90	267.37	320.85	374.32	427.80	481.27	534.75
2140	13.37	26.75	53.50	107.00	160.50	214.00	267.50	321.00	374.50	428.00	481.50	535.00
2141	13.38	26.76	53.52	107.05	160.57	214.10	267.62	321.15	374.67	428.20	481.72	535.25
2142	13.39	26.77	53.55	107.10	160.65	214.20	267.75	321.30	374.85	428.40	481.95	535.50
2143	13.39	26.79	53.57	107.15	160.72	214.30	267.87	321.45	375.02	428.60	482.17	535.75
2144	13.40	26.80	53.60	107.20	160.80	214.40	268.00	321.60	375.20	428.80	482.40	536.00
2145	13.41	26.81	53.62	107.25	160.87	214.50	268.12	321.75	375.37	429.00	482.62	536.25
2146	13.41	26.82	53.65	107.30	160.95	214.60	268.25	321.90	375.55	429.20	482.85	536.50
2147	13.42	26.84	53.67	107.35	161.02	214.70	268.37	322.05	375.72	429.40	483.07	536.75
2148	13.42	26.85	53.70	107.40	161.10	214.80	268.50	322.20	375.90	429.60	483.30	537.00
2149	13.43	26.86	53.72	107.45	161.17	214.90	268.62	322.35	376.07	429.80	483.52	537.25
2150	13.44	26.87	53.75	107.50	161.25	215.00	268.75	322.50	376.25	430.00	483.75	537.50

2150 FEET.

Per Ton,	$11	$12	$13	$14	$15	$16	$17	$18	$19	$20
Per Foot,	27½ cts.	30 cts.	32½ cts.	35 cts.	37½ cts.	40 cts.	42½ cts.	45 cts.	47½ cts.	50 cts.
Feet.										
2101	577.77	630.30	682.82	735.35	787.87	840.40	892.92	945.45	997.97	1050.50
2102	578.05	630.60	683.15	735.70	788.25	840.80	893.35	945.90	998.45	1051.00
2103	578.32	630.90	683.47	736.05	788.62	841.20	893.77	946.35	998.92	1051.50
2104	578.60	631.20	683.80	736.40	789.00	841.60	894.20	946.80	999.40	1052.00
2105	578.87	631.50	684.12	736.75	789.37	842.00	894.62	947.25	999.87	1052.50
2106	579.15	631.80	684.45	737.10	789.75	842.40	895.05	947.70	1000.35	1053.00
2107	579.42	632.10	684.77	737.45	790.12	842.80	895.47	948.15	1000.82	1053.50
2108	579.70	632.40	685.10	737.80	790.50	843.20	895.90	948.60	1001.30	1054.00
2109	579.97	632.70	685.42	738.15	790.87	843.60	896.32	949.05	1001.77	1054.50
2110	580.25	633.00	685.75	738.50	791.25	844.00	896.75	949.50	1002.25	1055.00
2111	580.52	633.30	686.07	738.85	791.62	844.40	897.17	949.95	1002.72	1055.50
2112	580.80	633.60	686.40	739.20	792.00	844.80	897.60	950.40	1003.20	1056.00
2113	581.07	633.90	686.72	739.55	792.37	845.20	898.02	950.85	1003.67	1056.50
2114	581.35	634.20	687.05	739.90	792.75	845.60	898.45	951.30	1004.15	1057.00
2115	581.62	634.50	687.37	740.25	793.12	846.00	898.87	951.75	1004.62	1057.50
2116	581.90	634.80	687.70	740.60	793.50	846.40	899.30	952.20	1005.10	1058.00
2117	582.17	635.10	688.02	740.95	793.87	846.80	899.72	952.65	1005.57	1058.50
2118	582.45	635.40	688.35	741.30	794.25	847.20	900.15	953.10	1006.05	1059.00
2119	582.72	635.70	688.67	741.65	794.62	847.60	900.57	953.55	1006.52	1059.50
2120	583.00	636.00	689.00	742.00	795.00	848.00	901.00	954.00	1007.00	1060.00
2121	583.27	636.30	689.32	742.35	795.37	848.40	901.42	954.45	1007.47	1060.50
2122	583.55	636.60	689.65	742.70	795.75	848.80	901.85	954.90	1007.95	1061.00
2123	583.82	636.90	689.97	743.05	796.12	849.20	902.27	955.35	1008.42	1061.50
2124	584.10	637.20	690.30	743.40	796.50	849.60	902.70	955.80	1008.90	1062.00
2125	584.37	637.50	690.62	743.75	796.87	850.00	903.12	956.25	1009.37	1062.50
2126	584.65	637.80	690.95	744.10	797.25	850.40	903.55	956.70	1009.85	1063.00
2127	584.92	638.10	691.27	744.45	797.62	850.80	903.97	957.15	1010.32	1063.50
2128	585.20	638.40	691.60	744.80	798.00	851.20	904.40	957.60	1010.80	1064.00
2129	585.47	638.70	691.92	745.15	798.37	851.60	904.82	958.05	1011.27	1064.50
2130	585.75	639.00	692.25	745.50	798.75	852.00	905.25	958.50	1011.75	1065.00
2131	586.02	639.30	692.57	745.85	799.12	852.40	905.67	958.95	1012.22	1065.50
2132	586.30	639.60	692.90	746.20	799.50	852.80	906.10	959.40	1012.70	1066.00
2133	586.57	639.90	693.22	746.55	799.87	853.20	906.52	959.85	1013.17	1066.50
2134	586.85	640.20	693.55	746.90	800.25	853.60	906.95	960.30	1013.65	1067.00
2135	587.12	640.50	693.87	747.25	800.62	854.00	907.37	960.75	1014.12	1067.50
2136	587.40	640.80	694.20	747.60	801.00	854.40	907.80	961.20	1014.60	1068.00
2137	587.67	641.10	694.52	747.95	801.37	854.80	908.22	961.65	1015.07	1068.50
2138	587.95	641.40	694.85	748.30	801.75	855.20	908.65	962.10	1015.55	1069.00
2139	588.22	641.70	695.17	748.65	802.12	855.60	909.07	962.55	1016.02	1069.50
2140	588.50	642.00	695.50	749.00	802.50	856.00	909.50	963.00	1016.50	1070.00
2141	588.77	642.30	695.82	749.35	802.87	856.40	909.92	963.45	1016.97	1070.50
2142	589.05	642.60	696.15	749.70	803.25	856.80	910.35	963.90	1017.45	1071.00
2143	589.32	642.90	696.47	750.05	803.62	857.20	910.77	964.35	1017.92	1071.50
2144	589.60	643.20	696.80	750.40	804.00	857.60	911.20	964.80	1018.40	1072.00
2145	589.87	643.50	697.12	750.75	804.37	858.00	911.62	965.25	1018.87	1072.50
2146	590.15	643.80	697.45	751.10	804.75	858.40	912.05	965.70	1019.35	1073.00
2147	590.42	644.10	697.77	751.45	805.12	858.80	912.47	966.15	1019.82	1073.50
2148	590.70	644.40	698.10	751.80	805.50	859.20	912.90	966.60	1020.30	1074.00
2149	590.97	644.70	698.42	752.15	805.87	859.60	913.32	967.05	1020.77	1074.50
2150	591.25	645.00	698.75	752.50	806.25	860.00	913.75	967.50	1021.25	1075.00

2200 FEET.

Per Ton,	25c.	50c.	$1	$2	$3	$4	$5	$6	$7	$8	$9	$10
Per Foot,			2¼ cts.	5 cts.	7½ cts.	10 cts.	12½ cts.	15 cts.	17½ cts.	20 cts.	22½ cts	25 cts.
Feet.												
2151	13.44	26.89	53.77	107.55	161.32	215.10	268.87	322.65	376.42	430.20	483.97	537.75
2152	13.45	26.90	53.80	107.60	161.40	215.20	269.00	322.80	376.60	430.40	484.20	538.00
2153	13.46	26.91	53.82	107.65	161.47	215.30	269.12	322.95	376.77	430.60	484.42	538.25
2154	13.46	26.92	53.85	107.70	161.55	215.40	269.25	323.10	376.95	430.80	484.65	538.50
2155	13.47	26.94	53.87	107.75	161.62	215.50	269.37	323.25	377.12	431.00	484.87	538.75
2156	13.47	26.95	53.90	107.80	161.70	215.60	269.50	323 40	377.30	431.20	485.10	539.00
2157	13.48	26.96	53.92	107.85	161.77	215.70	269.62	323.55	377.47	431.40	485.32	539.25
2158	13.49	26.97	53.95	107.90	161.85	215.80	269.75	323.70	377.65	431.60	485.55	539.50
2159	13.49	26.99	53.97	107.95	161.92	215.90	269.87	323.85	377.82	431.80	485.77	539.75
2160	13.50	27.00	54.00	108.00	162.00	216.00	270.00	324.00	378.00	432.00	486.00	540.00
2161	13.51	27.01	54.02	108.05	162.07	216.10	270.12	324.15	378.17	432.20	486.22	540.25
2162	13.51	27.02	54.05	108.10	162.15	216.20	270.25	324.30	378.35	432.40	486.45	540.50
2163	13.52	27.04	54.07	108.15	162.22	216.30	270.37	324.45	378.52	432.60	486.67	540.75
2164	13.52	27.05	54.10	108.20	162.30	216.40	270.50	324.60	378.70	432.80	486.90	541.00
2165	13.53	27.06	54.12	108.25	162.37	216.50	270.62	324.75	378.87	433.00	487.12	541.25
2166	13.54	27.07	54.15	108.30	162.45	216.60	270.75	324.90	379.05	433.20	487.35	541.50
2167	13.54	27.09	54.17	108.35	162.52	216.70	270.87	325.05	379.22	433.40	487.57	541.75
2168	13.55	27.10	54.20	108.40	162.60	216.80	271.00	325.20	379.40	433.60	487.80	542.00
2169	13.56	27.11	54.22	108.45	162.67	216.90	271.12	325.35	379.57	433.80	488.02	542.25
2170	13.56	27.12	54.25	108.50	162.75	217.00	271.25	325.50	379.75	434.00	488.25	542.50
2171	13.57	27.14	54.27	108.55	162.82	217.10	271.37	325.65	379.92	434.20	488.47	542.75
2172	13.57	27.15	54.30	108.60	162.90	217.20	271.50	325.80	380.10	434.40	488.70	543.00
2173	13.58	27.16	54.32	108.65	162.97	217.30	271.62	325.95	380.27	434.60	488.92	543.25
2174	13.59	27.17	54.35	108.70	163.05	217.40	271.75	326.10	380.45	434.80	489.15	543.50
2175	13.59	27.19	54.37	108.75	163.12	217.50	271.87	326.25	380.62	435.00	489.37	543.75
2176	13.60	27.20	54.40	108.80	163.20	217.60	272.00	326.40	380.80	435.20	489.60	544.00
2177	13.61	27.21	54.42	108.85	163.27	217.70	272.12	326.55	380.97	435.40	489.82	544.25
2178	13.61	27.22	54.45	108.90	163.35	217.80	272.25	326.70	381.15	435.60	490.05	544.50
2179	13.62	27.24	54.47	108.95	163.42	217.90	272.37	326.85	381.32	435.80	490.27	544.75
2180	13.62	27.25	54.50	109.00	163.50	218.00	272.50	327.00	381.50	436.00	490.50	545.00
2181	13.63	27.26	54.52	109.05	163.57	218.10	272.62	327.15	381.67	436.20	490.72	545.25
2182	13.64	27.27	54.55	109.10	163.65	218.20	272.75	327.30	381.85	436.40	490.95	545.50
2183	13.64	27.29	54.57	109.15	163.72	218.30	272.87	327.45	382.02	436.60	491.17	545.75
2184	13.65	27.30	54.60	109.20	163.80	218.40	273.00	327.60	382.20	436.80	491.40	546.00
2185	13.66	27.31	54.62	109.25	163.87	218.50	273.12	327.75	382.37	437.00	491.62	546.25
2186	13.66	27.32	54.65	109.30	163.95	218.60	273.25	327.90	382.55	437.20	491.85	546.50
2187	13.67	27.34	54.67	109.35	164.02	218.70	273.37	328.05	382.72	437.40	492.07	546.75
2188	13.67	27.35	54.70	109.40	164.10	218.80	273.50	328.20	382.90	437.60	492.30	547.00
2189	13.68	27.36	54.72	109.45	164.17	218.90	273.62	328.35	383.07	437.80	492.52	547.25
2190	13.69	27.37	54.75	109.50	164.25	219.00	273.75	328.50	383.25	438.00	492.75	547.50
2191	13.69	27.39	54.77	109.55	164.32	219.10	273.87	328.65	383.42	438.20	492.97	547.75
2192	13.70	27.40	54.80	109.60	164.40	219.20	274.00	328.80	383.60	438.40	493.20	548.00
2193	13.71	27.41	54.82	109.65	164.47	219.30	274.12	328.95	383.77	438.60	493.42	548.25
2194	13.71	27.42	54.85	109.70	164.55	219.40	274.25	329.10	383.95	438.80	493.65	548.50
2195	13.72	27.44	54.87	109.75	164.62	219.50	274.37	329.25	384.12	439.00	493.87	548.75
2196	13.72	27.45	54.90	109.80	164.70	219.60	274.50	329.40	384.30	439.20	494.10	549.00
2197	13.73	27.46	54.92	109.85	164.77	219.70	274.62	329.55	384.47	439.40	494.32	549.25
2198	13.74	27.47	54.95	109.90	164.85	219.80	274.75	329.70	384.65	439.60	494.55	549.50
2199	13.74	27.49	54.97	109.95	164.92	219.90	274.87	329.85	384.82	439.80	494.77	549.75
2200	13.75	27.50	55.00	110.00	165.00	220.00	275.00	330.00	385.00	440.00	495.00	550.00

2200 FEET.

Per Ton,	$11	$12	$13	$14	$15	$16	$17	$18	$19	$20
Per Foot,	27½ cts.	30 cts.	32½ cts.	35 cts.	37½ cts.	40 cts.	42½ cts.	45 cts.	47½ cts.	50 cts.
Feet.										
2151	591.52	645.30	699.07	752.85	806.62	860.40	914.17	967.95	1021.72	1075.50
2152	591.80	645.60	699.40	753.20	807.00	860.80	914.60	968.40	1022.20	1076.00
2153	592.07	645.90	699.72	753.55	807.37	861.20	915.02	968.85	1022.67	1076.50
2154	592.35	646.20	700.05	753.90	807.75	861.60	915.45	969.30	1023.15	1077.00
2155	592.62	646.50	700.37	754.25	808.12	862.00	915.87	969.75	1023.62	1077.50
2156	592.90	646.80	700.70	754.60	808.50	862.40	916.30	970.20	1024.10	1078.00
2157	593.17	647.10	701.02	754.95	808.87	862.80	916.72	970.65	1024.57	1078.50
2158	593.45	647.40	701.35	755.30	809.25	863.20	917.15	971.10	1025.05	1079.00
2159	593.72	647.70	701.67	755.65	809.62	863.60	917.57	971.55	1025.52	1079.50
2160	594.00	648.00	702.00	756.00	810.00	864.00	918.00	972.00	1026.00	1080.00
2161	594.27	648.30	702.32	756.35	810.37	864.40	918.42	972.45	1026.47	1080.50
2162	594.55	648.60	702.65	756.70	810.75	864.80	918.85	972.90	1026.95	1081.00
2163	594.82	648.90	702.97	757.05	811.12	865.20	919.27	973.35	1027.42	1081.50
2164	595.10	649.20	703.30	757.40	811.50	865.60	919.70	973.80	1027.90	1082.00
2165	595.37	649.50	703.62	757.75	811.87	866.00	920.12	974.25	1028.37	1082.50
2166	595.65	649.80	703.95	758.10	812.25	866.40	920.55	974.70	1028.85	1083.00
2167	595.92	650.10	704.27	758.45	812.62	866.80	920.97	975.15	1029.32	1083.50
2168	596.20	650.40	704.60	758.80	813.00	867.20	921.40	975.60	1029.80	1084.00
2169	596.47	650.70	704.92	759.15	813.37	867.60	921.82	976.05	1030.27	1084.50
2170	596.75	651.00	705.25	759.50	813.75	868.00	922.25	976.50	1030.75	1085.00
2171	597.02	651.30	705.57	759.85	814.12	868.40	922.67	976.95	1031.22	1085.50
2172	597.30	651.60	705.90	760.20	814.50	868.80	923.10	977.40	1031.70	1086.00
2173	597.57	651.90	706.22	760.55	814.87	869.20	923.52	977.85	1032.17	1086.50
2174	597.85	652.20	706.55	760.90	815.25	869.60	923.95	978.30	1032.65	1087.00
2175	598.12	652.50	706.87	761.25	815.62	870.00	924.37	978.75	1033.12	1087.50
2176	598.40	652.80	707.20	761.60	816.00	870.40	924.80	979.20	1033.60	1088.00
2177	598.67	653.10	707.52	761.95	816.37	870.80	925.22	979.65	1034.07	1088.50
2178	598.95	653.40	707.85	762.30	816.75	871.20	925.65	980.10	1034.55	1089.00
2179	599.22	653.70	708.17	762.65	817.12	871.60	926.07	980.55	1035.02	1089.50
2180	599.50	654.00	708.50	763.00	817.50	872.00	926.50	981.00	1035.50	1090.00
2181	599.77	654.30	708.82	763.35	817.87	872.40	926.92	981.45	1035.97	1090.50
2182	600.05	654.60	709.15	763.70	818.25	872.80	927.35	981.90	1036.45	1091.00
2183	600.32	654.90	709.47	764.05	818.62	873.20	927.77	982.35	1036.92	1091.50
2184	600.60	655.20	709.80	764.40	819.00	873.60	928.20	982.80	1037.40	1092.00
2185	600.87	655.50	710.12	764.75	819.37	874.00	928.62	983.25	1037.87	1092.50
2186	601.15	655.80	710.45	765.10	819.75	874.40	929.05	983.70	1038.35	1093.00
2187	601.42	656.10	710.77	765.45	820.12	874.80	929.47	984.15	1038.82	1093.50
2188	601.70	656.40	711.10	765.80	820.50	875.20	929.90	984.60	1039.30	1094.00
2189	601.97	656.70	711.42	766.15	820.87	875.60	930.32	985.05	1039.77	1094.50
2190	602.25	657.00	711.75	766.50	821.25	876.00	930.75	985.50	1040.25	1095.00
2191	602.52	657.30	712.07	766.85	821.62	876.40	931.17	985.95	1040.72	1095.50
2192	602.80	657.60	712.40	767.20	822.00	876.80	931.60	986.40	1041.20	1096.00
2193	603.07	657.90	712.72	767.55	822.37	877.20	932.02	986.85	1041.67	1096.50
2194	603.35	658.20	713.05	767.90	822.75	877.60	932.45	987.30	1042.15	1097.00
2195	603.62	658.50	713.37	768.25	823.12	878.00	932.87	987.75	1042.62	1097.50
2196	603.90	658.80	713.70	768.60	823.50	878.40	933.30	988.20	1043.10	1098.00
2197	604.17	659.10	714.02	768.95	823.87	878.80	933.72	988.65	1043.57	1098.50
2198	604.45	659.40	714.35	769.30	824.25	879.20	934.15	989.10	1044.05	1099.00
2199	604.72	659.70	714.67	769.65	824.62	879.60	934.57	989.55	1044.52	1099.50
2200	605.00	660.00	715.00	770.00	825.00	880.00	935.00	990.00	1045.00	1100.00

2250 FEET.

Per Ton, Per Foot,	25c.	50c.	$1 2½ cts.	$2 5 cts.	$3 7½ cts.	$4 10 cts.	$5 12½ cts.	$6 15 cts.	$7 17½ cts.	$8 20 cts.	$9 22½ cts	$10 25 cts.
Feet.												
2201	13.76	27.51	55.02	110.05	165.07	220.10	275.12	330.15	385.17	440.20	495.22	550.25
2202	13.76	27.52	55.05	110.10	165.15	220.20	275.25	330.30	385.35	440.40	495.45	550.50
2203	13.77	27.54	55.07	110.15	165.22	220.30	275.37	330.45	385.52	440.60	495.67	550.75
2204	13.77	27.55	55.10	110.20	165.30	220.40	275.50	330.60	385.70	440.80	495.90	551.00
2205	13.78	27.56	55.12	110.25	165.37	220.50	275.62	330.75	385.87	441.00	496.12	551.25
2206	13.79	27.57	55.15	110.30	165.45	220.60	275.75	330.90	386.05	441.20	496.35	551.50
2207	13.79	27.59	55.17	110.35	165.52	220.70	275.87	331.05	386.22	441.40	496.57	551.75
2208	13.80	27.60	55.20	110.40	165.60	220.80	276.00	331.20	386.40	441.60	496.80	552.00
2209	13.81	27.61	55.22	110.45	165.67	220.90	276.12	331.35	386.57	441.80	497.02	552.25
2210	13.81	27.62	55.25	110.50	165.75	221.00	276.25	331.50	386.75	442.00	497.25	552.50
2211	13.82	27.64	55.27	110.55	165.82	221.10	276.37	331.65	386.92	442.20	497.47	552.75
2212	13.82	27.65	55.30	110.60	165.90	221.20	276.50	331.80	387.10	442.40	497.70	553.00
2213	13.83	27.66	55.32	110.65	165.97	221.30	276.62	331.95	387.27	442.60	497.92	553.25
2214	13.84	27.67	55.35	110.70	166.05	221.40	276.75	332.10	387.45	442.80	498.15	553.50
2215	13.84	27.69	55.37	110.75	166.12	221.50	276.87	332.25	387.62	443.00	498.37	553.75
2216	13.85	27.70	55.40	110.80	166.20	221.60	277.00	332.40	387.80	443.20	498.60	554.00
2217	13.86	27.71	55.42	110.85	166.27	221.70	277.12	332.55	387.97	443.40	498.82	554.25
2218	13.86	27.72	55.45	110.90	166.35	221.80	277.25	332.70	388.15	443.60	499.05	554.50
2219	13.87	27.74	55.47	110.95	166.42	221.90	277.37	332.85	388.32	443.80	499.27	554.75
2220	13.87	27.75	55.50	111.00	166.50	222.00	277.50	333.00	388.50	444.00	499.50	555.00
2221	13.88	27.76	55.52	111.05	166.57	222.10	277.62	333.15	388.67	444.20	499.72	555.25
2222	13.89	27.77	55.55	111.10	166.65	222.20	277.75	333.30	388.85	444.40	499.95	555.50
2223	13.89	27.79	55.57	111.15	166.72	222.30	277.87	333.45	389.02	444.60	500.17	555.75
2224	13.90	27.80	55.60	111.20	166.80	222.40	278.00	333.60	389.20	444.80	500.40	556.00
2225	13.91	27.81	55.62	111.25	166.87	222.50	278.12	333.75	389.37	445.00	500.62	556.25
2226	13.91	27.82	55.65	111.30	166.95	222.60	278.25	333.90	389.55	445.20	500.85	556.50
2227	13.92	27.84	55.67	111.35	167.02	222.70	278.37	334.05	389.72	445.40	501.07	556.75
2228	13.92	27.85	55.70	111.40	167.10	222.80	278.50	334.20	389.90	445.60	501.30	557.00
2229	13.93	27.86	55.72	111.45	167.17	222.90	278.62	334.35	390.07	445.80	501.52	557.25
2230	13.94	27.87	55.75	111.50	167.25	223.00	278.75	334.50	390.25	446.00	501.75	557.50
2231	13.94	27.89	55.77	111.55	167.32	223.10	278.87	334.65	390.42	446.20	501.97	557.75
2232	13.95	27.90	55.80	111.60	167.40	223.20	279.00	334.80	390.60	446.40	502.20	558.00
2233	13.96	27.91	55.82	111.65	167.47	223.30	279.12	334.95	390.77	446.60	502.42	558.25
2234	13.96	27.92	55.85	111.70	167.55	223.40	279.25	335.10	390.95	446.80	502.65	558.50
2235	13.97	27.94	55.87	111.75	167.62	223.50	279.37	335.25	391.12	447.00	502.87	558.75
2236	13.97	27.95	55.90	111.80	167.70	223.60	279.50	335.40	391.30	447.20	503.10	559.00
2237	13.98	27.96	55.92	111.85	167.77	223.70	279.62	335.55	391.47	447.40	503.32	559.25
2238	13.99	27.97	55.95	111.90	167.85	223.80	279.75	335.70	391.65	447.60	503.55	559.50
2239	13.99	27.99	55.97	111.95	167.92	223.90	279.87	335.85	391.82	447.80	503.77	559.75
2240	14.00	28.00	56.00	112.00	168.00	224.00	280.00	336.00	392.00	448.00	504.00	560.00
2241	14.01	28.01	56.02	112.05	168.07	224.10	280.12	336.15	392.17	448.20	504.22	560.25
2242	14.01	28.02	56.05	112.10	168.15	224.20	280.25	336.30	392.35	448.40	504.45	560.50
2243	14.02	28.04	56.07	112.15	168.22	224.30	280.37	336.45	392.52	448.60	504.67	560.75
2244	14.02	28.05	56.10	112.20	168.30	224.40	280.50	336.60	392.70	448.80	504.90	561.00
2245	14.03	28.06	56.12	112.25	168.37	224.50	280.62	336.75	392.87	449.00	505.12	561.25
2246	14.04	28.07	56.15	112.30	168.45	224.60	280.75	336.90	393.05	449.20	505.35	561.50
2247	14.04	28.09	56.17	112.35	168.52	224.70	280.87	337.05	393.22	449.40	505.57	561.75
2248	14.05	28.10	56.20	112.40	168.60	224.80	281.00	337.20	393.40	449.60	505.80	562.00
2249	14.06	28.11	56.22	112.45	168.67	224.90	281.12	337.35	393.57	449.80	506.02	562.25
2250	14.06	28.12	56.25	112.50	168.75	225.00	281.25	337.50	393.75	450.00	506.25	562.50

2250 FEET.

Per Ton, Per Foot, Feet.	$11 27½ cts.	$12 30 cts.	$13 32½ cts.	$14 35 cts.	$15 37½ cts.	$16 40 cts.	$17 42½ cts.	$18 45 cts.	$19 47½ cts.	$20 50 cts.
2201	605.27	660.30	715.32	770.35	825.37	880.40	935.42	990.45	1045.47	1100.50
2202	605.55	660.60	715.65	770.70	825.75	880.80	935.85	990.90	1045.95	1101.00
2203	605.82	660.90	715.97	771.05	826.12	881.20	936.27	991.35	1046.42	1101.50
2204	606.10	661.20	716.30	771.40	826.50	881.60	936.70	991.80	1046.90	1102.00
2205	606.37	661.50	716.62	771.75	826.87	882.00	937.12	992.25	1047.37	1102.50
2206	606.65	661.80	716.95	772.10	827.25	882.40	937.55	992.70	1047.85	1103.00
2207	606.92	662.10	717.27	772.45	827.62	882.80	937.97	993.15	1048.32	1103.50
2208	607.20	662.40	717.60	772.80	828.00	883.20	938.40	993.60	1048.80	1104.00
2209	607.47	662.70	717.92	773.15	828.37	883.60	938.82	994.05	1049.27	1104.50
2210	607.75	663.00	718.25	773.50	828.75	884.00	939.25	994.50	1049.75	1105.00
2211	608.02	663.30	718.57	773.85	829.12	884.40	939.67	994.95	1050.22	1105.50
2212	608.30	663.60	718.90	774.20	829.50	884.80	940.10	995.40	1050.70	1106.00
2213	608.57	663.90	719.22	774.55	829.87	885.20	940.52	995.85	1051.17	1106.50
2214	608.85	664.20	719.55	774.90	830.25	885.60	940.95	996.30	1051.65	1107.00
2215	609.12	664.50	719.87	775.25	830.62	886.00	941.37	996.75	1052.12	1107.50
2216	609.40	664.80	720.20	775.60	831.00	886.40	941.80	997.20	1052.60	1108.00
2217	609.67	665.10	720.52	775.95	831.37	886.80	942.22	997.65	1053.07	1108.50
2218	609.95	665.40	720.85	776.30	831.75	887.20	942.65	998.10	1053.55	1109.00
2219	610.22	665.70	721.17	776.65	832.12	887.60	943.07	998.55	1054.02	1109.50
2220	610.50	666.00	721.50	777.00	832.50	888.00	943.50	999.00	1054.50	1110.00
2221	610.77	666.30	721.82	777.35	832.87	888.40	943.92	999.45	1054.97	1110.50
2222	611.05	666.60	722.15	777.70	833.25	888.80	944.35	999.90	1055.45	1111.00
2223	611.32	666.90	722.47	778.05	833.62	889.20	944.77	1000.35	1055.92	1111.50
2224	611.60	667.20	722.80	778.40	834.00	889.60	945.20	1000.80	1056.40	1112.00
2225	611.87	667.50	723.12	778.75	834.37	890.00	945.62	1001.25	1056.87	1112.50
2226	612.15	667.80	723.45	779.10	834.75	890.40	946.05	1001.70	1057.35	1113.00
2227	612.42	668.10	723.77	779.45	835.12	890.80	946.47	1002.15	1057.82	1113.50
2228	612.70	668.40	724.10	779.80	835.50	891.20	946.90	1002.60	1058.30	1114.00
2229	612.97	668.70	724.42	780.15	835.87	891.60	947.32	1003.05	1058.77	1114.50
2230	613.25	669.00	724.75	780.50	836.25	892.00	947.75	1003.50	1059.25	1115.00
2231	613.52	669.30	725.07	780.85	836.62	892.40	948.17	1003.95	1059.72	1115.50
2232	613.80	669.60	725.40	781.20	837.00	892.80	948.60	1004.40	1060.20	1116.00
2233	614.07	669.90	725.72	781.55	837.37	893.20	949.02	1004.85	1060.67	1116.50
2234	614.35	670.20	726.05	781.90	837.75	893.60	949.45	1005.30	1061.15	1117.00
2235	614.62	670.50	726.37	782.25	838.12	894.00	949.87	1005.75	1061.62	1117.50
2236	614.90	670.80	726.70	782.60	838.50	894.40	950.30	1006.20	1062.10	1118.00
2237	615.17	671.10	727.02	782.95	838.87	894.80	950.72	1006.65	1062.57	1118.50
2238	615.45	671.40	727.35	783.30	839.25	895.20	951.15	1007.10	1063.05	1119.00
2239	615.72	671.70	727.67	783.65	839.62	895.60	951.57	1007.55	1063.52	1119.50
2240	616.00	672.00	728.00	784.00	840.00	896.00	952.00	1008.00	1064.00	1120.00
2241	616.27	672.30	728.32	784.35	840.37	896.40	952.42	1008.45	1064.47	1120.50
2242	616.55	672.60	728.65	784.70	840.75	896.80	952.85	1008.90	1064.95	1121.00
2243	616.82	672.90	728.97	785.05	841.12	897.20	953.27	1009.35	1065.42	1121.50
2244	617.10	673.20	729.30	785.40	841.50	897.60	953.70	1009.80	1065.90	1122.00
2245	617.37	673.50	729.62	785.75	841.87	898.00	954.12	1010.25	1066.37	1122.50
2246	617.65	673.80	729.95	786.10	842.25	898.40	954.55	1010.70	1066.85	1123.00
2247	617.92	674.10	730.27	786.45	842.62	898.80	954.97	1011.15	1067.32	1123.50
2248	618.20	674.40	730.60	786.80	843.00	899.20	955.40	1011.60	1067.80	1124.00
2249	618.47	674.70	730.92	787.15	843.37	899.60	955.82	1012.05	1068.27	1124.50
2250	618.75	675.00	731.25	787.50	843.75	900.00	956.25	1012.50	1068.75	1125.00

2300 FEET.

Per Ton, Per Foot,	25c.	50c.	$1 2¼ cts.	$2 5 cts.	$3 7½ cts.	$4 10 cts.	$5 12½ cts.	$6 15 cts.	$7 17½ cts.	$8 20 cts.	$9 22½ cts	$10 25 cts.
Feet.												
2251	14.07	28.14	56.27	112.55	168.82	225.10	281.37	337.65	393.92	450.20	506.47	562.75
2252	14.07	28.15	56.30	112.60	168.90	225.20	281.50	337.80	394.10	450.40	506.70	563.00
2253	14.08	28.16	56.32	112.65	168.97	225.30	281.62	337.95	394.27	450.60	506.92	563.25
2254	14.09	28.17	56.35	112.70	169.05	225.40	281.75	338.10	394.45	450.80	507.15	563.50
2255	14.09	28.19	56.37	112.75	169.12	225.50	281.87	338.25	394.62	451.00	507.37	563.75
2256	14.10	28.20	56.40	112.80	169.20	225.60	282.00	338.40	394.80	451.20	507.60	564.00
2257	14.11	28.21	56.42	112.85	169.27	225.70	282.12	338.55	394.97	451.40	507.82	564.25
2258	14.11	28.22	56.45	112.90	169.35	225.80	282.25	338.70	395.15	451.60	508.05	564.50
2259	14.12	28.24	56.47	112.95	169.42	225.90	282.37	338.85	395.32	451.80	508.27	564.75
2260	14.12	28.25	56.50	113.00	169.50	226.00	282.50	339.00	395.50	452.00	508.50	565.00
2261	14.13	28.26	56.52	113.05	169.57	226.10	282.62	339.15	395.67	452.20	508.72	565.25
2262	14.14	28.27	56.55	113.10	169.65	226.20	282.75	339.30	395.85	452.40	508.95	565.50
2263	14.14	28.29	56.57	113.15	169.72	226.30	282.87	339.45	396.02	452.60	509.17	565.75
2264	14.15	28.30	56.60	113.20	169.80	226.40	283.00	339.60	396.20	452.80	509.40	566.00
2265	14.16	28.31	56.62	113.25	169.87	226.50	283.12	339.75	396.37	453.00	509.62	566.25
2266	14.16	28.32	56.65	113.30	169.95	226.60	283.25	339.90	396.55	453.20	509.85	566.50
2267	14.17	28.34	56.67	113.35	170.02	226.70	283.37	340.05	396.72	453.40	510.07	566.75
2268	14.17	28.35	56.70	113.40	170.10	226.80	283.50	340.20	396.90	453.60	510.30	567.00
2269	14.18	28.36	56.72	113.45	170.17	226.90	283.62	340.35	397.07	453.80	510.52	567.25
2270	14.19	28.37	56.75	113.50	170.25	227.00	283.75	340.50	397.25	454.00	510.75	567.50
2271	14.19	28.39	56.77	113.55	170.32	227.10	283.87	340.65	397.42	454.20	510.97	567.75
2272	14.20	28.40	56.80	113.60	170.40	227.20	284.00	340.80	397.60	454.40	511.20	568.00
2273	14.21	28.41	56.82	113.65	170.47	227.30	284.12	340.95	397.77	454.60	511.42	568.25
2274	14.21	28.42	56.85	113.70	170.55	227.40	284.25	341.10	397.95	454.80	511.65	568.50
2275	14.22	28.44	56.87	113.75	170.62	227.50	284.37	341.25	398.12	455.00	511.87	568.75
2276	14.22	28.45	56.90	113.80	170.70	227.60	284.50	341.40	398.30	455.20	512.10	569.00
2277	14.23	28.46	56.92	113.85	170.77	227.70	284.62	341.55	398.47	455.40	512.32	569.25
2278	14.24	28.47	56.95	113.90	170.85	227.80	284.75	341.70	398.65	455.60	512.55	569.50
2279	14.24	28.49	56.97	113.95	170.92	227.90	284.87	341.85	398.82	455.80	512.77	569.75
2280	14.25	28.50	57.00	114.00	171.00	228.00	285.00	342.00	399.00	456.00	513.00	570.00
2281	14.26	28.51	57.02	114.05	171.07	228.10	285.12	342.15	399.17	456.20	513.22	570.25
2282	14.26	28.52	57.05	114.10	171.15	228.20	285.25	342.30	399.35	456.40	513.45	570.50
2283	14.27	28.54	57.07	114.15	171.22	228.30	285.37	342.45	399.52	456.60	513.67	570.75
2284	14.27	28.55	57.10	114.20	171.30	228.40	285.50	342.60	399.70	456.80	513.90	571.00
2285	14.28	28.56	57.12	114.25	171.37	228.50	285.62	342.75	399.87	457.00	514.12	571.25
2286	14.29	28.57	57.15	114.30	171.45	228.60	285.75	342.90	400.05	457.20	514.35	571.50
2287	14.29	28.59	57.17	114.35	171.52	228.70	285.87	343.05	400.22	457.40	514.57	571.75
2288	14.30	28.60	57.20	114.40	171.60	228.80	286.00	343.20	400.40	457.60	514.80	572.00
2289	14.31	28.61	57.22	114.45	171.67	228.90	286.12	343.35	400.57	457.80	515.02	572.25
2290	14.31	28.62	57.25	114.50	171.75	229.00	286.25	343.50	400.75	458.00	515.25	572.50
2291	14.32	28.64	57.27	114.55	171.82	229.10	286.37	343.65	400.92	458.20	515.47	572.75
2292	14.32	28.65	57.30	114.60	171.90	229.20	286.50	343.80	401.10	458.40	515.70	573.00
2293	14.33	28.66	57.32	114.65	171.97	229.30	286.62	343.95	401.27	458.60	515.92	573.25
2294	14.34	28.67	57.35	114.70	172.05	229.40	286.75	344.10	401.45	458.80	516.15	573.50
2295	14.34	28.69	57.37	114.75	172.12	229.50	286.87	344.25	401.62	459.00	516.37	573.75
2296	14.35	28.70	57.40	114.80	172.20	229.60	287.00	344.40	401.80	459.20	516.60	574.00
2297	14.36	28.71	57.42	114.85	172.27	229.70	287.12	344.55	401.97	459.40	516.82	574.25
2298	14.36	28.72	57.45	114.90	172.35	229.80	287.25	344.70	402.15	459.60	517.05	574.50
2299	14.37	28.74	57.47	114.95	172.42	229.90	287.37	344.85	402.32	459.80	517.27	574.75
2300	14.37	28.75	57.50	115.00	172.50	230.00	287.50	345.00	402.50	460.00	517.50	575.00

2300 FEET.

Per Ton,	$11	$12	$13	$14	$15	$16	$17	$18	$19	$20
Per Foot,	27½ cts.	30 cts.	32½ cts.	35 cts.	37½ cts.	40 cts.	42½ cts.	45 cts.	47½ cts.	50 cts.
Feet.										
2251	619.02	675.30	731.57	787.85	844.12	900.40	956.67	1012.95	1069.22	1125.50
2252	619.30	675.60	731.90	788.20	844.50	900.80	957.10	1013.40	1069.70	1126.00
2253	619.57	675.90	732.22	788.55	844.87	901.20	957.52	1013.85	1070.17	1126.50
2254	619.85	676.20	732.55	788.90	845.25	901.60	957.95	1014.30	1070.65	1127.00
2255	620.12	676.50	732.87	789.25	845.62	902.00	958.37	1014.75	1071.12	1127.50
2256	620.40	676.80	733.20	789.60	846.00	902.40	958.80	1015.20	1071.60	1128.00
2257	620.67	677.10	733.52	789.95	846.37	902.80	959.22	1015.65	1072.07	1128.50
2258	620.95	677.40	733.85	790.30	846.75	903.20	959.65	1016.10	1072.55	1129.00
2259	621.22	677.70	734.17	790.65	847.12	903.60	960.07	1016.55	1073.02	1129.50
2260	621.50	678.00	734.50	791.00	847.50	904.00	960.50	1017.00	1073.50	1130.00
2261	621.77	678.30	734.82	791.35	847.87	904.40	960.92	1017.45	1073.97	1130.50
2262	622.05	678.60	735.15	791.70	848.25	904.80	961.35	1017.90	1074.45	1131.00
2263	622.32	678.90	735.47	792.05	848.62	905.20	961.77	1018.35	1074.92	1131.50
2264	622.60	679.20	735.80	792.40	849.00	905.60	962.20	1018.80	1075.40	1132.00
2265	622.87	679.50	736.12	792.75	849.37	906.00	962.62	1019.25	1075.87	1132.50
2266	623.15	679.80	736.45	793.10	849.75	906.40	963.05	1019.70	1076.35	1133.00
2267	623.42	680.10	736.77	793.45	850.12	906.80	963.47	1020.15	1076.82	1133.50
2268	623.70	680.40	737.10	793.80	850.50	907.20	963.90	1020.60	1077.30	1134.00
2269	623.97	680.70	737.42	794.15	850.87	907.60	964.32	1021.05	1077.77	1134.50
2270	624.25	681.00	737.75	794.50	851.25	908.00	964.75	1021.50	1078.25	1135.00
2271	624.52	681.30	738.07	794.85	851.62	908.40	965.17	1021.95	1078.72	1135.50
2272	624.80	681.60	738.40	795.20	852.00	908.80	965.60	1022.40	1079.20	1136.00
2273	625.07	681.90	738.72	795.55	852.37	909.20	966.02	1022.85	1079.67	1136.50
2274	625.35	682.20	739.05	795.90	852.75	909.60	966.45	1023.30	1080.15	1137.00
2275	625.62	682.50	739.37	796.25	853.12	910.00	966.87	1023.75	1080.62	1137.50
2276	625.90	682.80	739.70	796.60	853.50	910.40	967.30	1024.20	1081.10	1138.00
2277	626.17	683.10	740.02	796.95	853.87	910.80	967.72	1024.65	1081.57	1138.50
2278	626.45	683.40	740.35	797.30	854.25	911.20	968.15	1025.10	1082.05	1139.00
2279	626.72	683.70	740.67	797.65	854.62	911.60	968.57	1025.55	1082.52	1139.50
2280	627.00	684.00	741.00	798.00	855.00	912.00	969.00	1026.00	1083.00	1140.00
2281	627.27	684.30	741.32	798.35	855.37	912.40	969.42	1026.45	1083.47	1140.50
2282	627.55	684.60	741.65	798.70	855.75	912.80	969.85	1026.90	1083.95	1141.00
2283	627.82	684.90	741.97	799.05	856.12	913.20	970.27	1027.35	1084.42	1141.50
2284	628.10	685.20	742.30	799.40	856.50	913.60	970.70	1027.80	1084.90	1142.00
2285	628.37	685.50	742.62	799.75	856.87	914.00	971.12	1028.25	1085.37	1142.50
2286	628.65	685.80	742.95	800.10	857.25	914.40	971.55	1028.70	1085.85	1143.00
2287	628.92	686.10	743.27	800.45	857.62	914.80	971.97	1029.15	1086.32	1143.50
2288	629.20	686.40	743.60	800.80	858.00	915.20	972.40	1029.60	1086.80	1144.00
2289	629.47	686.70	743.92	801.15	858.37	915.60	972.82	1030.05	1087.27	1144.50
2290	629.75	687.00	744.25	801.50	858.75	916.00	973.25	1030.50	1087.75	1145.00
2291	630.02	687.30	744.57	801.85	859.12	916.40	973.67	1030.95	1088.22	1145.50
2292	630.30	687.60	744.90	802.20	859.50	916.80	974.10	1031.40	1088.70	1146.00
2293	630.57	687.90	745.22	802.55	859.87	917.20	974.52	1031.85	1089.17	1146.50
2294	630.85	688.20	745.55	802.90	860.25	917.60	974.95	1032.30	1089.65	1147.00
2295	631.12	688.50	745.87	803.25	860.62	918.00	975.37	1032.75	1090.12	1147.50
2296	631.40	688.80	746.20	803.60	861.00	918.40	975.80	1033.20	1090.60	1148.00
2297	631.67	689.10	746.52	803.95	861.37	918.80	976.22	1033.65	1091.07	1148.50
2298	631.95	689.40	746.85	804.30	861.75	919.20	976.65	1034.10	1091.55	1149.00
2299	632.22	689.70	747.17	804.65	862.12	919.60	977.07	1034.55	1092.02	1149.50
2300	632.50	690.00	747.50	805.00	862.50	920.00	977.50	1035.00	1092.50	1150.00

2350 FEET.

Per Ton, Per Foot,	25c.	50c.	$1 2½ cts.	$2 5 cts.	$3 7½ cts.	$4 10 cts.	$5 12½ cts.	$6 15 cts.	$7 17½ cts.	$8 20 cts.	$9 22½ cts.	$10 25 cts.
Feet.												
2301	14.38	28.76	57.52	115.05	172.57	230.10	287.62	345.15	402.67	460.20	517.72	575.25
2302	14.39	28.77	57.55	115.10	172.65	230.20	287.75	345.30	402.85	460.40	517.95	575.50
2303	14.39	28.79	57.57	115.15	172.72	230.30	287.87	345.45	403.02	460.60	518.17	575.75
2304	14.40	28.80	57.60	115.20	172.80	230.40	288.00	345.60	403.20	460.80	518.40	576.00
2305	14.41	28.81	57.62	115.25	172.87	230.50	288.12	345.75	403.37	461.00	518.62	576.25
2306	14.41	28.82	57.65	115.30	172.95	230.60	288.25	345.90	403.55	461.20	518.85	576.50
2307	14.42	28.84	57.67	115.35	173.02	230.70	288.37	346.05	403.72	461.40	519.07	576.75
2308	14.42	28.85	57.70	115.40	173.10	230.80	288.50	346.20	403.90	461.60	519.30	577.00
2309	14.43	28.86	57.72	115.45	173.17	230.90	288.62	346.35	404.07	461.80	519.52	577.25
2310	14.44	28.87	57.75	115.50	173.25	231.00	288.75	346.50	404.25	462.00	519.75	577.50
2311	14.44	28.89	57.77	115.55	173.32	231.10	288.87	346.65	404.42	462.20	519.97	577.75
2312	14.45	28.90	57.80	115.60	173.40	231.20	289.00	346.80	404.60	462.40	520.20	578.00
2313	14.46	28.91	57.82	115.65	173.47	231.30	289.12	346.95	404.77	462.60	520.42	578.25
2314	14.46	28.92	57.85	115.70	173.55	231.40	289.25	347.10	404.95	462.80	520.65	578.50
2315	14.47	28.94	57.87	115.75	173.62	231.50	289.37	347.25	405.12	463.00	520.87	578.75
2316	14.47	28.95	57.90	115.80	173.70	231.60	289.50	347.40	405.30	463.20	521.10	579.00
2317	14.48	28.96	57.92	115.85	173.77	231.70	289.62	347.55	405.47	463.40	521.32	579.25
2318	14.49	28.97	57.95	115.90	173.85	231.80	289.75	347.70	405.65	463.60	521.55	579.50
2319	14.49	28.99	57.97	115.95	173.92	231.90	289.87	347.85	405.82	463.80	521.77	579.75
2320	14.50	29.00	58.00	116.00	174.00	232.00	290.00	348.00	406.00	464.00	522.00	580.00
2321	14.51	29.01	58.02	116.05	174.07	232.10	290.12	348.15	406.17	464.20	522.22	580.25
2322	14.51	29.02	58.05	116.10	174.15	232.20	290.25	348.30	406.35	464.40	522.45	580.50
2323	14.52	29.04	58.07	116.15	174.22	232.30	290.37	348.45	406.52	464.60	522.67	580.75
2324	14.52	29.05	58.10	116.20	174.30	232.40	290.50	348.60	406.70	464.80	522.90	581.00
2325	14.53	29.06	58.12	116.25	174.37	232.50	290.62	348.75	406.87	465.00	523.12	581.25
2326	14.54	29.07	58.15	116.30	174.45	232.60	290.75	348.90	407.05	465.20	523.35	581.50
2327	14.54	29.09	58.17	116.35	174.52	232.70	290.87	349.05	407.22	465.40	523.57	581.75
2328	14.55	29.10	58.20	116.40	174.60	232.80	291.00	349.20	407.40	465.60	523.80	582.00
2329	14.56	29.11	58.22	116.45	174.67	232.90	291.12	349.35	407.57	465.80	524.02	582.25
2330	14.56	29.12	58.25	116.50	174.75	233.00	291.25	349.50	407.75	466.00	524.25	582.50
2331	14.57	29.14	58.27	116.55	174.82	233.10	291.37	349.65	407.92	466.20	524.47	582.75
2332	14.57	29.15	58.30	116.60	174.90	233.20	291.50	349.80	408.10	466.40	524.70	583.00
2333	14.58	29.16	58.32	116.65	174.97	233.30	291.62	349.95	408.27	466.60	524.92	583.25
2334	14.59	29.17	58.35	116.70	175.05	233.40	291.75	350.10	408.45	466.80	525.15	583.50
2335	14.59	29.19	58.37	116.75	175.12	233.50	291.87	350.25	408.62	467.00	525.37	583.75
2336	14.60	29.20	58.40	116.80	175.20	233.60	292.00	350.40	408.80	467.20	525.60	584.00
2337	14.61	29.21	58.42	116.85	175.27	233.70	292.12	350.55	408.97	467.40	525.82	584.25
2338	14.61	29.22	58.45	116.90	175.35	233.80	292.25	350.70	409.15	467.60	526.05	584.50
2339	14.62	29.24	58.47	116.95	175.42	233.90	292.37	350.85	409.32	467.80	526.27	584.75
2340	14.62	29.25	58.50	117.00	175.50	234.00	292.50	351.00	409.50	468.00	526.50	585.00
2341	14.63	29.26	58.52	117.05	175.57	234.10	292.62	351.15	409.67	468.20	526.72	585.25
2342	14.64	29.27	58.55	117.10	175.65	234.20	292.75	351.30	409.85	468.40	526.95	585.50
2343	14.64	29.29	58.57	117.15	175.72	234.30	292.87	351.45	410.02	468.60	527.17	585.75
2344	14.65	29.30	58.60	117.20	175.80	234.40	293.00	351.60	410.20	468.80	527.40	586.00
2345	14.66	29.31	58.62	117.25	175.87	234.50	293.12	351.75	410.37	469.00	527.62	586.25
2346	14.66	29.32	58.65	117.30	175.95	234.60	293.25	351.90	410.55	469.20	527.85	586.50
2347	14.67	29.34	58.67	117.35	176.02	234.70	293.37	352.05	410.72	469.40	528.07	586.75
2348	14.67	29.35	58.70	117.40	176.10	234.80	293.50	352.20	410.90	469.60	528.30	587.00
2349	14.68	29.36	58.72	117.45	176.17	234.90	293.62	352.35	411.07	469.80	528.52	587.25
2350	14.69	29.37	58.75	117.50	176.25	235.00	293.75	352.50	411.25	470.00	528.75	587.50

2350 FEET.

Per Ton,	$11	$12	$13	$14	$15	$16	$17	$18	$19	$20
Per Foot,	27½ cts.	30 cts.	32½ cts.	35 cts.	37½ cts.	40 cts.	42½ cts.	45 cts.	47½ cts.	50 cts.
Feet.										
2301	632.77	690.30	747.82	805.35	862.87	920.40	977.92	1035.45	1092.97	1150.50
2302	633.05	690.60	748.15	805.70	863.25	920.80	978.35	1035.90	1093.45	1151.00
2303	633.32	690.90	748.47	806.05	863.62	921.20	978.77	1036.35	1093.92	1151.50
2304	633.60	691.20	748.80	806.40	864.00	921.60	979.20	1036.80	1094.40	1152.00
2305	633.87	691.50	749.12	806.75	864.37	922.00	979.62	1037.25	1094.87	1152.50
2306	634.15	691.80	749.45	807.10	864.75	922.40	980.05	1037.70	1095.35	1153.00
2307	634.42	692.10	749.77	807.45	865.12	922.80	980.47	1038.15	1095.82	1153.50
2308	634.70	692.40	750.10	807.80	865.50	923.20	980.90	1038.60	1096.30	1154.00
2309	634.97	692.70	750.42	808.15	865.87	923.60	981.32	1039.05	1096.77	1154.50
2310	635.25	693.00	750.75	808.50	866.25	924.00	981.75	1039.50	1097.25	1155.00
2311	635.52	693.30	751.07	808.85	866.62	924.40	982.17	1039.95	1097.72	1155.50
2312	635.80	693.60	751.40	809.20	867.00	924.80	982.60	1040.40	1098.20	1156.00
2313	636.07	693.90	751.72	809.55	867.37	925.20	983.02	1040.85	1098.67	1156.50
2314	636.35	694.20	752.05	809.90	867.75	925.60	983.45	1041.30	1099.15	1157.00
2315	636.62	694.50	752.37	810.25	868.12	926.00	983.87	1041.75	1099.62	1157.50
2316	636.90	694.80	752.70	810.60	868.50	926.40	984.30	1042.20	1100.10	1158.00
2317	637.17	695.10	753.02	810.95	868.87	926.80	984.72	1042.65	1100.57	1158.50
2318	637.45	695.40	753.35	811.30	869.25	927.20	985.15	1043.10	1101.05	1159.00
2319	637.72	695.70	753.67	811.65	869.62	927.60	985.57	1043.55	1101.52	1159.50
2320	638.00	696.00	754.00	812.00	870.00	928.00	986.00	1044.00	1102.00	1160.00
2321	638.27	696.30	754.32	812.35	870.37	928.40	986.42	1044.45	1102.47	1160.50
2322	638.55	696.60	754.65	812.70	870.75	928.80	986.85	1044.90	1102.95	1161.00
2323	638.82	696.90	754.97	813.05	871.12	929.20	987.27	1045.35	1103.42	1161.50
2324	639.10	697.20	755.30	813.40	871.50	929.60	987.70	1045.80	1103.90	1162.00
2325	639.37	697.50	755.62	813.75	871.87	930.00	988.12	1046.25	1104.37	1162.50
2326	639.65	697.80	755.95	814.10	872.25	930.40	988.55	1046.70	1104.85	1163.00
2327	639.92	698.10	756.27	814.45	872.62	930.80	988.97	1047.15	1105.32	1163.50
2328	640.20	698.40	756.60	814.80	873.00	931.20	989.40	1047.60	1105.80	1164.00
2329	640.47	698.70	756.92	815.15	873.37	931.60	989.82	1048.05	1106.27	1164.50
2330	640.75	699.00	757.25	815.50	873.75	932.00	990.25	1048.50	1106.75	1165.00
2331	641.02	699.30	757.57	815.85	874.12	932.40	990.67	1048.95	1107.22	1165.50
2332	641.30	699.60	757.90	816.20	874.50	932.80	991.10	1049.40	1107.70	1166.00
2333	641.57	699.90	758.22	816.55	874.87	933.20	991.52	1049.85	1108.17	1166.50
2334	641.85	700.20	758.55	816.90	875.25	933.60	991.95	1050.30	1108.65	1167.00
2335	642.12	700.50	758.87	817.25	875.62	934.00	992.37	1050.75	1109.12	1167.50
2336	642.40	700.80	759.20	817.60	876.00	934.40	992.80	1051.20	1109.60	1168.00
2337	642.67	701.10	759.52	817.95	876.37	934.80	993.22	1051.65	1110.07	1168.50
2338	642.95	701.40	759.85	818.30	876.75	935.20	993.65	1052.10	1110.55	1169.00
2339	643.22	701.70	760.17	818.65	877.12	935.60	994.07	1052.55	1111.02	1169.50
2340	643.50	702.00	760.50	819.00	877.50	936.00	994.50	1053.00	1111.50	1170.00
2341	643.77	702.30	760.82	819.35	877.87	936.40	994.92	1053.45	1111.97	1170.50
2342	644.05	702.60	761.15	819.70	878.25	936.80	995.35	1053.90	1112.45	1171.00
2343	644.32	702.90	761.47	820.05	878.62	937.20	995.77	1054.35	1112.92	1171.50
2344	644.60	703.20	761.80	820.40	879.00	937.60	996.20	1054.80	1113.40	1172.00
2345	644.87	703.50	762.12	820.75	879.37	938.00	996.62	1055.25	1113.87	1172.50
2346	645.15	703.80	762.45	821.10	879.75	938.40	997.05	1055.70	1114.35	1173.00
2347	645.42	704.10	762.77	821.45	880.12	938.80	997.47	1056.15	1114.82	1173.50
2348	645.70	704.40	763.10	821.80	880.50	939.20	997.90	1056.60	1115.30	1174.00
2349	645.97	704.70	763.42	822.15	880.87	939.60	998.32	1057.05	1115.77	1174.50
2350	646.25	705.00	763.75	822.50	881.25	940.00	998.75	1057.50	1116.25	1175.00

2400 FEET.

Per Ton, Per Foot,	25c.	50c.	$1 2½ cts.	$2 5 cts.	$3 7½ cts.	$4 10 cts.	$5 12½ cts.	$6 15 cts.	$7 17½ cts.	$8 20 cts.	$9 22½ cts.	$10 25 cts.
Feet.												
2351	14.69	29.39	58.77	117.55	176.32	235.10	293.87	352.65	411.42	470.20	528.97	587.75
2352	14.70	29.40	58.80	117.60	176.40	235.20	294.00	352.80	411.60	470.40	529.20	588.00
2353	14.71	29.41	58.82	117.65	176.47	235.30	294.12	352.95	411.77	470.60	529.42	588.25
2354	14.71	29.42	58.85	117.70	176.55	235.40	294.25	353.10	411.95	470.80	529.65	588.50
2355	14.72	29.44	58.87	117.75	176.62	235.50	294.37	353.25	412.12	471.00	529.87	588.75
2356	14.72	29.45	58.90	117.80	176.70	235.60	294.50	353.40	412.30	471.20	530.10	589.00
2357	14.73	29.46	58.92	117.85	176.77	235.70	294.62	353.55	412.47	471.40	530.32	589.25
2358	14.74	29.47	58.95	117.90	176.85	235.80	294.75	353.70	412.65	471.60	530.55	589.50
2359	14.74	29.49	58.97	117.95	176.92	235.90	294.87	353.85	412.82	471.80	530.77	589.75
2360	14.75	29.50	59.00	118.00	177.00	236.00	295.00	354.00	413.00	472.00	531.00	590.00
2361	14.76	29.51	59.02	118.05	177.07	236.10	295.12	354.15	413.17	472.20	531.22	590.25
2362	14.76	29.52	59.05	118.10	177.15	236.20	295.25	354.30	413.35	472.40	531.45	590.50
2363	14.77	29.54	59.07	118.15	177.22	236.30	295.37	354.45	413.52	472.60	531.67	590.75
2364	14.77	29.55	59.10	118.20	177.30	236.40	295.50	354.60	413.70	472.80	531.90	591.00
2365	14.78	29.56	59.12	118.25	177.37	236.50	295.62	354.75	413.87	473.00	532.12	591.25
2366	14.79	29.57	59.15	118.30	177.45	236.60	295.75	354.90	414.05	473.20	532.35	591.50
2367	14.79	29.59	59.17	118.35	177.52	236.70	295.87	355.05	414.22	473.40	532.57	591.75
2368	14.80	29.60	59.20	118.40	177.60	236.80	296.00	355.20	414.40	473.60	532.80	592.00
2369	14.81	29.61	59.22	118.45	177.67	236.90	296.12	355.35	414.57	473.80	533.02	592.25
2370	14.81	29.62	59.25	118.50	177.75	237.00	296.25	355.50	414.75	474.00	533.25	592.50
2371	14.82	29.64	59.27	118.55	177.82	237.10	296.37	355.65	414.92	474.20	533.47	592.75
2372	14.82	29.65	59.30	118.60	177.90	237.20	296.50	355.80	415.10	474.40	533.70	593.00
2373	14.83	29.66	59.32	118.65	177.97	237.30	296.62	355.95	415.27	474.60	533.92	593.25
2374	14.84	29.67	59.35	118.70	178.05	237.40	296.75	356.10	415.45	474.80	534.15	593.50
2375	14.84	29.69	59.37	118.75	178.12	237.50	296.87	356.25	415.62	475.00	534.37	593.75
2376	14.85	29.70	59.40	118.80	178.20	237.60	297.00	356.40	415.80	475.20	534.60	594.00
2377	14.86	29.71	59.42	118.85	178.27	237.70	297.12	356.55	415.97	475.40	534.82	594.25
2378	14.86	29.72	59.45	118.90	178.35	237.80	297.25	356.70	416.15	475.60	535.05	594.50
2379	14.87	29.74	59.47	118.95	178.42	237.90	297.37	356.85	416.32	475.80	535.27	594.75
2380	14.87	29.75	59.50	119.00	178.50	238.00	297.50	357.00	416.50	476.00	535.50	595.00
2381	14.88	29.76	59.52	119.05	178.57	238.10	297.62	357.15	416.67	476.20	535.72	595.25
2382	14.89	29.77	59.55	119.10	178.65	238.20	297.75	357.30	416.85	476.40	535.95	595.50
2383	14.89	29.79	59.57	119.15	178.72	238.30	297.87	357.45	417.02	476.60	536.17	595.75
2384	14.90	29.80	59.60	119.20	178.80	238.40	298.00	357.60	417.20	476.80	536.40	596.00
2385	14.91	29.81	59.62	119.25	178.87	238.50	298.12	357.75	417.37	477.00	536.62	596.25
2386	14.91	29.82	59.65	119.30	178.95	238.60	298.25	357.90	417.55	477.20	536.85	596.50
2387	14.92	29.84	59.67	119.35	179.02	238.70	298.37	358.05	417.72	477.40	537.07	596.75
2388	14.92	29.85	59.70	119.40	179.10	238.80	298.50	358.20	417.90	477.60	537.30	597.00
2389	14.93	29.86	59.72	119.45	179.17	238.90	298.62	358.35	418.07	477.80	537.52	597.25
2390	14.94	29.87	59.75	119.50	179.25	239.00	298.75	358.50	418.25	478.00	537.75	597.50
2391	14.94	29.89	59.77	119.55	179.32	239.10	298.87	358.65	418.42	478.20	537.97	597.75
2392	14.95	29.90	59.80	119.60	179.40	239.20	299.00	358.80	418.60	478.40	538.20	598.00
2393	14.96	29.91	59.82	119.65	179.47	239.30	299.12	358.95	418.77	478.60	538.42	598.25
2394	14.96	29.92	59.85	119.70	179.55	239.40	299.25	359.10	418.95	478.80	538.65	598.50
2395	14.97	29.94	59.87	119.75	179.62	239.50	299.37	359.25	419.12	479.00	538.87	598.75
2396	14.97	29.95	59.90	119.80	179.70	239.60	299.50	359.40	419.30	479.20	539.10	599.00
2397	14.98	29.96	59.92	119.85	179.77	239.70	299.62	359.55	419.47	479.40	539.32	599.25
2398	14.99	29.97	59.95	119.90	179.85	239.80	299.75	359.70	419.65	479.60	539.55	599.50
2399	14.99	29.99	59.97	119.95	179.92	239.90	299.87	359.85	419.82	479.80	539.77	599.75
2400	15.00	30.00	60.00	120.00	180.00	240.00	300.00	360.00	420.00	480.00	540.00	600.00

2400 FEET.

Per Ton,	$11	$12	$13	$14	$15	$16	$17	$18	$19	$20
Per Foot,	27½ cts.	30 cts.	32½ cts.	35 cts.	37½ cts.	40 cts.	42½ cts.	45 cts.	47½ cts.	50 cts.
Feet.										
2351	646.52	705.30	764.07	822.85	881.62	940.40	999.17	1057.95	1116.72	1175.50
2352	646.80	705.60	764.40	823.20	882.00	940.80	999.60	1058.40	1117.20	1176.00
2353	647.07	705.90	764.72	823.55	882.37	941.20	1000.02	1058.85	1117.67	1176.50
2354	647.35	706.20	765.05	823.90	882.75	941.60	1000.45	1059.30	1118.15	1177.00
2355	647.62	706.50	765.37	824.25	883.12	942.00	1000.87	1059.75	1118.62	1177.50
2356	647.90	706.80	765.70	824.60	883.50	942.40	1001.30	1060.20	1119.10	1178.00
2357	648.17	707.10	766.02	824.95	883.87	942.80	1001.72	1060.65	1119.57	1178.50
2358	648.45	707.40	766.35	825.30	884.25	943.20	1002.15	1061.10	1120.05	1179.00
2359	648.72	707.70	766.67	825.65	884.62	943.60	1002.57	1061.55	1120.52	1179.50
2360	649.00	708.00	767.00	826.00	885.00	944.00	1003.00	1062.00	1121.00	1180.00
2361	649.27	708.30	767.32	826.35	885.37	944.40	1003.42	1062.45	1121.47	1180.50
2362	649.55	708.60	767.65	826.70	885.75	944.80	1003.85	1062.90	1121.95	1181.00
2363	649.82	708.90	767.97	827.05	886.12	945.20	1004.27	1063.35	1122.42	1181.50
2364	650.10	709.20	768.30	827.40	886.50	945.60	1004.70	1063.80	1122.90	1182.00
2365	650.37	709.50	768.62	827.75	886.87	946.00	1005.12	1064.25	1123.37	1182.50
2366	650.65	709.80	768.95	828.10	887.25	946.40	1005.55	1064.70	1123.85	1183.00
2367	650.92	710.10	769.27	828.45	887.62	946.80	1005.97	1065.15	1124.32	1183.50
2368	651.20	710.40	769.60	828.80	888.00	947.20	1006.40	1065.60	1124.80	1184.00
2369	651.47	710.70	769.92	829.15	888.37	947.60	1006.82	1066.05	1125.27	1184.50
2370	651.75	711.00	770.25	829.50	888.75	948.00	1007.25	1066.50	1125.75	1185.00
2371	652.02	711.30	770.57	829.85	889.12	948.40	1007.67	1066.95	1126.22	1185.50
2372	652.30	711.60	770.90	830.20	889.50	948.80	1008.10	1067.40	1126.70	1186.00
2373	652.57	711.90	771.22	830.55	889.87	949.20	1008.52	1067.85	1127.17	1186.50
2374	652.85	712.20	771.55	830.90	890.25	949.60	1008.95	1068.30	1127.65	1187.00
2375	653.12	712.50	771.87	831.25	890.62	950.00	1009.37	1068.75	1128.12	1187.50
2376	653.40	712.80	772.20	831.60	891.00	950.40	1009.80	1069.20	1128.60	1188.00
2377	653.67	713.10	772.52	831.95	891.37	950.80	1010.22	1069.65	1129.07	1188.50
2378	653.95	713.40	772.85	832.30	891.75	951.20	1010.65	1070.10	1129.55	1189.00
2379	654.22	713.70	773.17	832.65	892.12	951.60	1011.07	1070.55	1130.02	1189.50
2380	654.50	714.00	773.50	833.00	892.50	952.00	1011.50	1071.00	1130.50	1190.00
3381	654.77	714.30	773.82	833.35	892.87	952.40	1011.92	1071.45	1130.97	1190.50
2382	655.05	714.60	774.15	833.70	893.25	952.80	1012.35	1071.90	1131.45	1191.00
2383	655.32	714.90	774.47	834.05	893.62	953.20	1012.77	1072.35	1131.92	1191.50
2384	655.60	715.20	774.80	834.40	894.00	953.60	1013.20	1072.80	1132.40	1192.00
2385	655.87	715.50	775.12	834.75	894.37	954.00	1013.62	1073.25	1132.87	1192.50
2386	656.15	715.80	775.45	835.10	894.75	954.40	1014.05	1073.70	1133.35	1193.00
2387	656.42	716.10	775.77	835.45	895.12	954.80	1014.47	1074.15	1133.82	1193.50
2388	656.70	716.40	776.10	835.80	895.50	955.20	1014.90	1074.60	1134.30	1194.00
2389	656.97	716.70	776.42	836.15	895.87	955.60	1015.32	1075.05	1134.77	1194.50
2390	657.25	717.00	776.75	836.50	896.25	956.00	1015.75	1075.50	1135.25	1195.00
2391	657.52	717.30	777.07	836.85	896.62	956.40	1016.17	1075.95	1135.72	1195.50
2392	657.80	717.60	777.40	837.20	897.00	956.80	1016.60	1076.40	1136.20	1196.00
2393	658.07	717.90	777.72	837.55	897.37	957.20	1017.02	1076.85	1136.67	1196.50
2394	658.35	718.20	778.05	837.90	897.75	957.60	1017.45	1077.30	1137.15	1197.00
2395	658.62	718.50	778.37	838.25	898.12	958.00	1017.87	1077.75	1137.62	1197.50
2396	658.90	718.80	778.70	838.60	898.50	958.40	1018.30	1078.20	1138.10	1198.00
2397	659.17	719.10	779.02	838.95	898.87	958.80	1018.72	1078.65	1138.57	1198.50
2398	659.45	719.40	779.35	839.30	899.25	959.20	1019.15	1079.10	1139.05	1199.00
2399	659.72	719.70	779.67	839.65	899.62	959.60	1019.57	1079.55	1139.52	1199.50
2400	660.00	720.00	780.00	840.00	900.00	960.00	1020.00	1080.00	1140.00	1200.00

2450 FEET.

Per Ton, Per Foot, Feet.	25c.	50c.	$1 2½ cts.	$2 5 cts.	$3 7½ cts.	$4 10 cts.	$5 12½ cts.	$6 15 cts.	$7 17½ cts.	$8 20 cts.	$9 22½ cts.	$10 25 cts.
2401	15.01	30.01	60.02	120.05	180.07	240.10	300.12	360.15	420.17	480.20	540.22	600.25
2402	15.01	30.02	60.05	120.10	180.15	240.20	300.25	360.30	420.35	480.40	540.45	600.50
2403	15.02	30.04	60.07	120.15	180.22	240.30	300.37	360.45	420.52	480.60	540.67	600.75
2404	15.02	30.05	60.10	120.20	180.30	240.40	300.50	360.60	420.70	480.80	540.90	601.00
2405	15.03	30.06	60.12	120.25	180.37	240.50	300.62	360.75	420.87	481.00	541.12	601.25
2406	15.04	30.07	60.15	120.30	180.45	240.60	300.75	360.90	421.05	481.20	541.35	601.50
2407	15.04	30.09	60.17	120.35	180.52	240.70	300.87	361.05	421.22	481.40	541.57	601.75
2408	15.05	30.10	60.20	120.40	180.60	240.80	301.00	361.20	421.40	481.60	541.80	602.00
2409	15.06	30.11	60.22	120.45	180.67	240.90	301.12	361.35	421.57	481.80	542.02	602.25
2410	15.06	30.12	60.25	120.50	180.75	241.00	301.25	361.50	421.75	482.00	542.25	602.50
2411	15.07	30.14	60.27	120.55	180.82	241.10	301.37	361.65	421.92	482.20	542.47	602.75
2412	15.07	30.15	60.30	120.60	180.90	241.20	301.50	361.80	422.10	482.40	542.70	603.00
2413	15.08	30.16	60.32	120.65	180.97	241.30	301.62	361.95	422.27	482.60	542.92	603.25
2414	15.09	30.17	60.35	120.70	181.05	241.40	301.75	362.10	422.45	482.80	543.15	603.50
2415	15.09	30.19	60.37	120.75	181.12	241.50	301.87	362.25	422.62	483.00	543.37	603.75
2416	15.10	30.20	60.40	120.80	181.20	241.60	302.00	362.40	422.80	483.20	543.60	604.00
2417	15.11	30.21	60.42	120.85	181.27	241.70	302.12	362.55	422.97	483.40	543.82	604.25
2418	15.11	30.22	60.45	120.90	181.35	241.80	302.25	362.70	423.15	483.60	544.05	604.50
2419	15.12	30.24	60.47	120.95	181.42	241.90	302.37	362.85	423.32	483.80	544.27	604.75
2420	15.12	30.25	60.50	121.00	181.50	242.00	302.50	363.00	423.50	484.00	544.50	605.00
2421	15.13	30.26	60.52	121.05	181.57	242.10	302.62	363.15	423.67	484.20	544.72	605.25
2422	15.14	30.27	60.55	121.10	181.65	242.20	302.75	363.30	423.85	484.40	544.95	605.50
2423	15.14	30.29	60.57	121.15	181.72	242.30	302.87	363.45	424.02	484.60	545.17	605.75
2424	15.15	30.30	60.60	121.20	181.80	242.40	303.00	363.60	424.20	484.80	545.40	606.00
2425	15.16	30.31	60.62	121.25	181.87	242.50	303.12	363.75	424.37	485.00	545.62	606.25
2426	15.16	30.32	60.65	121.30	181.95	242.60	303.25	363.90	424.55	485.20	545.85	606.50
2427	15.17	30.34	60.67	121.35	182.02	242.70	303.37	364.05	424.72	485.40	546.07	606.75
2428	15.17	30.35	60.70	121.40	182.10	242.80	303.50	364.20	424.90	485.60	546.30	607.00
2429	15.18	30.36	60.72	121.45	182.17	242.90	303.62	364.35	425.07	485.80	546.52	607.25
2430	15.19	30.37	60.75	121.50	182.25	243.00	303.75	364.50	425.25	486.00	546.75	607.50
2431	15.19	30.39	60.77	121.55	182.32	243.10	303.87	364.65	425.42	486.20	546.97	607.75
2432	15.20	30.40	60.80	121.60	182.40	243.20	304.00	364.80	425.60	486.40	547.20	608.00
2433	15.21	30.41	60.82	121.65	182.47	243.30	304.12	364.95	425.77	486.60	547.42	608.25
2434	15.21	30.42	60.85	121.70	182.55	243.40	304.25	365.10	425.95	486.80	547.65	608.50
2435	15.22	30.44	60.87	121.75	182.62	243.50	304.37	365.25	426.12	487.00	547.87	608.75
2436	15.22	30.45	60.90	121.80	182.70	243.60	304.50	365.40	426.30	487.20	548.10	609.00
2437	15.23	30.46	60.92	121.85	182.77	243.70	304.62	365.55	426.47	487.40	548.32	609.25
2438	15.24	30.47	60.95	121.90	182.85	243.80	304.75	365.70	426.65	487.60	548.55	609.50
2439	15.24	30.49	60.97	121.95	182.92	243.90	304.87	365.85	426.82	487.80	548.77	609.75
2440	15.25	30.50	61.00	122.00	183.00	244.00	305.00	366.00	427.00	488.00	549.00	610.00
2441	15.26	30.51	61.02	122.05	183.07	244.10	305.12	366.15	427.17	488.20	549.22	610.25
2442	15.26	30.52	61.05	122.10	183.15	244.20	305.25	366.30	427.35	488.40	549.45	610.50
2443	15.27	30.54	61.07	122.15	183.22	244.30	305.37	366.45	427.52	488.60	549.67	610.75
2444	15.27	30.55	61.10	122.20	183.30	244.40	305.50	366.60	427.70	488.80	549.90	611.00
2445	15.28	30.56	61.12	122.25	183.37	244.50	305.62	366.75	427.87	489.00	550.12	611.25
2446	15.29	30.57	61.15	122.30	183.45	244.60	305.75	366.90	428.05	489.20	550.35	611.50
2447	15.29	30.59	61.17	122.35	183.52	244.70	305.87	367.05	428.22	489.40	550.57	611.75
2448	15.30	30.60	61.20	122.40	183.60	244.80	306.00	367.20	428.40	489.60	550.80	612.00
2449	15.31	30.61	61.22	122.45	183.67	244.90	306.12	367.35	428.57	489.80	551.02	612.25
2450	15.31	30.62	61.25	122.50	183.75	245.00	306.25	367.50	428.75	490.00	551.25	612.50

2450 FEET.

Per Ton,	$11	$12	$13	$14	$15	$16	$17	$18	$19	$20
Per Foot,	27½ cts.	30 cts.	32½ cts.	35 cts.	37½ cts.	40 cts.	42½ cts.	45 cts.	47½ cts.	50 cts.
Feet.										
2401	660.27	720.30	780.32	840.35	900.37	960.40	1020.42	1080.45	1140.47	1200.50
2402	660.55	720.60	780.65	840.70	900.75	960.80	1020.85	1080.90	1140.95	1201.00
2403	660.82	720.90	780.97	841.05	901.12	961.20	1021.27	1081.35	1141.42	1201.50
2404	661.10	721.20	781.30	841.40	901.50	961.60	1021.70	1081.80	1141.90	1202.00
2405	661.37	721.50	781.62	841.75	901.87	962.00	1022.12	1082.25	1142.37	1202.50
2406	661.65	721.80	781.95	842.10	902.25	962.40	1022.55	1082.70	1142.85	1203.00
2407	661.92	722.10	782.27	842.45	902.62	962.80	1022.97	1083.15	1143.32	1203.50
2408	662.20	722.40	782.60	842.80	903.00	963.20	1023.40	1083.60	1143.80	1204.00
2409	662.47	722.70	782.92	843.15	903.37	963.60	1023.82	1084.05	1144.27	1204.50
2410	662.75	723.00	783.25	843.50	903.75	964.00	1024.25	1084.50	1144.75	1205.00
2411	663.02	723.30	783.57	843.85	904.12	964.40	1024.67	1084.95	1145.22	1205.50
2412	663.30	723.60	783.90	844.20	904.50	964.80	1025.10	1085.40	1145.70	1206.00
2413	663.57	723.90	784.22	844.55	904.87	965.20	1025.52	1085.85	1146.17	1206.50
2414	663.85	724.20	784.55	844.90	905.25	965.60	1025.95	1086.30	1146.65	1207.00
2415	664.12	724.50	784.87	845.25	905.62	966.00	1026.37	1086.75	1147.12	1207.50
2416	664.40	724.80	785.20	845.60	906.00	966.40	1026.80	1087.20	1147.60	1208.00
2417	664.67	725.10	785.52	845.95	906.37	966.80	1027.22	1087.65	1148.07	1208.50
2418	664.95	725.40	785.85	846.30	906.75	967.20	1027.65	1088.10	1148.55	1209.00
2419	665.22	725.70	786.17	846.65	907.12	967.60	1028.07	1088.55	1149.02	1209.50
2420	665.50	726.00	786.50	847.00	907.50	968.00	1028.50	1089.00	1149.50	1210.00
2421	665.77	726.30	786.82	847.35	907.87	968.40	1028.92	1089.45	1149.97	1210.50
2422	666.05	726.60	787.15	847.70	908.25	968.80	1029.35	1089.90	1150.45	1211.00
2423	666.32	726.90	787.47	848.05	908.62	969.20	1029.77	1090.35	1150.92	1211.50
2424	666.60	727.20	787.80	848.40	909.00	969.60	1030.20	1090.80	1151.40	1212.00
2425	666.87	727.50	788.12	848.75	909.37	970.00	1030.62	1091.25	1151.87	1212.50
2426	667.15	727.80	788.45	849.10	909.75	970.40	1031.05	1091.70	1152.35	1213.00
2427	667.42	728.10	788.77	849.45	910.12	970.80	1031.47	1092.15	1152.82	1213.50
2428	667.70	728.40	789.10	849.80	910.50	971.20	1031.90	1092.60	1153.30	1214.00
2429	667.97	728.70	789.42	850.15	910.87	971.60	1032.32	1093.05	1153.77	1214.50
2430	668.25	729.00	789.75	850.50	911.25	972.00	1032.75	1093.50	1154.25	1215.00
2431	668.52	729.30	790.07	850.85	911.62	972.40	1033.17	1093.95	1154.72	1215.50
2432	668.80	729.60	790.40	851.20	912.00	972.80	1033.60	1094.40	1155.20	1216.00
2433	669.07	729.90	790.72	851.55	912.37	973.20	1034.02	1094.85	1155.67	1216.50
2434	669.35	730.20	791.05	851.90	912.75	973.60	1034.45	1095.30	1156.15	1217.00
2435	669.62	730.50	791.37	852.25	913.12	974.00	1034.87	1095.75	1156.62	1217.50
2436	669.90	730.80	791.70	852.60	913.50	974.40	1035.30	1096.20	1157.10	1218.00
2437	670.17	731.10	792.02	852.95	913.87	974.80	1035.72	1096.65	1157.57	1218.50
2438	670.45	731.40	792.35	853.30	914.25	975.20	1036.15	1097.10	1158.05	1219.00
2439	670.72	731.70	792.67	853.65	914.62	975.60	1036.57	1097.55	1158.52	1219.50
2440	671.00	732.00	793.00	854.00	915.00	976.00	1037.00	1098.00	1159.00	1220.00
2441	671.27	732.30	793.32	854.35	915.37	976.40	1037.42	1098.45	1159.47	1220.50
2442	671.55	732.60	793.65	854.70	915.75	976.80	1037.85	1098.90	1159.95	1221.00
2443	671.82	732.90	793.97	855.05	916.12	977.20	1038.27	1099.35	1160.42	1221.50
2444	672.10	733.20	794.30	855.40	916.50	977.60	1038.70	1099.80	1160.90	1222.00
2445	672.37	733.50	794.62	855.75	916.87	978.00	1039.12	1100.25	1161.37	1222.50
2446	672.65	733.80	794.95	856.10	917.25	978.40	1039.55	1100.70	1161.85	1223.00
2447	672.92	734.10	795.27	856.45	917.62	978.80	1039.97	1101.15	1162.32	1223.50
2448	673.20	734.40	795.60	856.80	918.00	979.20	1040.40	1101.60	1162.80	1224.00
2449	673.47	734.70	795.92	857.15	918.37	979.60	1040.82	1102.05	1163.27	1224.50
2450	673.75	735.00	796.25	857.50	918.75	980.00	1041.25	1102.50	1163.75	1225.00

2500 FEET.

Per Ton, Per Foot,	25c.	50c.	$1 2½ cts.	$2 5 cts.	$3 7½ cts.	$4 10 cts.	$5 12½ cts.	$6 15 cts.	$7 17½ cts.	$8 20 cts.	$9 22½ cts.	$10 25 cts.
Feet.												
2451	15.32	30.64	61.27	122.55	183.82	245.10	306.37	367.65	428.92	490.20	551.47	612.75
2452	15.32	30.65	61.30	122.60	183.90	245.20	306.50	367.80	429.10	490.40	551.70	613.00
2453	15.33	30.66	61.32	122.65	183.97	245.30	306.62	367.95	429.27	490.60	551.92	613.25
2454	15.34	30.67	61.35	122.70	184.05	245.40	306.75	368.10	429.45	490.80	552.15	613.50
2455	15.34	30.69	61.37	122.75	184.12	245.50	306.87	368.25	429.62	491.00	552.37	613.75
2456	15.35	30.70	61.40	122.80	184.20	245.60	307.00	368.40	429.80	491.20	552.60	614.00
2457	15.36	30.71	61.42	122.85	184.27	245.70	307.12	368.55	429.97	491.40	552.82	614.25
2458	15.36	30.72	61.45	122.90	184.35	245.80	307.25	368.70	430.15	491.60	553.05	614.50
2459	15.37	30.74	61.47	122.95	184.42	245.90	307.37	368.85	430.32	491.80	553.27	614.75
2460	15.37	30.75	61.50	123.00	184.50	246.00	307.50	369.00	430.50	492.00	553.50	615.00
2461	15.38	30.76	61.52	123.05	184.57	246.10	307.62	369.15	430.67	492.20	553.72	615.25
2462	15.39	30.77	61.55	123.10	184.65	246.20	307.75	369.30	430.85	492.40	553.95	615.50
2463	15.39	30.79	61.57	123.15	184.72	246.30	307.87	369.45	431.02	492.60	554.17	615.75
2464	15.40	30.80	61.60	123.20	184.80	246.40	308.00	369.60	431.20	492.80	554.40	616.00
2465	15.41	30.81	61.62	123.25	184.87	246.50	308.12	369.75	431.37	493.00	554.62	616.25
2466	15.41	30.82	61.65	123.30	184.95	246.60	308.25	369.90	431.55	493.20	554.85	616.50
2467	15.42	30.84	61.67	123.35	185.02	246.70	308.37	370.05	431.72	493.40	555.07	616.75
2468	15.42	30.85	61.70	123.40	185.10	246.80	308.50	370.20	431.90	493.60	555.30	617.00
2469	15.43	30.86	61.72	123.45	185.17	246.90	308.62	370.35	432.07	493.80	555.52	617.25
2470	15.44	30.87	61.75	123.50	185.25	247.00	308.75	370.50	432.25	494.00	555.75	617.50
2471	15.44	30.89	61.77	123.55	185.32	247.10	308.87	370.65	432.42	494.20	555.97	617.75
2472	15.45	30.90	61.80	123.60	185.40	247.20	309.00	370.80	432.60	494.40	556.20	618.00
2473	15.46	30.91	61.82	123.65	185.47	247.30	309.12	370.95	432.77	494.60	556.42	618.25
2474	15.46	30.92	61.85	123.70	185.55	247.40	309.25	371.10	432.95	494.80	556.65	618.50
2475	15.47	30.94	61.87	123.75	185.62	247.50	309.37	371.25	433.12	495.00	556.87	618.75
2476	15.47	30.95	61.90	123.80	185.70	247.60	309.50	371.40	433.30	495.20	557.10	619.00
2477	15.48	30.96	61.92	123.85	185.77	247.70	309.62	371.55	433.47	495.40	557.32	619.25
2478	15.49	30.97	61.95	123.90	185.85	247.80	309.75	371.70	433.65	495.60	557.55	619.50
2479	15.49	30.99	61.97	123.95	185.92	247.90	309.87	371.85	433.82	495.80	557.77	619.75
2480	15.50	31.00	62.00	124.00	186.00	248.00	310.00	372.00	434.00	496.00	558.00	620.00
2481	15.51	31.01	62.02	124.05	186.07	248.10	310.12	372.15	434.17	496.20	558.22	620.25
2482	15.51	31.02	62.05	124.10	186.15	248.20	310.25	372.30	434.35	496.40	558.45	620.50
2483	15.52	31.04	62.07	124.15	186.22	248.30	310.37	372.45	434.52	496.60	558.67	620.75
2484	15.52	31.05	62.10	124.20	186.30	248.40	310.50	372.60	434.70	496.80	558.90	621.00
2485	15.53	31.06	62.12	124.25	186.37	248.50	310.62	372.75	434.87	497.00	559.12	621.25
2486	15.54	31.07	62.15	124.30	186.45	248.60	310.75	372.90	435.05	497.20	559.35	621.50
2487	15.54	31.09	62.17	124.35	186.52	248.70	310.87	373.05	435.22	497.40	559.57	621.75
2488	15.55	31.10	62.20	124.40	186.60	248.80	311.00	373.20	435.40	497.60	559.80	622.00
2489	15.56	31.11	62.22	124.45	186.67	248.90	311.12	373.35	435.57	497.80	560.02	622.25
2490	15.56	31.12	62.25	124.50	186.75	249.00	311.25	373.50	435.75	498.00	560.25	622.50
2491	15.57	31.14	62.27	124.55	186.82	249.10	311.37	373.65	435.92	498.20	560.47	622.75
2492	15.57	31.15	62.30	124.60	186.90	249.20	311.50	373.80	436.10	498.40	560.70	623.00
2493	15.58	31.16	62.32	124.65	186.97	249.30	311.62	373.95	436.27	498.60	560.92	623.25
2494	15.59	31.17	62.35	124.70	187.05	249.40	311.75	374.10	436.45	498.80	561.15	623.50
2495	15.59	31.19	62.37	124.75	187.12	249.50	311.87	374.25	436.62	499.00	561.37	623.75
2496	15.60	31.20	62.40	124.80	187.20	249.60	312.00	374.40	436.80	499.20	561.60	624.00
2497	15.61	31.21	62.42	124.85	187.27	249.70	312.12	374.55	436.97	499.40	561.82	624.25
2498	15.61	31.22	62.45	124.90	187.35	249.80	312.25	374.70	437.15	499.60	562.05	624.50
2499	15.62	31.24	62.47	124.95	187.42	249.90	312.37	374.85	437.32	499.80	562.27	624.75
2500	15.62	31.25	62.50	125.00	187.50	250.00	312.50	375.00	437.50	500.00	562.50	625.00

2500 FEET.

Per Ton,	$11	$12	$13	$14	$15	$16	$17	$18	$19	$20
Per Foot,	27½ cts.	30 cts.	32½ cts.	35 cts.	37½ cts.	40 cts.	42½ cts.	45 cts.	47½ cts.	50 cts.
Feet.										
2451	674.02	735.30	796.57	857.85	919.12	980.40	1041.67	1102.95	1164.22	1225.50
2452	674.30	735.60	796.90	858.20	919.50	980.80	1042.10	1103.40	1164.70	1226.00
2453	674.57	735.90	797.22	858.55	919.87	981.20	1042.52	1103.85	1165.17	1226.50
2454	674.85	736.20	797.55	858.90	920.25	981.60	1042.95	1104.30	1165.65	1227.00
2455	675.12	736.50	797.87	859.25	920.62	982.00	1043.37	1104.75	1166.12	1227.50
2456	675.40	736.80	798.20	859.60	921.00	982.40	1043.80	1105.20	1166.60	1228.00
2457	675.67	737.10	798.52	859.95	921.37	982.80	1044.22	1105.65	1167.07	1228.50
2458	675.95	737.40	798.85	860.30	921.75	983.20	1044.65	1106.10	1167.55	1229.00
2459	676.22	737.70	799.17	860.65	922.12	983.60	1045.07	1106.55	1168.02	1229.50
2460	676.50	738.00	799.50	861.00	922.50	984.00	1045.50	1107.00	1168.50	1230.00
2461	676.77	738.30	799.82	861.35	922.87	984.40	1045.92	1107.45	1168.97	1230.50
2462	677.05	738.60	800.15	861.70	923.25	984.80	1046.35	1107.90	1169.45	1231.00
2463	677.32	738.90	800.47	862.05	923.62	985.20	1046.77	1108.35	1169.92	1231.50
2464	677.60	739.20	800.80	862.40	924.00	985.60	1047.20	1108.80	1170.40	1232.00
2465	677.87	739.50	801.12	862.75	924.37	986.00	1047.62	1109.25	1170.87	1232.50
2466	678.15	739.80	801.45	863.10	924.75	986.40	1048.05	1109.70	1171.35	1233.00
2467	678.42	740.10	801.77	863.45	925.12	986.80	1048.47	1110.15	1171.82	1233.50
2468	678.70	740.40	802.10	863.80	925.50	987.20	1048.90	1110.60	1172.30	1234.00
2469	678.97	740.70	802.42	864.15	925.87	987.60	1049.32	1111.05	1172.77	1234.50
2470	679.25	741.00	802.75	864.50	926.25	988.00	1049.75	1111.50	1173.25	1235.00
2471	679.52	741.30	803.07	864.85	926.62	988.40	1050.17	1111.95	1173.72	1235.50
2472	679.80	741.60	803.40	865.20	927.00	988.80	1050.60	1112.40	1174.20	1236.00
2473	680.07	741.90	803.72	865.55	927.37	989.20	1051.02	1112.85	1174.67	1236.50
2474	680.35	742.20	804.05	865.90	927.75	989.60	1051.45	1113.30	1175.15	1237.00
2475	680.62	742.50	804.37	866.25	928.12	990.00	1051.87	1113.75	1175.62	1237.50
2476	680.90	742.80	804.70	866.60	928.50	990.40	1052.30	1114.20	1176.10	1238.00
2477	681.17	743.10	805.02	866.95	928.87	990.80	1052.72	1114.65	1176.57	1238.50
2478	681.45	743.40	805.35	867.30	929.25	991.20	1053.15	1115.10	1177.05	1239.00
2479	681.72	743.70	805.67	867.65	929.62	991.60	1053.57	1115.55	1177.52	1239.50
2480	682.00	744.00	806.00	868.00	930.00	992.00	1054.00	1116.00	1178.00	1240.00
2481	682.27	744.30	806.32	868.35	930.37	992.40	1054.42	1116.45	1178.47	1240.50
2482	682.55	744.60	806.65	868.70	930.75	992.80	1054.85	1116.90	1178.95	1241.00
2483	682.82	744.90	806.97	869.05	931.12	993.20	1055.27	1117.35	1179.42	1241.50
2484	683.10	745.20	807.30	869.40	931.50	993.60	1055.70	1117.80	1179.90	1242.00
2485	683.37	745.50	807.62	869.75	931.87	994.00	1056.12	1118.25	1180.37	1242.50
2486	683.65	745.80	807.95	870.10	932.25	994.40	1056.55	1118.70	1180.85	1243.00
2487	683.92	746.10	808.27	870.45	932.62	994.80	1056.97	1119.15	1181.32	1243.50
2488	684.20	746.40	808.60	870.80	933.00	995.20	1057.40	1119.60	1181.80	1244.00
2489	684.47	746.70	808.92	871.15	933.37	995.60	1057.82	1120.05	1182.27	1244.50
2490	684.75	747.00	809.25	871.50	933.75	996.00	1058.25	1120.50	1182.75	1245.00
2491	685.02	747.30	809.57	871.85	934.12	996.40	1058.67	1120.95	1183.22	1245.50
2492	685.30	747.60	809.90	872.20	934.50	996.80	1059.10	1121.40	1183.70	1246.00
2493	685.57	747.90	810.22	872.55	934.87	997.20	1059.52	1121.85	1184.17	1246.50
2494	685.85	748.20	810.55	872.90	935.25	997.60	1059.95	1122.30	1184.65	1247.00
2495	686.12	748.50	810.87	873.25	935.62	998.00	1060.37	1122.75	1185.12	1247.50
2496	686.40	748.80	811.20	873.60	936.00	998.40	1060.80	1123.20	1185.60	1248.00
2497	686.67	749.10	811.52	873.95	936.37	998.80	1061.22	1123.65	1186.07	1248.50
2498	686.95	749.40	811.85	874.30	936.75	999.20	1061.65	1124.10	1186.55	1249.00
2499	687.22	749.70	812.17	874.65	937.12	999.60	1062.07	1124.55	1187.02	1249.50
2500	687.50	750.00	812.50	875.00	937.50	1000.00	1062.50	1125.00	1187.50	1250.00

2550 FEET.

Per Ton,	25c.	50c.	$1	$2	$3	$4	$5	$6	$7	$8	$9	$10
Per Foot,			2½ cts.	5 cts.	7½ cts.	10 cts.	12½ cts.	15 cts.	17½ cts.	20 cts.	22½ cts.	25 cts.
Feet.												
2501	15.63	31.26	62.52	125.05	187.57	250.10	312.62	375.15	437.67	500.20	562.72	625.25
2502	15.64	31.27	62.55	125.10	187.65	250.20	312.75	375.30	437.85	500.40	562.95	625.50
2503	15.64	31.29	62.57	125.15	187.72	250.30	312.87	375.45	438.02	500.60	563.17	625.75
2504	15.65	31.30	62.60	125.20	187.80	250.40	313.00	375.60	438.20	500.80	563.40	626.00
2505	15.66	31.31	62.62	125.25	187.87	250.50	313.12	375.75	438.37	501.00	563.62	626.25
2506	15.66	31.32	62.65	125.30	187.95	250.60	313.25	375.90	438.55	501.20	563.85	626.50
2507	15.67	31.34	62.67	125.35	188.02	250.70	313.37	376.05	438.72	501.40	564.07	626.75
2508	15.67	31.35	62.70	125.40	188.10	250.80	313.50	376.20	438.90	501.60	564.30	627.00
2509	15.68	31.36	62.72	125.45	188.17	250.90	313.62	376.35	439.07	501.80	564.52	627.25
2510	15.69	31.37	62.75	125.50	188.25	251.00	313.75	376.50	439.25	502.00	564.75	627.50
2511	15.69	31.39	62.77	125.55	188.32	251.10	313.87	376.65	439.42	502.20	564.97	627.75
2512	15.70	31.40	62.80	125.60	188.40	251.20	314.00	376.80	439.60	502.40	565.20	628.00
2513	15.71	31.41	62.82	125.65	188.47	251.30	314.12	376.95	439.77	502.60	565.42	628.25
2514	15.71	31.42	62.85	125.70	188.55	251.40	314.25	377.10	439.95	502.80	565.65	628.50
2515	15.72	31.44	62.87	125.75	188.62	251.50	314.37	377.25	440.12	503.00	565.87	628.75
2516	15.72	31.45	62.90	125.80	188.70	251.60	314.50	377.40	440.30	503.20	566.10	629.00
2517	15.73	31.46	62.92	125.85	188.77	251.70	314.62	377.55	440.47	503.40	566.32	629.25
2518	15.74	31.47	62.95	125.90	188.85	251.80	314.75	377.70	440.65	503.60	566.55	629.50
2519	15.74	31.49	62.97	125.95	188.92	251.90	314.87	377.85	440.82	503.80	566.77	629.75
2520	15.75	31.50	63.00	126.00	189.00	252.00	315.00	378.00	441.00	504.00	567.00	630.00
2521	15.76	31.51	63.02	126.05	189.07	252.10	315.12	378.15	441.17	504.20	567.22	630.25
2522	15.76	31.52	63.05	126.10	189.15	252.20	315.25	378.30	441.35	504.40	567.45	630.50
2523	15.77	31.54	63.07	126.15	189.22	252.30	315.37	378.45	441.52	504.60	567.67	630.75
2524	15.77	31.55	63.10	126.20	189.30	252.40	315.50	378.60	441.70	504.80	567.90	631.00
2525	15.78	31.56	63.12	126.25	189.37	252.50	315.62	378.75	441.87	505.00	568.12	631.25
2526	15.79	31.57	63.15	126.30	189.45	252.60	315.75	378.90	442.05	505.20	568.35	631.50
2527	15.79	31.59	63.17	126.35	189.52	252.70	315.87	379.05	442.22	505.40	568.57	631.75
2528	15.80	31.60	63.20	126.40	189.60	252.80	316.00	379.20	442.40	505.60	568.80	632.00
2529	15.81	31.61	63.22	126.45	189.67	252.90	316.12	379.35	442.57	505.80	569.02	632.25
2530	15.81	31.62	63.25	126.50	189.75	253.00	316.25	379.50	442.75	506.00	569.25	632.50
2531	15.82	31.64	63.27	126.55	189.82	253.10	316.37	379.65	442.92	506.20	569.47	632.75
2532	15.82	31.65	63.30	126.60	189.90	253.20	316.50	379.80	443.10	506.40	569.70	633.00
2533	15.83	31.66	63.32	126.65	189.97	253.30	316.62	379.95	443.27	506.60	569.92	633.25
2534	15.84	31.67	63.35	126.70	190.05	253.40	316.75	380.10	443.45	506.80	570.15	633.50
2535	15.84	31.69	63.37	126.75	190.12	253.50	316.87	380.25	443.62	507.00	570.37	633.75
2536	15.85	31.70	63.40	126.80	190.20	253.60	317.00	380.40	443.80	507.20	570.60	634.00
2537	15.86	31.71	63.42	126.85	190.27	253.70	317.12	380.55	443.97	507.40	570.82	634.25
2538	15.86	31.72	63.45	126.90	190.35	253.80	317.25	380.70	444.15	507.60	571.05	634.50
2539	15.87	31.74	63.47	126.95	190.42	253.90	317.37	380.85	444.32	507.80	571.27	634.75
2540	15.87	31.75	63.50	127.00	190.50	254.00	317.50	381.00	444.50	508.00	571.50	635.00
2541	15.88	31.76	63.52	127.05	190.57	254.10	317.62	381.15	444.67	508.20	571.72	635.25
2542	15.89	31.77	63.55	127.10	190.65	254.20	317.75	381.30	444.85	508.40	571.95	635.50
2543	15.89	31.79	63.57	127.15	190.72	254.30	317.87	381.45	445.02	508.60	572.17	635.75
2544	15.90	31.80	63.60	127.20	190.80	254.40	318.00	381.60	445.20	508.80	572.40	636.00
2545	15.91	31.81	63.62	127.25	190.87	254.50	318.12	381.75	445.37	509.00	572.62	636.25
2546	15.91	31.82	63.65	127.30	190.95	254.60	318.25	381.90	445.55	509.20	572.85	636.50
2547	15.92	31.84	63.67	127.35	191.02	254.70	318.37	382.05	445.72	509.40	573.07	636.75
2548	15.92	31.85	63.70	127.40	191.10	254.80	318.50	382.20	445.90	509.60	573.30	637.00
2549	15.93	31.86	63.72	127.45	191.17	254.90	318.62	382.35	446.07	509.80	573.52	637.25
2550	15.94	31.87	63.75	127.50	191.25	255.00	318.75	382.50	446.25	510.00	573.75	637.50

2550 FEET.

Per Ton, / Per Foot,	$11 27½ cts.	$12 30 cts.	$13 32½ cts.	$14 35 cts.	$15 37½ cts.	$16 40 cts.	$17 42½ cts.	$18 45 cts.	$19 47½ cts.	$20 50 cts.
Feet.										
2501	687.77	750.30	812.82	875.35	937.87	1000.40	1062.92	1125.45	1187.97	1250.50
2502	688.05	750.60	813.15	875.70	938.25	1000.80	1063.35	1125.90	1188.45	1251.00
2503	688.32	750.90	813.47	876.05	938.62	1001.20	1063.77	1126.35	1188.92	1251.50
2504	688.60	751.20	813.80	876.40	939.00	1001.60	1064.20	1126.80	1189.40	1252.00
2505	688.87	751.50	814.12	876.75	939.37	1002.00	1064.62	1127.25	1189.87	1252.50
2506	689.15	751.80	814.45	877.10	939.75	1002.40	1065.05	1127.70	1190.35	1253.00
2507	689.42	752.10	814.77	877.45	940.12	1002.80	1065.47	1128.15	1190.82	1253.50
2508	689.70	752.40	815.10	877.80	940.50	1003.20	1065.90	1128.60	1191.30	1254.00
2509	689.97	752.70	815.42	878.15	940.87	1003.60	1066.32	1129.05	1191.77	1254.50
2510	690.25	753.00	815.75	878.50	941.25	1004.00	1066.75	1129.50	1192.25	1255.00
2511	690.52	753.30	816.07	878.85	941.62	1004.40	1067.17	1129.95	1192.72	1255.50
2512	690.80	753.60	816.40	879.20	942.00	1004.80	1067.60	1130.40	1193.20	1256.00
2513	691.07	753.90	816.72	879.55	942.37	1005.20	1068.02	1130.85	1193.67	1256.50
2514	691.35	754.20	817.05	879.90	942.75	1005.60	1068.45	1131.30	1194.15	1257.00
2515	691.62	754.50	817.37	880.25	943.12	1006.00	1068.87	1131.75	1194.62	1257.50
2516	691.90	754.80	817.70	880.60	943.50	1006.40	1069.30	1132.20	1195.10	1258.00
2517	692.17	755.10	818.02	880.95	943.87	1006.80	1069.72	1132.65	1195.57	1258.50
2518	692.45	755.40	818.35	881.30	944.25	1007.20	1070.15	1133.10	1196.05	1259.00
2519	692.72	755.70	818.67	881.65	944.62	1007.60	1070.57	1133.55	1196.52	1259.50
2520	693.00	756.00	819.00	882.00	945.00	1008.00	1071.00	1134.00	1197.00	1260.00
2521	693.27	756.30	819.32	882.35	945.37	1008.40	1071.42	1134.45	1197.47	1260.50
2522	693.55	756.60	819.65	882.70	945.75	1008.80	1071.85	1134.90	1197.95	1261.00
2523	693.82	756.90	819.97	883.05	946.12	1009.20	1072.27	1135.35	1198.42	1261.50
2524	694.10	757.20	820.30	883.40	946.50	1009.60	1072.70	1135.80	1198.90	1262.00
2525	694.37	757.50	820.62	883.75	946.87	1010.00	1073.12	1136.25	1199.37	1262.50
2526	694.65	757.80	820.95	884.10	947.25	1010.40	1073.55	1136.70	1199.85	1263.00
2527	694.92	758.10	821.27	884.45	947.62	1010.80	1073.97	1137.15	1200.32	1263.50
2528	695.20	758.40	821.60	884.80	948.00	1011.20	1074.40	1137.60	1200.80	1264.00
2529	695.47	758.70	821.92	885.15	948.37	1011.60	1074.82	1138.05	1201.27	1264.50
2530	695.75	759.00	822.25	885.50	948.75	1012.00	1075.25	1138.50	1201.75	1265.00
2531	696.02	759.30	822.57	885.85	949.12	1012.40	1075.67	1138.95	1202.22	1265.50
2532	696.30	759.60	822.90	886.20	949.50	1012.80	1076.10	1139.40	1202.70	1266.00
2533	696.57	759.90	823.22	886.55	949.87	1013.20	1076.52	1139.85	1203.17	1266.50
2534	696.85	760.20	823.55	886.90	950.25	1013.60	1076.95	1140.30	1203.65	1267.00
2535	697.12	760.50	823.87	887.25	950.62	1014.00	1077.37	1140.75	1204.12	1267.50
2536	697.40	760.80	824.20	887.60	951.00	1014.40	1077.80	1141.20	1204.60	1268.00
2537	697.67	761.10	824.52	887.95	951.37	1014.80	1078.22	1141.65	1205.07	1268.50
2538	697.95	761.40	824.85	888.30	951.75	1015.20	1078.65	1142.10	1205.55	1269.00
2539	698.22	761.70	825.17	888.65	952.12	1015.60	1079.07	1142.55	1206.02	1269.50
2540	698.50	762.00	825.50	889.00	952.50	1016.00	1079.50	1143.00	1206.50	1270.00
2541	698.77	762.30	825.82	889.35	952.87	1016.40	1079.92	1143.45	1206.97	1270.50
2542	699.05	762.60	826.15	889.70	953.25	1016.80	1080.35	1143.90	1207.45	1271.00
2543	699.32	762.90	826.47	890.05	953.62	1017.20	1080.77	1144.35	1207.92	1271.50
2544	699.60	763.20	826.80	890.40	954.00	1017.60	1081.20	1144.80	1208.40	1272.00
2545	699.87	763.50	827.12	890.75	954.37	1018.00	1081.62	1145.25	1208.87	1272.50
2546	700.15	763.80	827.45	891.10	954.75	1018.40	1082.05	1145.70	1209.35	1273.00
2547	700.42	764.10	827.77	891.45	955.12	1018.80	1082.47	1146.15	1209.82	1273.50
2548	700.70	764.40	828.10	891.80	955.50	1019.20	1082.90	1146.60	1210.30	1274.00
2549	700.97	764.70	828.42	892.15	955.87	1019.60	1083.32	1147.05	1210.77	1274.50
2550	701.25	765.00	828.75	892.50	956.25	1020.00	1083.75	1147.50	1211.25	1275.00

2600 FEET.

Per Ton,	25c.	50c.	$1	$2	$3	$4	$5	$6	$7	$8	$9	$10
Per Foot,			2½ cts.	5 cts.	7½ cts.	10 cts.	12½ cts.	15 cts.	17½ cts.	20 cts.	22½ cts.	25 cts.
Feet.												
2551	15.94	31.89	63.77	127.55	191.32	255.10	318.87	382.65	446.42	510.20	573.97	637.75
2552	15.95	31.90	63.80	127.60	191.40	255.20	319.00	382.80	446.60	510.40	574.20	638.00
2553	15.96	31.91	63.82	127.65	191.47	255.30	319.12	382.95	446.77	510.60	574.42	638.25
2554	15.96	31.92	63.85	127.70	191.55	255.40	319.25	383.10	446.95	510.80	574.65	638.50
2555	15.97	31.94	63.87	127.75	191.62	255.50	319.37	383.25	447.12	511.00	574.87	638.75
2556	15.97	31.95	63.90	127.80	191.70	255.60	319.50	383.40	447.30	511.20	575.10	639.00
2557	15.98	31.96	63.92	127.85	191.77	255.70	319.62	383.55	447.47	511.40	575.32	639.25
2558	15.99	31.97	63.95	127.90	191.85	255.80	319.75	383.70	447.65	511.60	575.55	639.50
2559	15.99	31.99	63.97	127.95	191.92	255.90	319.87	383.85	447.82	511.80	575.77	639.75
2560	16.00	32.00	64.00	128.00	192.00	256.00	320.00	384.00	448.00	512.00	576.00	640.00
2561	16.01	32.01	64.02	128.05	192.07	256.10	320.12	384.15	448.17	512.20	576.22	640.25
2562	16.01	32.02	64.05	128.10	192.15	256.20	320.25	384.30	448.35	512.40	576.45	640.50
2563	16.02	32.04	64.07	128.15	192.22	256.30	320.37	384.45	448.52	512.60	576.67	640.75
2564	16.02	32.05	64.10	128.20	192.30	256.40	320.50	384.60	448.70	512.80	576.90	641.00
2565	16.03	32.06	64.12	128.25	192.37	256.50	320.62	384.75	448.87	513.00	577.12	641.25
2566	16.04	32.07	64.15	128.30	192.45	256.60	320.75	384.90	449.05	513.20	577.35	641.50
2567	16.04	32.09	64.17	128.35	192.52	256.70	320.87	385.05	449.22	513.40	577.57	641.75
2568	16.05	32.10	64.20	128.40	192.60	256.80	321.00	385.20	449.40	513.60	577.80	642.00
2569	16.06	32.11	64.22	128.45	192.67	256.90	321.12	385.35	449.57	513.80	578.02	642.25
2570	16.06	32.12	64.25	128.50	192.75	257.00	321.25	385.50	449.75	514.00	578.25	642.50
2571	16.07	32.14	64.27	128.55	192.82	257.10	321.37	385.65	449.92	514.20	578.47	642.75
2572	16.07	32.15	64.30	128.60	192.90	257.20	321.50	385.80	450.10	514.40	578.70	643.00
2573	16.08	32.16	64.32	128.65	192.97	257.30	321.62	385.95	450.27	514.60	578.92	643.25
2574	16.09	32.17	64.35	128.70	193.05	257.40	321.75	386.10	450.45	514.80	579.15	643.50
2575	16.09	32.19	64.37	128.75	193.12	257.50	321.87	386.25	450.62	515.00	579.37	643.75
2576	16.10	32.20	64.40	128.80	193.20	257.60	322.00	386.40	450.80	515.20	579.60	644.00
2577	16.11	32.21	64.42	128.85	193.27	257.70	322.12	386.55	450.97	515.40	579.82	644.25
2578	16.11	32.22	64.45	128.90	193.35	257.80	322.25	386.70	451.15	515.60	580.05	644.50
2579	16.12	32.24	64.47	128.95	193.42	257.90	322.37	386.85	451.32	515.80	580.27	644.75
2580	16.12	32.25	64.50	129.00	193.50	258.00	322.50	387.00	451.50	516.00	580.50	645.00
2581	16.13	32.26	64.52	129.05	193.57	258.10	322.62	387.15	451.67	516.20	580.72	645.25
2582	16.14	32.27	64.55	129.10	193.65	258.20	322.75	387.30	451.85	516.40	580.95	645.50
2583	16.14	32.29	64.57	129.15	193.72	258.30	322.87	387.45	452.02	516.60	581.17	645.75
2584	16.15	32.30	64.60	129.20	193.80	258.40	323.00	387.60	452.20	516.80	581.40	646.00
2585	16.16	32.31	64.62	129.25	193.87	258.50	323.12	387.75	452.37	517.00	581.62	646.25
2586	16.16	32.32	64.65	129.30	193.95	258.60	323.25	387.90	452.55	517.20	581.85	646.50
2587	16.17	32.34	64.67	129.35	194.02	258.70	323.37	388.05	452.72	517.40	582.07	646.75
2588	16.17	32.35	64.70	129.40	194.10	258.80	323.50	388.20	452.90	517.60	582.30	647.00
2589	16.18	32.36	64.72	129.45	194.17	258.90	323.62	388.35	453.07	517.80	582.52	647.25
2590	16.19	32.37	64.75	129.50	194.25	259.00	323.75	388.50	453.25	518.00	582.75	647.50
2591	16.19	32.39	64.77	129.55	194.32	259.10	323.87	388.65	453.42	518.20	582.97	647.75
2592	16.20	32.40	64.80	129.60	194.40	259.20	324.00	388.80	453.60	518.40	583.20	648.00
2593	16.21	32.41	64.82	129.65	194.47	259.30	324.12	388.95	453.77	518.60	583.42	648.25
2594	16.21	32.42	64.85	129.70	194.55	259.40	324.25	389.10	453.95	518.80	583.65	648.50
2595	16.22	32.44	64.87	129.75	194.62	259.50	324.37	389.25	454.12	519.00	583.87	648.75
2596	16.22	32.45	64.90	129.80	194.70	259.60	324.50	389.40	454.30	519.20	584.10	649.00
2597	16.23	32.46	64.92	129.85	194.77	259.70	324.62	389.55	454.47	519.40	584.32	649.25
2598	16.24	32.47	64.95	129.90	194.85	259.80	324.75	389.70	454.65	519.60	584.55	649.50
2599	16.24	32.49	64.97	129.95	194.92	259.90	324.87	389.85	454.82	519.80	584.77	649.75
2600	16.25	32.50	65.00	130.00	195.00	260.00	325.00	390.00	455.00	520.00	585.00	650.00

2600 FEET.

Per Ton,	$11	$12	$13	$14	$15	$16	$17	$18	$19	$20
Per Foot,	27½ cts.	30 cts.	32½ cts.	35 cts.	37½ cts.	40 cts.	42½ cts.	45 cts.	47½ cts.	50 cts.
Feet.										
2551	701.52	765.30	829.07	892.85	956.62	1020.40	1084.17	1147.95	1211.72	1275.50
2552	701.80	765.60	829.40	893.20	957.00	1020.80	1084.60	1148.40	1212.20	1276.00
2553	702.07	765.90	829.72	893.55	957.37	1021.20	1085.02	1148.85	1212.67	1276.50
2554	702.35	766.20	830.05	893.90	957.75	1021.60	1085.45	1149.30	1213.15	1277.00
2555	702.62	766.50	830.37	894.25	958.12	1022.00	1085.87	1149.75	1213.62	1277.50
2556	702.90	766.80	830.70	894.60	958.50	1022.40	1086.30	1150.20	1214.10	1278.00
2557	703.17	767.10	831.02	894.95	958.87	1022.80	1086.72	1150.65	1214.57	1278.50
2558	703.45	767.40	831.35	895.30	959.25	1023.20	1087.15	1151.10	1215.05	1279.00
2559	703.72	767.70	831.67	895.65	959.62	1023.60	1087.57	1151.55	1215.52	1279.50
2560	704.00	768.00	832.00	896.00	960.00	1024.00	1088.00	1152.00	1216.00	1280.00
2561	704.27	768.30	832.32	896.35	960.37	1024.40	1088.42	1152.45	1216.47	1280.50
2562	704.55	768.60	832.65	896.70	960.75	1024.80	1088.85	1152.90	1216.95	1281.00
2563	704.82	768.90	832.97	897.05	961.12	1025.20	1089.27	1153.35	1217.42	1281.50
2564	705.10	769.20	833.30	897.40	961.50	1025.60	1089.70	1153.80	1217.90	1282.00
2565	705.37	769.50	833.62	897.75	961.87	1026.00	1090.12	1154.25	1218.37	1282.50
2566	705.65	769.80	833.95	898.10	962.25	1026.40	1090.55	1154.70	1218.85	1283.00
2567	705.92	770.10	834.27	898.45	962.62	1026.80	1090.97	1155.15	1219.32	1283.50
2568	706.20	770.40	834.60	898.80	963.00	1027.20	1091.40	1155.60	1219.80	1284.00
2569	706.47	770.70	834.92	899.15	963.37	1027.60	1091.82	1156.05	1220.27	1284.50
2570	706.75	771.00	835.25	899.50	963.75	1028.00	1092.25	1156.50	1220.75	1285.00
2571	707.02	771.30	835.57	899.85	964.12	1028.40	1092.67	1156.95	1221.22	1285.50
2572	707.30	771.60	835.90	900.20	964.50	1028.80	1093.10	1157.40	1221.70	1286.00
2573	707.57	771.90	836.22	900.55	964.87	1029.20	1093.52	1157.85	1222.17	1286.50
2574	707.85	772.20	836.55	900.90	965.25	1029.60	1093.95	1158.30	1222.65	1287.00
2575	708.12	772.50	836.87	901.25	965.62	1030.00	1094.37	1158.75	1223.12	1287.50
2576	708.40	772.80	837.20	901.60	966.00	1030.40	1094.80	1159.20	1223.60	1288.00
2577	708.67	773.10	837.52	901.95	966.37	1030.80	1095.22	1159.65	1224.07	1288.50
2578	708.95	773.40	837.85	902.30	966.75	1031.20	1095.65	1160.10	1224.55	1289.00
2579	709.22	773.70	838.17	902.65	967.12	1031.60	1096.07	1160.55	1225.02	1289.50
2580	709.50	774.00	838.50	903.00	967.50	1032.00	1096.50	1161.00	1225.50	1290.00
2581	709.77	774.30	838.82	903.35	967.87	1032.40	1096.92	1161.45	1225.97	1290.50
2582	710.05	774.60	839.15	903.70	968.25	1032.80	1097.35	1161.90	1226.45	1291.00
2583	710.32	774.90	839.47	904.05	968.62	1033.20	1097.77	1162.35	1226.92	1291.50
2584	710.60	775.20	839.80	904.40	969.00	1033.60	1098.20	1162.80	1227.40	1292.00
2585	710.87	775.50	840.12	904.75	969.37	1034.00	1098.62	1163.25	1227.87	1292.50
2586	711.15	775.80	840.45	905.10	969.75	1034.40	1099.05	1163.70	1228.35	1293.00
2587	711.42	776.10	840.77	905.45	970.12	1034.80	1099.47	1164.15	1228.82	1293.50
2588	711.70	776.40	841.10	905.80	970.50	1035.20	1099.90	1164.60	1229.30	1294.00
2589	711.97	776.70	841.42	906.15	970.87	1035.60	1100.32	1165.05	1229.77	1294.50
2590	712.25	777.00	841.75	906.50	971.25	1036.00	1100.75	1165.50	1230.25	1295.00
2591	712.52	777.30	842.07	906.85	971.62	1036.40	1101.17	1165.95	1230.72	1295.50
2592	712.80	777.60	842.40	907.20	972.00	1036.80	1101.60	1166.40	1231.20	1296.00
2593	713.07	777.90	842.72	907.55	972.37	1037.20	1102.02	1166.85	1231.67	1296.50
2594	713.35	778.20	843.05	907.90	972.75	1037.60	1102.45	1167.30	1232.15	1297.00
2595	713.62	778.50	843.37	908.25	973.12	1038.00	1102.87	1167.75	1232.62	1297.50
2596	713.90	778.80	843.70	908.60	973.50	1038.40	1103.30	1168.20	1233.10	1298.00
2597	714.17	779.10	844.02	908.95	973.87	1038.80	1103.72	1168.65	1233.57	1298.50
2598	714.45	779.40	844.35	909.30	974.25	1039.20	1104.15	1169.10	1234.05	1299.00
2599	714.72	779.70	844.67	909.65	974.62	1039.60	1104.57	1169.55	1234.52	1299.50
2600	715.00	780.00	845.00	910.00	975.00	1040.00	1105.00	1170.00	1235.00	1300.00

2650 FEET.

Per Ton, Per Foot, Feet.	25c.	50c.	$1 2½ cts.	$2 5 cts.	$3 7½ cts.	$4 10 cts.	$5 12½ cts.	$6 15 cts.	$7 17½ cts.	$8 20 cts.	$9 22½ cts.	$10 25 cts.
2601	16.26	32.51	65.02	130.05	195.07	260.10	325.12	390.15	455.17	520.20	585.22	650.25
2602	16.26	32.52	65.05	130.10	195.15	260.20	325.25	390.30	455.35	520.40	585.45	650.50
2603	16.27	32.54	65.07	130.15	195.22	260.30	325.37	390.45	455.52	520.60	585.67	650.75
2604	16.27	32.55	65.10	130.20	195.30	260.40	325.50	390.60	455.70	520.80	585.90	651.00
2605	16.28	32.56	65.12	130.25	195.37	260.50	325.62	390.75	455.87	521.00	586.12	651.25
2606	16.29	32.57	65.15	130.30	195.45	260.60	325.75	390.90	456.05	521.20	586.35	651.50
2607	16.29	32.59	65.17	130.35	195.52	260.70	325.87	391.05	456.22	521.40	586.57	651.75
2608	16.30	32.60	65.20	130.40	195.60	260.80	326.00	391.20	456.40	521.60	586.80	652.00
2609	16.31	32.61	65.22	130.45	195.67	260.90	326.12	391.35	456.57	521.80	587.02	652.25
2610	16.31	32.62	65.25	130.50	195.75	261.00	326.25	391.50	456.75	522.00	587.25	652.50
2611	16.32	32.64	65.27	130.55	195.82	261.10	326.37	391.65	456.92	522.20	587.47	652.75
2612	16.32	32.65	65.30	130.60	195.90	261.20	326.50	391.80	457.10	522.40	587.70	653.00
2613	16.33	32.66	65.32	130.65	195.97	261.30	326.62	391.95	457.27	522.60	587.92	653.25
2614	16.34	32.67	65.35	130.70	196.05	261.40	326.75	392.10	457.45	522.80	588.15	653.50
2615	16.34	32.69	65.37	130.75	196.12	261.50	326.87	392.25	457.62	523.00	588.37	653.75
2616	16.35	32.70	65.40	130.80	196.20	261.60	327.00	392.40	457.80	523.20	588.60	654.00
2617	16.36	32.71	65.42	130.85	196.27	261.70	327.12	392.55	457.97	523.40	588.82	654.25
2618	16.36	32.72	65.45	130.90	196.35	261.80	327.25	392.70	458.15	523.60	589.05	654.50
2619	16.37	32.74	65.47	130.95	196.42	261.90	327.37	392.85	458.32	523.80	589.27	654.75
2620	16.37	32.75	65.50	131.00	196.50	262.00	327.50	393.00	458.50	524.00	589.50	655.00
2621	16.38	32.76	65.52	131.05	196.57	262.10	327.62	393.15	458.67	524.20	589.72	655.25
2622	16.39	32.77	65.55	131.10	196.65	262.20	327.75	393.30	458.85	524.40	589.95	655.50
2623	16.39	32.79	65.57	131.15	196.72	262.30	327.87	393.45	459.02	524.60	590.17	655.75
2624	16.40	32.80	65.60	131.20	196.80	262.40	328.00	393.60	459.20	524.80	590.40	656.00
2625	16.41	32.81	65.62	131.25	196.87	262.50	328.12	393.75	459.37	525.00	590.62	656.25
2626	16.41	32.82	65.65	131.30	196.95	262.60	328.25	393.90	459.55	525.20	590.85	656.50
2627	16.42	32.84	65.67	131.35	197.02	262.70	328.37	394.05	459.72	525.40	591.07	656.75
2628	16.42	32.85	65.70	131.40	197.10	262.80	328.50	394.20	459.90	525.60	591.30	657.00
2629	16.43	32.86	65.72	131.45	197.17	262.90	328.62	394.35	460.07	525.80	591.52	657.25
2630	16.44	32.87	65.75	131.50	197.25	263.00	328.75	394.50	460.25	526.00	591.75	657.50
2631	16.44	32.89	65.77	131.55	197.32	263.10	328.87	394.65	460.42	526.20	591.97	657.75
2632	16.45	32.90	65.80	131.60	197.40	263.20	329.00	394.80	460.60	526.40	592.20	658.00
2633	16.46	32.91	65.82	131.65	197.47	263.30	329.12	394.95	460.77	526.60	592.42	658.25
2634	16.46	32.92	65.85	131.70	197.55	263.40	329.25	395.10	460.95	526.80	592.65	658.50
2635	16.47	32.94	65.87	131.75	197.62	263.50	329.37	395.25	461.12	527.00	592.87	658.75
2636	16.47	32.95	65.90	131.80	197.70	263.60	329.50	395.40	461.30	527.20	593.10	659.00
2637	16.48	32.96	65.92	131.85	197.77	263.70	329.62	395.55	461.47	527.40	593.32	659.25
2638	16.49	32.97	65.95	131.90	197.85	263.80	329.75	395.70	461.65	527.60	593.55	659.50
2639	16.49	32.99	65.97	131.95	197.92	263.90	329.87	395.85	461.82	527.80	593.77	659.75
2640	16.50	33.00	66.00	132.00	198.00	264.00	330.00	396.00	462.00	528.00	594.00	660.00
2641	16.51	33.01	66.02	132.05	198.07	264.10	330.12	396.15	462.17	528.20	594.22	660.25
2642	16.51	33.02	66.05	132.10	198.15	264.20	330.25	396.30	462.35	528.40	594.45	660.50
2643	16.52	33.04	66.07	132.15	198.22	264.30	330.37	396.45	462.52	528.60	594.67	660.75
2644	16.52	33.05	66.10	132.20	198.30	264.40	330.50	396.60	462.70	528.80	594.90	661.00
2645	16.53	33.06	66.12	132.25	198.37	264.50	330.62	396.75	462.87	529.00	595.12	661.25
2646	16.54	33.07	66.15	132.30	198.45	264.60	330.75	396.90	463.05	529.20	595.35	661.50
2647	16.54	33.09	66.17	132.35	198.52	264.70	330.87	397.05	463.22	529.40	595.57	661.75
2648	16.55	33.10	66.20	132.40	198.60	264.80	331.00	397.20	463.40	529.60	595.80	662.00
2649	16.56	33.11	66.22	132.45	198.67	264.90	331.12	397.35	463.57	529.80	596.02	662.25
2650	16.56	33.12	66.25	132.50	198.75	265.00	331.25	397.50	463.75	530.00	596.25	662.50

2650 FEET.

Per Ton, Per Foot,	$11 27½ cts.	$12 30 cts.	$13 32½ cts.	$14 35 cts.	$15 37½ cts.	$16 40 cts.	$17 42½ cts.	$18 45 cts.	$19 47½ cts.	$20 50 cts.
Feet.										
2601	715.27	780.30	845.32	910.35	975.37	1040.40	1105.42	1170.45	1235.47	1300.50
2602	715.55	780.60	845.65	910.70	975.75	1040.80	1105.85	1170.90	1235.95	1301.00
2603	715.82	780.90	845.97	911.05	976.12	1041.20	1106.27	1171.35	1236.42	1301.50
2604	716.10	781.20	846.30	911.40	976.50	1041.60	1106.70	1171.80	1236.90	1302.00
2605	716.37	781.50	846.62	911.75	976.87	1042.00	1107.12	1172.25	1237.37	1302.50
2606	716.65	781.80	846.95	912.10	977.25	1042.40	1107.55	1172.70	1237.85	1303.00
2607	716.92	782.10	847.27	912.45	977.62	1042.80	1107.97	1173.15	1238.32	1303.50
2608	717.20	782.40	847.60	912.80	978.00	1043.20	1108.40	1173.60	1238.80	1304.00
2609	717.47	782.70	847.92	913.15	978.37	1043.60	1108.82	1174.05	1239.27	1304.50
2610	717.75	783.00	848.25	913.50	978.75	1044.00	1109.25	1174.50	1239.75	1305.00
2611	718.02	783.30	848.57	913.85	979.12	1044.40	1109.67	1174.95	1240.22	1305.50
2612	718.30	783.60	848.90	914.20	979.50	1044.80	1110.10	1175.40	1240.70	1306.00
2613	718.57	783.90	849.22	914.55	979.87	1045.20	1110.52	1175.85	1241.17	1306.50
2614	718.85	784.20	849.55	914.90	980.25	1045.60	1110.95	1176.30	1241.65	1307.00
2615	719.12	784.50	849.87	915.25	980.62	1046.00	1111.37	1176.75	1242.12	1307.50
2616	719.40	784.80	850.20	915.60	981.00	1046.40	1111.80	1177.20	1242.60	1308.00
2617	719.67	785.10	850.52	915.95	981.37	1046.80	1112.22	1177.65	1243.07	1308.50
2618	719.95	785.40	850.85	916.30	981.75	1047.20	1112.65	1178.10	1243.55	1309.00
2619	720.22	785.70	851.17	916.65	982.12	1047.60	1113.07	1178.55	1244.02	1309.50
2620	720.50	786.00	851.50	917.00	982.50	1048.00	1113.50	1179.00	1244.50	1310.00
2621	720.77	786.30	851.82	917.35	982.87	1048.40	1113.92	1179.45	1244.97	1310.50
2622	721.05	786.60	852.15	917.70	983.25	1048.80	1114.35	1179.90	1245.45	1311.00
2623	721.32	786.90	852.47	918.05	983.62	1049.20	1114.77	1180.35	1245.92	1311.50
2624	721.60	787.20	852.80	918.40	984.00	1049.60	1115.20	1180.80	1246.40	1312.00
2625	721.87	787.50	853.12	918.75	984.37	1050.00	1115.62	1181.25	1246.87	1312.50
2626	722.15	787.80	853.45	919.10	984.75	1050.40	1116.05	1181.70	1247.35	1313.00
2627	722.42	788.10	853.77	919.45	985.12	1050.80	1116.47	1182.15	1247.82	1313.50
2628	722.70	788.40	854.10	919.80	985.50	1051.20	1116.90	1182.60	1248.30	1314.00
2629	722.97	788.70	854.42	920.15	985.87	1051.60	1117.32	1183.05	1248.77	1314.50
2630	723.25	789.00	854.75	920.50	986.25	1052.00	1117.75	1183.50	1249.25	1315.00
2631	723.52	789.30	855.07	920.85	986.62	1052.40	1118.17	1183.95	1249.72	1315.50
2632	723.80	789.60	855.40	921.20	987.00	1052.80	1118.60	1184.40	1250.20	1316.00
2633	724.07	789.90	855.72	921.55	987.37	1053.20	1119.02	1184.85	1250.67	1316.50
2634	724.35	790.20	856.05	921.90	987.75	1053.60	1119.45	1185.30	1251.15	1317.00
2635	724.62	790.50	856.37	922.25	988.12	1054.00	1119.87	1185.75	1251.62	1317.50
2636	724.90	790.80	856.70	922.60	988.50	1054.40	1120.30	1186.20	1252.10	1318.00
2637	725.17	791.10	857.02	922.95	988.87	1054.80	1120.72	1186.65	1252.57	1318.50
2638	725.45	791.40	857.35	923.30	989.25	1055.20	1121.15	1187.10	1253.05	1319.00
2639	725.72	791.70	857.67	923.65	989.62	1055.60	1121.57	1187.55	1253.52	1319.50
2640	726.00	792.00	858.00	924.00	990.00	1056.00	1122.00	1188.00	1254.00	1320.00
2641	726.27	792.30	858.32	924.35	990.37	1056.40	1122.42	1188.45	1254.47	1320.50
2642	726.55	792.60	858.65	924.70	990.75	1056.80	1122.85	1188.90	1254.95	1321.00
2643	726.82	792.90	858.97	925.05	991.12	1057.20	1123.27	1189.35	1255.42	1321.50
2644	727.10	793.20	859.30	925.40	991.50	1057.60	1123.70	1189.80	1255.90	1322.00
2645	727.37	793.50	859.62	925.75	991.87	1058.00	1124.12	1190.25	1256.37	1322.50
2646	727.65	793.80	859.95	926.10	992.25	1058.40	1124.55	1190.70	1256.85	1323.00
2647	727.92	794.10	860.27	926.45	992.62	1058.80	1124.97	1191.15	1257.32	1323.50
2648	728.20	794.40	860.60	926.80	993.00	1059.20	1125.40	1191.60	1257.80	1324.00
2649	728.47	794.70	860.92	927.15	993.37	1059.60	1125.82	1192.05	1258.27	1324.50
2650	728.75	795.00	861.25	927.50	993.75	1060.00	1126.25	1192.50	1258.75	1325.00

2700 FEET.

Per Ton, Per Foot,	25c.	50c.	$1 2½ cts.	$2 5 cts.	$3 7½ cts.	$4 10 cts.	$5 12½ cts.	$6 15 cts.	$7 17½ cts.	$8 20 cts.	$9 22½ cts.	$10 25 cts.
Feet.												
2651	16.57	33.14	66.27	132.55	198.82	265.10	331.37	397.65	463.92	530.20	596.47	662.75
2652	16.57	33.15	66.30	132.60	198.90	265.20	331.50	397.80	464.10	530.40	596.70	663.00
2653	16.58	33.16	66.32	132.65	198.97	265.30	331.62	397.95	464.27	530.60	596.92	663.25
2654	16.59	33.17	66.35	132.70	199.05	265.40	331.75	398.10	464.45	530.80	597.15	663.50
2655	16.59	33.19	66.37	132.75	199.12	265.50	331.87	398.25	464.62	531.00	597.37	663.75
2656	16.60	33.20	66.40	132.80	199.20	265.60	332.00	398.40	464.80	531.20	597.60	664.00
2657	16.61	33.21	66.42	132.85	199.27	265.70	332.12	398.55	464.97	531.40	597.82	664.25
2658	16.61	33.22	66.45	132.90	199.35	265.80	332.25	398.70	465.15	531.60	598.05	664.50
2659	16.62	33.24	66.47	132.95	199.42	265.90	332.37	398.85	465.32	531.80	598.27	664.75
2660	16.62	33.25	66.50	133.00	199.50	266.00	332.50	399.00	465.50	532.00	598.50	665.00
2661	16.63	33.26	66.52	133.05	199.57	266.10	332.62	399.15	465.67	532.20	598.72	665.25
2662	16.64	33.27	66.55	133.10	199.65	266.20	332.75	399.30	465.85	532.40	598.95	665.50
2663	16.64	33.29	66.57	133.15	199.72	266.30	332.87	399.45	466.02	532.60	599.17	665.75
2664	16.65	33.30	66.60	133.20	199.80	266.40	333.00	399.60	466.20	532.80	599.40	666.00
2665	16.66	33.31	66.62	133.25	199.87	266.50	333.12	399.75	466.37	533.00	599.62	666.25
2666	16.66	33.32	66.65	133.30	199.95	266.60	333.25	399.90	466.55	533.20	599.85	666.50
2667	16.67	33.34	66.67	133.35	200.02	266.70	333.37	400.05	466.72	533.40	600.07	666.75
2668	16.67	33.35	66.70	133.40	200.10	266.80	333.50	400.20	466.90	533.60	600.30	667.00
2669	16.68	33.36	66.72	133.45	200.17	266.90	333.62	400.35	467.07	533.80	600.52	667.25
2670	16.69	33.37	66.75	133.50	200.25	267.00	333.75	400.50	467.25	534.00	600.75	667.50
2671	16.69	33.39	66.77	133.55	200.32	267.10	333.87	400.65	467.42	534.20	600.97	667.75
2672	16.70	33.40	66.80	133.60	200.40	267.20	334.00	400.80	467.60	534.40	601.20	668.00
2673	16.71	33.41	66.82	133.65	200.47	267.30	334.12	400.95	467.77	534.60	601.42	668.25
2674	16.71	33.42	66.85	133.70	200.55	267.40	334.25	401.10	467.95	534.80	601.65	668.50
2675	16.72	33.44	66.87	133.75	200.62	267.50	334.37	401.25	468.12	535.00	601.87	668.75
2676	16.72	33.45	66.90	133.80	200.70	267.60	334.50	401.40	468.30	535.20	602.10	669.00
2677	16.73	33.46	66.92	133.85	200.77	267.70	334.62	401.55	468.47	535.40	602.32	669.25
2678	16.74	33.47	66.95	133.90	200.85	267.80	334.75	401.70	468.65	535.60	602.55	669.50
2679	16.74	33.49	66.97	133.95	200.92	267.90	334.87	401.85	468.82	535.80	602.77	669.75
2680	16.75	33.50	67.00	134.00	201.00	268.00	335.00	402.00	469.00	536.00	603.00	670.00
2681	16.76	33.51	67.02	134.05	201.07	268.10	335.12	402.15	469.17	536.20	603.22	670.25
2682	16.76	33.52	67.05	134.10	201.15	268.20	335.25	402.30	469.35	536.40	603.45	670.50
2683	16.77	33.54	67.07	134.15	201.22	268.30	335.37	402.45	469.52	536.60	603.67	670.75
2684	16.77	33.55	67.10	134.20	201.30	268.40	335.50	402.60	469.70	536.80	603.90	671.00
2685	16.78	33.56	67.12	134.25	201.37	268.50	335.62	402.75	469.87	537.00	604.12	671.25
2686	16.79	33.57	67.15	134.30	201.45	268.60	335.75	402.90	470.05	537.20	604.35	671.50
2687	16.79	33.59	67.17	134.35	201.52	268.70	335.87	403.05	470.22	537.40	604.57	671.75
2688	16.80	33.60	67.20	134.40	201.60	268.80	336.00	403.20	470.40	537.60	604.80	672.00
2689	16.81	33.61	67.22	134.45	201.67	268.90	336.12	403.35	470.57	537.80	605.02	672.25
2690	16.81	33.62	67.25	134.50	201.75	269.00	336.25	403.50	470.75	538.00	605.25	672.50
2691	16.82	33.64	67.27	134.55	201.82	269.10	336.37	403.65	470.92	538.20	605.47	672.75
2692	16.82	33.65	67.30	134.60	201.90	269.20	336.50	403.80	471.10	538.40	605.70	673.00
2693	16.83	33.66	67.32	134.65	201.97	269.30	336.62	403.95	471.27	538.60	605.92	673.25
2694	16.84	33.67	67.35	134.70	202.05	269.40	336.75	404.10	471.45	538.80	606.15	673.50
2695	16.84	33.69	67.37	134.75	202.12	269.50	336.87	404.25	471.62	539.00	606.37	673.75
2696	16.85	33.70	67.40	134.80	202.20	269.60	337.00	404.40	471.80	539.20	606.60	674.00
2697	16.86	33.71	67.42	134.85	202.27	269.70	337.12	404.55	471.97	539.40	606.82	674.25
2698	16.86	33.72	67.45	134.90	202.35	269.80	337.25	404.70	472.15	539.60	607.05	674.50
2699	16.87	33.74	67.47	134.95	202.42	269.90	337.37	404.85	472.32	539.80	607.27	674.75
2700	16.87	33.75	67.50	135.00	202.50	270.00	337.50	405.00	472.50	540.00	607.50	675.00

2700 FEET.

Per Ton, / Per Foot, / Feet.	$11 27½ cts.	$12 30 cts.	$13 32½ cts.	$14 35 cts.	$15 37½ cts.	$16 40 cts.	$17 42½ cts.	$18 45 cts.	$19 47½ cts.	$20 50 cts.
2651	729.02	795.30	861.57	927.85	994.12	1060.40	1126.67	1192.95	1259.22	1325.50
2652	729.30	795.60	861.90	928.20	994.50	1060.80	1127.10	1193.40	1259.70	1326.00
2653	729.57	795.90	862.22	928.55	994.87	1061.20	1127.52	1193.85	1260.17	1326.50
2654	729.85	796.20	862.55	928.90	995.25	1061.60	1127.95	1194.30	1260.65	1327.00
2655	730.12	796.50	862.87	929.25	995.62	1062.00	1128.37	1194.75	1261.12	1327.50
2656	730.40	796.80	863.20	929.60	996.00	1062.40	1128.80	1195.20	1261.60	1328.00
2657	730.67	797.10	863.52	929.95	996.37	1062.80	1129.22	1195.65	1262.07	1328.50
2658	730.95	797.40	863.85	920.30	996.75	1063.20	1129.65	1196.10	1262.55	1329.00
2659	731.22	797.70	864.17	930.65	997.12	1063.60	1130.07	1196.55	1263.02	1329.50
2660	731.50	798.00	864.50	931.00	997.50	1064.00	1130.50	1197.00	1263.50	1330.00
2661	731.77	798.30	864.82	931.35	997.87	1064.40	1130.92	1197.45	1263.97	1330.50
2662	732.05	798.60	865.15	931.70	998.25	1064.80	1131.35	1197.90	1264.45	1331.00
2663	732.32	798.90	865.47	932.05	998.62	1065.20	1131.77	1198.35	1264.92	1331.50
2664	732.60	799.20	865.80	932.40	999.00	1065.60	1132.20	1198.80	1265.40	1332.00
2665	732.87	799.50	866.12	932.75	999.37	1066.00	1132.62	1199.25	1265.87	1332.50
2666	733.15	799.80	866.45	933.10	999.75	1066.40	1133.05	1199.70	1266.35	1333.00
2667	733.42	800.10	866.77	933.45	1000.12	1066.80	1133.47	1200.15	1266.82	1333.50
2668	733.70	800.40	867.10	933.80	1000.50	1067.20	1133.90	1200.60	1267.30	1334.00
2669	733.97	800.70	867.42	934.15	1000.87	1067.60	1134.32	1201.05	1267.77	1334.50
2670	734.25	801.00	867.75	934.50	1001.25	1068.00	1134.75	1201.50	1268.25	1335.00
2671	734.52	801.30	868.07	934.85	1001.62	1068.40	1135.17	1201.95	1268.72	1335.50
2672	734.80	801.60	868.40	935.20	1002.00	1068.80	1135.60	1202.40	1269.20	1336.00
2673	735.07	801.90	868.72	935.55	1002.37	1069.20	1136.02	1202.85	1269.67	1336.50
2674	735.35	802.20	869.05	935.90	1002.75	1069.60	1136.45	1203.30	1270.15	1337.00
2675	735.62	802.50	869.37	936.25	1003.12	1070.00	1136.87	1203.75	1270.62	1337.50
2676	735.90	802.80	869.70	936.60	1003.50	1070.40	1137.30	1204.20	1271.10	1338.00
2677	736.17	803.10	870.02	936.95	1003.87	1070.80	1137.72	1204.65	1271.57	1338.50
2678	736.45	803.40	870.35	937.30	1004.25	1071.20	1138.15	1205.10	1272.05	1339.00
2679	736.72	803.70	870.67	937.65	1004.62	1071.60	1138.57	1205.55	1272.52	1339.50
2680	737.00	804.00	871.00	938.00	1005.00	1072.00	1139.00	1206.00	1273.00	1340.00
2681	737.27	804.30	871.32	938.35	1005.37	1072.40	1139.42	1206.45	1273.47	1340.50
2682	737.55	804.60	871.65	938.70	1005.75	1072.80	1139.85	1206.90	1273.95	1341.00
2683	737.82	804.90	871.97	939.05	1006.12	1073.20	1140.27	1207.35	1274.42	1341.50
2684	738.10	805.20	872.30	939.40	1006.50	1073.60	1140.70	1207.80	1274.90	1342.00
2685	738.37	805.50	872.62	939.75	1006.87	1074.00	1141.12	1208.25	1275.37	1342.50
2686	738.65	805.80	872.95	940.10	1007.25	1074.40	1141.55	1208.70	1275.85	1343.00
2687	738.92	806.10	873.27	940.45	1007.62	1074.80	1141.97	1209.15	1276.32	1343.50
2688	739.20	806.40	873.60	940.80	1008.00	1075.20	1142.40	1209.60	1276.80	1344.00
2689	739.47	806.70	873.92	941.15	1008.37	1075.60	1142.82	1210.05	1277.27	1344.50
2690	739.75	807.00	874.25	941.50	1008.75	1076.00	1143.25	1210.50	1277.75	1345.00
2691	740.02	807.30	874.57	941.85	1009.12	1076.40	1143.67	1210.95	1278.22	1345.50
2692	740.30	807.60	874.90	942.20	1009.50	1076.80	1144.10	1211.40	1278.70	1346.00
2693	740.57	807.90	875.22	942.55	1009.87	1077.20	1144.52	1211.85	1279.17	1346.50
2694	740.85	808.20	875.55	942.90	1010.25	1077.60	1144.95	1212.30	1279.65	1347.00
2695	741.12	808.50	875.87	943.25	1010.62	1078.00	1145.37	1212.75	1280.12	1347.50
2696	741.40	808.80	876.20	943.60	1011.00	1078.40	1145.80	1213.20	1280.60	1348.00
2697	741.67	809.10	876.52	943.95	1011.37	1078.80	1146.22	1213.65	1281.07	1348.50
2698	741.95	809.40	876.85	944.30	1011.75	1079.20	1146.65	1214.10	1281.55	1349.00
2699	742.22	809.70	877.17	944.65	1012.12	1079.60	1147.07	1214.55	1282.02	1349.50
2700	742.50	810.00	877.50	945.00	1012.50	1080.00	1147.50	1215.00	1282.50	1350.00

2750 FEET.

Per Ton,	25c.	50c.	$1	$2	$3	$4	$5	$6	$7	$8	$9	$10
Per Foot,			2½ cts.	5 cts.	7½ cts.	10 cts.	12½ cts.	15 cts.	17½ cts.	20 cts.	22½ cts.	25 cts.
Feet.												
2701	16.88	33.76	67.52	135.05	202.57	270.10	337.62	405.15	472.67	540.20	607.72	675.25
2702	16.89	33.77	67.55	135.10	202.65	270.20	337.75	405.30	472.85	540.40	607.95	675.50
2703	16.89	33.79	67.57	135.15	202.72	270.30	337.87	405.45	473.02	540.60	608.17	675.75
2704	16.90	33.80	67.60	135.20	202.80	270.40	338.00	405.60	473.20	540.80	608.40	676.00
2705	16.91	33.81	67.62	135.25	202.87	270.50	338.12	405.75	473.37	541.00	608.62	676.25
2706	16.91	33.82	67.65	135.30	202.95	270.60	338.25	405.90	473.55	541.20	608.85	676.50
2707	16.92	33.84	67.67	135.35	203.02	270.70	338.37	406.05	473.72	541.40	609.07	676.75
2708	16.92	33.85	67.70	135.40	203.10	270.80	338.50	406.20	473.90	541.60	609.30	677.00
2709	16.93	33.86	67.72	135.45	203.17	270.90	338.62	406.35	474.07	541.80	609.52	677.25
2710	16.94	33.87	67.75	135.50	203.25	271.00	338.75	406.50	474.25	542.00	609.75	677.50
2711	16.94	33.89	67.77	135.55	203.32	271.10	338.87	406.65	474.42	542.20	609.97	677.75
2712	16.95	33.90	67.80	135.60	203.40	271.20	339.00	406.80	474.60	542.40	610.20	678.00
2713	16.96	33.91	67.82	135.65	203.47	271.30	339.12	406.95	474.77	542.60	610.42	678.25
2714	16.96	33.92	67.85	135.70	203.55	271.40	339.25	407.10	474.95	542.80	610.65	678.50
2715	16.97	33.94	67.87	135.75	203.62	271.50	339.37	407.25	475.12	543.00	610.87	678.75
2716	16.97	33.95	67.90	135.80	203.70	271.60	339.50	407.40	475.30	543.20	611.10	679.00
2717	16.98	33.96	67.92	135.85	203.77	271.70	339.62	407.55	475.47	543.40	611.32	679.25
2718	16.99	33.97	67.95	135.90	203.85	271.80	339.75	407.70	475.65	543.60	611.55	679.50
2719	16.99	33.99	67.97	135.95	203.92	271.90	339.87	407.85	475.82	543.80	611.77	679.75
2720	17.00	34.00	68.00	136.00	204.00	272.00	340.00	408.00	476.00	544.00	612.00	680.00
2721	17.01	34.01	68.02	136.05	204.07	272.10	340.12	408.15	476.17	544.20	612.22	680.25
2722	17.01	34.02	68.05	136.10	204.15	272.20	340.25	408.30	476.35	544.40	612.45	680.50
2723	17.02	34.04	68.07	136.15	204.22	272.30	340.37	408.45	476.52	544.60	612.67	680.75
2724	17.02	34.05	68.10	136.20	204.30	272.40	340.50	408.60	476.70	544.80	612.90	681.00
2725	17.03	34.06	68.12	136.25	204.37	272.50	340.62	408.75	476.87	545.00	613.12	681.25
2726	17.04	34.07	68.15	136.30	204.45	272.60	340.75	408.90	477.05	545.20	613.35	681.50
2727	17.04	34.09	68.17	136.35	204.52	272.70	340.87	409.05	477.22	545.40	613.57	681.75
2728	17.05	34.10	68.20	136.40	204.60	272.80	341.00	409.20	477.40	545.60	613.80	682.00
2729	17.06	34.11	68.22	136.45	204.67	272.90	341.12	409.35	477.57	545.80	614.02	682.25
2730	17.06	34.12	68.25	136.50	204.75	273.00	341.25	409.50	477.75	546.00	614.25	682.50
2731	17.07	34.14	68.27	136.55	204.82	273.10	341.37	409.65	477.92	546.20	614.47	682.75
2732	17.07	34.15	68.30	136.60	204.90	273.20	341.50	409.80	478.10	546.40	614.70	683.00
2733	17.08	34.16	68.32	136.65	204.97	273.30	341.62	409.95	478.27	546.60	614.92	683.25
2734	17.09	34.17	68.35	136.70	205.05	273.40	341.75	410.10	478.45	546.80	615.15	683.50
2735	17.09	34.19	68.37	136.75	205.12	273.50	341.87	410.25	478.62	547.00	615.37	683.75
2736	17.10	34.20	68.40	136.80	205.20	273.60	342.00	410.40	478.80	547.20	615.60	684.00
2737	17.11	34.21	68.42	136.85	205.27	273.70	342.12	410.55	478.97	547.40	615.82	684.25
2738	17.11	34.22	68.45	136.90	205.35	273.80	342.25	410.70	479.15	547.60	616.05	684.50
2739	17.12	34.24	68.47	136.95	205.42	273.90	342.37	410.85	479.32	547.80	616.27	684.75
2740	17.12	34.25	68.50	137.00	205.50	274.00	342.50	411.00	479.50	548.00	616.50	685.00
2741	17.13	34.26	68.52	137.05	205.57	274.10	342.62	411.15	479.67	548.20	616.72	685.25
2742	17.14	34.27	68.55	137.10	205.65	274.20	342.75	411.30	479.85	548.40	616.95	685.50
2743	17.14	34.29	68.57	137.15	205.72	274.30	342.87	411.45	480.02	548.60	617.17	685.75
2744	17.15	34.30	68.60	137.20	205.80	274.40	343.00	411.60	480.20	548.80	617.40	686.00
2745	17.16	34.31	68.62	137.25	205.87	274.50	343.12	411.75	480.37	549.00	617.62	686.25
2746	17.16	34.32	68.65	137.30	205.95	274.60	343.25	411.90	480.55	549.20	617.85	686.50
2747	17.17	34.34	68.67	137.35	206.02	274.70	343.37	412.05	480.72	549.40	618.07	686.75
2748	17.17	34.35	68.70	137.40	206.10	274.80	343.50	412.20	480.90	549.60	618.30	687.00
2749	17.18	34.36	68.72	137.45	206.17	274.90	343.62	412.35	481.07	549.80	618.52	687.25
2750	17.19	34.37	68.75	137.50	206.25	275.00	343.75	412.50	481.25	550.00	618.75	687.50

2750 FEET.

Per Ton,	$11	$12	$13	$14	$15	$16	$17	$18	$19	$20
Per Foot,	27½ cts.	30 cts.	32½ cts.	35 cts.	37½ cts.	40 cts.	42½ cts.	45 cts.	47½ cts.	50 cts.
Feet.										
2701	742.77	810.30	877.82	945.35	1012.87	1080.40	1147.92	1215.45	1282.97	1350.50
2702	743.05	810.60	878.15	945.70	1013.25	1080.80	1148.35	1215.90	1283.45	1351.00
2703	743.32	810.90	878.47	946.05	1013.62	1081.20	1148.77	1216.35	1283.92	1351.50
2704	743.60	811.20	878.80	946.40	1014.00	1081.60	1149.20	1216.80	1284.40	1352.00
2705	743.87	811.50	879.12	946.75	1014.37	1082.00	1149.62	1217.25	1284.87	1352.50
2706	744.15	811.80	879.45	947.10	1014.75	1082.40	1150.05	1217.70	1285.35	1353.00
2707	744.42	812.10	879.77	947.45	1015.12	1082.80	1150.47	1218.15	1285.82	1353.50
2708	744.70	812.40	880.10	947.80	1015.50	1083.20	1150.90	1218.60	1286.30	1354.00
2709	744.97	812.70	880.42	948.15	1015.87	1083.60	1151.32	1219.05	1286.77	1354.50
2710	745.25	813.00	880.75	948.50	1016.25	1084.00	1151.75	1219.50	1287.25	1355.00
2711	745.52	813.30	881.07	948.85	1016.62	1084.40	1152.17	1219.95	1287.72	1355.50
2712	745.80	813.60	881.40	949.20	1017.00	1084.80	1152.60	1220.40	1288.20	1356.00
2713	746.07	813.90	881.72	949.55	1017.37	1085.20	1153.02	1220.85	1288.67	1356.50
2714	746.35	814.20	882.05	949.90	1017.75	1085.60	1153.45	1221.30	1289.15	1357.00
2715	746.62	814.50	882.37	950.25	1018.12	1086.00	1153.87	1221.75	1289.62	1357.50
2716	746.90	814.80	882.70	950.60	1018.50	1086.40	1154.30	1222.20	1290.10	1358.00
2717	747.17	815.10	883.02	950.95	1018.87	1086.80	1154.72	1222.65	1290.57	1358.50
2718	747.45	815.40	883.35	951.30	1019.25	1087.20	1155.15	1223.10	1291.05	1359.00
2719	747.72	815.70	883.67	951.65	1019.62	1087.60	1155.57	1223.55	1291.52	1359.50
2720	748.00	816.00	884.00	952.00	1020.00	1088.00	1156.00	1224.00	1292.00	1360.00
2721	748.27	816.30	884.32	952.35	1020.37	1088.40	1156.42	1224.45	1292.47	1360.50
2722	748.55	816.60	884.65	952.70	1020.75	1088.80	1156.85	1224.90	1292.95	1361.00
2723	748.82	816.90	884.97	953.05	1021.12	1089.20	1157.27	1225.35	1293.42	1361.50
2724	749.10	817.20	885.30	953.40	1021.50	1089.60	1157.70	1225.80	1293.90	1362.00
2725	749.37	817.50	885.62	953.75	1021.87	1090.00	1158.12	1226.25	1294.37	1362.50
2726	749.65	817.80	885.95	954.10	1022.25	1090.40	1158.55	1226.70	1294.85	1363.00
2727	749.92	818.10	886.27	954.45	1022.62	1090.80	1158.97	1227.15	1295.32	1363.50
2728	750.20	818.40	886.60	954.80	1023.00	1091.20	1159.40	1227.60	1295.80	1364.00
2729	750.47	818.70	886.92	955.15	1023.37	1091.60	1159.82	1228.05	1296.27	1364.50
2730	750.75	819.00	887.25	955.50	1023.75	1092.00	1160.25	1228.50	1296.75	1365.00
2731	751.02	819.30	887.57	955.85	1024.12	1092.40	1160.67	1228.95	1297.22	1365.50
2732	751.30	819.60	887.90	956.20	1024.50	1092.80	1161.10	1229.40	1297.70	1366.00
2733	751.57	819.90	888.22	956.55	1024.87	1093.20	1161.52	1229.85	1298.17	1366.50
2734	751.85	820.20	888.55	956.90	1025.25	1093.60	1161.95	1230.30	1298.65	1367.00
2735	752.12	820.50	888.87	957.25	1025.62	1094.00	1162.37	1230.75	1299.12	1367.50
2736	752.40	820.80	889.20	957.60	1026.00	1094.40	1162.80	1231.20	1299.60	1368.00
2737	752.67	821.10	889.52	957.95	1026.37	1094.80	1163.22	1231.65	1300.07	1368.50
2738	752.95	821.40	889.85	958.30	1026.75	1095.20	1163.65	1232.10	1300.55	1369.00
2739	753.22	821.70	890.17	958.65	1027.12	1095.60	1164.07	1232.55	1301.02	1369.50
2740	753.50	822.00	890.50	959.00	1027.50	1096.00	1164.50	1233.00	1301.50	1370.00
2741	753.77	822.30	890.82	959.35	1027.87	1096.40	1164.92	1233.45	1301.97	1370.50
2742	754.05	822.60	891.15	959.70	1028.25	1096.80	1165.35	1233.90	1302.45	1371.00
2743	754.32	822.90	891.47	960.05	1028.62	1097.20	1165.77	1234.35	1302.92	1371.50
2744	754.60	823.20	891.80	960.40	1029.00	1097.60	1166.20	1234.80	1303.40	1372.00
2745	754.87	823.50	892.12	960.75	1029.37	1098.00	1166.62	1235.25	1303.87	1372.50
2746	755.15	823.80	892.45	961.10	1029.75	1098.40	1167.05	1235.70	1304.35	1373.00
2747	755.42	824.10	892.77	961.45	1030.12	1098.80	1167.47	1236.15	1304.82	1373.50
2748	755.70	824.40	893.10	961.80	1030.50	1099.20	1167.90	1236.60	1305.30	1374.00
2749	755.97	824.70	893.42	962.15	1030.87	1099.60	1168.32	1237.05	1305.77	1374.50
2750	756.25	825.00	893.75	962.50	1031.25	1100.00	1168.75	1237.50	1306.25	1375.00

2800 FEET.

Per Ton, Per Foot, Feet.	25c.	50c.	$1 2½ cts.	$2 5 cts.	$3 7½ cts.	$4 10 cts.	$5 12½ cts.	$6 15 cts.	$7 17½ cts.	$8 20 cts.	$9 22½ cts.	$10 25 cts.
2751	17.19	34.39	68.77	137.55	206.32	275.10	343.87	412.65	481.42	550.20	618.97	687.75
2752	17.20	34.40	68.80	137.60	206.40	275.20	344.00	412.80	481.60	550.40	619.20	688.00
2753	17.21	34.41	68.82	137.65	206.47	275.30	344.12	412.95	481.77	550.60	619.42	688.25
2754	17.21	34.42	68.85	137.70	206.55	275.40	344.25	413.10	481.95	550.80	619.65	688.50
2755	17.22	34.44	68.87	137.75	206.62	275.50	344.37	413.25	482.12	551.00	619.87	688.75
2756	17.22	34.45	68.90	137.80	206.70	275.60	344.50	413.40	482.30	551.20	620.10	689.00
2757	17.23	34.46	68.92	137.85	206.77	275.70	344.62	413.55	482.47	551.40	620.32	689.25
2758	17.24	34.47	68.95	137.90	206.85	275.80	344.75	413.70	482.65	551.60	620.55	689.50
2759	17.24	34.49	68.97	137.95	206.92	275.90	344.87	413.85	482.82	551.80	620.77	689.75
2760	17.25	34.50	69.00	138.00	207.00	276.00	345.00	414.00	483.00	552.00	621.00	690.00
2761	17.26	34.51	69.02	138.05	207.07	276.10	345.12	414.15	483.17	552.20	621.22	690.25
2762	17.26	34.52	69.05	138.10	207.15	276.20	345.25	414.30	483.35	552.40	621.45	690.50
2763	17.27	34.54	69.07	138.15	207.22	276.30	345.37	414.45	483.52	552.60	621.67	690.75
2764	17.27	34.55	69.10	138.20	207.30	276.40	345.50	414.60	483.70	552.80	621.90	691.00
2765	17.28	34.56	69.12	138.25	207.37	276.50	345.62	414.75	483.87	553.00	622.12	691.25
2766	17.29	34.57	69.15	138.30	207.45	276.60	345.75	414.90	484.05	553.20	622.35	691.50
2767	17.29	34.59	69.17	138.35	207.52	276.70	345.87	415.05	484.22	553.40	622.57	691.75
2768	17.30	34.60	69.20	138.40	207.60	276.80	346.00	415.20	484.40	553.60	622.80	692.00
2769	17.31	34.61	69.22	138.45	207.67	276.90	346.12	415.35	484.57	553.80	623.02	692.25
2770	17.31	34.62	69.25	138.50	207.75	277.00	346.25	415.50	484.75	554.00	623.25	692.50
2771	17.32	34.64	69.27	138.55	207.82	277.10	346.37	415.65	484.92	554.20	623.47	692.75
2772	17.32	34.65	69.30	138.60	207.90	277.20	346.50	415.80	485.10	554.40	623.70	693.00
2773	17.33	34.66	69.32	138.65	207.97	277.30	346.62	415.95	485.27	554.60	623.92	693.25
2774	17.34	34.67	69.35	138.70	208.05	277.40	346.75	416.10	485.45	554.80	624.15	693.50
2775	17.34	34.69	69.37	138.75	208.12	277.50	346.87	416.25	485.62	555.00	624.37	693.75
2776	17.35	34.70	69.40	138.80	208.20	277.60	347.00	416.40	485.80	555.20	624.60	694.00
2777	17.36	34.71	69.42	138.85	208.27	277.70	347.12	416.55	485.97	555.40	624.82	694.25
2778	17.36	34.72	69.45	138.90	208.35	277.80	347.25	416.70	486.15	555.60	625.05	694.50
2779	17.37	34.74	69.47	138.95	208.42	277.90	347.37	416.85	486.32	555.80	625.27	694.75
2780	17.37	34.75	69.50	139.00	208.50	278.00	347.50	417.00	486.50	556.00	625.50	695.00
2781	17.38	34.76	69.52	139.05	208.57	278.10	347.62	417.15	486.67	556.20	625.72	695.25
2782	17.39	34.77	69.55	139.10	208.65	278.20	347.75	417.30	486.85	556.40	625.95	695.50
2783	17.39	34.79	69.57	139.15	208.72	278.30	347.87	417.45	487.02	556.60	626.17	695.75
2784	17.40	34.80	69.60	139.20	208.80	278.40	348.00	417.60	487.20	556.80	626.40	696.00
2785	17.41	34.81	69.62	139.25	208.87	278.50	348.12	417.75	487.37	557.00	626.62	696.25
2786	17.41	34.82	69.65	139.30	208.95	278.60	348.25	417.90	487.55	557.20	626.85	696.50
2787	17.42	34.84	69.67	139.35	209.02	278.70	348.37	418.05	487.72	557.40	627.07	696.75
2788	17.42	34.85	69.70	139.40	209.10	278.80	348.50	418.20	487.90	557.60	627.30	697.00
2789	17.43	34.86	69.72	139.45	209.17	278.90	348.62	418.35	488.07	557.80	627.52	697.25
2790	17.44	34.87	69.75	139.50	209.25	279.00	348.75	418.50	488.25	558.00	627.75	697.50
2791	17.44	34.89	69.77	139.55	209.32	279.10	348.87	418.65	488.42	558.20	627.97	697.75
2792	17.45	34.90	69.80	139.60	209.40	279.20	349.00	418.80	488.60	558.40	628.20	698.00
2793	17.46	34.91	69.82	139.65	209.47	279.30	349.12	418.95	488.77	558.60	628.42	698.25
2794	17.46	34.92	69.85	139.70	209.55	279.40	349.25	419.10	488.95	558.80	628.65	698.50
2795	17.47	34.94	69.87	139.75	209.62	279.50	349.37	419.25	489.12	559.00	628.87	698.75
2796	17.47	34.95	69.90	139.80	209.70	279.60	349.50	419.40	489.30	559.20	629.10	699.00
2797	17.48	34.96	69.92	139.85	209.77	279.70	349.62	419.55	489.47	559.40	629.32	699.25
2798	17.49	34.97	69.95	139.90	209.85	279.80	349.75	419.70	489.65	559.60	629.55	699.50
2799	17.49	34.99	69.97	139.95	209.92	279.90	349.87	419.85	489.82	559.80	629.77	699.75
2800	17.50	35.00	70.00	140.00	210.00	280.00	350.00	420.00	490.00	560.00	630.00	700.00

2800 FEET.

Per Ton,	$11	$12	$13	$14	$15	$16	$17	$18	$19	$20
Per Foot,	27½ cts.	30 cts.	32½ cts.	35 cts.	37½ cts.	40 cts.	42½ cts.	45 cts.	47½ cts.	50 cts.
Feet.										
2751	756.52	825.30	894.07	962.85	1031.62	1100.40	1169.17	1237.95	1306.72	1375.50
2752	756.80	825.60	894.40	963.20	1032.00	1100.80	1169.60	1238.40	1307.20	1376.00
2753	757.07	825.90	894.72	963.55	1032.37	1101.20	1170.02	1238.85	1307.67	1376.50
2754	757.35	826.20	895.05	963.90	1032.75	1101.60	1170.45	1239.30	1308.15	1377.00
2755	757.62	826.50	895.37	964.25	1033.12	1102.00	1170.87	1239.75	1308.62	1377.50
2756	757.90	826.80	895.70	964.60	1033.50	1102.40	1171.30	1240.20	1309.10	1378.00
2757	758.17	827.10	896.02	964.95	1033.87	1102.80	1171.72	1240.65	1309.57	1378.50
2758	758.45	827.40	896.35	965.30	1034.25	1103.20	1172.15	1241.10	1310.05	1379.00
2759	758.72	827.70	896.67	965.65	1034.62	1103.60	1172.57	1241.55	1310.52	1379.50
2760	759.00	828.00	897.00	966.00	1035.00	1104.00	1173.00	1242.00	1311.00	1380.00
2761	759.27	828.30	897.32	966.35	1035.37	1104.40	1173.42	1242.45	1311.47	1380.50
2762	759.55	828.60	897.65	966.70	1035.75	1104.80	1173.85	1242.90	1311.95	1381.00
2763	759.82	828.90	897.97	967.05	1036.12	1105.20	1174.27	1243.35	1312.42	1381.50
2764	760.10	829.20	898.30	967.40	1036.50	1105.60	1174.70	1243.80	1312.90	1382.00
2765	760.37	829.50	898.62	967.75	1036.87	1106.00	1175.12	1244.25	1313.37	1382.50
2766	760.65	829.80	898.95	968.10	1037.25	1106.40	1175.55	1244.70	1313.85	1383.00
2767	760.92	830.10	899.27	968.45	1037.62	1106.80	1175.97	1245.15	1314.32	1383.50
2768	761.20	830.40	899.60	968.80	1038.00	1107.20	1176.40	1245.60	1314.80	1384.00
2769	761.47	830.70	899.92	969.15	1038.37	1107.60	1176.82	1246.05	1315.27	1384.50
2770	761.75	831.00	900.25	969.50	1038.75	1108.00	1177.25	1246.50	1315.75	1385.00
2771	762.02	831.30	900.57	969.85	1039.12	1108.40	1177.67	1246.95	1316.22	1385.50
2772	762.30	831.60	900.90	970.20	1039.50	1108.80	1178.10	1247.40	1316.70	1386.00
2773	762.57	831.90	901.22	970.55	1039.87	1109.20	1178.52	1247.85	1317.17	1386.50
2774	762.85	832.20	901.55	970.90	1040.25	1109.60	1178.95	1248.30	1317.65	1387.00
2775	763.12	832.50	901.87	971.25	1040.62	1110.00	1179.37	1248.75	1318.12	1387.50
2776	763.40	832.80	902.20	971.60	1041.00	1110.40	1179.80	1249.20	1318.60	1388.00
2777	763.67	833.10	902.52	971.95	1041.37	1110.80	1180.22	1249.65	1319.07	1388.50
2778	763.95	833.40	902.85	972.30	1041.75	1111.20	1180.65	1250.10	1319.55	1389.00
2779	764.22	833.70	903.17	972.65	1042.12	1111.60	1181.07	1250.55	1320.02	1389.50
2780	764.50	834.00	903.50	973.00	1042.50	1112.00	1181.50	1251.00	1320.50	1390.00
2781	764.77	834.30	903.82	973.35	1042.87	1112.40	1181.92	1251.45	1320.97	1390.50
2782	765.05	834.60	904.15	973.70	1043.25	1112.80	1182.35	1251.90	1321.45	1391.00
2783	765.32	834.90	904.47	974.05	1043.62	1113.20	1182.77	1252.35	1321.92	1391.50
2784	765.60	835.20	904.80	974.40	1044.00	1113.60	1183.20	1252.80	1322.40	1392.00
2785	765.87	835.50	905.12	974.75	1044.37	1114.00	1183.62	1253.25	1322.87	1392.50
2786	766.15	835.80	905.45	975.10	1044.75	1114.40	1184.05	1253.70	1323.35	1393.00
2787	766.42	836.10	905.77	975.45	1045.12	1114.80	1184.47	1254.15	1323.82	1393.50
2788	766.70	836.40	906.10	975.80	1045.50	1115.20	1184.90	1254.60	1324.30	1394.00
2789	766.97	836.70	906.42	976.15	1045.87	1115.60	1185.32	1255.05	1324.77	1394.50
2790	767.25	837.00	906.75	976.50	1046.25	1116.00	1185.75	1255.50	1325.25	1395.00
2791	767.52	837.30	907.07	976.85	1046.62	1116.40	1186.17	1255.95	1325.72	1395.50
2792	767.80	837.60	907.40	977.20	1047.00	1116.80	1186.60	1256.40	1326.20	1396.00
2793	768.07	837.90	907.72	977.55	1047.37	1117.20	1187.02	1256.85	1326.67	1396.50
2794	768.35	838.20	908.05	977.90	1047.75	1117.60	1187.45	1257.30	1327.15	1397.00
2795	768.62	838.50	908.37	978.25	1048.12	1118.00	1187.87	1257.75	1327.62	1397.50
2796	768.90	838.80	908.70	978.60	1048.50	1118.40	1188.30	1258.20	1328.10	1398.00
2797	769.17	839.10	909.02	978.95	1048.87	1118.80	1188.72	1258.65	1328.57	1398.50
2798	769.45	839.40	909.35	979.30	1049.25	1119.20	1189.15	1259.10	1329.05	1399.00
2799	769.72	839.70	909.67	979.65	1049.62	1119.60	1189.57	1259.55	1329.52	1399.50
2800	770.00	840.00	910.00	980.00	1050.00	1120.00	1190.00	1260.00	1330.00	1400.00

2850 FEET.

Per Ton, Per Foot,	25c.	50c.	$1 2½ cts.	$2 5 cts.	$3 7½ cts.	$4 10 cts.	$5 12½ cts.	$6 15 cts.	$7 17½ cts.	$8 20 cts.	$9 22½ cts.	$10 25 cts.
Feet.												
2801	17.51	35.01	70.02	140.05	210.07	280.10	350.12	420.15	490.17	560.20	630.22	700.25
2802	17.51	35.02	70.05	140.10	210.15	280.20	350.25	420.30	490.35	560.40	630.45	700.50
2803	17.52	35.04	70.07	140.15	210.22	280.30	350.37	420.45	490.52	560.60	630.67	700.75
2804	17.52	35.05	70.10	140.20	210.30	280.40	350.50	420.60	490.70	560.80	630.90	701.00
2805	17.53	35.06	70.12	140.25	210.37	280.50	350.62	420.75	490.87	561.00	631.12	701.25
2806	17.54	35.07	70.15	140.30	210.45	280.60	350.75	420.90	491.05	561.20	631.35	701.50
2807	17.54	35.09	70.17	140.35	210.52	280.70	350.87	421.05	491.22	561.40	631.57	701.75
2808	17.55	35.10	70.20	140.40	210.60	280.80	351.00	421.20	491.40	561.60	631.80	702.00
2809	17.56	35.11	70.22	140.45	210.67	280.90	351.12	421.35	491.57	561.80	632.02	702.25
2810	17.56	35.12	70.25	140.50	210.75	281.00	351.25	421.50	491.75	562.00	632.25	702.50
2811	17.57	35.14	70.27	140.55	210.82	281.10	351.37	421.65	491.92	562.20	632.47	702.75
2812	17.57	35.15	70.30	140.60	210.90	281.20	351.50	421.80	492.10	562.40	632.70	703.00
2813	17.58	35.16	70.32	140.65	210.97	281.30	351.62	421.95	492.27	562.60	632.92	703.25
2814	17.59	35.17	70.35	140.70	211.05	281.40	351.75	422.10	492.45	562.80	633.15	703.50
2815	17.59	35.19	70.37	140.75	211.12	281.50	351.87	422.25	492.62	563.00	633.37	703.75
2816	17.60	35.20	70.40	140.80	211.20	281.60	352.00	422.40	492.80	563.20	633.60	704.00
2817	17.61	35.21	70.42	140.85	211.27	281.70	352.12	422.55	492.97	563.40	633.82	704.25
2818	17.61	35.22	70.45	140.90	211.35	281.80	352.25	422.70	493.15	563.60	634.05	704.50
2819	17.62	35.24	70.47	140.95	211.42	281.90	352.37	422.85	493.32	563.80	634.27	704.75
2820	17.62	35.25	70.50	141.00	211.50	282.00	352.50	423.00	493.50	564.00	634.50	705.00
2821	17.63	35.26	70.52	141.05	211.57	282.10	352.62	423.15	493.67	564.20	634.72	705.25
2822	17.64	35.27	70.55	141.10	211.65	282.20	352.75	423.30	493.85	564.40	634.95	705.50
2823	17.64	35.29	70.57	141.15	211.72	282.30	352.87	423.45	494.02	564.60	635.17	705.75
2824	17.65	35.30	70.60	141.20	211.80	282.40	353.00	423.60	494.20	564.80	635.40	706.00
2825	17.66	35.31	70.62	141.25	211.87	282.50	353.12	423.75	494.37	565.00	635.62	706.25
2826	17.66	35.32	70.65	141.30	211.95	282.60	353.25	423.90	494.55	565.20	635.85	706.50
2827	17.67	35.34	70.67	141.35	212.02	282.70	352.37	424.05	494.72	565.40	636.07	706.75
2828	17.67	35.35	70.70	141.40	212.10	282.80	353.50	424.20	494.90	565.60	636.30	707.00
2829	17.68	35.36	70.72	141.45	212.17	282.90	353.62	424.35	495.07	565.80	636.52	707.25
2830	17.69	35.37	70.75	141.50	212.25	283.00	353.75	424.50	495.25	566.00	636.75	707.50
2831	17.69	35.39	70.77	141.55	212.32	283.10	353.87	424.65	495.42	566.20	636.97	707.75
2832	17.70	35.40	70.80	141.60	212.40	283.20	354.00	424.80	495.60	566.40	637.20	708.00
2833	17.71	35.41	70.82	141.65	212.47	283.30	354.12	424.95	495.77	566.60	637.42	708.25
2834	17.71	35.42	70.85	141.70	212.55	283.40	354.25	425.10	495.95	566.80	637.65	708.50
2835	17.72	35.44	70.87	141.75	212.62	283.50	354.37	425.25	496.12	567.00	637.87	708.75
2836	17.72	35.45	70.90	141.80	212.70	283.60	354.50	425.40	496.30	567.20	638.10	709.00
2837	17.73	35.46	70.92	141.85	212.77	283.70	354.62	425.55	496.47	567.40	638.32	709.25
2838	17.74	35.47	70.95	141.90	212.85	283.80	354.75	425.70	496.65	567.60	638.55	709.50
2839	17.74	35.49	70.97	141.95	212.92	283.90	354.87	425.85	496.82	567.80	638.77	709.75
2840	17.75	35.50	71.00	142.00	213.00	284.00	355.00	426.00	497.00	568.00	639.00	710.00
2841	17.76	35.51	71.02	142.05	213.07	284.10	355.12	426.15	497.17	568.20	639.22	710.25
2842	17.76	35.52	71.05	142.10	213.15	284.20	355.25	426.30	497.35	568.40	639.45	710.50
2843	17.77	35.54	71.07	142.15	213.22	284.30	355.37	426.45	497.52	568.60	639.67	710.75
2844	17.77	35.55	71.10	142.20	213.30	284.40	355.50	426.60	497.70	568.80	639.90	711.00
2845	17.78	35.56	71.12	142.25	213.37	284.50	355.62	426.75	497.87	569.00	640.12	711.25
2846	17.79	35.57	71.15	142.30	213.45	284.60	355.75	426.90	498.05	569.20	640.35	711.50
2847	17.79	35.59	71.17	142.35	213.52	284.70	355.87	427.05	498.22	569.40	640.57	711.75
2848	17.80	35.60	71.20	142.40	213.60	284.80	356.00	427.20	498.40	569.60	640.80	712.00
2849	17.81	35.61	71.22	142.45	213.67	284.90	356.12	427.35	498.57	569.80	641.02	712.25
2850	17.81	35.62	71.25	142.50	213.75	285.00	356.25	427.50	498.75	570.00	641.25	712.50

2850 FEET.

Per Ton,	$11	$12	$13	$14	$15	$16	$17	$18	$19	$20
Per Foot,	27½ cts.	30 cts.	32½ cts.	35 cts.	37½ cts.	40 cts.	42½ cts.	45 cts.	47½ cts.	50 cts.
Feet.										
2801	770.27	840.30	910.32	980.35	1050.37	1120.40	1190.42	1260.45	1330.47	1400.50
2802	770.55	840.60	910.65	980.70	1050.75	1120.80	1190.85	1260.90	1330.95	1401.00
2803	770.82	840.90	910.97	981.05	1051.12	1121.20	1191.27	1261.35	1331.42	1401.50
2804	771.10	841.20	911.30	981.40	1051.50	1121.60	1191.70	1261.80	1331.90	1402.00
2805	771.37	841.50	911.62	981.75	1051.87	1122.00	1192.12	1262.25	1332.37	1402.50
2806	771.65	841.80	911.95	982.10	1052.25	1122.40	1192.55	1262.70	1332.85	1403.00
2807	771.92	842.10	912.27	982.45	1052.62	1122.80	1192.97	1263.15	1333.32	1403.50
2808	772.20	842.40	912.60	982.80	1053.00	1123.20	1193.40	1263.60	1333.80	1404.00
2809	772.47	842.70	912.92	983.15	1053.37	1123.60	1193.82	1264.05	1334.27	1404.50
2810	772.75	843.00	913.25	983.50	1053.75	1124.00	1194.25	1264.50	1334.75	1405.00
2811	773.02	843.30	913.57	983.85	1054.12	1124.40	1194.67	1264.95	1335.22	1405.50
2812	773.30	843.60	913.90	984.20	1054.50	1124.80	1195.10	1265.40	1335.70	1406.00
2813	773.57	843.90	914.22	984.55	1054.87	1125.20	1195.52	1265.85	1336.17	1406.50
2814	773.85	844.20	914.55	984.90	1055.25	1125.60	1195.95	1266.30	1336.65	1407.00
2815	774.12	844.50	914.87	985.25	1055.62	1126.00	1196.37	1266.75	1337.12	1407.50
2816	774.40	844.80	915.20	985.60	1056.00	1126.40	1196.80	1267.20	1337.60	1408.00
2817	774.67	845.10	915.52	985.95	1056.37	1126.80	1197.22	1267.65	1338.07	1408.50
2818	774.95	845.40	915.85	986.30	1056.75	1127.20	1197.65	1268.10	1338.55	1409.00
2819	775.22	845.70	916.17	986.65	1057.12	1127.60	1198.07	1268.55	1339.02	1409.50
2820	775.50	846.00	916.50	987.00	1057.50	1128.00	1198.50	1269.00	1339.50	1410.00
2821	775.77	846.30	916.82	987.35	1057.87	1128.40	1198.92	1269.45	1339.97	1410.50
2822	776.05	846.60	917.15	987.70	1058.25	1128.80	1199.35	1269.90	1340.45	1411.00
2823	776.32	846.90	917.47	988.05	1058.62	1129.20	1199.77	1270.35	1340.92	1411.50
2824	776.60	847.20	917.80	988.40	1059.00	1129.60	1200.20	1270.80	1341.40	1412.00
2825	776.87	847.50	918.12	988.75	1059.37	1130.00	1200.62	1271.25	1341.87	1412.50
2826	777.15	847.80	918.45	989.10	1059.75	1130.40	1201.05	1271.70	1342.35	1413.00
2827	777.42	848.10	918.77	989.45	1060.12	1130.80	1201.47	1272.15	1342.82	1413.50
2828	777.70	848.40	919.10	989.80	1060.50	1131.20	1201.90	1272.60	1343.30	1414.00
2829	777.97	848.70	919.42	990.15	1060.87	1131.60	1202.32	1273.05	1343.77	1414.50
2830	778.25	849.00	919.75	990.50	1061.25	1132.00	1202.75	1273.50	1344.25	1415.00
2831	778.52	849.30	920.07	990.85	1061.62	1132.40	1203.17	1273.95	1344.72	1415.50
2832	778.80	849.60	920.40	991.20	1062.00	1132.80	1203.60	1274.40	1345.20	1416.00
2833	779.07	849.90	920.72	991.55	1062.37	1133.20	1204.02	1274.85	1345.67	1416.50
2834	779.35	850.20	921.05	991.90	1062.75	1133.60	1204.45	1275.30	1346.15	1417.00
2835	779.62	850.50	921.37	992.25	1063.12	1134.00	1204.87	1275.75	1346.62	1417.50
2836	779.90	850.80	921.70	992.60	1063.50	1134.40	1205.30	1276.20	1347.10	1418.00
2837	780.17	851.10	922.02	992.95	1063.87	1134.80	1205.72	1276.65	1347.57	1418.50
2838	780.45	851.40	922.35	993.30	1064.25	1135.20	1206.15	1277.10	1348.05	1419.00
2839	780.72	851.70	922.67	993.65	1064.62	1135.60	1206.57	1277.55	1348.52	1419.50
2840	781.00	852.00	923.00	994.00	1065.00	1136.00	1207.00	1278.00	1349.00	1420.00
2841	781.27	852.30	923.32	994.35	1065.37	1136.40	1207.42	1278.45	1349.47	1420.50
2842	781.55	852.60	923.65	994.70	1065.75	1136.80	1207.85	1278.90	1349.95	1421.00
2843	781.82	852.90	923.97	995.05	1066.12	1137.20	1208.27	1279.35	1350.42	1421.50
2844	782.10	853.20	924.30	995.40	1066.50	1137.60	1208.70	1279.80	1350.90	1422.00
2845	782.37	853.50	924.62	995.75	1066.87	1138.00	1209.12	1280.25	1351.37	1422.50
2846	782.65	853.80	924.95	996.10	1067.25	1138.40	1209.55	1280.70	1351.85	1423.00
2847	782.92	854.10	925.27	996.45	1067.62	1138.80	1209.97	1281.15	1352.32	1423.50
2848	783.20	854.40	925.60	996.80	1068.00	1139.20	1210.40	1281.60	1352.80	1424.00
2849	783.47	854.70	925.92	997.15	1068.37	1139.60	1210.82	1282.05	1353.27	1424.50
2850	783.75	855.00	926.25	997.50	1068.75	1140.00	1211.25	1282.50	1353.75	1425.00

2900 FEET.

Per Ton, Per Foot, Feet.	25c.	50c.	$1 2¼ cts.	$2 5 cts.	$3 7½ cts.	$4 10 cts.	$5 12½ cts.	$6 15 cts.	$7 17½ cts.	$8 20 cts.	$9 22½ cts.	$10 25 cts.
2851	17.82	35.64	71.27	142.55	213.82	285.10	356.37	427.65	498.92	570.20	641.47	712.75
2852	17.82	35.65	71.30	142.60	213.90	285.20	356.50	427.80	499.10	570.40	641.70	713.00
2853	17.83	35.66	71.32	142.65	213.97	285.30	356.62	427.95	499.27	570.60	641.92	713.25
2854	17.84	35.67	71.35	142.70	214.05	285.40	356.75	428.10	499.45	570.80	642.15	713.50
2855	17.84	35.69	71.37	142.75	214.12	285.50	356.87	428.25	499.62	571.00	642.37	713.75
2856	17.85	35.70	71.40	142.80	214.20	285.60	357.00	428.40	499.80	571.20	642.60	714.00
2857	17.86	35.71	71.42	142.85	214.27	285.70	357.12	428.55	499.97	571.40	642.82	714.25
2858	17.86	35.72	71.45	142.90	214.35	285.80	357.25	428.70	500.15	571.60	643.05	714.50
2859	17.87	35.74	71.47	142.95	214.42	285.90	357.37	428.85	500.32	571.80	643.27	714.75
2860	17.87	35.75	71.50	143.00	214.50	286.00	357.50	429.00	500.50	572.00	643.50	715.00
2861	17.88	35.76	71.52	143.05	214.57	286.10	357.62	429.15	500.67	572.20	643.72	715.25
2862	17.89	35.77	71.55	143.10	214.65	286.20	357.75	429.30	500.85	572.40	643.95	715.50
2863	17.89	35.79	71.57	143.15	214.72	286.30	357.87	429.45	501.02	572.60	644.17	715.75
2864	17.90	35.80	71.60	143.20	214.80	286.40	358.00	429.60	501.20	572.80	644.40	716.00
2865	17.91	35.81	71.62	143.25	214.87	286.50	358.12	429.75	501.37	573.00	644.62	716.25
2866	17.91	35.82	71.65	143.30	214.95	286.60	358.25	429.90	501.55	573.20	644.85	716.50
2867	17.92	35.84	71.67	143.35	215.02	286.70	358.37	430.05	501.72	573.40	645.07	716.75
2868	17.92	35.85	71.70	143.40	215.10	286.80	358.50	430.20	501.90	573.60	645.30	717.00
2869	17.93	35.86	71.72	143.45	215.17	286.90	358.62	430.35	502.07	573.80	645.52	717.25
2870	17.94	35.87	71.75	143.50	215.25	287.00	358.75	430.50	502.25	574.00	645.75	717.50
2871	17.94	35.89	71.77	143.55	215.32	287.10	358.87	430.65	502.42	574.20	645.97	717.75
2872	17.95	35.90	71.80	143.60	215.40	287.20	359.00	430.80	502.60	574.40	646.20	718.00
2873	17.96	35.91	71.82	143.65	215.47	287.30	359.12	430.95	502.77	574.60	646.42	718.25
2874	17.96	35.92	71.85	143.70	215.55	287.40	359.25	431.10	502.95	574.80	646.65	718.50
2875	17.97	35.94	71.87	143.75	215.62	287.50	359.37	431.25	503.12	575.00	646.87	718.75
2876	17.97	35.95	71.90	143.80	215.70	287.60	359.50	431.40	503.30	575.20	647.10	719.00
2877	17.98	35.96	71.92	143.85	215.77	287.70	359.62	431.55	503.47	575.40	647.32	719.25
2878	17.99	35.97	71.95	143.90	215.85	287.80	359.75	431.70	503.65	575.60	647.55	719.50
2879	17.99	35.99	71.97	143.95	215.92	287.90	359.87	431.85	503.82	575.80	647.77	719.75
2880	18.00	36.00	72.00	144.00	216.00	288.00	360.00	432.00	504.00	576.00	648.00	720.00
2881	18.01	36.01	72.02	144.05	216.07	288.10	360.12	432.15	504.17	576.20	648.22	720.25
2882	18.01	36.02	72.05	144.10	216.15	288.20	360.25	432.30	504.35	576.40	648.45	720.50
2883	18.02	36.04	72.07	144.15	216.22	288.30	360.37	432.45	504.52	576.60	648.67	720.75
2884	18.02	36.05	72.10	144.20	216.30	288.40	360.50	432.60	504.70	576.80	648.90	721.00
2885	18.03	36.06	72.12	144.25	216.37	288.50	360.62	432.75	504.87	577.00	649.12	721.25
2886	18.04	36.07	72.15	144.30	216.45	288.60	360.75	432.90	505.05	577.20	649.35	721.50
2887	18.04	36.09	72.17	144.35	216.52	288.70	360.87	433.05	505.22	577.40	649.57	721.75
2888	18.05	36.10	72.20	144.40	216.60	288.80	361.00	433.20	505.40	577.60	649.80	722.00
2889	18.06	36.11	72.22	144.45	216.67	288.90	361.12	433.35	505.57	577.80	650.02	722.25
2890	18.06	36.12	72.25	144.50	216.75	289.00	361.25	433.50	505.75	578.00	650.25	722.50
2891	18.07	36.14	72.27	144.55	216.82	289.10	361.37	433.65	505.92	578.20	650.47	722.75
2892	18.07	36.15	72.30	144.60	216.90	289.20	361.50	433.80	506.10	578.40	650.70	723.00
2893	18.08	36.16	72.32	144.65	216.97	289.30	361.62	433.95	506.27	578.60	650.92	723.25
2894	18.09	36.17	72.35	144.70	217.05	289.40	361.75	434.10	506.45	578.80	651.15	723.50
2895	18.09	36.19	72.37	144.75	217.12	289.50	361.87	434.25	506.62	579.00	651.37	723.75
2896	18.10	36.20	72.40	144.80	217.20	289.60	362.00	434.40	506.80	579.20	651.60	724.00
2897	18.11	36.21	72.42	144.85	217.27	289.70	362.12	434.55	506.97	579.40	651.82	724.25
2898	18.11	36.22	72.45	144.90	217.35	289.80	362.25	434.70	507.15	579.60	652.05	724.50
2899	18.12	36.24	72.47	144.95	217.42	289.90	362.37	434.85	507.32	579.80	652.27	724.75
2900	18.12	36.25	72.50	145.00	217.50	290.00	362.50	435.00	507.50	580.00	652.50	725.00

2900 FEET.

Per Ton,	$11	$12	$13	$14	$15	$16	$17	$18	$19	$20
Per Foot,	27½ cts.	30 cts.	32½ cts.	35 cts.	37½ cts.	40 cts.	42½ cts.	45 cts.	47½ cts.	50 cts.
Feet.										
2851	784.02	855.30	926.57	997.85	1069.12	1140.40	1211.67	1282.95	1354.22	1425.50
2852	784.30	855.60	926.90	998.20	1069.50	1140.80	1212.10	1283.40	1354.70	1426.00
2853	784.57	855.90	927.22	998.55	1069.87	1141.20	1212.52	1283.85	1355.17	1426.50
2854	784.85	856.20	927.55	998.90	1070.25	1141.60	1212.95	1284.30	1355.65	1427.00
2855	785.12	856.50	927.87	999.25	1070.62	1142.00	1213.37	1284.75	1356.12	1427.50
2856	785.40	856.80	928.20	999.60	1071.00	1142.40	1213.80	1285.20	1356.60	1428.00
2857	785.67	857.10	928.52	999.95	1071.37	1142.80	1214.22	1285.65	1357.07	1428.50
2858	785.95	857.40	928.85	1000.30	1071.75	1143.20	1214.65	1286.10	1357.55	1429.00
2859	786.22	857.70	929.17	1000.65	1072.12	1143.60	1215.07	1286.55	1358.02	1429.50
2860	786.50	858.00	929.50	1001.00	1072.50	1144.00	1215.50	1287.00	1358.50	1430.00
2861	786.77	858.30	929.82	1001.35	1072.87	1144.40	1215.92	1287.45	1358.97	1430.50
2862	787.05	858.60	930.15	1001.70	1073.25	1144.80	1216.35	1287.90	1359.45	1431.00
2863	787.32	858.90	930.47	1002.05	1073.62	1145.20	1216.77	1288.35	1359.92	1431.50
2864	787.60	859.20	930.80	1002.40	1074.00	1145.60	1217.20	1288.80	1360.40	1432.00
2865	787.87	859.50	931.12	1002.75	1074.37	1146.00	1217.62	1289.25	1360.87	1432.50
2866	788.15	859.80	931.45	1003.10	1074.75	1146.40	1218.05	1289.70	1361.35	1433.00
2867	788.42	860.10	931.77	1003.45	1075.12	1146.80	1218.47	1290.15	1361.82	1433.50
2868	788.70	860.40	932.10	1003.80	1075.50	1147.20	1218.90	1290.60	1362.30	1434.00
2869	788.97	860.70	932.42	1004.15	1075.87	1147.60	1219.32	1291.05	1362.77	1434.50
2870	789.25	861.00	932.75	1004.50	1076.25	1148.00	1219.75	1291.50	1363.25	1435.00
2871	789.52	861.30	933.07	1004.85	1076.62	1148.40	1220.17	1291.95	1363.72	1435.50
2872	789.80	861.60	933.40	1005.20	1077.00	1148.80	1220.60	1292.40	1364.20	1436.00
2873	790.07	861.90	933.72	1005.55	1077.37	1149.20	1221.02	1292.85	1364.67	1436.50
2874	790.35	862.20	934.05	1005.90	1077.75	1149.60	1221.45	1293.30	1365.15	1437.00
2875	790.62	862.50	934.37	1006.25	1078.12	1150.00	1221.87	1293.75	1365.62	1437.50
2876	790.90	862.80	934.70	1006.60	1078.50	1150.40	1222.30	1294.20	1366.10	1438.00
2877	791.17	863.10	935.02	1006.95	1078.87	1150.80	1222.72	1294.65	1366.57	1438.50
2878	791.45	863.40	935.35	1007.30	1079.25	1151.20	1223.15	1295.10	1367.05	1439.00
2879	791.72	863.70	935.67	1007.65	1079.62	1151.60	1223.57	1295.55	1367.52	1439.50
2880	792.00	864.00	936.00	1008.00	1080.00	1152.00	1224.00	1296.00	1368.00	1440.00
2881	792.27	864.30	936.32	1008.35	1080.37	1152.40	1224.42	1296.45	1368.47	1440.50
2882	792.55	864.60	936.65	1008.70	1080.75	1152.80	1224.85	1296.90	1368.95	1441.00
2883	792.82	864.90	936.97	1009.05	1081.12	1153.20	1225.27	1297.35	1369.42	1441.50
2884	793.10	865.20	937.30	1009.40	1081.50	1153.60	1225.70	1297.80	1369.90	1442.00
2885	793.37	865.50	937.62	1009.75	1081.87	1154.00	1226.12	1298.25	1370.37	1442.50
2886	793.65	865.80	937.95	1010.10	1082.25	1154.40	1226.55	1298.70	1370.85	1443.00
2887	793.92	866.10	938.27	1010.45	1082.62	1154.80	1226.97	1299.15	1371.32	1443.50
2888	794.20	866.40	938.60	1010.80	1083.00	1155.20	1227.40	1299.60	1371.80	1444.00
2889	794.47	866.70	938.92	1011.15	1083.37	1155.60	1227.82	1300.05	1372.27	1444.50
2890	794.75	867.00	939.25	1011.50	1083.75	1156.00	1228.25	1300.50	1372.75	1445.00
2891	795.02	867.30	939.57	1011.85	1084.12	1156.40	1228.67	1300.95	1373.22	1445.50
2892	795.30	867.60	939.90	1012.20	1084.50	1156.80	1229.10	1301.40	1373.70	1446.00
2893	795.57	867.90	940.22	1012.55	1084.87	1157.20	1229.52	1301.85	1374.17	1446.50
2894	795.85	868.20	940.55	1012.90	1085.25	1157.60	1229.95	1302.30	1374.65	1447.00
2895	796.12	868.50	940.87	1013.25	1085.62	1158.00	1230.37	1302.75	1375.12	1447.50
2896	796.40	868.80	941.20	1013.60	1086.00	1158.40	1230.80	1303.20	1375.60	1448.00
2897	796.67	869.10	941.52	1013.95	1086.37	1158.80	1231.22	1303.65	1376.07	1448.50
2898	796.95	869.40	941.85	1014.30	1086.75	1159.20	1231.65	1304.10	1376.55	1449.00
2899	797.22	869.70	942.17	1014.65	1087.12	1159.60	1232.07	1304.55	1377.02	1449.50
2900	797.50	870.00	942.50	1015.00	1087.50	1160.00	1232.50	1305.00	1377.50	1450.00

2950 FEET.

Per Ton, Per Foot, Feet.	25c.	50c.	$1 2½ cts.	$2 5 cts.	$3 7½ cts.	$4 10 cts.	$5 12½ cts.	$6 15 cts.	$7 17½ cts.	$8 20 cts.	$9 22½ cts.	$10 25 cts.
2901	18.13	36.26	72.52	145.05	217.57	290.10	362.62	435.15	507.67	580.20	652.72	725.25
2902	18.14	36.27	72.55	145.10	217.65	290.20	362.75	435.30	507.85	580.40	652.95	725.50
2903	18.14	36.29	72.57	145.15	217.72	290.30	362.87	435.45	508.02	580.60	653.17	725.75
2904	18.15	36.30	72.60	145.20	217.80	290.40	363.00	435.60	508.20	580.80	653.40	726.00
2905	18.16	36.31	72.62	145.25	217.87	290.50	363.12	435.75	508.37	581.00	653.62	726.25
2906	18.16	36.32	72.65	145.30	217.95	290.60	363.25	435.90	508.55	581.20	653.85	726.50
2907	18.17	36.34	72.67	145.35	218.02	290.70	363.37	436.05	508.72	581.40	654.07	726.75
2908	18.17	36.35	72.70	145.40	218.10	290.80	363.50	436.20	508.90	581.60	654.30	727.00
2909	18.18	36.36	72.72	145.45	218.17	290.90	363.62	436.35	509.07	581.80	654.52	727.25
2910	18.19	36.37	72.75	145.50	218.25	291.00	363.75	436.50	509.25	582.00	654.75	727.50
2911	18.19	36.39	72.77	145.55	218.32	291.10	363.87	436.65	509.42	582.20	654.97	727.75
2912	18.20	36.40	72.80	145.60	218.40	291.20	364.00	436.80	509.60	582.40	655.20	728.00
2913	18.21	36.41	72.82	145.65	218.47	291.30	364.12	436.95	509.77	582.60	655.42	728.25
2914	18.21	36.42	72.85	145.70	218.55	291.40	364.25	437.10	509.95	582.80	655.65	728.50
2915	18.22	36.44	72.87	145.75	218.62	291.50	364.37	437.25	510.12	583.00	655.87	728.75
2916	18.22	36.45	72.90	145.80	218.70	291.60	364.50	437.40	510.30	583.20	656.10	729.00
2917	18.23	36.46	72.92	145.85	218.77	291.70	364.62	437.55	510.47	583.40	656.32	729.25
2918	18.24	36.47	72.95	145.90	218.85	291.80	364.75	437.70	510.65	583.60	656.55	729.50
2919	18.24	36.49	72.97	145.95	218.92	291.90	364.87	437.85	510.82	583.80	656.77	729.75
2920	18.25	36.50	73.00	146.00	219.00	292.00	365.00	438.00	511.00	584.00	657.00	730.00
2921	18.26	36.51	73.02	146.05	219.07	292.10	365.12	438.15	511.17	584.20	657.22	730.25
2922	18.26	36.52	73.05	146.10	219.15	292.20	365.25	438.30	511.35	584.40	657.45	730.50
2923	18.27	36.54	73.07	146.15	219.22	292.30	365.37	438.45	511.52	584.60	657.67	730.75
2924	18.27	36.55	73.10	146.20	219.30	292.40	365.50	438.60	511.70	584.80	657.90	731.00
2925	18.28	36.56	73.12	146.25	219.37	292.50	365.62	438.75	511.87	585.00	658.12	731.25
2926	18.29	36.57	73.15	146.30	219.45	292.60	365.75	438.90	512.05	585.20	658.35	731.50
2927	18.29	36.59	73.17	146.35	219.52	292.70	365.87	439.05	512.22	585.40	658.57	731.75
2928	18.30	36.60	73.20	146.40	219.60	292.80	366.00	439.20	512.40	585.60	658.80	732.00
2929	18.31	36.61	73.22	146.45	219.67	292.90	366.12	439.35	512.57	585.80	659.02	732.25
2930	18.31	36.62	73.25	146.50	219.75	293.00	366.25	439.50	512.75	586.00	659.25	732.50
2931	18.32	36.64	73.27	146.55	219.82	293.10	366.37	439.65	512.92	586.20	659.47	732.75
2932	18.32	36.65	73.30	146.60	219.90	293.20	366.50	439.80	513.10	586.40	659.70	733.00
2933	18.33	36.66	73.32	146.65	219.97	293.30	366.62	439.95	513.27	586.60	659.92	733.25
2934	18.34	36.67	73.35	146.70	220.05	293.40	366.75	440.10	513.45	586.80	660.15	733.50
2935	18.34	36.69	73.37	146.75	220.12	293.50	366.87	440.25	513.62	587.00	660.37	733.75
2936	18.35	36.70	73.40	146.80	220.20	293.60	367.00	440.40	513.80	587.20	660.60	734.00
2937	18.36	36.71	73.42	146.85	220.27	293.70	367.12	440.55	513.97	587.40	660.82	734.25
2938	18.36	36.72	73.45	146.90	220.35	293.80	367.25	440.70	514.15	587.60	661.05	734.50
2939	18.37	36.74	73.47	146.95	220.42	293.90	367.37	440.85	514.32	587.80	661.27	734.75
2940	18.37	36.75	73.50	147.00	220.50	294.00	367.50	441.00	514.50	588.00	661.50	735.00
2941	18.38	36.76	73.52	147.05	220.57	294.10	367.62	441.15	514.67	588.20	661.72	735.25
2942	18.39	36.77	73.55	147.10	220.65	294.20	367.75	441.30	514.85	588.40	661.95	735.50
2943	18.39	36.79	73.57	147.15	220.72	294.30	367.87	441.45	515.02	588.60	662.17	735.75
2944	18.40	36.80	73.60	147.20	220.80	294.40	368.00	441.60	515.20	588.80	662.40	736.00
2945	18.41	36.81	73.62	147.25	220.87	294.50	368.12	441.75	515.37	589.00	662.62	736.25
2946	18.41	36.82	73.65	147.30	220.95	294.60	368.25	441.90	515.55	589.20	662.85	736.50
2947	18.42	36.84	73.67	147.35	221.02	294.70	368.37	442.05	515.72	589.40	663.07	736.75
2948	18.42	36.85	73.70	147.40	221.10	294.80	368.50	442.20	515.90	589.60	663.30	737.00
2949	18.43	36.86	73.72	147.45	221.17	294.90	368.62	442.35	516.07	589.80	663.52	737.25
2950	18.44	36.87	73.75	147.50	221.25	295.00	368.75	442.50	516.25	590.00	663.75	737.50

2950 FEET.

Per Ton, / Per Foot,	$11 / 27½ cts.	$12 / 30 cts.	$13 / 32½ cts.	$14 / 35 cts.	$15 / 37½ cts.	$16 / 40 cts.	$17 / 42½ cts.	$18 / 45 cts.	$19 / 47½ cts.	$20 / 50 cts.
Feet.										
2901	797.77	870.30	942.82	1015.35	1087.87	1160.40	1232.92	1305.45	1377.97	1450.50
2902	798.05	870.60	943.15	1015.70	1088.25	1160.80	1233.35	1305.90	1378.45	1451.00
2903	798.32	870.90	943.47	1016.05	1088.62	1161.20	1233.77	1306.35	1378.92	1451.50
2904	798.60	871.20	943.80	1016.40	1089.00	1161.60	1234.20	1306.80	1379.40	1452.00
2905	798.87	871.50	944.12	1016.75	1089.37	1162.00	1234.62	1307.25	1379.87	1452.50
2906	799.15	871.80	944.45	1017.10	1089.75	1162.40	1235.05	1307.70	1380.35	1453.00
2907	799.42	872.10	944.77	1017.45	1090.12	1162.80	1235.47	1308.15	1380.82	1453.50
2908	799.70	872.40	945.10	1017.80	1090.50	1163.20	1235.90	1308.60	1381.30	1454.00
2909	799.97	872.70	945.42	1018.15	1090.87	1163.60	1236.32	1309.05	1381.77	1454.50
2910	800.25	873.00	945.75	1018.50	1091.25	1164.00	1236.75	1309.50	1382.25	1455.00
2911	800.52	873.30	946.07	1018.85	1091.62	1164.40	1237.17	1309.95	1382.72	1455.50
2912	800.80	873.60	946.40	1019.20	1092.00	1164.80	1237.60	1310.40	1383.20	1456.00
2913	801.07	873.90	946.72	1019.55	1092.37	1165.20	1238.02	1310.85	1383.67	1456.50
2914	801.35	874.20	947.05	1019.90	1092.75	1165.60	1238.45	1311.30	1384.15	1457.00
2915	801.62	874.50	947.37	1020.25	1093.12	1166.00	1238.87	1311.75	1384.62	1457.50
2916	801.90	874.80	947.70	1020.60	1093.50	1166.40	1239.30	1312.20	1385.10	1458.00
2917	802.17	875.10	948.02	1020.95	1093.87	1166.80	1239.72	1312.65	1385.57	1458.50
2918	802.45	875.40	948.35	1021.30	1094.25	1167.20	1240.15	1313.10	1386.05	1459.00
2919	802.72	875.70	948.67	1021.65	1094.62	1167.60	1240.57	1313.55	1386.52	1459.50
2920	803.00	876.00	949.00	1022.00	1095.00	1168.00	1241.00	1314.00	1387.00	1460.00
2921	803.27	876.30	949.32	1022.35	1095.37	1168.40	1241.42	1314.45	1387.47	1460.50
2922	803.55	876.60	949.65	1022.70	1095.75	1168.80	1241.85	1314.90	1387.95	1461.00
2923	803.82	876.90	949.97	1023.05	1096.12	1169.20	1242.27	1315.35	1388.42	1461.50
2924	804.10	877.20	950.30	1023.40	1096.50	1169.60	1242.70	1315.80	1388.90	1462.00
2925	804.37	877.50	950.62	1023.75	1096.87	1170.00	1243.12	1316.25	1389.37	1462.50
2926	804.65	877.80	950.95	1024.10	1097.25	1170.40	1243.55	1316.70	1389.85	1463.00
2927	804.92	878.10	951.27	1024.45	1097.62	1170.80	1243.97	1317.15	1390.32	1463.50
2928	805.20	878.40	951.60	1024.80	1098.00	1171.20	1244.40	1317.60	1390.80	1464.00
2929	805.47	878.70	951.92	1025.15	1098.37	1171.60	1244.82	1318.05	1391.27	1464.50
2930	805.75	879.00	952.25	1025.50	1098.75	1172.00	1245.25	1318.50	1391.75	1465.00
2931	806.02	879.30	952.57	1025.85	1099.12	1172.40	1245.67	1318.95	1392.22	1465.50
2932	806.30	879.60	952.90	1026.20	1099.50	1172.80	1246.10	1319.40	1392.70	1466.00
2933	806.57	879.90	953.22	1026.55	1099.87	1173.20	1246.52	1319.85	1393.17	1466.50
2934	806.85	880.20	953.55	1026.90	1100.25	1173.60	1246.95	1320.30	1393.65	1467.00
2935	807.12	880.50	953.87	1027.25	1100.62	1174.00	1247.37	1320.75	1394.12	1467.50
2936	807.40	880.80	954.20	1027.60	1101.00	1174.40	1247.80	1321.20	1394.60	1468.00
2937	807.67	881.10	954.52	1027.95	1101.37	1174.80	1248.22	1321.65	1395.07	1468.50
2938	807.95	881.40	954.85	1028.30	1101.75	1175.20	1248.65	1322.10	1395.55	1469.00
2939	808.22	881.70	955.17	1028.65	1102.12	1175.60	1249.07	1322.55	1396.02	1469.50
2940	808.50	882.00	955.50	1029.00	1102.50	1176.00	1249.50	1323.00	1396.50	1470.00
2941	808.77	882.30	955.82	1029.35	1102.87	1176.40	1249.92	1323.45	1396.97	1470.50
2942	809.05	882.60	956.15	1029.70	1103.25	1176.80	1250.35	1323.90	1397.45	1471.00
2943	809.32	882.90	956.47	1030.05	1103.62	1177.20	1250.77	1324.35	1397.92	1471.50
2944	809.60	883.20	956.80	1030.40	1104.00	1177.60	1251.20	1324.80	1398.40	1472.00
2945	809.87	883.50	957.12	1030.75	1104.37	1178.00	1251.62	1325.25	1398.87	1472.50
2946	810.15	883.80	957.45	1031.10	1104.75	1178.40	1252.05	1325.70	1399.35	1473.00
2947	810.42	884.10	957.77	1031.45	1105.12	1178.80	1252.47	1326.15	1399.82	1473.50
2948	810.70	884.40	958.10	1031.80	1105.50	1179.20	1252.90	1326.60	1400.30	1474.00
2949	810.97	884.70	958.42	1032.15	1105.87	1179.60	1253.32	1327.05	1400.77	1474.50
2950	811.25	885.00	958.75	1032.50	1106.25	1180.00	1253.75	1327.50	1401.25	1475.00

3000 FEET.

Per Ton, Per Foot,	25c.	50c.	$1 2½ cts.	$2 5 cts.	$3 7½ cts.	$4 10 cts.	$5 12½ cts.	$6 15 cts.	$7 17½ cts.	$8 20 cts.	$9 22½ cts.	$10 25 cts.
Feet.												
2951	18.44	36.89	73.77	147.55	221.32	295.10	368.87	442.65	516.42	590.20	663.97	737.75
2952	18.45	36.90	73.80	147.60	221.40	295.20	369.00	442.80	516.60	590.40	664.20	738.00
2953	18.46	36.91	73.82	147.65	221.47	295.30	369.12	442.95	516.77	590.60	664.42	738.25
2954	18.46	36.92	73.85	147.70	221.55	295.40	369.25	443.10	516.95	590.80	664.65	738.50
2955	18.47	36.94	73.87	147.75	221.62	295.50	369.37	443.25	517.12	591.00	664.87	738.75
2956	18.47	36.95	73.90	147.80	221.70	295.60	369.50	443.40	517.30	591.20	665.10	739.00
2957	18.48	36.96	73.92	147.85	221.77	295.70	369.62	443.55	517.47	591.40	665.32	739.25
2958	18.49	36.97	73.95	147.90	221.85	295.80	369.75	443.70	517.65	591.60	665.55	739.50
2959	18.49	36.99	73.97	147.95	221.92	295.90	369.87	443.85	517.82	591.80	665.77	739.75
2960	18.50	37.00	74.00	148.00	222.00	296.00	370.00	444.00	518.00	592.00	666.00	740.00
2961	18.51	37.01	74.02	148.05	222.07	296.10	370.12	444.15	518.17	592.20	666.22	740.25
2962	18.51	37.02	74.05	148.10	222.15	296.20	370.25	444.30	518.35	592.40	666.45	740.50
2963	18.52	37.04	74.07	148.15	222.22	296.30	370.37	444.45	518.52	592.60	666.67	740.75
2964	18.52	37.05	74.10	148.20	222.30	296.40	370.50	444.60	518.70	592.80	666.90	741.00
2965	18.53	37.06	74.12	148.25	222.37	296.50	370.62	444.75	518.87	593.00	667.12	741.25
2966	18.54	37.07	74.15	148.30	222.45	296.60	370.75	444.90	519.05	593.20	667.35	741.50
2967	18.54	37.09	74.17	148.35	222.52	296.70	370.87	445.05	519.22	593.40	667.57	741.75
2968	18.55	37.10	74.20	148.40	222.60	296.80	371.00	445.20	519.40	593.60	667.80	742.00
2969	18.56	37.11	74.22	148.45	222.67	296.90	371.12	445.35	519.57	593.80	668.02	742.25
2970	18.56	37.12	74.25	148.50	222.75	297.00	371.25	445.50	519.75	594.00	668.25	742.50
2971	18.57	37.14	74.27	148.55	222.82	297.10	371.37	445.65	519.92	594.20	668.47	742.75
2972	18.57	37.15	74.30	148.60	222.90	297.20	371.50	445.80	520.10	594.40	668.70	743.00
2973	18.58	37.16	74.32	148.65	222.97	297.30	371.62	445.95	520.27	594.60	668.92	743.25
2974	18.59	37.17	74.35	148.70	223.05	297.40	371.75	446.10	520.45	594.80	669.15	743.50
2975	18.59	37.19	74.37	148.75	223.12	297.50	371.87	446.25	520.62	595.00	669.37	743.75
2976	18.60	37.20	74.40	148.80	223.20	297.60	372.00	446.40	520.80	595.20	669.60	744.00
2977	18.61	37.21	74.42	148.85	223.27	297.70	372.12	446.55	520.97	595.40	669.82	744.25
2978	18.61	37.22	74.45	148.90	223.35	297.80	372.25	446.70	521.15	595.60	670.05	744.50
2979	18.62	37.24	74.47	148.95	223.42	297.90	372.37	446.85	521.32	595.80	670.27	744.75
2980	18.62	37.25	74.50	149.00	223.50	298.00	372.50	447.00	521.50	596.00	670.50	745.00
2981	18.63	37.26	74.52	149.05	223.57	298.10	372.62	447.15	521.67	596.20	670.72	745.25
2982	18.64	37.27	74.55	149.10	223.65	298.20	372.75	447.30	521.85	596.40	670.95	745.50
2983	18.64	37.29	74.57	149.15	223.72	298.30	372.87	447.45	522.02	596.60	671.17	745.75
2984	18.65	37.30	74.60	149.20	223.80	298.40	373.00	447.60	522.20	596.80	671.40	746.00
2985	18.66	37.31	74.62	149.25	223.87	298.50	373.12	447.75	522.37	597.00	671.62	746.25
2986	18.66	37.32	74.65	149.30	223.95	298.60	373.25	447.90	522.55	597.20	671.85	746.50
2987	18.67	37.34	74.67	149.35	224.02	298.70	373.37	448.05	522.72	597.40	672.07	746.75
2988	18.67	37.35	74.70	149.40	224.10	298.80	373.50	448.20	522.90	597.60	672.30	747.00
2989	18.68	37.36	74.72	149.45	224.17	298.90	373.62	448.35	523.07	597.80	672.52	747.25
2990	18.69	37.37	74.75	149.50	224.25	299.00	373.75	448.50	523.25	598.00	672.75	747.50
2991	18.69	37.39	74.77	149.55	224.32	299.10	373.87	448.65	523.42	598.20	672.97	747.75
2992	18.70	37.40	74.80	149.60	224.40	299.20	374.00	448.80	523.60	598.40	673.20	748.00
2993	18.71	37.41	74.82	149.65	224.47	299.30	374.12	448.95	523.77	598.60	673.42	748.25
2994	18.71	37.42	74.85	149.70	224.55	299.40	374.25	449.10	523.95	598.80	673.65	748.50
2995	18.72	37.44	74.87	149.75	224.62	299.50	374.37	449.25	524.12	599.00	673.87	748.75
2996	18.72	37.45	74.90	149.80	224.70	299.60	374.50	449.40	524.30	599.20	674.10	749.00
2997	18.73	37.46	74.92	149.85	224.77	299.70	374.62	449.55	524.47	599.40	674.32	749.25
2998	18.74	37.47	74.95	149.90	224.85	299.80	374.75	449.70	524.65	599.60	674.55	749.50
2999	18.74	37.49	74.97	149.95	224.92	299.90	374.87	449.85	524.82	599.80	674.77	749.75
3000	18.75	37.50	75.00	150.00	225.00	300.00	375.00	450.00	525.00	600.00	675.00	750.00

3000 FEET.

Per Ton,	$11	$12	$13	$14	$15	$16	$17	$18	$19	$20
Per Foot,	27½ cts.	30 cts.	32½ cts.	35 cts.	37½ cts.	40 cts.	42½ cts.	45 cts.	47½ cts.	50 cts.
Feet.										
2951	811.52	885.30	959.07	1032.85	1106.62	1180.40	1254.17	1327.95	1401.72	1475.50
2952	811.80	885.60	959.40	1033.20	1107.00	1180.80	1254.60	1328.40	1402.20	1476.00
2953	812.07	885.90	959.72	1033.55	1107.37	1181.20	1255.02	1328.85	1402.67	1476.50
2954	812.35	886.20	960.05	1033.90	1107.75	1181.60	1255.45	1329.30	1403.15	1477.00
2955	812.62	886.50	960.37	1034.25	1108.12	1182.00	1255.87	1329.75	1403.62	1477.50
2956	812.90	886.80	960.70	1034.60	1108.50	1182.40	1256.30	1330.20	1404.10	1478.00
2957	813.17	887.10	961.02	1034.95	1108.87	1182.80	1256.72	1330.65	1404.57	1478.50
2958	813.45	887.40	961.35	1035.30	1109.25	1183.20	1257.15	1331.10	1405.05	1479.00
2959	813.72	887.70	961.67	1035.65	1109.62	1183.60	1257.57	1331.55	1405.52	1479.50
2960	814.00	888.00	962.00	1036.00	1110.00	1184.00	1258.00	1332.00	1406.00	1480.00
2961	814.27	888.30	962.32	1036.35	1110.37	1184.40	1258.42	1332.45	1406.47	1480.50
2962	814.55	888.60	962.65	1036.70	1110.75	1184.80	1258.85	1332.90	1406.95	1481.00
2963	814.82	888.90	962.97	1037.05	1111.12	1185.20	1259.27	1333.35	1407.42	1481.50
2964	815.10	889.20	963.30	1037.40	1111.50	1185.60	1259.70	1333.80	1407.90	1482.00
2965	815.37	889.50	963.62	1037.75	1111.87	1186.00	1260.12	1334.25	1408.37	1482.50
2966	815.65	889.80	963.95	1038.10	1112.25	1186.40	1260.55	1334.70	1408.85	1483.00
2967	815.92	890.10	964.27	1038.45	1112.62	1186.80	1260.97	1335.15	1409.32	1483.50
2968	816.20	890.40	964.60	1038.80	1113.00	1187.20	1261.40	1335.60	1409.80	1484.00
2969	816.47	890.70	964.92	1039.15	1113.37	1187.60	1261.82	1336.05	1410.27	1484.50
2970	816.75	891.00	965.25	1039.50	1113.75	1188.00	1262.25	1336.50	1410.75	1485.00
2971	817.02	891.30	965.57	1039.85	1114.12	1188.40	1262.67	1336.95	1411.22	1485.50
2972	817.30	891.60	965.90	1040.20	1114.50	1188.80	1263.10	1337.40	1411.70	1486.00
2973	817.57	891.90	966.22	1040.55	1114.87	1189.20	1263.52	1337.85	1412.17	1486.50
2974	817.85	892.20	966.55	1040.90	1115.25	1189.60	1263.95	1338.30	1412.65	1487.00
2975	818.12	892.50	966.87	1041.25	1115.62	1190.00	1264.37	1338.75	1413.12	1487.50
2976	818.40	892.80	967.20	1041.60	1116.00	1190.40	1264.80	1339.20	1413.60	1488.00
2977	818.67	893.10	967.52	1041.95	1116.37	1190.80	1265.22	1339.65	1414.07	1488.50
2978	818.95	893.40	967.85	1042.30	1116.75	1191.20	1265.65	1340.10	1414.55	1489.00
2979	819.22	893.70	968.17	1042.65	1117.12	1191.60	1266.07	1340.55	1415.02	1489.50
2980	819.50	894.00	968.50	1043.00	1117.50	1192.00	1266.50	1341.00	1415.50	1490.00
2981	819.77	894.30	968.82	1043.35	1117.87	1192.40	1266.92	1341.45	1415.97	1490.50
2982	820.05	894.60	969.15	1043.70	1118.25	1192.80	1267.35	1341.90	1416.45	1491.00
2983	820.32	894.90	969.47	1044.05	1118.62	1193.20	1267.77	1342.35	1416.92	1491.50
2984	820.60	895.20	969.80	1044.40	1119.00	1193.60	1268.20	1342.80	1417.40	1492.00
2985	820.87	895.50	970.12	1044.75	1119.37	1194.00	1268.62	1343.25	1417.87	1492.50
2986	821.15	895.80	970.45	1045.10	1119.75	1194.40	1269.05	1343.70	1418.35	1493.00
2987	821.42	896.10	970.77	1045.45	1120.12	1194.80	1269.47	1344.15	1418.82	1493.50
2988	821.70	896.40	971.10	1045.80	1120.50	1195.20	1269.90	1344.60	1419.30	1494.00
2989	821.97	896.70	971.42	1046.15	1120.87	1195.60	1270.32	1345.05	1419.77	1494.50
2990	822.25	897.00	971.75	1046.50	1121.25	1196.00	1270.75	1345.50	1420.25	1495.00
2991	822.52	897.30	972.07	1046.85	1121.62	1196.40	1271.17	1345.95	1420.72	1495.50
2992	822.80	897.60	972.40	1047.20	1122.00	1196.80	1271.60	1346.40	1421.20	1496.00
2993	823.07	897.90	972.72	1047.55	1122.37	1197.20	1272.02	1346.85	1421.67	1496.50
2994	823.35	898.20	973.05	1047.90	1122.75	1197.60	1272.45	1347.30	1422.15	1497.00
2995	823.62	898.50	973.37	1048.25	1123.12	1198.00	1272.87	1347.75	1422.62	1497.50
2996	823.90	898.80	973.70	1048.60	1123.50	1198.40	1273.30	1348.20	1423.10	1498.00
2997	824.17	899.10	974.02	1048.95	1123.87	1198.80	1273.72	1348.65	1423.57	1498.50
2998	824.45	899.40	974.35	1049.30	1124.25	1199.20	1274.15	1349.10	1424.05	1499.00
2999	824.72	899.70	974.67	1049.65	1124.62	1199.60	1274.57	1349.55	1424.52	1499.50
3000	825.00	900.00	975.00	1050.00	1125.00	1200.00	1275.00	1350.00	1425.00	1500.00

Per Ton,	25c.	50c.	$1	$2	$3	$4	$5	$6	$7	$8	$9	$10
Per Foot,			2½ cts.	5 cts.	7½ cts.	10 cts.	12½ cts.	15 cts.	17½ cts.	20 cts.	22½ cts.	25 cts.
Feet.												
3001	18.76	37.51	75.02	150.05	225.07	300.10	375.12	450.15	525.17	600.20	675.22	750.25
3002	18.76	37.52	75.05	150.10	225.15	300.20	375.25	450.30	525.35	600.40	675.45	750.50
3003	18.77	37.54	75.07	150.15	225.22	300.30	375.37	450.45	525.52	600.60	675.67	750.75
3004	18.77	37.55	75.10	150.20	225.30	300.40	375.50	450.60	525.70	600.80	675.90	751.00
3005	18.78	37.56	75.12	150.25	225.37	300.50	375.62	450.75	525.87	601.00	676.12	751.25
3006	18.79	37.57	75.15	150.30	225.45	300.60	375.75	450.90	526.05	601.20	676.35	751.50
3007	18.79	37.59	75.17	150.35	225.52	300.70	375.87	451.05	526.22	601.40	676.57	751.75
3008	18.80	37.60	75.20	150.40	225.60	300.80	376.00	451.20	526.40	601.60	676.80	752.00
3009	18.81	37.61	75.22	150.45	225.67	300.90	376.12	451.35	526.57	601.80	677.02	752.25
3010	18.81	37.62	75.25	150.50	225.75	301.00	376.25	451.50	526.75	602.00	677.25	752.50
3011	18.82	37.64	75.27	150.55	225.82	301.10	376.37	451.65	526.92	602.20	677.47	752.75
3012	18.82	37.65	75.30	150.60	225.90	301.20	376.50	451.80	527.10	602.40	677.70	753.00
3013	18.83	37.66	75.32	150.65	225.97	301.30	376.62	451.95	527.27	602.60	677.92	753.25
3014	18.84	37.67	75.35	150.70	226.05	301.40	376.75	452.10	527.45	602.80	678.15	753.50
3015	18.84	37.69	75.37	150.75	226.12	301.50	376.87	452.25	527.62	603.00	678.37	753.75
3016	18.85	37.70	75.40	150.80	226.20	301.60	377.00	452.40	527.80	603.20	678.60	754.00
3017	18.86	37.71	75.42	150.85	226.27	301.70	377.12	452.55	527.97	603.40	678.82	754.25
3018	18.86	37.72	75.45	150.90	226.35	301.80	377.25	452.70	528.15	603.60	679.05	754.50
3019	18.87	37.74	75.47	150.95	226.42	301.90	377.37	452.85	528.32	603.80	679.27	754.75
3020	18.87	37.75	75.50	151.00	226.50	302.00	377.50	453.00	528.50	604.00	679.50	755.00
3021	18.88	37.76	75.52	151.05	226.57	302.10	377.62	453.15	528.67	604.20	679.72	755.25
3022	18.89	37.77	75.55	151.10	226.65	302.20	377.75	453.30	528.85	604.40	679.95	755.50
3023	18.89	37.79	75.57	151.15	226.72	302.30	377.87	453.45	529.02	604.60	680.17	755.75
3024	18.90	37.80	75.60	151.20	226.80	302.40	378.00	453.60	529.20	604.80	680.40	756.00
3025	18.91	37.81	75.62	151.25	226.87	302.50	378.12	453.75	529.37	605.00	680.62	756.25
3026	18.91	37.82	75.65	151.30	226.95	302.60	378.25	453.90	529.55	605.20	680.85	756.50
3027	18.92	37.84	75.67	151.35	227.02	302.70	378.37	454.05	529.72	605.40	681.07	756.75
3028	18.92	37.85	75.70	151.40	227.10	302.80	378.50	454.20	529.90	605.60	681.30	757.00
3029	18.93	37.86	75.72	151.45	227.17	302.90	378.62	454.35	530.07	605.80	681.52	757.25
3030	18.94	37.87	75.75	151.50	227.25	303.00	378.75	454.50	530.25	606.00	681.75	757.50
3031	18.94	37.89	75.77	151.55	227.32	303.10	378.87	454.65	530.42	606.20	681.97	757.75
3032	18.95	37.90	75.80	151.60	227.40	303.20	379.00	454.80	530.60	606.40	682.20	758.00
3033	18.96	37.91	75.82	151.65	227.47	303.30	379.12	454.95	530.77	606.60	682.42	758.25
3034	18.96	37.92	75.85	151.70	227.55	303.40	379.25	455.10	530.95	606.80	682.65	758.50
3035	18.97	37.94	75.87	151.75	227.62	303.50	379.37	455.25	531.12	607.00	682.87	758.75
3036	18.97	37.95	75.90	151.80	227.70	303.60	379.50	455.40	531.30	607.20	683.10	759.00
3037	18.98	37.96	75.92	151.85	227.77	303.70	379.62	455.55	531.47	607.40	683.32	759.25
3038	18.99	37.97	75.95	151.90	227.85	303.80	379.75	455.70	531.65	607.60	683.55	759.50
3039	18.99	37.99	75.97	151.95	227.92	303.90	379.87	455.85	531.82	607.80	683.77	759.75
3040	19.00	38.00	76.00	152.00	228.00	304.00	380.00	456.00	532.00	608.00	684.00	760.00
3041	19.01	38.01	76.02	152.05	228.07	304.10	380.12	456.15	532.17	608.20	684.22	760.25
3042	19.01	38.02	76.05	152.10	228.15	304.20	380.25	456.30	532.35	608.40	684.45	760.50
3043	19.02	38.04	76.07	152.15	228.22	304.30	380.37	456.45	532.52	608.60	684.67	760.75
3044	19.02	38.05	76.10	152.20	228.30	304.40	380.50	456.60	532.70	608.80	684.90	761.00
3045	19.03	38.06	76.12	152.25	228.37	304.50	380.62	456.75	532.87	609.00	685.12	761.25
3046	19.04	38.07	76.15	152.30	228.45	304.60	380.75	456.90	533.05	609.20	685.35	761.50
3047	19.04	38.09	76.17	152.35	228.52	304.70	380.87	457.05	533.22	609.40	685.57	761.75
3048	19.05	38.10	76.20	152.40	228.60	304.80	381.00	457.20	533.40	609.60	685.80	762.00
3049	19.06	38.11	76.22	152.45	228.67	304.90	381.12	457.35	533.57	609.80	686.02	762.25
3050	19.06	38.12	76.25	152.50	228.75	305.00	381.25	457.50	533.75	610.00	686.25	762.50

3050 FEET.

Per Ton,	$11	$12	$13	$14	$15	$16	$17	$18	$19	$20
Per Foot,	27½ cts.	30 cts.	32½ cts.	35 cts.	37½ cts.	40 cts.	42½ cts.	45 cts.	47½ cts.	50 cts.
Feet.										
3001	825.27	900.30	975.32	1050.35	1125.37	1200.40	1275.42	1350.45	1425.47	1500.50
3002	825.55	900.60	975.65	1050.70	1125.75	1200.80	1275.85	1350.90	1425.95	1501.00
3003	825.82	900.90	975.97	1051.05	1126.12	1201.20	1276.27	1351.35	1426.42	1501.50
3004	826.10	901.20	976.30	1051.40	1126.50	1201.60	1276.70	1351.80	1426.90	1502.00
3005	826.37	901.50	976.62	1051.75	1126.87	1202.00	1277.12	1352.25	1427.37	1502.50
3006	826.65	901.80	976.95	1052.10	1127.25	1202.40	1277.55	1352.70	1427.85	1503.00
3007	826.92	902.10	977.27	1052.45	1127.62	1202.80	1277.97	1353.15	1428.32	1503.50
3008	827.20	902.40	977.60	1052.80	1128.00	1203.20	1278.40	1353.60	1428.80	1504.00
3009	827.47	902.70	977.92	1053.15	1128.37	1203.60	1278.82	1354.05	1429.27	1504.50
3010	827.75	903.00	978.25	1053.50	1128.75	1204.00	1279.25	1354.50	1429.75	1505.00
3011	828.02	903.30	978.57	1053.85	1129.12	1204.40	1279.67	1354.95	1430.22	1505.50
3012	828.30	903.60	978.90	1054.20	1129.50	1204.80	1280.10	1355.40	1430.70	1506.00
3013	828.57	903.90	979.22	1054.55	1129.87	1205.20	1280.52	1355.85	1431.17	1506.50
3014	828.85	904.20	979.55	1054.90	1130.25	1205.60	1280.95	1356.30	1431.65	1507.00
3015	829.12	904.50	979.87	1055.25	1130.62	1206.00	1281.37	1356.75	1432.12	1507.50
3016	829.40	904.80	980.20	1055.60	1131.00	1206.40	1281.80	1357.20	1432.60	1508.00
3017	829.67	905.10	980.52	1055.95	1131.37	1206.80	1282.22	1357.65	1433.07	1508.50
3018	829.95	905.40	980.85	1056.30	1131.75	1207.20	1282.65	1358.10	1433.55	1509.00
3019	830.22	905.70	981.17	1056.65	1132.12	1207.60	1283.07	1358.55	1434.02	1509.50
3020	830.50	906.00	981.50	1057.00	1132.50	1208.00	1283.50	1359.00	1434.50	1510.00
3021	830.77	906.30	981.82	1057.35	1132.87	1208.40	1283.92	1359.45	1434.97	1510.50
3022	831.05	906.60	982.15	1057.70	1133.25	1208.80	1284.35	1359.90	1435.45	1511.00
3023	831.32	906.90	982.47	1058.05	1133.62	1209.20	1284.77	1360.35	1435.92	1511.50
3024	831.60	907.20	982.80	1058.40	1134.00	1209.60	1285.20	1360.80	1436.40	1512.00
3025	831.87	907.50	983.12	1058.75	1134.37	1210.00	1285.62	1361.25	1436.87	1512.50
3026	832.15	907.80	983.45	1059.10	1134.75	1210.40	1286.05	1361.70	1437.35	1513.00
3027	832.42	908.10	983.77	1059.45	1135.12	1210.80	1286.47	1362.15	1437.82	1513.50
3028	832.70	908.40	984.10	1059.80	1135.50	1211.20	1286.90	1362.60	1438.30	1514.00
3029	832.97	908.70	984.42	1060.15	1135.87	1211.60	1287.32	1363.05	1438.77	1514.50
3030	833.25	909.00	984.75	1060.50	1136.25	1212.00	1287.75	1363.50	1439.25	1515.00
3031	833.52	909.30	985.07	1060.85	1136.62	1212.40	1288.17	1363.95	1439.72	1515.50
3032	833.80	909.60	985.40	1061.20	1137.00	1212.80	1288.60	1364.40	1440.20	1516.00
3033	834.07	909.90	985.72	1061.55	1137.37	1213.20	1289.02	1364.85	1440.67	1516.50
3034	834.35	910.20	986.05	1061.90	1137.75	1213.60	1289.45	1365.30	1441.15	1517.00
3035	834.62	910.50	986.37	1062.25	1138.12	1214.00	1289.87	1365.75	1441.62	1517.50
3036	834.90	910.80	986.70	1062.60	1138.50	1214.40	1290.30	1366.20	1442.10	1518.00
3037	835.17	911.10	987.02	1062.95	1138.87	1214.80	1290.72	1366.65	1442.57	1518.50
3038	835.45	911.40	987.35	1063.30	1139.25	1215.20	1291.15	1367.10	1443.05	1519.00
3039	835.72	911.70	987.67	1063.65	1139.62	1215.60	1291.57	1367.55	1443.52	1519.50
3040	836.00	912.00	988.00	1064.00	1140.00	1216.00	1292.00	1368.00	1444.00	1520.00
3041	836.27	912.30	988.32	1064.35	1140.37	1216.40	1292.42	1368.45	1444.47	1520.50
3042	836.55	912.60	988.65	1064.70	1140.75	1216.80	1292.85	1368.90	1444.95	1521.00
3043	836.82	912.90	988.97	1065.05	1141.12	1217.20	1293.27	1369.35	1445.42	1521.50
3044	837.10	913.20	989.30	1065.40	1141.50	1217.60	1293.70	1369.80	1445.90	1522.00
3045	837.37	913.50	989.62	1065.75	1141.87	1218.00	1294.12	1370.25	1446.37	1522.50
3046	837.65	913.80	989.95	1066.10	1142.25	1218.40	1294.55	1370.70	1446.85	1523.00
3047	837.92	914.10	990.27	1066.45	1142.62	1218.80	1294.97	1371.15	1447.32	1523.50
3048	838.20	914.40	990.60	1066.80	1143.00	1219.20	1295.40	1371.60	1447.80	1524.00
3049	838.47	914.70	990.92	1067.15	1143.37	1219.60	1295.82	1372.05	1448.27	1524.50
3050	838.75	915.00	991.25	1067.50	1143.75	1220.00	1296.25	1372.50	1448.75	1525.00

Per Ton,	25c.	50c.	$1	$2	$3	$4	$5	$6	$7	$8	$9	$10
Per Foot,			2¼ cts.	5 cts.	7½ cts.	10 cts.	12½ cts.	15 cts.	17½ cts.	20 cts.	22½ cts.	25 cts.
Feet.												
3051	19.07	38.14	76.27	152.55	228.82	305.10	381.37	457.65	533.92	610.20	686.47	762.75
3052	19.07	38.15	76.30	152.60	228.90	305.20	381.50	457.80	534.10	610.40	686.70	763.00
3053	19.08	38.16	76.32	152.65	228.97	305.30	381.62	457.95	534.27	610.60	686.92	763.25
3054	19.09	38.17	76.35	152.70	229.05	305.40	381.75	458.10	534.45	610.80	687.15	763.50
3055	19.09	38.19	76.37	152.75	229.12	305.50	381.87	458.25	534.62	611.00	687.37	763.75
3056	19.10	38.20	76.40	152.80	229.20	305.60	382.00	458.40	534.80	611.20	687.60	764.00
3057	19.11	38.21	76.42	152.85	229.27	305.70	382.12	458.55	534.97	611.40	687.82	764.25
3058	19.11	38.22	76.45	152.90	229.35	305.80	382.25	458.70	535.15	611.60	688.05	764.50
3059	19.12	38.24	76.47	152.95	229.42	305.90	382.37	458.85	535.32	611.80	688.27	764.75
3060	19.12	38.25	76.50	153.00	229.50	306.00	382.50	459.00	535.50	612.00	688.50	765.00
3061	19.13	38.26	76.52	153.05	229.57	306.10	382.62	459.15	535.67	612.20	688.72	765.25
3062	19.14	38.27	76.55	153.10	229.65	306.20	382.75	459.30	535.85	612.40	688.95	765.50
3063	19.14	38.29	76.57	153.15	229.72	306.30	382.87	459.45	536.02	612.60	689.17	765.75
3064	19.15	38.30	76.60	153.20	229.80	306.40	383.00	459.60	536.20	612.80	689.40	766.00
3065	19.16	38.31	76.62	153.25	229.87	306.50	383.12	459.75	536.37	613.00	689.62	766.25
3066	19.16	38.32	76.65	153.30	229.95	306.60	383.25	459.90	536.55	613.20	689.85	766.50
3067	19.17	38.34	76.67	153.35	230.02	306.70	383.37	460.05	536.72	613.40	690.07	766.75
3068	19.17	38.35	76.70	153.40	230.10	306.80	383.50	460.20	536.90	613.60	690.30	767.00
3069	19.18	38.36	76.72	153.45	230.17	306.90	383.62	460.35	537.07	613.80	690.52	767.25
3070	19.19	38.37	76.75	153.50	230.25	307.00	383.75	460.50	537.25	614.00	690.75	767.50
3071	19.19	38.39	76.77	153.55	230.32	307.10	383.87	460.65	537.42	614.20	690.97	767.75
3072	19.20	38.40	76.80	153.60	230.40	307.20	384.00	460.80	537.60	614.40	691.20	768.00
3073	19.21	38.41	76.82	153.65	230.47	307.30	384.12	460.95	537.77	614.60	691.42	768.25
3074	19.21	38.42	76.85	153.70	230.55	307.40	384.25	461.10	537.95	614.80	691.65	768.50
3075	19.22	38.44	76.87	153.75	230.62	307.50	384.37	461.25	538.12	615.00	691.87	768.75
3076	19.22	38.45	76.90	153.80	230.70	307.60	384.50	461.40	538.30	615.20	692.10	769.00
3077	19.23	38.46	76.92	153.85	230.77	307.70	384.62	461.55	538.47	615.40	692.32	769.25
3078	19.24	38.47	76.95	153.90	230.85	307.80	384.75	461.70	538.65	615.60	692.55	769.50
3079	19.24	38.49	76.97	153.95	230.92	307.90	384.87	461.85	538.82	615.80	692.77	769.75
3080	19.25	38.50	77.00	154.00	231.00	308.00	385.00	462.00	539.00	616.00	693.00	770.00
3081	19.26	38.51	77.02	154.05	231.07	308.10	385.12	462.15	539.17	616.20	693.22	770.25
3082	19.26	38.52	77.05	154.10	231.15	308.20	385.25	462.30	539.35	616.40	693.45	770.50
3083	19.27	38.54	77.07	154.15	231.22	308.30	385.37	462.45	539.52	616.60	693.67	770.75
3084	19.27	38.55	77.10	154.20	231.30	308.40	385.50	462.60	539.70	616.80	693.90	771.00
3085	19.28	38.56	77.12	154.25	231.37	308.50	385.62	462.75	539.87	617.00	694.12	771.25
3086	19.29	38.57	77.15	154.30	231.45	308.60	385.75	462.90	540.05	617.20	694.35	771.50
3087	19.29	38.59	77.17	154.35	231.52	308.70	385.87	463.05	540.22	617.40	694.57	771.75
3088	19.30	38.60	77.20	154.40	231.60	308.80	386.00	463.20	540.40	617.60	694.80	772.00
3089	19.31	38.61	77.22	154.45	231.67	308.90	386.12	463.35	540.57	617.80	695.02	772.25
3090	19.31	38.62	77.25	154.50	231.75	309.00	386.25	463.50	540.75	618.00	695.25	772.50
3091	19.32	38.64	77.27	154.55	231.82	309.10	386.37	463.65	540.92	618.20	695.47	772.75
3092	19.32	38.65	77.30	154.60	231.90	309.20	386.50	463.80	541.10	618.40	695.70	773.00
3093	19.33	38.66	77.32	154.65	231.97	309.30	386.62	463.95	541.27	618.60	695.92	773.25
3094	19.34	38.67	77.35	154.70	232.05	309.40	386.75	464.10	541.45	618.80	696.15	773.50
3095	19.34	38.69	77.37	154.75	232.12	309.50	386.87	464.25	541.62	619.00	696.37	773.75
3096	19.35	38.70	77.40	154.80	232.20	309.60	387.00	464.40	541.80	619.20	696.60	774.00
3097	19.36	38.71	77.42	154.85	232.27	309.70	387.12	464.55	541.97	619.40	696.82	774.25
3098	19.36	38.72	77.45	154.90	232.35	309.80	387.25	464.70	542.15	619.60	697.05	774.50
3099	19.37	38.74	77.47	154.95	232.42	309.90	387.37	464.85	542.32	619.80	697.27	774.75
3100	19.37	38.75	77.50	155.00	232.50	310.00	387.50	465.00	542.50	620.00	697.50	775.00

3100 FEET.

Per Ton,	$11	$12	$13	$14	$15	$16	$17	$18	$19	$20
Per Foot,	27½ cts.	30 cts.	32½ cts.	35 cts.	37½ cts.	40 cts.	42½ cts.	45 cts.	47½ cts.	50 cts.
Feet.										
3051	839.02	915.30	991.57	1067.85	1144.12	1220.40	1296.67	1372.95	1449.22	1525.50
3052	839.30	915.60	991.90	1068.20	1144.50	1220.80	1297.10	1373.40	1449.70	1526.00
3053	839.57	915.90	992.22	1068.55	1144.87	1221.20	1297.52	1373.85	1450.17	1526.50
3054	839.85	916.20	992.55	1068.90	1145.25	1221.60	1297.95	1374.30	1450.65	1527.00
3055	840.12	916.50	992.87	1069.25	1145.62	1222.00	1298.37	1374.75	1451.12	1527.50
3056	840.40	916.80	993.20	1069.60	1146.00	1222.40	1298.80	1375.20	1451.60	1528.00
3057	840.67	917.10	993.52	1069.95	1146.37	1222.80	1299.22	1375.65	1452.07	1528.50
3058	840.95	917.40	993.85	1070.30	1146.75	1223.20	1299.65	1376.10	1452.55	1529.00
3059	841.22	917.70	994.17	1070.65	1147.12	1223.60	1300.07	1376.55	1453.02	1529.50
3060	841.50	918.00	994.50	1071.00	1147.50	1224.00	1300.50	1377.00	1453.50	1530.00
3061	841.77	918.30	994.82	1071.35	1147.87	1224.40	1300.92	1377.45	1453.97	1530.50
3062	842.05	918.60	995.15	1071.70	1148.25	1224.80	1301.35	1377.90	1454.45	1531.00
3063	842.32	918.90	995.47	1072.05	1148.62	1225.20	1301.77	1378.35	1454.92	1531.50
3064	842.60	919.20	995.80	1072.40	1149.00	1225.60	1302.20	1378.80	1455.40	1532.00
3065	842.87	919.50	996.12	1072.75	1149.37	1226.00	1302.62	1379.25	1455.87	1532.50
3066	843.15	919.80	996.45	1073.10	1149.75	1226.40	1303.05	1379.70	1456.35	1533.00
3067	843.42	920.10	996.77	1073.45	1150.12	1226.80	1303.47	1380.15	1456.82	1533.50
3068	843.70	920.40	997.10	1073.80	1150.50	1227.20	1303.90	1380.60	1457.30	1534.00
3069	843.97	920.70	997.42	1074.15	1150.87	1227.60	1304.32	1381.05	1457.77	1534.50
3070	844.25	921.00	997.75	1074.50	1151.25	1228.00	1304.75	1381.50	1458.25	1535.00
3071	844.52	921.30	998.07	1074.85	1151.62	1228.40	1305.17	1381.95	1458.72	1535.50
3072	844.80	921.60	998.40	1075.20	1152.00	1228.80	1305.60	1382.40	1459.20	1536.00
3073	845.07	921.90	998.72	1075.55	1152.37	1229.20	1306.02	1382.85	1459.67	1536.50
3074	845.35	922.20	999.05	1075.90	1152.75	1229.60	1306.45	1383.30	1460.15	1537.00
3075	845.62	922.50	999.37	1076.25	1153.12	1230.00	1306.87	1383.75	1460.62	1537.50
3076	845.90	922.80	999.70	1076.60	1153.50	1230.40	1307.30	1384.20	1461.10	1538.00
3077	846.17	923.10	1000.02	1076.95	1153.87	1230.80	1307.72	1384.65	1461.57	1538.50
3078	846.45	923.40	1000.35	1077.30	1154.25	1231.20	1308.15	1385.10	1462.05	1539.00
3079	846.72	923.70	1000.67	1077.65	1154.62	1231.60	1308.57	1385.55	1462.52	1539.50
3080	847.00	924.00	1001.00	1078.00	1155.00	1232.00	1309.00	1386.00	1463.00	1540.00
3081	847.27	924.30	1001.32	1078.35	1155.37	1232.40	1309.42	1386.45	1463.47	1540.50
3082	847.55	924.60	1001.65	1078.70	1155.75	1232.80	1309.85	1386.90	1463.95	1541.00
3083	847.82	924.90	1001.97	1079.05	1156.12	1233.20	1310.27	1387.35	1464.42	1541.50
3084	848.10	925.20	1002.30	1079.40	1156.50	1233.60	1310.70	1387.80	1464.90	1542.00
3085	848.37	925.50	1002.62	1079.75	1156.87	1234.00	1311.12	1388.25	1465.37	1542.50
3086	848.65	925.80	1002.95	1080.10	1157.25	1234.40	1311.55	1388.70	1465.85	1543.00
3087	848.92	926.10	1003.27	1080.45	1157.62	1234.80	1311.97	1389.15	1466.32	1543.50
3088	849.20	926.40	1003.60	1080.80	1158.00	1235.20	1312.40	1389.60	1466.80	1544.00
3089	849.47	926.70	1003.92	1081.15	1158.37	1235.60	1312.82	1390.05	1467.27	1544.50
3090	849.75	927.00	1004.25	1081.50	1158.75	1236.00	1313.25	1390.50	1467.75	1545.00
3091	850.02	927.30	1004.57	1081.85	1159.12	1236.40	1313.67	1390.95	1468.22	1545.50
3092	850.30	927.60	1004.90	1082.20	1159.50	1236.80	1314.10	1391.40	1468.70	1546.00
3093	850.57	927.90	1005.22	1082.55	1159.87	1237.20	1314.52	1391.85	1469.17	1546.50
3094	850.85	928.20	1005.55	1082.90	1160.25	1237.60	1314.95	1392.30	1469.65	1547.00
3095	851.12	928.50	1005.87	1083.25	1160.62	1238.00	1315.37	1392.75	1470.12	1547.50
3096	851.40	928.80	1006.20	1083.60	1161.00	1238.40	1315.80	1393.20	1470.60	1548.00
3097	851.67	929.10	1006.52	1083.95	1161.37	1238.80	1316.22	1393.65	1471.07	1548.50
3098	851.95	929.40	1006.85	1084.30	1161.75	1239.20	1316.65	1394.10	1471.55	1549.00
3099	852.22	929.70	1007.17	1084.65	1162.12	1239.60	1317.07	1394.55	1472.02	1549.50
3100	852.50	930.00	1007.50	1085.00	1162.50	1240.00	1317.50	1395.00	1472.50	1550.00

3150 FEET.

Per Ton,	25c.	50c.	$1	$2	$3	$4	$5	$6	$7	$8	$9	$10
Per Foot,			2½ cts.	5 cts.	7½ cts.	10 cts.	12½ cts.	15 cts.	17½ cts.	20 cts.	22½ cts.	25 cts.
Feet.												
3101	19.38	38.76	77.52	155.05	232.57	310.10	387.62	465.15	542.67	620.20	697.72	775.25
3102	19.39	38.77	77.55	155.10	232.65	310.20	387.75	465.30	542.85	620.40	697.95	775.50
3103	19.39	38.79	77.57	155.15	232.72	310.30	387.87	465.45	543.02	620.60	698.17	775.75
3104	19.40	38.80	77.60	155.20	232.80	310.40	388.00	465.60	543.20	620.80	698.40	776.00
3105	19.41	38.81	77.62	155.25	232.87	310.50	388.12	465.75	543.37	621.00	698.62	776.25
3106	19.41	38.82	77.65	155.30	232.95	310.60	388.25	465.90	543.55	621.20	698.85	776.50
3107	19.42	38.84	77.67	155.35	233.02	310.70	388.37	466.05	543.72	621.40	699.07	776.75
3108	19.42	38.85	77.70	155.40	233.10	310.80	388.50	466.20	543.90	621.60	699.30	777.00
3109	19.43	38.86	77.72	155.45	233.17	310.90	388.62	466.35	544.07	621.80	699.52	777.25
3110	19.44	38.87	77.75	155.50	233.25	311.00	388.75	466.50	544.25	622.00	699.75	777.50
3111	19.44	38.89	77.77	155.55	233.32	311.10	388.87	466.65	544.42	622.20	699.97	777.75
3112	19.45	38.90	77.80	155.60	233.40	311.20	389.00	466.80	544.60	622.40	700.20	778.00
3113	19.46	38.91	77.82	155.65	233.47	311.30	389.12	466.95	544.77	622.60	700.42	778.25
3114	19.46	38.92	77.85	155.70	233.55	311.40	389.25	467.10	544.95	622.80	700.65	778.50
3115	19.47	38.94	77.87	155.75	233.62	311.50	389.37	467.25	545.12	623.00	700.87	778.75
3116	19.47	38.95	77.90	155.80	233.70	311.60	389.50	467.40	545.30	623.20	701.10	779.00
3117	19.48	38.96	77.92	155.85	233.77	311.70	389.62	467.55	545.47	623.40	701.32	779.25
3118	19.49	38.97	77.95	155.90	233.85	311.80	389.75	467.70	545.65	623.60	701.55	779.50
3119	19.49	38.99	77.97	155.95	233.92	311.90	389.87	467.85	545.82	623.80	701.77	779.75
3120	19.50	39.00	78.00	156.00	234.00	312.00	390.00	468.00	546.00	624.00	702.00	780.00
3121	19.51	39.01	78.02	156.05	234.07	312.10	390.12	468.15	546.17	624.20	702.22	780.25
3122	19.51	39.02	78.05	156.10	234.15	312.20	390.25	468.30	546.35	624.40	702.45	780.50
3123	19.52	39.04	78.07	156.15	234.22	312.30	390.37	468.45	546.52	624.60	702.67	780.75
3124	19.52	39.05	78.10	156.20	234.30	312.40	390.50	468.60	546.70	624.80	702.90	781.00
3125	19.53	39.06	78.12	156.25	234.37	312.50	390.62	468.75	546.87	625.00	703.12	781.25
3126	19.54	39.07	78.15	156.30	234.45	312.60	390.75	468.90	547.05	625.20	703.35	781.50
3127	19.54	39.09	78.17	156.35	234.52	312.70	390.87	469.05	547.22	625.40	703.57	781.75
3128	19.55	39.10	78.20	156.40	234.60	312.80	391.00	469.20	547.40	625.60	703.80	782.00
3129	19.56	39.11	78.22	156.45	234.67	312.90	391.12	469.35	547.57	625.80	704.02	782.25
3130	19.56	39.12	78.25	156.50	234.75	313.00	391.25	469.50	547.75	626.00	704.25	782.50
3131	19.57	39.14	78.27	156.55	234.82	313.10	391.37	469.65	547.92	626.20	704.47	782.75
3132	19.57	39.15	78.30	156.60	234.90	313.20	391.50	469.80	548.10	626.40	704.70	783.00
3133	19.58	39.16	78.32	156.65	234.97	313.30	391.62	469.95	548.27	626.60	704.92	783.25
3134	19.59	39.17	78.35	156.70	235.05	313.40	391.75	470.10	548.45	626.80	705.15	783.50
3135	19.59	39.19	78.37	156.75	235.12	313.50	391.87	470.25	548.62	627.00	705.37	783.75
3136	19.60	39.20	78.40	156.80	235.20	313.60	392.00	470.40	548.80	627.20	705.60	784.00
3137	19.61	39.21	78.42	156.85	235.27	313.70	392.12	470.55	548.97	627.40	705.82	784.25
3138	19.61	39.22	78.45	156.90	235.35	313.80	392.25	470.70	549.15	627.60	706.05	784.50
3139	19.62	39.24	78.47	156.95	235.42	313.90	392.37	470.85	549.32	627.80	706.27	784.75
3140	19.62	39.25	78.50	157.00	235.50	314.00	392.50	471.00	549.50	628.00	706.50	785.00
3141	19.63	39.26	78.52	157.05	235.57	314.10	392.62	471.15	549.67	628.20	706.72	785.25
3142	19.64	39.27	78.55	157.10	235.65	314.20	392.75	471.30	549.85	628.40	706.95	785.50
3143	19.64	39.29	78.57	157.15	235.72	314.30	392.87	471.45	550.02	628.60	707.17	785.75
3144	19.65	39.30	78.60	157.20	235.80	314.40	393.00	471.60	550.20	628.80	707.40	786.00
3145	19.66	39.31	78.62	157.25	235.87	314.50	393.12	471.75	550.37	629.00	707.62	786.25
3146	19.66	39.32	78.65	157.30	235.95	314.60	393.25	471.90	550.55	629.20	707.85	786.50
3147	19.67	39.34	78.67	157.35	236.02	314.70	393.37	472.05	550.72	629.40	708.07	786.75
3148	19.67	39.35	78.70	157.40	236.10	314.80	393.50	472.20	550.90	629.60	708.30	787.00
3149	19.68	39.36	78.72	157.45	236.17	314.90	393.62	472.35	551.07	629.80	708.52	787.25
3150	19.69	39.37	78.75	157.50	236.25	315.00	393.75	472.50	551.25	630.00	708.75	787.50

3150 FEET.

Per Ton	$11	$12	$13	$14	$15	$16	$17	$18	$19	$20
Per Foot,	27½ cts.	30 cts.	32½ cts.	35 cts.	37½ cts.	40 cts.	42½ cts.	45 cts.	47½ cts.	50 cts.
Feet.										
3101	852.77	930.30	1007.82	1085.35	1162.87	1240.40	1317.92	1395.45	1472.97	1550.50
3102	853.05	930.60	1008.15	1085.70	1163.25	1240.80	1318.35	1395.90	1473.45	1551.00
3103	853.32	930.90	1008.47	1086.05	1163.62	1241.20	1318.77	1396.35	1473.92	1551.50
3104	853.60	931.20	1008.80	1086.40	1164.00	1241.60	1319.20	1396.80	1474.40	1552.00
3105	853.87	931.50	1009.12	1086.75	1164.37	1242.00	1319.62	1397.25	1474.87	1552.50
3106	854.15	931.80	1009.45	1087.10	1164.75	1242.40	1320.05	1397.70	1475.35	1553.00
3107	854.42	932.10	1009.77	1087.45	1165.12	1242.80	1320.47	1398.15	1475.82	1553.50
3108	854.70	932.40	1010.10	1087.80	1165.50	1243.20	1320.90	1398.60	1476.30	1554.00
3109	854.97	932.70	1010.42	1088.15	1165.87	1243.60	1321.32	1399.05	1476.77	1554.50
3110	855.25	933.00	1010.75	1088.50	1166.25	1244.00	1321.75	1399.50	1477.25	1555.00
3111	855.52	933.30	1011.07	1088.85	1166.62	1244.40	1322.17	1399.95	1477.72	1555.50
3112	855.80	933.60	1011.40	1089.20	1167.00	1244.80	1322.60	1400.40	1478.20	1556.00
3113	856.07	933.90	1011.72	1089.55	1167.37	1245.20	1323.02	1400.85	1478.67	1556.50
3114	856.35	934.20	1012.05	1089.90	1167.75	1245.60	1323.45	1401.30	1479.15	1557.00
3115	856.62	934.50	1012.37	1090.25	1168.12	1246.00	1323.87	1401.75	1479.62	1557.50
3116	856.90	934.80	1012.70	1090.60	1168.50	1246.40	1324.30	1402.20	1480.10	1558.00
3117	857.17	935.10	1013.02	1090.95	1168.87	1246.80	1324.72	1402.65	1480.57	1558.50
3118	857.45	935.40	1013.35	1091.30	1169.25	1247.20	1325.15	1403.10	1481.05	1559.00
3119	857.72	935.70	1013.67	1091.65	1169.62	1247.60	1325.57	1403.55	1481.52	1559.50
3120	858.00	936.00	1014.00	1092.00	1170.00	1248.00	1326.00	1404.00	1482.00	1560.00
3121	858.27	936.30	1014.32	1092.35	1170.37	1248.40	1326.42	1404.45	1482.47	1560.50
3122	858.55	936.60	1014.65	1092.70	1170.75	1248.80	1326.85	1404.90	1482.95	1561.00
3123	858.82	936.90	1014.97	1093.05	1171.12	1249.20	1327.27	1405.35	1483.42	1561.50
3124	859.10	937.20	1015.30	1093.40	1171.50	1249.60	1327.70	1405.80	1483.90	1562.00
3125	859.37	937.50	1015.62	1093.75	1171.87	1250.00	1328.12	1406.25	1484.37	1562.50
3126	859.65	937.80	1015.95	1094.10	1172.25	1250.40	1328.55	1406.70	1484.85	1563.00
3127	859.92	938.10	1016.27	1094.45	1172.62	1250.80	1328.97	1407.15	1485.32	1563.50
3128	860.20	938.40	1016.60	1094.80	1173.00	1251.20	1329.40	1407.60	1485.80	1564.00
3129	860.47	938.70	1016.92	1095.15	1173.37	1251.60	1329.82	1408.05	1486.27	1564.50
3130	860.75	939.00	1017.25	1095.50	1173.75	1252.00	1330.25	1408.50	1486.75	1565.00
3131	861.02	939.30	1017.57	1095.85	1174.12	1252.40	1330.67	1408.95	1487.22	1565.50
3132	861.30	939.60	1017.90	1096.20	1174.50	1252.80	1331.10	1409.40	1487.70	1566.00
3133	861.57	939.90	1018.22	1096.55	1174.87	1253.20	1331.52	1409.85	1488.17	1566.50
3134	861.85	940.20	1018.55	1096.90	1175.25	1253.60	1331.95	1410.30	1488.65	1567.00
3135	862.12	940.50	1018.87	1097.25	1175.62	1254.00	1332.37	1410.75	1489.12	1567.50
3136	862.40	940.80	1019.20	1097.60	1176.00	1254.40	1332.80	1411.20	1489.60	1568.00
3137	862.67	941.10	1019.52	1097.95	1176.37	1254.80	1333.22	1411.65	1490.07	1568.50
3138	862.95	941.40	1019.85	1098.30	1176.75	1255.20	1333.65	1412.10	1490.55	1569.00
3139	863.22	941.70	1020.17	1098.65	1177.12	1255.60	1334.07	1412.55	1491.02	1569.50
3140	863.50	942.00	1020.50	1099.00	1177.50	1256.00	1334.50	1413.00	1491.50	1570.00
3141	863.77	942.30	1020.82	1099.35	1177.87	1256.40	1334.92	1413.45	1491.97	1570.50
3142	864.05	942.60	1021.15	1099.70	1178.25	1256.80	1335.35	1413.90	1492.45	1571.00
3143	864.32	942.90	1021.47	1100.05	1178.62	1257.20	1335.77	1414.35	1492.92	1571.50
3144	864.60	943.20	1021.80	1100.40	1179.00	1257.60	1336.20	1414.80	1493.40	1572.00
3145	864.87	943.50	1022.12	1100.75	1179.37	1258.00	1336.62	1415.25	1493.87	1572.50
3146	865.15	943.80	1022.45	1101.10	1179.75	1258.40	1337.05	1415.70	1494.35	1573.00
3147	865.42	944.10	1022.77	1101.45	1180.12	1258.80	1337.47	1416.15	1494.82	1573.50
3148	865.70	944.40	1023.10	1101.80	1180.50	1259.20	1337.90	1416.60	1495.30	1574.00
3149	865.97	944.70	1023.42	1102.15	1180.87	1259.60	1338.32	1417.05	1495.77	1574.50
3150	866.25	945.00	1023.75	1102.50	1181.25	1260.00	1338.75	1417.50	1496.25	1575.00

3200 FEET.

Per Ton, Per Foot,	25c.	50c.	$1 2½ cts.	$2 5 cts.	$3 7½ cts.	$4 10 cts.	$5 12½ cts.	$6 15 cts.	$7 17½ cts.	$8 20 cts.	$9 22½ cts.	$10 25 cts.
Feet.												
3151	19.69	39.39	78.77	157.55	236.32	315.10	393.87	472.65	551.42	630.20	708.97	787.75
3152	19.70	39.40	78.80	157.60	236.40	315.20	394.00	472.80	551.60	630.40	709.20	788.00
3153	19.71	39.41	78.82	157.65	236.47	315.30	394.12	472.95	551.77	630.60	709.42	788.25
3154	19.71	39.42	78.85	157.70	236.55	315.40	394.25	473.10	551.95	630.80	709.65	788.50
3155	19.72	39.44	78.87	157.75	236.62	315.50	394.37	473.25	552.12	631.00	709.87	788.75
3156	19.72	39.45	78.90	157.80	236.70	315.60	394.50	473.40	552.30	631.20	710.10	789.00
3157	19.73	39.46	78.92	157.85	236.77	315.70	394.62	473.55	552.47	631.40	710.32	789.25
3158	19.74	39.47	78.95	157.90	236.85	315.80	394.75	473.70	552.65	631.60	710.55	789.50
3159	19.74	39.49	78.97	157.95	236.92	315.90	394.87	473.85	552.82	631.80	710.77	789.75
3160	19.75	39.50	79.00	158.00	237.00	316.00	395.00	474.00	553.00	632.00	711.00	790.00
3161	19.76	39.51	79.02	158.05	237.07	316.10	395.12	474.15	553.17	632.20	711.22	790.25
3162	19.76	39.52	79.05	158.10	237.15	316.20	395.25	474.30	553.35	632.40	711.45	790.50
3163	19.77	39.54	79.07	158.15	237.22	316.30	395.37	474.45	553.52	632.60	711.67	790.75
3164	19.77	39.55	79.10	158.20	237.30	316.40	395.50	474.60	553.70	632.80	711.90	791.00
3165	19.78	39.56	79.12	158.25	237.37	316.50	395.62	474.75	553.87	633.00	712.12	791.25
3166	19.79	39.57	79.15	158.30	237.45	316.60	395.75	474.90	554.05	633.20	712.35	791.50
3167	19.79	39.59	79.17	158.35	237.52	316.70	395.87	475.05	554.22	633.40	712.57	791.75
3168	19.80	39.60	79.20	158.40	237.60	316.80	396.00	475.20	554.40	633.60	712.80	792.00
3169	19.81	39.61	79.22	158.45	237.67	316.90	396.12	475.35	554.57	633.80	713.02	792.25
3170	19.81	39.62	79.25	158.50	237.75	317.00	396.25	475.50	554.75	634.00	713.25	792.50
3171	19.82	39.64	79.27	158.55	237.82	317.10	396.37	475.65	554.92	634.20	713.47	792.75
3172	19.82	39.65	79.30	158.60	237.90	317.20	396.50	475.80	555.10	634.40	713.70	793.00
3173	19.83	39.66	79.32	158.65	237.97	317.30	396.62	475.95	555.27	634.60	713.92	793.25
3174	19.84	39.67	79.35	158.70	238.05	317.40	396.75	476.10	555.45	634.80	714.15	793.50
3175	19.84	39.69	79.37	158.75	238.12	317.50	396.87	476.25	555.62	635.00	714.37	793.75
3176	19.85	39.70	79.40	158.80	238.20	317.60	397.00	476.40	555.80	635.20	714.60	794.00
3177	19.86	39.71	79.42	158.85	238.27	317.70	397.12	476.55	555.97	635.40	714.82	794.25
3178	19.86	39.72	79.45	158.90	238.35	317.80	397.25	476.70	556.15	635.60	715.05	794.50
3179	19.87	39.74	79.47	158.95	238.42	317.90	397.37	476.85	556.32	635.80	715.27	794.75
3180	19.87	39.75	79.50	159.00	238.50	318.00	397.50	477.00	556.50	636.00	715.50	795.00
3181	19.88	39.76	79.52	159.05	238.57	318.10	397.62	477.15	556.67	636.20	715.72	795.25
3182	19.89	39.77	79.55	159.10	238.65	318.20	397.75	477.30	556.85	636.40	715.95	795.50
3183	19.89	39.79	79.57	159.15	238.72	318.30	397.87	477.45	557.02	636.60	716.17	795.75
3184	19.90	39.80	79.60	159.20	238.80	318.40	398.00	477.60	557.20	636.80	716.40	796.00
3185	19.91	39.81	79.62	159.25	238.87	318.50	398.12	477.75	557.37	637.00	716.62	796.25
3186	19.91	39.82	79.65	159.30	238.95	318.60	398.25	477.90	557.55	637.20	716.85	796.50
3187	19.92	39.84	79.67	159.35	239.02	318.70	398.37	478.05	557.72	637.40	717.07	796.75
3188	19.92	39.85	79.70	159.40	239.10	318.80	398.50	478.20	557.90	637.60	717.30	797.00
3189	19.93	39.86	79.72	159.45	239.17	318.90	398.62	478.35	558.07	637.80	717.52	797.25
3190	19.94	39.87	79.75	159.50	239.25	319.00	398.75	478.50	558.25	638.00	717.75	797.50
3191	19.94	39.89	79.77	159.55	239.32	319.10	398.87	478.65	558.42	638.20	717.97	797.75
3192	19.95	39.90	79.80	159.60	239.40	319.20	399.00	478.80	558.60	638.40	718.20	798.00
3193	19.96	39.91	79.82	159.65	239.47	319.30	399.12	478.95	558.77	638.60	718.42	798.25
3194	19.96	39.92	79.85	159.70	239.55	319.40	399.25	479.10	558.95	638.80	718.65	798.50
3195	19.97	39.94	79.87	159.75	239.62	319.50	399.37	479.25	559.12	639.00	718.87	798.75
3196	19.97	39.95	79.90	159.80	239.70	319.60	399.50	479.40	559.30	639.20	719.10	799.00
3197	19.98	39.96	79.92	159.85	239.77	319.70	399.62	479.55	559.47	639.40	719.32	799.25
3198	19.99	39.97	79.95	159.90	239.85	319.80	399.75	479.70	559.65	639.60	719.55	799.50
3199	19.99	39.99	79.97	159.95	239.92	319.90	399.87	479.85	559.82	639.80	719.77	799.75
3200	20.00	40.00	80.00	160.00	240.00	320.00	400.00	480.00	560.00	640.00	720.00	800.00

3200 FEET.

Per Ton / Per Foot, Feet.	$11 27½ cts.	$12 30 cts.	$13 32½ cts.	$14 35 cts.	$15 37½ cts.	$16 40 cts.	$17 42½ cts.	$18 45 cts.	$19 47½ cts.	$20 50 cts.
3151	866.52	945.30	1024.07	1102.85	1181.62	1260.40	1339.17	1417.95	1496.72	1575.50
3152	866.80	945.60	1024.40	1103.20	1182.00	1260.80	1339.60	1418.40	1497.20	1576.00
3153	867.07	945.90	1024.72	1103.55	1182.37	1261.20	1340.02	1418.85	1497.67	1576.50
3154	867.35	946.20	1025.05	1103.90	1182.75	1261.60	1340.45	1419.30	1498.15	1577.00
3155	867.62	946.50	1025.37	1104.25	1183.12	1262.00	1340.87	1419.75	1498.62	1577.50
3156	867.90	946.80	1025.70	1104.60	1183.50	1262.40	1341.30	1420.20	1499.10	1578.00
3157	868.17	947.10	1026.02	1104.95	1183.87	1262.80	1341.72	1420.65	1499.57	1578.50
3158	868.45	947.40	1026.35	1105.30	1184.25	1263.20	1342.15	1421.10	1500.05	1579.00
3159	868.72	947.70	1026.67	1105.65	1184.62	1263.60	1342.57	1421.55	1500.52	1579.50
3160	869.00	948.00	1027.00	1106.00	1185.00	1264.00	1343.00	1422.00	1501.00	1580.00
3161	869.27	948.30	1027.32	1106.35	1185.37	1264.40	1343.42	1422.45	1501.47	1580.50
3162	869.55	948.60	1027.65	1106.70	1185.75	1264.80	1343.85	1422.90	1501.95	1581.00
3163	869.82	948.90	1027.97	1107.05	1186.12	1265.20	1344.27	1423.35	1502.42	1581.50
3164	870.10	949.20	1028.30	1107.40	1186.50	1265.60	1344.70	1423.80	1502.90	1582.00
3165	870.37	949.50	1028.62	1107.75	1186.87	1266.00	1345.12	1424.25	1503.37	1582.50
3166	870.65	949.80	1028.95	1108.10	1187.25	1266.40	1345.55	1424.70	1503.85	1583.00
3167	870.92	950.10	1029.27	1108.45	1187.62	1266.80	1345.97	1425.15	1504.32	1583.50
3168	871.20	950.40	1029.60	1108.80	1188.00	1267.20	1346.40	1425.60	1504.80	1584.00
3169	871.47	950.70	1029.92	1109.15	1188.37	1267.60	1346.82	1426.05	1505.27	1584.50
3170	871.75	951.00	1030.25	1109.50	1188.75	1268.00	1347.25	1426.50	1505.75	1585.00
3171	872.02	951.30	1030.57	1109.85	1189.12	1268.40	1347.67	1426.95	1506.22	1585.50
3172	872.30	951.60	1030.90	1110.20	1189.50	1268.80	1348.10	1427.40	1506.70	1586.00
3173	872.57	951.90	1031.22	1110.55	1189.87	1269.20	1348.52	1427.85	1507.17	1586.50
3174	872.85	952.20	1031.55	1110.90	1190.25	1269.60	1348.95	1428.30	1507.65	1587.00
3175	873.12	952.50	1031.87	1111.25	1190.62	1270.00	1349.37	1428.75	1508.12	1587.50
3176	873.40	952.80	1032.20	1111.60	1191.00	1270.40	1349.80	1429.20	1508.60	1588.00
3177	873.67	953.10	1032.52	1111.95	1191.37	1270.80	1350.22	1429.65	1509.07	1588.50
3178	873.95	953.40	1032.85	1112.30	1191.75	1271.20	1350.65	1430.10	1509.55	1589.00
3179	874.22	953.70	1033.17	1112.65	1192.12	1271.60	1351.07	1430.55	1510.02	1589.50
3180	874.50	954.00	1033.50	1113.00	1192.50	1272.00	1351.50	1431.00	1510.50	1590.00
3181	874.77	954.30	1033.82	1113.35	1192.87	1272.40	1351.92	1431.45	1510.97	1590.50
3182	875.05	954.60	1034.15	1113.70	1193.25	1272.80	1352.35	1431.90	1511.45	1591.00
3183	875.32	954.90	1034.47	1114.05	1193.62	1273.20	1352.77	1432.35	1511.92	1591.50
3184	875.60	955.20	1034.80	1114.40	1194.00	1273.60	1353.20	1432.80	1512.40	1592.00
3185	875.87	955.50	1035.12	1114.75	1194.37	1274.00	1353.62	1433.25	1512.87	1592.50
3186	876.15	955.80	1035.45	1115.10	1194.75	1274.40	1354.05	1433.70	1513.35	1593.00
3187	876.42	956.10	1035.77	1115.45	1195.12	1274.80	1354.47	1434.15	1513.82	1593.50
3188	876.70	956.40	1036.10	1115.80	1195.50	1275.20	1354.90	1434.60	1514.30	1594.00
3189	876.97	956.70	1036.42	1116.15	1195.87	1275.60	1355.32	1435.05	1514.77	1594.50
3190	877.25	957.00	1036.75	1116.50	1196.25	1276.00	1355.75	1435.50	1515.25	1595.00
3191	877.52	957.30	1037.07	1116.85	1196.62	1276.40	1356.17	1435.95	1515.72	1595.50
3192	877.80	957.60	1037.40	1117.20	1197.00	1276.80	1356.60	1436.40	1516.20	1596.00
3193	878.07	957.90	1037.72	1117.55	1197.37	1277.20	1357.02	1436.85	1516.67	1596.50
3194	878.35	958.20	1038.05	1117.90	1197.75	1277.60	1357.45	1437.30	1517.15	1597.00
3195	878.62	958.50	1038.37	1118.25	1198.12	1278.00	1357.87	1437.75	1517.62	1597.50
3196	878.90	958.80	1038.70	1118.60	1198.50	1278.40	1358.30	1438.20	1518.10	1598.00
3197	879.17	959.10	1039.02	1118.95	1198.87	1278.80	1358.72	1438.65	1518.57	1598.50
3198	879.45	959.40	1039.35	1119.30	1199.25	1279.20	1359.15	1439.10	1519.05	1599.00
3199	879.72	959.70	1039.67	1119.65	1199.62	1279.60	1359.57	1439.55	1519.52	1599.50
3200	880.00	960.00	1040.00	1120.00	1200.00	1280.00	1360.00	1440.00	1520.00	1600.00

3250 FEET.

Per Ton, Per Foot, Feet.	25c.	50c.	$1 2½ cts.	$2 5 cts.	$3 7½ cts.	$4 10 cts.	$5 12½ cts.	$6 15 cts.	$7 17½ cts.	$8 20 cts.	$9 22½ cts.	$10 25 cts.
3201	20.01	40.01	80.02	160.05	240.07	320.10	400.12	480.15	560.17	640.20	720.22	800.25
3202	20.01	40.02	80.05	160.10	240.15	320.20	400.25	480.30	560.35	640.40	720.45	800.50
3203	20.02	40.04	80.07	160.15	240.22	320.30	400.37	480.45	560.52	640.60	720.67	800.75
3204	20.02	40.05	80.10	160.20	240.30	320.40	400.50	480.60	560.70	640.80	720.90	801.00
3205	20.03	40.06	80.12	160.25	240.37	320.50	400.62	480.75	560.87	641.00	721.12	801.25
3206	20.04	40.07	80.15	160.30	240.45	320.60	400.75	480.90	561.05	641.20	721.35	801.50
3207	20.04	40.09	80.17	160.35	240.52	320.70	400.87	481.05	561.22	641.40	721.57	801.75
3208	20.05	40.10	80.20	160.40	240.60	320.80	401.00	481.20	561.40	641.60	721.80	802.00
3209	20.06	40.11	80.22	160.45	240.67	320.90	401.12	481.35	561.57	641.80	722.02	802.25
3210	20.06	40.12	80.25	160.50	240.75	321.00	401.25	481.50	561.75	642.00	722.25	802.50
3211	20.07	40.14	80.27	160.55	240.82	321.10	401.37	481.65	561.92	642.20	722.47	802.75
3212	20.07	40.15	80.30	160.60	240.90	321.20	401.50	481.80	562.10	642.40	722.70	803.00
3213	20.08	40.16	80.32	160.65	240.97	321.30	401.62	481.95	562.27	642.60	722.92	803.25
3214	20.09	40.17	80.35	160.70	241.05	321.40	401.75	482.10	562.45	642.80	723.15	803.50
3215	20.09	40.19	80.37	160.75	241.12	321.50	401.87	482.25	562.62	643.00	723.37	803.75
3216	20.10	40.20	80.40	160.80	241.20	321.60	402.00	482.40	562.80	643.20	723.60	804.00
3217	20.11	40.21	80.42	160.85	241.27	321.70	402.12	482.55	562.97	643.40	723.82	804.25
3218	20.11	40.22	80.45	160.90	241.35	321.80	402.25	482.70	563.15	643.60	724.05	804.50
3219	20.12	40.24	80.47	160.95	241.42	321.90	402.37	482.85	563.32	643.80	724.27	804.75
3220	20.12	40.25	80.50	161.00	241.50	322.00	402.50	483.00	563.50	644.00	724.50	805.00
3221	20.13	40.26	80.52	161.05	241.57	322.10	402.62	483.15	563.67	644.20	724.72	805.25
3222	20.14	40.27	80.55	161.10	241.65	322.20	402.75	483.30	563.85	644.40	724.95	805.50
3223	20.14	40.29	80.57	161.15	241.72	322.30	402.87	483.45	564.02	644.60	725.17	805.75
3224	20.15	40.30	80.60	161.20	241.80	322.40	403.00	483.60	564.20	644.80	725.40	806.00
3225	20.16	40.31	80.62	161.25	241.87	322.50	403.12	483.75	564.37	645.00	725.62	806.25
3226	20.16	40.32	80.65	161.30	241.95	322.60	403.25	483.90	564.55	645.20	725.85	806.50
3227	20.17	40.34	80.67	161.35	242.02	322.70	403.37	484.05	564.72	645.40	726.07	806.75
3228	20.17	40.35	80.70	161.40	242.10	322.80	403.50	484.20	564.90	645.60	726.30	807.00
3229	20.18	40.36	80.72	161.45	242.17	322.90	403.62	484.35	565.07	645.80	726.52	807.25
3230	20.19	40.37	80.75	161.50	242.25	323.00	403.75	484.50	565.25	646.00	726.75	807.50
3231	20.19	40.39	80.77	161.55	242.32	323.10	403.87	484.65	565.42	646.20	726.97	807.75
3232	20.20	40.40	80.80	161.60	242.40	323.20	404.00	484.80	565.60	646.40	727.20	808.00
3233	20.21	40.41	80.82	161.65	242.47	323.30	404.12	484.95	565.77	646.60	727.42	808.25
3234	20.21	40.42	80.85	161.70	242.55	323.40	404.25	485.10	565.95	646.80	727.65	808.50
3235	20.22	40.44	80.87	161.75	242.62	323.50	404.37	485.25	566.12	647.00	727.87	808.75
3236	20.22	40.45	80.90	161.80	242.70	323.60	404.50	485.40	566.30	647.20	728.10	809.00
3237	20.23	40.46	80.92	161.85	242.77	323.70	404.62	485.55	566.47	647.40	728.32	809.25
3238	20.24	40.47	80.95	161.90	242.85	323.80	404.75	485.70	566.65	647.60	728.55	809.50
3239	20.24	40.49	80.97	161.95	242.92	323.90	404.87	485.85	566.82	647.80	728.77	809.75
3240	20.25	40.50	81.00	162.00	243.00	324.00	405.00	486.00	567.00	648.00	729.00	810.00
3241	20.26	40.51	81.02	162.05	243.07	324.10	405.12	486.15	567.17	648.20	729.22	810.25
3242	20.26	40.52	81.05	162.10	243.15	324.20	405.25	486.30	567.35	648.40	729.45	810.50
3243	20.27	40.54	81.07	162.15	243.22	324.30	405.37	486.45	567.52	648.60	729.67	810.75
3244	20.27	40.55	81.10	162.20	243.30	324.40	405.50	486.60	567.70	648.80	729.90	811.00
3245	20.28	40.56	81.12	162.25	243.37	324.50	405.62	486.75	567.87	649.00	730.12	811.25
3246	20.29	40.57	81.15	162.30	243.45	324.60	405.75	486.90	568.05	649.20	730.35	811.50
3247	20.29	40.59	81.17	162.35	243.52	324.70	405.87	487.05	568.22	649.40	730.57	811.75
3248	20.30	40.60	81.20	162.40	243.60	324.80	406.00	487.20	568.40	649.60	730.80	812.00
3249	20.31	40.61	81.22	162.45	243.67	324.90	406.12	487.35	568.57	649.80	731.02	812.25
3250	20.31	40.62	81.25	162.50	243.75	325.00	406.25	487.50	568.75	650.00	731.25	812.50

3250 FEET.

Per Ton	$11	$12	$13	$14	$15	$16	$17	$18	$19	$20
Per Foot,	27½ cts.	30 cts.	32½ cts.	35 cts.	37½ cts.	40 cts.	42½ cts.	45 cts.	47½ cts.	50 cts.
Feet.										
3201	880.27	960.30	1040.32	1120.35	1200.37	1280.40	1360.42	1440.45	1520.47	1600.50
3202	880.55	960.60	1040.65	1120.70	1200.75	1280.80	1360.85	1440.90	1520.95	1601.00
3203	880.82	960.90	1040.97	1121.05	1201.12	1281.20	1361.27	1441.35	1521.42	1601.50
3204	881.10	961.20	1041.30	1121.40	1201.50	1281.60	1361.70	1441.80	1521.90	1602.00
3205	881.37	961.50	1041.62	1121.75	1201.87	1282.00	1362.12	1442.25	1522.37	1602.50
3206	881.65	961.80	1041.95	1122.10	1202.25	1282.40	1362.55	1442.70	1522.85	1603.00
3207	881.92	962.10	1042.27	1122.45	1202.62	1282.80	1362.97	1443.15	1523.32	1603.50
3208	882.20	962.40	1042.60	1122.80	1203.00	1283.20	1363.40	1443.60	1523.80	1604.00
3209	882.47	962.70	1042.92	1123.15	1203.37	1283.60	1363.82	1444.05	1524.27	1604.50
3210	882.75	963.00	1043.25	1123.50	1203.75	1284.00	1364.25	1444.50	1524.75	1605.00
3211	883.02	963.30	1043.57	1123.85	1204.12	1284.40	1364.67	1444.95	1525.22	1605.50
3212	883.30	963.60	1043.90	1124.20	1204.50	1284.80	1365.10	1445.40	1525.70	1606.00
3213	883.57	963.90	1044.22	1124.55	1204.87	1285.20	1365.52	1445.85	1526.17	1606.50
3214	883.85	964.20	1044.55	1124.90	1205.25	1285.60	1365.95	1446.30	1526.65	1607.00
3215	884.12	964.50	1044.87	1125.25	1205.62	1286.00	1366.37	1446.75	1527.12	1607.50
3216	884.40	964.80	1045.20	1125.60	1206.00	1286.40	1366.80	1447.20	1527.60	1608.00
3217	884.67	965.10	1045.52	1125.95	1206.37	1286.80	1367.22	1447.65	1528.07	1608.50
3218	884.95	965.40	1045.85	1126.30	1206.75	1287.20	1367.65	1448.10	1528.55	1609.00
3219	885.22	965.70	1046.17	1126.65	1207.12	1287.60	1368.07	1448.55	1529.02	1609.50
3220	885.50	966.00	1046.50	1127.00	1207.50	1288.00	1368.50	1449.00	1529.50	1610.00
3221	885.77	966.30	1046.82	1127.35	1207.87	1288.40	1368.92	1449.45	1529.97	1610.50
3222	886.05	966.60	1047.15	1127.70	1208.25	1288.80	1369.35	1449.90	1530.45	1611.00
3223	886.32	966.90	1047.47	1128.05	1208.62	1289.20	1369.77	1450.35	1530.92	1611.50
3224	886.60	967.20	1047.80	1128.40	1209.00	1289.60	1370.20	1450.80	1531.40	1612.00
3225	886.87	967.50	1048.12	1128.75	1209.37	1290.00	1370.62	1451.25	1531.87	1612.50
3226	887.15	967.80	1048.45	1129.10	1209.75	1290.40	1371.05	1451.70	1532.35	1613.00
3227	887.42	968.10	1048.77	1129.45	1210.12	1290.80	1371.47	1452.15	1532.82	1613.50
3228	887.70	968.40	1049.10	1129.80	1210.50	1291.20	1371.90	1452.60	1533.30	1614.00
3229	887.97	968.70	1049.42	1130.15	1210.87	1291.60	1372.32	1453.05	1533.77	1614.50
3230	888.25	969.00	1049.75	1130.50	1211.25	1292.00	1372.75	1453.50	1534.25	1615.00
3231	888.52	969.30	1050.07	1130.85	1211.62	1292.40	1373.17	1453.95	1534.72	1615.50
3232	888.80	969.60	1050.40	1131.20	1212.00	1292.80	1373.60	1454.40	1535.20	1616.00
3233	889.07	969.90	1050.72	1131.55	1212.37	1293.20	1374.02	1454.85	1535.67	1616.50
3234	889.35	970.20	1051.05	1131.90	1212.75	1293.60	1374.45	1455.30	1536.15	1617.00
3235	889.62	970.50	1051.37	1132.25	1213.12	1294.00	1374.87	1455.75	1536.62	1617.50
3236	889.90	970.80	1051.70	1132.60	1213.50	1294.40	1375.30	1456.20	1537.10	1618.00
3237	890.17	971.10	1052.02	1132.95	1213.87	1294.80	1375.72	1456.65	1537.57	1618.50
3238	890.45	971.40	1052.35	1133.30	1214.25	1295.20	1376.15	1457.10	1538.05	1619.00
3239	890.72	971.70	1052.67	1133.65	1214.62	1295.60	1376.57	1457.55	1538.52	1619.50
3240	891.00	972.00	1053.00	1134.00	1215.00	1296.00	1377.00	1458.00	1539.00	1620.00
3241	891.27	972.30	1053.32	1134.35	1215.37	1296.40	1377.42	1458.45	1539.47	1620.50
3242	891.55	972.60	1053.65	1134.70	1215.75	1296.80	1377.85	1458.90	1539.95	1621.00
3243	891.82	972.90	1053.97	1135.05	1216.12	1297.20	1378.27	1459.35	1540.42	1621.50
3244	892.10	973.20	1054.30	1135.40	1216.50	1297.60	1378.70	1459.80	1540.90	1622.00
3245	892.37	973.50	1054.62	1135.75	1216.87	1298.00	1379.12	1460.25	1541.37	1622.50
3246	892.65	973.80	1054.95	1136.10	1217.25	1298.40	1379.55	1460.70	1541.85	1623.00
3247	892.92	974.10	1055.27	1136.45	1217.62	1298.80	1379.97	1461.15	1542.32	1623.50
3248	893.20	974.40	1055.60	1136.80	1218.00	1299.20	1380.40	1461.60	1542.80	1624.00
3249	893.47	974.70	1055.92	1137.15	1218.37	1299.60	1380.82	1462.05	1543.27	1624.50
3250	893.75	975.00	1056.25	1137.50	1218.75	1300.00	1381.25	1462.50	1543.75	1625.00

3300 FEET.

Per Ton,	25c.	50c.	$1	$2	$3	$4	$5	$6	$7	$8	$9	$10
Per Foot,			2½ cts.	5 cts.	7½ cts.	10 cts.	12½ cts.	15 cts.	17½ cts.	20 cts.	22½ cts.	25 cts.
Feet.												
3251	20.32	40.64	81.27	162.55	243.82	325.10	406.37	487.65	568.92	650.20	731.47	812.75
3252	20.32	40.65	81.30	162.60	243.90	325.20	406.50	487.80	569.10	650.40	731.70	813.00
3253	20.33	40.66	81.32	162.65	243.97	325.30	406.62	487.95	569.27	650.60	731.92	813.25
3254	20.34	40.67	81.35	162.70	244.05	325.40	406.75	488.10	569.45	650.80	732.15	813.50
3255	20.34	40.69	81.37	162.75	244.12	325.50	406.87	488.25	569.62	651.00	732.37	813.75
3256	20.35	40.70	81.40	162.80	244.20	325.60	407.00	488.40	569.80	651.20	732.60	814.00
3257	20.36	40.71	81.42	162.85	244.27	325.70	407.12	488.55	569.97	651.40	732.82	814.25
3258	20.36	40.72	81.45	162.90	244.35	325.80	407.25	488.70	570.15	651.60	733.05	814.50
3259	20.37	40.74	81.47	162.95	244.42	325.90	407.37	488.85	570.32	651.80	733.27	814.75
3260	20.37	40.75	81.50	163.00	244.50	326.00	407.50	489.00	570.50	652.00	733.50	815.00
3261	20.38	40.76	81.52	163.05	244.57	326.10	407.62	489.15	570.67	652.20	733.72	815.25
3262	20.39	40.77	81.55	163.10	244.65	326.20	407.75	489.30	570.85	652.40	733.95	815.50
3263	20.39	40.79	81.57	163.15	244.72	326.30	407.87	489.45	571.02	652.60	734.17	815.75
3264	20.40	40.80	81.60	163.20	244.80	326.40	408.00	489.60	571.20	652.80	734.40	816.00
3265	20.41	40.81	81.62	163.25	244.87	326.50	408.12	489.75	571.37	653.00	734.62	816.25
3266	20.41	40.82	81.65	163.30	244.95	326.60	408.25	489.90	571.55	653.20	734.85	816.50
3267	20.42	40.84	81.67	163.35	245.02	326.70	408.37	490.05	571.72	653.40	735.07	816.75
3268	20.42	40.85	81.70	163.40	245.10	326.80	408.50	490.20	571.90	653.60	735.30	817.00
3269	20.43	40.86	81.72	163.45	245.17	326.90	408.62	490.35	572.07	653.80	735.52	817.25
3270	20.44	40.87	81.75	163.50	245.25	327.00	408.75	490.50	572.25	654.00	735.75	817.50
3271	20.44	40.89	81.77	163.55	245.32	327.10	408.87	490.65	572.42	654.20	735.97	817.75
3272	20.45	40.90	81.80	163.60	245.40	327.20	409.00	490.80	572.60	654.40	736.20	818.00
3273	20.46	40.91	81.82	163.65	245.47	327.30	409.12	490.95	572.77	654.60	736.42	818.25
3274	20.46	40.92	81.85	163.70	245.55	327.40	409.25	491.10	572.95	654.80	736.65	818.50
3275	20.47	40.94	81.87	163.75	245.62	327.50	409.37	491.25	573.12	655.00	736.87	818.75
3276	20.47	40.95	81.90	163.80	245.70	327.60	409.50	491.40	573.30	655.20	737.10	819.00
3277	20.48	40.96	81.92	163.85	245.77	327.70	409.62	491.55	573.47	655.40	737.32	819.25
3278	20.49	40.97	81.95	163.90	245.85	327.80	409.75	491.70	573.65	655.60	737.55	819.50
3279	20.49	40.99	81.97	163.95	245.92	327.90	409.87	491.85	573.82	655.80	737.77	819.75
3280	20.50	41.00	82.00	164.00	246.00	328.00	410.00	492.00	574.00	656.00	738.00	820.00
3281	20.51	41.01	82.02	164.05	246.07	328.10	410.12	492.15	574.17	656.20	738.22	820.25
3282	20.51	41.02	82.05	164.10	246.15	328.20	410.25	492.30	574.35	656.40	738.45	820.50
3283	20.52	41.04	82.07	164.15	246.22	328.30	410.37	492.45	574.52	656.60	738.67	820.75
3284	20.52	41.05	82.10	164.20	246.30	328.40	410.50	492.60	574.70	656.80	738.90	821.00
3285	20.53	41.06	82.12	164.25	246.37	328.50	410.62	492.75	574.87	657.00	739.12	821.25
3286	20.54	41.07	82.15	164.30	246.45	328.60	410.75	492.90	575.05	657.20	739.35	821.50
3287	20.54	41.09	82.17	164.35	246.52	328.70	410.87	493.05	575.22	657.40	739.57	821.75
3288	20.55	41.10	82.20	164.40	246.60	328.80	411.00	493.20	575.40	657.60	739.80	822.00
3289	20.56	41.11	82.22	164.45	246.67	328.90	411.12	493.35	575.57	657.80	740.02	822.25
3290	20.56	41.12	82.25	164.50	246.75	329.00	411.25	493.50	575.75	658.00	740.25	822.50
3291	20.57	41.14	82.27	164.55	246.82	329.10	411.37	493.65	575.92	658.20	740.47	822.75
3292	20.57	41.15	82.30	164.60	246.90	329.20	411.50	493.80	576.10	658.40	740.70	823.00
3293	20.58	41.16	82.32	164.65	246.97	329.30	411.62	493.95	576.27	658.60	740.92	823.25
3294	20.59	41.17	82.35	164.70	247.05	329.40	411.75	494.10	576.45	658.80	741.15	823.50
3295	20.59	41.19	82.37	164.75	247.12	329.50	411.87	494.25	576.62	659.00	741.37	823.75
3296	20.60	41.20	82.40	164.80	247.20	329.60	412.00	494.40	576.80	659.20	741.60	824.00
3297	20.61	41.21	82.42	164.85	247.27	329.70	412.12	494.55	576.97	659.40	741.82	824.25
3298	20.61	41.22	82.45	164.90	247.35	329.80	412.25	494.70	577.15	659.60	742.05	824.50
3299	20.62	41.24	82.47	164.95	247.42	329.90	412.37	494.85	577.32	659.80	742.27	824.75
3300	20.62	41.25	82.50	165.00	247.50	330.00	412.50	495.00	577.50	660.00	742.50	825.00

3300 FEET.

Per Ton	$11	$12	$13	$14	$15	$16	$17	$18	$19	$20
Per Foot,	27½ cts.	30 cts.	32½ cts.	35 cts.	37½ cts.	40 cts.	42½ cts.	45 cts.	47½ cts.	50 cts.
Feet.										
3251	894.02	975.30	1056.57	1137.85	1219.12	1300.40	1381.67	1462.95	1544.22	1625.50
3252	894.30	975.60	1056.90	1138.20	1219.50	1300.80	1382.10	1463.40	1544.70	1626.00
3253	894.57	975.90	1057.22	1138.55	1219.87	1301.20	1382.52	1463.85	1545.17	1626.50
3254	894.85	976.20	1057.55	1138.90	1220.25	1301.60	1382.95	1464.30	1545.65	1627.00
3255	895.12	976.50	1057.87	1139.25	1220.62	1302.00	1383.37	1464.75	1546.12	1627.50
3256	895.40	976.80	1058.20	1139.60	1221.00	1302.40	1383.80	1465.20	1546.60	1628.00
3257	895.67	977.10	1058.52	1139.95	1221.37	1302.80	1384.22	1465.65	1547.07	1628.50
3258	895.95	977.40	1058.85	1140.30	1221.75	1303.20	1384.65	1466.10	1547.55	1629.00
3259	896.22	977.70	1059.17	1140.65	1222.12	1303.60	1385.07	1466.55	1548.02	1629.50
3260	896.50	978.00	1059.50	1141.00	1222.50	1304.00	1385.50	1467.00	1548.50	1630.00
3261	896.77	978.30	1059.82	1141.35	1222.87	1304.40	1385.92	1467.45	1548.97	1630.50
3262	897.05	978.60	1060.15	1141.70	1223.25	1304.80	1386.35	1467.90	1549.45	1631.00
3263	897.32	978.90	1060.47	1142.05	1223.62	1305.20	1386.77	1468.35	1549.92	1631.50
3264	897.60	979.20	1060.80	1142.40	1224.00	1305.60	1387.20	1468.80	1550.40	1632.00
3265	897.87	979.50	1061.12	1142.75	1224.37	1306.00	1387.62	1469.25	1550.87	1632.50
3266	898.15	979.80	1061.45	1143.10	1224.75	1306.40	1388.05	1469.70	1551.35	1633.00
3267	898.42	980.10	1061.77	1143.45	1225.12	1306.80	1388.47	1470.15	1551.82	1633.50
3268	898.70	980.40	1062.10	1143.80	1225.50	1307.20	1388.90	1470.60	1552.30	1634.00
3269	898.97	980.70	1062.42	1144.15	1225.87	1307.60	1389.32	1471.05	1552.77	1634.50
3270	899.25	981.00	1062.75	1144.50	1226.25	1308.00	1389.75	1471.50	1553.25	1635.00
3271	899.52	981.30	1063.07	1144.85	1226.62	1308.40	1390.17	1471.95	1553.72	1635.50
3272	899.80	981.60	1063.40	1145.20	1227.00	1308.80	1390.60	1472.40	1554.20	1636.00
3273	900.07	981.90	1063.72	1145.55	1227.37	1309.20	1391.02	1472.85	1554.67	1636.50
3274	900.35	982.20	1064.05	1145.90	1227.75	1309.60	1391.45	1473.30	1555.15	1637.00
3275	900.62	982.50	1064.37	1146.25	1228.12	1310.00	1391.87	1473.75	1555.62	1637.50
3276	900.90	982.80	1064.70	1146.60	1228.50	1310.40	1392.30	1474.20	1556.10	1638.00
3277	901.17	983.10	1065.02	1146.95	1228.87	1310.80	1392.72	1474.65	1556.57	1638.50
3278	901.45	983.40	1065.35	1147.30	1229.25	1311.20	1393.15	1475.10	1557.05	1639.00
3279	901.72	983.70	1065.67	1147.65	1229.62	1311.60	1393.57	1475.55	1557.52	1639.50
3280	902.00	984.00	1066.00	1148.00	1230.00	1312.00	1394.00	1476.00	1558.00	1640.00
3281	902.27	984.30	1066.32	1148.35	1230.37	1312.40	1394.42	1476.45	1558.47	1640.50
3282	902.55	984.60	1066.65	1148.70	1230.75	1312.80	1394.85	1476.90	1558.95	1641.00
3283	902.82	984.90	1066.97	1149.05	1231.12	1313.20	1395.27	1477.35	1559.42	1641.50
3284	903.10	985.20	1067.30	1149.40	1231.50	1313.60	1395.70	1477.80	1559.90	1642.00
3285	903.37	985.50	1067.62	1149.75	1231.87	1314.00	1396.12	1478.25	1560.37	1642.50
3286	903.65	985.80	1067.95	1150.10	1232.25	1314.40	1396.55	1478.70	1560.85	1643.00
3287	903.92	986.10	1068.27	1150.45	1232.62	1314.80	1396.97	1479.15	1561.32	1643.50
3288	904.20	986.40	1068.60	1150.80	1233.00	1315.20	1397.40	1479.60	1561.80	1644.00
3289	904.47	986.70	1068.92	1151.15	1233.37	1315.60	1397.82	1480.05	1562.27	1644.50
3290	904.75	987.00	1069.25	1151.50	1233.75	1316.00	1398.25	1480.50	1562.75	1645.00
3291	905.02	987.30	1069.57	1151.85	1234.12	1316.40	1398.67	1480.95	1563.22	1645.50
3292	905.30	987.60	1069.90	1152.20	1234.50	1316.80	1399.10	1481.40	1563.70	1646.00
3293	905.57	987.90	1070.22	1152.55	1234.87	1317.20	1399.52	1481.85	1564.17	1646.50
3294	905.85	988.20	1070.55	1152.90	1235.25	1317.60	1399.95	1482.30	1564.65	1647.00
3295	906.12	988.50	1070.87	1153.25	1235.62	1318.00	1400.37	1482.75	1565.12	1647.50
3296	906.40	988.80	1071.20	1153.60	1236.00	1318.40	1400.80	1483.20	1565.60	1648.00
3297	906.67	989.10	1071.52	1153.95	1236.37	1318.80	1401.22	1483.65	1566.07	1648.50
3298	906.95	989.40	1071.85	1154.30	1236.75	1319.20	1401.65	1484.10	1566.55	1649.00
3299	907.22	989.70	1072.17	1154.65	1237.12	1319.60	1402.07	1484.55	1567.02	1649.50
3300	907.50	990.00	1072.50	1155.00	1237.50	1320.00	1402.50	1485.00	1567.50	1650.00

Per Ton,	25c.	50c.	$1	$2	$3	$4	$5	$6	$7	$8	$9	$10
Per Foot,			2½ cts.	5 cts.	7½ cts.	10 cts.	12½ cts.	15 cts.	17½ cts.	20 cts.	22½ cts.	25 cts.
Feet.												
3301	20.63	41.26	82.52	165.05	247.57	330.10	412.62	495.15	577.67	660.20	742.72	825.25
3302	20.64	41.27	82.55	165.10	247.65	330.20	412.75	495.30	577.85	660.40	742.95	825.50
3303	20.64	41.29	82.57	165.15	247.72	330.30	412.87	495.45	578.02	660.60	743.17	825.75
3304	20.65	41.30	82.60	165.20	247.80	330.40	413.00	495.60	578.20	660.80	743.40	826.00
3305	20.66	41.31	82.62	165.25	247.87	330.50	413.12	495.75	578.37	661.00	743.62	826.25
3306	20.66	41.32	82.65	165.30	247.95	330.60	413.25	495.90	578.55	661.20	743.85	826.50
3307	20.67	41.34	82.67	165.35	248.02	330.70	413.37	496.05	578.72	661.40	744.07	826.75
3308	20.67	41.35	82.70	165.40	248.10	330.80	413.50	496.20	578.90	661.60	744.30	827.00
3309	20.68	41.36	82.72	165.45	248.17	330.90	413.62	496.35	579.07	661.80	744.52	827.25
3310	20.69	41.37	82.75	165.50	248.25	331.00	413.75	496.50	579.25	662.00	744.75	827.50
3311	20.69	41.39	82.77	165.55	248.32	331.10	413.87	496.65	579.42	662.20	744.97	827.75
3312	20.70	41.40	82.80	165.60	248.40	331.20	414.00	496.80	579.60	662.40	745.20	828.00
3313	20.71	41.41	82.82	165.65	248.47	331.30	414.12	496.95	579.77	662.60	745.42	828.25
3314	20.71	41.42	82.85	165.70	248.55	331.40	414.25	497.10	579.95	662.80	745.65	828.50
3315	20.72	41.44	82.87	165.75	248.62	331.50	414.37	497.25	580.12	663.00	745.87	828.75
3316	20.72	41.45	82.90	165.80	248.70	331.60	414.50	497.40	580.30	663.20	746.10	829.00
3317	20.73	41.46	82.92	165.85	248.77	331.70	414.62	497.55	580.47	663.40	746.32	829.25
3318	20.74	41.47	82.95	165.90	248.85	331.80	414.75	497.70	580.65	663.60	746.55	829.50
3319	20.74	41.49	82.97	165.95	248.92	331.90	414.87	497.85	580.82	663.80	746.77	829.75
3320	20.75	41.50	83.00	166.00	249.00	332.00	415.00	498.00	581.00	664.00	747.00	830.00
3321	20.76	41.51	83.02	166.05	249.07	332.10	415.12	498.15	581.17	664.20	747.22	830.25
3322	20.76	41.52	83.05	166.10	249.15	332.20	415.25	498.30	581.35	664.40	747.45	830.50
3323	20.77	41.54	83.07	166.15	249.22	332.30	415.37	498.45	581.52	664.60	747.67	830.75
3324	20.77	41.55	83.10	166.20	249.30	332.40	415.50	498.60	581.70	664.80	747.90	831.00
3325	20.78	41.56	83.12	166.25	249.37	332.50	415.62	498.75	581.87	665.00	748.12	831.25
3326	20.79	41.57	83.15	166.30	249.45	332.60	415.75	498.90	582.05	665.20	748.35	831.50
3327	20.79	41.59	83.17	166.35	249.52	332.70	415.87	499.05	582.22	665.40	748.57	831.75
3328	20.80	41.60	83.20	166.40	249.60	332.80	416.00	499.20	582.40	665.60	748.80	832.00
3329	20.81	41.61	83.22	166.45	249.67	332.90	416.12	499.35	582.57	665.80	749.02	832.25
3330	20.81	41.62	83.25	166.50	249.75	333.00	416.25	499.50	582.75	666.00	749.25	832.50
3331	20.82	41.64	83.27	166.55	249.82	333.10	416.37	499.65	582.92	666.20	749.47	832.75
3332	20.82	41.65	83.30	166.60	249.90	333.20	416.50	499.80	583.10	666.40	749.70	833.00
3333	20.83	41.66	83.32	166.65	249.97	333.30	416.62	499.95	583.27	666.60	749.92	833.25
3334	20.84	41.67	83.35	166.70	250.05	333.40	416.75	500.10	583.45	666.80	750.15	833.50
3335	20.84	41.69	83.37	166.75	250.12	333.50	416.87	500.25	583.62	667.00	750.37	833.75
3336	20.85	41.70	83.40	166.80	250.20	333.60	417.00	500.40	583.80	667.20	750.60	834.00
3337	20.86	41.71	83.42	166.85	250.27	333.70	417.12	500.55	583.97	667.40	750.82	834.25
3338	20.86	41.72	83.45	166.90	250.35	333.80	417.25	500.70	584.15	667.60	751.05	834.50
3339	20.87	41.74	83.47	166.95	250.42	333.90	417.37	500.85	584.32	667.80	751.27	834.75
3340	20.87	41.75	83.50	167.00	250.50	334.00	417.50	501.00	584.50	668.00	751.50	835.00
3341	20.88	41.76	83.52	167.05	250.57	334.10	417.62	501.15	584.67	668.20	751.72	835.25
3342	20.89	41.77	83.55	167.10	250.65	334.20	417.75	501.30	584.85	668.40	751.95	835.50
3343	20.89	41.79	83.57	167.15	250.72	334.30	417.87	501.45	585.02	668.60	752.17	835.75
3344	20.90	41.80	83.60	167.20	250.80	334.40	418.00	501.60	585.20	668.80	752.40	836.00
3345	20.91	41.81	83.62	167.25	250.87	334.50	418.12	501.75	585.37	669.00	752.62	836.25
3346	20.91	41.82	83.65	167.30	250.95	334.60	418.25	501.90	585.55	669.20	752.85	836.50
3347	20.92	41.84	83.67	167.35	251.02	334.70	418.37	502.05	585.72	669.40	753.07	836.75
3348	20.92	41.85	83.70	167.40	251.10	334.80	418.50	502.20	585.90	669.60	753.30	837.00
3349	20.93	41.86	83.72	167.45	251.17	334.90	418.62	502.35	586.07	669.80	753.52	837.25
3350	20.94	41.87	83.75	167.50	251.25	335.00	418.75	502.50	586.25	670.00	753.75	837.50

3350 FEET.

Per Ton Per Foot,	$11 27½ cts.	$12 30 cts.	$13 32½ cts.	$14 35 cts.	$15 37½ cts.	$16 40 cts.	$17 42½ cts.	$18 45 cts.	$19 47½ cts.	$20 50 cts.
Feet.										
3301	907.77	990.30	1072.82	1155.35	1237.87	1320.40	1402.92	1485.45	1567.97	1650.50
3302	908.05	990.60	1073.15	1155.70	1238.25	1320.80	1403.35	1485.90	1568.45	1651.00
3303	908.32	990.90	1073.47	1156.05	1238.62	1321.20	1403.77	1486.35	1568.92	1651.50
3304	908.60	991.20	1073.80	1156.40	1239.00	1321.60	1404.20	1486.80	1569.40	1652.00
3305	908.87	991.50	1074.12	1156.75	1239.37	1322.00	1404.62	1487.25	1569.87	1652.50
3306	909.15	991.80	1074.45	1157.10	1239.75	1322.40	1405.05	1487.70	1570.35	1653.00
3307	909.42	992.10	1074.77	1157.45	1240.12	1322.80	1405.47	1488.15	1570.82	1653.50
3308	909.70	992.40	1075.10	1157.80	1240.50	1323.20	1405.90	1488.60	1571.30	1654.00
3309	909.97	992.70	1075.42	1158.15	1240.87	1323.60	1406.32	1489.05	1571.77	1654.50
3310	910.25	993.00	1075.75	1158.50	1241.25	1324.00	1406.75	1489.50	1572.25	1655.00
3311	910.52	993.30	1076.07	1158.85	1241.62	1324.40	1407.17	1489.95	1572.72	1655.50
3312	910.80	993.60	1076.40	1159.20	1242.00	1324.80	1407.60	1490.40	1573.20	1656.00
3313	911.07	993.90	1076.72	1159.55	1242.37	1325.20	1408.02	1490.85	1573.67	1656.50
3314	911.35	994.20	1077.05	1159.90	1242.75	1325.60	1408.45	1491.30	1574.15	1657.00
3315	911.62	994.50	1077.37	1160.25	1243.12	1326.00	1408.87	1491.75	1574.62	1657.50
3316	911.90	994.80	1077.70	1160.60	1243.50	1326.40	1409.30	1492.20	1575.10	1658.00
3317	912.17	995.10	1078.02	1160.95	1243.87	1326.80	1409.72	1492.65	1575.57	1658.50
3318	912.45	995.40	1078.35	1161.30	1244.25	1327.20	1410.15	1493.10	1576.05	1659.00
3319	912.72	995.70	1078.67	1161.65	1244.62	1327.60	1410.57	1493.55	1576.52	1659.50
3320	913.00	996.00	1079.00	1162.00	1245.00	1328.00	1411.00	1494.00	1577.00	1660.00
3321	913.27	996.30	1079.32	1162.35	1245.37	1328.40	1411.42	1494.45	1577.47	1660.50
3322	913.55	996.60	1079.65	1162.70	1245.75	1328.80	1411.85	1494.90	1577.95	1661.00
3323	913.82	996.90	1079.97	1163.05	1246.12	1329.20	1412.27	1495.35	1578.42	1661.50
3324	914.10	997.20	1080.30	1163.40	1246.50	1329.60	1412.70	1495.80	1578.90	1662.00
3325	914.37	997.50	1080.62	1163.75	1246.87	1330.00	1413.12	1496.25	1579.37	1662.50
3326	914.65	997.80	1080.95	1164.10	1247.25	1330.40	1413.55	1496.70	1579.85	1663.00
3327	914.92	998.10	1081.27	1164.45	1247.62	1330.80	1413.97	1497.15	1580.32	1663.50
3328	915.20	998.40	1081.60	1164.80	1248.00	1331.20	1414.40	1497.60	1580.80	1664.00
3329	915.47	998.70	1081.92	1165.15	1248.37	1331.60	1414.82	1498.05	1581.27	1664.50
3330	915.75	999.00	1082.25	1165.50	1248.75	1332.00	1415.25	1498.50	1581.75	1665.00
3331	916.02	999.30	1082.57	1165.85	1249.12	1332.40	1415.67	1498.95	1582.22	1665.50
3332	916.30	999.60	1082.90	1166.20	1249.50	1332.80	1416.10	1499.40	1582.70	1666.00
3333	916.57	999.90	1083.22	1166.55	1249.87	1333.20	1416.52	1499.85	1583.17	1666.50
3334	916.85	1000.20	1083.55	1166.90	1250.25	1333.60	1416.95	1500.30	1583.65	1667.00
3335	917.12	1000.50	1083.87	1167.25	1250.62	1334.00	1417.37	1500.75	1584.12	1667.50
3336	917.40	1000.80	1084.20	1167.60	1251.00	1334.40	1417.80	1501.20	1584.60	1668.00
3337	917.67	1001.10	1084.52	1167.95	1251.37	1334.80	1418.22	1501.65	1585.07	1668.50
3338	917.95	1001.40	1084.85	1168.30	1251.75	1335.20	1418.65	1502.10	1585.55	1669.00
3339	918.22	1001.70	1085.17	1168.65	1252.12	1335.60	1419.07	1502.55	1586.02	1669.50
3340	918.50	1002.00	1085.50	1169.00	1252.50	1336.00	1419.50	1503.00	1586.50	1670.00
3341	918.77	1002.30	1085.82	1169.35	1252.87	1336.40	1419.92	1503.45	1586.97	1670.50
3342	919.05	1002.60	1086.15	1169.70	1253.25	1336.80	1420.35	1503.90	1587.45	1671.00
3343	919.32	1002.90	1086.47	1170.05	1253.62	1337.20	1420.77	1504.35	1587.92	1671.50
3344	919.60	1003.20	1086.80	1170.40	1254.00	1337.60	1421.20	1504.80	1588.40	1672.00
3345	919.87	1003.50	1087.12	1170.75	1254.37	1338.00	1421.62	1505.25	1588.87	1672.50
3346	920.15	1003.80	1087.45	1171.10	1254.75	1338.40	1422.05	1505.70	1589.35	1673.00
3347	920.42	1004.10	1087.77	1171.45	1255.12	1338.80	1422.47	1506.15	1589.82	1673.50
3348	920.70	1004.40	1088.10	1171.80	1255.50	1339.20	1422.90	1506.60	1590.30	1674.00
3349	920.97	1004.70	1088.42	1172.15	1255.87	1339.60	1423.32	1507.05	1590.77	1674.50
3350	921.25	1005.00	1088.75	1172.50	1256.25	1340.00	1423.75	1507.50	1591.25	1675.00

3400 FEET.

Per Ton,	25c.	50c.	$1	$2	$3	$4	$5	$6	$7	$8	$9	$10
Per Foot,			2½ cts.	5 cts.	7½ cts.	10 cts.	12½ cts.	15 cts.	17½ cts.	20 cts.	22½ cts.	25 cts.
Feet.												
3351	20.94	41.89	83.77	167.55	251.32	335.10	418.87	502.65	586.42	670.20	753.97	837.75
3352	20.95	41.90	83.80	167.60	251.40	335.20	419.00	502.80	586.60	670.40	754.20	838.00
3353	20.96	41.91	83.82	167.65	251.47	335.30	419.12	502.95	586.77	670.60	754.42	838.25
3354	20.96	41.92	83.85	167.70	251.55	335.40	419.25	503.10	586.95	670.80	754.65	838.50
3355	20.97	41.94	83.87	167.75	251.62	335.50	419.37	503.25	587.12	671.00	754.87	838.75
3356	20.97	41.95	83.90	167.80	251.70	335.60	419.50	503.40	587.30	671.20	755.10	839.00
3357	20.98	41.96	83.92	167.85	251.77	335.70	419.62	503.55	587.47	671.40	755.32	839.25
3358	20.99	41.97	83.95	167.90	251.85	335.80	419.75	503.70	587.65	671.60	755.55	839.50
3359	20.99	41.99	83.97	167.95	251.92	335.90	419.87	503.85	587.82	671.80	755.77	839.75
3360	21.00	42.00	84.00	168.00	252.00	336.00	420.00	504.00	588.00	672.00	756.00	840.00
3361	21.01	42.01	84.02	168.05	252.07	336.10	420.12	504.15	588.17	672.20	756.22	840.25
3362	21.01	42.02	84.05	168.10	252.15	336.20	420.25	504.30	588.35	672.40	756.45	840.50
3363	21.02	42.04	84.07	168.15	252.22	336.30	420.37	504.45	588.52	672.60	756.67	840.75
3364	21.02	42.05	84.10	168.20	252.30	336.40	420.50	504.60	588.70	672.80	756.90	841.00
3365	21.03	42.06	84.12	168.25	252.37	336.50	420.62	504.75	588.87	673.00	757.12	841.25
3366	21.04	42.07	84.15	168.30	252.45	336.60	420.75	504.90	589.05	673.20	757.35	841.50
3367	21.04	42.09	84.17	168.35	252.52	336.70	420.87	505.05	589.22	673.40	757.57	841.75
3368	21.05	42.10	84.20	168.40	252.60	336.80	421.00	505.20	589.40	673.60	757.80	842.00
3369	21.06	42.11	84.22	168.45	252.67	336.90	421.12	505.35	589.57	673.80	758.02	842.25
3370	21.06	42.12	84.25	168.50	252.75	337.00	421.25	505.50	589.75	674.00	758.25	842.50
3371	21.07	42.14	84.27	168.55	252.82	337.10	421.37	505.65	589.92	674.20	758.47	842.75
3372	21.07	42.15	84.30	168.60	252.90	337.20	421.50	505.80	590.10	674.40	758.70	843.00
3373	21.08	42.16	84.32	168.65	252.97	337.30	421.62	505.95	590.27	674.60	758.92	843.25
3374	21.09	42.17	84.35	168.70	253.05	337.40	421.75	506.10	590.45	674.80	759.15	843.50
3375	21.09	42.19	84.37	168.75	253.12	337.50	421.87	506.25	590.62	675.00	759.37	843.75
3376	21.10	42.20	84.40	168.80	253.20	337.60	422.00	506.40	590.80	675.20	759.60	844.00
3377	21.11	42.21	84.42	168.85	253.27	337.70	422.12	506.55	590.97	675.40	759.82	844.25
3378	21.11	42.22	84.45	168.90	253.35	337.80	422.25	506.70	591.15	675.60	760.05	844.50
3379	21.12	42.24	84.47	168.95	253.42	337.90	422.37	506.85	591.32	675.80	760.27	844.75
3380	21.12	42.25	84.50	169.00	253.50	338.00	422.50	507.00	591.50	676.00	760.50	845.00
3381	21.13	42.26	84.52	169.05	253.57	338.10	422.62	507.15	591.67	676.20	760.72	845.25
3382	21.14	42.27	84.55	169.10	253.65	338.20	422.75	507.30	591.85	676.40	760.95	845.50
3383	21.14	42.29	84.57	169.15	253.72	338.30	422.87	507.45	592.02	676.60	761.17	845.75
3384	21.15	42.30	84.60	169.20	253.80	338.40	423.00	507.60	592.20	676.80	761.40	846.00
3385	21.16	42.31	84.62	169.25	253.87	338.50	423.12	507.75	592.37	677.00	761.62	846.25
3386	21.16	42.32	84.65	169.30	253.95	338.60	423.25	507.90	592.55	677.20	761.85	846.50
3387	21.17	42.34	84.67	169.35	254.02	338.70	423.37	508.05	592.72	677.40	762.07	846.75
3388	21.17	42.35	84.70	169.40	254.10	338.80	423.50	508.20	592.90	677.60	762.30	847.00
3389	21.18	42.36	84.72	169.45	254.17	338.90	423.62	508.35	593.07	677.80	762.52	847.25
3390	21.19	42.37	84.75	169.50	254.25	339.00	423.75	508.50	593.25	678.00	762.75	847.50
3391	21.19	42.39	84.77	169.55	254.32	339.10	423.87	508.65	593.42	678.20	762.97	847.75
3392	21.20	42.40	84.80	169.60	254.40	339.20	424.00	508.80	593.60	678.40	763.20	848.00
3393	21.21	42.41	84.82	169.65	254.47	339.30	424.12	508.95	593.77	678.60	763.42	848.25
3394	21.21	42.42	84.85	169.70	254.55	339.40	424.25	509.10	593.95	678.80	763.65	848.50
3395	21.22	42.44	84.87	169.75	254.62	339.50	424.37	509.25	594.12	679.00	763.87	848.75
3396	21.22	42.45	84.90	169.80	254.70	339.60	424.50	509.40	594.30	679.20	764.10	849.00
3397	21.23	42.46	84.92	169.85	254.77	339.70	424.62	509.55	594.47	679.40	764.32	849.25
3398	21.24	42.47	84.95	169.90	254.85	339.80	424.75	509.70	594.65	679.60	764.55	849.50
3399	21.24	42.49	84.97	169.95	254.92	339.90	424.87	509.85	594.82	679.80	764.77	849.75
3400	21.25	42.50	85.00	170.00	255.00	340.00	425.00	510.00	595.00	680.00	765.00	850.00

3400 FEET.

Per Ton / Per Foot,	$11 / 27½ cts.	$12 / 30 cts.	$13 / 32½ cts.	$14 / 35 cts.	$15 / 37½ cts.	$16 / 40 cts.	$17 / 42½ cts.	$18 / 45 cts.	$19 / 47½ cts.	$20 / 50 cts.
Feet.										
3351	921.52	1005.30	1089.07	1172.85	1256.62	1340.40	1424.17	1507.95	1591.72	1675.50
3352	921.80	1005.60	1089.40	1173.20	1257.00	1340.80	1424.60	1508.40	1592.20	1676.00
3353	922.07	1005.90	1089.72	1173.55	1257.37	1341.20	1425.02	1508.85	1592.67	1676.50
3354	922.35	1006.20	1090.05	1173.90	1257.75	1341.60	1425.45	1509.30	1593.15	1677.00
3355	922.62	1006.50	1090.37	1174.25	1258.12	1342.00	1425.87	1509.75	1593.62	1677.50
3356	922.90	1006.80	1090.70	1174.60	1258.50	1342.40	1426.30	1510.20	1594.10	1678.00
3357	923.17	1007.10	1091.02	1174.95	1258.87	1342.80	1426.72	1510.65	1594.57	1678.50
3358	923.45	1007.40	1091.35	1175.30	1259.25	1343.20	1427.15	1511.10	1595.05	1679.00
3359	923.72	1007.70	1091.67	1175.65	1259.62	1343.60	1427.57	1511.55	1595.52	1679.50
3360	924.00	1008.00	1092.00	1176.00	1260.00	1344.00	1428.00	1512.00	1596.00	1680.00
3361	924.27	1008.30	1092.32	1176.35	1260.37	1344.40	1428.42	1512.45	1596.47	1680.50
3362	924.55	1008.60	1092.65	1176.70	1260.75	1344.80	1428.85	1512.90	1596.95	1681.00
3363	924.82	1008.90	1092.97	1177.05	1261.12	1345.20	1429.27	1513.35	1597.42	1681.50
3364	925.10	1009.20	1093.30	1177.40	1261.50	1345.60	1429.70	1513.80	1597.90	1682.00
3365	925.37	1009.50	1093.62	1177.75	1261.87	1346.00	1430.12	1514.25	1598.37	1682.50
3366	925.65	1009.80	1093.95	1178.10	1262.25	1346.40	1430.55	1514.70	1598.85	1683.00
3367	925.92	1010.10	1094.27	1178.45	1262.62	1346.80	1430.97	1515.15	1599.32	1683.50
3368	926.20	1010.40	1094.60	1178.80	1263.00	1347.20	1431.40	1515.60	1599.80	1684.00
3369	926.47	1010.70	1094.92	1179.15	1263.37	1347.60	1431.82	1516.05	1600.27	1684.50
3370	926.75	1011.00	1095.25	1179.50	1263.75	1348.00	1432.25	1516.50	1600.75	1685.00
3371	927.02	1011.30	1095.57	1179.85	1264.12	1348.40	1432.67	1516.95	1601.22	1685.50
3372	927.30	1011.60	1095.90	1180.20	1264.50	1348.80	1433.10	1517.40	1601.70	1686.00
3373	927.57	1011.90	1096.22	1180.55	1264.87	1349.20	1433.52	1517.85	1602.17	1686.50
3374	927.85	1012.20	1096.55	1180.90	1265.25	1349.60	1433.95	1518.30	1602.65	1687.00
3375	928.12	1012.50	1096.87	1181.25	1265.62	1350.00	1434.37	1518.75	1603.12	1687.50
3376	928.40	1012.80	1097.20	1181.60	1266.00	1350.40	1434.80	1519.20	1603.60	1688.00
3377	928.67	1013.10	1097.52	1181.95	1266.37	1350.80	1435.22	1519.65	1604.07	1688.50
3378	928.95	1013.40	1097.85	1182.30	1266.75	1351.20	1435.65	1520.10	1604.55	1689.00
3379	929.22	1013.70	1098.17	1182.65	1267.12	1351.60	1436.07	1520.55	1605.02	1689.50
3380	929.50	1014.00	1098.50	1183.00	1267.50	1352.00	1436.50	1521.00	1605.50	1690.00
3381	929.77	1014.30	1098.82	1183.35	1267.87	1352.40	1436.92	1521.45	1605.97	1690.50
3382	930.05	1014.60	1099.15	1183.70	1268.25	1352.80	1437.35	1521.90	1606.45	1691.00
3383	930.32	1014.90	1099.47	1184.05	1268.62	1353.20	1437.77	1522.35	1606.92	1691.50
3384	930.60	1015.20	1099.80	1184.40	1269.00	1353.60	1438.20	1522.80	1607.40	1692.00
3385	930.87	1015.50	1100.12	1184.75	1269.37	1354.00	1438.62	1523.25	1607.87	1692.50
3386	931.15	1015.80	1100.45	1185.10	1269.75	1354.40	1439.05	1523.70	1608.35	1693.00
3387	931.42	1016.10	1100.77	1185.45	1270.12	1354.80	1439.47	1524.15	1608.82	1693.50
3388	931.70	1016.40	1101.10	1185.80	1270.50	1355.20	1439.90	1524.60	1609.30	1694.00
3389	931.97	1016.70	1101.42	1186.15	1270.87	1355.60	1440.32	1525.05	1609.77	1694.50
3390	932.25	1017.00	1101.75	1186.50	1271.25	1356.00	1440.75	1525.50	1610.25	1695.00
3391	932.52	1017.30	1102.07	1186.85	1271.62	1356.40	1441.17	1525.95	1610.72	1695.50
3392	932.80	1017.60	1102.40	1187.20	1272.00	1356.80	1441.60	1526.40	1611.20	1696.00
3393	933.07	1017.90	1102.72	1187.55	1272.37	1357.20	1442.02	1526.85	1611.67	1696.50
3394	933.35	1018.20	1103.05	1187.90	1272.75	1357.60	1442.45	1527.30	1612.15	1697.00
3395	933.62	1018.50	1103.37	1188.25	1273.12	1358.00	1442.87	1527.75	1612.62	1697.50
3396	933.90	1018.80	1103.70	1188.60	1273.50	1358.40	1443.30	1528.20	1613.10	1698.00
3397	934.17	1019.10	1104.02	1188.95	1273.87	1358.80	1443.72	1528.65	1613.57	1698.50
3398	934.45	1019.40	1104.35	1189.30	1274.25	1359.20	1444.15	1529.10	1614.05	1699.00
3399	934.72	1019.70	1104.67	1189.65	1274.62	1359.60	1444.57	1529.55	1614.52	1699.50
3400	935.00	1020.00	1105.00	1190.00	1275.00	1360.00	1445.00	1530.00	1615.00	1700.00

3450 FEET.

Per Ton, Per Foot, Feet.	25c.	50c.	$1 2½ cts.	$2 5 cts.	$3 7½ cts.	$4 10 cts.	$5 12½ cts.	$6 15 cts.	$7 17½ cts.	$8 20 cts.	$9 22½ cts.	$10 25 cts.
3401	21.26	42.51	85.02	170.05	255.07	340.10	425.12	510.15	595.17	680.20	765.22	850.25
3402	21.26	42.52	85.05	170.10	255.15	340.20	425.25	510.30	595.35	680.40	765.45	850.50
3403	21.27	42.54	85.07	170.15	255.22	340.30	425.37	510.45	595.52	680.60	765.67	850.75
3404	21.27	42.55	85.10	170.20	255.30	340.40	425.50	510.60	595.70	680.80	765.90	851.00
3405	21.28	42.56	85.12	170.25	255.37	340.50	425.62	510.75	595.87	681.00	766.12	851.25
3406	21.29	42.57	85.15	170.30	255.45	340.60	425.75	510.90	596.05	681.20	766.35	851.50
3407	21.29	42.59	85.17	170.35	255.52	340.70	425.87	511.05	596.22	681.40	766.57	851.75
3408	21.30	42.60	85.20	170.40	255.60	340.80	426.00	511.20	596.40	681.60	766.80	852.00
3409	21.31	42.61	85.22	170.45	255.67	340.90	426.12	511.35	596.57	681.80	767.02	852.25
3410	21.31	42.62	85.25	170.50	255.75	341.00	426.25	511.50	596.75	682.00	767.25	852.50
3411	21.32	42.64	85.27	170.55	255.82	341.10	426.37	511.65	596.92	682.20	767.47	852.75
3412	21.32	42.65	85.30	170.60	255.90	341.20	426.50	511.80	597.10	682.40	767.70	853.00
3413	21.33	42.66	85.32	170.65	255.97	341.30	426.62	511.95	597.27	682.60	767.92	853.25
3414	21.34	42.67	85.35	170.70	256.05	341.40	426.75	512.10	597.45	682.80	768.15	853.50
3415	21.34	42.69	85.37	170.75	256.12	341.50	426.87	512.25	597.62	683.00	768.37	853.75
3416	21.35	42.70	85.40	170.80	256.20	341.60	427.00	512.40	597.80	683.20	768.60	854.00
3417	21.36	42.71	85.42	170.85	256.27	341.70	427.12	512.55	597.97	683.40	768.82	854.25
3418	21.36	42.72	85.45	170.90	256.35	341.80	427.25	512.70	598.15	683.60	769.05	854.50
3419	21.37	42.74	85.47	170.95	256.42	341.90	427.37	512.85	598.32	683.80	769.27	854.75
3420	21.37	42.75	85.50	171.00	256.50	342.00	427.50	513.00	598.50	684.00	769.50	855.00
3421	21.38	42.76	85.52	171.05	256.57	342.10	427.62	513.15	598.67	684.20	769.72	855.25
3422	21.39	42.77	85.55	171.10	256.65	342.20	427.75	513.30	598.85	684.40	769.95	855.50
3423	21.39	42.79	85.57	171.15	256.72	342.30	427.87	513.45	599.02	684.60	770.17	855.75
3424	21.40	42.80	85.60	171.20	256.80	342.40	428.00	513.60	599.20	684.80	770.40	856.00
3425	21.41	42.81	85.62	171.25	256.87	342.50	428.12	513.75	599.37	685.00	770.62	856.25
3426	21.41	42.82	85.65	171.30	256.95	342.60	428.25	513.90	599.55	685.20	770.85	856.50
3427	21.42	42.84	85.67	171.35	257.02	342.70	428.37	514.05	599.72	685.40	771.07	856.75
3428	21.42	42.85	85.70	171.40	257.10	342.80	428.50	514.20	599.90	685.60	771.30	857.00
3429	21.43	42.86	85.72	171.45	257.17	342.90	428.62	514.35	600.07	685.80	771.52	857.25
3430	21.44	42.87	85.75	171.50	257.25	343.00	428.75	514.50	600.25	686.00	771.75	857.50
3431	21.44	42.89	85.77	171.55	257.32	343.10	428.87	514.65	600.42	686.20	771.97	857.75
3432	21.45	42.90	85.80	171.60	257.40	343.20	429.00	514.80	600.60	686.40	772.20	858.00
3433	21.46	42.91	85.82	171.65	257.47	343.30	429.12	514.95	600.77	686.60	772.42	858.25
3434	21.46	42.92	85.85	171.70	257.55	343.40	429.25	515.10	600.95	686.80	772.65	858.50
3435	21.47	42.94	85.87	171.75	257.62	343.50	429.37	515.25	601.12	687.00	772.87	858.75
3436	21.47	42.95	85.90	171.80	257.70	343.60	429.50	515.40	601.30	687.20	773.10	859.00
3437	21.48	42.96	85.92	171.85	257.77	343.70	429.62	515.55	601.47	687.40	773.32	859.25
3438	21.49	42.97	85.95	171.90	257.85	343.80	429.75	515.70	601.65	687.60	773.55	859.50
3439	21.49	42.99	85.97	171.95	257.92	343.90	429.87	515.85	601.82	687.80	773.77	859.75
3440	21.50	43.00	86.00	172.00	258.00	344.00	430.00	516.00	602.00	688.00	774.00	860.00
3441	21.51	43.01	86.02	172.05	258.07	344.10	430.12	516.15	602.17	688.20	774.22	860.25
3442	21.51	43.02	86.05	172.10	258.15	344.20	430.25	516.30	602.35	688.40	774.45	860.50
3443	21.52	43.04	86.07	172.15	258.22	344.30	430.37	516.45	602.52	688.60	774.67	860.75
3444	21.52	43.05	86.10	172.20	258.30	344.40	430.50	516.60	602.70	688.80	774.90	861.00
3445	21.53	43.06	86.12	172.25	258.37	344.50	430.62	516.75	602.87	689.00	775.12	861.25
3446	21.54	43.07	86.15	172.30	258.45	344.60	430.75	516.90	603.05	689.20	775.35	861.50
3447	21.54	43.09	86.17	172.35	258.52	344.70	430.87	517.05	603.22	689.40	775.57	861.75
3448	21.55	43.10	86.20	172.40	258.60	344.80	431.00	517.20	603.40	689.60	775.80	862.00
3449	21.56	43.11	86.22	172.45	258.67	344.90	431.12	517.35	603.57	689.80	776.02	862.25
3450	21.56	43.12	86.25	172.50	258.75	345.00	431.25	517.50	603.75	690.00	776.25	862.50

3450 FEET.

Per Ton / Per Foot, Feet.	$11 27½ cts.	$12 30 cts.	$13 32½ cts.	$14 35 cts.	$15 37½ cts.	$16 40 cts.	$17 42½ cts.	$18 45 cts.	$19 47½ cts.	$20 50 cts.
3401	935.27	1020.30	1105.32	1190.35	1275.37	1360.40	1445.42	1530.45	1615.47	1700.50
3402	935.55	1020.60	1105.65	1190.70	1275.75	1360.80	1445.85	1530.90	1615.95	1701.00
3403	935.82	1020.90	1105.97	1191.05	1276.12	1361.20	1446.27	1531.35	1616.42	1701.50
3404	936.10	1021.20	1106.30	1191.40	1276.50	1361.60	1446.70	1531.80	1616.90	1702.00
3405	936.37	1021.50	1106.62	1191.75	1276.87	1362.00	1447.12	1532.25	1617.37	1702.50
3406	936.65	1021.80	1106.95	1192.10	1277.25	1362.40	1447.55	1532.70	1617.85	1703.00
3407	936.92	1022.10	1107.27	1192.45	1277.62	1362.80	1447.97	1533.15	1618.32	1703.50
3408	937.20	1022.40	1107.60	1192.80	1278.00	1363.20	1448.40	1533.60	1618.80	1704.00
3409	937.47	1022.70	1107.92	1193.15	1278.37	1363.60	1448.82	1534.05	1619.27	1704.50
3410	937.75	1023.00	1108.25	1193.50	1278.75	1364.00	1449.25	1534.50	1619.75	1705.00
3411	938.02	1023.30	1108.57	1193.85	1279.12	1364.40	1449.67	1534.95	1620.22	1705.50
3412	938.30	1023.60	1108.90	1194.20	1279.50	1364.80	1450.10	1535.40	1620.70	1706.00
3413	938.57	1023.90	1109.22	1194.55	1279.87	1365.20	1450.52	1535.85	1621.17	1706.50
3414	938.85	1024.20	1109.55	1194.90	1280.25	1365.60	1450.95	1536.30	1621.65	1707.00
3415	939.12	1024.50	1109.87	1195.25	1280.62	1366.00	1451.37	1536.75	1622.12	1707.50
3416	939.40	1024.80	1110.20	1195.60	1281.00	1366.40	1451.80	1537.20	1622.60	1708.00
3417	939.67	1025.10	1110.52	1195.95	1281.37	1366.80	1452.22	1537.65	1623.07	1708.50
3418	939.95	1025.40	1110.85	1196.30	1281.75	1367.20	1452.65	1538.10	1623.55	1709.00
3419	940.22	1025.70	1111.17	1196.65	1282.12	1367.60	1453.07	1538.55	1624.02	1709.50
3420	940.50	1026.00	1111.50	1197.00	1282.50	1368.00	1453.50	1539.00	1624.50	1710.00
3421	940.77	1026.30	1111.82	1197.35	1282.87	1368.40	1453.92	1539.45	1624.97	1710.50
3422	941.05	1026.60	1112.15	1197.70	1283.25	1368.80	1454.35	1539.90	1625.45	1711.00
3423	941.32	1026.90	1112.47	1198.05	1283.62	1369.20	1454.77	1540.35	1625.92	1711.50
3424	941.60	1027.20	1112.80	1198.40	1284.00	1369.60	1455.20	1540.80	1626.40	1712.00
3425	941.87	1027.50	1113.12	1198.75	1284.37	1370.00	1455.62	1541.25	1626.87	1712.50
3426	942.15	1027.80	1113.45	1199.10	1284.75	1370.40	1456.05	1541.70	1627.35	1713.00
3427	942.42	1028.10	1113.77	1199.45	1285.12	1370.80	1456.47	1542.15	1627.82	1713.50
3428	942.70	1028.40	1114.10	1199.80	1285.50	1371.20	1456.90	1542.60	1628.30	1714.00
3429	942.97	1028.70	1114.42	1200.15	1285.87	1371.60	1457.32	1543.05	1628.77	1714.50
3430	943.25	1029.00	1114.75	1200.50	1286.25	1372.00	1457.75	1543.50	1629.25	1715.00
3431	943.52	1029.30	1115.07	1200.85	1286.62	1372.40	1458.17	1543.95	1629.72	1715.50
3432	943.80	1029.60	1115.40	1201.20	1287.00	1372.80	1458.60	1544.40	1630.20	1716.00
3433	944.07	1029.90	1115.72	1201.55	1287.37	1373.20	1459.02	1544.85	1630.67	1716.50
3434	944.35	1030.20	1116.05	1201.90	1287.75	1373.60	1459.45	1545.30	1631.15	1717.00
3435	944.62	1030.50	1116.37	1202.25	1288.12	1374.00	1459.87	1545.75	1631.62	1717.50
3436	944.90	1030.80	1116.70	1202.60	1288.50	1374.40	1460.30	1546.20	1632.10	1718.00
3437	945.17	1031.10	1117.02	1202.95	1288.87	1374.80	1460.72	1546.65	1632.57	1718.50
3438	945.45	1031.40	1117.35	1203.30	1289.25	1375.20	1461.15	1547.10	1633.05	1719.00
3439	945.72	1031.70	1117.67	1203.65	1289.62	1375.60	1461.57	1547.55	1633.52	1719.50
3440	946.00	1032.00	1118.00	1204.00	1290.00	1376.00	1462.00	1548.00	1634.00	1720.00
3441	946.27	1032.30	1118.32	1204.35	1290.37	1376.40	1462.42	1548.45	1634.47	1720.50
3442	946.55	1032.60	1118.65	1204.70	1290.75	1376.80	1462.85	1548.90	1634.95	1721.00
3443	946.82	1032.90	1118.97	1205.05	1291.12	1377.20	1463.27	1549.35	1635.42	1721.50
3444	947.10	1033.20	1119.30	1205.40	1291.50	1377.60	1463.70	1549.80	1635.90	1722.00
3445	947.37	1033.50	1119.62	1205.75	1291.87	1378.00	1464.12	1550.25	1636.37	1722.50
3446	947.65	1033.80	1119.95	1206.10	1292.25	1378.40	1464.55	1550.70	1636.85	1723.00
3447	947.92	1034.10	1120.27	1206.45	1292.62	1378.80	1464.97	1551.15	1637.32	1723.50
3448	948.20	1034.40	1120.60	1206.80	1293.00	1379.20	1465.40	1551.60	1637.80	1724.00
3449	948.47	1034.70	1120.92	1207.15	1293.37	1379.60	1465.82	1552.05	1638.27	1724.50
3450	948.75	1035.00	1121.25	1207.50	1293.75	1380.00	1466.25	1552.50	1638.75	1725.00

3500 FEET.

Per Ton, 25c. Per Foot,		50c.	$1 2½ cts.	$2 5 cts.	$3 7½ cts.	$4 10 cts.	$5 12½ cts.	$6 15 cts.	$7 17½ cts.	$8 20 cts.	$9 22½ cts.	$10 25 cts.
Feet.												
3451	21.57	43.14	86.27	172.55	258.82	345.10	431.37	517.65	603.92	690.20	776.47	862.75
3452	21.57	43.15	86.30	172.60	258.90	345.20	431.50	517.80	604.10	690.40	776.70	863.00
3453	21.58	43.16	86.32	172.65	258.97	345.30	431.62	517.95	604.27	690.60	776.92	863.25
3454	21.59	43.17	86.35	172.70	259.05	345.40	431.75	518.10	604.45	690.80	777.15	863.50
3455	21.59	43.19	86.37	172.75	259.12	345.50	431.87	518.25	604.62	691.00	777.37	863.75
3456	21.60	43.20	86.40	172.80	259.20	345.60	432.00	518.40	604.80	691.20	777.60	864.00
3457	21.61	43.21	86.42	172.85	259.27	345.70	432.12	518.55	604.97	691.40	777.82	864.25
3458	21.61	43.22	86.45	172.90	259.35	345.80	432.25	518.70	605.15	691.60	778.05	864.50
3459	21.62	43.24	86.47	172.95	259.42	345.90	432.37	518.85	605.32	691.80	778.27	864.75
3460	21.62	43.25	86.50	173.00	259.50	346.00	432.50	519.00	605.50	692.00	778.50	865.00
3461	21.63	43.26	86.52	173.05	259.57	346.10	432.62	519.15	605.67	692.20	778.72	865.25
3462	21.64	43.27	86.55	173.10	259.65	346.20	432.75	519.30	605.85	692.40	778.95	865.50
3463	21.64	43.29	86.57	173.15	259.72	346.30	432.87	519.45	606.02	692.60	779.17	865.75
3464	21.65	43.30	86.60	173.20	259.80	346.40	433.00	519.60	606.20	692.80	779.40	866.00
3465	21.66	43.31	86.62	173.25	259.87	346.50	433.12	519.75	606.37	693.00	779.62	866.25
3466	21.66	43.32	86.65	173.30	259.95	346.60	433.25	519.90	606.55	693.20	779.85	866.50
3467	21.67	43.34	86.67	173.35	260.02	346.70	433.37	520.05	606.72	693.40	780.07	866.75
3468	21.67	43.35	86.70	173.40	260.10	346.80	433.50	520.20	606.90	693.60	780.30	867.00
3469	21.68	43.36	86.72	173.45	260.17	346.90	433.62	520.35	607.07	693.80	780.52	867.25
3470	21.69	43.37	86.75	173.50	260.25	347.00	433.75	520.50	607.25	694.00	780.75	867.50
3471	21.69	43.39	86.77	173.55	260.32	347.10	433.87	520.65	607.42	694.20	780.97	867.75
3472	21.70	43.40	86.80	173.60	260.40	347.20	434.00	520.80	607.60	694.40	781.20	868.00
3473	21.71	43.41	86.82	173.65	260.47	347.30	434.12	520.95	607.77	694.60	781.42	868.25
3474	21.71	43.42	86.85	173.70	260.55	347.40	434.25	521.10	607.95	694.80	781.65	868.50
3475	21.72	43.44	86.87	173.75	260.62	347.50	434.37	521.25	608.12	695.00	781.87	868.75
3476	21.72	43.45	86.90	173.80	260.70	347.60	434.50	521.40	608.30	695.20	782.10	869.00
3477	21.73	43.46	86.92	173.85	260.77	347.70	434.62	521.55	608.47	695.40	782.32	869.25
3478	21.74	43.47	86.95	173.90	260.85	347.80	434.75	521.70	608.65	695.60	782.55	869.50
3479	21.74	43.49	86.97	173.95	260.92	347.90	434.87	521.85	608.82	695.80	782.77	869.75
3480	21.75	43.50	87.00	174.00	261.00	348.00	435.00	522.00	609.00	696.00	783.00	870.00
3481	21.76	43.51	87.02	174.05	261.07	348.10	435.12	522.15	609.17	696.20	783.22	870.25
3482	21.76	43.52	87.05	174.10	261.15	348.20	435.25	522.30	609.35	696.40	783.45	870.50
3483	21.77	43.54	87.07	174.15	261.22	348.30	435.37	522.45	609.52	696.60	783.67	870.75
3484	21.77	43.55	87.10	174.20	261.30	348.40	435.50	522.60	609.70	696.80	783.90	871.00
3485	21.78	43.56	87.12	174.25	261.37	348.50	435.62	522.75	609.87	697.00	784.12	871.25
3486	21.79	43.57	87.15	174.30	261.45	348.60	435.75	522.90	610.05	697.20	784.35	871.50
3487	21.79	43.59	87.17	174.35	261.52	348.70	435.87	523.05	610.22	697.40	784.57	871.75
3488	21.80	43.60	87.20	174.40	261.60	348.80	436.00	523.20	610.40	697.60	784.80	872.00
3489	21.81	43.61	87.22	174.45	261.67	348.90	436.12	523.35	610.57	697.80	785.02	872.25
3490	21.81	43.62	87.25	174.50	261.75	349.00	436.25	523.50	610.75	698.00	785.25	872.50
3491	21.82	43.64	87.27	174.55	261.82	349.10	436.37	523.65	610.92	698.20	785.47	872.75
3492	21.82	43.65	87.30	174.60	261.90	349.20	436.50	523.80	611.10	698.40	785.70	873.00
3493	21.83	43.66	87.32	174.65	261.97	349.30	436.62	523.95	611.27	698.60	785.92	873.25
3494	21.84	43.67	87.35	174.70	262.05	349.40	436.75	524.10	611.45	698.80	786.15	873.50
3495	21.84	43.69	87.37	174.75	262.12	349.50	436.87	524.25	611.62	699.00	786.37	873.75
3496	21.85	43.70	87.40	174.80	262.20	349.60	437.00	524.40	611.80	699.20	786.60	874.00
3497	21.86	43.71	87.42	174.85	262.27	349.70	437.12	524.55	611.97	699.40	786.82	874.25
3498	21.86	43.72	87.45	174.90	262.35	349.80	437.25	524.70	612.15	699.60	787.05	874.50
3499	21.87	43.74	87.47	174.95	262.42	349.90	437.37	524.85	612.32	699.80	787.27	874.75
3500	21.87	43.75	87.50	175.00	262.50	350.00	437.50	525.00	612.50	700.00	787.50	875.00

3500 FEET.

Per Ton Per Foot,	$11 27½ cts.	$12 30 cts.	$13 32½ cts.	$14 35 cts.	$15 37½ cts.	$16 40 cts.	$17 42½ cts.	$18 45 cts.	$19 47½ cts.	$20 50 cts.
Feet.										
3451	949.02	1035.30	1121.57	1207.85	1294.12	1380.40	1466.67	1552.95	1639.22	1725.50
3452	949.30	1035.60	1121.90	1208.20	1294.50	1380.80	1467.10	1553.40	1639.70	1726.00
3453	949.57	1035.90	1122.22	1208.55	1294.87	1381.20	1467.52	1553.85	1640.17	1726.50
3454	949.85	1036.20	1122.55	1208.90	1295.25	1381.60	1467.95	1554.30	1640.65	1727.00
3455	950.12	1036.50	1122.87	1209.25	1295.62	1382.00	1468.37	1554.75	1641.12	1727.50
3456	950.40	1036.80	1123.20	1209.60	1296.00	1382.40	1468.80	1555.20	1641.60	1728.00
3457	950.67	1037.10	1123.52	1209.95	1296.37	1382.80	1469.22	1555.65	1642.07	1728.50
3458	950.95	1037.40	1123.85	1210.30	1296.75	1383.20	1469.65	1556.10	1642.55	1729.00
3459	951.22	1037.70	1124.17	1210.65	1297.12	1383.60	1470.07	1556.55	1643.02	1729.50
3460	951.50	1038.00	1124.50	1211.00	1297.50	1384.00	1470.50	1557.00	1643.50	1730.00
3461	951.77	1038.30	1124.82	1211.35	1297.87	1384.40	1470.92	1557.45	1643.97	1730.50
3462	952.05	1038.60	1125.15	1211.70	1298.25	1384.80	1471.35	1557.90	1644.45	1731.00
3463	952.32	1038.90	1125.47	1212.05	1298.62	1385.20	1471.77	1558.35	1644.92	1731.50
3464	952.60	1039.20	1125.80	1212.40	1299.00	1385.60	1472.20	1558.80	1645.40	1732.00
3465	952.87	1039.50	1126.12	1212.75	1299.37	1386.00	1472.62	1559.25	1645.87	1732.50
3466	953.15	1039.80	1126.45	1213.10	1299.75	1386.40	1473.05	1559.70	1646.35	1733.00
3467	953.42	1040.10	1126.77	1213.45	1300.12	1386.80	1473.47	1560.15	1646.82	1733.50
3468	953.70	1040.40	1127.10	1213.80	1300.50	1387.20	1473.90	1560.60	1647.30	1734.00
3469	953.97	1040.70	1127.42	1214.15	1300.87	1387.60	1474.32	1561.05	1647.77	1734.50
3470	954.25	1041.00	1127.75	1214.50	1301.25	1388.00	1474.75	1561.50	1648.25	1735.00
3471	954.52	1041.30	1128.07	1214.85	1301.62	1388.40	1475.17	1561.95	1648.72	1735.50
3472	954.80	1041.60	1128.40	1215.20	1302.00	1388.80	1475.60	1562.40	1649.20	1736.00
3473	955.07	1041.90	1128.72	1215.55	1302.37	1389.20	1476.02	1562.85	1649.67	1736.50
3474	955.35	1042.20	1129.05	1215.90	1302.75	1389.60	1476.45	1563.30	1650.15	1737.00
3475	955.62	1042.50	1129.37	1216.25	1303.12	1390.00	1476.87	1563.75	1650.62	1737.50
3476	955.90	1042.80	1129.70	1216.60	1303.50	1390.40	1477.30	1564.20	1651.10	1738.00
3477	956.17	1043.10	1130.02	1216.95	1303.87	1390.80	1477.72	1564.65	1651.57	1738.50
3478	956.45	1043.40	1130.35	1217.30	1304.25	1391.20	1478.15	1565.10	1652.05	1739.00
3479	956.72	1043.70	1130.67	1217.65	1304.62	1391.60	1478.57	1565.55	1652.52	1739.50
3480	957.00	1044.00	1131.00	1218.00	1305.00	1392.00	1479.00	1566.00	1653.00	1740.00
3481	957.27	1044.30	1131.32	1218.35	1305.37	1392.40	1479.42	1566.45	1653.47	1740.50
3482	957.55	1044.60	1131.65	1218.70	1305.75	1392.80	1479.85	1566.90	1653.95	1741.00
3483	957.82	1044.90	1131.97	1219.05	1306.12	1393.20	1480.27	1567.35	1654.42	1741.50
3484	958.10	1045.20	1132.30	1219.40	1306.50	1393.60	1480.70	1567.80	1654.90	1742.00
3485	958.37	1045.50	1132.62	1219.75	1306.87	1394.00	1481.12	1568.25	1655.37	1742.50
3486	958.65	1045.80	1132.95	1220.10	1307.25	1394.40	1481.55	1568.70	1655.85	1743.00
3487	958.92	1046.10	1133.27	1220.45	1307.62	1394.80	1481.97	1569.15	1656.32	1743.50
3488	959.20	1046.40	1133.60	1220.80	1308.00	1395.20	1482.40	1569.60	1656.80	1744.00
3489	959.47	1046.70	1133.92	1221.15	1308.37	1395.60	1482.82	1570.05	1657.27	1744.50
3490	959.75	1047.00	1134.25	1221.50	1308.75	1396.00	1483.25	1570.50	1657.75	1745.00
3491	960.02	1047.30	1134.57	1221.85	1309.12	1396.40	1483.67	1570.95	1658.22	1745.50
3492	960.30	1047.60	1134.90	1222.20	1309.50	1396.80	1484.10	1571.40	1658.70	1746.00
3493	960.57	1047.90	1135.22	1222.55	1309.87	1397.20	1484.52	1571.85	1659.17	1746.50
3494	960.85	1048.20	1135.55	1222.90	1310.25	1397.60	1484.95	1572.30	1659.65	1747.00
3495	961.12	1048.50	1135.87	1223.25	1310.62	1398.00	1485.37	1572.75	1660.12	1747.50
3496	961.40	1048.80	1136.20	1223.60	1311.00	1398.40	1485.80	1573.20	1660.60	1748.00
3497	961.67	1049.10	1136.52	1223.95	1311.37	1398.80	1486.22	1573.65	1661.07	1748.50
3498	961.95	1049.40	1136.85	1224.30	1311.75	1399.20	1486.65	1574.10	1661.55	1749.00
3499	962.22	1049.70	1137.17	1224.65	1312.12	1399.60	1487.07	1574.55	1662.02	1749.50
3500	962.50	1050.00	1137.50	1225.00	1312.50	1400.00	1487.50	1575.00	1662.50	1750.00

3550 FEET.

Per Ton,	25c.	50c.	$1	$2	$3	$4	$5	$6	$7	$8	$9	$10
Per Foot,			2½ cts.	5 cts.	7½ cts.	10 cts.	12½ cts.	15 cts.	17½ cts.	20 cts.	22½ cts.	25 cts.
Feet.												
3501	21.88	43.76	87.52	175.05	262.57	350.10	437.62	525.15	612.67	700.20	787.72	875.25
3502	21.89	43.77	87.55	175.10	262.65	350.20	437.75	525.30	612.85	700.40	787.95	875.50
3503	21.89	43.79	87.57	175.15	262.72	350.30	437.87	525.45	613.02	700.60	788.17	875.75
3504	21.90	43.80	87.60	175.20	262.80	350.40	438.00	525.60	613.20	700.80	788.40	876.00
3505	21.91	43.81	87.62	175.25	262.87	350.50	438.12	525.75	613.37	701.00	788.62	876.25
3506	21.91	43.82	87.65	175.30	262.95	350.60	438.25	525.90	613.55	701.20	788.85	876.50
3507	21.92	43.84	87.67	175.35	263.02	350.70	438.37	526.05	613.72	701.40	789.07	876.75
3508	21.92	43.85	87.70	175.40	263.10	350.80	438.50	526.20	613.90	701.60	789.30	877.00
3509	21.93	43.86	87.72	175.45	263.17	350.90	438.62	526.35	614.07	701.80	789.52	877.25
3510	21.94	43.87	87.75	175.50	263.25	351.00	438.75	526.50	614.25	702.00	789.75	877.50
3511	21.94	43.89	87.77	175.55	263.32	351.10	438.87	526.65	614.42	702.20	789.97	877.75
3512	21.95	43.90	87.80	175.60	263.40	351.20	439.00	526.80	614.60	702.40	790.20	878.00
3513	21.96	43.91	87.82	175.65	263.47	351.30	439.12	526.95	614.77	702.60	790.42	878.25
3514	21.96	43.92	87.85	175.70	263.55	351.40	439.25	527.10	614.95	702.80	790.65	878.50
3515	21.97	43.94	87.87	175.75	263.62	351.50	439.37	527.25	615.12	703.00	790.87	878.75
3516	21.97	43.95	87.90	175.80	263.70	351.60	439.50	527.40	615.30	703.20	791.10	879.00
3517	21.98	43.96	87.92	175.85	263.77	351.70	439.62	527.55	615.47	703.40	791.32	879.25
3518	21.99	43.97	87.95	175.90	263.85	351.80	439.75	527.70	615.65	703.60	791.55	879.50
3519	21.99	43.99	87.97	175.95	263.92	351.90	439.87	527.85	615.82	703.80	791.77	879.75
3520	22.00	44.00	88.00	176.00	264.00	352.00	440.00	528.00	616.00	704.00	792.00	880.00
3521	22.01	44.01	88.02	176.05	264.07	352.10	440.12	528.15	616.17	704.20	792.22	880.25
3522	22.01	44.02	88.05	176.10	264.15	352.20	440.25	528.30	616.35	704.40	792.45	880.50
3523	22.02	44.04	88.07	176.15	264.22	352.30	440.37	528.45	616.52	704.60	792.67	880.75
3524	22.02	44.05	88.10	176.20	264.30	352.40	440.50	528.60	616.70	704.80	792.90	881.00
3525	22.03	44.06	88.12	176.25	264.37	352.50	440.62	528.75	616.87	705.00	793.12	881.25
3526	22.04	44.07	88.15	176.30	264.45	352.60	440.75	528.90	617.05	705.20	793.35	881.50
3527	22.04	44.09	88.17	176.35	264.52	352.70	440.87	529.05	617.22	705.40	793.57	881.75
3528	22.05	44.10	88.20	176.40	264.60	352.80	441.00	529.20	617.40	705.60	793.80	882.00
3529	22.06	44.11	88.22	176.45	264.67	352.90	441.12	529.35	617.57	705.80	794.02	882.25
3530	22.06	44.12	88.25	176.50	264.75	353.00	441.25	529.50	617.75	706.00	794.25	882.50
3531	22.07	44.14	88.27	176.55	264.82	353.10	441.37	529.65	617.92	706.20	794.47	882.75
3532	22.07	44.15	88.30	176.60	264.90	353.20	441.50	529.80	618.10	706.40	794.70	883.00
3533	22.08	44.16	88.32	176.65	264.97	353.30	441.62	529.95	618.27	706.60	794.92	883.25
3534	22.09	44.17	88.35	176.70	265.05	353.40	441.75	530.10	618.45	706.80	795.15	883.50
3535	22.09	44.19	88.37	176.75	265.12	353.50	441.87	530.25	618.62	707.00	795.37	883.75
3536	22.10	44.20	88.40	176.80	265.20	353.60	442.00	530.40	618.80	707.20	795.60	884.00
3537	22.11	44.21	88.42	176.85	265.27	353.70	442.12	530.55	618.97	707.40	795.82	884.25
3538	22.11	44.22	88.45	176.90	265.35	353.80	442.25	530.70	619.15	707.60	796.05	884.50
3539	22.12	44.24	88.47	176.95	265.42	353.90	442.37	530.85	619.32	707.80	796.27	884.75
3540	22.12	44.25	88.50	177.00	265.50	354.00	442.50	531.00	619.50	708.00	796.50	885.00
3541	22.13	44.26	88.52	177.05	265.57	354.10	442.62	531.15	619.67	708.20	796.72	885.25
3542	22.14	44.27	88.55	177.10	265.65	354.20	442.75	531.30	619.85	708.40	796.95	885.50
3543	22.14	44.29	88.57	177.15	265.72	354.30	442.87	531.45	620.02	708.60	797.17	885.75
3544	22.15	44.30	88.60	177.20	265.80	354.40	443.00	531.60	620.20	708.80	797.40	886.00
3545	22.16	44.31	88.62	177.25	265.87	354.50	443.12	531.75	620.37	709.00	797.62	886.25
3546	22.16	44.32	88.65	177.30	265.95	354.60	443.25	531.90	620.55	709.20	797.85	886.50
3547	22.17	44.34	88.67	177.35	266.02	354.70	443.37	532.05	620.72	709.40	798.07	886.75
3548	22.17	44.35	88.70	177.40	266.10	354.80	443.50	532.20	620.90	709.60	798.30	887.00
3549	22.18	44.36	88.72	177.45	266.17	354.90	443.62	532.35	621.07	709.80	798.52	887.25
3550	22.19	44.37	88.75	177.50	266.25	355.00	443.75	532.50	621.25	710.00	798.75	887.50

3550 FEET.

Per Ton	$11	$12	$13	$14	$15	$16	$17	$18	$19	$20
Per Foot,	27½ cts.	30 cts.	32½ cts.	35 cts.	37½ cts.	40 cts.	42½ cts.	45 cts.	47½ cts.	50 cts.
Feet.										
3501	962.77	1050.30	1137.82	1225.35	1312.87	1400.40	1487.92	1575.45	1662.97	1750.50
3502	963.05	1050.60	1138.15	1225.70	1313.25	1400.80	1488.35	1575.90	1663.45	1751.00
3503	963.32	1050.90	1138.47	1226.05	1313.62	1401.20	1488.77	1576.35	1663.92	1751.50
3504	963.60	1051.20	1138.80	1226.40	1314.00	1401.60	1489.20	1576.80	1664.40	1752.00
3505	963.87	1051.50	1139.12	1226.75	1314.37	1402.00	1489.62	1577.25	1664.87	1752.50
3506	964.15	1051.80	1139.45	1227.10	1314.75	1402.40	1490.05	1577.70	1665.35	1753.00
3507	964.42	1052.10	1139.77	1227.45	1315.12	1402.80	1490.47	1578.15	1665.82	1753.50
3508	964.70	1052.40	1140.10	1227.80	1315.50	1403.20	1490.90	1578.60	1666.30	1754.00
3509	964.97	1052.70	1140.42	1228.15	1315.87	1403.60	1491.32	1579.05	1666.77	1754.50
3510	965.25	1053.00	1140.75	1228.50	1316.25	1404.00	1491.75	1579.50	1667.25	1755.00
3511	965.52	1053.30	1141.07	1228.85	1316.62	1404.40	1492.17	1579.95	1667.72	1755.50
3512	965.80	1053.60	1141.40	1229.20	1317.00	1404.80	1492.60	1580.40	1668.20	1756.00
3513	966.07	1053.90	1141.72	1229.55	1317.37	1405.20	1493.02	1580.85	1668.67	1756.50
3514	966.35	1054.20	1142.05	1229.90	1317.75	1405.60	1493.45	1581.30	1669.15	1757.00
3515	966.62	1054.50	1142.37	1230.25	1318.12	1406.00	1493.87	1581.75	1669.62	1757.50
3516	966.90	1054.80	1142.70	1230.60	1318.50	1406.40	1494.30	1582.20	1670.10	1758.00
3517	967.17	1055.10	1143.02	1230.95	1318.87	1406.80	1494.72	1582.65	1670.57	1758.50
3518	967.45	1055.40	1143.35	1231.30	1319.25	1407.20	1495.15	1583.10	1671.05	1759.00
3519	967.72	1055.70	1143.67	1231.65	1319.62	1407.60	1495.57	1583.55	1671.52	1759.50
3520	968.00	1056.00	1144.00	1232.00	1320.00	1408.00	1496.00	1584.00	1672.00	1760.00
3521	968.27	1056.30	1144.32	1232.35	1320.37	1408.40	1496.42	1584.45	1672.47	1760.50
3522	968.55	1056.60	1144.65	1232.70	1320.75	1408.80	1496.85	1584.90	1672.95	1761.00
3523	968.82	1056.90	1144.97	1233.05	1321.12	1409.20	1497.27	1585.35	1673.42	1761.50
3524	969.10	1057.20	1145.30	1233.40	1321.50	1409.60	1497.70	1585.80	1673.90	1762.00
3525	969.37	1057.50	1145.62	1233.75	1321.87	1410.00	1498.12	1586.25	1674.37	1762.50
3526	969.65	1057.80	1145.95	1234.10	1322.25	1410.40	1498.55	1586.70	1674.85	1763.00
3527	969.92	1058.10	1146.27	1234.45	1322.62	1410.80	1498.97	1587.15	1675.32	1763.50
3528	970.20	1058.40	1146.60	1234.80	1323.00	1411.20	1499.40	1587.60	1675.80	1764.00
3529	970.47	1058.70	1146.92	1235.15	1323.37	1411.60	1499.82	1588.05	1676.27	1764.50
3530	970.75	1059.00	1147.25	1235.50	1323.75	1412.00	1500.25	1588.50	1676.75	1765.00
3531	971.02	1059.30	1147.57	1235.85	1324.12	1412.40	1500.67	1588.95	1677.22	1765.50
3532	971.30	1059.60	1147.90	1236.20	1324.50	1412.80	1501.10	1589.40	1677.70	1766.00
3533	971.57	1059.90	1148.22	1236.55	1324.87	1413.20	1501.52	1589.85	1678.17	1766.50
3534	971.85	1060.20	1148.55	1236.90	1325.25	1413.60	1501.95	1590.30	1678.65	1767.00
3535	972.12	1060.50	1148.87	1237.25	1325.62	1414.00	1502.37	1590.75	1679.12	1767.50
3536	972.40	1060.80	1149.20	1237.60	1326.00	1414.40	1502.80	1591.20	1679.60	1768.00
3537	972.67	1061.10	1149.52	1237.95	1326.37	1414.80	1503.22	1591.65	1680.07	1768.50
3538	972.95	1061.40	1149.85	1238.30	1326.75	1415.20	1503.65	1592.10	1680.55	1769.00
3539	973.22	1061.70	1150.17	1238.65	1327.12	1415.60	1504.07	1592.55	1681.02	1769.50
3540	973.50	1062.00	1150.50	1239.00	1327.50	1416.00	1504.50	1593.00	1681.50	1770.00
3541	973.77	1062.30	1150.82	1239.35	1327.87	1416.40	1504.92	1593.45	1681.97	1770.50
3542	974.05	1062.60	1151.15	1239.70	1328.25	1416.80	1505.35	1593.90	1682.45	1771.00
3543	974.32	1062.90	1151.47	1240.05	1328.62	1417.20	1505.77	1594.35	1682.92	1771.50
3544	974.60	1063.20	1151.80	1240.40	1329.00	1417.60	1506.20	1594.80	1683.40	1772.00
3545	974.87	1063.50	1152.12	1240.75	1329.37	1418.00	1506.62	1595.25	1683.87	1772.50
3546	975.15	1063.80	1152.45	1241.10	1329.75	1418.40	1507.05	1595.70	1684.35	1773.00
3547	975.42	1064.10	1152.77	1241.45	1330.12	1418.80	1507.47	1596.15	1684.82	1773.50
3548	975.70	1064.40	1153.10	1241.80	1330.50	1419.20	1507.90	1596.60	1685.30	1774.00
3549	975.97	1064.70	1153.42	1242.15	1330.87	1419.60	1508.32	1597.05	1685.77	1774.50
3550	976.25	1065.00	1153.75	1242.50	1331.25	1420.00	1508.75	1597.50	1686.25	1775.00

Per Ton, / Per Foot,	25c.	50c.	$1 2½ cts.	$2 5 cts.	$3 7½ cts.	$4 10 cts.	$5 12½ cts.	$6 15 cts.	$7 17½ cts.	$8 20 cts.	$9 22½ cts.	$10 25 cts.
Feet.												
3551	22.19	44.39	88.77	177.55	266.32	355.10	443.87	532.65	621.42	710.20	798.97	887.75
3552	22.20	44.40	88.80	177.60	266.40	355.20	444.00	532.80	621.60	710.40	799.20	888.00
3553	22.21	44.41	88.82	177.65	266.47	355.30	444.12	532.95	621.77	710.60	799.42	888.25
3554	22.21	44.42	88.85	177.70	266.55	355.40	444.25	533.10	621.95	710.80	799.65	888.50
3555	22.22	44.44	88.87	177.75	266.62	355.50	444.37	533.25	622.12	711.00	799.87	888.75
3556	22.22	44.45	88.90	177.80	266.70	355.60	444.50	533.40	622.30	711.20	800.10	889.00
3557	22.23	44.46	88.92	177.85	266.77	355.70	444.62	533.55	622.47	711.40	800.32	889.25
3558	22.24	44.47	88.95	177.90	266.85	355.80	444.75	533.70	622.65	711.60	800.55	889.50
3559	22.24	44.49	88.97	177.95	266.92	355.90	444.87	533.85	622.82	711.80	800.77	889.75
3560	22.25	44.50	89.00	178.00	267.00	356.00	445.00	534.00	623.00	712.00	801.00	890.00
3561	22.26	44.51	89.02	178.05	267.07	356.10	445.12	534.15	623.17	712.20	801.22	890.25
3562	22.26	44.52	89.05	178.10	267.15	356.20	445.25	534.30	623.35	712.40	801.45	890.50
3563	22.27	44.54	89.07	178.15	267.22	356.30	445.37	534.45	623.52	712.60	801.67	890.75
3564	22.27	44.55	89.10	178.20	267.30	356.40	445.50	534.60	623.70	712.80	801.90	891.00
3565	22.28	44.56	89.12	178.25	267.37	356.50	445.62	534.75	623.87	713.00	802.12	891.25
3566	22.29	44.57	89.15	178.30	267.45	356.60	445.75	534.90	624.05	713.20	802.35	891.50
3567	22.29	44.59	89.17	178.35	267.52	356.70	445.87	535.05	624.22	713.40	802.57	891.75
3568	22.30	44.60	89.20	178.40	267.60	356.80	446.00	535.20	624.40	713.60	802.80	892.00
3569	22.31	44.61	89.22	178.45	267.67	356.90	446.12	535.35	624.57	713.80	803.02	892.25
3570	22.31	44.62	89.25	178.50	267.75	357.00	446.25	535.50	624.75	714.00	803.25	892.50
3571	22.32	44.64	89.27	178.55	267.82	357.10	446.37	535.65	624.92	714.20	803.47	892.75
3572	22.32	44.65	89.30	178.60	267.90	357.20	446.50	535.80	625.10	714.40	803.70	893.00
3573	22.33	44.66	89.32	178.65	267.97	357.30	446.62	535.95	625.27	714.60	803.92	893.25
3574	22.34	44.67	89.35	178.70	268.05	357.40	446.75	536.10	625.45	714.80	804.15	893.50
3575	22.34	44.69	89.37	178.75	268.12	357.50	446.87	536.25	625.62	715.00	804.37	893.75
3576	22.35	44.70	89.40	178.80	268.20	357.60	447.00	536.40	625.80	715.20	804.60	894.00
3577	22.36	44.71	89.42	178.85	268.27	357.70	447.12	536.55	625.97	715.40	804.82	894.25
3578	22.36	44.72	89.45	178.90	268.35	357.80	447.25	536.70	626.15	715.60	805.05	894.50
3579	22.37	44.74	89.47	178.95	268.42	357.90	447.37	536.85	626.32	715.80	805.27	894.75
3580	22.37	44.75	89.50	179.00	268.50	358.00	447.50	537.00	626.50	716.00	805.50	895.00
3581	22.38	44.76	89.52	179.05	268.57	358.10	447.62	537.15	626.67	716.20	805.72	895.25
3582	22.39	44.77	89.55	179.10	268.65	358.20	447.75	537.30	626.85	716.40	805.95	895.50
3583	22.39	44.79	89.57	179.15	268.72	358.30	447.87	537.45	627.02	716.60	806.17	895.75
3584	22.40	44.80	89.60	179.20	268.80	358.40	448.00	537.60	627.20	716.80	806.40	896.00
3585	22.41	44.81	89.62	179.25	268.87	358.50	448.12	537.75	627.37	717.00	806.62	896.25
3586	22.41	44.82	89.65	179.30	268.95	358.60	448.25	537.90	627.55	717.20	806.85	896.50
3587	22.42	44.84	89.67	179.35	269.02	358.70	448.37	538.05	627.72	717.40	807.07	896.75
3588	22.42	44.85	89.70	179.40	269.10	358.80	448.50	538.20	627.90	717.60	807.30	897.00
3589	22.43	44.86	89.72	179.45	269.17	358.90	448.62	538.35	628.07	717.80	807.52	897.25
3590	22.44	44.87	89.75	179.50	269.25	359.00	448.75	538.50	628.25	718.00	807.75	897.50
3591	22.44	44.89	89.77	179.55	269.32	359.10	448.87	538.65	628.42	718.20	807.97	897.75
3592	22.45	44.90	89.80	179.60	269.40	359.20	449.00	538.80	628.60	718.40	808.20	898.00
3593	22.46	44.91	89.82	179.65	269.47	359.30	449.12	538.95	628.77	718.60	808.42	898.25
3594	22.46	44.92	89.85	179.70	269.55	359.40	449.25	539.10	628.95	718.80	808.65	898.50
3595	22.47	44.94	89.87	179.75	269.62	359.50	449.37	539.25	629.12	719.00	808.87	898.75
3596	22.47	44.95	89.90	179.80	269.70	359.60	449.50	539.40	629.30	719.20	809.10	899.00
3597	22.48	44.96	89.92	179.85	269.77	359.70	449.62	539.55	629.47	719.40	809.32	899.25
3598	22.49	44.97	89.95	179.90	269.85	359.80	449.75	539.70	629.65	719.60	809.55	899.50
3599	22.49	44.99	89.97	179.95	269.92	359.90	449.87	539.85	629.82	719.80	809.77	899.75
3600	22.50	45.00	90.00	180.00	270.00	360.00	450.00	540.00	630.00	720.00	810.00	900.00

3600 FEET.

Feet.	Per Ton $11 Per Foot, 27½ cts.	$12 30 cts.	$13 32½ cts.	$14 35 cts.	$15 37½ cts.	$16 40 cts.	$17 42½ cts.	$18 45 cts.	$19 47½ cts.	$20 50 cts.
3551	976.52	1065.30	1154.07	1242.85	1331.62	1420.40	1509.17	1597.95	1686.72	1775.50
3552	976.80	1065.60	1154.40	1243.20	1332.00	1420.80	1509.60	1598.40	1687.20	1776.00
3553	977.07	1065.90	1154.72	1243.55	1332.37	1421.20	1510.02	1598.85	1687.67	1776.50
3554	977.35	1066.20	1155.05	1243.90	1332.75	1421.60	1510.45	1599.30	1688.15	1777.00
3555	977.62	1066.50	1155.37	1244.25	1333.12	1422.00	1510.87	1599.75	1688.62	1777.50
3556	977.90	1066.80	1155.70	1244.60	1333.50	1422.40	1511.30	1600.20	1689.10	1778.00
3557	978.17	1067.10	1156.02	1244.95	1333.87	1422.80	1511.72	1600.65	1689.57	1778.50
3558	978.45	1067.40	1156.35	1245.30	1334.25	1423.20	1512.15	1601.10	1690.05	1779.00
3559	978.72	1067.70	1156.67	1245.65	1334.62	1423.60	1512.57	1601.55	1690.52	1779.50
3560	979.00	1068.00	1157.00	1246.00	1335.00	1424.00	1513.00	1602.00	1691.00	1780.00
3561	979.27	1068.30	1157.32	1246.35	1335.37	1424.40	1513.42	1602.45	1691.47	1780.50
3562	979.55	1068.60	1157.65	1246.70	1335.75	1424.80	1513.85	1602.90	1691.95	1781.00
3563	979.82	1068.90	1157.97	1247.05	1336.12	1425.20	1514.27	1603.35	1692.42	1781.50
3564	980.10	1069.20	1158.30	1247.40	1336.50	1425.60	1514.70	1603.80	1692.90	1782.00
3565	980.37	1069.50	1158.62	1247.75	1336.87	1426.00	1515.12	1604.25	1693.37	1782.50
3566	980.65	1069.80	1158.95	1248.10	1337.25	1426.40	1515.55	1604.70	1693.85	1783.00
3567	980.92	1070.10	1159.27	1248.45	1337.62	1426.80	1515.97	1605.15	1694.32	1783.50
3568	981.20	1070.40	1159.60	1248.80	1338.00	1427.20	1516.40	1605.60	1694.80	1784.00
3569	981.47	1070.70	1159.92	1249.15	1338.37	1427.60	1516.82	1606.05	1695.27	1784.50
3570	981.75	1071.00	1160.25	1249.50	1338.75	1428.00	1517.25	1606.50	1695.75	1785.00
3571	982.02	1071.30	1160.57	1249.85	1339.12	1428.40	1517.67	1606.95	1696.22	1785.50
3572	982.30	1071.60	1160.90	1250.20	1339.50	1428.80	1518.10	1607.40	1696.70	1786.00
3573	982.57	1071.90	1161.22	1250.55	1339.87	1429.20	1518.52	1607.85	1697.17	1786.50
3574	982.85	1072.20	1161.55	1250.90	1340.25	1429.60	1518.95	1608.30	1697.65	1787.00
3575	983.12	1072.50	1161.87	1251.25	1340.62	1430.00	1519.37	1608.75	1698.12	1787.50
3576	983.40	1072.80	1162.20	1251.60	1341.00	1430.40	1519.80	1609.20	1698.60	1788.00
3577	983.67	1073.10	1162.52	1251.95	1341.37	1430.80	1520.22	1609.65	1699.07	1788.50
3578	983.95	1073.40	1162.85	1252.30	1341.75	1431.20	1520.65	1610.10	1699.55	1789.00
3579	984.22	1073.70	1163.17	1252.65	1342.12	1431.60	1521.07	1610.55	1700.02	1789.50
3580	984.50	1074.00	1163.50	1253.00	1342.50	1432.00	1521.50	1611.00	1700.50	1790.00
3581	984.77	1074.30	1163.82	1253.35	1342.87	1432.40	1521.92	1611.45	1700.97	1790.50
3582	985.05	1074.60	1164.15	1253.70	1343.25	1432.80	1522.35	1611.90	1701.45	1791.00
3583	985.32	1074.90	1164.47	1254.05	1343.62	1433.20	1522.77	1612.35	1701.92	1791.50
3584	985.60	1075.20	1164.80	1254.40	1344.00	1433.60	1523.20	1612.80	1702.40	1792.00
3585	985.87	1075.50	1165.12	1254.75	1344.37	1434.00	1523.62	1613.25	1702.87	1792.50
3586	986.15	1075.80	1165.45	1255.10	1344.75	1434.40	1524.05	1613.70	1703.35	1793.00
3587	986.42	1076.10	1165.77	1255.45	1345.12	1434.80	1524.47	1614.15	1703.82	1793.50
3588	986.70	1076.40	1166.10	1255.80	1345.50	1435.20	1524.90	1614.60	1704.30	1794.00
3589	986.97	1076.70	1166.42	1256.15	1345.87	1435.60	1525.32	1615.05	1704.77	1794.50
3590	987.25	1077.00	1166.75	1256.50	1346.25	1436.00	1525.75	1615.50	1705.25	1795.00
3591	987.52	1077.30	1167.07	1256.85	1346.62	1436.40	1526.17	1615.95	1705.72	1795.50
3592	987.80	1077.60	1167.40	1257.20	1347.00	1436.80	1526.60	1616.40	1706.20	1796.00
3593	988.07	1077.90	1167.72	1257.55	1347.37	1437.20	1527.02	1616.85	1706.67	1796.50
3594	988.35	1078.20	1168.05	1257.90	1347.75	1437.60	1527.45	1617.30	1707.15	1797.00
3595	988.62	1078.50	1168.37	1258.25	1348.12	1438.00	1527.87	1617.75	1707.62	1797.50
3596	988.90	1078.80	1168.70	1258.60	1348.50	1438.40	1528.30	1618.20	1708.10	1798.00
3597	989.17	1079.10	1169.02	1258.95	1348.87	1438.80	1528.72	1618.65	1708.57	1798.50
3598	989.45	1079.40	1169.35	1259.30	1349.25	1439.20	1529.15	1619.10	1709.05	1799.00
3599	989.72	1079.70	1169.67	1259.65	1349.62	1439.60	1529.57	1619.55	1709.52	1799.50
3600	990.00	1080.00	1170.00	1260.00	1350.00	1440.00	1530.00	1620.00	1710.00	1800.00

3650 FEET.

Per Ton,	25c.	50c.	$1	$2	$3	$4	$5	$6	$7	$8	$9	$10
Per Foot,			2½ cts.	5 cts.	7½ cts.	10 cts.	12½ cts.	15 cts.	17½ cts.	20 cts.	22½ cts.	25 cts.
Feet.												
3601	22.51	45.01	90.02	180.05	270.07	360.10	450.12	540.15	630.17	720.20	810.22	900.25
3602	22.51	45.02	90.05	180.10	270.15	360.20	450.25	540.30	630.35	720.40	810.45	900.50
3603	22.52	45.04	90.07	180.15	270.22	360.30	450.37	540.45	630.52	720.60	810.67	900.75
3604	22.52	45.05	90.10	180.20	270.30	360.40	450.50	540.60	630.70	720.80	810.90	901.00
3605	22.53	45.06	90.12	180.25	270.37	360.50	450.62	540.75	630.87	721.00	811.12	901.25
3606	22.54	45.07	90.15	180.30	270.45	360.60	450.75	540.90	631.05	721.20	811.35	901.50
3607	22.54	45.09	90.17	180.35	270.52	360.70	450.87	541.05	631.22	721.40	811.57	901.75
3608	22.55	45.10	90.20	180.40	270.60	360.80	451.00	541.20	631.40	721.60	811.80	902.00
3609	22.56	45.11	90.22	180.45	270.67	360.90	451.12	541.35	631.57	721.80	812.02	902.25
3610	22.56	45.12	90.25	180.50	270.75	361.00	451.25	541.50	631.75	722.00	812.25	902.50
3611	22.57	45.14	90.27	180.55	270.82	361.10	451.37	541.65	631.92	722.20	812.47	902.75
3612	22.57	45.15	90.30	180.60	270.90	361.20	451.50	541.80	632.10	722.40	812.70	903.00
3613	22.58	45.16	90.32	180.65	270.97	361.30	451.62	541.95	632.27	722.60	812.92	903.25
3614	22.59	45.17	90.35	180.70	271.05	361.40	451.75	542.10	632.45	722.80	813.15	903.50
3615	22.59	45.19	90.37	180.75	271.12	361.50	451.87	542.25	632.62	723.00	813.37	903.75
3616	22.60	45.20	90.40	180.80	271.20	361.60	452.00	542.40	632.80	723.20	813.60	904.00
3617	22.61	45.21	90.42	180.85	271.27	361.70	452.12	542.55	632.97	723.40	813.82	904.25
3618	22.61	45.22	90.45	180.90	271.35	361.80	452.25	542.70	633.15	723.60	814.05	904.50
3619	22.62	45.24	90.47	180.95	271.42	361.90	452.37	542.85	633.32	723.80	814.27	904.75
3620	22.62	45.25	90.50	181.00	271.50	362.00	452.50	543.00	633.50	724.00	814.50	905.00
3621	22.63	45.26	90.52	181.05	271.57	362.10	452.62	543.15	633.67	724.20	814.72	905.25
3622	22.64	45.27	90.55	181.10	271.65	362.20	452.75	543.30	633.85	724.40	814.95	905.50
3623	22.64	45.29	90.57	181.15	271.72	362.30	452.87	543.45	634.02	724.60	815.17	905.75
3624	22.65	45.30	90.60	181.20	271.80	362.40	453.00	543.60	634.20	724.80	815.40	906.00
3625	22.66	45.31	90.62	181.25	271.87	362.50	453.12	543.75	634.37	725.00	815.62	906.25
3626	22.66	45.32	90.65	181.30	271.95	362.60	453.25	543.90	634.55	725.20	815.85	906.50
3627	22.67	45.34	90.67	181.35	272.02	362.70	453.37	544.05	634.72	725.40	816.07	906.75
3628	22.67	45.35	90.70	181.40	272.10	362.80	453.50	544.20	634.90	725.60	816.30	907.00
3629	22.68	45.36	90.72	181.45	272.17	362.90	453.62	544.35	635.07	725.80	816.52	907.25
3630	22.69	45.37	90.75	181.50	272.25	363.00	453.75	544.50	635.25	726.00	816.75	907.50
3631	22.69	45.39	90.77	181.55	272.32	363.10	453.87	544.65	635.42	726.20	816.97	907.75
3632	22.70	45.40	90.80	181.60	272.40	363.20	454.00	544.80	635.60	726.40	817.20	908.00
3633	22.71	45.41	90.82	181.65	272.47	363.30	454.12	544.95	635.77	726.60	817.42	908.25
3634	22.71	45.42	90.85	181.70	272.55	363.40	454.25	545.10	635.95	726.80	817.65	908.50
3635	22.72	45.44	90.87	181.75	272.62	363.50	454.37	545.25	636.12	727.00	817.87	908.75
3636	22.72	45.45	90.90	181.80	272.70	363.60	454.50	545.40	636.30	727.20	818.10	909.00
3637	22.73	45.46	90.92	181.85	272.77	363.70	454.62	545.55	636.47	727.40	818.32	909.25
3638	22.74	45.47	90.95	181.90	272.85	363.80	454.75	545.70	636.65	727.60	818.55	909.50
3639	22.74	45.49	90.97	181.95	272.92	363.90	454.87	545.85	636.82	727.80	818.77	909.75
3640	22.75	45.50	91.00	182.00	273.00	364.00	455.00	546.00	637.00	728.00	819.00	910.00
3641	22.76	45.51	91.02	182.05	273.07	364.10	455.12	546.15	637.17	728.20	819.22	910.25
3642	22.76	45.52	91.05	182.10	273.15	364.20	455.25	546.30	637.35	728.40	819.45	910.50
3643	22.77	45.54	91.07	182.15	273.22	364.30	455.37	546.45	637.52	728.60	819.67	910.75
3644	22.77	45.55	91.10	182.20	273.30	364.40	455.50	546.60	637.70	728.80	819.90	911.00
3645	22.78	45.56	91.12	182.25	273.37	364.50	455.62	546.75	637.87	729.00	820.12	911.25
3646	22.79	45.57	91.15	182.30	273.45	364.60	455.75	546.90	638.05	729.20	820.35	911.50
3647	22.79	45.59	91.17	182.35	273.52	364.70	455.87	547.05	638.22	729.40	820.57	911.75
3648	22.80	45.60	91.20	182.40	273.60	364.80	456.00	547.20	638.40	729.60	820.80	912.00
3649	22.81	45.61	91.22	182.45	273.67	364.90	456.12	547.35	638.57	729.80	821.02	912.25
3650	22.81	45.62	91.25	182.50	273.75	365.00	456.25	547.50	638.75	730.00	821.25	912.50

3650 FEET.

Per Ton	$11	$12	$13	$14	$15	$16	$17	$18	$19	$20
Per Foot,	27¼ cts.	30 cts.	32½ cts.	35 cts.	37½ cts.	40 cts.	42½ cts.	45 cts.	47½ cts.	50 cts.
Feet.										
3601	990.27	1080.30	1170.32	1260.35	1350.37	1440.40	1530.42	1620.45	1710.47	1800.50
3602	990.55	1080.60	1170.65	1260.70	1350.75	1440.80	1530.85	1620.90	1710.95	1801.00
3603	990.82	1080.90	1170.97	1261.05	1351.12	1441.20	1531.27	1621.35	1711.42	1801.50
3604	991.10	1081.20	1171.30	1261.40	1351.50	1441.60	1531.70	1621.80	1711.90	1802.00
3605	991.37	1081.50	1171.62	1261.75	1351.87	1442.00	1532.12	1622.25	1712.37	1802.50
3606	991.65	1081.80	1171.95	1262.10	1352.25	1442.40	1532.55	1622.70	1712.85	1803.00
3607	991.92	1082.10	1172.27	1262.45	1352.62	1442.80	1532.97	1623.15	1713.32	1803.50
3608	992.20	1082.40	1172.60	1262.80	1353.00	1443.20	1533.40	1623.60	1713.80	1804.00
3609	992.47	1082.70	1172.92	1263.15	1353.37	1443.60	1533.82	1624.05	1714.27	1804.50
3610	992.75	1083.00	1173.25	1263.50	1353.75	1444.00	1534.25	1624.50	1714.75	1805.00
3611	993.02	1083.30	1173.57	1263.85	1354.12	1444.40	1534.67	1624.95	1715.22	1805.50
3612	993.30	1083.60	1173.90	1264.20	1354.50	1444.80	1535.10	1625.40	1715.70	1806.00
3613	993.57	1083.90	1174.22	1264.55	1354.87	1445.20	1535.52	1625.85	1716.17	1806.50
3614	993.85	1084.20	1174.55	1264.90	1355.25	1445.60	1535.95	1626.30	1716.65	1807.00
3615	994.12	1084.50	1174.87	1265.25	1355.62	1446.00	1536.37	1626.75	1717.12	1807.50
3616	994.40	1084.80	1175.20	1265.60	1356.00	1446.40	1536.80	1627.20	1717.60	1808.00
3617	994.67	1085.10	1175.52	1265.95	1356.37	1446.80	1537.22	1627.65	1718.07	1808.50
3618	994.95	1085.40	1175.85	1266.30	1356.75	1447.20	1537.65	1628.10	1718.55	1809.00
3619	995.22	1085.70	1176.17	1266.65	1357.12	1447.60	1538.07	1628.55	1719.02	1809.50
3620	995.50	1086.00	1176.50	1267.00	1357.50	1448.00	1538.50	1629.00	1719.50	1810.00
3621	995.77	1086.30	1176.82	1267.35	1357.87	1448.40	1538.92	1629.45	1719.97	1810.50
3622	996.05	1086.60	1177.15	1267.70	1358.25	1448.80	1539.35	1629.90	1720.45	1811.00
3623	996.32	1086.90	1177.47	1268.05	1358.62	1449.20	1539.77	1630.35	1720.92	1811.50
3624	996.60	1087.20	1177.80	1268.40	1359.00	1449.60	1540.20	1630.80	1721.40	1812.00
3625	996.87	1087.50	1178.12	1268.75	1359.37	1450.00	1540.62	1631.25	1721.87	1812.50
3626	997.15	1087.80	1178.45	1269.10	1359.75	1450.40	1541.05	1631.70	1722.35	1813.00
3627	997.42	1088.10	1178.77	1269.45	1360.12	1450.80	1541.47	1632.15	1722.82	1813.50
3628	997.70	1088.40	1179.10	1269.80	1360.50	1451.20	1541.90	1632.60	1723.30	1814.00
3629	997.97	1088.70	1179.42	1270.15	1360.87	1451.60	1542.32	1633.05	1723.77	1814.50
3630	998.25	1089.00	1179.75	1270.50	1361.25	1452.00	1542.75	1633.50	1724.25	1815.00
3631	998.52	1089.30	1180.07	1270.85	1361.62	1452.40	1543.17	1633.95	1724.72	1815.50
3632	998.80	1089.60	1180.40	1271.20	1362.00	1452.80	1543.60	1634.40	1725.20	1816.00
3633	999.07	1089.90	1180.72	1271.55	1362.37	1453.20	1544.02	1634.85	1725.67	1816.50
3634	999.35	1090.20	1181.05	1271.90	1362.75	1453.60	1544.45	1635.30	1726.15	1817.00
3635	999.62	1090.50	1181.37	1272.25	1363.12	1454.00	1544.87	1635.75	1726.62	1817.50
3636	999.90	1090.80	1181.70	1272.60	1363.50	1454.40	1545.30	1636.20	1727.10	1818.00
3637	1000.17	1091.10	1182.02	1272.95	1363.87	1454.80	1545.72	1636.65	1727.57	1818.50
3638	1000.45	1091.40	1182.35	1273.30	1364.25	1455.20	1546.15	1637.10	1728.05	1819.00
3639	1000.72	1091.70	1182.67	1273.65	1364.62	1455.60	1546.57	1637.55	1728.52	1819.50
3640	1001.00	1092.00	1183.00	1274.00	1365.00	1456.00	1547.00	1638.00	1729.00	1820.00
3641	1001.27	1092.30	1183.32	1274.35	1365.37	1456.40	1547.42	1638.45	1729.47	1820.50
3642	1001.55	1092.60	1183.65	1274.70	1365.75	1456.80	1547.85	1638.90	1729.95	1821.00
3643	1001.82	1092.90	1183.97	1275.05	1366.12	1457.20	1548.25	1639.35	1730.42	1821.50
3644	1002.10	1093.20	1184.30	1275.40	1366.50	1457.60	1548.70	1639.80	1730.90	1822.00
3645	1002.37	1093.50	1184.62	1275.75	1366.87	1458.00	1549.12	1640.25	1731.37	1822.50
3646	1002.65	1093.80	1184.95	1276.10	1367.25	1458.40	1549.55	1640.70	1731.85	1823.00
3647	1002.92	1094.10	1185.27	1276.45	1367.62	1458.80	1549.97	1641.15	1732.32	1823.50
3648	1003.20	1094.40	1185.60	1276.80	1368.00	1459.20	1550.40	1641.60	1732.80	1824.00
3649	1003.47	1094.70	1185.92	1277.15	1368.37	1459.60	1550.82	1642.05	1733.27	1824.50
3650	1003.75	1095.00	1186.25	1277.50	1368.75	1460.00	1551.25	1642.50	1733.75	1825.00

3700 FEET.

Per Ton,	25c.	50c.	$1	$2	$3	$4	$5	$6	$7	$8	$9	$10
Per Foot,			2½ cts.	5 cts.	7½ cts.	10 cts.	12½ cts.	15 cts.	17½ cts.	20 cts.	22½ cts.	25 cts.
Feet.												
3651	22.82	45.64	91.27	182.55	273.82	365.10	456.37	547.65	638.92	730.20	821.47	912.75
3652	22.82	45.65	91.30	182.60	273.90	365.20	456.50	547.80	639.10	730.40	821.70	913.00
3653	22.83	45.66	91.32	182.65	273.97	365.30	456.62	547.95	639.27	730.60	821.92	913.25
3654	22.84	45.67	91.35	182.70	274.05	365.40	456.75	548.10	639.45	730.80	822.15	913.50
3655	22.84	45.69	91.37	182.75	274.12	365.50	456.87	548.25	639.62	731.00	822.37	913.75
3656	22.85	45.70	91.40	182.80	274.20	365.60	457.00	548.40	639.80	731.20	822.60	914.00
3657	22.86	45.71	91.42	182.85	274.27	365.70	457.12	548.55	639.97	731.40	822.82	914.25
3658	22.86	45.72	91.45	182.90	274.35	365.80	457.25	548.70	640.15	731.60	823.05	914.50
3659	22.87	45.74	91.47	182.95	274.42	365.90	457.37	548.85	640.32	731.80	823.27	914.75
3660	22.87	45.75	91.50	183.00	274.50	366.00	457.50	549.00	640.50	732.00	823.50	915.00
3661	22.88	45.76	91.52	183.05	274.57	366.10	457.62	549.15	640.67	732.20	823.72	915.25
3662	22.89	45.77	91.55	183.10	274.65	366.20	457.75	549.30	640.85	732.40	823.95	915.50
3663	22.89	45.79	91.57	183.15	274.72	366.30	457.87	549.45	641.02	732.60	824.17	915.75
3664	22.90	45.80	91.60	183.20	274.80	366.40	458.00	549.60	641.20	732.80	824.40	916.00
3665	22.91	45.81	91.62	183.25	274.87	366.50	458.12	549.75	641.37	733.00	824.62	916.25
3666	22.91	45.82	91.65	183.30	274.95	366.60	458.25	549.90	641.55	733.20	824.85	916.50
3667	22.92	45.84	91.67	183.35	275.02	366.70	458.37	550.05	641.72	733.40	825.07	916.75
3668	22.92	45.85	91.70	183.40	275.10	366.80	458.50	550.20	641.90	733.60	825.30	917.00
3669	22.93	45.86	91.72	183.45	275.17	366.90	458.62	550.35	642.07	733.80	825.52	917.25
3670	22.94	45.87	91.75	183.50	275.25	367.00	458.75	550.50	642.25	734.00	825.75	917.50
3671	22.94	45.89	91.77	183.55	275.32	367.10	458.87	550.65	642.42	734.20	825.97	917.75
3672	22.95	45.90	91.80	183.60	275.40	367.20	459.00	550.80	642.60	734.40	826.20	918.00
3673	22.96	45.91	91.82	183.65	275.47	367.30	459.12	550.95	642.77	734.60	826.42	918.25
3674	22.96	45.92	91.85	183.70	275.55	367.40	459.25	551.10	642.95	734.80	826.65	918.50
3675	22.97	45.94	91.87	183.75	275.62	367.50	459.37	551.25	643.12	735.00	826.87	918.75
3676	22.97	45.95	91.90	183.80	275.70	367.60	459.50	551.40	643.30	735.20	827.10	919.00
3677	22.98	45.96	91.92	183.85	275.77	367.70	459.62	551.55	643.47	735.40	827.32	919.25
3678	22.99	45.97	91.95	183.90	275.85	367.80	459.75	551.70	643.65	735.60	827.55	919.50
3679	22.99	45.99	91.97	183.95	275.92	367.90	459.87	551.85	643.82	735.80	827.77	919.75
3680	23.00	46.00	92.00	184.00	276.00	368.00	460.00	552.00	644.00	736.00	828.00	920.00
3681	23.01	46.01	92.02	184.05	276.07	368.10	460.12	552.15	644.17	736.20	828.22	920.25
3682	23.01	46.02	92.05	184.10	276.15	368.20	460.25	552.30	644.35	736.40	828.45	920.50
3683	23.02	46.04	92.07	184.15	276.22	368.30	460.37	552.45	644.52	736.60	828.67	920.75
3684	23.02	46.05	92.10	184.20	276.30	368.40	460.50	552.60	644.70	736.80	828.90	921.00
3685	23.03	46.06	92.12	184.25	276.37	368.50	460.62	552.75	644.87	737.00	829.12	921.25
3686	23.04	46.07	92.15	184.30	276.45	368.60	460.75	552.90	645.05	737.20	829.35	921.50
3687	23.04	46.09	92.17	184.35	276.52	368.70	460.87	553.05	645.22	737.40	829.57	921.75
3688	23.05	46.10	92.20	184.40	276.60	368.80	461.00	553.20	645.40	737.60	829.80	922.00
3689	23.06	46.11	92.22	184.45	276.67	368.90	461.12	553.35	645.57	737.80	830.02	922.25
3690	23.06	46.12	92.25	184.50	276.75	369.00	461.25	553.50	645.75	738.00	830.25	922.50
3691	23.07	46.14	92.27	184.55	276.82	369.10	461.37	553.65	645.92	738.20	830.47	922.75
3692	23.07	46.15	92.30	184.60	276.90	369.20	461.50	553.80	646.10	738.40	830.70	923.00
3693	23.08	46.16	92.32	184.65	276.97	369.30	461.62	553.95	646.27	738.60	830.92	923.25
3694	23.09	46.17	92.35	184.70	277.05	369.40	461.75	554.10	646.45	738.80	831.15	923.50
3695	23.09	46.19	92.37	184.75	277.12	369.50	461.87	554.25	646.62	739.00	831.37	923.75
3696	23.10	46.20	92.40	184.80	277.20	369.60	462.00	554.40	646.80	739.20	831.60	924.00
3697	23.11	46.21	92.42	184.85	277.27	369.70	462.12	554.55	646.97	739.40	831.82	924.25
3698	23.11	46.22	92.45	184.90	277.35	369.80	462.25	554.70	647.15	739.60	832.05	924.50
3699	23.12	46.24	92.47	184.95	277.42	369.90	462.37	554.85	647.32	739.80	832.27	924.75
3700	23.12	46.25	92.50	185.00	277.50	370.00	462.50	555.00	647.50	740.00	832.50	925.00

3700 FEET.

Per Ton, Per Foot,	$11 27½ cts.	$12 30 cts.	$13 32½ cts.	$14 35 cts.	$15 37½ cts.	$16 40 cts.	$17 42½ cts.	$18 45 cts.	$19 47½ cts.	$20 50 cts.
Feet.										
3651	1004.02	1095.30	1186.57	1277.85	1369.12	1460.40	1551.67	1642.95	1734.22	1825.50
3652	1004.30	1095.60	1186.90	1278.20	1369.50	1460.80	1552.10	1643.40	1734.70	1826.00
3653	1004.57	1095.90	1187.22	1278.55	1369.87	1461.20	1552.52	1643.85	1735.17	1826.50
3654	1004.85	1096.20	1187.55	1278.90	1370.25	1461.60	1552.95	1644.30	1735.65	1827.00
3655	1005.12	1096.50	1187.87	1279.25	1370.62	1462.00	1553.37	1644.75	1736.12	1827.50
3656	1005.40	1096.80	1188.20	1279.60	1371.00	1462.40	1553.80	1645.20	1736.60	1828.00
3657	1005.67	1097.10	1188.52	1279.95	1371.37	1462.80	1554.22	1645.65	1737.07	1828.50
3658	1005.95	1097.40	1188.85	1280.30	1371.75	1463.20	1554.65	1646.10	1737.55	1829.00
3659	1006.22	1097.70	1189.17	1280.65	1372.12	1463.60	1555.07	1646.55	1738.02	1829.50
3660	1006.50	1098.00	1189.50	1281.00	1372.50	1464.00	1555.50	1647.00	1738.50	1830.00
3661	1006.77	1098.30	1189.82	1281.35	1372.87	1464.40	1555.92	1647.45	1738.97	1830.50
3662	1007.05	1098.60	1190.15	1281.70	1373.25	1464.80	1556.35	1647.90	1739.45	1831.00
3663	1007.32	1098.90	1190.47	1282.05	1373.62	1465.20	1556.77	1648.35	1739.92	1831.50
3664	1007.60	1099.20	1190.80	1282.40	1374.00	1465.60	1557.20	1648.80	1740.40	1832.00
3665	1007.87	1099.50	1191.12	1282.75	1374.37	1466.00	1557.62	1649.25	1740.87	1832.50
3666	1008.15	1099.80	1191.45	1283.10	1374.75	1466.40	1558.05	1649.70	1741.35	1833.00
3667	1008.42	1100.10	1191.77	1283.45	1375.12	1466.80	1558.47	1650.15	1741.82	1833.50
3668	1008.70	1100.40	1192.10	1283.80	1375.50	1467.20	1558.90	1650.60	1742.30	1834.00
3669	1008.97	1100.70	1192.42	1284.15	1375.87	1467.60	1559.32	1651.05	1742.77	1834.50
3670	1009.25	1101.00	1192.75	1284.50	1376.25	1468.00	1559.75	1651.50	1743.25	1835.00
3671	1009.52	1101.30	1193.07	1284.85	1376.62	1468.40	1560.17	1651.95	1743.72	1835.50
3672	1009.80	1101.60	1193.40	1285.20	1377.00	1468.80	1560.60	1652.40	1744.20	1836.00
3673	1010.07	1101.90	1193.72	1285.55	1377.37	1469.20	1561.02	1652.85	1744.67	1836.50
3674	1010.35	1102.20	1194.05	1285.90	1377.75	1469.60	1561.45	1653.30	1745.15	1837.00
3675	1010.62	1102.50	1194.37	1286.25	1378.12	1470.00	1561.87	1653.75	1745.62	1837.50
3676	1010.90	1102.80	1194.70	1286.60	1378.50	1470.40	1562.30	1654.20	1746.10	1838.00
3677	1011.17	1103.10	1195.02	1286.95	1378.87	1470.80	1562.72	1654.65	1746.57	1838.50
3678	1011.45	1103.40	1195.35	1287.30	1379.25	1471.20	1563.15	1655.10	1747.05	1839.00
3679	1011.72	1103.70	1195.67	1287.65	1379.62	1471.60	1563.57	1655.55	1747.52	1839.50
3680	1012.00	1104.00	1196.00	1288.00	1380.00	1472.00	1564.00	1656.00	1748.00	1840.00
3681	1012.27	1104.30	1196.32	1288.35	1380.37	1472.40	1564.42	1656.45	1748.47	1840.50
3682	1012.55	1104.60	1196.65	1288.70	1380.75	1472.80	1564.85	1656.90	1748.95	1841.00
3683	1012.82	1104.90	1196.97	1289.05	1381.12	1473.20	1565.27	1657.35	1749.42	1841.50
3684	1013.10	1105.20	1197.30	1289.40	1381.50	1473.60	1565.70	1657.80	1749.90	1842.00
3685	1013.37	1105.50	1197.62	1289.75	1381.87	1474.00	1566.12	1658.25	1750.37	1842.50
3686	1013.65	1105.80	1197.95	1290.10	1382.25	1474.40	1566.55	1658.70	1750.85	1843.00
3687	1013.92	1106.10	1198.27	1290.45	1382.62	1474.80	1566.97	1659.15	1751.32	1843.50
3688	1014.20	1106.40	1198.60	1290.80	1383.00	1475.20	1567.40	1659.60	1751.80	1844.00
3689	1014.47	1106.70	1198.92	1291.15	1383.37	1475.60	1567.82	1660.05	1752.27	1844.50
3690	1014.75	1107.00	1199.25	1291.50	1383.75	1476.00	1568.25	1660.50	1752.75	1845.00
3691	1015.02	1107.30	1199.57	1291.85	1384.12	1476.40	1568.67	1660.95	1753.22	1845.50
3692	1015.30	1107.60	1199.90	1292.20	1384.50	1476.80	1569.10	1661.40	1753.70	1846.00
3693	1015.57	1107.90	1200.22	1292.55	1384.87	1477.20	1569.52	1661.85	1754.17	1846.50
3694	1015.85	1108.20	1200.55	1292.90	1385.25	1477.60	1569.95	1662.30	1754.65	1847.00
3695	1016.12	1108.50	1200.87	1293.25	1385.62	1478.00	1570.37	1662.75	1755.12	1847.50
3696	1016.40	1108.80	1201.20	1293.60	1386.00	1478.40	1570.80	1663.20	1755.60	1848.00
3697	1016.67	1109.10	1201.52	1293.95	1386.37	1478.80	1571.22	1663.65	1756.07	1848.50
3698	1016.95	1109.40	1201.85	1294.30	1386.75	1479.20	1571.65	1664.10	1756.55	1849.00
3699	1017.22	1109.70	1202.17	1294.65	1387.12	1479.60	1572.07	1664.55	1757.02	1849.50
3700	1017.50	1110.00	1202.50	1295.00	1387.50	1480.00	1572.50	1665.00	1757.50	1850.00

3750 FEET.

Per Ton, Per Foot,	25c.	50c.	$1 2½ cts.	$2 5 cts.	$3 7½ cts.	$4 10 cts.	$5 12½ cts.	$6 15 cts.	$7 17½ cts.	$8 20 cts.	$9 22½ cts.	$10 25 cts.
Feet.												
3701	23.13	46.26	92.52	185.05	277.57	370.10	462.62	555.15	647.67	740.20	832.72	925.25
3702	23.14	46.27	92.55	185.10	277.65	370.20	462.75	555.30	647.85	740.40	832.95	925.50
3703	23.14	46.29	92.57	185.15	277.72	370.30	462.87	555.45	648.02	740.60	833.17	925.75
3704	23.15	46.30	92.60	185.20	277.80	370.40	463.00	555.60	648.20	740.80	833.40	926.00
3705	23.16	46.31	92.62	185.25	277.87	370.50	463.12	555.75	648.37	741.00	833.62	926.25
3706	23.16	46.32	92.65	185.30	277.95	370.60	463.25	555.90	648.55	741.20	833.85	926.50
3707	23.17	46.34	92.67	185.35	278.02	370.70	463.37	556.05	648.72	741.40	834.07	926.75
3708	23.17	46.35	92.70	185.40	278.10	370.80	463.50	556.20	648.90	741.60	834.30	927.00
3709	23.18	46.36	92.72	185.45	278.17	370.90	463.62	556.35	649.07	741.80	834.52	927.25
3710	23.19	46.37	92.75	185.50	278.25	371.00	463.75	556.50	649.25	742.00	834.75	927.50
3711	23.19	46.39	92.77	185.55	278.32	371.10	463.87	556.65	649.42	742.20	834.97	927.75
3712	23.20	46.40	92.80	185.60	278.40	371.20	464.00	556.80	649.60	742.40	835.20	928.00
3713	23.21	46.41	92.82	185.65	278.47	371.30	464.12	556.95	649.77	742.60	835.42	928.25
3714	23.21	46.42	92.85	185.70	278.55	371.40	464.25	557.10	649.95	742.80	835.65	928.50
3715	23.22	46.44	92.87	185.75	278.62	371.50	464.37	557.25	650.12	743.00	835.87	928.75
3716	23.22	46.45	92.90	185.80	278.70	371.60	464.50	557.40	650.30	743.20	836.10	929.00
3717	23.23	46.46	92.92	185.85	278.77	371.70	464.62	557.55	650.47	743.40	836.32	929.25
3718	23.24	46.47	92.95	185.90	278.85	371.80	464.75	557.70	650.65	743.60	836.55	929.50
3719	23.24	46.49	92.97	185.95	278.92	371.90	464.87	557.85	650.82	743.80	836.77	929.75
3720	23.25	46.50	93.00	186.00	279.00	372.00	465.00	558.00	651.00	744.00	837.00	930.00
3721	23.26	46.51	93.02	186.05	279.07	372.10	465.12	558.15	651.17	744.20	837.22	930.25
3722	23.26	46.52	93.05	186.10	279.15	372.20	465.25	558.30	651.35	744.40	837.45	930.50
3723	23.27	46.54	93.07	186.15	279.22	372.30	465.37	558.45	651.52	744.60	837.67	930.75
3724	23.27	46.55	93.10	186.20	279.30	372.40	465.50	558.60	651.70	744.80	837.90	931.00
3725	23.28	46.56	93.12	186.25	279.37	372.50	465.62	558.75	651.87	745.00	838.12	931.25
3726	23.29	46.57	93.15	186.30	279.45	372.60	465.75	558.90	652.05	745.20	838.35	931.50
3727	23.29	46.59	93.17	186.35	279.52	372.70	465.87	559.05	652.22	745.40	838.57	931.75
3728	23.30	46.60	93.20	186.40	279.60	372.80	466.00	559.20	652.40	745.60	838.80	932.00
3729	23.31	46.61	93.22	186.45	279.67	372.90	466.12	559.35	652.57	745.80	839.02	932.25
3730	23.31	46.62	93.25	186.50	279.75	373.00	466.25	559.50	652.75	746.00	839.25	932.50
3731	23.32	46.64	93.27	186.55	279.82	373.10	466.37	559.65	652.92	746.20	839.47	932.75
3732	23.32	46.65	93.30	186.60	279.90	373.20	466.50	559.80	653.10	746.40	839.70	933.00
3733	23.33	46.66	93.32	186.65	279.97	373.30	466.62	559.95	653.27	746.60	839.92	933.25
3734	23.34	46.67	93.35	186.70	280.05	373.40	466.75	560.10	653.45	746.80	840.15	933.50
3735	23.34	46.69	93.37	186.75	280.12	373.50	466.87	560.25	653.62	747.00	840.37	933.75
3736	23.35	46.70	93.40	186.80	280.20	373.60	467.00	560.40	653.80	747.20	840.60	934.00
3737	23.36	46.71	93.42	186.85	280.27	373.70	467.12	560.55	653.97	747.40	840.82	934.25
3738	23.36	46.72	93.45	186.90	280.35	373.80	467.25	560.70	654.15	747.60	841.05	934.50
3739	23.37	46.74	93.47	186.95	280.42	373.90	467.37	560.85	654.32	747.80	841.27	934.75
3740	23.37	46.75	93.50	187.00	280.50	374.00	467.50	561.00	654.50	748.00	841.50	935.00
3741	23.38	46.76	93.52	187.05	280.57	374.10	467.62	561.15	654.67	748.20	841.72	935.25
3742	23.39	46.77	93.55	187.10	280.65	374.20	467.75	561.30	654.85	748.40	841.95	935.50
3743	23.39	46.79	93.57	187.15	280.72	374.30	467.87	561.45	655.02	748.60	842.17	935.75
3744	23.40	46.80	93.60	187.20	280.80	374.40	468.00	561.60	655.20	748.80	842.40	936.00
3745	23.41	46.81	93.62	187.25	280.87	374.50	468.12	561.75	655.37	749.00	842.62	936.25
3746	23.41	46.82	93.65	187.30	280.95	374.60	468.25	561.90	655.55	749.20	842.85	936.50
3747	23.42	46.84	93.67	187.35	281.02	374.70	468.37	562.05	655.72	749.40	843.07	936.75
3748	23.42	46.85	93.70	187.40	281.10	374.80	468.50	562.20	655.90	749.60	843.30	937.00
3749	23.43	46.86	93.72	187.45	281.17	374.90	468.62	562.35	656.07	749.80	843.52	937.25
3750	23.44	46.87	93.75	187.50	281.25	375.00	468.75	562.50	656.25	750.00	843.75	937.50

Per Ton,	$11	$12	$13	$14	$15	$16	$17	$18	$19	$20
Per Foot,	27½ cts.	30 cts.	32½ cts.	35 cts.	37½ cts.	40 cts.	42½ cts.	45 cts.	47½ cts.	50 cts.
Feet.										
3701	1017.77	1110.30	1202.82	1295.35	1387.87	1480.40	1572.92	1665.45	1757.97	1850.50
3702	1018.05	1110.60	1203.15	1295.70	1388.25	1480.80	1573.35	1665.90	1758.45	1851.00
3703	1018.32	1110.90	1203.47	1296.05	1388.62	1481.20	1573.77	1666.35	1758.92	1851.50
3704	1018.60	1111.20	1203.80	1296.40	1389.00	1481.60	1574.20	1666.80	1759.40	1852.00
3705	1018.87	1111.50	1204.12	1296.75	1389.37	1482.00	1574.62	1667.25	1759.87	1852.50
3706	1019.15	1111.80	1204.45	1297.10	1389.75	1482.40	1575.05	1667.70	1760.35	1853.00
3707	1019.42	1112.10	1204.77	1297.45	1390.12	1482.80	1575.47	1668.15	1760.82	1853.50
3708	1019.70	1112.40	1205.10	1297.80	1390.50	1483.20	1575.90	1668.60	1761.30	1854.00
3709	1019.97	1112.70	1205.42	1298.15	1390.87	1483.60	1576.32	1669.05	1761.77	1854.50
3710	1020.25	1113.00	1205.75	1298.50	1391.25	1484.00	1576.75	1669.50	1762.25	1855.00
3711	1020.52	1113.30	1206.07	1298.85	1391.62	1484.40	1577.17	1669.95	1762.72	1855.50
3712	1020.80	1113.60	1206.40	1299.20	1392.00	1484.80	1577.60	1670.40	1763.20	1856.00
3713	1021.07	1113.90	1206.72	1299.55	1392.37	1485.20	1578.02	1670.85	1763.67	1856.50
3714	1021.35	1114.20	1207.05	1299.90	1392.75	1485.60	1578.45	1671.30	1764.15	1857.00
3715	1021.62	1114.50	1207.37	1300.25	1393.12	1486.00	1578.87	1671.75	1764.62	1857.50
3716	1021.90	1114.80	1207.70	1300.60	1393.50	1486.40	1579.30	1672.20	1765.10	1858.00
3717	1022.17	1115.10	1208.02	1300.95	1393.87	1486.80	1579.72	1672.65	1765.57	1858.50
3718	1022.45	1115.40	1208.35	1301.30	1394.25	1487.20	1580.15	1673.10	1766.05	1859.00
3719	1022.72	1115.70	1208.67	1301.65	1394.62	1487.60	1580.57	1673.55	1766.52	1859.50
3720	1023.00	1116.00	1209.00	1302.00	1395.00	1488.00	1581.00	1674.00	1767.00	1860.00
3721	1023.27	1116.30	1209.32	1302.35	1395.37	1488.40	1581.42	1674.45	1767.47	1860.50
3722	1023.55	1116.60	1209.65	1302.70	1395.75	1488.80	1581.85	1674.90	1767.95	1861.00
3723	1023.82	1116.90	1209.97	1303.05	1396.12	1489.20	1582.27	1675.35	1768.42	1861.50
3724	1024.10	1117.20	1210.30	1303.40	1396.50	1489.60	1582.70	1675.80	1768.90	1862.00
3725	1024.37	1117.50	1210.62	1303.75	1396.87	1490.00	1583.12	1676.25	1769.37	1862.50
3726	1024.65	1117.80	1210.95	1304.10	1397.25	1490.40	1583.55	1676.70	1769.85	1863.00
3727	1024.92	1118.10	1211.27	1304.45	1397.62	1490.80	1583.97	1677.15	1770.32	1863.50
3728	1025.20	1118.40	1211.60	1304.80	1398.00	1491.20	1584.40	1677.60	1770.80	1864.00
3729	1025.47	1118.70	1211.92	1305.15	1398.37	1491.60	1584.82	1678.05	1771.27	1864.50
3730	1025.75	1119.00	1212.25	1305.50	1398.75	1492.00	1585.25	1678.50	1771.75	1865.00
3731	1026.02	1119.30	1212.57	1305.85	1399.12	1492.40	1585.67	1678.95	1772.22	1865.50
3732	1026.30	1119.60	1212.90	1306.20	1399.50	1492.80	1586.10	1679.40	1772.70	1866.00
3733	1026.57	1119.90	1213.22	1306.55	1399.87	1493.20	1586.52	1679.85	1773.17	1866.50
3734	1026.85	1120.20	1213.55	1306.90	1400.25	1493.60	1586.95	1680.30	1773.65	1867.00
3735	1027.12	1120.50	1213.87	1307.25	1400.62	1494.00	1587.37	1680.75	1774.12	1867.50
3736	1027.40	1120.80	1214.20	1307.60	1401.00	1494.40	1587.80	1681.20	1774.60	1868.00
3737	1027.67	1121.10	1214.52	1307.95	1401.37	1494.80	1588.22	1681.65	1775.07	1868.50
3738	1027.95	1121.40	1214.85	1308.30	1401.75	1495.20	1588.65	1682.10	1775.55	1869.00
3739	1028.22	1121.70	1215.17	1308.65	1402.12	1495.60	1589.07	1682.55	1776.02	1869.50
3740	1028.50	1122.00	1215.50	1309.00	1402.50	1496.00	1589.50	1683.00	1776.50	1870.00
3741	1028.77	1122.30	1215.82	1309.35	1402.87	1496.40	1589.92	1683.45	1776.97	1870.50
3742	1029.05	1122.60	1216.15	1309.70	1403.25	1496.80	1590.35	1683.90	1777.45	1871.00
3743	1029.32	1122.90	1216.47	1310.05	1403.62	1497.20	1590.77	1684.35	1777.92	1871.50
3744	1029.60	1123.20	1216.80	1310.40	1404.00	1497.60	1591.20	1684.80	1778.40	1872.00
3745	1029.87	1123.50	1217.12	1310.75	1404.37	1498.00	1591.62	1685.25	1778.87	1872.50
3746	1030.15	1123.80	1217.45	1311.10	1404.75	1498.40	1592.05	1685.70	1779.35	1873.00
3747	1030.42	1124.10	1217.77	1311.45	1405.12	1498.80	1592.47	1686.15	1779.82	1873.50
3748	1030.70	1124.40	1218.10	1311.80	1405.50	1499.20	1592.90	1686.60	1780.30	1874.00
3749	1030.97	1124.70	1218.42	1312.15	1405.87	1499.60	1593.32	1687.05	1780.77	1874.50
3750	1031.25	1125.00	1218.75	1312.50	1406.25	1500.00	1593.75	1687.50	1781.25	1875.00

3800 FEET.

Per Ton, Per Foot, Feet.	25c.	50c.	$1 2½ cts.	$2 5 cts.	$3 7½ cts.	$4 10 cts.	$5 12½ cts.	$6 15 cts.	$7 17½ cts.	$8 20 cts.	$9 22½ cts.	$10 25 cts.
3751	23.44	46.89	93.77	187.55	281.32	375.10	468.87	562.65	656.42	750.20	843.97	937.75
3752	23.45	46.90	93.80	187.60	281.40	375.20	469.00	562.80	656.60	750.40	844.20	938.00
3753	23.46	46.91	93.82	187.65	281.47	375.30	469.12	562.95	656.77	750.60	844.42	938.25
3754	23.46	46.92	93.85	187.70	281.55	375.40	469.25	563.10	656.95	750.80	844.65	938.50
3755	23.47	46.94	93.87	187.75	281.62	375.50	469.37	563.25	657.12	751.00	844.87	938.75
3756	23.47	46.95	93.90	187.80	281.70	375.60	469.50	563.40	657.30	751.20	845.10	939.00
3757	23.48	46.96	93.92	187.85	281.77	375.70	469.62	563.55	657.47	751.40	845.32	939.25
3758	23.49	46.97	93.95	187.90	281.85	375.80	469.75	563.70	657.65	751.60	845.55	939.50
3759	23.49	46.99	93.97	187.95	281.92	375.90	469.87	563.85	657.82	751.80	845.77	939.75
3760	23.50	47.00	94.00	188.00	282.00	376.00	470.00	564.00	658.00	752.00	846.00	940.00
3761	23.51	47.01	94.02	188.05	282.07	376.10	470.12	564.15	658.17	752.20	846.22	940.25
3762	23.51	47.02	94.05	188.10	282.15	376.20	470.25	564.30	658.35	752.40	846.45	940.50
3763	23.52	47.04	94.07	188.15	282.22	376.30	470.37	564.45	658.52	752.60	846.67	940.75
3764	23.52	47.05	94.10	188.20	282.30	376.40	470.50	564.60	658.70	752.80	846.90	941.00
3765	23.53	47.06	94.12	188.25	282.37	376.50	470.62	564.75	658.87	753.00	847.12	941.25
3766	23.54	47.07	94.15	188.30	282.45	376.60	470.75	564.90	659.05	753.20	847.35	941.50
3767	23.54	47.09	94.17	188.35	282.52	376.70	470.87	565.05	659.22	753.40	847.57	941.75
3768	23.55	47.10	94.20	188.40	282.60	376.80	471.00	565.20	659.40	753.60	847.80	942.00
3769	23.56	47.11	94.22	188.45	282.67	376.90	471.12	565.35	659.57	753.80	848.02	942.25
3770	23.56	47.12	94.25	188.50	282.75	377.00	471.25	565.50	659.75	754.00	848.25	942.50
3771	23.57	47.14	94.27	188.55	282.82	377.10	471.37	565.65	659.92	754.20	848.47	942.75
3772	23.57	47.15	94.30	188.60	282.90	377.20	471.50	565.80	660.10	754.40	848.70	943.00
3773	23.58	47.16	94.32	188.65	282.97	377.30	471.62	565.95	660.27	754.60	848.92	943.25
3774	23.59	47.17	94.35	188.70	283.05	377.40	471.75	566.10	660.45	754.80	849.15	943.50
3775	23.59	47.19	94.37	188.75	283.12	377.50	471.87	566.25	660.62	755.00	849.37	943.75
3776	23.60	47.20	94.40	188.80	283.20	377.60	472.00	566.40	660.80	755.20	849.60	944.00
3777	23.61	47.21	94.42	188.85	283.27	377.70	472.12	566.55	660.97	755.40	849.82	944.25
3778	23.61	47.22	94.45	188.90	283.35	377.80	472.25	566.70	661.15	755.60	850.05	944.50
3779	23.62	47.24	94.47	188.95	283.42	377.90	472.37	566.85	661.32	755.80	850.27	944.75
3780	23.62	47.25	94.50	189.00	283.50	378.00	472.50	567.00	661.50	756.00	850.50	945.00
3781	23.63	47.26	94.52	189.05	283.57	378.10	472.62	567.15	661.67	756.20	850.72	945.25
3782	23.64	47.27	94.55	189.10	283.65	378.20	472.75	567.30	661.85	756.40	850.95	945.50
3783	23.64	47.29	94.57	189.15	283.72	378.30	472.87	567.45	662.02	756.60	851.17	945.75
3784	23.65	47.30	94.60	189.20	283.80	378.40	473.00	567.60	662.20	756.80	851.40	946.00
3785	23.66	47.31	94.62	189.25	283.87	378.50	473.12	567.75	662.37	757.00	851.62	946.25
3786	23.66	47.32	94.65	189.30	283.95	378.60	473.25	567.90	662.55	757.20	851.85	946.50
3787	23.67	47.34	94.67	189.35	284.02	378.70	473.37	568.05	662.72	757.40	852.07	946.75
3788	23.67	47.35	94.70	189.40	284.10	378.80	473.50	568.20	662.90	757.60	852.30	947.00
3789	23.68	47.36	94.72	189.45	284.17	378.90	473.62	568.35	663.07	757.80	852.52	947.25
3790	23.69	47.37	94.75	189.50	284.25	379.00	473.75	568.50	663.25	758.00	852.75	947.50
3791	23.69	47.39	94.77	189.55	284.32	379.10	473.87	568.65	663.42	758.20	852.97	947.75
3792	23.70	47.40	94.80	189.60	284.40	379.20	474.00	568.80	663.60	758.40	853.20	948.00
3793	23.71	47.41	94.82	189.65	284.47	379.30	474.12	568.95	663.77	758.60	853.42	948.25
3794	23.71	47.42	94.85	189.70	284.55	379.40	474.25	569.10	663.95	758.80	853.65	948.50
3795	23.72	47.44	94.87	189.75	284.62	379.50	474.37	569.25	664.12	759.00	853.87	948.75
3796	23.72	47.45	94.90	189.80	284.70	379.60	474.50	569.40	664.30	759.20	854.10	949.00
3797	23.73	47.46	94.92	189.85	284.77	379.70	474.62	569.55	664.47	759.40	854.32	949.25
3798	23.74	47.47	94.95	189.90	284.85	379.80	474.75	569.70	664.65	759.60	854.55	949.50
3799	23.74	47.49	94.97	189.95	284.92	379.90	474.87	569.85	664.82	759.80	854.77	949.75
3800	23.75	47.50	95.00	190.00	285.00	380.00	475.00	570.00	665.00	760.00	855.00	950.00

3800 FEET.

Per Ton,	$11	$12	$13	$14	$15	$16	$17	$18	$19	$20
Per Foot,	27½ cts.	30 cts.	32½ cts.	35 cts.	37½ cts.	40 cts.	42½ cts.	45 cts.	47½ cts.	50 cts.
Feet.										
3751	1031.52	1125.30	1219.07	1312.85	1406.62	1500.40	1594.17	1687.95	1781.72	1875.50
3752	1031.80	1125.60	1219.40	1313.20	1407.00	1500.80	1594.60	1688.40	1782.20	1876.00
3753	1032.07	1125.90	1219.72	1313.55	1407.37	1501.20	1595.02	1688.85	1782.67	1876.50
3754	1032.35	1126.20	1220.05	1313.90	1407.75	1501.60	1595.45	1689.30	1783.15	1877.00
3755	1032.62	1126.50	1220.37	1314.25	1408.12	1502.00	1595.87	1689.75	1783.62	1877.50
3756	1032.90	1126.80	1220.70	1314.60	1408.50	1502.40	1596.30	1690.20	1784.10	1878.00
3757	1033.17	1127.10	1221.02	1314.95	1408.87	1502.80	1596.72	1690.65	1784.57	1878.50
3758	1033.45	1127.40	1221.35	1315.30	1409.25	1503.20	1597.15	1691.10	1785.05	1879.00
3759	1033.72	1127.70	1221.67	1315.65	1409.62	1503.60	1597.57	1691.55	1785.52	1879.50
3760	1034.00	1128.00	1222.00	1316.00	1410.00	1504.00	1598.00	1692.00	1786.00	1880.00
3761	1034.27	1128.30	1222.32	1316.35	1410.37	1504.40	1598.42	1692.45	1786.47	1880.50
3762	1034.55	1128.60	1222.65	1316.70	1410.75	1504.80	1598.85	1692.90	1786.95	1881.00
3763	1034.82	1128.90	1222.97	1317.05	1411.12	1505.20	1599.27	1693.35	1787.42	1881.50
3764	1035.10	1129.20	1223.30	1317.40	1411.50	1505.60	1599.70	1693.80	1787.90	1882.00
3765	1035.37	1129.50	1223.62	1317.75	1411.87	1506.00	1600.12	1694.25	1788.37	1882.50
3766	1035.65	1129.80	1223.95	1318.10	1412.25	1506.40	1600.55	1694.70	1788.85	1883.00
3767	1035.92	1130.10	1224.27	1318.45	1412.62	1506.80	1600.97	1695.15	1789.32	1883.50
3768	1036.20	1130.40	1224.60	1318.80	1413.00	1507.20	1601.40	1695.60	1789.80	1884.00
3769	1036.47	1130.70	1224.92	1319.15	1413.37	1507.60	1601.82	1696.05	1790.27	1884.50
3770	1036.75	1131.00	1225.25	1319.50	1413.75	1508.00	1602.25	1696.50	1790.75	1885.00
3771	1037.02	1131.30	1225.57	1319.85	1414.12	1508.40	1602.67	1696.95	1791.22	1885.50
3772	1037.30	1131.60	1225.90	1320.20	1414.50	1508.80	1603.10	1697.40	1791.70	1886.00
3773	1037.57	1131.90	1226.22	1320.55	1414.87	1509.20	1603.52	1697.85	1792.17	1886.50
3774	1037.85	1132.20	1226.55	1320.90	1415.25	1509.60	1603.95	1698.30	1792.65	1887.00
3775	1038.12	1132.50	1226.87	1321.25	1415.62	1510.00	1604.37	1698.75	1793.12	1887.50
3776	1038.40	1132.80	1227.20	1321.60	1416.00	1510.40	1604.80	1699.20	1793.60	1888.00
3777	1038.67	1133.10	1227.52	1321.95	1416.37	1510.80	1605.22	1699.65	1794.07	1888.50
3778	1038.95	1133.40	1227.85	1322.30	1416.75	1511.20	1605.65	1700.10	1794.55	1889.00
3779	1039.22	1133.70	1228.17	1322.65	1417.12	1511.60	1606.07	1700.55	1795.02	1889.50
3780	1039.50	1134.00	1228.50	1323.00	1417.50	1512.00	1606.50	1701.00	1795.50	1890.00
3781	1039.77	1134.30	1228.82	1323.35	1417.87	1512.40	1606.92	1701.45	1795.97	1890.50
3782	1040.05	1134.60	1229.15	1323.70	1418.25	1512.80	1607.35	1701.90	1796.45	1891.00
3783	1040.32	1134.90	1229.47	1324.05	1418.62	1513.20	1607.77	1702.35	1796.92	1891.50
3784	1040.60	1135.20	1229.80	1324.40	1419.00	1513.60	1608.20	1702.80	1797.40	1892.00
3785	1040.87	1135.50	1230.12	1324.75	1419.37	1514.00	1608.62	1703.25	1797.87	1892.50
3786	1041.15	1135.80	1230.45	1325.10	1419.75	1514.40	1609.05	1703.70	1798.35	1893.00
3787	1041.42	1136.10	1230.77	1325.45	1420.12	1514.80	1609.47	1704.15	1798.82	1893.50
3788	1041.70	1136.40	1231.10	1325.80	1420.50	1515.20	1609.90	1704.60	1799.30	1894.00
3789	1041.97	1136.70	1231.42	1326.15	1420.87	1515.60	1610.32	1705.05	1799.77	1894.50
3790	1042.25	1137.00	1231.75	1326.50	1421.25	1516.00	1610.75	1705.50	1800.25	1895.00
3791	1042.52	1137.30	1232.07	1326.85	1421.62	1516.40	1611.17	1705.95	1800.72	1895.50
3792	1042.80	1137.60	1232.40	1327.20	1422.00	1516.80	1611.60	1706.40	1801.20	1896.00
3793	1043.07	1137.90	1232.72	1327.55	1422.37	1517.20	1612.02	1706.85	1801.67	1896.50
3794	1043.35	1138.20	1233.05	1327.90	1422.75	1517.60	1612.45	1707.30	1802.15	1897.00
3795	1043.62	1138.50	1233.37	1328.25	1423.12	1518.00	1612.87	1707.75	1802.62	1897.50
3796	1043.90	1138.80	1233.70	1328.60	1423.50	1518.40	1613.30	1708.20	1803.10	1898.00
3797	1044.17	1139.10	1234.02	1328.95	1423.87	1518.80	1613.72	1708.65	1803.57	1898.50
3798	1044.45	1139.40	1234.35	1329.30	1424.25	1519.20	1614.15	1709.10	1804.05	1899.00
3799	1044.72	1139.70	1234.67	1329.65	1424.62	1519.60	1614.57	1709.55	1804.52	1899.50
3800	1045.00	1140.00	1235.00	1330.00	1425.00	1520.00	1615.00	1710.00	1805.00	1900.00

Per Ton,	25c.	50c.	$1	$2	$3	$4	$5	$6	$7	$8	$9	$10
Per Foot,			2¼ cts.	5 cts.	7½ cts.	10 cts.	12½ cts.	15 cts.	17½ cts.	20 cts.	22½ cts.	25 cts.
Feet.												
3801	23.76	47.51	95.02	190.05	285.07	380.10	475.12	570.15	665.17	760.20	855.22	950.25
3802	23.76	47.52	95.05	190.10	285.15	380.20	475.25	570.30	665.35	760.40	855.45	950.50
3803	23.77	47.54	95.07	190.15	285.22	380.30	475.37	570.45	665.52	760.60	855.67	950.75
3804	23.77	47.55	95.10	190.20	285.30	380.40	475.50	570.60	665.70	760.80	855.90	951.00
3805	23.78	47.56	95.12	190.25	285.37	380.50	475.62	570.75	665.87	761.00	856.12	951.25
3806	23.79	47.57	95.15	190.30	285.45	380.60	475.75	570.90	666.05	761.20	856.35	951.50
3807	23.79	47.59	95.17	190.35	285.52	380.70	475.87	571.05	666.22	761.40	856.57	951.75
3808	23.80	47.60	95.20	190.40	285.60	380.80	476.00	571.20	666.40	761.60	856.80	952.00
3809	23.81	47.61	95.22	190.45	285.67	380.90	476.12	571.35	666.57	761.80	857.02	952.25
3810	23.81	47.62	95.25	190.50	285.75	381.00	476.25	571.50	666.75	762.00	857.25	952.50
3811	23.82	47.64	95.27	190.55	285.82	381.10	476.37	571.65	666.92	762.20	857.47	952.75
3812	23.82	47.65	95.30	190.60	285.90	381.20	476.50	571.80	667.10	762.40	857.70	953.00
3813	23.83	47.66	95.32	190.65	285.97	381.30	476.62	571.95	667.27	762.60	857.92	953.25
3814	23.84	47.67	95.35	190.70	286.05	381.40	476.75	572.10	667.45	762.80	858.15	953.50
3815	23.84	47.69	95.37	190.75	286.12	381.50	476.87	572.25	667.62	763.00	858.37	953.75
3816	23.85	47.70	95.40	190.80	286.20	381.60	477.00	572.40	667.80	763.20	858.60	954.00
3817	23.86	47.71	95.42	190.85	286.27	381.70	477.12	572.55	667.97	763.40	858.82	954.25
3818	23.86	47.72	95.45	190.90	286.35	381.80	477.25	572.70	668.15	763.60	859.05	954.50
3819	23.87	47.74	95.47	190.95	286.42	381.90	477.37	572.85	668.32	763.80	859.27	954.75
3820	23.87	47.75	95.50	191.00	286.50	382.00	477.50	573.00	668.50	764.00	859.50	955.00
3821	23.88	47.76	95.52	191.05	286.57	382.10	477.62	573.15	668.67	764.20	859.72	955.25
3822	23.89	47.77	95.55	191.10	286.65	382.20	477.75	573.30	668.85	764.40	859.95	955.50
3823	23.89	47.79	95.57	191.15	286.72	382.30	477.87	573.45	669.02	764.60	860.17	955.75
3824	23.90	47.80	95.60	191.20	286.80	382.40	478.00	573.60	669.20	764.80	860.40	956.00
3825	23.91	47.81	95.62	191.25	286.87	382.50	478.12	573.75	669.37	765.00	860.62	956.25
3826	23.91	47.82	95.65	191.30	286.95	382.60	478.25	573.90	669.55	765.20	860.85	956.50
3827	23.92	47.84	95.67	191.35	287.02	382.70	478.37	574.05	669.72	765.40	861.07	956.75
3828	23.92	47.85	95.70	191.40	287.10	382.80	478.50	574.20	669.90	765.60	861.30	957.00
3829	23.93	47.86	95.72	191.45	287.17	382.90	478.62	574.35	670.07	765.80	861.52	957.25
3830	23.94	47.87	95.75	191.50	287.25	383.00	478.75	574.50	670.25	766.00	861.75	957.50
3831	23.94	47.89	95.77	191.55	287.32	383.10	478.87	574.65	670.42	766.20	861.97	957.75
3832	23.95	47.90	95.80	191.60	287.40	383.20	479.00	574.80	670.60	766.40	862.20	958.00
3833	23.96	47.91	95.82	191.65	287.47	383.30	479.12	574.95	670.77	766.60	862.42	958.25
3834	23.96	47.92	95.85	191.70	287.55	383.40	479.25	575.10	670.95	766.80	862.65	958.50
3835	23.97	47.94	95.87	191.75	287.62	383.50	479.37	575.25	671.12	767.00	862.87	958.75
3836	23.97	47.95	95.90	191.80	287.70	383.60	479.50	575.40	671.30	767.20	863.10	959.00
3837	23.98	47.96	95.92	191.85	287.77	383.70	479.62	575.55	671.47	767.40	863.32	959.25
3838	23.99	47.97	95.95	191.90	287.85	383.80	479.75	575.70	671.65	767.60	863.55	959.50
3839	23.99	47.99	95.97	191.95	287.92	383.90	479.87	575.85	671.82	767.80	863.77	959.75
3840	24.00	48.00	96.00	192.00	288.00	384.00	480.00	576.00	672.00	768.00	864.00	960.00
3841	24.01	48.01	96.02	192.05	288.07	384.10	480.12	576.15	672.17	768.20	864.22	960.25
3842	24.01	48.02	96.05	192.10	288.15	384.20	480.25	576.30	672.35	768.40	864.45	960.50
3843	24.02	48.04	96.07	192.15	288.22	384.30	480.37	576.45	672.52	768.60	864.67	960.75
3844	24.02	48.05	96.10	192.20	288.30	384.40	480.50	576.60	672.70	768.80	864.90	961.00
3845	24.03	48.06	96.12	192.25	288.37	384.50	480.62	576.75	672.87	769.00	865.12	961.25
3846	24.04	48.07	96.15	192.30	288.45	384.60	480.75	576.90	673.05	769.20	865.35	961.50
3847	24.04	48.09	96.17	192.35	288.52	384.70	480.87	577.05	673.22	769.40	865.57	961.75
3848	24.05	48.10	96.20	192.40	288.60	384.80	481.00	577.20	673.40	769.60	865.80	962.00
3849	24.06	48.11	96.22	192.45	288.67	384.90	481.12	577.35	673.57	769.80	866.02	962.25
3850	24.06	48.12	96.25	192.50	288.75	385.00	481.25	577.50	673.75	770.00	866.25	962.50

3850 FEET.

Per Ton,	$11	$12	$13	$14	$15	$16	$17	$18	$19	$20
Per Foot,	27½ cts.	30 cts.	32½ cts.	35 cts.	37½ cts.	40 cts.	42½ cts.	45 cts.	47½ cts.	50 cts.
Feet.										
3801	1045.27	1140.30	1235.32	1330.35	1425.37	1520.40	1615.42	1710.45	1805.47	1900.50
3802	1045.55	1140.60	1235.65	1330.70	1425.75	1520.80	1615.85	1710.90	1805.95	1901.00
3803	1045.82	1140.90	1235.97	1331.05	1426.12	1521.20	1616.27	1711.35	1806.42	1901.50
3804	1046.10	1141.20	1236.30	1331.40	1426.50	1521.60	1616.70	1711.80	1806.90	1902.00
3805	1046.37	1141.50	1236.62	1331.75	1426.87	1522.00	1617.12	1712.25	1807.37	1902.50
3806	1046.65	1141.80	1236.95	1332.10	1427.25	1522.40	1617.55	1712.70	1807.85	1903.00
3807	1046.92	1142.10	1237.27	1332.45	1427.62	1522.80	1617.97	1713.15	1808.32	1903.50
3808	1047.20	1142.40	1237.60	1332.80	1428.00	1523.20	1618.40	1713.60	1808.80	1904.00
3809	1047.47	1142.70	1237.92	1333.15	1428.37	1523.60	1618.82	1714.05	1809.27	1904.50
3810	1047.75	1143.00	1238.25	1333.50	1428.75	1524.00	1619.25	1714.50	1809.75	1905.00
3811	1048.02	1143.30	1238.57	1333.85	1429.12	1524.40	1619.67	1714.95	1810.22	1905.50
3812	1048.30	1143.60	1238.90	1334.20	1429.50	1524.80	1620.10	1715.40	1810.70	1906.00
3813	1048.57	1143.90	1239.22	1334.55	1429.87	1525.20	1620.52	1715.85	1811.17	1906.50
3814	1048.85	1144.20	1239.55	1334.90	1430.25	1525.60	1620.95	1716.30	1811.65	1907.00
3815	1049.12	1144.50	1239.87	1335.25	1430.62	1526.00	1621.37	1716.75	1812.12	1907.50
3816	1049.40	1144.80	1240.20	1335.60	1431.00	1526.40	1621.80	1717.20	1812.60	1908.00
3817	1049.67	1145.10	1240.52	1335.95	1431.37	1526.80	1622.22	1717.65	1813.07	1908.50
3818	1049.95	1145.40	1240.85	1336.30	1431.75	1527.20	1622.65	1718.10	1813.55	1909.00
3819	1050.22	1145.70	1241.17	1336.65	1432.12	1527.60	1623.07	1718.55	1814.02	1909.50
3820	1050.50	1146.00	1241.50	1337.00	1432.50	1528.00	1623.50	1719.00	1814.50	1910.00
3821	1050.77	1146.30	1241.82	1337.35	1432.87	1528.40	1623.92	1719.45	1814.97	1910.50
3822	1051.05	1146.60	1242.15	1337.70	1433.25	1528.80	1624.35	1719.90	1815.45	1911.00
3823	1051.32	1146.90	1242.47	1338.05	1433.62	1529.20	1624.77	1720.35	1815.92	1911.50
3824	1051.60	1147.20	1242.80	1338.40	1434.00	1529.60	1625.20	1720.80	1816.40	1912.00
3825	1051.87	1147.50	1243.12	1338.75	1434.37	1530.00	1625.62	1721.25	1816.87	1912.50
3826	1052.15	1147.80	1243.45	1339.10	1434.75	1530.40	1626.05	1721.70	1817.35	1913.00
3827	1052.42	1148.10	1243.77	1339.45	1435.12	1530.80	1626.47	1722.15	1817.82	1913.50
3828	1052.70	1148.40	1244.10	1339.80	1435.50	1531.20	1626.90	1722.60	1818.30	1914.00
3829	1052.97	1148.70	1244.42	1340.15	1435.87	1531.60	1627.32	1723.05	1818.77	1914.50
3830	1053.25	1149.00	1244.75	1340.50	1436.25	1532.00	1627.75	1723.50	1819.25	1915.00
3831	1053.52	1149.30	1245.07	1340.85	1436.62	1532.40	1628.17	1723.95	1819.72	1915.50
3832	1053.80	1149.60	1245.40	1341.20	1437.00	1532.80	1628.60	1724.40	1820.20	1916.00
3833	1054.07	1149.90	1245.72	1341.55	1437.37	1533.20	1629.02	1724.85	1820.67	1916.50
3834	1054.35	1150.20	1246.05	1341.90	1437.75	1533.60	1629.45	1725.30	1821.15	1917.00
3835	1054.62	1150.50	1246.37	1342.25	1438.12	1534.00	1629.87	1725.75	1821.62	1917.50
3836	1054.90	1150.80	1246.70	1342.60	1438.50	1534.40	1630.30	1726.20	1822.10	1918.00
3837	1055.17	1151.10	1247.02	1342.95	1438.87	1534.80	1630.72	1726.65	1822.57	1918.50
3838	1055.45	1151.40	1247.35	1343.30	1439.25	1535.20	1631.15	1727.10	1823.05	1919.00
3839	1055.72	1151.70	1247.67	1343.65	1439.62	1535.60	1631.57	1727.55	1823.52	1919.50
3840	1056.00	1152.00	1248.00	1344.00	1440.00	1536.00	1632.00	1728.00	1824.00	1920.00
3841	1056.27	1152.30	1248.32	1344.35	1440.37	1536.40	1632.42	1728.45	1824.47	1920.50
3842	1057.55	1152.60	1248.65	1344.70	1440.75	1536.80	1632.85	1728.90	1824.95	1921.00
3843	1057.82	1152.90	1248.97	1345.05	1441.12	1537.20	1633.27	1729.35	1825.42	1921.50
3844	1058.10	1153.20	1249.30	1345.40	1441.50	1537.60	1633.70	1729.80	1825.90	1922.00
3845	1058.37	1153.50	1249.62	1345.75	1441.87	1538.00	1634.12	1730.25	1826.37	1922.50
3846	1058.65	1153.80	1249.95	1346.10	1442.25	1538.40	1634.55	1730.70	1826.85	1923.00
3847	1058.92	1154.10	1250.27	1346.45	1442.62	1538.80	1634.97	1731.15	1827.32	1923.50
3848	1058.20	1154.40	1250.60	1346.80	1443.00	1539.20	1635.40	1731.60	1827.80	1924.00
3849	1058.47	1154.70	1250.92	1347.15	1443.37	1539.60	1635.82	1732.05	1828.27	1924.50
3850	1058.75	1155.00	1251.25	1347.50	1443.75	1540.00	1636.25	1732.50	1828.75	1925.00

3900 FEET.

Per Ton,	25c.	50c.	$1	$2	$3	$4	$5	$6	$7	$8	$9	$10
Per Foot,			2½ cts.	5 cts.	7½ cts.	10 cts.	12½ cts.	15 cts.	17½ cts.	20 cts.	22½ cts.	25 cts.
Feet.												
3851	24.07	48.14	96.27	192.55	288.82	385.10	481.37	577.65	673.92	770.20	866.47	962.75
3852	24.07	48.15	96.30	192.60	288.90	385.20	481.50	577.80	674.10	770.40	866.70	963.00
3853	24.08	48.16	96.32	192.65	288.97	385.30	481.62	577.95	674.27	770.60	866.92	963.25
3854	24.09	48.17	96.35	192.70	289.05	385.40	481.75	578.10	674.45	770.80	867.15	963.50
3855	24.09	48.19	96.37	192.75	289.12	385.50	481.87	578.25	674.62	771.00	867.37	963.75
3856	24.10	48.20	96.40	192.80	289.20	385.60	482.00	578.40	674.80	771.20	867.60	964.00
3857	24.11	48.21	96.42	192.85	289.27	385.70	482.12	578.55	674.97	771.40	867.82	964.25
3858	24.11	48.22	96.45	192.90	289.35	385.80	482.25	578.70	675.15	771.60	868.05	964.50
3859	24.12	48.24	96.47	192.95	289.42	385.90	482.37	578.85	675.32	771.80	868.27	964.75
3860	24.12	48.25	96.50	193.00	289.50	386.00	482.50	579.00	675.50	772.00	868.50	965.00
3861	24.13	48.26	96.52	193.05	289.57	386.10	482.62	579.15	675.67	772.20	868.72	965.25
3862	24.14	48.27	96.55	193.10	289.65	386.20	482.75	579.30	675.85	772.40	868.95	965.50
3863	24.14	48.29	96.57	193.15	289.72	386.30	482.87	579.45	676.02	772.60	869.17	965.75
3864	24.15	48.30	96.60	193.20	289.80	386.40	483.00	579.60	676.20	772.80	869.40	966.00
3865	24.16	48.31	96.62	193.25	289.87	386.50	483.12	579.75	676.37	773.00	869.62	966.25
3866	24.16	48.32	96.65	193.30	289.95	386.60	483.25	579.90	676.55	773.20	869.85	966.50
3867	24.17	48.34	96.67	193.35	290.02	386.70	483.37	580.05	676.72	773.40	870.07	966.75
3868	24.17	48.35	96.70	193.40	290.10	386.80	483.50	580.20	676.90	773.60	870.30	967.00
3869	24.18	48.36	96.72	193.45	290.17	386.90	483.62	580.35	677.07	773.80	870.52	967.25
3870	24.19	48.37	96.75	193.50	290.25	387.00	483.75	580.50	677.25	774.00	870.75	967.50
3871	24.19	48.39	96.77	193.55	290.32	387.10	483.87	580.65	677.42	774.20	870.97	967.75
3872	24.20	48.40	96.80	193.60	290.40	387.20	484.00	580.80	677.60	774.40	871.20	968.00
3873	24.21	48.41	96.82	193.65	290.47	387.30	484.12	580.95	677.77	774.60	871.42	968.25
3874	24.21	48.42	96.85	193.70	290.55	387.40	484.25	581.10	677.95	774.80	871.65	968.50
3875	24.22	48.44	96.87	193.75	290.62	387.50	484.37	581.25	678.12	775.00	871.87	968.75
3876	24.22	48.45	96.90	193.80	290.70	387.60	484.50	581.40	678.30	775.20	872.10	969.00
3877	24.23	48.46	96.92	193.85	290.77	387.70	484.62	581.55	678.47	775.40	872.32	969.25
3878	24.24	48.47	96.95	193.90	290.85	387.80	484.75	581.70	678.65	775.60	872.55	969.50
3879	24.24	48.49	96.97	193.95	290.92	387.90	484.87	581.85	678.82	775.80	872.77	969.75
3880	24.25	48.50	97.00	194.00	291.00	388.00	485.00	582.00	679.00	776.00	873.00	970.00
3881	24.26	48.51	97.02	194.05	291.07	388.10	485.12	582.15	679.17	776.20	873.22	970.25
3882	24.26	48.52	97.05	194.10	291.15	388.20	485.25	582.30	679.35	776.40	873.45	970.50
3883	24.27	48.54	97.07	194.15	291.22	388.30	485.37	582.45	679.52	776.60	873.67	970.75
3884	24.27	48.55	97.10	194.20	291.30	388.40	485.50	582.60	679.70	776.80	873.90	971.00
3885	24.28	48.56	97.12	194.25	291.37	388.50	485.62	582.75	679.87	777.00	874.12	971.25
3886	24.29	48.57	97.15	194.30	291.45	388.60	485.75	582.90	680.05	777.20	874.35	971.50
3887	24.29	48.59	97.17	194.35	291.52	388.70	485.87	583.05	680.22	777.40	874.57	971.75
3888	24.30	48.60	97.20	194.40	291.60	388.80	486.00	583.20	680.40	777.60	874.80	972.00
3889	24.31	48.61	97.22	194.45	291.67	388.90	486.12	583.35	680.57	777.80	875.02	972.25
3890	24.31	48.62	97.25	194.50	291.75	389.00	486.25	583.50	680.75	778.00	875.25	972.50
3891	24.32	48.64	97.27	194.55	291.82	389.10	486.37	583.65	680.92	778.20	875.47	972.75
3892	24.32	48.65	97.30	194.60	291.90	389.20	486.50	583.80	681.10	778.40	875.70	973.00
3893	24.33	48.66	97.32	194.65	291.97	389.30	486.62	583.95	681.27	778.60	875.92	973.25
3894	24.34	48.67	97.35	194.70	292.05	389.40	486.75	584.10	681.45	778.80	876.15	973.50
3895	24.34	48.69	97.37	194.75	292.12	389.50	486.87	584.25	681.62	779.00	876.37	973.75
3896	24.35	48.70	97.40	194.80	292.20	389.60	487.00	584.40	681.80	779.20	876.60	974.00
3897	24.36	48.71	97.42	194.85	292.27	389.70	487.12	584.55	681.97	779.40	876.82	974.25
3898	24.36	48.72	97.45	194.90	292.35	389.80	487.25	584.70	682.15	779.60	877.05	974.50
3899	24.37	48.74	97.47	194.95	292.42	389.90	487.37	584.85	682.32	779.80	877.27	974.75
3900	24.37	48.75	97.50	195.00	292.50	390.00	487.50	585.00	682.50	780.00	877.50	975.00

3900 FEET.

Per Ton,	$11	$12	$13	$14	$15	$16	$17	$18	$19	$20
Per Foot,	27½ cts.	30 cts.	32½ cts.	35 cts.	37½ cts.	40 cts.	42½ cts.	45 cts.	47½ cts.	50 cts.
Feet.										
3851	1059.02	1155.30	1251.57	1347.85	1444.12	1540.40	1636.67	1732.95	1829.22	1925.50
3852	1059.30	1155.60	1251.90	1348.20	1444.50	1540.80	1637.10	1733.40	1829.70	1926.00
3853	1059.57	1155.90	1252.22	1348.55	1444.87	1541.20	1637.52	1733.85	1830.17	1926.50
3854	1059.85	1156.20	1252.55	1348.90	1445.25	1541.60	1637.95	1734.30	1830.65	1927.00
3855	1060.12	1156.50	1252.87	1349.25	1445.62	1542.00	1638.37	1734.75	1831.12	1927.50
3856	1060.40	1156.80	1253.20	1349.60	1446.00	1542.40	1638.80	1735.20	1831.60	1928.00
3857	1060.67	1157.10	1253.52	1349.95	1446.37	1542.80	1639.22	1735.65	1832.07	1928.50
3858	1060.95	1157.40	1253.85	1350.30	1446.75	1543.20	1639.65	1736.10	1832.55	1929.00
3859	1031.22	1157.70	1254.17	1350.65	1447.12	1543.60	1640.07	1736.55	1833.02	1929.50
3860	1061.50	1158.00	1254.50	1351.00	1447.50	1544.00	1640.50	1737.00	1833.50	1930.00
3861	1061.77	1158.30	1254.82	1351.35	1447.87	1544.40	1640.92	1737.45	1833.97	1930.50
3862	1062.05	1158.60	1255.15	1351.70	1448.25	1544.80	1641.35	1737.90	1834.45	1931.00
3863	1062.32	1158.90	1255.47	1352.05	1448.62	1545.20	1641.77	1738.25	1834.92	1931.50
3864	1062.60	1159.20	1255.80	1352.40	1449.00	1545.60	1642.20	1738.80	1835.40	1932.00
3865	1062.87	1159.50	1256.12	1352.75	1449.37	1546.00	1642.62	1739.25	1835.87	1932.50
3866	1063.15	1159.80	1256.45	1353.10	1449.75	1546.40	1643.05	1739.70	1836.35	1933.00
3867	1063.42	1160.10	1256.77	1353.45	1450.12	1546.80	1643.47	1740.15	1836.82	1933.50
3868	1063.70	1160.40	1257.10	1353.80	1450.50	1547.20	1643.90	1740.60	1837.30	1934.00
3869	1063.97	1160.70	1257.42	1354.15	1450.87	1547.60	1644.32	1741.05	1837.77	1934.50
3870	1064.25	1161.00	1257.75	1354.50	1451.25	1548.00	1644.75	1741.50	1838.25	1935.00
3871	1064.52	1161.30	1258.07	1354.85	1451.62	1548.40	1645.17	1741.95	1838.72	1935.50
3872	1064.80	1161.60	1258.40	1355.20	1452.00	1548.80	1645.60	1742.40	1839.20	1936.00
3873	1065.07	1161.90	1258.72	1355.55	1452.37	1549.20	1646.02	1742.85	1839.67	1936.50
3874	1065.35	1162.20	1259.05	1355.90	1452.75	1549.60	1646.45	1743.30	1840.15	1937.00
3875	1065.62	1162.50	1259.37	1356.25	1453.12	1550.00	1646.87	1743.75	1840.62	1937.50
3876	1065.90	1162.80	1259.70	1356.60	1453.50	1550.40	1647.30	1744.20	1841.10	1938.00
3877	1066.17	1163.10	1260.02	1356.95	1453.87	1550.80	1647.72	1744.65	1841.57	1938.50
3878	1066.45	1163.40	1260.35	1357.30	1454.25	1551.20	1648.15	1745.10	1842.05	1939.00
3879	1066.72	1163.70	1260.67	1357.65	1454.62	1551.60	1648.57	1745.55	1842.52	1939.50
3880	1067.00	1164.00	1261.00	1358.00	1455.00	1552.00	1649.00	1746.00	1843.00	1940.00
3881	1067.27	1164.30	1261.32	1358.35	1455.37	1552.40	1649.42	1746.45	1843.47	1940.50
3882	1067.55	1164.60	1261.65	1358.70	1455.75	1552.80	1649.85	1746.90	1843.95	1941.00
3883	1067.82	1164.90	1261.97	1359.05	1456.12	1553.20	1650.27	1747.35	1844.42	1941.50
3884	1068.10	1165.20	1262.30	1359.40	1456.50	1553.60	1650.70	1747.80	1844.90	1942.00
3885	1068.37	1165.50	1262.62	1359.75	1456.87	1554.00	1651.12	1748.25	1845.37	1942.50
3886	1068.65	1165.80	1262.95	1360.10	1457.25	1554.40	1651.55	1748.70	1845.85	1943.00
3887	1068.92	1166.10	1263.27	1360.45	1457.62	1554.80	1651.97	1749.15	1846.32	1943.50
3888	1069.20	1166.40	1263.60	1360.80	1458.00	1555.20	1652.40	1749.60	1846.80	1944.00
3889	1069.47	1166.70	1263.92	1361.15	1458.37	1555.60	1652.82	1750.05	1847.27	1944.50
3890	1069.75	1167.00	1264.25	1361.50	1458.75	1556.00	1653.25	1750.50	1847.75	1945.00
3891	1070.02	1167.30	1264.57	1361.85	1459.12	1556.40	1653.67	1750.95	1848.22	1945.50
3892	1070.30	1167.60	1264.90	1362.20	1459.50	1556.80	1654.10	1751.40	1848.70	1946.00
3893	1070.57	1167.90	1265.22	1362.55	1459.87	1557.20	1654.52	1751.85	1849.17	1946.50
3894	1070.85	1168.20	1265.55	1362.90	1460.25	1557.60	1654.95	1752.30	1849.65	1947.00
3895	1071.12	1168.50	1265.87	1363.25	1460.62	1558.00	1655.37	1752.75	1850.12	1947.50
3896	1071.40	1168.80	1266.20	1363.60	1461.00	1558.40	1655.80	1753.20	1850.60	1948.00
3897	1071.67	1169.10	1266.52	1363.95	1461.37	1558.80	1656.22	1753.65	1851.07	1948.50
3898	1071.95	1169.40	1266.85	1364.30	1461.75	1559.20	1656.65	1754.10	1851.55	1949.00
3899	1072.22	1169.70	1267.17	1364.65	1462.12	1559.60	1657.07	1754.55	1852.02	1949.50
3900	1072.50	1170.00	1267.50	1365.00	1462.50	1560.00	1657.50	1755.00	1852.50	1950.00

3950 FEET.

Per Ton,	25c.	50c.	$1	$2	$3	$4	$5	$6	$7	$8	$9	$10
Per Foot,			2½ cts.	5 cts.	7½ cts.	10 cts.	12½ cts.	15 cts.	17½ cts.	20 cts.	22½ cts.	25 cts.
Feet.												
3901	24.38	48.76	97.52	195.05	292.57	390.10	487.62	585.15	682.67	780.20	877.72	975.25
3902	24.39	48.77	97.55	195.10	292.65	390.20	487.75	585.30	682.85	780.40	877.95	975.50
3903	24.39	48.79	97.57	195.15	292.72	390.30	487.87	585.45	683.02	780.60	878.17	975.75
3904	24.40	48.80	97.60	195.20	292.80	390.40	488.00	585.60	683.20	780.80	878.40	976.00
3905	24.41	48.81	97.62	195.25	292.87	390.50	488.12	585.75	683.37	781.00	878.62	976.25
3906	24.41	48.82	97.65	195.30	292.95	390.60	488.25	585.90	683.55	781.20	878.85	976.50
3907	24.42	48.84	97.67	195.35	293.02	390.70	488.37	586.05	683.72	781.40	879.07	976.75
3908	24.42	48.85	97.70	195.40	293.10	390.80	488.50	586.20	683.90	781.60	879.30	977.00
3909	24.43	48.86	97.72	195.45	293.17	390.90	488.62	586.35	684.07	781.80	879.52	977.25
3910	24.44	48.87	97.75	195.50	293.25	391.00	488.75	586.50	684.25	782.00	879.75	977.50
3911	24.44	48.89	97.77	195.55	293.32	391.10	488.87	586.65	684.42	782.20	879.97	977.75
3912	24.45	48.90	97.80	195.60	293.40	391.20	489.00	586.80	684.60	782.40	880.20	978.00
3913	24.46	48.91	97.82	195.65	293.47	391.30	489.12	586.95	684.77	782.60	880.42	978.25
3914	24.46	48.92	97.85	195.70	293.55	391.40	489.25	587.10	684.95	782.80	880.65	978.50
3915	24.47	48.94	97.87	195.75	293.62	391.50	489.37	587.25	685.12	783.00	880.87	978.75
3916	24.47	48.95	97.90	195.80	293.70	391.60	489.50	587.40	685.30	783.20	881.10	979.00
3917	24.48	48.96	97.92	195.85	293.77	391.70	489.62	587.55	685.47	783.40	881.32	979.25
3918	24.49	48.97	97.95	195.90	293.85	391.80	489.75	587.70	685.65	783.60	881.55	979.50
3919	24.49	48.99	97.97	195.95	293.92	391.90	489.87	587.85	685.82	783.80	881.77	979.75
3920	24.50	49.00	98.00	196.00	294.00	392.00	490.00	588.00	686.00	784.00	882.00	980.00
3921	24.51	49.01	98.02	196.05	294.07	392.10	490.12	588.15	686.17	784.20	882.22	980.25
3922	24.51	49.02	98.05	196.10	294.15	392.20	490.25	588.30	686.35	784.40	882.45	980.50
3923	24.52	49.04	98.07	196.15	294.22	392.30	490.37	588.45	686.52	784.60	882.67	980.75
3924	24.52	49.05	98.10	196.20	294.30	392.40	490.50	588.60	686.70	784.80	882.90	981.00
3925	24.53	49.06	98.12	196.25	294.37	392.50	490.62	588.75	686.87	785.00	883.12	981.25
3926	24.54	49.07	98.15	196.30	294.45	392.60	490.75	588.90	687.05	785.20	883.35	981.50
3927	24.54	49.09	98.17	196.35	294.52	392.70	490.87	589.05	687.22	785.40	883.57	981.75
3928	24.55	49.10	98.20	196.40	294.60	392.80	491.00	589.20	687.40	785.60	883.80	982.00
3929	24.56	49.11	98.22	196.45	294.67	392.90	491.12	589.35	687.57	785.80	884.02	982.25
3930	24.56	49.12	98.25	196.50	294.75	393.00	491.25	589.50	687.75	786.00	884.25	982.50
3931	24.57	49.14	98.27	196.55	294.82	393.10	491.37	589.65	687.92	786.20	884.47	982.75
3932	24.57	49.15	98.30	196.60	294.90	393.20	491.50	589.80	688.10	786.40	884.70	983.00
3933	24.58	49.16	98.32	196.65	294.97	393.30	491.62	589.95	688.27	786.60	884.92	983.25
3934	24.59	49.17	98.35	196.70	295.05	393.40	491.75	590.10	688.45	786.80	885.15	983.50
3935	24.59	49.19	98.37	196.75	295.12	393.50	491.87	590.25	688.62	787.00	885.37	983.75
3936	24.60	49.20	98.40	196.80	295.20	393.60	492.00	590.40	688.80	787.20	885.60	984.00
3937	24.61	49.21	98.42	196.85	295.27	393.70	492.12	590.55	688.97	787.40	885.82	984.25
3938	24.61	49.22	98.45	196.90	295.35	393.80	492.25	590.70	689.15	787.60	886.05	984.50
3939	24.62	49.24	98.47	196.95	295.42	393.90	492.37	590.85	689.32	787.80	886.27	984.75
3940	24.62	49.25	98.50	197.00	295.50	394.00	492.50	591.00	689.50	788.00	886.50	985.00
3941	24.63	49.26	98.52	197.05	295.57	394.10	492.62	591.15	689.67	788.20	886.72	985.25
3942	24.64	49.27	98.55	197.10	295.65	394.20	492.75	591.30	689.85	788.40	886.95	985.50
3943	24.64	49.29	98.57	197.15	295.72	394.30	492.87	591.45	690.02	788.60	887.17	985.75
3944	24.65	49.30	98.60	197.20	295.80	394.40	493.00	591.60	690.20	788.80	887.40	986.00
3945	24.66	49.31	98.62	197.25	295.87	394.50	493.12	591.75	690.37	789.00	887.62	986.25
3946	24.66	49.32	98.65	197.30	295.95	394.60	493.25	591.90	690.55	789.20	887.85	986.50
3947	24.67	49.34	98.67	197.35	296.02	394.70	493.37	592.05	690.72	789.40	888.07	986.75
3948	24.67	49.35	98.70	197.40	296.10	394.80	493.50	592.20	690.90	789.60	888.30	987.00
3949	24.68	49.36	98.72	197.45	296.17	394.90	493.62	592.35	691.07	789.80	888.52	987.25
3950	24.69	49.37	98.75	197.50	296.25	395.00	493.75	592.50	691.25	790.00	888.75	987.50

Per Ton,	$11	$12	$13	$14	$15	$16	$17	$18	$19	$20
Per Foot,	27½ cts.	30 cts.	32½ cts.	35 cts.	37½ cts.	40 cts.	42½ cts.	45 cts.	47½ cts.	50 cts.
Feet.										
3901	1072.77	1170.30	1267.82	1365.35	1462.87	1560.40	1657.92	1755.45	1852.97	1950.50
3902	1073.05	1170.60	1268.15	1365.70	1463.25	1560.80	1658.35	1755.90	1853.45	1951.00
3903	1073.32	1170.90	1268.47	1366.05	1463.62	1561.20	1658.77	1756.35	1853.92	1951.50
3904	1073.60	1171.20	1268.80	1366.40	1464.00	1561.60	1659.20	1756.80	1854.40	1952.00
3905	1073.87	1171.50	1269.12	1366.75	1464.37	1562.00	1659.62	1757.25	1854.87	1952.50
3906	1074.15	1171.80	1269.45	1367.10	1464.75	1562.40	1660.05	1757.70	1855.35	1953.00
3907	1074.42	1172.10	1269.77	1367.45	1465.12	1562.80	1660.47	1758.15	1855.82	1953.50
3908	1074.70	1172.40	1270.10	1367.80	1465.50	1563.20	1660.90	1758.60	1856.30	1954.00
3909	1074.97	1172.70	1270.42	1368.15	1465.87	1563.60	1661.32	1759.05	1856.77	1954.50
3910	1075.25	1173.00	1270.75	1368.50	1466.25	1564.00	1661.75	1759.50	1857.25	1955.00
3911	1075.52	1173.30	1271.07	1368.85	1466.62	1564.40	1662.17	1759.95	1857.72	1955.50
3912	1075.80	1173.60	1271.40	1369.20	1467.00	1564.80	1662.60	1760.40	1858.20	1956.00
3913	1076.07	1173.90	1271.72	1369.55	1467.37	1565.20	1663.02	1760.85	1858.67	1956.50
3914	1076.35	1174.20	1272.05	1369.90	1467.75	1565.60	1663.45	1761.30	1859.15	1957.00
3915	1076.62	1174.50	1272.37	1370.25	1468.12	1566.00	1663.87	1761.75	1859.62	1957.50
3916	1076.90	1174.80	1272.70	1370.60	1468.50	1566.40	1664.30	1762.20	1860.10	1958.00
3917	1077.17	1175.10	1273.02	1370.95	1468.87	1566.80	1664.72	1762.65	1860.57	1958.50
3918	1077.45	1175.40	1273.35	1371.30	1469.25	1567.20	1665.15	1763.10	1861.05	1959.00
3919	1077.72	1175.70	1273.67	1371.65	1469.62	1567.60	1665.57	1763.55	1861.52	1959.50
3920	1078.00	1176.00	1274.00	1372.00	1470.00	1568.00	1666.00	1764.00	1862.00	1960.00
3921	1078.27	1176.30	1274.32	1372.35	1470.37	1568.40	1666.42	1764.45	1862.47	1960.50
3922	1078.55	1176.60	1274.65	1372.70	1470.75	1568.80	1666.85	1764.90	1862.95	1961.00
3923	1078.82	1176.90	1274.97	1373.05	1471.12	1569.20	1667.27	1765.35	1863.42	1961.50
3924	1079.10	1177.20	1275.30	1373.40	1471.50	1569.60	1667.70	1765.80	1863.90	1962.00
3925	1079.37	1177.50	1275.62	1373.75	1471.87	1570.00	1668.12	1766.25	1864.37	1962.50
3926	1079.65	1177.80	1275.95	1374.10	1472.25	1570.40	1668.55	1766.70	1864.85	1963.00
3927	1079.92	1178.10	1276.27	1374.45	1472.62	1570.80	1668.97	1767.15	1865.32	1963.50
3928	1080.20	1178.40	1276.60	1374.80	1473.00	1571.20	1669.40	1767.60	1865.80	1964.00
3929	1080.47	1178.70	1276.92	1375.15	1473.37	1571.60	1669.82	1768.05	1866.27	1964.50
3930	1080.75	1179.00	1277.25	1375.50	1473.75	1572.00	1670.25	1768.50	1866.75	1965.00
3931	1081.02	1179.30	1277.57	1375.85	1474.12	1572.40	1670.67	1768.95	1867.22	1965.50
3932	1081.30	1179.60	1277.90	1376.20	1474.50	1572.80	1671.10	1769.40	1867.70	1966.00
3933	1081.57	1179.90	1278.22	1376.55	1474.87	1573.20	1671.52	1769.85	1868.17	1966.50
3934	1081.85	1180.20	1278.55	1376.90	1475.25	1573.60	1671.95	1770.30	1868.65	1967.00
3935	1082.12	1180.50	1278.87	1377.25	1475.62	1574.00	1672.37	1770.75	1869.12	1967.50
3936	1082.40	1180.80	1279.20	1377.60	1476.00	1574.40	1672.80	1771.20	1869.60	1968.00
3937	1082.67	1181.10	1279.52	1377.95	1476.37	1574.80	1673.22	1771.65	1870.07	1968.50
3938	1082.95	1181.40	1279.85	1378.30	1476.75	1575.20	1673.65	1772.10	1870.55	1969.00
3939	1083.22	1181.70	1280.17	1378.65	1477.12	1575.60	1674.07	1772.55	1871.02	1969.50
3940	1083.50	1182.00	1280.50	1379.00	1477.50	1576.00	1674.50	1773.00	1871.50	1970.00
3941	1083.77	1182.30	1280.82	1379.35	1477.87	1576.40	1674.92	1773.45	1871.97	1970.50
3942	1084.05	1182.60	1281.15	1379.70	1478.25	1576.80	1675.35	1773.90	1872.45	1971.00
3943	1084.32	1182.90	1281.47	1380.05	1478.62	1577.20	1675.77	1774.35	1872.92	1971.50
3944	1084.60	1183.20	1281.80	1380.40	1479.00	1577.60	1676.20	1774.80	1873.40	1972.00
3945	1084.87	1183.50	1282.12	1380.75	1479.37	1578.00	1676.62	1775.25	1873.87	1972.50
3946	1085.15	1183.80	1282.45	1381.10	1479.75	1578.40	1677.05	1775.70	1874.35	1973.00
3947	1085.42	1184.10	1282.77	1381.45	1480.12	1578.80	1677.47	1776.15	1874.82	1973.50
3948	1085.70	1184.40	1283.10	1381.80	1480.50	1579.20	1677.90	1776.60	1875.30	1974.00
3949	1085.97	1184.70	1283.42	1382.15	1480.87	1579.60	1678.32	1777.05	1875.77	1974.50
3950	1086.25	1185.00	1283.75	1382.50	1481.25	1580.00	1678.75	1777.50	1876.25	1975.00

4000 FEET.

Per Ton, Per Foot,	25c.	50c.	$1 2½ cts.	$2 5 cts.	$3 7½ cts.	$4 10 cts.	$5 12½ cts.	$6 15 cts.	$7 17½ cts.	$8 20 cts.	$9 22½ cts.	$10 25 cts.
Feet.												
3951	24.69	49.39	98.77	197.55	296.32	395.10	493.87	592.65	691.42	790.20	888.97	987.75
3952	24.70	49.40	98.80	197.60	296.40	395.20	494.00	592.80	691.60	790.40	889.20	988.00
3953	24.71	49.41	98.82	197.65	296.47	395.30	494.12	592.95	691.77	790.60	889.42	988.25
3954	24.71	49.42	98.85	197.70	296.55	395.40	494.25	593.10	691.95	790.80	889.65	988.50
3955	24.72	49.44	98.87	197.75	296.62	395.50	494.37	593.25	692.12	791.00	889.87	988.75
3956	24.72	49.45	98.90	197.80	296.70	395.60	494.50	593.40	692.30	791.20	890.10	989.00
3957	24.73	49.46	98.92	197.85	296.77	395.70	494.62	593.55	692.47	791.40	890.32	989.25
3958	24.74	49.47	98.95	197.90	296.85	395.80	494.75	593.70	692.65	791.60	890.55	989.50
3959	24.74	49.49	98.97	197.95	296.92	395.90	494.87	593.85	692.82	791.80	890.77	989.75
3960	24.75	49.50	99.00	198.00	297.00	396.00	495.00	594.00	693.00	792.00	891.00	990.00
3961	24.76	49.51	99.02	198.05	297.07	396.10	495.12	594.15	693.17	792.20	891.22	990.25
3962	24.76	49.52	99.05	198.10	297.15	396.20	495.25	594.30	693.35	792.40	891.45	990.50
3963	24.77	49.54	99.07	198.15	297.22	396.30	495.37	594.45	693.52	792.60	891.67	990.75
3964	24.77	49.55	99.10	198.20	297.30	396.40	495.50	594.60	693.70	792.80	891.90	991.00
3965	24.78	49.56	99.12	198.25	297.37	396.50	495.62	594.75	693.87	793.00	892.12	991.25
3966	24.79	49.57	99.15	198.30	297.45	396.60	495.75	594.90	694.05	793.20	892.35	991.50
3967	24.79	49.59	99.17	198.35	297.52	396.70	495.87	595.05	694.22	793.40	892.57	991.75
3968	24.80	49.60	99.20	198.40	297.60	396.80	496.00	595.20	694.40	793.60	892.80	992.00
3969	24.81	49.61	99.22	198.45	297.67	396.90	496.12	595.35	694.57	793.80	893.02	992.25
3970	24.81	49.62	99.25	198.50	297.75	397.00	496.25	595.50	694.75	794.00	893.25	992.50
3971	24.82	49.64	99.27	198.55	297.82	397.10	496.37	595.65	694.92	794.20	893.47	992.75
3972	24.82	49.65	99.30	198.60	297.90	397.20	496.50	595.80	695.10	794.40	893.70	993.00
3973	24.83	49.66	99.32	198.65	297.97	397.30	496.62	595.95	695.27	794.60	893.92	993.25
3974	24.84	49.67	99.35	198.70	298.05	397.40	496.75	596.10	695.45	794.80	894.15	993.50
3975	24.84	49.69	99.37	198.75	298.12	397.50	496.87	596.25	695.62	795.00	894.37	993.75
3976	24.85	49.70	99.40	198.80	298.20	397.60	497.00	596.40	695.80	795.20	894.60	994.00
3977	24.86	49.71	99.42	198.85	298.27	397.70	497.12	596.55	695.97	795.40	894.82	994.25
3978	24.86	49.72	99.45	198.90	298.35	397.80	497.25	596.70	696.15	795.60	895.05	994.50
3979	24.87	49.74	99.47	198.95	298.42	397.90	497.37	596.85	696.32	795.80	895.27	994.75
3980	24.87	49.75	99.50	199.00	298.50	398.00	497.50	597.00	696.50	796.00	895.50	995.00
3981	24.88	49.76	99.52	199.05	298.57	398.10	497.62	597.15	696.67	796.20	895.72	995.25
3982	24.89	49.77	99.55	199.10	298.65	398.20	497.75	597.30	696.85	796.40	895.95	995.50
3983	24.89	49.79	99.57	199.15	298.72	398.30	497.87	597.45	697.02	796.60	896.17	995.75
3984	24.90	49.80	99.60	199.20	298.80	398.40	498.00	597.60	697.20	796.80	896.40	996.00
3985	24.91	49.81	99.62	199.25	298.87	398.50	498.12	597.75	697.37	797.00	896.62	996.25
3986	24.91	49.82	99.65	199.30	298.95	398.60	498.25	597.90	697.55	797.20	896.85	996.50
3987	24.92	49.84	99.67	199.35	299.02	398.70	498.37	598.05	697.72	797.40	897.07	996.75
3988	24.92	49.85	99.70	199.40	299.10	398.80	498.50	598.20	697.90	797.60	897.30	997.00
3989	24.93	49.86	99.72	199.45	299.17	398.90	498.62	598.35	698.07	797.80	897.52	997.25
3990	24.94	49.87	99.75	199.50	299.25	399.00	498.75	598.50	698.25	798.00	897.75	997.50
3991	24.94	49.89	99.77	199.55	299.32	399.10	498.87	598.65	698.42	798.20	897.97	997.75
3992	24.95	49.90	99.80	199.60	299.40	399.20	499.00	598.80	698.60	798.40	898.20	998.00
3993	24.96	49.91	99.82	199.65	299.47	399.30	499.12	598.95	698.77	798.60	898.42	998.25
3994	24.96	49.92	99.85	199.70	299.55	399.40	499.25	599.10	698.95	798.80	898.65	998.50
3995	24.97	49.94	99.87	199.75	299.62	399.50	499.37	599.25	699.12	799.00	898.87	998.75
3996	24.97	49.95	99.90	199.80	299.70	399.60	499.50	599.40	699.30	799.20	899.10	999.00
3997	24.98	49.96	99.92	199.85	299.77	399.70	499.62	599.55	699.47	799.40	899.32	999.25
3998	24.99	49.97	99.95	199.90	299.85	399.80	499.75	599.70	699.65	799.60	899.55	999.50
3999	24.99	49.99	99.97	199.95	299.92	399.90	499.87	599.85	699.82	799.80	899.77	999.75
4000	25.00	50.00	100.00	200.00	300.00	400.00	500.00	600.00	700.00	800.00	900.00	1000.00

Per Ton, Per Foot,	$11 27½ cts.	$12 30 cts.	$13 32½ cts.	$14 35 cts.	$15 37½ cts.	$16 40 cts.	$17 42½ cts.	$18 45 cts.	$19 47½ cts.	$20 50 cts.
Feet.										
3951	1086.52	1185.30	1284.07	1382.85	1481.62	1580.40	1679.17	1777.95	1876.72	1975.50
3952	1086.80	1185.60	1284.40	1383.20	1482.00	1580.80	1679.60	1778.40	1877.20	1976.00
3953	1087.07	1185.90	1284.72	1383.55	1482.37	1581.20	1680.02	1778.85	1877.67	1976.50
3954	1087.35	1186.20	1285.05	1383.90	1482.75	1581.60	1680.45	1779.30	1878.15	1977.00
3955	1087.62	1186.50	1285.37	1384.25	1483.12	1582.00	1680.87	1779.75	1878.62	1977.50
3956	1087.90	1186.80	1285.70	1384.60	1483.50	1582.40	1681.30	1780.20	1879.10	1978.00
3957	1088.17	1187.10	1286.02	1384.95	1483.87	1582.80	1681.72	1780.65	1879.57	1978.50
3958	1088.45	1187.40	1286.35	1385.30	1484.25	1583.20	1682.15	1781.10	1880.05	1979.00
3959	1088.72	1187.70	1286.67	1385.65	1484.62	1583.60	1682.57	1781.55	1880.52	1979.50
3960	1089.00	1188.00	1287.00	1386.00	1485.00	1584.00	1683.00	1782.00	1881.00	1980.00
3961	1089.27	1188.30	1287.32	1386.35	1485.37	1584.40	1683.42	1782.45	1881.47	1980.50
3962	1089.55	1188.60	1287.65	1386.70	1485.75	1584.80	1683.85	1782.90	1881.95	1981.00
3963	1089.82	1188.90	1287.97	1387.05	1486.12	1585.20	1684.27	1783.35	1882.42	1981.50
3964	1090.10	1189.20	1288.30	1387.40	1486.50	1585.60	1684.70	1783.80	1882.90	1982.00
3965	1090.37	1189.50	1288.62	1387.75	1486.87	1586.00	1685.12	1784.25	1883.37	1982.50
3966	1090.65	1189.80	1288.95	1388.10	1487.25	1586.40	1685.55	1784.70	1883.85	1983.00
3967	1090.92	1190.10	1289.27	1388.45	1487.62	1586.80	1685.97	1785.15	1884.32	1983.50
3968	1091.20	1190.40	1289.60	1388.80	1488.00	1587.20	1686.40	1785.60	1884.80	1984.00
3969	1091.47	1190.70	1289.92	1389.15	1488.37	1587.60	1686.82	1786.05	1885.27	1984.50
3970	1091.75	1191.00	1290.25	1389.50	1488.75	1588.00	1687.25	1786.50	1885.75	1985.00
3971	1092.02	1191.30	1290.57	1389.85	1489.12	1588.40	1687.67	1786.95	1886.22	1985.50
3972	1092.30	1191.60	1290.90	1390.20	1489.50	1588.80	1688.10	1787.40	1886.70	1986.00
3973	1092.57	1191.90	1291.22	1390.55	1489.87	1589.20	1688.52	1787.85	1887.17	1986.50
3974	1092.85	1192.20	1291.55	1390.90	1490.25	1589.60	1688.95	1788.30	1887.65	1987.00
3975	1093.12	1192.50	1291.87	1391.25	1490.62	1590.00	1689.37	1788.75	1888.12	1987.50
3976	1093.40	1192.80	1292.20	1391.60	1491.00	1590.40	1689.80	1789.20	1888.60	1988.00
3977	1093.67	1193.10	1292.52	1391.95	1491.37	1590.80	1690.22	1789.65	1889.07	1988.50
3978	1093.95	1193.40	1292.85	1392.30	1491.75	1591.20	1690.65	1790.10	1889.55	1989.00
3979	1094.22	1193.70	1293.17	1392.65	1492.12	1591.60	1691.07	1790.55	1890.02	1989.50
3980	1094.50	1194.00	1293.50	1393.00	1492.50	1592.00	1691.50	1791.00	1890.50	1990.00
3981	1094.77	1194.30	1293.82	1393.35	1492.87	1592.40	1691.92	1791.45	1890.97	1990.50
3982	1095.05	1194.60	1294.15	1393.70	1493.25	1592.80	1692.35	1791.90	1891.45	1991.00
3983	1095.32	1194.90	1294.47	1394.05	1493.62	1593.20	1692.77	1792.35	1891.92	1991.50
3984	1095.60	1195.20	1294.80	1394.40	1494.00	1593.60	1693.20	1792.80	1892.40	1992.00
3985	1095.87	1195.50	1295.12	1394.75	1494.37	1594.00	1693.62	1793.25	1892.87	1992.50
3986	1096.15	1195.80	1295.45	1395.10	1494.75	1594.40	1694.05	1793.70	1893.35	1993.00
3987	1096.42	1196.10	1295.77	1395.45	1495.12	1594.80	1694.47	1794.15	1893.82	1993.50
3988	1096.70	1196.40	1296.10	1395.80	1495.50	1595.20	1694.90	1794.60	1894.30	1994.00
3989	1096.97	1196.70	1296.42	1396.15	1495.87	1595.60	1695.32	1795.05	1894.77	1994.50
3990	1097.25	1197.00	1296.75	1396.50	1496.25	1596.00	1695.75	1795.50	1895.25	1995.00
3991	1097.52	1197.30	1297.07	1396.85	1496.62	1596.40	1696.17	1795.95	1895.72	1995.50
3992	1097.80	1197.60	1297.40	1397.20	1497.00	1596.80	1696.60	1796.40	1896.20	1996.00
3993	1098.07	1197.90	1297.72	1397.55	1497.37	1597.20	1697.02	1796.85	1896.67	1996.50
3994	1098.35	1198.20	1298.05	1397.90	1497.75	1597.60	1697.45	1797.30	1897.15	1997.00
3995	1098.62	1198.50	1298.37	1398.25	1498.12	1598.00	1697.87	1797.75	1897.62	1997.50
3996	1098.90	1198.80	1298.70	1398.60	1498.50	1598.40	1698.30	1798.20	1898.10	1998.00
3997	1099.17	1199.10	1299.02	1398.95	1498.87	1598.80	1698.72	1798.65	1898.57	1998.50
3998	1099.45	1199.40	1299.35	1399.30	1499.25	1599.20	1699.15	1799.10	1899.05	1999.00
3999	1099.72	1199.70	1299.67	1399.65	1499.62	1599.60	1699.57	1799.55	1899.52	1999.50
4000	1100.00	1200.00	1300.00	1400.00	1500.00	1600.00	1700.00	1800.00	1900.00	2000.00

www.ingramcontent.com/pod-product-compliance
Lightning Source LLC
LaVergne TN
LVHW021400110826
845150LV00007B/1733

* 9 7 8 1 4 2 5 5 1 2 9 8 9 *